Materials on Intellectual Property

Materials on Intellectual Property

Edited by

W.R. Cornish

Professor of Law
University of Cambridge

ESC Publishing Limited
Oxford
1990

Statutes quoted in the Materials appear in bold type. The texts of judicial decisions appear in roman type, and commentary and editorial notes appear in italics.

The Editor and Publishers gratefully acknowledge the kind permission of the following publishers for allowing the reproduction of extracts from their law reports: Butterworths, Sweet & Maxwell, European Patent Office and Her Majesty's Stationery Office.

ISBN 0 906214 67 X

Published by ESC Publishing Limited
Mill Street
Oxford OX2 0JU
United Kingdom

Typeset by VAP Publishing Services, Kidlington
Printed by Dotesios Limited, Trowbridge

PREFACE

These *Materials*, which are appearing as a single volume in 1990, have grown out of three smaller Casebooks: on *Patents and Confidential Information, Copyright and Designs* and *Trade Marks and Names*. In the new *Materials* selected statutory provisions are included for the first time. Students of intellectual property law will thus have available the major sections from United Kingdom statutes, as well as leading provisions from EC and other European Treaties, Conventions and Regulations, in a volume which also gives substantial extracts from many judicial decisions of UK, European and Commonwealth courts.

The main range of intellectual property law is now covered. The book contains the following major Parts:

1. Patents
2. Confidential Information
3. Copyright
4. Industrial Designs
5. Trade Marks and Names
6. European Community Law and Intellectual Property
7. Enforcement and Remedies

The book is entirely given over to source materials. There has been no room for linking commentaries or teasing questions. In the UK the subject is now well provided with texts at every level of advance, from which the meaning and problems of the subject can be gathered. I have naturally had in mind my own book, *Intellectual Property* (2nd edition, 1990), as a volume to be read in tandem with these *Materials*.

I hope that in its new form, the present volume will be useful to students of a subject whose popularity seems to be steadily on the increase.

My thanks go, first, to the Max-Planck Institute for Foreign and International Patent, Copyright and Competition Law, Munich – as an external member of the Institute I have been given much assistance in preparing the book; and, secondly, to my publishers, who have been most supportive at all stages of the venture.

W.R. Cornish
Professor of Law
University of Cambridge 1990

CONTENTS

Table of Cases Included in the Materials

Spycatcher

Table of Statutes and Like Material

1. PATENTS FOR INVENTIONS

1.1 Granting and Maintenance of Patents

1.1.1 International Connections

1.1.1.1 Patents Act 1977, s.130(7): Interpretation of 1977 Act

S.130(7) Whereas by a resolution made on the signature of the Community Patent Convention the governments of the member states of the European Economic Community resolved to adjust their laws relating to patents so as (among other things) to bring those laws into conformity with the corresponding provisions of the European Patent Convention, the Community Patent Convention and the Patent Cooperation Treaty, it is hereby declared that the following provisions of this Act, this is to say, sections 1(1) to (4), ? to 6, 14(3), (5) and (6), 37(5), 54, 60, 69, 72(1) and (2), 74(4), 82, 83, 88(6) and (7), 100 and 125, are so framed as to have, as nearly as practicable, the same effects in the United Kingdom as the corresponding provisions of the European Patent Convention, the Community Patent Convention and the Patent Cooperation Treaty have in the territories to which those Conventions apply.

1.1.1.2 Patents Act 1977, s.5: Priority under the Paris Industrial Property Convention

S.5(1) For the purposes of this Act the priority date of an invention to which an application for a patent relates and also of any matter (whether or not the same as the invention) contained in any such application is, except as provided by the following provisions of this Act, the date of filing the application.

(2) If in or in connection with an application for a patent (the application in suit) a declaration is made, whether by the applicant or any predecessor in title of his, complying with the relevant requirements of rules and specifying one or more earlier relevant applications for the purposes of this section made by the applicant or a predecessor in title of his and each having a date of filing during the period of twelve months immediately preceding the date of filing the application in suit, then –

    (a) if an invention to which the application in suit relates is supported by matter disclosed in the earlier relevant application or applications, the priority date of that invention shall instead of being the date of filing the application in suit be the date of filing the relevant application in which that matter was disclosed or, if it was disclosed in more than one relevant application, the earliest of them;

(b) the priority date of any matter contained in the application in suit which was also disclosed in the earlier relevant application or applications shall be the date of filing the relevant application in which that matter was disclosed or, if it was disclosed in more than one relevant application, the earliest of them.

(3) Where an invention or other matter contained in the application in suit is also disclosed in two earlier relevant applications filed by the same applicant as in the case of the application in suit of a predecessor in title of his and the second of those relevant applications was specified in or in connection with the application in suit, the second of those relevant applications shall, so far as concerns that invention or matter, be disregarded unless –

(a) it was filed in or in respect of the same country as the first; and

(b) not later than the date of filing the second, the first (whether or not so specified) was unconditionally withdrawn, or was abandoned or refused, without –

(i) having been made available to the public (whether in the United Kingdom or elsewhere);

(ii) leaving any rights outstanding; and

(iii) having served to establish a priority date in relation to another application, wherever made.

(4) The foregoing provisions of this section shall apply for determining the priority date of an invention for which a patent has been granted as they apply for determining the priority date of an invention to which an application for that patent relates.

(5) In this section "relevant application" means any of the following applications which has a date of filing, namely –

(a) an application for a patent under this Act;

(b) an application in or for a convention country (specified under section 90 below) for protection in respect of an invention or an application which, in accordance with the law of a convention country or a treaty or international convention to which a convention country is a party, is equivalent to such an application.

For the equivalent provision in the EPC, see Art. 88. Note also: PA 1977 s.6 – Disclosure of matter between earlier and later appl cations.

1.1.1.3   Patents Act 1977, s.77: Effect of European Patent (UK)

S.77(1) Subject to the provisions of this Act, a European patent (UK) shall, as from the publication of the mention of its grant in the European Patent Bulletin, be treated for the purposes of Parts I and III of this Act as if it were a patent under this Act granted in pursuance of an application made under this Act and as if notice of the grant of the patent had, on the date of that publication, been published under section 24 above in the journal; and –

(a) the proprietor of a European patent (UK) shall accordingly as respects the United Kingdom have the same rights and remedies, subject to the same conditions, as the proprietor of a patent under this Act;

    (b) references in Parts I and III of this Act to a patent shall be construed accordingly; and

    (c) any statement made and any certificate filed for the purposes of the provision of the convention corresponding to section 2(4)(c) above shall be respectively treated as a statement made and written evidence filed for the purposes of the said paragraph (c).

(2) Subsection (1) above shall not affect the operation in relation to a European patent (UK) of any provisions for the European Patent Convention relating to the amendment or revocation of such a patent in proceedings before the European Patent Office.

(3) Sections 58(7) to (9) and 63 above shall apply to the case where, after proceedings for the infringement of a European patent have been commenced before the court or the comptroller but have not been finally disposed of, it is established in proceedings before the European Patent Office that the patent is only partially valid as those provisions apply to proceedings in which the validity of a patent is put in issue and in which it is found that the patent is only partially valid.

(4) Subject to subsection (6) below, where a European patent (UK) is amended or revoked in accordance with the Euroepan Patent Convention, the amendment shall be treated for the purposes of Parts I and III of this Act as if it had been made, or as the case may be the patent shall be treated for those purposes as having been revoked, under this Act.

(5) Where –

    (a) under the European Patent Convention a European patent (UK) is revoked for failure to observe a time limit and is subsequently restored; and

    (b) between the revocation and publication of the fact that it has been restored a person begins in good faith to do an act which would, apart from section 55 above, constitute an infringement of the patent or makes in good faith effective and serious preparations to do such an act;

he shall have the rights conferred by section 28(6) above, and subsections (8) and (9) of that section shall apply accordingly.

(6) While this subsection is in force –

    (a) subsection (1) above shall not apply to a European patent (UK) the specification of which was published in French or German, unless a translation of the specification into English is filed at the Patent Office and the prescribed fee is paid before the end of the prescribed period;

    (b) subsection (4) above shall not apply to an amendment made in French or German unless a translation of the amendment into English is filed at the Patent Office and the prescribed fee is paid before the end of the prescribed period.

(7) Where a translation of a specification or amendment into English is not filed in accordance with subsection 6(a) or (b) above, the patent shall be treated as always having been void.

(8) The comptroller shall publish any translation filed at the Patent Office under subsection (6) above.

(9) Subsection (6) above shall come into force on a day appointed for the purpose by rules and shall cease to have effect on a day so appointed, without prejudice, however, to the power to bring it into force again.

Note also: s.78 – European patent (UK) applications.

1.1.1.4   Patents Act 1977, s.89: International Application under the Patent Cooperation Treaty

S.89(1) Subject to the provisions of this Act, an international application for a patent (UK) for which a date of filing has been accorded (whether by the Patent Office or by any other body) under the Patent Cooperation Treaty (in this section referred to as the Treaty) shall, until this subsection ceases to apply to the application be treated for the purposes of Parts I and III of this Act as an applicaton for a patent under this Act having that date as its date of filing and –

- (a)   the application, if published in accordance with the Treaty and if it satisfies relevant conditions, shall be so treated as published under section 16 above, subject, however, to subsection (7) below;
- (b)   where the date of filing an application is re-dated under the Treaty to a later date, that date shall be so treated as the date of filing the application;
- (c)   any declaration of priority made under the Treaty shall be so treated as a declaration made under section 5(2) above;
- (d)   where a period of time relevant to priority is extended under the Treaty, the period of twelve months specified in section 5(2) above shall be treated as altered correspondingly;
- (e)   any statement of the name of the inventor under the Treaty shall be so treated as a statement filed under section 13(2) above; and
- (f)   an amendment of the application made in accordance with the Treaty shall, if it satisfies the relevant conditions, be so treated as made under this Act.

(2) Accordingly until subsection (1) above ceases to apply to an application filed or published in accordance with the Treaty the applicant shall, subject to subsection (7) below, have the same rights and remedies in relation to the application as an applicant for a patent under this Act has in relation to a filed or, as the case may be, a published application for such a patent.

(3) Notwithstanding anything in subsection (1) above, the provisions of the Treaty and not those of this Act relating to publication, search, examination and amendment shall apply to any such application until all the relevant conditions are satisfied and, if those conditions are not satisfied before the end of the prescribed period, the application shall be taken to be withdrawn.

(4) The relevant conditions –

- (a)   in the case of an application, are that a copy of the application and, if it is not in English, a translation into English have been filed at the Patent Office and the filing fee has been paid to the Patent Office by the applicant; and
- (b)   in the case of an amendment, are that a copy of the amendment and, if it is not in English, a translation into English have been filed at the Patent Office.

Of the remaining subsections, note especially s.89(9), giving the Comptroller power to order additional search and examination; and s.89(10), excluding from the effects of the section an international application for a European patent (UK).

1.1.2 Patent Granting Procedure: Basic Provisions of UK Act

1.1.2.1 Patents Act 1977, s.14: Making of Application

S.14(1) Every application for a patent –
  - (a) shall be made in the prescribed form and shall be filed at the Patent Office in the prescribed manner; and
  - (b) shall be accompanied by the fee prescribed for the purposes of this subsection (hereafter in this Act referred to as the filing fee).

(2) Every application for a patent shall contain –
  - (a) a request for the grant of a patent;
  - (b) a specification containing a description of the invention, a claim or claims and any drawing referred to in the description of any claim; and
  - (c) an abstract;

but the foregoing provision shall not prevent an application being initiated by documents complying with section 15(1) below.

(3) The specification of an application shall disclose the invention in a manner which is clear enough and complete enough for the invention to be performed by a person skilled in the art.

(4) Without prejudice to subsection (3) above, rules may prescribe the circumstances in which the specification of an application which requires for its performance the use of a micro-organism is to be treated for the purposes of this Act as complying with that subsection.

(5) The claim or claims shall –
  - (a) define the matter for which the applicant seeks protection;
  - (b) be clear and concise;
  - (c) be supported by the description; and
  - (d) relate to one invention or to a group of inventions which are so linked as to form a single inventive concept.

(6) Without prejudice to the generality of subsection (5)(d) above, rules may provide for treating two or more inventions as being so linked as to form a single inventive concept for the purposes of this Act.

(7) The purpose of the abstract is to give technical information and on publication it shall not form part of the state of the art by virtue of section 2(3) above, and the comptroller may determine whether the abstract adequately fulfils its purpose and, if it does not, may reframe it so that it does.

(8) Rules may require a person who has made an application for a patent for an invention which requires for its performance the use of a micro-organism not to impose or maintain in the prescribed circumstances any restrictions on the availability to the public of samples of the micro-organism and the uses to which they may be put, subject, however, to any prescribed exceptions, and rules may provide that in the event of a contra-vention of any provision included in the rules by virtue of this subsection the specification shall be treated for the purposes of this Act as not disclosing the invention in a manner required by subsection (3) above.

(9) An application for a patent may be withdrawn at any time before the

patent is granted and any withdrawal of such an application may not be revoked.

Note also: s.13 – Mention of inventor; s.15 – Date of filing application; s.16 – Early publication of application; s.17 – Preliminary examination. For the equivalent steps in applying for a European patent through the EPO, see EPC Arts. 75–86 and EPC Rules 13–19, 24–36.

For international applications, see PCT, Chap.1 and PCT Rules 3–52.

1.1.2.2 Patents Act 1977, s.18: Substantive examination and grant or refusal of patent

S.18(1) Where the conditions imposed by section 17(1) above for the comptroller to refer an application to an examiner for a preliminary examination and search are satisfied and at the time of the request under that subsection or within the prescribed period –

    (a) a request is made by the applicant to the Patent Office in the prescribed form for a substantive examination; and

    (b) the prescribed fee is paid for the examination;

the comptroller shall refer the application to an examiner for a substantive examination; and if no such request is made or the prescribed fee is not paid within that period, the application shall be treated as having been withdrawn at the end of that period.

(2) On a substantive examination of an application the examiner shall investigate, to such extent as he considers necessary in view of any examination and search carried out under section 17 above, whether the application complies with the requirements of this Act and the rules and shall determine that question and report his determination to the comptroller.

(3) If the examiner reports that any of those requirements are not complied with, the comptroller shall give the applicant an opportunity within a specified period to make observations on the report and to amend the application so as to comply with those requirements (subject, however, to section 76 below), and if the applicant fails to satisfy the comptroller that those requirements are complied with, or to amend the application so as to comply with them, the comptroller may refuse the application.

(4) If the examiner reports that the application, whether as originally filed or as amended in pursuance of section 17 above, this section or section 19 below, complies with those requirements at any time before the end of the prescribed period, the comptroller shall notify the applicant of that fact and, subject to subsection (5) and sections 19 and 22 below and on payment within the prescribed period of any fee prescribed for the grant, grant him a patent.

(5) Where two or more applications for a patent for the same invention having the same priority date are filed by the same applicant or his successor in title, the comptroller may on that ground refuse to grant a patent in pursuance of more than one of the applications.

Note also: s.20 – Failure of application; s.21 – Observations by third party on patentability; s.22 – National security and public safety; s.23 – Restrictions on UK residents making applications abroad. For the equivalent steps in EPO procedure, see EPC Arts. 90–98 and EPC Rules 39–54.

For international preliminary examination, PCT Chap.II and PCT Rules 53–75.

1.1.3 Grant and Term

1.1.3.1 Patents Act 1977, s.24: Publication and certificate of grant

S.24(1) As soon as practicable after a patent has been granted under this Act the comptroller shall publish in the journal a notice that it has been granted.

(2) The comptroller shall, as soon as practicable after he publishes a notice under subsection (1) above, send the proprietor of the patent a certificate in the prescribed form that the patent has been granted to the proprietor.

(3) The comptroller shall, at the same time as he publishes a notice under subsection (1) above in relation to a patent publish the specification of the patent, the names of the proprietor and (if different) the inventor and any other matters constituting or relating to the patent which in the comptroller's opinion it is desirable to publish.

1.1.3.2 Patents Act 1977, s.25: Term of patent

S.25(1) A patent granted under this Act shall be treated for the purposes of the following provisions of this Act as having been granted, and shall take effect, on the date on which notice of its grant is published in the journal and, subject to subsection (3) below, shall continue in force until the end of the period of 20 years beginning with the date of filing the application for the patent or with such other date as may be prescribed.

(2) A rule prescribing any such other date under this section shall not be made unless a draft of the rule has been laid before, and approved by resolution of, each House of Parliament.

(3) A patent shall cease to have effect at the end of the period prescribed for the payment of any renewal fee if it is not paid within that period.

(4) If during the period of six months immediately following the end of the prescribed period the renewal fee and any prescribed additional fee are paid, the patent shall be treated for the purposes of this Act as if it had never expired, and accordingly –

    (a) anything done under or in relation to it during that further period shall be valid;

    (b) an act which would constitute an infringement of it if it had not expired shall constitute such an infringement; and

    (c) an act which would constitute the use of the patented invention for the services of the Crown if the patent had not expired shall constitute that use.

(5) Rules shall include provision requiring the comptroller to notify the registered proprietor of a patent that a renewal fee has not been received from him in the Patent Office before the end of the prescribed period and before the framing of the notification.

Note also: s.26 – Patent not to be impugned for lack of unity; s.28 – Restoration of lapsed patents; s.29 – Surrender of patents.

1.1.4 Amendment

1.1.4.1 Patents Act 1977, s.19: General power to amend application before grant

S.19(1) At any time before a patent is granted in pursuance of an application the applicant may, in accordance with the prescribed conditions and subject to section 76 below, amend the application of his own volition.

(2) The comptroller may, without an application being made to him for the purpose, amend the specification and abstract contained in an application for a patent so as to acknowledge a registered trade mark.

1.1.4.2 Patents Act 1977, s.27: General power to amend specification after grant

S.27(1) Subject to the following provisions of this section and to section 76 below, the comptroller may, on an application made by the proprietor of a patent, allow the specification of the patent to be amended subject to such conditions, if any, as he thinks fit.

(2) No such amendment shall be allowed under this section where there are pending before the court or the comptroller proceedings in which the validity of the patent may be put in issue.

(3) An amendment of a specification of a patent under this section shall have effect and be deemed always to have had effect from the grant of the patent.

(4) The comptroller may, without an application being made to him for the purpose, amend the specification of a patent so as to acknowledge a registered trade mark.

(5) A person may give notice to the comptroller of his opposition to an application under this section by the proprietor of a patent, and if he does so the comptroller shall notify the proprietor and consider the opposition in deciding whether to grant the application.

1.1.4.3 Patents Act 1977, s.75: Amendment of patent in infringement or revocation proceedings

S.75(1) In any proceedings before the court or the comptroller in which the validity of a patent is put in issue the court or, as the case may be, the comptroller may, subject to section 76 below, allow the proprietor of the patent to amend the specification of the patent in such manner, and subject to such terms as to advertising the proposed amendment and as to costs, expenses or otherwise, as the court or comptroller thinks fit.

(2) A person may give notice to the court or the comptroller of his opposition to an amendment proposed by the proprietor of the patent under this section, and if he does so the court or the comptroller shall notify the proprietor and consider the opposition in deciding whether the amendment or any amendment should be allowed.

(3) An amendment of a specification of a patent under this section shall have effect and be deemed always to have had effect from the grant of the patent.

(4) Where an application for an order under this section is made to the court, the applicant shall notify the comptroller, who shall be entitled to appear and be heard and shall appear if so directed by the court.

1.1.4.4   Patents Act 1977, s.76: Amendments of applications and patents not to include added matter

S.76(1) An application for a patent (the later application) shall not be allowed to be filed under section 8(3), 12, or 37(4) above or as mentioned in section 15(4) above, in respect of any matter disclosed in an earlier application or the specification of a patent which has been granted, if the later application discloses matter which extends beyond that disclosed in the earlier application, as filed, or the application for the patent, as filed.

(2) No amendment of an application or the specification of a patent shall be allowed under any of the provisions of this Act to which this subsection applies if it –

   (a) results in the application or specification disclosing any such matter, or

   (b) (where a patent has been granted) extends the protection conferred by the patent.

(3) Subsection (2) above applies to the following provisions of this Act, namely, sections 17(3), 18(3), 19(1), 27(1), 73 and 75.

1.1.5   Revocation and Opposition

1.1.5.1   Patents Act 1977, s.72: Power to revoke patents on application

S.72(1) Subject to the following provisions of this Act, the court or the comptroller may on the application of any person by order revoke a patent for an invention on (but only on) any of the following grounds, that is to say –

(a) the invention is not a patentable invention;

(b) the patent was granted to a person who was not the only person entitled under section 7(2) above to be granted that patent or to two or more persons who were not the only persons so entitled;

(c) the specification of the patent does not disclose the invention clearly enough and completely enough for it to be performed by a person skilled in the art;

(d) the matter disclosed in the specification of the patent extends beyond that disclosed in the application for the patent, as filed, or, if the patent was granted on a new application filed under section 8(3), 12 or 37(4) above or as mentioned in section 15(4) above, in the earlier application, as filed;

(e) the protection conferred by the patent has been extended by an amendment which should not have been allowed.

(2) An application for the revocation of a patent on the ground mentioned in subsection (1)(b) above –

(a) may only be made by a person found by the court in an action for a declaration or declarator, or found by the court or the comptroller on a reference under section 37 above, to be entitled to be granted that patent or to be granted a patent for part of the matter comprised in the specification of the patent sought to be revoked; and

(b) may not be made if that action was commenced or that reference was made after the end of the period of two years beginning with the date of the grant of the patent sought to be revoked, unless it is shown that any person registered as a proprietor of the patent knew at the time of the grant or of the transfer of the patent to him that he was not entitled to the patent.

(3) Rules under section 14(4) and (8) above shall, with any necessary modifications, apply for the purposes of subsection (1)(c) above as they apply for the purposes of section 14(3) above.

(4) An order under this section may be an order for the unconditional revocation of the patent or, where the court or the comptroller determines that one of the grounds mentioned in subsection (1) above has been established, but only so as to invalidate the patent to a limited extent, an order that the patent should be revoked unless within a specified time the specification is amended under section 75 below to the satisfaction of the court or the comptroller, as the case may be.

(5) A decision of the comptroller or on appeal from the comptroller shall not estop any party to civil proceedings in which infringement of a patent is in issue from alleging invalidity of the patent on any of the grounds referred to in subsection (1) above, whether or not any of the issues involved were decided in the said decision.

(6) Where the comptroller refuses to grant an application made to him by any person under this section, no application (otherwise than by way of appeal or by way of putting validity in issue in proceedings for infringement) may be made to the court by that person under this section in relation to the patent concerned, without the leave of the court.

(7) Where the comptroller has not disposed of an application made to him under this section, the applicant may not apply to the court under this section in respect of the patent concerned unless either –

  (a) the proprietor of the patent agrees that the applicant may so apply, or

  (b) the comptroller certifies in writing that it appears to him that the question whether the patent should be revoked is one which would more properly be determined by the court.

Note also: s.73 – Comptroller's power to revoke patents of his own initiative; s.74 – Proceedings in which validity of patent may be put in issue.

1.1.5.2   European Patent Convention, Arts.99, 100: Opposition

Art.99 (1) Within nine months from the publication of the mention of the grant of the European patent, any person may give notice to the European Patent Office of opposition to the European patent granted. Notice of opposition shall be filed in a written reasoned statement. It shall not be deemed to have been filed until the opposition fee has been paid.

(2) The opposition shall apply to the European patent in all the Contracting States in which that patent has effect.

(3) An opposition may be filed even if the European patent has been surrendered or has lapsed for all the designated States.

(4) Opponents shall be parties to the opposition proceedings as well as the proprietor of the patent.

(5) Where a person provides evidence that in a Contracting State, following a final decision, he has been entered in the patent register of such State instead of the previous proprietor, such person shall, at his request, replace the previous proprietor in respect of such State. By derogation from Article 118, the previous proprietor and the person making the request shall not be deemed to be joint proprietors unless both so request.

Art.100 Opposition may only be filed on the grounds that:

  (a) the subject-matter of the European patent is not patentable within the terms of Articles 52 to 57;

  (b) the European patent does not disclose the invention in a manner sufficiently clear and complete for it to be carried out by a person skilled in the art;

  (c) the subject-matter of the European patent extends beyond the content of the application as filed, or, if the patent was granted on a divisional application or on a new application filed in accordance with Article 61, beyond the content of the earlier application as filed.

Note also EPC Arts. 101–105 and EPC rules 55–63 on opposition proceedings; and EPC Arts. 106–112 and EPC rules 64–67 on appeals from decisions of EPO Divisions.

1.2 Validity

1.2.1 Novelty

1.2.1.1 Patents Act 1977, s.1(1), 2: Statutory provisions

S.1(1) A patent may be granted only for an invention in respect of which the following conditions are satisfied, that is to say –
  (a) the invention is new;
  (b) it involves an inventive step;
  (c) it is capable of industrial application;
  (d) the grant of a patent for it is not excluded by subsections (2) and (3) below; and references in this Act to a patentable invention shall be construed accordingly.

For s.1(2)–(5), see below, 1.2.3.1. S.1(1) corresponds in large measure to EPC, Art.52(1).

S.2(1) An invention shall be taken to be new if it does not form part of the state of the art.

(2) The state of the art in the case of an invention shall be taken to comprise all matter (whether a product, a process, information about either, or anything else) which has at any time before the priority date of that invention been made available to the public (whether in the United Kingdom or elsewhere) by written or oral description, by use or in any other way.

(3) The state of the art in the case of an invention to which an application for a patent or a patent relates shall be taken also to comprise matter contained in an application for another patent which was published on or after the priority date of that invention, if the following conditions are satisfied, that is to say –
  (a) that matter was contained in the application for that other patent both as filed and as published; and
  (b) the priority date of that matter is earlier than that of the invention.

(4) For the purposes of this section the disclosure of matter constituting an invention shall be disregarded in the case of a patent or an application for a patent if occurring later than the beginning of the period of six months immediately preceding the date of filing the application for the patent and either –
  (a) the disclosure was due to, or made in consequence of, the matter having been obtained unlawfully or in breach of confidence by any person –
    (i) from the inventor or from any other person to whom the matter was made available in confidence by the inventor or who obtained it from the inventor because he or the inventor believed that he was entitled to obtain it; or
    (ii) from any other person to whom the matter was made available in confidence by any person mentioned in sub-paragraph (i) above or in this sub-paragraph or who obtained it from any person so mentioned because he or the person from whom he obtained it believed that he was entitled to obtain it;

    (b) the disclosure was made in breach of confidence by any person who obtained the matter in confidence from the inventor or from any other person to whom it was made available, or who obtained it, from the inventor; or

    (c) the disclosure was due to, or made in consequence of the inventor displaying the invention at an international exhibition and the applicant states, on filing the application, that the invention has been so displayed and also, within the prescribed period, files written evidence in support of the statement complying with any prescribed conditions.

(5) In this section references to the inventor include references to any proprietor of the invention for the time being.

(6) In the case of an invention consisting of a substance or composition for use in a method of treatment of the human or animal body by surgery or therapy or of diagnosis practised on the human or animal body, the fact that the substance or composition forms part of the state of the art shall not prevent the invention from being taken to be new if the use of the substance or composition in any such method does not form part of the state of the art.

S.2 corresponds broadly to EPC, Arts.54, 55. But compare, in particular, EPC, Art.54(2):

The state of the art shall be held to comprise everything made available to the public by means of a written or oral description, by use, or in any other way, before the date of filing of the European patent application. EPC, Art.55(1): For the application of Article 54 a disclosure of the invention shall not be taken into consideration if it occurred no earlier than six months preceding the filing of the European patent application and if it was due to, or in consequence of:

    (a) an evident abuse in relation to the applicant or his legal predecessor, or

    (b) the fact that the applicant or his legal predecessor has displayed the invention at an official, or officially recognised, international exhibition falling within the terms of the Convention on international exhibitions signed at Paris on 22 November 1928 and last revised on 30 November 1972.

1.2.1.2   *Fomento v Mentmore* [1956] R.P.C. 87 (C.A.)

The plaintiff's patent, No 609,817, was for an improvement to the nib of a ball-point pen designed to make the flow of ink continuous and uniform. The essence of the invention can best be appreciated by imagining a ball sitting on a rather wide golf-tee; round the side of the ball is placed a metal housing, but between the housing and the tee is a gap forming a horizontal ring. In terms of the specification, the tee is the base seat through which the supply of ink from the reservoir is fed. The housing is the lateral seat. The crux of the invention was said to be the discovery that if the ring-gap between lateral and base seat comes below the equator of the ball the ink flows better.

The attack on the validity of the patent arose from the claim that the patentees themselves had both published a description of making ball-point pens which would mean performing the invention, and that they had made pens embodying the invention available to the public before the priority date of the patent.

The common technique for inserting the ball in a ball-point nib, and then closing the

*housing around it so that it was kept in at the top, was called peining. The housing was
formed into a cylinder at the top end, the ball was dropped into it and the house was then
hit with a peining tool shaped to close the cylinder up. The force of this last step had the
effect of deforming the housing so as to produce a ring gap. The defendants alleged that
the ring gap would occur below the equatorial line and that the plaintiffs had been peining
in this way before they appreciated that the ring gave them a better flow of ink.*

*The plaintiff's activities were said to amount to an anticipation by virtue of (1) publication
and (2) use.*

*Publication: This was alleged to have been made in a prior UK Patent No 564,172. The
patent was concerned with improvements to the base-seat and made no mention of the
ring-gap as such, nor did it give explicit instructions as to how a nib would be made
embodying its special base-seat.*

Of this Jenkins L.J. said:

Mr Mould for the Defendants submitted that, even if none of the specific instances of
publication by prior user was held to have been made out, the Defendants would,
nevertheless, still be entitled to succeed on the following grounds. Firstly, he
propounded the general proposition that, when a man publishes a specification
describing an article but containing no directions as to how it is to be made, and the
article when made by a normal method will necessarily possess a particular characteristic not mentioned in the specification, a man entering the field thereafter cannot validly
claim a patent in respect of that same article on the strength of its possession of that
particular characteristic, for in such a case the second comer has invented nothing; he
has merely discovered that the article already described will, when made in a normal
way, possess that particular characteristic, and a mere discovery is not an invention
within the meaning of the Act, because it is not a manner of new manufacture within
the meaning of the Statute of Monopolies. (See Sec 32(1) (d) of the Act and the
definition of "invention" by reference to the Statute of Monopolies contained in Sec
101(1).) Mr Mould contended that this proposition applied to the present case so as to
invalidate the patent in suit, because peining was a normal, and indeed obvious, method
of performing an operation such as the closing of the ball housing of the pen described
in the prior specification No 564,172 and peining would necessarily produce the
particular characteristic of a lower lateral seat separated from the base seat by an
annular space. . . .

As to Mr Mould's first proposition, Mr Shelley submitted, firstly, that peining was not a
normal or obvious method of closing the ball housing, and, secondly, that, even if it was,
it would not necessarily produce the relevant characteristic of a lower lateral seat
separated from the base seat by an annular space. I agree with the Judge and with my
Lord that peining must be taken to have been a normal, and indeed obvious, method of
closing the ball housing, in view of the evidence of Dr Aitchison and the assumption to
this effect clearly made in the specification of the patent in suit. On the other hand, I
also agree with the learned Judge and my Lord that the evidence of Dr Aitchison and the
experimental peining operations of Messrs Moss and Leistikow fall short, having regard
to the evidence of Mr Wicks of establishing that peining must necessarily produce the
relevant characteristic, though, as the learned Judge said, it "might well" do so if the
operator was merely seeking to make a pen that would write, without any intention one
way or the other on the question of lateral seating.

Mr Mould submitted that, if peining "might well" produce a lower lateral seat, that was
enough for his purpose: and he relied on the case of *British Thomson-Houston v
Charlesworth, Peebles & Coy* [1925] 42 R.P.C. 180, and particularly on the speech of
Lord Shaw at p. 206. With respect, that seems to me to have been an entirely different

case. The earlier patent there related to treating tungsten so as to make it ductile when hot, while the later patent related to the subjecting of tungsten to a similar but somewhat more protracted treatment so as to make it ductile when cold; and Lord Shaw held that the later patent involved no inventive step. Here, the alleged invention resides in a particular characteristic in a given article, which characteristic is a new departure in the sense that it has never before been described or claimed. If in fact the article has never been made so as to possess that characteristic, and the characteristic is a useful or potentially useful one, I do not think that the Plaintiffs' patent is to be held invalid because a person working a prior specification in which, so far from being described or claimed, the relevant characteristic seems inferentially to have been excluded, might unwittingly produce it.

Lord Evershed, in arriving at the same conclusion, remarked:

I think therefore notwithstanding the passage to which Mr Mould referred, that it is necessary, if he is to establish his first and broadest proposition, to show not only that peining was at the relevant date a normal method of manufacture to employ, but that if peining were employed it would, save in exceptional cases (as one might say, in 99 cases out of 100) produce the lower lateral seat.

Use: This was alleged to have occurred by manufacture and sale of peined pens having annular spaces below the equator before the priority date. Proof was also proffered of particular instances in which such pens had been given away before that date.

The law on this aspect of the case was discussed only by Evershed M.R.:

Of the various attacks in the way of prior publication made upon the patent in the Court below, the learned Judge, Lloyd-Jacob, J., rejected all the attacks but one. But he came to the conclusion that there had been proved publication by prior user in certain very few specific cases: in the case of two pens supplied to a Mr Hogan and in the case of two pens supplied one each to a Mrs MacLean and a Mr Hulme.

Now, there is, I apprehend, no dispute about the law; and indeed Mr Shelley has not, as I have followed him, contended otherwise than that, if the Judge came to a right conclusion as to the facts or inferences of fact in regard to these cases of supply to Hogan, MacLean and Hulme, then indeed there had been prior publication by user and the patent failed in validity.

The matter is dealt with in the case of *Humpherson v Syer* [1887] 4 R.P.C. 407. I will read a short passage from the judgment of Bowen, L.J., and another short passage from the judgment of Fry, L.J. The case, I should say, was one which concerned a device for preventing water waste, and the passage I am about to read related to the effect of the patentee having asked a gentleman named Widner to make one of the devices. Lord Justice Bowen at p. 413 said: "Was Widner a person to whom this communication had been made in a manner which left him free both in law and equity to do what he like with the information? If so, the information, of course, had been given to a member of the public, and there was nothing further to serve as consideration for any patent."

To the same purpose Fry, L.J., at p. 414 referred to the language of Lindley, L.J., and Cotton, L.J., in an earlier case. In that case, Lindley, L.J., delivering the judgment both of himself and of Cotton, L.J., said: "'On the present occasion it is unnecessary to decide this' – that is another point – 'and without going so far as to say that the judge ought to give such a direction, I am clearly of opinion that the judge ought at least to tell the jury to find for the defendant on the issue that the patentee was the first and true inventor if they thought that the German specification had been so published in this country as to have become known to any one here'". Therefore, in the view of the Lords Justices, the knowledge of any one here was enough to give the public the possession of the invention.

It may seem at first sight a hard result for the patentee; but in light of that authority it is I think clear that if the cases of these few pens were proved, pens having the necessary characteristics so as to bring them with scope of 609,817 – if those few pens came to the hand of Hogan, MacLean and Hulme in circumstances which left them free at law and equity to do whatever they liked with them and what they discovered from them (subject only, of course, to the effect of Patent 564,172) then it would appear to follow that the Plaintiffs must in this case fail.

The Court of Appeal placed no reliance on the case of Hulme, but each member gave substantially similar reasons for agreeing with the trial judge that there had been prior publication through use in the cases of MacLean and Hogan.

Jenkins L.J.:

As to Mrs MacLean, it will be remembered that her story was that a Canadian Air Force man came into her shop and asked her if he could write on the counter. She gave him permission, and he did his writing, and went away, leaving his pen behind. When he returned some time later, she gave him his pen and said that it was a nice one, or something of the sort, and the Canadian then said, "I will get you one for your birthday". This, according to Mrs MacLean, took place in October, 1944, her birthday being on the 28th of that month. In November 1944, according to Mrs MacLean she removed to another shop, and the Canadian redeemed his promise as to the pen by coming to the new shop and presenting her with one. That was some time in November, and she fixed it by the fact that she had moved from one shop to another in November, 1944. There was no doubt as to the provenance of the pen or that it embodied the relevant features of the lower lateral seat and the annular space. The contest centred round the actual date of acquisition. The learned Judge assessed Mrs MacLean's evidence in these words: "The evidence of Mrs MacLean completely satisfied me that the Exhibit V.A.T.B. was acquired by her as and when she asserted".

1.2.1.3 *Bayer's Application* (G 6/88 [1990] O.J. EPO 114 (**Enlarged Board of Appeal**)

This case referred to the Enlarged Board the question whether it was permissible to seek claims in the form "use of compound X for a stated purpose", in order to protect the discovery that the compound, already known for one use, has a further useful characteristic that previously was unknown.

1. Having regard to the purpose for which questions are referred to the Enlarged Board as set out in Article 112 EPC, it is appropriate that the Enlarged Board should not take too narrow a view of the question which has been referred but should consider and answer it in such a way as to clarify the points of law which lie behind it.

2. Prior to the entry into force of the EPC in 1978, the role of patent claims in determining the protection conferred by a patent had developed differently within the national patent systems of the countries that are now Contracting States. Such different developments reflected somewhat different national philosophies underlying the concept of patent protection.

In particular, the extent to which the wording of the claims determined the scope of protection varied considerably from country to country, and this factor significantly affected drafting practice.

In some countries, in particular Germany, in practice the protection conferred by a patent depended more upon what was perceived to be the inventor's contribution to the art, as disclosed in the patent, by way of the general inventive concept, than upon the wording of the claims. In other countries, in particular the United Kingdom, the precise wording of the claims was regarded as crucial, because the claims were required to define the boundary between what was protected and what was not, for purposes of legal certainty.

2.1 The manner in which claims were drafted naturally developed differently in the different countries, depending upon the relative importance of their function. Clearly in a country such as the United Kingdom, the wording of a claim had to provide a much more precise definition of what was sought to be protected than in countries such as Germany, where a statement of the essence of the inventive concept was more appropriate.

2.2 There are basically two different types of claim, namely a claim to a physical entity (e.g. product, apparatus) and a claim to a physical activity (e.g. method, process, use).

Various sub-classes are possible (e.g. a compound, a composition, a machine; or a manufacturing method, a process of producing a compound, a method of testing, etc.). Furthermore, claims including both features relating to physical activities and features relating to physical entities are also possible. There are no rigid lines of demarcation between the various possible forms of claim.

2.3 The question which has been referred to the Enlarged Board is concerned with "use" claims: that is, with claims defining a "use of compound X for a particular purpose", or similar wording.

The recognition or discovery of a previously unknown property of a known compound, such property providing a new technical effect, can clearly involve a valuable and inventive contribution to the art.

In countries such as Germany, such inventions have for many years commonly been sought to be protected by means of "use" claims.

In countries such as the United Kingdom, prior to 1978 such use claims were rarely found in patent applications and patents; a claim to an invention of such a character would normally have been defined in terms of the essential physical steps comprising the "activity" to be protected.

2.4 Despite the entry into force of the EPC, European patent applications originating in the different Contracting States have continued commonly to include claims drafted in accordance with the traditional practices of such Contracting States discussed above.

However, the requirements for drafting claims in respect of inventions which are the subject of European patent applications and patents, and the patentability of such inventions, are all matters which must be decided upon the basis of the law under the EPC. The function of the claims is central to the operation of the European patent system.

2.5 Article 84 EPC provides that the claims of a European patent application "shall define the matter for which protection is sought". Rule 29(1) EPC further requires that the claims "shall define the matter for which protection is sought in terms of the technical features of the invention". The primary aim of the wording used in a claim must therefore be to satisfy such requirements, having regard to the particular nature of the subject invention, and having regard also to the purpose of such claims.

The purpose of claims under the EPC is to enable the protection conferred by the patent (or patent application) to be determined (Article 69 EPC), and thus the rights of the patent owner within the designated Contracting States (Article 64 EPC), having regard to the patentability requirements of Articles 52 to 57 EPC. It follows that the technical features of the invention are the physical features which are essential to it.

When considering the two basic types of claim referred to in paragraph 2.2 above the technical features of a claim to a physical entity are the physical parameters of the entity, and the technical features of a claim to an activity are the physical steps which define such activity. A number of decisions of the Boards of Appeal have held that in appropriate cases technical features may be defined functionally (see e.g. T 68/85, OJ EPO, 1987, 228; T 139/85 EPOR 1987, 229).

3. For the purpose of determining their technical features, the claims must be interpreted in accordance with Article 69(1) EPC and its Protocol. The Protocol was adopted by the Contracting States as an integral part of the EPC in order to provide a mechanism for harmonisation of the various national approaches to the drafting and interpretation of claims discussed in paragraph 2.1 above. The central role of the claims under the EPC would clearly be undermined if the protection and consequently the rights conferred within individual designated Contracting States varied widely as a result of purely national traditions of claim interpretation: and the Protocol was added to the EPC as a supplement primarily directed to providing an intermediate method of interpretation of claims of European patents throughout their life, as a compromise between the various national approaches to interpretation and determination of the protection conferred ("... so as to combine a fair protection for the patentee with a reasonable degree of certainty for third parties").

The object of the Protocol is clearly to avoid too much emphasis on the literal wording of the claims when considered in isolation from the remainder of the text of the patent in which they appear; and also to avoid too much emphasis upon the general inventive concept disclosed in the text of the patent as compared to the relevant prior art, without sufficient regard also to the wording of the claims as a means of definition.

4. The legal problems associated with the patent-ability of claims to the new use of a known compound provided the subject-matter for the first seven Decisions to be issued by the Enlarged Board of Appeal, namely G 1–7/83 (three of which, G 1/83, G 5/83 and G 6/83 in German, English and French respectively, are published in OJ EPO 1985, 60, 64, 67). Such Decisions were all concerned with the patentability of further medical uses for a substance already known to have one medical use; and with the appropriate form of claim in respect of such an invention. All such Decisions have essentially the same content. In this Decision, it is only necessary to refer to the relevant German language Decision, G 1/83.

The present Enlarged Board has considered how far the reasoning there set out bears upon the point of law to be decided in the present case.

The question of law which was referred to the Enlarged Board in G 5/83 arose essentially because of the particular exclusion from patentability in relation to "methods of treatment of the human or animal body" set out in the first sentence of Article 52 (4) EPC, and the exception to that exclusion set out in Article 54 (5) EPC. The reasoning in G 5/83 is therefore primarily directed to answering a question of law concerning the allowability of claims whose subject-matter is a particular kind of medical or veterinary invention. The *ratio decidendi* of that Decision is essentially confined to the proper interpretation of Articles 52(4) and 54(5) EPC in their context.

In that field of technology, the normal type of use claim is prohibited by Article 52(4) EPC, but Article 54(5) EPC expressly provides for an exception to the general rules for novelty (Articles 54(1) to (5) EPC) in respect of the first medical or veterinary use of a substance or composition, by allowing a claim to the substances or compositions for that use. G 1/83 applied this to cases of second and subsequent therapeutic use, but expressly indicated that such a special approach to the derivation of novelty could only be applied to claims to the use of substances or compositions intended for use in a method referred to in Article 52(4) EPC. The present Enlarged Board of Appeal endorses that view.

G 1/83 has the effect of giving to the inventor of a new use for a known medicament a protection analogous to but restricted in comparison with the protection normally allowable for a new non-medical use. The patentability of a second non-medical new and non-obvious use of a product is clearly recognised in principle (see Reasons 21). The patentability of "the (second or subsequent) use of a substance or composition for the manufacture of a medicament for a specified new and inventive therapeutic application" was accepted, because although the exclusion of therapeutic methods from patentability provided in Article 52(4) (on the ground that then these are not susceptible of industrial application) has the effect of excluding from patentability a claim directed to the use of a substance for therapy (see Reasons 13), this type of claim would be clearly allowable (as susceptible of industrial application) for a non-medical use. Compare: "The use of X for treating disease A in mammals" (not allowed), with "The use of X for treating disease B in cereal drops" (allowed).

In contrast, the question of law which has been referred to the Enlarged Board in the present case is not related to medical inventions but is of a general nature, being primarily concerned with the question of interpretation of Article 54(1) and (2) EPC.

5. The question referred assumes that the only novel feature in the claim under consideration is the purpose for which the compound is to be used. However, insofar as the question of interpretation of Article 54(1) and (2) EPC and the question of the allowable scope of protection (if any) of inventions concerning a further non-medical use are matters of general importance, it will be appropriate for this Board to consider the question raised more generally, and in particular to consider other possible constructions for such use claims.

6. As discussed at paragraphs 2 to 2.5 above, the claims of a European patent should clearly define the technical features of the subject invention and thus its technical subject-matter, in order that the protection conferred by the patent can be determined and a comparison can be made with the state of the art to ensure that the claimed invention is *inter alia* novel. A claimed invention lacks novelty unless it includes at least one essential technical feature which distinguishes it from the state of the art.

When deciding upon the novelty of a claim, a basic initial consideration is therefore to construe the claim in order to determine its technical features.

7. In relation to a claim whose wording clearly defines a new use of a known compound, depending upon its particular wording in the context of the remainder of the patent, the proper interpretation of the claim will normally be such that the attaining of a new technical effect which underlies the new use is a technical feature of the claimed invention. In this connection, and with reference to the discussion in paragraphs 2.1

and 2.2 above, it is necessary to bear in mind the Protocol to Article 69 EPC, as discussed in paragraph 4 above. Thus with such a claim, where a particular technical effect which underlies such use is described in the patent, having regard to the Protocol, the proper interpretation of the claim will require that a functional feature should be implied into the claim, as a technical feature; for example, that the compound actually achieves the particular effect.

7.1 An example of such a claim which should be so interpreted can be given by reference to the facts in Decision T 231/85 (OJ EPO 1989, 74). The claims in question define "Use of (certain compounds) . . . for controlling fungi and for preventive fungus control" – and the application contained teaching as to how to carry this out so as to achieve this effect. Prior published document (1) described the use of the same compounds for influencing plant growth. In both application T 231/85 and document (1), the respective treatments were carried out in the same way (so the means of realisation was the same).

The Examining Division held that the claimed invention lacked novelty, apparently on the basis that the means of realisation was the same in document (1), and so the claimed effect underlying the use for fungus control must have been achieved in the treatment described in document (1). The Board of Appeal on the other hand held that the claimed invention was novel, on the basis that the technical teaching ("Lehre") in the application was different from that in document (1), and that the use was hitherto unknown, even though the means of realisation was the same.

In the view of the Enlarged Board, with reference to the discussion concerning the interpretation of claims in paragraph 7, the claim in question should properly be construed, having regard to the Protocol to Article 69 EPC, as implicitly including the following functional technical feature: that the named compounds, when used in accordance with the described means of realisation, in fact achieve the effect (i.e. perform the function) of controlling fungus. Such a functional feature is a technical feature which qualifies the invention: and the use claim is properly to be considered as a claim containing technical features both to the physical entity (the compound and its nature), and to a physical activity (the means of realisation). In other words, when following the method of interpretation of claims set out in the Protocol, what is required in the context of a claim to the "use of a compound A for purpose B" is that such a claim should not be interpreted literally, as only including by way of technical features "the compound" and "the means of realisation of purpose B"; it should be interpreted (in appropriate cases) as also including as a technical feature the function of achieving purpose B (because this is the technical result). Such a method of interpretation, in the view of the Enlarged Board, is in accordance with the object and intention of the Protocol to Article 69 EPC.

If the proper construction of such a claim in the context of a particular patent is such as to include such a functional technical feature, the question which remains to be considered is whether such claimed invention is novel.

8. Article 54(2) EPC defines the state of the art as comprising "everything made available to the public by means of a written or oral description, by use, or in any other way". Thus, whatever the physical means by which information is made available to the public (e.g. written description, oral description, use, pictorial description on a film or in a photograph, etc., or a combination of such means), the question of what has been made available to the public is one of fact in each case.

The word "available" carries with it the idea that, for lack of novelty to be found, all the technical features of the claimed invention in combination must have been communicated to the public, or laid open for inspection.

In the case of a "written description" which is open for inspection, what is made available in particular is the information content of the written description. Furthermore, in some cases, the information which the written description actually contains, teaching the carrying out of a process for example, also makes available further information which is the inevitable result of carrying out such teaching (see in this respect Decision T 12/81 Diastereomers, OJ EPO 1982, 296, Reasons paragraphs 7 to 10, Decision T 124/87, Copolymers EPOR 1989, 33 and Decision T 303/86 Flavour concentrates, EPOR 1989, 95 for example).

In each such case, however, a line must be drawn between what is in fact made available, and what remains hidden or otherwise has not been made available. In this connection the distinction should also be emphasised between lack of novelty and lack of inventive step: information equivalent to a claimed invention may be "made available" (lack of novelty), or may not have been made available but obvious (novel, but lack of inventive step), or not made available and not obvious (novel and inventive). Thus, in particular, what is hidden may still be obvious.

8.1 In cases where, for example, a compound has previously been described as having been used, but for a different purpose from the claimed use, and the previously described use had inherently had the same technical effect as the claimed use, the question arises as to whether there is a lack of novelty. In this connection problems in relation to infringement can also arise if there is no finding of lack of novelty in such circumstances, since a user of the previously described use would risk infringement of a later filed patent.

In respect of this submission, the Enlarged Board would emphasise that under Article 54(2) EPC the question to be decided is what has been "made available" to the public: the question is not what may have been "inherent" in what was made available (by a prior written description, or in what has previously been used (prior use), for example). Under the EPC, a hidden or secret use, because it has not been made available to the public, is not a ground of objection to validity of a European patent. In this respect, the provisions of the EPC may differ from the previous national laws of some Contracting States, and even from the current national laws of some non-Contracting States. Thus, the question of "inherency" does not arise as such under Article 54 EPC. Any vested right derived from prior use of an invention is a matter for national law (see, in this connection, e.g. Article 38 of the Community Patent Convention, not yet in force). Furthermore, as to the suggested problems concerning infringement referred to above, it is to be noted that analogous problems would result from G 1/83 in the medical area.

8.2 This point may be illustrated by a further reference to the facts of Decision T 231/85. If the claims are interpreted as discussed in paragraph 7.1, the question in relation to novelty is whether document (1) made available to the public the technical feature that the compounds, when used as described, achieved the effect of controlling fungus.

The Board of Appeal there referred in its decision to the "hitherto unknown" use of such compounds for controlling fungi and the "unnoticed protective effect" (even though the means of application of such compounds to plants (the "technical realisation") was the same). Thus, although document (1) described a method of treating plants with compounds in order to regulate their growth which, when carried out, would inevitably have been inherently a use of such compounds for controlling fungi, nevertheless it appears that the technical feature of the claim set out above and underlying such use was not "made available" to the public by the prior written description in document (1).

9. The answer to the question referred may therefore be summarised as follows: with respect to a claim to a new use of a known compound, such new use may reflect a newly discovered technical effect described in the patent. The attaining of such a technical effect should then be considered as a functional technical feature of the claim (e.g. the achievement in a particular context of that technical effect). If that technical feature has not been previously made available to the public by any of the means as set out in Article 54(2) EPC, then the claimed invention is novel, even though such technical effect may have inherently taken place in the course of carrying out what has previously been made available to the public.

1.2.1.4   *Catnic Components v C. Evans & Co* **[1983] F.S.R. 401 (Falconer J.)**

The action concerned the lintels that were the subject of Catnic v Hill & Smith *(below, 1.3.1.6), Evans having bought them from Hill & Smith. Evans attacked the validity of the patent (under the Patents Act 1949, s.32(1)) on the basis of prior discovery of the invention by an architect, Edmonds. Some years before the priority date of the patent, Edmonds made a drawing in cross-section for such a lintel and had arranged for a portion of it (not long enough for use) to be made up.*

Falconer J. found that all persons to whom Edmonds had shown his drawings and section were bound by implied obligations of confidence, so that the invention had not been made available to the public. Equally there had been no prior use, since the model did not itself constitute a lintel. The defendant, however, argued that, under the 1949 Act, prior invention was of itself a ground of invalidity, provided that the inventor was himself free in law and equity to use it as he pleased. Reliance was placed particularly on Bristol-Myers' Application *[1969] R.P.C. 146.*

Falconer J.:

That was a case in which the Queen's Bench Divisional Court considered an application for certiorari to set aside a decision of the Patent Appeal Tribunal in an appeal in an opposition to a patent application. The matter in issue was whether a particular prior document, admittedly relevant to its contents, had been published before the priority date of the patent application so as to be available as a prior publication under section 14(1)(e) of the 1949 Act. The document in question was a South African patent specification which had been received from South Africa but in this country by an employee of Boots Pure Drug Company in his capacity as such employee.

I should point out that "published" in the 1949 Act is defined as meaning "made available to the public". Lord Parker C.J., giving the judgment of the court, referred to the decision of the Court of Appeal in the *Fomento* case (above, 1.2.1.2) and, after pointing out (at p. 155) that in the *Fomento* case the Court of Appeal had treated the question of prior user as equivalent to the question whether the giving of the pens had been a publication which made available to the public the means of knowledge of the invention, continued:

> "It seems to us that we are bound by this authority to reject the contention that publication depends either upon anything in the nature of a dedication to the public or upon the degree of dissemination of the information alleged to have been published. On the contrary, if the information, whether in documentary form or in the form of the invention itself, has been communicated to a single

member of the public without inhibiting fetter, that is enough to amount to a making available to the public and we do not think it is open to us to construe the words 'made available to the public' in section 101 in a sense which conflicts with this decision".

It will be noted that the Divisional Court in that case was dealing with a communication to the Boots Pure Drug Company in this country as making available to the public the contents of the document in question, but was not considering any question as to the knowledge of the communicator.

Both those cases derive the principle applied from the early case of *Humpherson v Syer*; but reference to that case shows that it is no authority for the proposition that Mr Jacob seeks to establish in this case, namely, that the knowledge of Mr Edmonds, whom he refers to, and I think rightly, as a "prior inventor", is knowledge which is available to anticipate the plaintiffs' patent. In that case (which is reported in (1887) 4 R.P.C. 184 at first instance and in the same volume at p. 407 in the Court of Appeal) the case concerned a device called a "waste-water preventer". The plaintiff's patent which the defendant was alleged to infringe was for a waste-water preventer without an air valve. The defendant, himself an inventor, had a patent earlier in date for a waste-water preventer with an air valve. Some time before the date of the plaintiff's patent the defendant had given instructions to one Widmer to make up a waste-water preventer and this was made up and the model made was without an air valve, that is to say, was the same as the plaintiff's patented device. One question was whether the disclosure in the instructions to Widmer constituted a publication of the plaintiff's invention or whether it was made in confidence and the passage cited by the Master of the Rolls in the *Fomento* case as the test from the *Humpherson v Syer* case is dealing with that question. In fact, the model in question was apparently also exhibited in the defendant's shop and seen by several people, and that was held to be a prior use which invalidated the plaintiff's patent.

But it is important to notice that it was nowhere suggested either in the case at first instance or in the Court of Appeal, so far as any indication in the two reports goes, that the knowledge of the defendant of the device which anticipated the plaintiff's patent was itself sufficient to invalidate the plaintiff's patent. It seems to me that it must follow that the authority relied upon in the *Fomento* and *Bristol-Myers'* cases, cannot go to the extent of supporting Mr Jacob's proposition that Mr Edmonds' knowledge alone is sufficient to anticipate the plaintiffs' patent in the present case.

However that may be, Mr Bateson for the plaintiffs submits that the defendants are not entitled to rely on Mr Edmonds' own knowledge of his concept and his model. Apart from pointing out that Mr Edmonds' knowledge was confidential to himself, Mr Bateson referred me to a number of authorities, some of which I must refer to now, although I do not propose to refer to all of them. Before I go to them, however, I must state that I apprehend that it has long been well-settled law that a patent is not invalidated for anticipation by reason of the prior knowledge of a third person who, prior to the date of the patent, has himself invented the same invention but has kept it to himself, not making any non-confidential disclosure of it and not attempting to patent it himself, so that the public has had no way of learning of it from him.

As further support, Falconer J. referred to a number of early authorities relied on by counsel for the plaintiff. The first was *Dolland's Case* [1776] 1 W.P.C. 43, of which Buller J. remarked in *Boulton & Watt v Bull* [1795] 2 Hy.Bl.463:

"The objection to Dollond's Patent was that he was not the inventor of the new method of making object glasses, but that Dr Hall had made the same discovery before him. But it was holden that, as Dr Hall had confined it to his closet and the public were not acquainted with it, Dollond was to be considered as the inventor".

Mr Bateson also referred to the notes on that case in Webster at p. 44.

"The preceding would appear to be the first decision on the meaning of the statute in the case of two rival inventors within the realm; the case of *Edgebury v Stephens* [1693] 1 W.P.C. 35, ante p. 35, had decided that the introducer from foreign parts of an invention within the realm is the true and first inventor within the meaning of the statute, and this case decides that publication is essential to the acquiring that character; that user in private, without some publication, will not defeat the claim of the subsequent independent inventor and publisher of his invention under letters patent for the benefit of the public; the question then arises, what user is such a publication as will defeat a patent, and two cases of user present themselves; first, by the patentee; second, by a stranger.

The words of the statute are "The working or making of any manner of new manufactures, which others, at the time of making such letters patent and grant, shall not use; the words of the letters patent are 'new invention as to the public use and exercise thereof'".

I point out that the statue there referred to is, of course, section 6 of the Statute of Monopolies. . . .

After references to a number of cases, the note in Webster continues with a citation from the direction to the jury of Sir N Tindal C.J. – I think in the Court of Common Pleas – in the case of *Cornish v Keene*, and I should read it. Sir N Tindal said:

"It will be for the jury to say whether the invention was or was not in public use and operation at the time the patent was granted. There are certain limits to this question. A man may make experiments in his own closet; if he never communicates these experiments to the world, and lays them by, and another person has made the same experiments, and, being satisfied, takes a patent, it would be no answer to say that another person had made the same experiments: there may be several rivals starting at the same time; the first who comes and takes a patent, it not being generally known to the public, that man has a right to clothe himself with the authority of the patent, and enjoys the benefit of it. If the evidence, when properly considered, classes itself under the description of experiment only, that would be no answer. On the other hand, the use of an article might be so general as to be almost universal; then you can hardly suppose anybody would take a patent. Between these two limits most cases will range themselves; and it must be for the jury to say whether the evidence convinces their understanding that the subject of the patent was in public use and operation at the time when the patent was granted". . . .

The next case cited by Mr Bateson to which I wish to refer is that of *Gadd v Mayor of Manchester* [1892] 9 R.P.C. 516. In that case the plaintiffs' patent related to a construction of gas-holder and the defendants who were sued for infringement attacked its validity on a number of grounds, one of which was that the invention had been prior published by one Terrace, who had invented the same device, and the question was whether Terrace had prior published the invention. . . .

On this issue the decision of the court was unanimous. It is important to note the criterion applied by Lindley L.J. . . . :

"Terrace's invention was never used in public, nor indeed at all; and such knowledge of it as the persons to whom it was communicated really had, cannot be regarded as knowledge acquired by or open to the public in any sense whatever. The public had no access to Mr Terrace's description of his invention. No one had access to that who was not confidentially consulted respecting it." . . .

In my judgment, *Dollond's* case, *Cornish v Keene* and *Gadd's* case, as well as, indeed, *Humpherson v Syer* are sufficient authorities (although that list is not exhaustive) to establish the principles which I stated earlier that I apprehend to have long been well-settled law, namely, that a patent is not invalid by reason of the fact that, before the inventor applied for the patent, another person had independently made the same invention if that earlier inventor has kept his knowledge of it to himself. (I am, of course, considering in this case a patent under the Patents Act 1949, and I say nothing about a patent under the Act of 1977). The later inventor, who applies for the patent for the invention and thus is the first to publish the invention, is the "true and first inventor" in patent law.

It was argued for the defendant that, since the grounds of invalidity had been entirely codified by the Act of 1949 (American Cyanamid's (Dann) Patent [1971] R.P.C. 425 (H.L.)), the need to show consideration for a patent grant had disappeared and the case-law just referred to was no longer applicable. Falconer J. rejected this, relying upon views expressed by Lords Wilberforce, Guest and Diplock in the Dann case and Lord Diplock in Bristol-Myers' (Johnson) Application [1975] R.P.C. 127 that the concept of consideration for the grant underlay several of the statutory grounds of invalidity, including the requirements of novelty and lack of obviousness.

1.2.1.5   *Du Pont's (Witsiepe) Application* [1982] F.S.R. 303 (H.L.)

The application in suit concerned the discovery of a plastic co-polymer which, because of its rapid hardening rate, was specially suited to injection moulding and high-speed extrusion. The co-polymer comprised:

> *(a) terephthalic acid (TPA)*
> *(b) 1, 4-butanediol*
> *(c) a poly (alkylene oxide) glycol*

The opponent asserted that (under the Patents Act 1949, s 14 (1) (b)) the claimed invention had been published in a prior British specification, an ICI patent (No 682,866). This related to a co-polymer for textile fibre with an improved absorption of water, making for easier dyeing. It consisted of elements (a) and (c) in the Du Pont specification together with one of nine glycols, (five of which were specifically named). Among these five was tetramethylene glycol, another name for (b) 1, 4-butanediol. All the examples given in the specification, however, made use of another of the glycols – ethylene glycol. Accordingly the alleged anticipation was a purely paper suggestion.

Lord Wilberforce:

The opponents' case is simply put. The ICI specification gave sufficient directions to enable a chemist to make any of the indicated nine copolyesters. Each and all of these was therefore available to the public. All that is required by the law is that a person of ordinary knowledge and skill in the subject would be able to make the product without the necessity of making further experiments and without taking any new inventive step. This requirement, they claim, was amply satisfied by the ICI specification.

In order to consider whether this argument is correct, or whether it is too simplistic, it is necessary to look more closely at the process by which an invention is disclosed in a document, and the nature of the identification required. There are several principles here involved. First, it may be true to say as a general rule that where an invention for a substance is specifically disclosed, with a claim for particular advantages, or where a substance is already known, a discovery that the disclosed or known substance has some advantage or useful quality not previously recognised does not give a right to a patent. The difficulty arises when disclosure is made of a group or class of substances for which some advantage is claimed, and later it is found that one or more of this group or class possesses special advantages not belonging to the rest of the group or class, and not previously identified. This situation arises particularly in relation to inventions in the chemical field, particularly where molecular combinations are involved. In many fields, of which those concerned with polymeric chains are a good example, the number of combinations of chains, sub-chains, rings, individual molecules, may be very large. When a researcher is able to discover that a particular combination produces advantageous results he will most probably be able to assert, and will assert in the specification of his invention, that the same qualities will be produced by a number of variants or homologues described by a formula, or formulae. Moreover, having described how to produce the particular combination, he may well be able to assert, with truth, that productions of any of the combinations can be made by any skilled chemist, following the indications he has given. Is, then, the mere fact that he has disclosed or published in general terms the possibility of these combinations, in such a way that they can be made, a disclosure or publication of unrecognised advantages which may be found to be possessed by one or some of them?

The law regarding selection patents has been developed to deal with this problem. It has done so in the direction of recognising two objectives, first to protect the original inventor, as regards the invention which he has made, but secondly, to encourage other researchers in the field to use their inventive powers so as to discover fresh advantages and to treat the discovery of such advantages as inherent in selected members of the group or class as a patentable invention. The modern statement of this part of the law as regards chemical patents is the judgment of Maugham J. in *I. G. Farbenindustrie A.G.'s Patents* [1930] 47 R.P.C. 289, a case concerned with chemical combinations for the production of dyes. It has been approved and carried forward in cases concerned with the production of synthetic penicillins, where again the number of possible molecular variations is very large. The present position was compendiously stated by Lord Diplock:

"The patents at any rate to the extent that they claim the products para-hydroxy-penicillin and Amoxycillin respectively, are selection patents.

The inventive step in a selection patent lies in the discovery that one or more members of a previously known class of products possess some special advantage for a particular purpose, which could not be predicted before the discovery was made (In *re I.G. Farbenindustrie A.G.'s Patents* [1930] 47 R.P.C. 283 per Maugham J. at pp 322/3). The *quid pro quo* for the monopoly granted to the inventor is the public disclosure by him in his specification of the special advantages that the selected members of the class possess." (*Beecham Group Ltd v Bristol Laboratories International S.A.* [1978] R.P.C. 521 at 579).

My own opinion contains observations to a similar effect – l.c.p.568.

That case was concerned not with any question as to validity, but with one arising under a contract, but it has been applied to a validity issue by the New Zealand Court of Appeal in a judgment dated 22nd December 1981. The general principle is now securely part of the law and needs no fresh discussion in the present case. I confine myself to such aspects as are necessary for our decision.

In the first place, in order to leave open a field for selection by a subsequent inventor, it does not matter whether the original field is described by formula or by enumeration. A skilled chemist could, in most cases, quite easily transform the one into the other and the rights of the subsequent inventor cannot depend upon the notation used. In the present case, the ICI specification uses both a formula, and, to some extent, an enumeration: it does not matter to which one directs attention.

Secondly, the size of the initial group or class is not in itself decisive as to a question of prior publication of an invention related to a selected member or members. A selection patent might be claimed for one or several out of a class of 10 million (cf *I.G. Farbenindustrie A.G.'s Patents* at p. 321) or for one out of two (cf the selection of one of two epimers of a synthetic penicillin combination). The size of the class may be relevant to a question of obviousness, and that question in turn may depend, in part, upon whether the later invention relates to the same field as that occupied by the prior invention, or to a different field. If an ordinary uninventive man would not be likely to look for the advantages he desires to produce in the area occupied by the prior invention, a decision to do so may well amount to the beginning of an inventive step. Here, to look for a product possessing special thermoplastic and elastomeric qualities in a 20-year old patent concerned with producing dyeable fibres involves, *prima facie*, an inventive approach.

Thirdly, disclosing a prior invention does not amount to prior publication of a later invention if the former merely points the way which might lead to the latter. A much quoted and useful passage is that from the judgment of the Court of Appeal in *General Tire & Rubber Co v Firestone Tyre & Rubber Co* [1972] R.P.C. 456 at 486. There Sachs L.J. said:

> "A signpost, however, clear, upon the road to the patentee's invention will not suffice. The prior inventor must be clearly shown to have planted his flag at the precise destination before the patentee."

Attractive metaphors may be dangerous for those in search of precision, but the passage illustrates the necessity that the alleged prior disclosure must clearly indicate that use of the relevant material (ie that ultimately selected) does result in a product having the advantages predicted for the class. The point is well put by the New Zealand Court of Appeal. Dealing with semi-synthetic penicillin, the court (per Cooke J.) said:

> "If such a compound has not been made before, its properties often cannot be predicted with any confidence: and where that is the case we do not consider that the invention claimed can fairly or accurately be described as 'published,' even if a skilled chemist would realise that to make the compound by routine means would be practicable. A making of the compound and a discovery of its properties is necessary before the 'invention' has occurred and can be published." (My emphasis).

This is in line with, but adds a useful precision to what was said by Maugham J.:

> "It must be remembered, of course, that the selected compounds have not been made before, or the patent would fail for want of novelty." (*I.G. Farbenindustrie A.G.'s Patents*, at p.321).

In *Kaye v Chubb & Sons Ltd* [1887] 4 R.P.C. 289, Lord Esher, M.R., too, had referred to "any clear conclusion ... either as to the result or as to the means" (my emphasis) at p.298.

I do not think that there is any inconsistency between the principle so stated and those authorities which are concerned with the degree of information necessary to enable a product to be made (see *Gillette Safety Razor Co v Anglo-American Trading Co Ltd*, 30 R.P.C. 465; *C Van Der Lely N.V. v Bamfords Ltd* [1963] R.P.C. 61; *Ransburg Co v Aerostyle Ltd* [1968] R.P.C. 287). When one is dealing with this question, the fact that the product has not been made or tested may well be irrelevant, but different considerations arise when the issue is as to the field left open for subsequent researchers.

It is the absence of the discovery of the special advantages, as well as the fact of non-making, that makes it possible for such persons to make an invention related to a member of the class.

Applying the law as I have endeavoured to state it, I have no doubt that the invention made by Du Pont was not disclosed or published by ICI. The latter merely indicated that the use, with other ingredients, of one preferred glycol would produce a compound with particular qualities, suggesting at the same time that use of any one of the other eight glycols would produce the same result. There was no statement that any of these others had in fact been used or that the product resulting therefrom had been found to have any particular advantages. That left it open to Du Pont to select one of them, to exercise upon it inventive research, and to discover that the product so made had valuable properties in a different field. I do not therefore understand how it can be claimed that this product, with its advantages, had been anticipated by ICI.

It is said by the opponents that it is wrong for Du Pont to seek to monopolise one of the products envisaged by ICI which has now passed into the public domain through expiry of the ICI patent. If the Du Pont invention had been made during the currency of the ICI patent, Du Pont, though entitled to exploit its invention, would have had to obtain a licence from ICI to make a product covered by ICI's patent. Now that ICI's invention is in the public domain, there is no need for such a licence and there is no basis in law on which Du Pont's monopoly can be cut down. That Du Pont is able to carve out a new monopoly out of the area claimed by ICI is an inevitable consequence of the doctrine of selection patents. In spite of this, ICI would have been able during the currency of its patent to exploit its preferred product, and variants of it, by use of any of the other diols (other than 1, 4-butanediol). And similarly such use remains available to the public. There is no reason why either ICI or the public should be able to prevent Du Pont from using its own invention: so to prevent it would remove the possibility of selection patents.

For these reasons I agree with the judgments of Whitford J. and the Court of Appeal and would dismiss the appeal.

Lord Simon of Glaisdale after referring, inter alia, to the doctrine of selection patents as formulated by Maugham J. in I.G. Farbenindustrie and Evershed J. in Dreyfus' Application (1945) 62 R.P.C. 125 at 133 continued:

These citations suggest what is the meaning of "class" for the purpose of the law of selection patents. It is a group of products or processes from all of which some particular result or results may be predicted. So, too, products or processes are "related" or "homologous" if some similar result may be predicted of them as may be predicted of other members of the class, and especially of any product or process (also a member of the class) for which a given result has been claimed. If from such a class of related or homologous products or processes a property, quality or use is discovered which could not have been predicted by anyone ordinarily skilled in the art in question, that discovery may be an invention giving rise to a valid selection patent.

If such is the nature of the "class" for the purpose of selection patent law, "specific" must for the purpose of that law stand in contradistinction. The product or process will be specifically patented and as such published in priority, so as to be effectively monopolised and unavailable for any later patent, if it is identified in the earlier specification but is not in that specification a member of a "class" (in the sense suggested above). Even then it will not bar a later patent if it is no more than a starting point on the road to a new invention – is merely what counsel for the appellants called an "enabling disclosure."

In *Hill v Evans* [1862] 4 De G.F. & J. 288, Lord Westbury said at pp. 307, 308:

> "I cannot find in any of those [earlier] patents a clear, distinct and definite indication of the admittedly beneficial discovery that was afterwards made by the Plaintiff."

And in *General Tire & Rubber Co v Firestone Tyre & Rubber Co Ltd* [1972] R.P.C. 457 at 486, Sachs L.J. said:

> "A signpost, however clear, upon the road to the patentee's invention will not suffice. The prior inventor must be clearly shown to have planted his flag at the precise destination before the patentee."

It is not necessary to decide what is the consequence of a new quality or property or use being found in or for a product or process part of a class given in a previous specification but therein also made the subject matter of a formal example. Counsel for the respondents was prepared to concede that the product or process would thereby be so successfully monopolised as to be unavailable as the subject of a valid selection patent. It seemed to Buckley L.J. in the Court of Appeal (p. 395) that such a concession might be necessary, though he refrained from expressing a concluded view. I would myself prefer to leave the point open.

Counsel for the appellants urged powerfully that, if the respondents' general contention was correct, then the polyester using 1, 4-butanediol would be effectively monopolised for all purposes; so that it could be taken out of the public domain at the end of the monopoly period – in the instant case, for example, remonopolised to be used by Du Pont even for dyeing purposes. This point may to some extent be bound up with the question whether the concession I have just referred to had to be made. You cannot obtain a valid patent generally for the discovery of a new quality in or use of a known product or process. But, as Lord Wilberforce pointed out, this does not apply when the new quality or use is discovered in or for a product or process which is merely a member of a class (in the sense used in selection patent law). The subject of the selection patent is the inventive step as described by Lord Diplock. I am not convinced that this necessarily involves that the different inventive step the subject matter of the earlier patent is subsumed. But, if it were, that would be something inherent in the very concept of selection patents, which inevitably involve the taking over by a later patent of part of an area previously claimed in an earlier one for a "class."

Applying the foregoing to the instant appeal, the compound of TPA and 1, 4-butanediol was a member of a class of nine glycol compounds in the ICI patent. It could not have predicted that this class of nine glycols, singly or *seriatim*, named or innominate, would have any property or quality giving novel utility in injection moulding etc. The compound in the ICI patent was not "specific" within the meaning of selection patent law. Du Pont's discovery that the compound of TPA and 1, 4-butanediol had the said unpredictable property or quality meant that the discovery was an inventive step such as would give rise to a valid selection patent. Until it had been made and tested for such property or quality it was not "known or used" within the meaning of section 32(1)(e) of the Patents Act 1949.

It follows that I respectfully agree with the judgments of the courts below; and I would dismiss the appeal.

Lord Keith of Kinkel:

I have had the benefit of reading in draft the speeches prepared by my noble and learned friends Lord Wilberforce and Lord Simon of Glaisdale, and I am in agreement with the reasoning therein contained. I share the doubts expressed by my noble and learned friend Lord Simon of Glaisdale as to whether upholding the validity of the respondents' patent necessarily involves that the use of their compound for producing fibres capable of being readily dyed will be included in their monopoly, and I do not consider it necessary or appropriate that any concluded opinion on that matter should be expressed.

My Lords, I too would dismiss the appeal.

Lord Russell of Killowen and Lord Bridge of Harwich concurred in both these speeches.

1.2.2   Inventive Step

1.2.2.1   Patents Act 1977, s.3 Inventive step

S.3 An invention shall be taken to involve an inventive step if it is not obvious to a person skilled in the art, having regard to any matter which forms part of the state of the art by virtue only of section 2(2) above (and disregarding section 2(3) above).

1.2.2.2   *Williams v Nye* (1890) 7 R.P.C. 62 (C.A.)

The plaintiff patented a machine for making sausages which was in effect a combination of a mincing machine and a filling machine, both of which were old. He brought an action for infringement against the defendant who put in issue the validity of the patent on the ground that the alleged invention consisted simply in joining two well-known machines, and therefore lacked subject matter.

Lindley L.J.:

I also think that, having regard to Gilbert and Nye's patent, the present Appeal cannot be supported. Gilbert and Nye's patent consisted of two things: first of all there was the cutting part: and then there was the filling part, that filling part being a screw which operated upon the cut meat and forced it along into the skin which had to be filled. Donald improved the cutting part. He did nothing to the filling part, but left it out. Therefore what has the Plaintiff done? He has simply taken, so far as I can see, Gilbert and Nye's invention, and has substituted Donald's cutter for Gilbert's cutter. That is the whole of what he has done. I do not think a patent can be granted for that considering that the object was perfectly well known; that the utility of the forcing nozzle was known; that the object of it had been attained before, and there is nothing which amounts to what is understood by an invention. I think in principle the decision in *Harwood v The Great Northern Railway Company* (1864) 11 H.L. (at 654) governs this case, and that the patent must be held invalid.

Cotton L.J. delivered a longer judgment to similar effect and Lopes L.J. agreed.

1.2.2.3   *General Tire v Firestone* [1972] R.P.C. 457 at 484–6, 497–500 (C.A.)

Sachs L.J.:

ANTICIPATION

(1) General

The word "Anticipation" is not used in the text of the Patents Act, 1949, although it appears in the side notes to sections 7 and 8 of the Act. The language of section 32 (1)(e), with which we are concerned on this aspect of this case, is as follows:

"That the invention, so far as claimed in any claim of the complete specification, is not new having regard to what was known or used, before the priority date of the claim, in the United Kingdom."

Stated in the shortest terms, the problem is to determine whether the device, to use a neutral expression, has been forestalled in this country. For the sake of clarity we will refer to the patentee or would-be patentee of the device which is alleged to have been anticipated as the "patentee" and to the inventor of the device which is alleged to constitute anticipation as the "prior inventor".

In the present case we are not concerned with anticipation by earlier use of the patentee's device but with anticipation by prior publication: that is to say, it is contended that the plaintiffs' invention as claimed in their patent was at the priority date of their claim something which was known in the United Kingdom by reason of prior publications. To determine whether a patentee's claim has been anticipated by an earlier publication it is necessary to compare the earlier publication with the patentee's claim. The earlier publication must, for this purpose, be interpreted as at the date of its publication, having regard to the relevant surrounding circumstances which then existed, and without regard to subsequent events. The patentee's claim must similarly be construed as at its own date of publication having regard to the relevant surrounding circumstances then existing. If the earlier publication, so construed, discloses the same device as the device which the patentee by his claim, so construed, asserts that he has invented, the patentee's claim has been anticipated, but not otherwise. In such circumstances the patentee is not the true and first inventor of the device and his claimed invention is not new within the terms of section 32(1)(e).

The earlier publication and the patentee's claim must each be construed as they would be at the respective relevant dates by a reader skilled in the art to which they relate having regard to the state of knowledge in such art at the relevant date. The construction of these documents is a function of the court, being a matter of law, but, since documents of this nature are almost certain to contain technical material, the court must, by evidence, be put in the position of a person of the kind to whom the document is addressed, that is to say, a person skilled in the relevant art at the relevant date. If the art is one having a highly developed technology, the notional skilled reader to whom the document is addressed may not be a single person but a team, whose combined skills would normally be employed in that art in interpreting and carrying into effect instructions such as those which are contained in the document to be construed. We have already described the composite entity deemed to constitute the notional skilled addressee.

When the prior inventor's publication and the patentee's claim have respectively been construed by the court in the light of all properly admissible evidence as to technical matters, the meaning of words and expressions used in the art and so forth, the question whether the patentee's claim is new for the purposes of section 32(1)(e) falls to be decided as a question of fact. If the prior inventor's publication contains a clear description of, or clear instructions to do or make, something that would infringe the patentee's claim if carried out after the grant of the patentee's patent, the patentee's claim will have been shown to lack the necessary novelty, that is to say, it will have been anticipated. The prior inventor, however, and the patentee may have approached the same device from different starting points and may for this reason, or it may be for other reasons, have so described their devices that it cannot be immediately discerned from a reading of the language which they have respectively used that they have discovered in truth the same device; but if carrying out the directions contained in the prior inventor's publication will inevitably result in something being made or done which, if the patentee's patent were valid, would constitute an infringement of the patentee's claim, this circumstance demonstrates that the patentee's claim has in fact been anticipated.

If, on the other hand, the prior publication contains a direction which is capable of being carried out in a manner which would infringe the patentee's claim, but would be at least as likely to be carried out in a way which would not do so, the patentee's claim will not have been anticipated, although it may fail on the ground of obviousness. To anticipate the patentee's claim the prior publication must contain clear and unmistakable directions to do what the patentee claims to have invented: *Flour Oxidizing Co Ltd v Carr & Co Ltd* [1908] 25 R.P.C. 428 at 457, line 34, approved in *B.T.H. Co Ltd v Metropolitan Vickers Electrical Co Ltd* [1928] 45 R.P.C. 1 at 24, line 1. A signpost, however clear, upon the road to the patentee's invention will not suffice. The prior inventor must be clearly shown to have planted his flag at the precise destination before the patentee. . . .

OBVIOUSNESS

(1) General

Section 32(1), head (f), reads:

> "that the invention, so far as claimed in any claim of the complete specification, is obvious and does not involve any inventive step having regard to what was known or used before the priority date of the claim in the United Kingdom."

In relation to the word "obvious" we were assisted by Sir Lionel Heald reminding us as to how this word came to be introduced into patent law – referring us to the speeches of Lord Herschell in the *American Braided Wire* case [1889] 6 R.P.C. 518 at 528 and in *Vickers v Siddell* [1890] 7 R.P.C. 292 at 305. There were also cited to us a considerable number of cases in which the meaning of this word was discussed in relation to particular facts. We agree, however, with what was said by Diplock, L.J. (as he then was) and Willmer, L.J. in the *Johns-Manville* case [1967] R.P.C. 479 at 493 and 496 deprecating "coining" phrases which may later be suggested to be of general application. "Obvious" is, after all, a much-used word and it does not seem to us that there is any need to go beyond the primary dictionary meaning of "very plain".

When head (f) is invoked it is, of course, as previously indicated, for whoever seeks revocation of a patent to show that the alleged inventive step was obvious to a normally skilled addressee in the art. On the way to that end there are here a number of preliminary questions to be resolved. These include the common general knowledge to be imputed to that addressee; whether what had to be done to achieve the step was truly a matter of inventive experiment or merely a matter of that type of trial and error which forms part of the normal industrial function of such an addressee; what documents he would find in the course of such researches as he would be expected to make; and how he would regard those documents in the light of common general knowledge. Then finally one has to consider whether the step is properly described as a new combination of integers or merely as a collocation of old ones. None of these questions, some of which inevitably overlap, is easy to resolve, and on each it is for the appellants to establish their contentions.

As regards obviousness as a whole the trial judge approached the matter correctly when he said, [1970] F.S.R. at 302:

> "The question of obviousness is seldom easy to decide. It has been said to be a kind of jury question and, in the days when patent actions were tried before a judge and jury, was treated so. The decision is ultimately one for the court which cannot let its function in this respect be usurped by the witnesses, though undoubtedly the evidence of the witnesses may help the court to arrive at its decision. It must be decided objectively and, being a jury question, it is right that all the relevant circumstances of the case should be taken into account. That this is the correct view of the matter is clear both from the old cases and the new."

His observations naturally apply with equal force to each of the questions which need resolution on the way to giving a final answer on the issue.

It is as well in relation to the evidence in the instant case at this point to refer to the need for objective as opposed to subjective tests. The question is whether the step was obvious to a normally qualified skilled addressee in 1950 – as opposed to the person who in fact claims to be the inventor or to any particular rival of his. Indeed, it is not infrequent that the inventor is not himself called as a witness in a patent action. That, however, does not rule out evidence as to how the problems were in fact approached at the relevant time by the patentee, by his rivals, or by others. What they did may provide significant signposts leading to the answer to the objective test. In this behalf the literature – both the widely read documents and the internal memoranda of Goodyear and the Office of Rubber Reserve already mentioned provide valuable evidence as also do the actual experiments carried out by the plaintiffs in the year preceding the date of the patent-in-suit – though this material happens originally to have been admitted into evidence on an issue other than obviousness.

(2) The Semperit and Wilmington Specifications

With those preliminary observations it is convenient at the outset to consider Mr Templeman's strongly pressed submission that although the Semperit and Wilmington specifications formed no part of the common general knowledge of the skilled addressee, yet when we consider the issue of obviousness he must be deemed to have seen and read every word of them.

His primary contention was that the addressee must be deemed to be a man who as regards every potentially relevant specification "sits down, reads and knows every word in it" and is a man with an "enormous memory". In the alternative he argued that the addressee must be taken to have made a diligent search (see the *Technograph* case, per Lord Reid, [1971] F.S.R. at 193–D) for all relevant documents including specifications, and that upon such a search he would have come across Semperit (a), Semperit (c) and Wilmington. In either case it was urged that this addressee must be deemed to have fully read the three specifications and that, keeping them simultaneously in mind, in addition to the widely read publications, the alleged inventive step or steps would have been obvious to him.

If the primary submission is correct then as regards specifications the word "known" in head (f) of section 32(1) includes all public knowledge and thus embraces everything that is "published" within the meaning of that word as defined in section 101 of the 1949 Act: moreover, it makes the words "known or used" in relation to obviousness have the same meaning as in head (e) which deals with anticipation. On this point there was a divergence of opinion in the *Technograph* case between Lord Reid (with whom Lord Morris of Borth-y-Gest agreed) and Lord Diplock. The former at page 193 said:

> "Attention was drawn to the fact that both heads (e) and (f) in section 32 contain the words 'having regard to what was known or used . . . in the United Kingdom'. I doubt whether they were intended to mean the same in each case. If they were there would now be little, if any, difference between novelty and obviousness",

and a little later stated:

> "I think that in head (f) the words should have the more natural meaning of what was or ought to have been known to a diligent searcher."

Lord Diplock, on the other hand, when discussing head (f) said at page 201:

"I do not, as at present advised, think that the meaning of those words is any different in paragraph (e)."

Both opinions were *obiter* in view of concessions made in their Lordships' House, and having regard to what we are about to determine on the assumption that Lord Diplock's view is correct we do not find it necessary to decide between them on this important question, which manifestly needs an authoritative answer in due course. In case, however, this matter goes further and our determination on that assumption is found not to be correct, we think it apposite to say that as at present advised we would, if it is open to us, have been disposed to hold that "known" in head (f) does not include everything that comes within the definition of "published" in section 101: and we note that the word "published", although it appears in section 14(1)(e) (which deals with obviousness in relation to oppositions to grants), is not incorporated into head (f) of section 32(1), which incidentally uses language very different to that in head (a).

We would add that we find some cogency in the observation in Halsbury's Laws of England, Vol. 29, page 30, para 63:

"It would be absurd to presume that knowledge of every publication affecting any branch of industry or art must be simultaneously in the mind of a person engaged therein"

although those words relate to common general knowledge. No authority binding on us was cited which states in general terms any proposition as wide as that of Mr Templeman's primary submission, nor indeed any which seems to make it necessary to give the word "known" in head (f) a meaning other than one natural in relation to a real person who is a skilled addressee – and that meaning would include what a competent addressee ought to know, but would not burden him with anything further in the nature of constructive notice.

As regards diligent search, a phrase which we were given to understand originates from Lord Reid in *Technograph* (above), we take this as apt to describe what research groups employed by large-scale concerns, such as those in the *Technograph* case and in the instant case, ought to know. Such researches, however, can involve not only heavy expenditure but also questions of priorities in the use of available manpower. What extent of search is appropriate in a given case and what would be its probable results are questions of fact. On these we have not the advantage of the views of the trial judge, who delivered judgment before the date of the *Technograph* decision in the House of Lords.

We have already referred to the location of the Semperit specifications and to the main clues to their existence. We also have before us some evidence from the appellants' witnesses as to searches made with a view to finding material with which to attack the patent-in-suit. Those searches were, of course, initiated with advance knowledge that those concerned were looking for "material relating to oil-extended rubber". The person who actually found the Semperit documents was not called: but a Mr Jackson, employed to make such searches, was in fact occupied upon them in various directions for some four to six weeks. Dr Duck expressed the view that whilst he might have got "an enormous fee" for the search, yet if one is determined enough one can find anything, and did not consider that there would have been difficulty in bringing the Semperit specifications to light.

Taking the evidence as a whole, and having looked at the terms of the abridgements (G.S.p.8,220 and 8,217) available in Book 8 of Vol. 3 of the Patent Office, we doubt whether, on balance of probabilities, a normally diligent search by persons seeking a solution to the problem of the "gap" mentioned earlier in this judgment but not knowing the answer in advance would have brought Semperit (a) or Semperit (c) to attention as potentially useful material. It may perhaps be pertinent to note that these applications, unlike the Wilmington specification, were not mentioned to us as having been relied upon in the course of the lengthy opposition proceedings which, as previously mentioned, occupied some five or six years.

1.2.2.4 *Bayer's (Baatz – Carbonless Copying Paper) Application* [1982] O.J. EPO 206 (Tech. Bd. App.)

The application concerned a carbonless copying paper. The material on the surface of the paper which would act in place of a carbon sheet was a dye contained in micro-capsules. An earlier published specification (German application, No. 2,251,381) revealed that the walls of the capsules could be made of a particular class of polyisocyanates. The claimed invention was said to lie in the selection of a sub-group of this class. The Examining Division held the selection obvious. But on appeal, the applicant produced evidence of comparative tests showing, as the advantage of the selection, that the paper did not so rapidly lose its copying capacity.

Referring to this prior art, the Board of Appeal stated:

6 The indisputably *novel* carbonless copying papers according to the application differ from these in that a more precisely presented oxadiazinetrione diisocyanate is employed as polyisocyanate. To this extent the problem could be seen as the mere preparation of another carbonless copying paper ...

8 As shown in comparative experiments 20–22, the applicant had defined the *problem*, vis-a-vis the nearest prior art as not just preparing other copying papers but *improved* copying papers.

Referring to the prior art already mentioned, the Board stated:

11 But from the point of view of the problem of preparing copying paper having improved storage stability, the prior art cited by the Examining Division did not give any indication for selection of the more precisely prescribed oxadiazinetrione diisocyanate according to the claim from the enormous number of possible polyisocyanates for the micro-encapsulation of dyestuff-intermediates.

Referring to another similar prior specification, the Board said:

12 The document does not furnish any inducement to employ the oxadiazinetrione diisocyanates for the production of *improved* copying papers: since this special class of compounds is merely mentioned incidentally and not emphasised by an example. Mere mention of a group of substances amongst numerous other groups of substances permits at best a surmise of comparable suitability and effectiveness for the purpose in hand if these groups of substances are interchanged.

A further prior specification covered (inter alia) polyisocyanates within the current application for use as coatings for wood, metal and the like and for mouldings and foam. The Board commented:

13 Even with knowledge of this prior art the person skilled in the art could at the most expect that if he were to use these oxadiazinetrione diisocyanates to produce wall material for micro-capsules he would get only qualitatively and quantitatively

similar results as in German unexamined application 2,251,381. Thus the person skilled in the art who – as in this case – had tried to improve the copying papers specified in German unexamined application 2,251,381 would, on the basis of the prior art cited, not have arrived at the solution claimed in the application. The teaching of the present application, that the employment of the oxadiazinetrione diisocyanates as claimed leads to significantly improved copying papers must – independently of whether it is expressed in the form of the product claim 1 or the use claim 2 – be regarded as surprising, and hence involving an inventive step within the meaning of Article 56 EPC.

1.2.2.5   *Fives-Cail Babcock's Application* [1982] O.J. EPO 225 (Tech. Bd. App.)

The applicant for a European patent claimed to have discovered that scrapers for cleaning an endless conveyor belt could be effectively supported by rods made of plastic reinforced by glass fibre. In the prior art, these rods were made of metal and had a tendency to break. Claim 1 was in the following form:

1 Cleaning apparatus for endless conveyor belt, comprising a set of independent scrapers connected to a support by means of elastic elements, characterised in that each elastic element is composed of a glass-fibre-reinforced plastics rod.

The main issue on appeal to the EPO Technical Board of Appeal was whether this involved an inventive step over the prior art:

4.1 According to what the applicant says in his submission received on 30 December 1981, there are disadvantages in using elastic elements made of metal as a means of supporting the scrapers, because such metal components often break.

Considering that the rod-shaped design of elastic elements in an apparatus possessing the features indicated in the first part of Claim 1 was already known (see the drawing in patent specification DT 58900, particularly reference symbol 5), the problem to be solved in connection with the apparatus according to Claim 1 consists in discovering a rod-shaped elastic element which is less prone to breakage.

4.2 This problem undeniably confronts the conveying equipment specialist: however, it prompts him at the same time to seek its solution in the field of materials science. Consequently, the skilled person qualified to solve the problem cannot be a conveying equipment specialist, but has to be a materials specialist alone. Therefore, the assessment of whether the problem's solution (which, according to Claim 1, consists in replacing metal by a synthetic resin reinforced with glass fibres) involves an inventive step must be made by reference to the knowledge and ability of a materials specialist, not a conveying equipment specialist.

4.3 A materials specialist customarily uses plastics in place of traditional materials, particularly in cases where traditional materials would not function satisfactorily, in the present case. The skilled person knows that the only suitable possibility is a synthetic material of sufficient elasticity and fatigue strength. He also knows that synthetic resins reinforced with glass fibres meet those requirements. It thus immediately occurs to him to suggest using a synthetic resin reinforced with glass fibres as the material for rod-shaped elastic elements.

If the skilled person is unsure whether glass fibre rods break less easily than the known springy strips or rods, he can simply conduct an experiment.

4.4 For the foregoing reasons, the Board cannot agree with the applicant that the skilled person relevant in the assessment whether the invention involves an inventive step is the specialist in the technical field indicated in the preamble of the claim.

4.5 Thus, the subject-matter of Claim 1 does not involve an inventive step (Article 56 EPC).

Claim 1 is therefore not allowable under Article 52(1) EPC.

1.2.2.6 *Mobey Chemical's Application* [1982] O.J. EPO 394 (Tech. Bd. App.)

The applicant claimed a process for producing MBP (methylenebis phenyl isocyanate) which was liquid and stable in storage by heating the substance in the presence of a catalyst (PO – phosopholine acid) to a temperature of 180° to 300°C and then quenching it to 100°C or less. This was said to be an improvement over the prior art in which quenching was not used and the catalyst had to be removed by the use of a poison which itself had undesirable consequences. Alternatively higher temperatures had to be used.

6 In summary it is clear that, given the problem to be solved, neither the methods of the prior art individually, nor their respective combination with the generally available specialist knowledge, would make the solution according to the invention with the advantageous effects achieved foreseeable. While it is inadmissible to combine unrelated or conflicting documents in order to deny inventive step, it is indeed permissible to consider various documents together mosaically in order to prove a prejudice or a general trend pointing away from the invention. The idea of departing from the catalyst poison regarded as indispensable, in conjunction with the teaching that the PO catalysts decompose at higher temperature, represents a valuable simplification of the state of the art which could not have been found without an inventive step.

1.2.2.7 *Beecham Group's (Amoxycillin) Application* [1980] R.P.C. 261 (C.A.)

In 1958 Beechams discovered and claimed (873,049) a very large class of penicillins – the aminoacyl derivatives of 6 amino-penicillanic acid (6,APA) – as being compounds valuable as antibiotics. In 1960 and 1962 they obtained two patents of addition (902,703 and 978,178) claiming one and then nine members of the wide class as having particularly desirable properties especially in respect of their activity against gram-negative bacteria. These specifications did disclose that each penicillin had two "mirror image" (stereo-isometric) forms, the l(+) and d(−) epimers; and that production of these would normally appear in mixed (racemic (dl)) form, though they could subsequently be separated.

When 978,178 was applied for, the only tests reported were upon racemic para-hydroxy penicillin and racemic meta-hydroxy penicillin; both were stated to give better results than the compound in 902,703 (Ampicillin), the meta-hydroxy being more successful than the para-hydroxy. Nothing specific was said about the d(−) epimer of the para-hydroxy penicillin because no work had yet been done on it. Subsequent tests eventually revealed that this particular form was exceptionally well absorbed into the bloodstream. Accordingly Beechams applied (1,241,844) to patent this under an (amended) claim to "a pharmaceutical composition adapted for oral administration to human beings containing as an active ingredient [the d(−) epimer – amoxycillin] or a non-toxic salt thereof, the said acid or non-toxic salt being subsequently free of the corresponding l(+) epimeric form".

Bristol Myers opposed this application under the Patents Act 1949, s 14(1), on grounds of anticipation and obviousness in the light of the earlier specification.

On the question of novelty, Buckley L.J. said:

In *Flour Oxidizing Co Ltd v Carr & Co Ltd* [1908] 25 R.P.C. 428, Parker J., a judge of great authority in this branch of the law, said that to anticipate a claim in a later patent an earlier publication must contain clear and unmistakable directions to do something falling within the later claim, ie something which, if carried out after the date of the later patent would amount to an infringement of it. When considering whether a claim has been anticipated, all other possible grounds of invalidity should, in my opinion, be disregarded. The claim should, for that purpose, be treated as valid unless anticipated. Anticipation and obviousness should be kept distinct (see per Lindley L.J. in *Gadd & Mason v Mayor etc of Manchester* [1892] 9 R.P.C. 516 at 525. If the later claim is for something which is no more than an obvious development or application of the earlier publication, it may well be invalid on the ground of obviousness, or lack of invention, but not of anticipation. 978,178 does not in terms tell the reader to combine Amoxycillin with a suitable carrier so as to produce a composition suitable for administration to humans. It does not in terms comply with Parker J.'s test of giving clear and unmistakable directions. But Mr Hirst says – and I hope that I summarise his argument fairly – that *sub silentio* 978,178 does tell the reader to make a composition suitable for administration to man. Mr Hirst says that 978,178 taught the reader that, amongst other penicillins claimed by that patent, Amoxycillin was valuable for, *inter alia*, therapeutic treatment of infectious diseases caused by gram-positive and gram-negative bacteria in man. It was then common knowledge how to harness such a compound to a suitable carrier for oral administration to humans. Therefore, says Mr Hirst, 978,178 taught all that was necessary to enable a skilled man to make such a composition. 978,178 consequently, in Mr Hirst's submission, anticipates claim 1 of the patent in suit. This argument, in my opinion, confuses anticipation with obviousness, but in case I am wrong in that view let me consider the contention. . . .

Dr Rolinson (Beecham's senior micro-biologist) goes on to discuss the tests to which any new semi-synthetic penicillin must be subjected before it can be submitted to the Committee on Safety of Medicines for permission to carry out clinical trials in hospitals or general medical practice. The programme of testing adopted by Beecham falls under six heads, viz: (1) initial tests in vitro for anti-bacterial activity; (2) further in vitro evaluation involving a large number of strains of particular bacteria tested under various conditions; (3) evaluation in vivo for determining the activity of the product against experimental bacterial infection in animals; the value of the initial test in animals lies primarily in the fact that it can show that the penicillin is capable of functioning against an infection in a living body; more detailed tests in animals are required in order to interpret activity in vivo in a quantitative sense and to make comparisons with other penicillins and other antibiotics; (4) pharmacological tests in animals involving the study of the absorption, distribution, metabolism and excretion of the penicillin in experimental animals; (5) pharmacological tests in human volunteers, at which stage the absorption, metabolism and excretion of the penicillin is studied in humans, one of the most important aspects being the level of absorption of the penicillin into the blood; (6) full toxicological studies and clinical trials. At this final stage the way in which the drug affects the test animals is studied in great depth. Animals are dosed with the drug in small and large amounts. Any adverse effects in the living animal are noted, some animals are killed and their organs examined for damage caused by the drug. All possible adverse effects are looked for. The drug is again tested in human volunteers and the metabolic products, if any, obtained from the urine of the volunteers are identified and themselves looked at for toxic effects. When all these studies are completed satisfactorily, a dossier is compiled summarising the results and is sent to the Committee on the Safety of Medicines with a request for permission to carry out clinical trials in hospitals or in general practice. . . .

It is apparent from 978,178 that at the date of that patent the testing of the penicillins claimed by that patent had only been taken to Dr Rolinson's stage 3. That patent made no disclosure or promise, and contained no teaching, about the characteristics of the penicillins which it covered beyond those contained in the table at page 3, which relates to stage 3 tests in vivo in mice against only two gram-negative bacteria. In my judgment, therefore, it is not correct to say that 978,178 taught that Amoxycillin would necessarily prove suitable for treatment of humans. The patent in suit, on the other hand, as amended, claims a pharmaceutical composition for oral administration to human beings. For these reasons I agree with the learned judge's conclusion that Beechams succeed on the issue of anticipation. I proceed to consider the question of obviousness. . . .

It is clearly established that, for a particular step or process to be obvious for the purpose of either section, it is not necessary to establish that its success is clearly predictable (*Johns-Manville Corporation's Patent* [1967] R.P.C. 479 at 494 line 10). It will suffice if it is shown that it would appear to anyone skilled in the art but lacking in inventive capacity that to try the step or process would be worthwhile (*Technograph Printed Circuits Ltd v Mills & Rockley (Electronics) Ltd* [1972] R.P.C. 346, per Lord Reid at 355 line 37 and 356 line 3; *Johns-Manville*, above, per Diplock L.J. at 493 and 494; *Tetra Molectric Ltd v Japan Imports Ltd* [1976] R.P.C. 547 at 581 line 41, 583 line 37, 584 line 2). Worthwhile to what end? It must, in my opinion, be shown to be worth trying in order to solve some recognised problem or meet some recognised need. The uninventive expert (see [1972] R.P.C. page 355, line 5) should not be supposed to be attempting to discover something new, that is, to be striving for inventiveness. Having been shown what was disclosed by the prior art, he must be supposed to be attempting to solve some problem or fulfil some need which has not been resolved or satisfied by the prior art but which appears to his uninventive mind to be possibly capable of solution or satisfaction by taking the step or doing the thing under consideration. This, seems to me, must involve the uninventive but skilled man having a particular problem or need in mind. If on carrying out his test he finds that the new step has the sort of consequence he had hoped but in an unexpectedly high degree, this would or might not mean that the new step was inventive or other than obvious; it might merely mean that a new and obvious step has solved the problem or met the need unexpectedly well. The question would, I think, be one of degree. If, on the other hand, the new step produces some unexpected result productive of an improvement or benefit of an unexpected kind it may well be held to be inventive, the association of the new step with its result not having been obvious. Where, however, the skilled man has no particular problem or need in mind but merely regards some part of the known art as giving a good lead for further research, which may result in the discovery of some useful further knowledge, can the result of that research and its ascertainment by carrying out the research be obvious in the relevant sense? I think not, although this also may be a question of degree. By selecting the research, the researcher is, in my view, demonstrating that he is not wholly devoid of inventive capacity. He is not merely employing an obvious technique to get round an awkward corner; he is seeking to extend the field of human knowledge. The distinction is between a mere exercise of ingenuity and a voyage of discovery.

Buckley L.J. then reviewed the evidence in detail and concluded:

I am fully prepared to assume on the evidence before the court that 978,178 should be regarded as having made clear to one skilled in the field of penicillins that the epimers of the para-hydroxy and the meta-hydroxy compounds were likely to prove fruitful avenues of research, possibly the most promising avenues known to exist. I accept that the lines which that research would follow would be what Bristol witnesses described as "routine", ie well-known. I accept that anyone experienced in penicillin research who pursued research along those avenues would probably have found what Beecham found. But with great deference to the learned judge, I do not agree that this is enough to constitute the claim to Amoxycillin as a penicillin for administration to humans obvious for the purposes of section 14(1)(e) of the Act. To reach the discovery of the particular characteristics of Amoxycillin and its suitability for treating humans the research worker would have had to embark upon a voyage of discovery. It is possible now to see that his voyage would have been short and perhaps uneventfully straightforward, but where each of his two, or possibly more, vessels would make landfall and what those places would be like would not have been obvious to him at the outset. The voyage might have been clearly worth trying but not as a means of reaching a specific hoped-for destination.

On this ground and with diffidence I venture to differ from Graham J. and to hold that the opponents have not established that claim 1 of 1,241,844 as amended was obvious having regard to the disclosures in 978,178.

Browne and Templeman L.JJ. delivered concurring judgments.

1.2.2.8 *Johns-Manville's Patent* [1967] R.P.C. 479 (C.A.)

Asbestos cement (a mixture of asbestos, cement and silica) was prepared from a slurry – a concentrated aqueous suspension of finely divided particles – of these ingredients. The process of producing shaped asbestos cement articles, such as pipes, from this slurry was well known and widely used at the priority date of the patent. The first step was to pick up from a cylinder rotating in the wet mixing vat a thin skin of the slurry on a moving belt made of felt which acted as a filter through which the water was drained from the solids until the mixture had reached the right consistency to enable the skin of asbestos cement on the felt to be transferred mechanically to a revolving cylinder upon which it built up in spiral layers or laminations.

The use of flocculating agents to aid filtration was well known. But the flocculating agents previously available had not been found effective for use in the production of shaped asbestos cement articles. The alleged invention in the patent in suit consisted simply of adding to the mixture of suspended solids to be filtered in the process of manufacturing asbestos cement pipes the known, but recently developed, flocculating agent, polyacrylamide, in the proportions recommended by the manufacturers of that product. The respondents claimed that the patent was invalid for obviousness.

Diplock L.J. (for the court):

The successful use of this flocculating agent in the process called for some adjustment in the operation of the manufacturing plant such as increasing the speed of movement of the felt filter, or adding more water to the slurry. Those adjustments are not referred to in the specification, and it is now common ground that it was unnecessary to do so, for the need for adjustments and the nature of those required would be obvious to anyone skilled in the industry. Their introduction would accordingly involve no inventive step.

If there is any inventive step involved in the appellants' claim, it is in the idea of using a known, but recently developed, flocculating agent in a known filtration process in which it had not been used before. This idea, when put into practice as indicated in the specification, with the necessary but unspecified adjustments to the plant, does produce substantial economies of manufacture. If the idea was not obvious, the invention claimed is patentable.

The respondents' case was simply that "a person versed in the art" of manufacturing asbestos cement pipes (which nowadays means a hypothetical and highly qualified technologist in the research department of asbestos cement pipe manufacturers) would be likely to read the two publications referred to, and that if he did so the information which they contained about polyacrylamides would make him realise that here was a flocculating agent which was well worth trying out in the filtration process used in his own industry in order to see whether it would have beneficial results. If that had been established, the respondents in my view have made out their case that the idea of using polyacrylamides as flocculating agents in the manufacture of cement asbestos pipes was, at the priority date, "obvious and clearly did not involve any inventive step."

I have endeavoured to refrain from coining a definition of "obviousness" which counsel may be tempted to cite in subsequent cases relating to different types of claims. Patent law can too easily be bedevilled by linguistics, and the citation of a plethora of cases about other inventions of different kinds. The correctness of a decision upon an issue of obviousness does not depend upon whether or not the decider has paraphrased the words of the Act in some particular verbal formula. I doubt whether there is any verbal formula which is appropriate to all classes of claims. The superintending examiner used the expression "alerted to the possibilities" of using polyacrylamides in improving the filterability of asbestos cement slurries. I find no fault with this phrase in the context of the claim in the appellants' specification. The learned judge preferred the expression "see without difficulty that these newly-introduced polymers would be of advantage in his filtration step." I think that "would be" puts it too high if it postulates prior certainty of success before actually testing the polymers in the filtration process; it is enough that the person versed in the art would assess the likelihood of success as sufficient to warrant actual trial. I do not, however, understand that the learned judge meant more than this, for he did not consider that there was any genuine difference between his phrase and that used by the superintending examiner.

The publications relied upon are a sales pamphlet entitled "Aerofloc Reagents", which contains the manufacturers' particulars of polyacrylamide flocculating agents, and directions for their use. It does not refer specifically to their potential value in asbestos cement manufacturing, but deals primarily with their commercial application in various kinds of mining industries in which the flocculation of mineral particles in aqueous solution can be of advantage. Asbestos, cement and silica are, all three, minerals. The second document, an article by Mr A.M. Swift in a technical journal of the pulp and paper industries, refers specifically to the flocculating effect of polyacrylamides upon (*inter alia*) cement and clay particles. The polyacrylamides were stated to be effective in very small quantities. As compared with other flocculating agents they would thus be present in minute quantities only in the filtered product. The superintending examiner and the Patents Appeal Tribunal were both of opinion that, filtration processes being common to many industries, these documents, although addressed primarily to the mining and paper industries respectively, were likely to be read by those concerned with the asbestos cement industry, and that such readers would have realised that here was a newly introduced flocculating agent which it was well worth trying out in their own filtration process. I can see no grounds which would justify this court in reversing this concurrent finding by two expert tribunals. And there, but for an argument to which I must now advert, is an end of this appeal.

It has been contended with protracted vigour in this court, as it was before both tribunals below, that the action which was in fact taken by a particular witness, who was an actual research worker in the asbestos cement manufacturing industry, when polyacrylamides were first drawn to his attention, demonstrates that these concurrent findings were wrong. The individual was the manager of the respondents' own research department, who made a statutory declaration in support of their application. His evidence discloses that when he first heard of polyacrylamides (which was before the documents relied upon were published) he sought to obtain samples in order to see whether they would be effective flocculating agents for use in the filtration process involved in the manufacture of asbestos cement pipes. As a result of his inquiries he obtained trial quantities of polyacrylamide from the manufacturers, and subsequently received from them the documents relied on when they were published in 1957. In 1956 he carried out experiments with a polyacrylamide and asbestos cement slurry. He "found that it improved the filtration of the slurry, but that this resulted in the formation of a thicker skin of asbestos cement being transferred from the felt filter belt to the revolving cylinder, and a corresponding reduction in the number of laminations for a given thickness in the final product. This had an adverse effect upon its quality." He accordingly abandoned his experiments in 1957, and did not resume them until 1960 (that is, after the priority date of the applicants' specification). He then found out for himself that by speeding up the rate of travel of the belt, the thickness of the skin of asbestos cement upon the felt could be reduced, and the number of laminations correspondingly increased so that the quality of the final product was unimpaired.

In so far as this witness obtained literature about flocculating agents used in other industries, and realised, as soon as he heard of them, that polyacrylamides were well worth trying out as flocculating agents in his own industry of manufacturing asbestos cement pipes, his evidence confirms the opinion of the superintending examiner and the Patents Appeal Tribunal that the idea of trying out these newly introduced flocculating agents in the filtration process in that industry would be obvious to persons "versed in the art." His failure to persevere with his experiments, when he found that the skin of asbestos cement upon the felt filter was too thick, would be cogent evidence for the appellants if the invention claimed in their specification included an adjustment to the speed of the filter belt. But there is not a word about this in their specification. If, appreciating the necessity for such an adjustment involved any inventive step, the specification could be attacked upon the alternative ground set out in section 14(1)(g), namely, that it "does not sufficiently and fairly describe the invention or the method by which it is to be performed." But it is (and so far as the appellants are concerned, it has to be) common ground that, once the idea of adding polyacrylamides to the asbestos cement slurry used in the manufacture of asbestos cement pipes has been tried out, and the thicker skin of asbestos resulting from the improved filtration observed, the necessary adjustment to the speed of the filter belt to obviate any deleterious effect upon the quality of the final product would be obvious, notwithstanding that the respondents' own research manager did not find it so.

All that this evidence shows is that this particular witness's glimpse of the obvious was spasmodic. To this extent he was atypical of the hypothetical person "versed in the art" of manufacturing asbestos cement pipes, whom the superintending examiner, the Patents Appeal Tribunal and this court must postulate as reading the publications relied upon, and drawing from them those conclusions about the likelihood of poly-acrylamides being useful in that manufacture, to which his skill, his knowledge and his experience would lead him. Like the learned judge, I see nothing in this evidence to throw doubt upon the conclusions reached by the superintending examiner and by the Patents Appeal Tribunal itself that the idea of adding a polyacrylamide to the asbestos cement slurry in the manufacture of shaped asbestos cement articles was obvious having regard to the information published in the two documents relied upon.

I would dismiss the appeal.

Russell and Willmer L.JJ. delivered brief concurring judgments.

1.2.2.9 *Olin Mathieson Chemical v Biorex Laboratories* [1970] R.P.C. 157 (Graham J.)

The phenothiazines are a vast group of organic substances with a basically similar chemical structure. Certain members of the class were first known as useful dyes and then as anti-malarial drugs. One sub-class, having as its principal characteristic a chlorine radical, was later found to contain a member that was useful as a tranquilliser: chlorpromazine. The plaintiffs experimented upon another sub-class, in which the chlorine radical (−Cl) was replaced by a trifluoromethyl radical (−CF3). They too found that one member, trifluoroperazine, was a useful tranquilliser and they could predict that other members of the sub-class (which was itself very large) would have a similar characteristic. (The basic chemistry of the whole group is outlined in an Appendix to the judgment: [1970] R.P.C. at 197–200).

In relation to the legal test of obviousness, Graham J. said:

It is, however, most important, in my judgment, to remember that during the years covered by this history a very large number of patents and proposals, the vast majority of which came to nothing, were made in this general field in the endeavour to find really useful drugs. This can probably best be appreciated from a study of documents prepared by Dr Margaret Simkins, the head of the Research Information Department at Smith, Kline & French. She gave evidence, the effect of which was that, if asked at the relevant date to provide information to a research team faced with the problem of producing an alternative for or better drug than chlorpromazine, she would produce all the information on phenothlazines and methods of making them which she could find had been recorded to date, together with any other useful information on the subject such as which other companies had patents in the field and for what drugs. This would result in extracts and tabulations such as M.A.S.7 and other documents.

That this was what she would have done was not really disputed, and I accept her evidence in this respect. This would have meant that the research group would have information about, *inter alia*, all the Rhone-Poulenc patents and work in this field, the Smith papers and a great number of other patents and papers covering a very wide variety of suggestions for substitutions in the side chains and in the phenothiazyl ring and at the "2", "3", and "4" positions. If interest was shown by the research group in the use of −CF, substitution, and this would be one possibility brought to their attention by the first search, and asked for further information on this topic, then it seems certain that papers mentioning this substituent, such as Caldwell, Lindenstruth, Nes and Burger, and Walborsky, would be found and brought to their attention. For the purposes of answering the question of obviousness, I have assumed that such papers would be so produced.

In testing the validity of claim 1, and this, of course, is the most vulnerable claim, the vital question which must then be answered, in my judgment, can perhaps best be expressed as follows:

"Would the notional research group at the relevant date, in all the circumstances, which include a knowledge of all the relevant prior art and of the facts of the nature and success of chlorpromazine, directly be led as a matter of course to try the −CF, substitution in the '2' position in place of the −Cl atom in chlorpromazine or in any other body which, apart from the −CF, substitution, has the other characteristics of the formula of claim 1, in the expectation that it might well produce a useful alternative to or better drug than chlorpromazine or a body useful for any other purpose?"

This question is in fact a sort of jury question, and must be decided objectively, and the judge cannot surrender his decision to the witnesses, though their evidence may be of assistance in placing him in a better position to come to the right answer.

1.2.3   Patentable Subject-matter

1.2.3.1   Patents Act 1977, s.1(2)–(5), 4: Excluded Subject-matter; Industrial Application

S.1(2) It is hereby declared that the following (among other things) are not inventions for the purposes of this Act, that is to say, anything which consists of –

(a) a discovery, scientific theory or mathematical method;

(b) a literary, dramatic, musical or artistic work or any other aesthetic creation whatsoever;

(c) a scheme, rule or method for performing a mental act, playing a game or doing business, or a program for a computer;

(d) the presentation of information;

but the foregoing provision shall prevent anything from being treated as an invention for the purposes of this Act only to the extent that a patent or application for a patent relates to that thing as such.

(3) A patent shall not be granted –

(a) for an invention the publication or exploitation of which would be generally expected to encourage offensive, immoral or anti-social behaviour;

(b) for any variety of animal or plant or any essentially biological process for the production of animals or plants, not being a micro-biological process or the product of such a process.

(4) For the purposes of subsection (3) above behaviour shall not be regarded as offensive, immoral or anti-social only because it is prohibited by any law in force in the United Kingdom or any part of it.

(5) The Secretary of State may by order vary the provisions of subsection (2) above for the purpose of maintaining them in conformity with developments in science and technology; and no such order shall be made unless a draft of the order has been laid before, and approved by resolution of, each House of Parliament.

S.4(1) Subject to subsection (2) below, an invention shall be taken to be capable of industrial application if it can be made or used in any kind of industry, including agriculture.

(2) An invention of a method of treatment of the human or animal body by surgery or therapy or of diagnosis practised on the human or animal body shall not be taken to be capable of industrial application.

(3) Subsection (2) above shall not prevent a product consisting of a substance or composition being treated as capable of industrial application merely because it is invented for use in any such method.

S.1(2) corresponds in general to EPC Art. 52(2), (3); s.1(3) to Art 53; s.4(1) to Art. 57; and s.4(2) and (3) to Art. 52(4).

1.2.3.2 *National Research and Development Corp's Application* [1961] R.P.C. 134 (H.C. Australia)

In this decision, the High Court of Australia upheld claims to a method of eradicating weeds from crop areas by applying a weed-killer from a specific class of chemicals (which were themselves assumed to be known substances).

Dixon C.J., Kitto and Windeyer J.:

Section 6 of the Statute of Monopolies provides that the declarations of invalidity contained in the preceding provisions of the Act "shall not extend to any letters patents and graunts of privilege . . . hereafter to be made of the sole working or makinge of any manner of new manufactures within this realme, to the true and first inventor and inventors of such manufactures, which others at the tyme of makinge such letters patents and graunts shall not use, soe as alsoe they be not contrary to the lawe or mischievous to the state by raisinge prices by comodities at home, or hurt of trade, or generallie inconvenient": Halsbury's Statutes of England, 2nd ed. vol 17 (1950) p 619. It is of the first importance to remember always that the Patents Act 1952–1955 (Cth) like its predecessor the Patents Act 1903 (Cth) and corresponding statutes of the United Kingdom (see the Patents, Designs and Trade Marks Act, 1883, s 46: the Patents Act, 1907 s 93: and the Patents Act, 1949, s 101), defines the word "invention", not by direct explication and in the language of its own day, nor yet by carrying forward the usage of the period in which the Statute of Monopolies was passed, but by reference to the established ambit of s 6 of that Statute. The inquiry which the definition demands is an inquiry into the scope of the permissible subject matter of letters patent and grants of privilege protected by the section. It is an inquiry not into the meaning of a word so much as into the breadth of the concept which the law has developed by its consideration of the text and purpose of the Statute of Monopolies. One may remark that although the Statute spoke of the inventor it nowhere spoke of the invention; all that is nowadays understood by the latter word as used in patent law it comprehended in "new manufactures". The word "manufacture" finds a place in the present Act, not as a word intended to reduce a question of patentability to a question of verbal interpretation, but simply as the general title found in the Statute of Monopolies for the whole category under which all grants of patents which may be made in accordance with the developed principles of patent law are to be subsumed. It is therefore a mistake, and a mistake likely to lead to an incorrect conclusion, to treat the question whether a given process or product is within the definition as if that question could be restated in the form: "Is this a manner (or kind) of manufacture?". It is a mistake which tends to limit one's thinking by reference to the idea of making tangible goods by hand or by machine, because "manufacture" as a word of everyday speech generally conveys that idea. The right question is: "Is this a proper subject of letters patent according to the principles which have been developed for the application of s 6 of the Statute of Monopolies?"

It is a very different question. A perusal of the definitions and quotations appearing in the Oxford English Dictionary under "manufacture" will show that the word has always admitted of applications beyond the limits which a strict observance of its etymology would suggest, and, as the present Chief Justice said in *Maeder v Busch* (1938) 59 C.L.R. 684 at p 706, a widening conception of the notion has been a characteristic of the growth of patent law. As early as 1795 it was possible for Eyre, C.J., to say that "the exposition of the statute as far as usage will expound it, has gone much beyond the letter;" and the width of the meaning that had already been accepted may be gauged from the statement of the same learned judge that "manufacture" extended "to any new results of principles carried into practice . . . new processes in any art producing effects useful to the public": *Boulton v Bull* (1795) 1 H. Bl. 463 at pp 492, 493; 126 E.R. 651 at p 666. By 1842 it was finally settled that "manufacture" was used in the Statute of Monopolies in the dual sense which comprehends both a process and a product: *Crane v Price* (1842) 1 W.P.C. 393; 4 M & G 580; 134 E.R. 239. But a question which appears still to await final decision is whether it is enough that a process produces a useful result or whether it is necessary that some physical thing is either brought into existence or so affected as the better to serve man's purposes. In some of the cases it is suggested that the process must issue in some "vendible matter" or a "vendible product". The former expression was used by Heath, J. in *Boulton v Bull* (1795) 1 H. Bl. 463 at p 482; 126 E.R. 651 at p 661, in the course of maintaining the opinion, which must now be considered heretical, that there could not be a patent for a method; but no such expression appears in the powerful judgment in which Eyre, C.J., maintained the opposite view and reached the conclusion in the particular case which was ultimately upheld in *Hornblower v Boulton* (1799) 8 T.R. 95; 101 E.R. 1235. Abbott C.J. in *The King v Wheeler* (1819) 2 B & Ald. 345 at p 349; 106 E.R. 392 at p 394 having spoken of a "thing made, which is useful for its own sake, and vendible as such", went on to show that he did not find in such expressions as those any absolute test. He said (the italics are ours): "Something of a corporeal and substantial nature, something that can be made by man from the matters subjected to his art and skill, or at the least some new mode of employing practically his art and skill, is requisite to satisfy this word". It is of course not possible to treat such a statement as conclusive of the question. The need for qualification must be confessed, even if only in order to put aside, as they apparently must be put aside, processes for treating diseases of the human body: see C. & W.'s Application (1914) 31 R.P.C. 235; *Maeder v Busch* (1938) 59 C.L.R. 684. When appearing as counsel in the case last cited (59 C.L.R. 684 at p 696), Sir George Ligertwood made a helpful suggestion which in effect amended the statement of Abbott, C.J., to read ". . . or at least some new method of employing practically the art and skill of the workman in a manual art". But even so comprehensive a statement needs to be given a somewhat flexible meaning to allow for long-standing authorities such as *Forsyth v Riviere* (1819) 1 W.P.C., 95 (where the patent was for a method of discharging firearms), and *Electric Telegraph Company v Brett* (1851) 10 C.B. 838; 138 E.R. 331, (where the patent was for a method of giving duplicate electric signals). The truth is that any attempt to state the ambit of s 6 of the Statute of Monopolies by precisely defining "manufacture" is bound to fail. The purpose of s 6, it must be remembered, was to allow the use of the prerogative to encourage national development in a field which already, in 1623, was seen to be excitingly unpredictable. To attempt to place upon the idea the fetters of an exact verbal formula could never have been sound. It would be unsound to the point of folly to attempt to do so now, when science has made such advances that the concrete applications of the notion which were familiar in 1623 can be seen to provide only the more obvious, not to say the more primitive, illustrations of the broad sweep of the concept.

In a case which has been much cited in recent times, the *G.E.C.* case (1942) 60 R.P.C. 1, Morton J., as he then was, while disclaiming the intention of laying down any hard and fast rule applicable to all cases, put forward a proposition which, if literally applied, would have a narrowing effect on the law and indeed has already been found to stand as much in need as the Statute itself of a generous interpretation. The proposition was that "a method or process is a manner of manufacture if it (a) results in the production of some vendible product, or (b) improves or restores to its former condition a vendible product, or (c) has the effect of preserving from deterioration some vendible product to which it is applied". Any criticism to which this is open, as Lord Jenkins remarked in

Reitzman v Grahame – Chapman and Derustit Limited (1950) 68 R.P.C. 25 at p 32, is certainly not on the score of its being too wide. It is valuable for its insistence that in patent law at the present day a process may be within the concept of "manufacture" notwithstanding that it merely improves, restores, or preserves some antecedently existing thing; but in so far as it may appear to restrict the concept by its use of the expression "vendible product", it must be considered now as substantially qualified by the comments made upon it by Evershed J. (as he then was), in the *Cementation* case (1945) 62 R.P.C. 151 and in *Rantzen's* case (1946) 64 R.P.C. 63 at p 65 and by Lloyd-Jacob J., in *Elton and Leda Chemicals Limited's Application* [1957] R.P.C. 267.

The *Cementation* case has importance here, because it decided that a process of treating a stratum of subterranean soil with chemicals may be patentable, the word "product" in Morton J.'s formulation being understood in a sense wide enough to include such a subject matter. The process in question consisted in drilling holes from the surface to a subterranean formation which was liable to combustion, and introducing through the holes material of such a nature that it would dissociate upon the initiation of combustion, with liberation of carbon dioxide and the consequential extinguishing of the fire. For this process, Evershed J., granted a patent, observing that the emphasis in Morton J.'s "rule" was upon the three activities of production, improvement or restoration, and prevention from deterioration, and that the word "product" was used in a sense which included "that which is produced by any action, operation or work; a production; the result;" so that it denoted the subject matter of each of the three forms of activity referred to, and was not intended to limit the conception by reference to the common acceptation of "product".

A little later, in *Bovingdon's* case (1946) 64 R.P.C. 20, Evershed J., refused a patent for a process of fumigating buildings, on the ground that the killing of insects in a building is not a process of manufacture; but he appears to have thought that if the process had involved the impregnation of the fabric it would have been a manufacture.

In *Rantzen's* case (1946) 64 R.P.C., 63, the same learned judge had before him an application for a patent for a method of electrical transmission. The process was one which affected nothing but electrical oscillations, that is to say (as they were defined in the evidence) "the manner in which electrical energy exists when being transmitted either by means of wires or other conducting media or through space". The method was held to be a "manufacture", not by rejecting Morton J.'s mode of describing the ambit of the word, but by interpreting his expression "vendible product" in a sense wide enough to include electrical energy, despite its non-material character, because of its analogy, in commercial respects, with material commodities. That this was sound is hardly to be doubted. In the varying applications of which the word "manufacture" is capable analogy has always played a considerable part.

In this state of the authorities the *Standard Oil Development Company's* (1951) 68 R.P.C. 144 arose for decision. It was a case which resembled the present in that a patent was sought for a selective herbicide. Apparently the claims in the specification as originally drawn resembled those in the specification before us. There were claims for the herbicidal compounds, and also claims for the application of those compounds to vegetable plots in order to eliminate weeds. But after the examiner had made an objection the exact nature of which does not appear, the claims were amended by a draftsman who had his eye on the "rule" formulated by Morton J., in the *G.E.C.* case. The invention was described as "a method for the production of an improved tract of arable land from a tract which contains growing vegetables of the Umbelliferae family together with weeds of the type of grasses and/or clover, which comprises applying to the land

and to the vegetation therein a herbicidal composition (the ingredients and temperature range being stated) in such an amount, that the weeds are substantially completely killed while the vegetables are substantially unharmed, whereby there is obtained an improved tract of substantially weed-free vegetable-containing land".

The case came before Lloyd-Jacob J., who refused a patent. The judgment deals with two contentions by which the application had been supported. One was that the method resulted in the production, improvement, or prevention from deterioration, of a vendible product, namely the growing crop; and his Lordship disposed of it by pointing out, first, that it was not the treatment that produced the crop; secondly that any resulting improvement was not in the crop but in the cultivation, though of course that might ultimately be reflected in the quality and condition of the crop; and thirdly that since the only direct effect of the process was upon the weeds there was no justification for saying that it preserved the crop from deterioration. The other contention seems to have been that it was sufficient ground for holding the process to be a "manufacture" that it resulted in a product consisting of "arable land treated with selective herbicides for the raising of vegetables". To this his Lordship gave two answers. First he said that it was beyond the capacity of the applicants to provide arable land. "Given the arable land, they can doubtless treat it, but their contribution does not embrace the making of the land". The observation may be permitted that what had to be considered was not a contention that the process was within the first limb of Morton J.'s, "rule" as being a process which produced arable land, but a contention that it was within the second limb as being a process which improved arable land. The learned Judge's second answer so understood the argument. The answer was that the land remained unaltered. "Some of the herbs in or upon it are affected", his Lordship said. "The land is merely the carrier both of crop and herbage and plays no part in the operation by which they are selectively affected". No doubt the use of the adjective "arable" in the specification had fastened attention on the nature or composition of the soil itself, and invited the answer that the soil was not made arable by the process of killing the weeds. But it seems hardly sufficient to treat a case like this as if it were covered by the reasoning of *Bovingdon's* case (1946) 64 R.P.C. 20, and to dismiss it by saying that, since the structure of the soil is unaffected by the killing of weeds, the process of converting a weed-infested area into a weed-free area is not within the notion of "manufacture". Why is it not as completely within it as the process of converting a combustible subterranean formation into a noncombustible formation, or making a building fire-proof? Once it is conceded that land may be a "product" within the sense of Morton J.'s "rule" as now understood, and that accordingly a process for improving it may be a "manufacture" in the relevant sense of the word – and Lloyd-Jacob J., did not question this – a considerable step seems to have been taken towards establishing that an artificial process for suppressing unwanted forms of growth which impede the profitable use of land may be within the concept. There is of course this point of distinction in fact from the illustrations mentioned, that here the improvement is negative, consisting of the elimination of what had formed a prejudicial element in the growth upon the land of the products of agriculture, whereas there the improvement is positive, consisting of the addition to the land of a new advantageous feature. But that can hardly be a valid objection. As Eyre C.J., pointed out in *Boulton v Bull* (1795) 2 H.Bl. 463 at p 494; 126 E.R. 651 at p 667, though the patent in *Hartley's* case (for the fire-proofing of a building or ship) could not have been for the effect produced, because the effect was merely negative, it was none the less validly granted for the process. In *Hall v Jarvis* (1822) 1 W.P.C. 100 the patent was upheld although it was for a process which did nothing more than remove superfluous and loose fibres, or ends of fibres, from lace: see Webster's note 1 W.P.C. p 97. If a new process for chemically cleaning dirty linen would be good subject matter for a patent – and we have the authority of Parker J., in *Alsop's Patent* (1907) 24 R.P.C. 733 at 752 for believing that it would – why not a new process for chemically ridding land of unwanted growth?

In the next case which calls for attention it was found necessary, as was sure to happen sooner or later, to emphasise the inconclusiveness of Morton J.'s "rule". The case was *Elton and Leda Chemicals Limited's Application* [1957] R.P.C. 267. A patent was sought for a method of dispersing fog, consisting in introducing a surface-active agent in the form of a smoke or spray into the fog in order to remove or lower the electric charge carried by the surfaces of the droplets of the fog, whereby coalescence of the droplets would take place and they would precipitate as rain or drizzle. Lloyd-Jacob J., allowed the application to proceed, not being satisfied that a sustainable claim could not be based on the specification. The Patents Office had relied on Morton J.'s, "rule", and the argument on the appeal was directed both to "vendible" and to "product". As to the former word the learned Judge made the comment that the convenience of the vendibility test was obvious, and "in the majority of cases" plainly applicable. "Applied with a little latitude", he said, "it might afford some assistance in the present case, for a fog-free atmosphere or a deliberately induced rainfall could be a factor in the site value of the land whereon the Applicant's process was applied". Whether or not one would be prepared to put the matter quite in that way, the underlying idea seems to be the same as that which Evershed J., suggested in *Rantzen's* case (1946) 64 R.P.C. 63 at p 66, where he spoke of the expression "vendible product" as laying proper emphasis upon the trading or industrial character of the processes intended to be comprehended by the Acts – their "industrial or commercial or trading character" as Lloyd-Jacob J., himself described it in *Lenard's Application* (1954) 71 R.P.C. 190 at p 192. The point is that a process, to fall within the limits of patentability which the context of the Statute of Monopolies has supplied, must be one that offers some advantage which is material, in the sense that the process belongs to a useful art as distinct from a fine art (see *Virginia-Carolina Chemical Corporation's Application* [1958] R.P.C. 35 at p 36) that its value to the country is in the field of economic endeavour. (The exclusion of methods of surgery and other processes for treating the human body may well lie outside the concept of invention because the whole subject is conceived as essentially non-economic: see *Maeder v Busch* (1938) 59 C.L.R. 684 at p 706).

But the judgment in the *Elton and Leda Chemicals* case [1957] R.P.C. 267 is also valuable for present purposes by reason of a suggestion which it contains as to the true office of the word "product" in such contexts as that of Morton J.'s, "rule". The learned Judge said: "There has been no question, at any rate since before the year 1800, that the expression 'manner of manufacture' in the Statute of James I must be construed in the sense of including a practice of making as well as the means of making and the product of making. It has thus been appreciated that, although an inventor may use no newly devised mechanism, nor produce a new substance, none the less he may, by providing some new and useful effect, appropriate for himself a patent monopoly in such improved result by covering the mode or manner by means of which his result is secured. Seeing that the promise which he offers is some new and useful effect, there must of necessity be some product whereby the validity of his promise can be "tested". Notwithstanding the use of the word "making", which but for the context might have been taken to indicate the narrow view that an article or material must result if a process is to be a "manufacture", the tenor of the passage seems to be that what is meant by a "product" in relation to a process is only something in which the new and useful effect may be observed. Sufficient authority has been cited to show that the "something" need not be a "thing" in the sense of an article; it may be any physical phenomenon in which the effect, be it creation or merely alteration, may be observed: a building (for example), a tract or stratum of land, an explosion, an electrical oscillation. It is, we think, only by understanding the word "product" as covering every end produced, and treating the word "vendible" as pointing only to the requirement of utility in practical affairs, that the language of Morton J.'s, "rule" may be accepted as wide enough to convey the broad idea which the long line of decisions on the subject has shown to be comprehended by the Statute.

To the decision of Lloyd-Jacob J., in the *Standard Oil Development Company's* case (1951) 68 R.P.C. 114, there must be added, as tending against the appellant's case in this appeal, his Lordship's more recent decisions denying patentability in the *Virginia-Carolina Chemical Corporation's Application* [1958] R.P.C. 38 (a process for destroying nematodes in soil) and the *American Chemical Paint Company's Application* [1958] R.P.C. 47 (a process for defoliating cotton plants before harvesting in order to save the cotton from contamination).

Notwithstanding the tendency of these decisions, the view which we think is correct in the present case is that the method the subject of the relevant claims has as its end result an artificial effect falling squarely within the true concept of what must be produced by a process if it is to be held patentable. This view is, we think, required by a sound understanding of the lines along which patent law has developed and necessarily must develop in a modern society. The effect produced by the appellant's method exhibits the two essential qualities upon which "product" and "vendible" seem designed to insist. It is a "product" because it consists in an artificially created state of affairs, discernible by observing over a period the growth of weeds and crops respectively on sown land on which the method has been put into practice. And the significance of the product is economic; for it provides a remarkable advantage, indeed to the lay mind a sensational advantage, for one of the most elemental activities by which man has served his material needs, the cultivation of the soil for the production of its fruits. Recognition that the relevance of the process is to this economic activity old as it is, need not be inhibited by any fear of inconsistency with the claim to novelty which the specification plainly makes. The method cannot be classed as a variant of ancient procedures. It is additional to the cultivation. It achieves a separate result, and the result possesses its own economic utility consisting in an important improvement in the conditions in which the crop is to grow, whereby it is afforded a better opportunity to flourish and yield a good harvest.

There remains for consideration the Commissioner's contention that, even apart from the considerations which have been discussed, agricultural or horticultural processes are, by reason of their nature, outside the limits of patentable inventions. Only in comparatively recent times have statements appeared which explicitly support the contention. In the *Rau Gesellschaft* case (1935) 52 R.P.C. 362, an application for a patent in respect of the production by selective cultivation of lupin seeds having certain characteristics was rejected. Luxmore J., approved a statement by the examiner in terms which seem to run together the question whether such a process can be novel and the question whether it can be a "manufacture". It reads: "Selective breeding of animals and cultivation of plants for the obtainment of improved stocks by the rigorous selection of and breeding from the few individuals which are nearest the ideal has, as is well known, been practised from the earliest times as a part of agricultural or horticultural development, as for example in the production of improved flowers or fruit with desired characteristics in the progeny, and the exercise of art or skill in these directions has not been regarded as coming within the term "manufacture". (There had been earlier cases in which applications relating to agriculture had been refused on other grounds; for instance, *Hamilton-Adams'* case (1918) 35 R.P.C. 90, where the process was one for rotation of crops, and the ground taken was that although there was a discovery there was no improvement in the method of carrying out any agricultural operations.) It must often happen in a sphere of human endeavour as old as that of primary production that a newly-devised procedure amounts to nothing more than an analogous application of age old techniques; and where that is the case, want of novelty is a fatal objection to a patent. It may be conceded, however, that if there were nothing that could properly be called a "product" of the process, even an ingenious new departure would be outside the limits of patentability. In *R.H.F.'s Application* (1944) 61 R.P.C. 49, Morton J., approved a statement of the examiner which had been made to illustrate that the vendible product test enunciated in the *G.E.C.* case (1942) 50 R.P.C., 1, was not definitive. The statement was that fruit and other growing crops, although the assistance of man may be invoked for their planting and cultivation, do not result from a process which is a "manner of manufacture". This may be agreed. However advantageously man may alter the conditions of growth, the fruit is still not produced by his action. But in the *Standard Oil Development Company's* case (1951) 68 R.P.C. 144, where a patent was sought for a selective herbicidal process, it emerged from the examiner's report that an "established office practice" had grown up of denying that any agricultural or horticultural process could be a "manner of manufacture". Upon this, Lloyd-Jacob J. made no comment, and the office view has since been adhered to: *Dow Chemical Company's Application* [1956] R.P.C. 247; *Canterbury Agricultural College's Application* [1958] R.P.C. 85. The proposition seems an example of a generalisation not supported by the reasons leading to the conclusions in the particular instances from which the generalisation is drawn. If it means that there is some consideration wrapped up in the label "agricultural or horticultural" which necessarily takes a process outside the area of patentability even though it is a novel process and of sufficient inventiveness, the consideration is not easy to identify. There seems to be here a classic illustration of thinking in terms of the everyday concept of manufacture instead of following the lines along which, over a long period, the courts have given effect to the real purpose and operation of s 6 of the Statute of Monopolies. The cases of *Lenard's Application* (1954) 71 R.P.C. 190 (pruning to reduce mortality from disease in clove trees) and *N V Philips' Gloeilampenfabrieken's Application* (1954) 71 R.P.C. 192 (a method for producing a new form of poinsettia) both seem to depend on the view that the process in question was only one for altering the conditions of growth, so that the contemplated end result would not be a result of the process but would be "the inevitable result of that which is inherent in the plant" (as it was expressed in the case last cited [1954] 71 R.P.C. 192 at p 194). A distinction has necessarily to be drawn between cases of this class and cases of methods employing micro-organisms: see the *Commercial Solvent's* case (1926) 43 R.P.C. 185 and *Adhesives Pty Ltd v Aktieselskabet Dansk Gaerings-Industri and Another* (1935) 55 C.L.R. 523; *Virginia-Carolina Chemical Corporation's Application* [1958] R.P.C. 35 at p 37, for in the latter class of cases the process is analogous to a chemical process in that, given the micro-organisms and the appropriate conditions, the desired result inevitably follows from the working of the process: see *Szuec's* case [1956] R.P.C. 25.

We are here concerned with a process producing its effect by means of a chemical reaction, and the ultimate weed-free, or comparatively weed-free condition of the crop-bearing land is properly described as produced by the process. The fact that the relevance of the process is to agricultural or horticultural enterprises does not in itself supply or suggest any consideration not already covered in this judgment for denying that the process is a patentable invention.

For these reasons we allow the appeal.

1.2.3.3   *Vicom's Application* [1987] O.J. EPO 14 (Tech. Bd. App.)

An applicant sought in particular to procure the following amended claims:

1. A method of digitally processing images in the form of a two-dimensional data array having elements arranged in rows and columns in which an operator matrix of a size substantially smaller than the size of the data array is convolved with the data array, including sequentially scanning the elements of the data array with the operator matrix, characterised in that the method includes repeated cycles of sequentially scanning the entire data array with a small generating kernel operator matrix to generate a convolved array and then replacing the data array as a new data array; the small generating kernel remaining the same for any single scan of the entire data array and although comprising at least a multiplicity of elements, nevertheless being of a size substantially smaller than is required of a conventional operator matrix in which the operator matrix is convolved with the data array only once, and the cycle being repeated for each previous new data array by selecting the small generating kernel operator matrices and the number of cycles according to conventional error minimisation techniques until the last new data array generated is substantially the required convolution of the original data array with the conventional operator matrix.

8. Apparatus for carrying out the method in Claim 1 including data input means (10) for receiving said data array, and said data array to generate an operator matrix for scanning said data array to generate the required convolution of the operator matrix and the data array, characterised in that there are provided feedback means (50) for transferring the output of the mask means (20) to the data input means, and control means (30) for causing the scanning and transferring of the output of the mask means (20) to the data input means to be repeated a predetermined number of times.

The Examining Division rejected these as constituting a mathematical method which did not define new technical subject-matter in terms of technical features. The Technical Board of Appeal disagreed.

After holding that the claimed invention was susceptible of industrial application (Art. 57), it considered both whether the claims were excluded as being for a mathematical method as such and a computer program as such:

5. There can be little doubt that any processing operation on an electric signal can be described in mathematical terms. The characteristic of a filter, for example, can be expressed in terms of a mathematical formula. A basic difference between a mathematical method and a technical process can be seen, however, in the fact that a mathematical method or a mathematical algorithm is carried out on numbers (whatever these numbers may represent) and provides a result also in numerical form, the mathematical method or algorithm being only an abstract concept prescribing how to operate on the numbers. No direct technical result is produced by the method as such. In contrast thereto, if a mathematical method is used in a technical process, that process is carried out on a physical entity (which may be a material object but equally an image stored as an electric signal) by some technical means implementing the method and provides as its result a certain change in that entity. The technical means might include a computer comprising suitable hardware or an appropriately programmed general purpose computer.

6. The Board, therefore, is of the opinion that even if the idea underlying an invention may be considered to reside in a mathematical method a claim directed to a technical process in which the method is used does not seek protection for the mathematical method **as such**.

7. In contrast, a "method for digitally filtering data" remains an abstract notion not

distinguished from a mathematical method so long as it is not specified what physical entity is represented by the data and forms the subject of a technical process i.e. a process which is susceptible of industrial application. . . .

11. The appellants have stressed that the application discloses new hardware for carrying out the claimed methods but admit on the other hand that at least in principle it is possible to implement the method and apparatus according to the application by a suitably programmed conventional computer although such a computer may not be optimised for carrying out digital image processing (cf. page A–2 of the Statement of Grounds).

12. The Board is of the opinion that a claim directed to a technical process which process is carried out under the control of a program (be this implemented in hardware or in software, cannot be regarded as relating to a computer program **as such** within the meaning of Article 52(3) EPC, as it is the application of the program for determining the sequence of steps in the process for which in effect protection is sought. Consequently, such a claim is allowable under Article 52(2)(c) and (3) EPC.

13. Concerning the apparatus Claim 8, the Examining Division has held that it is not acceptable because a new apparatus is not clearly disclosed. According to the decision under appeal, the claim when interpreted in the light of the description and the drawings seems to imply only the use of a conventional computer which could not provide the basis of an acceptable product claim in view of Articles 52(1) and 54 EPC. The Board understands this as meaning that the Examining Division was of the opinion that a conventional computer programmed so as to carry out a method according to one or more of the method claims is not novel.

14. In the view of the Board, however, Article 54 EPC leaves no room for such an interpretation. A computer of known type set up to operate according to a new program cannot be considered as forming part of the state of the art as defined by Article 54(2) EPC.

This is particularly apparent in the present case as Claims 8–11 clearly embrace also the use of special hardware, for which some indications are given in the description and also mixed solutions combining some special hardware with an appropriate program.

15. In view of certain considerations by the Examining Division which appear to apply to the apparatus claims as well (cf. paragraph 10 above) it remains to be examined if the present apparatus Claim 8 would be objectionable under Article 52(2)(c) as qualified by (3) EPC. For reasons analogous to these given in paragraph 12 above, the Board holds that this is not the case and the same applies to the other appratus Claims 9–11. Generally claims which can be considered as being directed to a computer set up to operate in accordance with a specified program (whether by means of hardware or software) for controlling or carrying out a technical process cannot be regarded as relating to a computer program **as such** and thus are not objectionable under Article 52(2)(c) and (3) EPC.

16. In arriving at this conclusion the Board has additionally considered that making a distinction between embodiments of the same invention carried out in hardware or in software is inappropriate as it can fairly be said that the choice between these two possibilities is not of an essential nature but is based on technical and economical considerations which bear no relationship to the inventive concept as such.

Generally speaking, an invention which would be patentable in accordance with conventional patentability criteria should not be excluded from protection by the mere fact that for its implementation modern technical means in the form of a computer program are used. Decisive is what technical contribution the invention is defined in the claim when considered as a whole makes to the known art.

Finally, it would seem illogical to grant protection for a technical process controlled by a suitably programmed computer but not for the computer itself when set up to execute the control.

1.2.3.4   *Merrill Lynch's Application* [1989] R.P.C. 561 (C.A.)

The application concerned a data processing system for making a trading market in securities, which deployed a known computer system programmed in a standard language. Claim 1 was as follows:

"In combination in a data processing system for making a trading market in at least one security in which the system proprietor is acting as principal; said system including means for receiving trade orders for said at least one security from system customers, said trade orders including fields identifying the stock to be traded and characterisation of the trade as a customer purchase or sale, and the number of shares for the transaction; means for retrieving and for storing operative bid and asked prices for said at least one security; means for entering and for storing order qualification parameters, said parameters and said stored prices determining which received orders and qualified for execution; means for storing data characterising position, cost and profit for said at least one security; qualifying means responsive to said received trade orders and said stored prices and order qualification parameters for qualifying a trade order for execution when the received trade order fields do not violate the stored prices and qualification parameters; means for executing each trade order qualified by said qualification means; and post-execution updating means for updating said position and at least one of said stored parameters upon execution of a trade order".

At first instance, Falconer J. rejected the claim as being for a computer program as such (s.1(2)(c)) and in doing so placed emphasis on the phrase "to the extent that" which introduces the whole of s.1(2):

It seems to me that the words "to the extent that" contemplate that the subsection is also to be applicable to cases where the invention involves one of the excluding matters (specified in paragraphs (a), (b), (c) and (d)), but does not relate to it only. Using the exemplification of an invention involving a computer program, Mr Thorley submitted that the wording 'only to the extent that' means that there cannot be a patentable invention in so far as the invention resides in the computer program itself, but if some practical (i.e. technical) effect is achieved by the computer or machine operating according to the instructions contained in the program and such effect is novel and inventive (i.e. not obvious), a claim directed to that practical effect will be patentable, notwithstanding it is defined by that computer program. In my judgment, Mr Thorley was right in that submission.

In Genentech's Patent (below, 1.2.5.1), Whitford J., at first instance, took a different view, holding that the prohibition in s.1(2) was limited to inventions which related to the matters there specified and did not include modes of using these matters in a process or in relation to an artefact. In Genentech, the Court of Appeal preferred this view and refused to accept Falconer J.'s reasoning above, while being careful to cast no doubt on the actual result reached by Falconer J. in the present case which was then also taken on appeal. The C.A. followed its view in Genentech. Fox L.J. (for the Court) proceeded to quote from Vicom's Application (above, 1.2.3.3). He concluded:

The position seems to me to be this, *Genentech* decides that the reasoning of Falconer J.

is wrong. On the other hand, it seems to me to be clear, for the reasons indicated by Dillon L.J., that it cannot be permissible to patent an item excluded by section 1(2) under the guise of an article which contains that item – that is to say, in the case of a computer program, the patenting of a conventional computer containing that program. Something further is necessary. The nature of that addition is, I think, to be found in the *Vicom* case where it is stated: "Decisive is what technical contribution the invention makes to the known art". There must, I think, be some technical advance on the prior art in the form of a new result (e.g. a substantial increase in processing speed as in *Vicom*).

Now let it be supposed that claim 1 can be regarded as producing a new result in the form of a technical contribution to the prior art. That result, whatever the technical advance may be, is simply the production of a trading system. It is a data-processing system for doing a specific business, that is to say, making a trading market in securities. The end result, therefore, is simply "a method . . . of doing business", and is excluded by section 1(2)(c). The fact that the method of doing business may be an improvement on previous methods of doing business does not seem to me to be material. The prohibition in section 1(2)(c) is generic; qualitative considerations do not enter into the matter. The section draws no distinction between the method by which the mode of doing business is achieved. If what is produced in the end is itself an item excluded from patentability by section 1(2), the matter can go no further. Claim 1, after all, is directed to "a data processing system for making a trading market". That is simply a method of doing business. A data processing system operating to produce a novel technical result would normally be patentable. But it cannot, it seems to me, be patentable if the result itself is a prohibited item under section 1(2). In the present case it is such a prohibited item.

We were referred to *International Business Machines Corp's Application* [1980] F.S.R. 564, as being on all fours with the present case, but it was decided under the 1949 Act, which is not in the same form as the 1977 Act.

In the end, therefore, for the reasons which I have indicated, I reach the same result as Falconer J., namely that there is not a patentable invention here. I would dismiss the appeal.

1.2.3.5 *Ciba-Geigy's Propagating Material Application* [1984] O.J. EPO 112 (Tech. Bd. App.)

An Applicant sought to procure the following (amended) claims:

"Claim 13: Propagating material for cultivated plants, treated with an oxime derivative according to formula 1 in claim 1.
Claim 14: Propagating material according to claim 13, characterised in that it consists of seed".

The Examining Division rejected them as debarred by EPC, Art. 53(b); but the Technical Board of Appeal disagreed:

2. No general exclusion of inventions in the sphere of animate nature can be inferred from the European Patent Convention (cf. Art. 52(1) in conjunction with Art. 53(b) after the semi-colon, and Rules 28 and 28a EPC). However, Article 53(b) EPC before the semi-colon prohibits the granting of patents for certain biological inventions. This provision, which needs to be examined more closely in the present case, says that patents shall not be granted in respect of plant varieties or essentially biological

processes for the production of plants. The skilled person understands the term "plant varieties" to mean a multiplicity of plants which are largely the same in their characteristics and remain the same within specific tolerances after every propagation or every propagation cycle. This definition is reflected in the International Convention for the Protection of New Varieties of Plants of 2 December 1961, which is intended to give the breeder of a new plant variety a protective right (Art. 1(1)) extending both to the reproductive or vegetative propagating material and also to the whole plant (Art. 5(1)). Plant varieties in this sense are all cultivated varieties, clones, lines, strains and hybrids which can be grown in such a way that they are clearly distinguishable from other varieties, sufficiently homogeneous, and stable in their essential characteristics (Art. 2(2) in conjunction with Art. 6(1)(a), (c) and (d)). The legislator did not wish to afford patent protection under the European Patent Convention to plant varieties of this kind, whether in the form of propagating material or of the plant itself.

3. Claims 13 and 14, whose maintenance resulted in the refusal of the present application, concern propagating material, in particular seeds of cultivated plants, treated with a sulphurous oxime derivative which is characterised in greater detail in claim 1. A definition of cultivated plants in the description (cf. page 9, paragraph 3) shows that this includes all plants which yield substances in any form. Examples of known plants are listed. Propagating material from such cultivated plants comprises all reproductive plant components, including plants and plantlings which have begun to be germinated, but particularly seeds (cf. page 10, paragraph 2, of the description).

Even if certain known varieties of wheat, millet and barley are mentioned in the examples in connection with oxime treatment (cf. pages 35 and 36 of the description), the subject-matter of claims 13 and 14 is not an individual variety of plant distinguishable from any other variety, but the claims relate to any cultivated plants in the form of their propagating material which have been chemically treated in a certain way. However, Article 53(b) EPC prohibits only the patenting of plants or their propagating material in the genetically fixed form of the plant variety.

4. The very wording of Article 53(b) EPC before the semi-colon precludes the equation of plants and plant varieties, which would also be at variance with the general sense of the provision. Plant varieties were excluded from European patent protection mainly because several of the signatory States to the European Patent Convention have developed special protection for plant breeding at national and international level (R. Singer, *The New European Patent System*, Seminar Services International, page 22, paragraph 6).

In Article 53(b) EPC before the semi-colon the authors adhered strictly to the wording of Article 2(b) of the Strasbourg Patent Convention of 27 November 1963, in which the Contracting States to that Convention were given the opportunity to exclude plant varieties, amongst other things, from patent protection. Even at that time the majority of the States represented on the Council of Europe were already of the opinion that plant varieties should be protected not by patents but by a special industrial property right (Pfanner, *Vereinheitlichung des materiellen Patentrechts im Rahmen des Europarats*, GRUR Int. 1962, 545, 547).

By contrast, the innovation claimed here does not lie within the sphere of plant breeding, which is concerned with the genetic modification of plants. Rather, it acts on the propagating material by means of chemical agents in order to make it resistant to agricultural chemicals. The new parameter for the propagating material, namely treatment with an oxime derivative, is not a criterion which can be characteristic of a plant variety as far as the protection of varieties is concerned. There is therefore no conflict between the protection of varieties or the patent as different forms of protection for propagating material treated in this way. In fact, patent protection is the only possibility.

Technologically, the treatment with an oxime derivative is a plant protection measure which, in contrast to other cases, is carried out on a marketable object, namely the propagating material. It is not necessary for the object of the treatment always to be a plant variety, since the treatment can also be carried out on propagating material which does not meet the essential criteria of homogeneity or stability characteristic of a plant variety. Conversely, it is immaterial to the question of patentability that the propagating material which is treated can also be, or is primarily, a plant variety. If plant varieties have been excluded from patent protection because specifically the achievement involved in breeding a new variety is to have its own form of protection, it is perfectly sufficient for the exclusion to be left restricted, in conformity with its wording, to cases in which plants are characterised precisely by the genetically determined peculiarities of their natural phenotype. In this respect there is no conflict between areas reserved for national protection of varieties and the field of application of the EPC. On the other hand, innovations which cannot be given the protection afforded to varieties are still patentable if the general prerequisites are met.

5. Moreover, the propagating material claimed is not the result of an essentially biological process for the breeding of plants – which would be excluded from patent protection – but the result of treatment with chemical agents (e.g. dressing agents, seed-dressing processes, immersion of the plantling in an oxime solution, cf. page 6, line 23, page 9, line 8 and page 10, lines 17–20). To summarise, therefore, Article 53(b) EPC is not an obstacle to the patenting of the propagating material claimed in the present case.

1.2.3.6 *Harvard College's Onco-Mouse Application* [1989] O.J. EPO 451 (Ex. Div.)

The application derives from experiments which demonstrated that particular oncogenes (malignancy-creating genes) could be introduced into a mouse by a technique such as micro-injection. The probability of the mouse then developing neoplasms (tumours) was thereby increased and the mouse acquired an enhanced value in cancer research.

Claim 1 was as follows:

1. A method for producing a transgenic non-human mammalian animal having an increased probability of developing neoplasms, said method comprising introducing an activated oncogene sequence into a non-human mammalian animal at a stage no later than the 8-cell stage.

Amongst other consequential claims, Claim 17 was to a non-human mammalian animal treated as in Claim 1; and Claim 18 was to such an animal when it was a rodent. The Examining Division rejected these and other claims for failure to comply (i) with Art. 53(b) and (ii) with Art. 83 (insufficient disclosure – Judgment not here included):

7. Considerations under Article 53(b) EPC
In defence of his position the Applicant essentially points out that
– the claims are not directed to an animal variety,
– the claimed process (which is also used for defining the animals claimed *per se*) is not essentially biological, and that
– consequently, the animals of Claims 17 and 18 are to be considered patentable subject-matter as they represent the product of a microbiological process.

7.1 Animal varieties

7.1.1 In interpreting Article 53(b) EPC it has to be borne in mind that the language of the article goes back to the Strasbourg Patent Convention which was conceived in 1962 and that at that time the question of patenting transgenic animals was scarcely conceivable. In interpreting the article, it is therefore necessary to consider what the intentions of the legislator were at that time.

7.1.2 In Article 53(b) EPC it is stated that European patents shall not be granted in respect of animal varieties. This provision is interpreted by the Examining Division to refer not only to these cases where a specifically designated variety is claimed but also to cases where varities are covered by a claim.

7.1.3 It is true that the Board of Appeal has interpreted the term plant variety in the same paragraph as excluding from patentability only plants in the genetically fixed form of a plant variety (T 49/83, OJ EPO 1984, 112, later confirmed in T 320/87, as yet unpublished).

This conclusion was based on the purpose of the provision. The legislator of the EPC wanted to have plant varieties protected by a special industrial property right according to the International Convention for the Protection of New Varieties of Plants (UPOV Convention). Double protection was to be excluded according to Article 2(1) of the UPOV Convention. The restrictive interpretation of the exclusion of plant varieties is therefore justified by the limited purpose of the provision to exclude from patent protection only such subject-matter which is eligible for plant variety protection.

7.1.4 No similar situation exists in the field of animals. The exclusion of animal varieties in Article 53(b) EPC was taken over unchanged from Article 2(b) of the Strasbourg Patent Convention, in which the Contracting States were given the opportunity to exclude animal varieties from patent protection. The idea behind this exclusion was that animal varieties are not an appropriate subject-matter for patent protection (Pfanner, *Vereinheitlichung des materiellen Patentrechts im Rahmen des Europarats*, GRUR Int. 1962, 545, at page 547).

Moreover, if Article 53(b) EPC is considered in the three official languages it is apparent that with regard to plants the legislator used identical designations in all three languages whereas this is not the case with respect to animals. The German version "Tierarten" is definitely different from the English "animal varieties" and the French "races animales". This is a further indication that the legislator's intention was not the exclusion of some particular group of animals but rather the exclusion of animals in general.

7.1.5 It is therefore quite in conformity with the purpose of the law to reject not only claims to a specific variety but also claims covering an animal variety. Claims 17 and 18 refer to "A . . . mammalian animal" and to "rodent", respectively, and thus any individual animal/rodent having the oncogene in question is covered by these claims.

Moreover, groups of individual animals having the same or a very similar appearance are covered by the claim and therefore also groups of animals forming varieties.

7.1.6 In addition, the term animal **variety** is not a criterion sufficient to delineate patentable from non-patentable subject-matter. Whereas the UPOV Convention, especially in Article 6, gives a legal definition for plant varieties which can also be applied to Article 53(b) EPC (see also Decision T 320/87, item 13), no similar definition exists for animal varieties.

Furthermore, there is no uniform use of this term in scientific language which would give a clear and reliable basis for the application of Article 53(b) EPC.

Applicant's argument that the EPO has no difficulty in distinguishing between deposited strains of micro-organisms and general claims to classes of micro-organisms and that a parallel can be drawn to animal varieties and animals is not convincing because in the present situation "animal varieties" is something which is clearly excluded whereas, in the comparison, deposited strains are not.

Moreover, strains of micro-organisms and taxonomic classes thereof are well known and accepted in biology whereas, as pointed out above, no good and generally accepted definition of animal varieties exists.

7.1.7 At the oral proceedings the Applicant has offered a definition of the term "animal variety". According to this definition an animal variety shall be understood to be the result of the mere breeding of animals. Claims 17 and 18 contain process features ("or an ancestor of said animal") which are concerned with the mere breeding of animals, namely animals which already have the oncogene incorporated in their genome. Thus, if the above definition is applied to the animals of Claims 17 and 18, it also follows that animal varieties are covered by these claims.

7.1.8 In summarising, Claims 17 and 18 embrace subject-matter excluded from patentability by Article 53(b) EPC and are not allowable for this reason.

7.2 Essentially biological processes, microbiological processes and the products of the latter

7.2.1 As pointed out in Decision T 320/87 in paragraph 6 the exclusion of "essentially biological" has to be construed narrowly and this question has to be judged on the basis of the essence of the invention. The essence of the present process invention is the introduction of an oncogene into an animal by technical means, e.g. micro-injection. This clearly is not "essentially biological" and therefore an objection under Article 53(b) first part EPC was not raised having regard to the process claims.

7.2.2 Therefore, it is not a point at issue for the patentability of the claimed **process**, whether it is of a microbiological character or not (for the product claims see 7.2.4 below).

7.2.3 In considering the product Claims 17 and 18 it is noted that these claims contain two different process steps, namely the non-biological step referred to in the preceding paragraph 7.2.1 and the breeding step as referred to in paragraph 7.1.7 in order to extend the claims to generations of animals which were not themselves genetically manipulated. The two steps result in two different products. Animals which were genetically manipulated themselves are products of a non-essentially biological process, whereas further generations are the product of sexual reproduction which is exclusively biological; therefore, the latter products do not fall under Article 53(b) second part EPT. The artificial connection of the two steps aims at circumventing the exclusion provision in Article 53(b) first part EPC. This does, however, not dispense with the need to evaluate the biological or non-biological character of each step according to its own merits.

7.2.4 Even if the Division followed the arguments of the Applicant and regarded the process as a whole and accepted its character as being essentially non-biological, this would not make the product claims allowable. In general, products of microbiological process are accessible to protection under Article 53(b) EPC, second part. This part has to be interpreted in the light of the first part; if the product of a process is something which falls under the manifest exclusion of the first part of said article, the second part cannot be interpreted as setting aside the first part. This means that at the least, processes producing plant or animal varieties in the sense of the first part are not to be regarded as microbiological processes. This seems to be quite in conformity with scientific terminology which uses microbiology in relation to micro-organisms and biology in relation to plants or animals even at the cellular stage. Both the main and the auxiliary request are therefore not acceptable.

1.2.3.7   *American Cyanamid v Berk* [1976] R.P.C. 231 (Whitford J.)

The plaintiffs had isolated strains of the micro-organism, Streptomyces aureofaciens, which could be used to produce the antibiotic, tetracycline, with almost no admixture of chlortetracycline. The form of S. aureofaciens (A–377) had produced the two substances together and it was by experimentation with mutations of this isolate that the plaintiff's invention had been reached. Claim 1 of its patent read: "The process of producing tetracycline which comprises cultivating a strain of S. aureofaciens" having the ability to produce the drug to the virtual exclusion of chlortetracycline and have certain colour patterns in their reflectant spectra.

The defendants, when sued for infringement, counter-claimed, inter alia, that the invention was not patentable under the Patents Act 1949. On this issue, Whitford J. said:

In support of his proposition that a biochemical process is outside the scope of the Patents Act, counsel for the defendants made reference to the fact that Parliament thought it necessary to pass a special Act – I quote from the words of the preamble –

"to provide for the granting of proprietary rights to persons who breed or discover plant varieties and for the issue of compulsory licences in respect thereof".

This Act was the Plant Varieties and Seeds Act, 1964. It provided for plant breeders' rights, and certain conditions were laid down which had to be fulfilled by those who wished to take advantage of the statute. Only certain persons were entitled to make application for protection, and it was a specific provision of the Act that varieties which were to be the subject of protection under the Act should comply with certain rules. The rules provided that the variety must be clearly distinguishable by one or more important morphological, physiological or other characteristics from any other variety whose existence was a matter of common knowledge at the date of the application. If the applicant was able to satisfy the registering authority that he had in fact a new variety, he could secure protection for a specified period; but specific provision was made in the Act that the holder of rights under the Act should ensure that, throughout the period during which the rights were exercisable, he would be in a position to produce to the authority reproductive material capable of producing the variety to which the rights related.

The submission of counsel was that in substance the type of process with which I am now concerned is really one which is very akin in many respects, so far as relevant protection is concerned, to plants and new varieties of plants. These micro-organisms, it was said, are merely carrying out a natural function; they are found by the investigator in nature; they are subject to mutation so that new varieties are derived, as may be the case with plants. When these new varieties have been derived by mutation, they may be found to have particularly desirable properties, as may be the case with new plants producing blooms of particular colours or of especial fragrance or improved fruit. What was suggested was that the Patents Act is really not of sufficient breadth to cover a process using a micro-organism growing in the natural way; and that, if protection is to be given for processes based on the use of micro-organisms of this kind, it can only be through the passage of some legislation comparable with the Plant Varieties and Seeds Act 1964.

I decline so to hold. These Streptomyces, to take merely the example of the micro-organisms with which I am particularly concerned, do not, so far as is known, produce antibiotics in nature at all. They have to be transferred to some appropriate medium, selected, mutated, re-selected and so on, before they produce any, still less any appreciable, quantity of antibiotic. Production of the required antibiotic may, indeed will, require a whole series of selection and mutation steps, and the whole process is one which at the end, before the antibiotic which goes on the market is produced, will involve a great variety of manufacturing techniques. Such a process is, to my mind, in no way analogous to the production by selective breeding of, for example a better tomato, an example chosen by counsel for the plaintiffs. It appears to me to use the present case as an example, that the work of Dr Growich and his assistant, Mr Deduck, in the production of mutant strains which produce nearly 100 per cent tetracycline – the four T-strains and the two S-strains – was as much, and the use of the specific strains in a process such as is claimed by the subsidiary claims of the Growich patent can be considered as much, a method for producing a new and salutary effect intimately connected with trade and manufacture as was the method involving the operation of James Watt's condenser. I reject this attack.

1.2.3.8 *Schering's Application* [1971] R.P.C. 337 (Patents Appeal Tribunal in banc)

The applicant sought to patent its discovery that a known type of oral contraceptive, a particular gestagen, could effectively be administered in much smaller doses than had previously been given. This reduced undesirable side-effects.

Claim 1 read:
"A method of contraception without suppression of ovulation, wherein there is administered to a human female parenterally or by implantation a gestagen as hereinbefore defined, the gestagen being free from oestrogens and being administered in a dose as hereinbefore defined".

Whitford J. (for the Tribunal) reviewed the authorities under the pre-1977 law which precluded methods of medical treatment from the scope of the patent system and held them to be good law. He continued:

On a narrower line of defence the applicants say that a process for contraception is not a process for "medical treatment" in the sense of treatment to cure or prevent disease and that the established practice relates only to medical treatment. In the broader sense this does not, of course, meet the point that in the *C. and W.* case the Solicitor-General, while endorsing the Patent Office refusal of the application on the ground that it related to medical treatment, in fact rejected the application because it was not directed to the making of an object of commercial value.

Reference has, however, already been made to the fact that today it is recognised that the vendible product "test", though sometimes useful, is not conclusive. The numerous authorities touching this question have been recently reviewed most comprehensively and lucidly in the decision of the High Court of Australia in *N.R.D.C's Application* (above, 1.2.3.2) and it is unnecessary to go through them again in detail. We agree fully with the reasons and conclusions in that case on this point and note that the desirability of having a homogeneous development of the law in all countries which have adopted our system of patent legislation was emphasised by Lord Parker, L.C.J., in the *Swift* case [1962] R.P.C. 47.

In *Cementation Co's Application* (1945) 62 R.P.C. 151 claims to a method of treating subterranean formations by the injection of chemicals so as to avoid or suppress underground combustion were allowed in this Tribunal. The present claim is to a process involving a chemical treatment which will avoid or suppress conception. Unless any treatment of the human body, as opposed to medical treatment to cure or prevent disease, is to be considered as being outside the scope of patent protection, there seems to be no reason why such a claim should not be allowed. The process is in the field of the useful as opposed to the fine arts. It is of commercial significance because it will produce a result which people are going to be prepared to pay for and which is widely considered desirable in the present climate of public opinion. It ought to be protected if it is, as must be accepted for the present purposes, of inventive merit and because it is a process which others no doubt would be only too anxious to adopt, if they could, without paying tribute to anyone.

The application was accordingly permitted to proceed to grant.

1.2.3.9   *Unilever's (Davis) Application* [1983] R.P.C. 219 (Falconer J.)

Under the Patents Act 1977, an application was lodged of which Claim 1 was as follows:

"A method for immunising poultry against coccidiosis, wherein the poultry are reared on a diet comprising nutrient feed material containing added viable sporulated oocysts of at least one species of coccidia to which the poultry are susceptible, the oocysts being present in a concentration sufficient only to induce sub-clinical infection in the poultry."

The Patent Office objected that this could not be taken to be capable of industrial application, since (under s 4(2)) it was "an invention of a method of treatment of the human or animal body by surgery or therapy or of diagnosis practised on the human or animal body". The applicant, relying on medical works, argued that "therapy" related only to curative and not to prophylactic treatment. After reviewing the arguments in detail, Falconer J. concluded:

Thus far I am firmly of the view that the word "therapy" in section 4(2) is to be construed in its wider sense as meaning the medical treatment of disease, including preventive treatment, as well as curative treatment, and it is not to be construed in the narrower sense of meaning curative treatment only.

Mr Watson relied strongly on the principle of construction that, where the wording of a statute is *prima facie* ambiguous, there is a presumption against any change in the existing law. The principle is stated in the twelfth edition of Maxwell at page 116 thus:

> "It is presumed that the legislature does not intend to make any change in the existing law beyond that which is expressly stated in, or follows by implication from, the language in the statute in question. It is thought to be in the highest degree improbable that Parliament would depart from the general system of law without expressing its intention with irresistible clearness, and to give any such effect to general words merely because this would be their widest, usual, natural or literal meaning would be to place on them a construction other than that which Parliament must be supposed to have intended. If the arguments on a question of interpretation are 'fairly evenly balanced, that interpretation should be chosen which involves the least alteration of the existing law'."

That is a quotation from Lord Reid in *George Wimpey & Co Ltd v British Overseas Airways Corporation* [1955] A.C. 169 at 191.

Under that principle Mr Watson submitted that, if the word "therapy" can be regarded as having either the wider or the narrower meaning in section 4(2) and there is no other guidance, as he submits, in the Act to which one can refer, the court should construe it a way which would least prevent a person from obtaining a patent. He pointed out that in the prior art the medical treatment of persons, not only curative but prophylactic or preventive, was not patentable. He referred to *Schering A.G.'s Application* [1971] R.P.C. 337 and the dictum in the decision therein in the passage bridging pages 343 and 344, where it was authoritatively stated that methods for the medical treatment of human beings to cure or prevent disease were not patentable. Although this was so stated in that case, which was a case in the Patents Appeal Tribunal where both patent judges Graham J. and Whitford J. were sitting, the principle had long been established before that case.

Mr Watson submitted further that, in contradistinction to the position with regard to medical treatment for human beings, up to 1977 there had been many patents accepted and many granted for methods of medical treatment of animals. Mr Watson referred me to the decision in *Swift & Co's Application* [1962] R.P.C. 37, a case in which the invention was a method of improving the tenderness of meat by injecting an enzyme solution into the live animal shortly before slaughter, in which the Divisional Court quashed the decision of the Patents Appeal Tribunal which had upheld the Comptroller in refusing the application. It is correct, as Mr Watson submitted, that, as far as animals are concerned, such patents for the treatment of animals have been allowed to proceed to grant, and in particular following the decision of the Patent Office, given in the light of the *Swift* case, in *United States Rubber Company's Application* [1964] R.P.C. 104, which related to a method of medically treating an animal where it was stated it would be acceptable, though not acceptable in respect of human beings. That being the position with regard to patent applications in respect of methods of treatment of animals as distinct from human beings, Mr Watson submitted that the principle under which he brought this argument should be applied, namely, that in the absence of clear wording the legislature must be presumed not to have intended to change the law, in particular the law he is referring to as to the patentability of methods of treatment in respect of animals.

I do not see how the argument can begin to run in this particular case. It seems to me that there is no basis for the operation of that principle which Mr Watson invoked because Parliament made it abundantly clear in the long title to the Act which I have read that the old law of patents is being swept away. I have already read the title of the statute. Right at the beginning of that long title, the Act is described as "An Act to establish a new law of patents applicable to future patents". And again as I have already pointed out, this application is an application under the 1977 Act. I have already referred to section 130(7) which includes within its terms the very section with which we are now concerned, namely, section 4. One of the striking changes in the 1977 Act was to include for the first time in our patent law in section 1, as qualified by section 4, a statutory definition of what constituted a patentable invention.

But apart from that there is another difficulty inherent in this argument advanced by Mr Watson. Section 4(2) draws no distinction between the treatment of the human body and the treatment of the animal body. If "therapy" were to be read narrowly so as to include prophylactic treatment as the applicants contend it should, at least in relation to the treatment of animals, that narrow construction of "therapy" would apply equally to the treatment of human beings, or, as it is put in the section, to the human body, thus rendering patentable methods of prophylactic treatment of diseases of human beings. That would be a change in the law as it is stated in *Schering's* case which, as I have pointed out already, although stated clearly in that state, it had been a long-established principle before that case was decided.

Realising that difficulty, I think, Mr Watson submitted, as I understood him, that in section 4(2) the word "therapy" in relation to the treatment of human beings could have a different meaning from that which it bore in relation to the treatment of animals. I cannot think that Parliament intended the word "therapy" to be used in two different senses in section 4(2), one in relation to the treatment of the human and another in relation to the treatment of the animal body. The very language of the subsection it seems to me negates such a dual construction. I think there is much force in the observation of the principal examiner in the last sentence of the second complete paragraph of page 3 of his decision, where he says:

"Similarly if prophylactic treatments in the veterinary field were to be regarded as an exception, then section 4(2) would surely have made this clear."

In my judgment the word "therapy" in section 4(2) is to be construed in its wide meaning as including preventive, that is to say, prophylactic, treatment as well as curative treatment of disease of the human body and the animal body. Accordingly under the terms of section 4(2) the applicants' invention is not to be taken as being capable of industrial application, and is therefore not a patentable invention. Accordingly the appeal falls to be dismissed.

1.2.3.10 *T 245/87 (Siemens – Flow Measurement)* [1989] O.J. EPO 171 (Ex. Div.)

The applicant sought a patent for a method of measuring the flow of small quantities of liquid through a tube by injecting a bubble into the liquid and then measuring its rate of progression between two points on the tube. The technique could be applied in particular in a device planted in the human or animal body for the administration of a drug such as insulin. Claims 1–3 claimed the device without requiring that means be provided for linking the flow time thus ascertained to a control signal in order to control a device for conveying the liquid. Claim 4 covered this additional element.

The EPO Examining Division rejected all the claims by reference to EPC, Art. 52(4). Allowing the appeal, the Appeal Board offered the following comments:

In the Board's opinion the introduction of a drug into the human body by means of a device for controlled drug administration that has already been implanted is clearly unconnected with either a surgical or a diagnostic method.

The check on the operation of the device therefore requires no medical knowledge whatsoever as regards the behaviour of the body into which the device is introduced. For this reason the Board is satisfied that the problem objectively inferable from the application documents is addressed solely to the engineer designing the device for controlled drug administration and not to the doctor using the finished product.

Of Claims 1–3 the Appeal Board stated:

3.2.2 The Board regards such a method as solely matter for the apparatus designer. The operating parameters measured according to the method claimed allow the doctor complete liberty to plan the operating timetable of the pump – and thus the drug intake required for treatment – with medical discretion. Hence, even if under Claim 1 protection is granted for a method of measurement carried out in relation to an implanted device for controlled drug administration, the doctor is in no way hindered in exercising his professional skills, i.e. preventing, curing or alleviating illness; cf. also the definition of therapeutic action in point 3 of Decision T 144/83 of EPO Technical

Board of Appeal 3.3.1 dated 27 March 1986 (OJ EPO 1986, 301, 304). Non-commercial and non-industrial medical and veterinary activities are therefore not restricted by patent rights in this case; cf. in this connection point 22 of Decision G 1/83 of the EPO Enlarged Board of Appeal dated 5 December 1984 (OJ EPO 1985, 60–63).

3.2.3 A method therefore does not fall within the scope of the first sentence of Article 52(4) EPC if there is no functional link and hence no physical causality between its constituent steps carried out in relation to a therapy device and the therapeutic effect produced on the body by that device.

Of Claim 4 the Appeal Board stated:

5.2 In the Board's opinion, a finding that a claim seeks protection *inter alia* for a therapeutic method covered by Article 52(4) EPC is not warranted unless the said claim defines a control mechanism in full technical detail which, when embodied in an implanted device for controlled drug administration, clearly determines when what volume of which drug fluid is fed to the body within what period of time. Only then would the controlling action claimed, when featured in an implanted device for controlled drug administration, have any functional connection with the quality and quantity of the drug dose and a direct causal influence on the therapeutic effect produced, thus hindering the doctor in the exercise of his professional skill. The derivation and use of the control signal as specified in Claim 4, however, merely enhances the technical capabilities of the device and does not cause any such hindrance.

1.2.3.11 *T 116/85 (Wellcome-Pigs I)* [1989] O.J. EPO 13 (Tech. Bd. App.)

Pig mange is caused by an infestation of ectoparasites. The applicants for a European patent claimed a method of controlling such an infestation by applying a pesticide (admixed with an aliphatic hydrocarbon oil, in order to prevent the pesticide from being absorbed) to areas of a pig's body. The EPO refused the claim, relying upon EPC, Art. 52(4).

The Technical Board of Appeal upheld this view, but on a somewhat different basis. It reviewed Arts. 52–57 and concluded:

However, the scheme of Articles 52 to 57 as set out above makes it quite clear that even though agricultural methods in general are potentially patentable subject-matter, the particular methods defined in Article 52(4) EPC are excluded from patentability. In other words, for the particular methods defined in Article 52(4) EPC, Article 52(4) takes precedence over Article 57 EPC.

3.6 The excluded methods are:
(i) methods for treatment of the human or animal body by surgery or therapy;
(ii) diagnostic methods practised on the human or animal body.

3.7 The exclusion of such methods from patentability is not a new provision under the EPC. Prior to the coming into force of the EPC, such methods were excluded from patentability under the national laws of many European countries. The policy behind the exclusion of such methods is clearly in order to ensure that those who carry out such methods as part of the medical treatment of humans or the veterinary treatment of animals should not be inhibited by patents.

3.8 The Board has considered the relevant preparatory documents which led to the EPC. The interpretation of the Articles 52 and 57 EPC set out above appears to be fully consistent with such documents, in that the object of the provision of Article 52(4) EPC was to exclude from patentability 'treatment intended to cure or alleviate the suffering of animals' (see in particular Conference document BR/219/72, paragraph 27). . . .

In relation to the particular claim, the Board held:

4.3 Therefore, to summarise, if a claimed method requires the treatment of an animal body by therapy, it is a method which falls within the prohibition on patentability set out in Article 52(4) EPC. It is not possible as a matter of law to draw a distinction between such a method as carried out by a farmer and the same method as carried out by a veterinarian, and to say that the method when carried out by a farmer is an industrial activity and therefore patentable under Article 57, and when carried out by a veterinarian is a therapeutic treatment not patentable under Article 52(4). Nor is it possible as a matter of law to distinguish between the use of such a method for the treatment of ectoparasites and endoparasites.

4.4 A further question to be decided in this appeal is whether, as a matter of fact, the treatment of pigs infested with pig mange is treatment of a disease. The appellant has submitted that mange is not a disease. However, in the Board's view it is clear that, contrary to the submission of the appellant, mange is a disease of the skin which is caused by the presence of parasites. Thus the Shorter Oxford English Dictionary defines mange as 'A cutaneous disease occurring in many . . . animals, caused by an arachnidan parasite'. Furthermore, effective treatment of this disease is only possibly by treatment of the infected body so as to eradicate the ectoparasites which caused it.

The Examples in the descriptive part of the application in suit are all concerned with the treatment of pigs infested with pig mange (sarcoptes scabei). It is noted that the reference cited by the appellant – Monnig's *Veterinary Helminthology and Entomology*, London 1962 – at page 516 states that 'Sarcoptic mange is a scheduled disease in most countries'.

As a matter of fact, the Board therefore considers that the Examples in the application in suit are each carrying out a method of treatment of diseased pigs' bodies, and that such a method is a method for treatment of the animal body by therapy.

The Board refused to reach the opposite conclusion on the basis of Stafford-Miller's Application *[1984] F.S.R. 258, which it distinguished on two grounds:*

6.2 As to (i), the Board's finding set out in paragraph 4.4 above that the treatment of pigs infected with a pig mange is a therapeutic treatment of a disease is made on the basis of the evidence before it. The finding of the UK Patents Court to the effect that an infestation of lice on human beings is not a disease was based on different evidence, and is therefore not persuasive to the Board.

As to (ii) the legal framework in which the *Stafford-Miller* case was decided must be distinguished from that of the present appeal on the following basis . . . . Thus the function of the Patents Court in the *Stafford-Miller* case was only to decide whether the claimed invention in that case was possibly patentable: not whether it was actually patentable. The Court's conclusion in the penultimate sentence on page 261 reflects this function: '. . . I am not sufficiently satisfied that these claims fall on the wrong side of the line as to justify saying at this stage in their life that these patents are incapable of providing a good basis for a sound claim'. The Court thus gave the applicants the benefit of the doubt.

In contrast to the function of the UK Patents Court in the *Stafford-Miller* case, in the present case the function of this Board is to decide the question of actual patentability of the claims having regard to Article 52(4) EPC. Thus the decision in the present case would not cause any lack of uniformity in the law of the EPC countries.

The Board also held that there was no justification for taking a "special view" of the relation between Art. 52(4) and Art. 57, similar to that taken of "second medical applications" in the Eisai *case (see above).*

1.2.3.12   *T 58/87 (Salminen – Pigs III)* [1989] E.P.O.R. 125 (Tech. Bd. App.)

The patentee claimed a method and apparatus for preventing piglets from suffocating under the dam in a brooding pen, in which a sensor, such as a photo-electric cell, was placed to detect when the dam stood up; hot air could then be blown beneath her so as to discourage the piglets from going to her.

The Opposition Division and the Board of Appeal were united in upholding the claims, despite the opponent's objection that they fell within EPC Art. 52(4). The Board of Appeal stated:

The Board agrees in that the word 'therapy'

— covers any non-surgical treatment which is designed to cure, alleviate, remove or lessen the symptoms of, or prevent or reduce the possibility of contracting any malfunction of the animal body (cf. *Patent Law of Europe and the United Kingdom* by A.M. Walton, H.I.L. Laddie, J.P. Baldwin and D.J.T. Kitchin, 1983, page II [684]), and also
— relates to the treatment of a disease in general or to a curative treatment in the narrow sense as well as the alleviation of the symptoms of pain and suffering (cf. *Chambers Twentieth Century Dictionary*, 1399, 'Therapy'; *The Oxford English Dictionary*, Vol. XI, 280, 'Therapy'; and, for example, T144/83 (point 3) – OJ, EPO 1986, 301).

The behaviour of newborn piglets to creep under the dam standing up to eat and drink either during or after farrowing cannot be fairly regarded as a malfunction of piglets whose instinct is not adequately developed. Furthermore, as far as the language of Claim 1 is concerned, it clearly covers a method for protection of piglets from the disadvantageous consequences of this behaviour, such as suffocating under the dam, by blowing air under the standing dam thus creating unpleasant conditions for the piglets. This cannot reasonably be called a treatment by therapy, which is practised on the bodies of piglets, within the meaning of Article 52(4) EPC. As the Opposition Division rightly considered, the invention is concerned with preventing accidents, analogous to a method of preventing a worker from trapping his hand in machinery.

1.2.3.13   *Organon Laboratories' Application* [1970] R.P.C. 574 (Patents Appeal Tribunal) (Graham J.)

These proceedings tested the validity of a "pack claim" for the administration of a drug, as oral contraceptive for women. The claim read:

"A pack of between 20 and 27 discrete dosage units such as tablets, pills or capsules for human oral administration at the rate of one unit per day over a period of between 20 and 27 successive days in order to stimulate anovulatory cycles, comprising a tube, box or chart in or on which units of two different kinds are packed in a particular order together with written or printed indications or directions, the indications or directions and the manner of packing being such as to provide guidance in relation to and to facilitate the

taking at the said rate first of 6 to 13 units containing an oestrogenic compound only as a hormonal substance and consequently 14 to 16 units containing a combination of an oestrogenic compound and a progestative compound".

Graham J.:

The applicants claim to have discovered an improvement in the so-called and known "sequential" treatment to prevent conception. This known treatment involves the taking of an oestrogenic compound from the 2nd to 5th day after the beginning of the menstrual period until the 20th day and then taking a combination of oestrogenic and progestative compounds from the 20th to the 25th day. The applicants' improvement, which they have christened the "Normophasic" method, involves also two successive phases and preferably lasts for 22 days, beginning not later than the 5th day after the onset of the last menstruation, the first period during which an oestrogenic compound is taken lasting 7 days, and the second phase during which a combined oestrogenic and progestative compound is taken lasting 15 days. The Normophasic method is claimed to be "fully reliable", and if it turns out to be so it will no doubt be recognised as a valuable new weapon in the armoury of our female population. For present purposes, it will be assumed to be a novel discovery.

The invention claimed, however, is not the discovery of the Normophasic method, but is the box or card in or on which the pills suitable for taking during one menstrual period are arranged in no doubt a convenient order for following the accompanying instructions, and the question for decision is whether such a box or card with the pills so arranged is a manner of new manufacture within the section. . . .

The discovery of a new method of treatment, which may itself be very meritorious even though not patentable, may it seems to me give subject matter to a pack or card of pills suitable for the carrying out of that method if, first, there is something novel in the constitution of the pack or card itself. Thus there might be something novel and not obvious in the particular physical form or structure of the pack or card, such as for example in the method of attachment of the pills to the card in order to ensure that they cannot be taken in the wrong order or in the physical structure of the parts or construction of the pack, which has the same effect. Secondly, however, even though, as in the case here, the general public are in possession of the idea that pills can usefully be arranged on a card or in a pack with suitable instructions to enable any particular course of treatment to be carried out, there may also be room for an invention or manner of new manufacture within the section consisting of the mere idea of a new card with the particular pills arranged in the new order suitable for the newly discovered method of treatment if there is no reason why anyone would be likely to want to arrange those pills in that order, unless and until they had learned of the new method. Though the truth may be that the basic discovery lies in the method of treatment and not in the arrangement of the pills on the card and though the arrangement itself is not in any way a guarantee that the treatment must or will be followed, the card itself cannot unequivocally be said to be obvious if no-one would be likely to want to make it except for the treatment in question.

1.2.3.14   *Ciba-Geigy (Dürr) Application* [1977] R.P.C. 83 (C.A.)

The plaintiff discovered that a known chemical could be used as a selective weed-killer to kill monocotyledinous weeds (such as grasses) occurring in a monocotyledinous crop. In order to secure effective protection against competitors it sought a "pack claim" in the following terms:

"12. A compound of the formula defined in claim 1 in a container which bears instructions for use in selectively combating weeds at a locus comprising wheat, barley, rye, oats, rice, maize, cotton or soya".

Russell L.J. (for the C.A.):

At the outset of the argument we were startled by the proposition that it can be an invention to state in writing that which has been discovered; that is to say, that the known material can be used to combat selectively weeds in the loci described. It is however clear that if the claim can be sustained so that rival manufacturers of the substance cannot without infringement or licence sell in containers bearing the information in question, it will contribute greatly to the solution of the policing problem. Graham J. after discussing the cases of *L'Oreal* [1970] R.P.C. 565 and *Organon* [1970] R.P.C. 574 and *Dow Corning* [1974] R.P.C. 235 and after referring to a passage from the opinion of Lord Roche in the *Mullard* case [1936] R.P.C. 323 with a comment thereon with which we agree, summarised his decision as follows:

> "Applying the principles of those cases ... it seems quite impossible to say that by the claim (claim 12) ... the applicants here are doing any more than claiming any package of any shape or size which will not in any way be modified by any instructions also included, that pack containing only a well-known and admittedly old material ... they have not by the words used in any way modified their pack or qualified it so that it has a particular shape or construction or is particularly suitable for the purpose for which the material is intended to be used. It is really in effect only claiming the old material as such".

We find ourselves entirely in agreement with the decision of the Patents Appeal Tribunal. We cannot see that it can sensibly be said that there is any invention involved in claim 12, any manner of new manufacture. The invention is the discovery that this known substance may be used without harm to the stated crops for the purpose of selectively combating weeds. There seems to us to be nothing inventive about parcelling up the known material in any and every convenient package or container having written thereon the information that it can be used for the stated purpose in the stated loci. There is no interaction between the container with its contents and the writing thereon. The mere writing cannot make the contents in the container a manner of new manufacture. There is nothing novel in the mere presentation of information by ordinary writing or printing on a container.

1.2.3.15 *Schering's and Wyeth's Applications* [1985] R.P.C. L 545 (Patents Court: Whitford and Falconer J.J.)

The decision considered the patentability and novelty of claims involving the discovery of a second medical use for a known substance. The proposed claims were in two main forms: (i) use of the substance for the new purpose; and (ii) use of the substance for manufacturing a medicament for the new purpose (the "Swiss form", since its recognition by the Swiss Patent Office). The Patents Court rejected the claims of the first type, but allowed those of the second.

(i) Substance-for-new-use claims
Claim 1 of Wyeth's Application read: "The use of a guanidine of [given formula] or a pharmaceutically acceptable acid addition salt thereof in treating diarrhoea in mammals or poultry". The substances were already known to be effective for lowering blood pressure, as hyperglycaemic agents and for anti-ulcer treatment. The UK Patent Office had already rejected similar claims in the "Hydropyridine" decision (Bayer's Application [1984] R.P.C. 11). But the German Supreme Court had allowed them in the equivalent German

application (OJ EPO 1983, p.26). The Enlarged Board of Appeal of the EPO, in Eisai's Application *(see below), had chosen to pronounce it "unfortunate" that in consequence Bayer had not appealed to the Patents Court in the UK, because "the decisions of the national courts of two Contracting States tending in the same direction might have had great weight".*

In the present application, Falconer J. stated:

While, of course, this court will desire at all times to pay respect to the decisions of the Federal Court of Justice of the Federal Republic of Germany, the Federal Court's Hydropyridine decision appears to be based on earlier German national case law whereas this court (as also the Comptroller) has to apply the United Kingdom statute, the relevant provisions of which, as already indicated, we think have been correctly applied by the Principal Examiner in refusing to allow claims worded in the form of Wyeth claims 1 and 2.

(ii) Swiss form of claim
Claim 3 of Wyeth's Application read: "The use of a guanadine of [given formula] or a pharmaceutically acceptable acid salt thereof in the preparation of an antidiarrhoeal agent in ready-to-use drug form for treating or preventing diarrhoea in mammals or poultry". The Schering application contained equivalent claims. In rejecting them, the Hearing Officer relied upon Ciba-Geigy's (Dürr) Application *[1977] R.P.C. 83 and* Adhesive Dry Mounting v Trapp *(1910) 27 R.P.C. 341. Falconer J. held that such an invention was capable of industrial application (Patents Act 1977, s.1(1)(c), 4) and was not merely the presentation of information (s.1(2)); but that, if the matter were one purely of interpreting s.1–4 of that Act (and especially s.2(6)), it would be difficult to conclude that the invention was novel. However he continued:*

But the matter is not to be considered without regard to the position, as it has developed, under the corresponding provisions of the E.P.C. As pointed out earlier, by section 130(7) of the 1977 Act, it is declared that certain sections, including, *inter alia,* section 4(2), 4(3) and 2(6), of the Act are so framed as to have the same effects in the United Kingdom as the corresponding provisions of the E.P.C. (respectively Articles 52(4) and 54(5)) have in the territories to which the E.P.C. applies, which territories include the United Kingdom. It is, therefore, convenient at this point to consider the decision of the Enlarged Board of Appeal of the E.P.O. in the *Eisai* case in respect of the Swiss form of claim.

In paragraph 21 the Board states:

"... Article 52(1) E.P.C. expresses a general principle of patentability for inventions which are industrially applicable, new and inventive and it is clear that in all fields of industrial activity other than those of making products for use in surgery, therapy and diagnostic methods, a new use for a known product can be fully protected as such by claims directed to that use.

"This is in fact the appropriate form of protection in such cases as the new and non-obvious use of the known product constitutes the invention and it is the clear intention of the European Patent Convention that a patent be granted for the invention to which a European patent application relates (compare Articles 52(1), 69, 84 and Rule 29 E.P.C. read together). Article 54(5) E.P.C. provides an exception to this general rule, however, so far as the first use of medicaments is concerned, in respect of which the normal type of use claim is prohibited by Article 52(4) E.P.C. In effect, in this case the required novelty for the medicament which forms the subject-matter of the claim is derived from the new pharmaceutical use".

"It seems justifiable by analogy to derive the novelty for the process which forms the subject-matter of the type of use claim now being considered from the new therapeutic use of the medicament and this irrespective of the fact whether any pharmaceutical use of the medicament was already known or not. It is to be clearly understood that the application of this special approach to the derivation of novelty can only be applied to claims to the use of substances or compositions intended for use in a method referred to in Article 52(4) E.P.C."

"The intention of Article 52(4) E.P.C., ... is only to free from restraint non-commercial and non-industrial medical and veterinary activities. To prevent the exclusion from going beyond its proper limits, it seems appropriate to take a special view of the concept of the 'state of the art' defined in Article 54(2) E.P.C. Article 54(5) E.P.C. alone provides only a partial compensation for the restriction on patent rights in the industrial and commercial field resulting from Article 52(4) E.P.C., first sentence. It should be added that the Enlarged Board does not deduce from the special provision of Article 54(5) E.P.C. that there was any intention to exclude second (and further) medical indications from patent protection other than by a purpose-limited product claim. ... No intention to exclude second (and further) medical indications generally from patent protection can be deduced from the terms of the European Patent Convention; nor can it be deduced from the legislative history of the articles in question."

"For these reasons, the Enlarged Board considers that it is legitimate in principle to allow claims directed to the use of a substance or composition for the manufacture of a medicament for a specified new and inventive therapeutic application, even in a case in which the process of manufacture as such does not differ from known processes using the same active ingredient.". . .

That approach to the novelty of the Swiss type of use claim directed to a second, or subsequent, therapeutic use if equally possible under the corresponding provisions of the 1977 Act and, notwithstanding the opinion expressed earlier as to the better view of the patentability of such a Swiss type claim under the material provisions of the Act considered without regard to the position, as it has developed, under the corresponding provisions of the E.P.C., having regard to the desirability of achieving conformity the same approach should be adopted to the novelty of the Swiss type of claim now under consideration under the material provisions of the Act.

1.2.4   Adequate Disclosure

1.2.4.1   *No Fume v Pitchford* [1935] 52 R.P.C. 231 (C.A.)

The plaintiff claimed a "smokeless" ashtray in the following terms:

"An ash receptacle which, without the use of moveable parts, retains the smoke rising from objects thrown into it, characterised by the fact that it consists of a closed container into which extends a shaft of substantially constant cross section, the sides of which, with the sides of the receptacle, form a trapped space closed above, whilst wholly beneath the shaft is provided a deflecting member, which deflects objects thrown in wholly to one side of the lower mouth of the shaft".

Romer L.J.:

Let me deal with the question of sufficiency first. Be it observed from the very words I have used, that the Patentee fulfils his duty if in his complete specification he describes and ascertains the nature of the invention, and the manner in which the invention is to be performed, sufficiently and fairly. It is not necessary that he should describe in his specification the manner in which the invention is to be performed, with that wealth of detail with which the specification of the manufacturer of something is usually put before the workman who is engaged to manufacture it. Specifications very frequently contain mistakes; they also have omissions. But if a man skilled in the art can easily rectify the mistakes and can readily supply the omissions, the patent will not be held to be invalid. The test to be applied for the purpose of ascertaining whether a man skilled in the art can readily correct the mistakes or readily supply the omissions, has been stated to be this: Can he rectify the mistakes and supply the omissions without the exercise of any inventive faculty? If he can, then the description of the specification is sufficient. If he cannot, the patent will be void for insufficiency.

That principle was laid down – I do not know whether for the first time or not in a reported case – in the case of *The King v Arkwright* reported in the first volume of Webster's Patent Cases p.64. There Mr Justice Buller, in summing up to the Jury, said this: "It has been truly said by the counsel, that if the specification be such that mechanical men of common understanding can comprehend it, to make a machine by it, it is sufficient; but then it must be such that the mechanics may be able to make the machine by following the directions of the specification, without any new inventions or additions of their own." It is plain, I think, that by the word "additions" the learned Judge meant inventive additions. That principle has been applied in numerous cases, to which Mr Whitehead called our attention in his opening and to which the Master of the Rolls has already referred. In those circumstances, I should only desire to refer to a short passage in the Judgment of Sir George Jessel in *Otto v Linford*, (46 Law Times N.S. 35). That was a case relating to the Otto gas engine; and it had been alleged, among other things, that the patent was void for insufficiency, inasmuch as the specification did not show the proportions in which the air was to be put in as regards the combustible mixture. Sir George Jessel said this, on page 41:

> "The first thing to be remembered, in specifications of patents, is that they are addressed to those who know something about the matter. A specification for improvements in gas motor engines is addressed to gas-motor engine-makers and workers, not to the public outside. Consequently you do not require the same amount of minute information that you would in the case of a totally new invention, applicable to a totally new kind of manufacture. In this case the inventor says this: 'I am going to turn that which was a sudden explosion of gas into a gradual explosion of gas, and I am going to do that by the introduction of a

cushion of air in one place between the piston and the combustible mixture'. If a man is left without any more information he asks: 'How much air am I to let in?' He lets in a little air, and he finds that the thing explodes as before; and he lets in some more, and he finds directly, on the mere regulation of his stop-cock, how much is required; and he finds very soon that he has let in enough, and now there is a gradual expansion, and no longer a sudden and explosive expansion. It does not appear to me that that requires invention. It requires a little care and watching, and that is all."

That being the principle to be applied, we turn to the specification of the Patent in suit. I am not going to read it again; but the Patentee tells us that he has discovered that, if an ash-tray be made so that it consists of "a closed container, into which extends an inlet shaft of substantially constant cross section, the sides of which, with the sides of the container form a trapped space completely closed above, whilst wholly beneath the shaft is provided a deflecting member which deflects everything that is thrown into the container away from and to one side of the lower mouth of the shaft", the smoke of a cigarette thrown into the shaft will not come out through the shaft but will be retained in the receptacle: subject, however, to this, that you must not make the container too large or too small, or the other integers he has mentioned too large or too small. You will not get the result of the smoke being contained, if you do. But once given the fact that, if the thing be made in the way mentioned, the desired result will be obtained if the various integers bear one to another the proper relative proportion, it requires no invention or inventive study further to discover within what limits those proportions should lie. That can be done easily enough by a series of experiments similar to the experiment Sir George Jessel referred to as necessarily being made by a workman who wanted to find, in the case of the Otto gas-engine, how much air he should let in to produce the result that the patentee said would be produced.

The Specification as has been pointed out by the Master of the Rolls, expressly says this:

"The dimensions of the shaft and of the deflecting member, relatively to one another and to the sides of the closed container, being so selected that the smoke rising from objects thrown into the container is collected entirely in the enclosed space, and upon cooling is again thrown down without, however, during its movement being able to pass the lower mouth of the shaft".

In other words, the Patentee does not tell the world within what limits the relative proportions of the integers he has mentioned must be kept to produce the desired result. If, however, a workman skilled in the art can by trial and error readily discover for himself what the proportions should be in order to give the desired result, then, inasmuch as I have already pointed out, that to discover those proportions requires the exercise of no inventive faculty at all, the Patentee has complied with his obligation.

It is further to be observed in this case that the Patentee does show a drawing illustrating, as he says, one construction of the ash-tray by way of example. So the workman has not only the common knowledge of his trade to help him, but he has also the example shown by the figure attached by the Patentee to the specification. Further, Mr Gill stated in his evidence that he found no difficulty whatsoever, by following the directions contained in the Specification, in making an ash-tray which had the desired result. On page 7 of the First Day of the evidence, he was asked this. Reading from the Defence, this question is put to him:

"It is impossible to discover from the specification what relative dimensions of the shaft, deflecting member and closed container, will satisfy the requirements of the invention".

That is from the Particulars of Objection. He was asked: "Do you find any such impossibility? (A.) No; I find no difficulty, following the Specification, in arriving at suitable dimensions, and nothing which I have done in attempting to carry out the invention has led me to any such difficulty as is suggested in this paragraph". It is established by the authorities that the question of sufficiency or non-sufficiency is a question of fact. That is the only evidence that has been given in this case upon this question. For that reason and for the other reasons which I have mentioned, I am of opinion that this Patent is not void for want of sufficiency.

Romer L.J. proceeded to hold the claims not unnecessarily ambiguous. Lord Hanworth M.R. and Maugham L.J. delivered judgments upholding the validity of the patent.

1.2.5 Synthesis

1.2.5.1 *Genentech's Patent* **[1989] R.P.C. 147 (C.A.)**

Where a patentee describes a new method of producing a known substance, there is an issue of fundamental importance concerning the permissible scope of monopoly to be granted. The issue may be raised under various grounds of invalidity, as this case amply demonstrates. Accordingly, it is presented here by way of summation to this section. The extracts from the judgments are placed under three heads: (i) patentable subject-matter: discovery "as such"; (ii) inventive step; (iii) the claims and insufficient disclosure.

The facts in outline: the patent was granted by the UK Patent Office and its validity attacked under the Patents Act 1977, s.72(1). Principal claims of the patent in suit related to human tissue plasminogen activator (t-PA). t-PA, a protein, was known to occur in very small amounts in human tissue. Its function was to activate the conversion of existing precursor plasminogen into plasmin, an enzyme capable of dissolving fibrin in blood clots. t-PA was obviously desirable as a therapeutic agent if it could be produced in quantity. Cells of Bowes melanoma, a human tumour cell line, were known to secrete t-PA. By means of genetic engineering, using a particular route of recombinant DNA technology, the pai.ntees took the relevant genetic information from the cell line and expressed it in micro-organisms capable of producing t-PA as a therapeutically acceptable product. The background was briefly as follows.

A protein such as t-PA was known to consist of certain amino acids arranged in a particular sequence, and techniques for establishing the sequence were known, although the whole sequence of t-PA itself was not. The sequence of amino acids was known to correspond to a sequence of nucleotides in the essential genetic material (DNA) of the cell in which the protein was made according to a known code associating each triplet of nucleotides with an amino acid. It was known that, in forming protein, the information in the DNA was first transcribed into messenger RNA (mRNA) of a complementary nucleotide sequence and then translated from the mRNA into the amino acid sequence of the newly formed protein. It was also known that complementary DNA (cDNA) could be formed by reverse transcription from the mRNA, that this cDNA could be inserted into plasmids, that the plasmids could be used to transform suitable micro-organisms or other hosts, and that growth of the latter could replicate the cDNA and produce the protein free of other proteins of the cell from which the genetic information orginated.

Reverse transcription of a population of mRNAs from Bowes melanoma cells formed a corresponding population of cDNAs. The technique used by the patentees to identify and isolate the individual cDNA corresponding to t-PA involved making short lengths of synthetic DNA which contained the nucleotide sequences corresponding to known fragments of the amino acid sequence of t-PA. Synthetic DNA having a nucleotide sequence identical with part of the sequence in the desired c-DNA would be expected to bind to it and could therefore be used to identify it.

On the evidence, at least five teams embarked independently on research in this direction. It involved laborious and costly effort and success was not certain. The patentees had been the first to discover the nucleotide sequence of the cDNA corresponding to t-PA (and hence the amino acid sequence of t-PA itself), and this discovery formed the basis of the alleged invention of the patent in suit.

Since there were many potential variations that could be introduced in the production of t-PA by recombinant DNA technology, claims merely to the particular route described in the patent were of no commercial significance. The following proved to be the claims of most significance in the litigation:

3. Human tissue plasminogen activator as produced by recombinant DNA technology.

7. A recombinant cloning vector comprising a DNA sequence encoding human tissue plasminogen activator.

8. A replicable expression vector capable, in a transformant micro-organism or cell culture, of expressing a DNA sequence according to claim 7.

16. A process which comprises expressing DNA encoding human tissue plasminogen activator in a recombinant host cell.

17. A process for producing human t-PA, which process comprises:
   a. preparing a replicable expression vector capable of expressing the DNA sequence encoding human t-PA in a host cell;
   b. transforming a host cell culture to obtain a recombinant host cell;
   c. culturing said recombinant host cells under conditions permitting expression of said t-PA encoding DNA sequence to produce human t-PA;
   d. recovering said human t-PA.

These should be compared with the narrow claims:

9. The plasmid > RIPA or pt-PAtrp12.

19. A process for producing human tissue plasminogen activator, substantially as described herein.

(i) The attack that the claims were to a discovery "as such" and so excluded by the Patents Act 1977, s.1(2)(a).

Purchas L.J.:

12.09 In my judgment the plain and ordinary interpretation to be given to the words "only to the extent that" in conjunction with "relates to that thing as such" is derived from taking the two phrases together as meaning that any of the matters listed in sub-paragraphs (a) to (d) shall not be an invention for the purposes of the Act. *Semble*, otherwise they would have constituted inventions and shall only to the extent that the application or patent relates to that step as such be disqualified. Applying this approach to the facts of the present case, a claim for the figure 5 data would be a claim to a discovery as such and only to that extent would be disqualified by section 1(2). If, on the other hand, the discovery is one that was not known in the state of the art at the material date and was not obvious to a person skilled in the art, then it is capable of forming the substratum of invention so that if it is applied in a technique or process or incorporated in a product then it would be patentable. This is in line with the judgments in *Hickton's* case [(1909) 26 R.P.C. 339] and the opinions expressed by the Technical Board of Appeal in *Vicom's* case [above, 1.2.3.3]. It is also what I believe to have been the view of Whitford J. [at first instance]:

> "It is trite law that you cannot patent a discovery, but if on the basis of that discovery you can tell people how it can be usefully employed then a patent or invention may result. This in my view would be the case even though once you have made the discovery the way in which it can be usefully employed is obvious enough".

Purchas L.J. accordingly rejected the contrary proposition adopted by Falconer J. (Merrill Lynch's Application (above, 1.2.3.4) first instance) that "an invention was unpatentable if the inventiveness was contributed only by matters excluded under s.1(2)"; and that therefore it was necessary to take into account "whether the non-excluded features were already known or obvious".

Dillon L.J. agreed with Purchas L.J. on the general principle. However, in applying it to the facts, Dillon L.J. found that only two of the broadest claims (Claims 2 and 4, neither of which the patentee sought to rely upon) were for discoveries as such. Purchas L.J., on the contrary, considered that, as currently drafted, all the claims failed under this head:

The "vehicle" by which the "discovery" can become an invention need not itself be "new" in the sense of section 2(1) in order to escape the disqualification in section 1(2)(a) if the principles in *Hickton's* case apply. . . .

I am able to accept part of Mr Gratwick's submission that Genentech should be entitled to protection not only in respect of their plasmids detailed in their specification but also in respect of plasmids or vectors readily available within the state of the art, or immediate derivations or variations thereof. I would extend this to include plasmids or vectors incorporating genes resulting from minor adjustments to the molecular structure of the gene disclosed in figures 4, 5 and 12 of the patent. I think that this accords with the sense of the Protocol to Article 69.

However, as I have already indicated, Mr Gratwick's contention that Genentech should be protected against any use of this information, howsoever this may be achieved in the future, is, in my view, not a claim to a method embracing the discovery but rather a claim for protection of the discovery as such. There are two reasons for this: first, the claim is speculative as to the method by which the discovery is to be embraced; secondly, the method is not capable of description and it must fail under section 72(1)(c). Again, I believe that this limitation does justice between the patentee and the public and is in accordance with the Protocol to Article 69.

On the interpretation of s.1(2)(a), Mustill L.J. remained in doubt. His uncertainty related to an entirely general objection arising under s.1(2) – that a patent could be held invalid if it was not granted for an "invention", as distinct from an invention patentable in accordance with the four criteria prescribed in s.1(1). Mustill L.J. doubted in particular that there could ever be a patent for finding out previously unknown properties of a known substance. With this radical view, Dillon L.J. expressly disagreed. He pointed out that it would render invalid patents for much successful pharmaceutical research currently thought to be within the scope of the system.

(ii) The attack on lack of inventive step.

Dillon L.J.:

The next question, which is fundamental to this appeal, is whether the invention involved an inventive step or was obvious to persons skilled in the art.

This is always a difficult question where highly specialised science or technology is involved. The judge was of the view that there was an inventive step – see his judgment at page 596 lines 14 to 21. Otherwise he could not have been prepared to uphold even claims 9 and 19. But it is clear that in this court we have to evaluate the evidence afresh and form our own independent opinion, as is explained in *Benmax v Austin Motor Co Ltd* (1955) 72 R.P.C. 39.

It is common ground that the persons skilled in the art in the present case, for the purposes of section 3 of the 1977 Act and the test of obviousness, would be a team of persons, each of whom would be the holder of a PhD in a relevant field of science. They are thus necessarily persons of very considerable intellectual capacity, but by force of the terms of the section whatever is obvious to them has to be obvious without any inventive step of their part.

It is agreed between the experts that at the relevant time, in early May 1982, the production of quantities of t-PA adequate to treat human patients suffering from blood clots was known to be a desirable objective and it is further agreed that the Bowes melanoma cell-line was then available and was known to be a source of t-PA and of the corresponding mRNA. It was of course then known that the nucleotide and amino-acid sequences of t-PA existed, though their composition was not known. All the steps taken by Genentech in finding out the composition of the sequences and applying that knowledge to produce human t-PA, as defined in the specification, by recombinant DNA technology were applications of known technology, and no step was by itself inventive.

It is not in doubt that empirical research industriously pursued may lead to a patentable invention. This was stated by Lord Simonds in *May & Baker Ltd v Boots Pure Drug Co Ltd* (1950) 67 R.P.C. 23 at 34, a case concerned with the discovery of two new sulphathiazole drugs, and the application of those drugs for medicinal purposes. What Lord Simonds said was amplified by Lord MacDermott at page 50 as follows:

> "The problem was to find some substance at once less toxic and more effectual against certain infections than sulphanilamide. Each of the new compounds provided a solution. They were produced by known methods from known materials and the inventive step lay in the discovery of their virtue as drugs. This achievement was not the result of applying any known principle or law of nature. It was entirely empirical. No doubt the inventors used skill and experience of a high order in selecting a profitable line of research. But they had not means of knowing that success had crowned their efforts until the new products had been tested by experiment".

The patent merited by such empirical research ought to have been limited to the actual new drugs discovered. No question of obviousness was however raised in that case, but that, as it seems to me, was because the drugs discovered were indeed new and the profitable line of research selected by the inventors was not obvious.

There are also observations in relation to scientific discoveries, in particular in the field of antibiotics, by Lord Diplock in his dissenting speech in *American Cyanamid Co (Dann's) Patent* [1971] R.P.C. 425, where he said at page 451:

> "Since the original discovery of the therapeutic uses of antibiotics and of the methods of aerobic fermentation by which they can be produced from micro-organisms to be found in nature, further advances in this field of medicines have been achieved by searching for and finding hitherto unidentified strains of micro-organisms existing in the natural state from which useful new antibiotics can be prepared by what is now a well-known standard process. The task of finding such a strain of micro-organism, calls for the exercise of technical proficiency and is laborious and very costly, for the odds against success are large. It is not easy to see what inventive step, as distinct from the mere exercise of proficiency and practice, is involved in this kind of research, but the result of success in it is a new product useful to humanity which does not exist in nature. If such research is to be encouraged in a competitive society, the monetary rewards of success must be assured to those who undertake the expense; and the means of doing so in this and in most other countries with comparable social systems is by according to the successful discoverer of the new product the controlled and limited monopoly granted for inventions under the national patent laws".

and at page 452:

> "It is in my view consistent with this basic policy to treat the kind of research involved in the discovery of a strain of micro-organism from which a new and useful antibiotic can be prepared as an activity which entitles the person who undertakes it to a temporary monopoly under the Patents Act 1949, of the product of his success. I accept, therefore, the extension of the concept of 'invention' to include antibiotics which are discovered through this kind of

research. But if this is to be done without defeating the basic policy of the Act one must also accept the necessary corollaries in the interpretation of those parts of it which deal with the information to be provided as the counterpart of the temporary monopoly granted to the inventor".

These observations were adopted by Whitford J. in the present case, and, as general statements of the law they are not challenged by Mr Jacob for the respondents. They were however *obiter*, in that there was no issue in the *American Cyanamid* case as to the patentability, as such, of the new antibiotic which had been discovered; the question was whether the disclosure in the patent was inadequate because strains of the newly discovered micro-organism had not been deposited and so were not available to the reader of the patent. Lord Diplock was therefore not concerned with any question of obviousness. Whitford J. seems however to have deduced in the present case from Lord Diplock's observations that as the work of Genentech involved, as he put it at page 596, laborious and costly effort amounting to rather more than the exercise of proficiency, it therefore involved an inventive step and cannot have been obvious to persons skilled in the art, within the meaning of section 3 of the 1977 Act. I have great difficulty in seeing the logic of this, since (as I have already said) Lord Diplock was not concerned with obviousness, and in the *American Cyanamid* case a new product had been found by following a line of empirical research which may well not have been obvious to anyone.

Lord Diplock was indeed concerned with obviousness, as Diplock L.J., in the case of *Johns-Manville Corp's Patent* [1967] R.P.C. 479. At pages 493–4 he expressed the view that the case that an allegedly inventive idea was at the priority date "obvious and clearly did not involve any inventive step" would have been made out if before the priority date the man skilled in the art would have thought the idea well worth trying out in order to see whether it would have beneficial results. He took the view that it would be enough that the person skilled in the art would assess the likelihood of success as sufficient to warrant actual trial, without postulating prior certainty of success. In *Olin Mathieson Chemical Corp v Biorex Laboratories Ltd* [1970] R.P.C. 157, Graham J., formulated the question at pages 187–8 as being whether a notional research group at the relevant date would have been directly led to try a certain idea, in the expectation that it might well produce a useful result. Again certainty of success was not postulated. In *Philips (Bosgra's) Application* [1974] R.P.C. 241 at 251, Whitford J. held that to render an invention obvious it was not necessary that the materials in question should have been the first choice of the notional research worker; it was enough that the materials were "lying in the road" and there for the research worker to use.

By the various tests set out in the immediately foregoing paragraph it was indeed obvious, in my judgment, to the person skilled in the art to set out to produce human t-PA by recombinant DNA technology. At least four teams did just that at about the same time. The evidence of those at Leuven and Umea as to their choice of projects is particularly relevant. The end was a known desiderandum, and to produce by oligonucleotide probing was, if not the first choice of each team, an early choice which lay in the way, ready to hand. It was indeed at one stage submitted for Genentech, as I understood Mr Gratwick, that it was not made out that the person skilled in the art would have known of the process of screening a library by the use of oligonucleotide probes, but in my judgment the evidence is ample that the process was well-known.

If indeed no one else had set to clone t-PA and produce human t-PA by recombinant DNA technology, the position on obviousness would, I apprehend, have been very different, and it could then have been said that a novel idea for a project, carried through with painstaking skill and proficiency to a successful end, involved an inventive step and merited patent protection. Even so, there would have been scope for much argument on the proper width of the claim.

As it is, however, the main argument for Genentech on the question of obviousness to persons skilled in the art has been that the hypothetical team of persons skilled in the art, even if they had thought of trying to do so, would not have succeeded in discovering the sequences. This is put, not on the basis that there was anything novel or original in the technology used by Genentech in discovering the sequences (since admittedly there was not) but on the basis that the person "skilled in the art" has come by judicial interpretation to mean the person only moderately skilled in the art. Indeed the running thread that showed through Mr Gratwick's very detailed analysis of the evidence was that in his submission whenever anything was required to be done, in the discovery of the sequences, that required skill in the art, the "person skilled in the art" would, almost *ex hypothesi*, have been able to do it.

The foundation for this submission appeared to be the decision of this court in *Valensi v British Radio Corp* [1973] R.P.C. 337. That case was however concerned with a different question, namely, the question, which now arises under sections 14(3) and 72(1)(c) of the 1977 Act, whether the specification of a patent, or application, discloses the invention clearly enough and completely enough for it to be performed by a person skilled in the art. It was held, and the good sense of the conclusion is obvious, that the hypothetical addressees were not – or were not merely – persons of exceptional skill and knowledge, like the expert witnesses in that case, but skilled technicians from whom a team could be constituted which would possess the common knowledge of those in the relevant arts but would not have the capacity to make elaborate additions to or modifications of what was disclosed in a specification. The application of that to the question of obviousness and inventive step under section 3 of the 1977 Act might in an appropriate case be that if a new line of research or some other original step would only have occurred to a particularly brilliant or inventive person in the art, and not to persons skilled in the art generally, then that line of research or original step was inventive and not obvious. That is not, however, this case since the production of human t-PA by recombinant DNA technology was an obvious choice as a line of research, and the discovery of the sequences was achieved by known technology without any original step. In such a case as the present, the ability of the person skilled in the art, or moderately skilled in the art, to perform known techniques has, in my judgment, nothing to do with the question of obviousness or inventive step under section 3. I cannot see that there is an inventive step in the use by Genentech among the processes by which they discovered the sequences of a known process not devised by Genentech which only persons of high skill in the art – of whom there are many – have the ability to perform.

In agreeing with Dillon L.J. that the case on obviousness was made out, Mustill L.J. stated:

I now turn to the second group of problems arising under section 3, which concern the meaning of "a person skilled in the art". The trouble is, of course, that in a case like this no such person exists. The successful pursuit of Genentech's research required the deployment of techniques in more than one field: for example, protein sequencing, handling mRNA, building a library, making a probe. I am satisfied on the evidence that there was nobody who united in himself (or herself) all the knowledge and practical skills in each field to a sufficient extent to carry out any kindred project, even if assumed to be non-inventive, on his own. This fact has two corollaries, neither of which I understood to be in dispute. First, that the hypothetical person is a team of persons. Second, that since the search embraced a series of arts, the obviousness of any particular contribution to the ultimate success must be adjudged by reference individually to the hypothetical members of the team, attributing to each the appropriate degree of skill.

The next question relates to the staffing and equipment of the team, a topic on which there appears to be no authority. As to staffing, this arises because some of the teams sent the work of sequencing or probe manufacturing to workers or laboratories outside. I see no problem here. Once it is accepted that the hypothetical team is practising a variety of arts through a variety of individuals, it seems to me that it makes no difference whether they are conceived to be working together as a single unit, or whether the notional individuals against whose notional skills the obviousness of the invention is to be tested are regarded as sub-contractors. The standard for skills is the same.

The question of equipment is more puzzling, largely, I believe, because traditional patent law, and indeed the current legislation, is ill at ease with this type of complex and rapidly developing new technology. It seems to me, however, that since we are looking to distinguish the inventive spark from a triumph of method, we should credit the hypothetical team with the best available equipment to see whether, so equipped, they could have found their way to a solution without exceeding the permitted maximum of inventive thinking.

On this issue, Purchas L.J. dissented (hence the importance of his broad view of "discovery as such".)

(iii) The attack concerning the scope of the claims in relation to the invention disclosed.

At first instance, Whitford J. found against validity of the patent solely on the ground that the claims were "not supported by the description". He held that this requirement, which must be applied by the Patent Office during the course of considering an application (see s.14(5)), must also be treated as a ground for revocation after grant within s.72, despite the absence of any express reference to it there. The members of the C.A. refused to adopt this view.

Dillon L.J.:

The 1977 Act was enacted to give effect to this country's adherence to the European Patent Convention, and that in turn was entered into by the contracting countries in order to establish a unified patent law throughout all those countries. Although there had been previous international patent conventions, there is no reason whatever to suppose that that unified patent law, as enacted in the 1977 Act, would be in all respects identical with the previous United Kingdom patent law, Section 72 of the 1977 Act is categorical in providing that a patent may be revoked on (but only on) any of the grounds specified in the section. Furthermore section 74 specifies in subsection (1) the only proceedings in which the validity of a patent may be put in issue, including proceedings for revocation under section 72, and then categorically provides in subsection (2) that the validity of a patent may not be put in issue in any other proceedings, and in subsection (3) that the only grounds on which the validity of a patent may be put in issue (whether in proceedings for revocation under section 72 or otherwise) are the grounds on which the patent may be revoked under that section. There is no general or inherent power in the court to revoke a patent if the court feels that it should not have been granted, or should not have been granted in such wide terms.

One of the other permissible grounds for revocation in section 72 is ground (c): "the specification of the patent does not disclose the invention clearly enough and completely enough for it to be performed by a person skilled in the art". That clearly reflects section 14(3) of the 1977 Act, but there is nothing in section 72 to reflect section 14(5), and the fact that section 14(3) is deliberately picked up in section 72, while section 14(5) is not, makes it impossible to imply that failure to comply with section 14(5) in relation to the claims in a patent is to provide grounds for revocation under section 72. Ground (a) of the grounds for revocation in section 72 "that the invention is not a patentable invention" refers back to section 1, which defines what is a patentable invention, and to sections, 2, 3 and 4 which explain that definition, but it does not, in my judgment, refer back to section 14(5).

If, therefore, there is a patentable invention and a patent is granted, that patent cannot be revoked – nor can its validity be disputed – on the grounds that the claims in the patent as granted do not comply with section 14(5). Section 14(5) reflects the provisions of Article 84 of the European Patents Convention. I see no escape, on the scheme Convention and of the 1977 Act, from the conclusion of the appeals board of the European Patent Office in the cases of *Naimer's Patent (Decision T23/86)* [1987] Official Journal, E.P.O. 316, and *Mobil Oil Corp's Patent (Decision Gr01/84)* [1985] Official Journal E.P.O. 299, decided on 24 July 1985 that in the absence of any application by the patentee to introduce amended claims an objection under Article 84 is inadmissible in opposition or revocation proceedings, and that opposition, or revocation, proceedings are not a continuation, involving third parties, of the examination proceedings in the Patent Office.

It follows, incidentally, that in considering in the course of the examination of an application in the Patent Office, whether the claims satisfy the requirements of section 14(5) of the 1977 Act, the Patent Office ought to have very clearly in mind that it is undesirable to allow claims the object of which is to cover a wide and unexplored field or where there is no disclosure in the specification which is in any way coterminous with the monopoly indicated in the claims.

This appeal must therefore be decided on grounds other than those on which the judge based his decision in the court below.

Mustill L.J. concluded similarly, but added the following:

There remains, however, one further possibility, namely that the specification does not disclose the invention clearly enough and completely enough for it to be performed by a person skilled in the art. That this differs from an allegation that the claim is not supported by the description, and in that (unlike such an allegation) it may be brought forward in revocation proceedings, is clear from sections 14(3), 14(5) and 72(1). Significantly, the Guidelines say this, at D-III, 5:

> "The following allegations, for example, do not constitute grounds for opposition: that the proprietor of the patent is not entitled to the European patent, that the subject matter of the patent lacks unity, that the claims are not supported by the description (unless it is also argued that the claims are so broadly worded that the description in the specification does not sufficiently disclose the subject-matter within the meaning of Article 100, sub-paragraph (b)). ..."

One must, therefore, ask this: Given the benefit of the specification to work from, could a person ordinarily skilled in the art create without a further inventive act all the products stipulated in claim 8? If I have correctly interpreted this claim, at an earlier stage of the present judgment, it seems to me that the answer must be negative. Indeed,

I believe that even an inventive person could not be guaranteed to construct all these products in the present state of the technology. If this is so, claim 8 and also the associated claim 7 must be apt for revocation.

I have hesitated before expressing this conclusion, partly because I am conscious of the risk that to allow the objection would let back into the case the trial judge's ground for decision, which all are agreed is excluded by section 72(1), and partly because this way of putting the matter was not foreshadowed in the respondents' Particulars of Objections. As to the former, however, it is undeniable that a patent, and an application for a patent, may be invalid on grounds which give different statutory labels to what are essentially the same flaws: and any qualms are largely allayed by my strong impression that, by whatever route attained, the conclusion is fair. As to the question of pleading, I entirely endorse the view that in the interests of an orderly and just trial an objector should, as a rule, be held to the case which he has reduced to writing. But the present litigation is out of the ordinary. Against the background of a complex and unfamiliar technology the parties have had to address a series of legal concepts which, to me at least, have seemed remarkably elusive. In the event there have throughout the proceedings been substantial reformulations and shifts on both sides. This is not a matter for surprise or criticism, but it does suggest that insistence to what would otherwise be healthy formalities would be out of place. I am satisfied that counsel for Genentech have been able to muster a full response to this line of argument, and that there will be no injustice if it is given its full weight.

1.3 Infringement

1.3.1 Scope of Monopoly

1.3.1.1 European Patent Convention, Art. 69 and Protocol; Patents Act 1977, s.125, 130(7): Extent of protection

European Patent Convention
Art.69(1) The extent of the protection conferred by a European patent or a European patent application shall be determined by the terms of the claims. Nevertheless, the description and drawings shall be used to interpret the claims.

(2) For the period up to grant of the European patent, the extent of the protection conferred by the European patent application shall be determined by the latest filed claims contained in the publication under Article 93. However, the European patent as granted or as amended in opposition proceedings shall determine retroactively the protection conferred by the European patent application, in so far as such protection is not thereby extended.

Protocol on the Interpretation of Article 69
Article 69 should not be interpreted in the sense that the extent of the protection conferred by a European patent is to be understood as that defined by the strict, literal meaning of the wording used in the claims, the description and drawings being employed only for the purpose of resolving an ambiguity found in the claims. Neither should it be interpreted in the sense that the claims serve only as a guideline and that the actual protection conferred may extend to what, from a consideration of the description and drawings by a person skilled in the art, the patentee has contemplated. On the contrary, it is to be interpreted as defining a position between these extremes which combines a fair protection for the patentee with a reasonable degree of certainty for third parties.

Patents Act 1977
S.125(1) For the purposes of this Act an invention for a patent for which an application has been made or for which a patent has been granted shall, unless the context otherwise requires, be taken to be that specified in a claim of the specification of the application or patent, as the case may be, as interpreted by the description and any drawings contained in that specification, and the extent of the protection conferred by a patent or application for a patent shall be determined accordingly.

(2) It is hereby declared for the avoidance of doubt that where more than one invention is specified in any such claim, each invention may have a different priority date under section 5 above.

(3) The Protocol on the Interpretation of Article 69 of the European Patent Convention (which Article contains a provision corresponding to subsection (1) above) shall, as for the time being in force, apply for the purposes of subsection (1) above as it applies for the purposes of that Article.

S.130(7) Whereas by a resolution made on the signature of the Community

Patent Convention the governments of the member states of the European Economic Community resolved to adjust their laws relating to patents so as (among other things) to bring those laws into conformity with the corresponding provisions of the European Patent Convention, the Community Patent Convention and the Patent Cooperation Treaty, it is hereby declared that the following provisions of this Act, this is to say, sections 1(1) to (4), 2 to 6, 14(3), (5) and (6), 37(5), 54, 60, 69, 72(1) and (2), 74(4), 82, 83, 88(6) and (7), 100 and 125, are so framed as to have, as nearly as practicable, the same effects in the United Kingdom as the corresponding provisions of the European Patent Convention, the Community Patent Convention and the Patent Cooperation Treaty have in the territories to which those Conventions apply.

1.3.1.2 *Electrical and Musical Industries Ltd v Lissen* [1939] 56 R.P.C. 23 at 39–42 (H.L.)

Lord Russell:

The Court of Appeal have stated that in their opinion no special rules are applicable to the construction of a specification, that it must be read as a whole and in the light of surrounding circumstances; that it may be gathered from the specification that particular words bear an unusual meaning; and that, if possible, a specification should be construed so as not to lead to a foolish result or one which the patentee could not have contemplated. They further have pointed out that the claims have a particular function to discharge. With every word of this I agree; but I desire to add something further in regard to the claim in a specification.

The function of the claims is to define clearly and with precision the monopoly claimed, so that others may know the exact boundaries of the area within which they will be trespassers. Their primary object is to limit and not to extend the monopoly. What is not claimed is disclaimed. The claims must undoubtedly be read as part of the entire document, and not as a separate document; but the forbidden field must be found in the language of the claims and not elsewhere. It is not permissible, in my opinion, by reference to some language used in the earlier part of the specification, to change a claim which by its own language is a claim for one subject-matter, which is what you do when you alter the boundaries of the forbidden territory. A patentee who describes an invention in the body of a specification obtains no monopoly unless it is claimed in the claims. As Lord Cairns said, there is no such thing as infringement of the equity of a patent, *Dudgeon v Thomson*, (1877) 3 App.C. as 34. . . .

I would point out that there is no question here of words in Claim 1 bearing any special or unusual meaning by reason either of a dictionary found elsewhere in the specification or of technical knowledge possessed by persons skilled in the art. The *prima facie* meaning of words used in a claim may not be their true meaning when read in the light of such a dictionary or of such technical knowledge; and in those circumstances a claim, when so construed, may bear a meaning different from that which it would have borne had no such assisting light been available. That is construing a document in accordance with the recognised canons of construction. But I know of no canon or principle which will justify one in departing from the unambiguous and grammatical meaning of a claim and narrowing or extending its scope by reading into it words which are not in it; or will justify one in using stray phrases in the body of a specification for the purpose of narrowing or widening the boundaries of the monopoly fixed by the plain words of a claim.

A claim is a portion of the specification which fulfils a separate and distinct function. It, and it alone, defines the monopoly; and the patentee is under a statutory obligation to state in the claims clearly and distinctly what is the invention which he desires to protect. As Lord Chelmsford said in this House many years ago: 'The office of a claim is to define and limit with precision what it is which is claimed to have been invented and therefore patented.' (*Harrison v Anderston Foundry Co.*, (1876) 1 App. (as 574)). If the patentee has done this in a claim the language of which is plain and unambiguous, it is not open to your lordships to restrict or expand or qualify its scope by reference to the body of the specification. Lord Loreburn emphasised this when he said: 'The idea of allowing a patentee to use perfectly general language in the claim and subsequently to restrict or expand or qualify what is therein expressed by borrowing this or that gloss from other parts of the specification is wholly inadmissible.' *Ingersoll Sergeant Drill Co v Consolidated Pneumatic Tool Co.*, (1907) 25 R.P.C. 61 at p.83. Sir Mark Romer expressed the same view in the following felicitous language: 'One may and one ought to refer to the body of the specification for the purpose of ascertaining the meaning of words and phrases used in the claims, or for the purpose of resolving difficulties of construction occasioned by the claims when read by themselves. But where the construction of a claim when read by itself is plain, it is not in my opinion, legitimate to diminish the ambit of the monopoly claimed merely because in the body of the specification the patentee has described his invention in more restricted terms than in the claim itself.'

1.3.1.3   *Van der Lely v Bamfords* [1963] R.P.C. 61 (H.L.)

The plaintiff company developed a mechanised hay-rake whose rake wheels, instead of being driven round mechanically, were moved by contact with the ground. This was the principal feature of the invention as patented, but it was found to have been anticipated by a photograph of an American hay-rake having the same characteristic. Claims 1–10, which referred to this feature, were accordingly invalid.

A second inventive feature claimed in the plaintiff's specification allowed the rake to be converted for the purpose of turning swathes of crop (as distinct from raking the crop together). In the embodiment first described, the rake wheels were ranged down the side of the mechanism, so that they were parallel and slightly overlapping. To convert to a swathe-turner, the hindmost wheels were moved forward to a position, side by side with the foremost wheels. Claim 11 read:

'A device as claimed in claim 10 wherein of the row or each row one or more of the rake wheels situated hindmost in the direction of motion of the vehicular frame is/are separately or jointly dismountable from the said row, and means is provided to carry the dismounted wheels in one or more groups adjacent the foremost rake wheels of the original row and parallel thereto'.

This claim was held valid. The defendant company, however, produced a rake in which the three foremost wheels were dismounted, and remounted beside the hindmost wheels.

Viscount Radcliffe:

I do not say that what is called in legal jargon the "pith and marrow" principle has no longer any status in patent law. To the extent I disagree with the argument put before us by Sir Lionel Heald on behalf of the respondents and, with all respect to that argument, I think that he attributes a general significance to the decision of this House in *E.M.I. v Lissen*, (above, 1.3.1.2) which is greater than it is capable of sustaining. On the other hand, the application of this principle is from first to last directed to the prevention of abuse of patent rights by colourable evasion: it is not a special or "benevolent" method of construing an uncertain claim; and I think that he is right to remind us that the basic duty of the patentee to state clearly what is the invention for which he seeks protection and the modern practice of building up patent claims by a meticulous accumulation of separate or combined elements has left a good deal less room for a patentee to complain of abuse, where there is no textual infringement, than may have been allowed to him at some periods in the past.

When, therefore, one speaks of theft or piracy of another's invention or says that it has been "taken" by an alleged infringer and this "pith and marrow" principle is invoked to support the accusation, I think that one must be very careful to see that the inventor has not by the actual form of his claim left open to the world the appropriation of just that property that he says has been filched from him by piracy or theft. After all, it is he who has committed himself to the unequivocal description of what he claims to have invented, and he must submit in the first place to be judged by his own action and words.

If he is so judged, I cannot for my part see what inventive idea is claimed by claim 11, regarded as a separate claim, except the idea of dismounting the hindmost wheels and bringing them forwards to a position adjacent to and parallel with the foremost wheels. Without that claim 11 adds nothing material to what is contained in claim 10; and claim 10, it is agreed, fails because it is only a statement of a general principle and is too wide and vague for enforceability. I cannot, therefore, embark upon an enquiry whether the dismountability of the hindmost wheels is an essential or unessential element of the invention claimed, because it seems to me that the patentee himself has told us by the way that he has drawn up claim 11 that this dismountability of the hindmost wheels is the very element of his idea that makes it an invention. When one says, then, as has been said by the majority of the Court of Appeal, that the appellants have "deliberately chosen to make it an essential feature of the claim that the hindmost wheels should be detachable," what one means is not merely that the wording of this claim has been carefully selected, as has all the rest of the patent document, to put the appellants in as strong a position as their expert advisers thought attainable or desirable, but also that the appellants have stated clearly and without equivocation that the point of their invention lies in its application to the hindmost wheels. The case has not revealed why they decided to concentrate on this aspect. It may be, as the trial judge thought, that they simply had not realised that the required vehicular frame could be devised which allowed for the retention in position of the hindmost wheels. If so, it does not seem to me unfair to say that the respondents' device of bringing the foremost wheels back contains an element of inventive ingenuity. But however that may be, I think that, as the Court of Appeal thought, "why they so confined the claim is not for us to speculate." The fact is that they did; and it is not open to them to complain if others are found to have occupied the ground that they so deliberately refrained from enclosing.

Lords Jenkins, Hodson and Devlin concurred, Lord Reid dissented.

1.3.1.4 *Rodi & Wienenberger v Showell* (H.L.) [1969] R.P.C. 367 (H.L.)

The plaintiff company held a patent for an expandable watch-strap made up of two layers of sleeves. Each sleeve was connected to two sleeves in the layer above or below by "U-shaped connecting bows" as Claim 1 described them. These bows were inserted along each side of the strap and were themselves held in place by means of springs within each sleeve. The rotation of the bows allowed the strap to expand. The defendants' straps replaced each pair of U-shaped bows (one on each side) with a single C-shaped bow which ran right across the sleeve.

Lord Upjohn:

First, the question is whether the relevant claim has been infringed. This is purely a question of construction of the claim read as a matter of ordinary language, in the light of the complete specification taken as a whole, but the claim must be construed as a document without having in mind the alleged infringement. What is not claimed is disclaimed. The claim must be read through the eyes of the notional addressee, the man who is going to carry out the invention described. There are many authorities on this, but it is unnecessary to review them, for I have already said enough to show that, in my view, this document must be read through the eyes of the common man at his bench.

In considering the claim the court must ascertain what are the essential integers of the claim: this remains a question of construction and no general principles can be laid down (see my observations in *Van der Lely v Bamfords Ltd* [1961] R.P.C. 296 at 313 approved on appeal to this House).

Secondly, the essential integers having been ascertained, the infringing article must be considered. To constitute infringement the article must take each and every one of the essential integers of the claim. Non-essential integers may be omitted or replaced by mechanical equivalents; there will still be infringement. I believe that this states the whole substance of the "pith and marrow" theory of infringement. Furthermore, where the invention as in this case, resides in a new combination of known integers but also merely in a new arrangement and interaction of ordinary working parts it is not sufficient to show that the same result is reached; the working parts must act on one another in the way claimed in the claim of this patent. This is well illustrated by *Birmingham Sound Reproduce Ltd v Collaro Ltd* [1956] R.P.C. 232 where Lord Evershed M.R. delivering the judgment of the court said at page 245:

> "Thus the essence of the invention resides wholly in the selection and arrangement of the parts and the manner in which they interact when arranged in accordance with the invention. It is therefore essential to the invention that it should consist of the particular parts described in the claim arranged and acting upon each other in the way described in the claim."

The question therefore appears to be whether the allegedly infringing apparatus consists of substantially the same parts acting upon each other in substantially the same way as the apparatus claimed as constituting the invention. It is not enough to find that the parts comprised in the respondents' apparatus individually or collectively perform substantially similar functions to those performed individually or collectively by the parts comprised in the apparatus claimed as the appellants' invention, or that the respondents' apparatus produces the same result as the appellants' apparatus. It must be shown that the respondents' selection and arrangements of parts is substantially the same as the appellants' selection and arrangement of parts, for it is in such selection and arrangement that the appellants' invention resides.

So if the patentee has in his specification limited the essential features of his claim in a manner that may appear to be unnecessary, it may be that the copier can escape infringement by adopting some simple mechanical equivalents so that it cannot be said that every essential integer of the claim has been taken: the *Van der Lely* case (above, 1.3.1.3) (admittedly a borderline case which led to a conflict of judicial opinion upon its facts) affords a very good example. But it must be remembered that unlike a conveyance or commercial document which is normally *inter partes* and must be interpreted, frequently very broadly, so far as possible to give effect to what appears to have been the intentions of the parties, a patent is a grant of a monopoly forbidding others to enter a part of the general commercial territory open to all of Her Majesty's subjects and so in the interests of those subjects that territory must be marked out with reasonable clarity by the claim, construing it fairly in the light of the relevant art.

Together with Lords Morris of Borth-y-Gest, Hodson and Guest, Lord Upjohn found that U-shaped bows were essential integers and that accordingly there was no infringement.

Lords Reid and Pearce dissented, Lord Pearce saying:

It is not enough to say that the U-shaped bow was an essential integer and that the respondents have not got two U-shaped bows but only one C-shaped connector. For the question is whether the essential part of the essential integer is taken although the inessential parts of it have been omitted. Neither the individual U-shape (as opposed to any other alphabetical shape) nor its lack of attachment to the connector at the other end is its essential quality. Its essential feature lies in that it connects two adjacent sleeves by a bridge between two parallel limbs that lie in the sleeves and pivots on the spring. The C-shaped connector has this feature too, since it has at each end a U-shape which performs the functions of the plaintiffs' U-shaped bows and it pivots on the spring in precisely the same way. In all essential respects, therefore it is the same.

1.3.1.5 *Beecham v Bristol* [1978] R.P.C. 153 (H.L.)

The plaintiff owned four patents relating to a new class of semi-synthetic penicillins and to methods for their manufacture. One such penicillin was known as Ampicillin and proved to be a valuable antibiotic. The patentee owned similar patents in the USA where the second defendants were licensees. The first defendant, a wholly-owned subsidiary of the second defendant, imported and sold in the UK an antibiotic known as Hetacillin which was an acetone derivative of Ampicillin. It was not disputed that the clinical effectiveness of Hetacillin was due entirely to the Ampicillin into which it reverted in the presence of water. Whenever it was administered as an antibiotic it accordingly reverted to Ampicillin in the bloodstream. In response to this importation, the plaintiff sued the defendants for infringement of various claims of the four patents and by earlier proceedings had secured interim relief preventing further importation. One basis of claim was a "pith and marrow" infringement of the claim to Ampicillin. This succeeded and the extract here given relates to this.

It was also alleged that manufacture of intermediate substances in the US and subsequent importation of Hetacillin derived from them infringed claims to those intermediate substances by virtue of the doctrine of infringing importation in Saccharin Corp v Anglo-Continental Chemical *(1900) 17 R.P.C. 307. Infringement on this ground was also found, but it is not clear whether, by virtue of the Patents Act 1977, s.60 (1)(c), the decision is still applicable in any respect on this question.*

Lord Diplock (for the H.L.):

Contemporaneously with the rise of the doctrine of infringing importation there was developing another doctrine known by the phrase adopted by Lord Cairns L.C. in *Clark v Adie* (1877) 2 App. Cas. 315 as that of "pith and marrow." It first arose in connection with mechanical patents for machines or processes which made use of novel combinations of known mechanical principles. Regarded separately each element or integer in the machine or process might not be new; the novelty and accordingly the invention lay in the particular combination of them. When *Clark v Adie* was in the Court of Appeal (1875) L.R. 10 Ch. 667) James L.J. was able to say: "In fact, every, or almost every, patent is a patent for a new combination." The doctrine which, in the case of mechanical patents to which it has principally been applied, is also known as the doctrine of "equivalents", was lucidly stated by Lord Parker, then Parker J., in *Marconi v British Radio Telegraph and Telephone Co Ltd* (1911) 28 R.P.C. 181 at p 217, where he said: "Where ... the combination or process, besides being itself new, produces new and useful results, everyone who produces the same results by using the essential parts of the combination or process is an infringer, even though he has, in fact, altered the combination or process by omitting some unessential part or step and substituting another part or step which is equivalent to the part or step that he has omitted."

The increasing particularity with which the claims are drafted and multiplied in modern specifications may have reduced the scope of application of the doctrine of pith and marrow, but I am unable to accept the argument advanced by Bristol that this has made the doctrine obsolete. It still remains a part of patent law as is acknowledged in speeches delivered in this House as recently as *C. Van der Lely N.V. v Bamfords Ltd* [1963] R.P.C. 61; *Rodi & Weinberger A.G. v Henry Showell Ltd* [1969] R.P.C. 367. Directed as it is against colourable evasion of a patent it is not in my view confined to mechanical inventions or to claims for new combinations of integers, but in appropriate cases, though they may be rare, is applicable to claims for new products. ...

I turn first to the contention by Beechams that under the pith and marrow doctrine the product Hetacillin was an infringement of their claim to Ampicillin as a product. At the hearing before Mr Falconer this contention was much more extensive and covered all claims in the patents to all products made from 6-APA by acylation and to the product 6-APA itself. This may account for his rejection of it. The Court of Appeal in their judgment dealt only with the application of the doctrine to the claim to Ampicillin itself. This they held to be infringed under the pith and marrow doctrine.

I have already expressed my opinion that the pith and marrow doctrine is applicable to claims for new products as well as to new processes; and I agree with the Court of Appeal that the relationship of Hetacillin to Ampicillin provides a clear case for its application. It was argued that what is claimed in the patents as an essential feature of the class of products to which Ampicillin belongs is the presence of an amino group in the alpha position, and that this feature is absent in Hetacillin. This is literally true at the time of importation and sale but it ceases to be true as soon as Hetacillin is put to use for the only purpose for which it is intended. The substitution for the postulated amino group of the variant incorporated in Hetacillin is evanescent and reversible and for all practical purposes of use can be regarded as the equivalent of the amino group in Ampicillin. In the apt phrase used by the Court of Appeal, it is the reproduction of the substance Ampicillin, albeit temporarily masked.

1.3.1.6 *Catnic Components v Hill & Smith* [1982] R.P.C. 183 (H.L.)

The plaintiff's patented invention concerned galvanised steel lintels for doors and windows for use in cavity walls. It was a breakthrough in the industry and a considerable commercial success, providing a substitute for solid, much heavier lintels. It depended for its resilience upon the particular formation of steel plates, which in cross-section appeared as in Figure 1.

The element chiefly in dispute in the infringement proceedings (italicised in Claim 1) is marked "105" on the drawing, which is Figure 1 in the plaintiff's specification. Claim 1 read:

"A lintel for use over apertures in cavity walls having an inner and outer skin comprising a first horizontal plate or part adapted to support a course or a plurality of superimposed units forming part of the inner skin and a second horizontal plate or part substantially parallel to the first and spaced therefrom in a downward vertical direction and adapted to

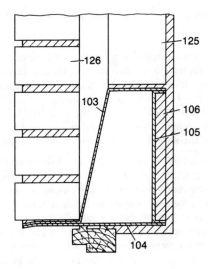

Figure 1

span the cavity in the cavity wall and be supported at least at each end thereof upon courses forming parts of the outer and inner skins respectively of the cavity wall adjacent an aperture, and a first rigid inclined support member extending downwardly and forwardly from or near the front edge adjacent the cavity of the first horizontal plate or part and joining with the second plate or part at an intermediate position which lies between the front and rear edge of the second plate or part and adapted to extend across the cavity, and a second rigid support member extending vertically from or from near the rear edge of the first horizontal plate or part to join with the second plate or part adjacent its rear edge." (Emphasis added).

The variation which the defendant introduced into its lintel with a view to avoiding infringement of this claim appeared as follows (for a lintel three bricks high – if of two bricks, the angle is increased to 8°): see Figure 2.

Figure 2

Lord Diplock (in whose speech Lords Keith of Kinkel, Scarman, Lowry and Roskill concurred):

My Lords, in their closely reasoned written cases in this House and in the oral argument, both parties to this appeal have tended to treat "textual infringement" and infringement of the "pith and marrow" of an invention as if they were separate causes of action, the existence of the former to be determined as a matter of construction only and of the latter upon some broader principle of colourable evasion. There is, in my view, no such dichotomy; there is but a single cause of action and to treat it otherwise, particularly in cases like that which is the subject of the instant appeal, is liable to lead to confusion.

The expression "no textual infringement" has been borrowed from the speeches in this House in the hay-rake case, *Van der Lely v Bamfords*, (above, 1.3.1.3) where it was used by several of their Lordships as a convenient way of saying that the word "hindmost" as descriptive of rake wheels to be dismounted could not as a matter of linguistics mean "foremost": but this did not exhaust the question of construction of the specification that was determinative of whether there had been an infringement of the claim or not. It left open the question whether the patentee had made his reference to the "hindmost" (rather than any other wheels) as those to be dismounted, an essential feature of the monopoly that he claimed. It was on this question that there was a division of opinion in this House and in the Court of Appeal in the hay-rake case.

My Lords, a patent specification is a unilateral statement by the patentee, in words of his own choosing, addressed to those likely to have a practical interest in the subject matter of his invention (ie "skilled in the art"), by which he informs them what he claims to be the essential features of the new product or process for which the letters patent grant him a monopoly. It is those novel features only that he claims to be essential that constitute the so-called "pith and marrow" of the claim. A patent specification should be given a purposive construction rather than a purely literal one derived from applying to it the kind of meticulous verbal analysis in which lawyers are too often tempted by their training to indulge. The question in each case is: whether persons with practical knowledge and experience of the kind of work in which the invention was intended to be used, would understand that strict compliance with a particular descriptive word or phrase appearing in a claim was intended by the patentee to be an essential requirement of the invention so that any variant would fall outside the monopoly claimed, even though it could have no material effect upon the way the invention worked.

The question, of course, does not arise where the variant would in fact have a material effect upon the way the invention worked. Nor does it arise unless at the date of publication of the specification it would be obvious to the informed reader that this was so. Where it is not obvious, in the light of then existing knowledge, the reader is entitled to assume that the patentee thought at the time of the specification that he had good reason for limiting his monopoly so strictly and had intended to do so, even though subsequent work by him or others in the field of the invention might show the limitation to have been unnecessary. It is to be answered in the negative only when it would be apparent to any reader skilled in the art that a particular descriptive word or phrase used in a claim cannot have been intended by a patentee, who was also skilled in the art, to exclude minor variants which, to the knowledge of both him and the readers to whom the patent was addressed, could have no material effect upon the way in which the invention worked.

My Lords, upon analysis of the speeches in this House in *Van Der Lely v Bamfords* the division of opinion between Lord Reid and the remainder of their Lordships appears to have been due to his thinking that it would be obvious to the informed reader that dismounting the "foremost" rather than the "hindmost" wheels was an immaterial variant, whereas the majority were not satisfied that this was even the fact, let alone that it was obviously so. In the bracelet case, *Rodi and Wienenberger A.G. v Henry Showell Ltd* where this House was more evenly divided, the difference between the majority and the minority appears to have turned upon their respective views as to whether the particular variant alleged to be an infringement, had a material effect upon what were claimed to be the advantages obtained by the patented invention – as to which they differed. In the third of the trilogy of leading cases in this House upon this topic, the Ampicillin case, *Beecham Group Ltd v Bristol Laboratories Ltd* [1977] F.S.R. 215; [1978] R.P.C. 153, the descriptive phrase was "an amino group in the alpha position." In the alleged infringing antibiotic, Hetacillin, this amino group had been temporarily converted by a further chemical reaction into a molecular structure that was no longer an amino group, but the reaction was reversible and upon being put to use as an antibiotic, (which necessitated contact with water) it reverted to its original form as an amino group and in that form produced its prophylactic effects. This House unanimously held that this temporary masking of the amino group amounted to an immaterial variant. It would be obvious to anyone skilled in the specialised art of selecting and synthesising polymers for use as antibiotics that the essential feature of the invention was that when put to use for its intended purpose, the product should have an amino group in the alpha position; and that, accordingly, the patentee's reference to this feature of his claim cannot have been intended by him to exclude products in which the amino group in that position was temporarily displaced during a period before the product was put to any prophylactic use.

The essential features of the invention that is the subject of claim 1 of the patent in suit in the instant appeal are much easier to understand than those of any of the three patents to which I have just referred; and this makes the question of its construction simpler. Put in a nutshell the question to be answered is: Would the specification make it obvious to a builder familiar with ordinary building operations that the description of a lintel in the form of a weight-bearing box girder of which the back plate was referred to as "extending vertically" from one of the two horizontal plates to join the other, could not have been intended to exclude lintels, in which the back plate although not positioned at precisely 90° to both horizontal plates was close enough to 90° to make no material difference to the way the lintel worked when used in building operations? No plausible reason has been advanced why any rational patentee should want a place so narrow a limitation on his invention. On the contrary, to do so would render his monopoly for practical purposes worthless, since any imitator could avoid it and take all the benefit of the invention by the simple expedient of positioning the back plate a degree or two from the exact vertical.

It may be that when used by a geometer addressing himself to fellow geometers, such expressions descriptive of relative position as "horizontal", "parallel", "vertical" and "vertically" are to be understood as words of precision only; but when used in a description of a manufactured product intended to perform the practical function of a weight-bearing box girder in supporting courses of brickwork over window and door spaces in buildings, it seems to me that the expression "extending vertically" as descriptive of the position of what in use will be the upright member of a trapezoid-shaped box girder, is perfectly capable of meaning positioned near enough to the exact geometrical vertical to enable it in actual use to perform satisfactorily all the functions that it could perform if it were precisely vertical; and having regard to those considerations to which I have just referred that is the sense in which in my opinion "extending vertically" would be understood by a builder familiar with ordinary building operation. Or, putting the same thing in another way, it would be obvious to him that the patentee did not intend to make exact verticality in the positioning of the back plate an essential feature of the invention claimed.

My Lords, if one analyses line by line the ways in which the various expressions are used in the specification, one can find pointers either way as to whether in particular lines various adjectives and adverbs descriptive of relative position are used as words of precision or not. Some of these are discussed in the judgments of the majority of the Court of Appeal who found the pointers in favour of precision stronger than those to the contrary, of which one example is the description of the two "horizontal" plates as being only "substantially parallel". For my part I find the result of such analysis inconclusive and of little weight as compared with the broad considerations to which I have referred and which are a consequence of giving as I think one should, a purposive construction to the specification. It follows that I have reached the same conclusion as the trial judge and Sir David Cairns, although not by the route of drawing a distinction between "textual infringement" and infringement of the "pith and marrow" of the invention. Accordingly I would allow the appeal.

1.3.1.7   *Improver Corp v Remington* [1990] F.S.R. 181 (Hoffmann J.)

The plaintiffs' European patent (UK) was for an electrical device for plucking hairs from the body. Its principal element consisted of a helical spring bent to form an arc which was rotated at a high speed. Because of the arcuate form, on the convex side the spring would open out, while on the concave side it would close together. Hairs would accordingly be captured and then plucked with the rotation of the spring. The result was less painful than waxing, and more longlasting than shaving. The plaintiffs' own device, "Epilady", was a great commercial success.

The claims in the patent were defined by reference to a "helical spring". Because the principle of the invention could be embodied in springs in many configurations, the description ended with an "equivalents clause":

"It will be evident to those skilled in the art that the invention is not limited to the details of the foregoing illustrative embodiments, and that the present invention may be embodied in other specific forms without departing from the essential attributes thereof, and it is therefore desired that the present embodiments be considered in all respects as illustrative and not restrictive, reference being made to the appended claims, rather than to the foregoing description, and all variations which come within the meaning and range of equivalency of the claims are therefore intended to be embraced therein".

The defendants' device was designed as a less painful alternative to "Epilady". In place of a helical spring it had a tube of synthetic rubber, partly cut through by slits. When rotated, hair was drawn into the slits and then plucked, as the slits squeezed together. For this variant, a US patent had been secured. It was marketed as "Smooth & Silky", with additional tubes for replacement after some seven hours use.

Hoffmann J. introduced the issue of infringement thus:

The question of infringement turns upon a short but undoubtedly difficult point of construction, namely whether the rubber rod is a "helical spring" as that expression is used in the claims of the patent in suit. In the Court of Appeal at the interlocutory injunction stage of this action Dillon L.J. said that a more attractive way of putting the question, from the plaintiff's point of view, was to ask whether the rod was a "mechanical equivalent" for a helical spring. But I think with respect, for reasons which I shall explain, that these are different ways of saying the same thing.

The proper approach to the interpretation of English patents registered under the Patents Act 1949 was explained by Lord Diplock in *Catnic Components Ltd v Hill & Smith Ltd*. The language should be given a "purposive" and not necessarily a literal construction. If the issue was whether a feature embodied in an alleged infringement which fell outside the primary, literal or a contextual meaning of a descriptive word or phrase in the claim ("a variant") was nevertheless within its language as properly interpreted, the court should ask itself the following three questions:

(1) Does the variant have a material effect upon the way the invention works? If yes, the variant is outside the claim. If no –

(2) Would this (i.e. that the variant had no material effect) have been obvious at the date of publication of the patent to a reader skilled in the art. If no, the variant is outside the claim. If yes –

(3) Would the reader skilled in the art nevertheless have understood from the language of the claim that the patentee intended that strict compliance with the primary meaning was an essential requirement of the invention. If yes, the variant is outside the claim.

On the other hand, a negative answer to the last question would lead to the conclusion that the patentee was intending the word or phrase to have not a literal but a figurative meaning (the figure being a form of synecdoche or metonymy) denoting a class of things which included the variant and the literal meaning, the latter being perhaps the most perfect, best-known or striking example of the class.

After further observations on the law, he examined the evidence of the rival experts in relation to the first and second questions, and found that the defendants' variant had no material effect on the way the invention worked, and that this would have been obvious to the skilled reader. On the latter issue, he remarked:

Mr Young [for the Defendants] interpreted this question to mean that the variant must be one which would have suggested itself to the skilled man as an obvious alternative to the thing denoted by the literal meaning. In this case, he said, the term "helical spring" did not suggest a rubber rod as an obvious alternative. On the contrary, it was an inventive step. He relied upon the evidence of Dr Laming who said that mention of a helical spring would not have made him think of a rubber rod and that the choice of the latter was innovative.

I do not think that this is what Lord Diplock meant by the question and I think that Mr Young has been misled by Lord Diplock's use of the word "obvious" into thinking that he must have been intending to refer to the rule that an obvious improvement is not an inventive step. In my view the question supposes that the skilled man is told of both the invention and the variant and asked whether the variant would obviously work in the same way. An affirmative answer would not be inconsistent with the variant being an inventive step. For example, the choice of some material for the bendy rod which was *a priori* improbable (e.g. on account of its expense) but had been discovered to give some additional advantage (e.g painless extraction) might be a variant which obviously worked in the same way as the invention and yet be an inventive step. Nor would it matter that the material in question, being improbable, would not have suggested itself to the skilled man as an obvious alternative. Questions such as these may be relevant to the question of construction (Lord Diplock's third question) but not at this stage of the inquiry.

On the third question, Hoffmann J. referred in detail to the views of the experts – Dr Sharpe for the plaintiffs and Dr Laming for the defendants. He concluded:

In my judgment the different between the experts depends upon how one construes the equivalents clause. The first part of the clause merely says that the description should not be used to restrict the meaning of the language used in the claims. That is not the question here. What matters is the final words: "and all variations which come within the meaning and range of equivalency of the claims are therefore intended to be embraced therein". If this means: "whatever contrary impression the skilled man may be given by the language of the claims read in the context of the rest of the description, all references in the claims to hardware are deemed to include any other hardware which would in any circumstances function in the same way" then I think Dr Sharpe must be right. In my judgment, however, the clause does not have so wide an effect. The words I have quoted say that the variation must still come within the meaning of the claims and the reference to "range of equivalency" means in my judgment no more than "don't forget that the claims must be interpreted in accordance with *Catnic* and the Protocol".

Thus interpreted, I do not think that "helical spring" can reasonably be given a wide generic construction and I accept Dr Laming's reasons for thinking that a skilled man would not understand it in this sense. This is not a case like *Catnic* in which the angle of the support member can be regarded as an approximation to the vertical. The rubber rod is not an approximation to a helical spring. It is a different thing which can in limited circumstances work in the same way. Nor can the spring be regarded as an "inessential" or the change from metal spring to rubber rod as a minor variant. In *Catnic* Lord Diplock asked rhetorically whether there was any reason why the patentee should wish to restrict his invention to a support angled at precisely 90°, thereby making avoidance easy. In this case I think that a similar question would receive a ready answer. It would be obvious that the rubber had problems of hysteresis which might be very difficult to overcome. The plaintiff's inventors had done no work on rubber rods. Certainly the rubber rod cannot be used in the loop configuration which is the plaintiff's preferred embodiment. On the other hand, drafting the claim in wide generic terms to cover alternatives like the rubber rod might be unacceptable to the patent office. I do not think that the hypothetical skilled man is also assumed to be skilled in patent law and he would in my judgment be entitled to think that patentee had good reasons for limiting himself, as he obviously appeared to have done, to a helical coil. To derive a different meaning solely from the equivalents clause would in my view be denying third parties that reasonable degree of certainty to which they are entitled under the Protocol.

The German Decisions

The patent in suit is being litigated in a number of countries but the only one in which the action has come to trial is in Germany, where the Landgericht of Düsseldorf found in favour of the plaintiff. This naturally causes me concern because the Landgericht was interpreting the same patent according to the same Protocol and came to a different conclusion. It seems to me that the reason for the difference between me and my colleagues in Düsseldorf is that, having answered what I have labelled as Lord Diplock's first two questions in the same way as I have, they treated those answers as concluding the matter in favour of the plaintiff and did not find it necessary to ask the third question at all. The specification, they said, conveyed to the expert "the understanding that the configuration of the hair engaging portion as helical spring has to be understood functionally" and that the expert to whom the patent was directed would have "no difficulties in perceiving and understanding this meaning of the teaching of the invention". This does seem to me with respect to be an interpretation closer to treating the language of the claims as a "guideline" than the median course required by the Protocol. I also detect some difference in approach between the Landgericht and the

Oberlandesgericht (Court of Appeal) which had previously discharged an interlocutory injunction granted by the Landgericht. The Court of Appeal placed much more emphasis upon the language of the specification. Its view on the primary meaning of a helical spring was as follows:

"A spiral or helical shape is characterised by curved lines such as those showing on the level a spiral and, three-dimensionally, more or less the rising turns of a screw. Nothing else is meant by the theory of the [plantiff's] patent and this is made clear to a person skilled in the art by the state of the art to which the patent refers and on which its proposition is undoubtedly based. A solid roller-shaped hair-engaging part with vertical incisions at a distance from each other can therefore at the most constitute an equivalent means of replacement for the helical spring".

The Court went on to say that the rubber rod undoubtedly worked in the same way as the helical spring (i.e. it answered Lord Diplock's first question in the same way as I have). Although it does not specifically say so, I think it may be assumed that it would have regarded this as equally obvious to anyone skilled in the art. But when dealing with the question of whether this would affect the question of construction, i.e. whether the skilled man would have regarded the rubber rod as included in the claims of the patent, the Court of Appeal expressed considerable doubt. He could have done so if he had analysed the function of the spring in the invention and then set about thinking of equivalents to perform the same function. But the Court doubted whether –

"the average person skilled in the art thinks in such a theoretical way. This applies particularly to the present case because there appeared to be no need for theorising in view of the fact that a normal helical spring was known as a perfectly suitable means for plucking".

It may be said that the expert evidence before the Landgericht at the trial was different, but I doubt whether this could have been so. There was no real difference between the views of Dr Sharpe and Dr Laming on questions of engineering: the difference lay in the approach to construction, which is really a question of law.

1.3.2   Acts Constituting Infringement

1.3.2.1   Patents Act, s.60

Meaning of infringement

S.60(1) Subject to the provisions of this section, a person infringes a patent for an invention if, but only if, while the patent is in force, he does any of the following things in the United Kingdom in relation to the invention without the consent of the proprietor of the patent, that is to say –

(a) where the invention is a product, he makes, disposes of, offers to dispose of, uses or imports the product or keeps it whether for disposal of otherwise;

(b) where the invention is a process, he uses the process or he offers it for use in the United Kingdom when he knows, or it is obvious to a reasonable person in the circumstances, that its use there without the consent of the proprietor would be an infringement of the patent;

(c) where the invention is a process, he disposes of, offers to dispose of, uses or imports any product obtained directly by means of that process or keeps any such product whether for disposal or otherwise.

(2) Subject to the following provisions of this section, a person (other than the proprietor of the patent) also infringes a patent for an invention if, while the patent is in force and without the consent of the proprietor, he supplies or offers to supply in the United Kingdom a person other than a licensee or other person entitled to work the invention with any of the means, relating to an essential element of the invention, for putting the invention into effect when he knows, or it is obvious to a reasonable person in the circumstances, that those means are suitable for putting, and are intended to put, the invention into effect in the United Kingdom.

(3) Subsection (2) above shall not apply to the supply or offer of a staple commercial product unless the supply or the offer is made for the purpose of inducing the person supplied or, as the case may be, the person to whom the offer is made to do an act which constitutes an infringement of the patent by virtue of subsection (1) above.

(4) Without prejudice to section 86 below, subsections (1) and (2) above shall not apply to any act which, under any provision of the Community Patent Convention relating to the exhaustion of the rights of the proprietor of a patent, as that provision applies by virtue of that section, cannot be prevented by the proprietor of the patent.

(5) An act which, apart from this subsection, would constitute an infringement of a patent for an invention shall not do so if –

(a) it is done privately and for purposes which are not commercial;

(b) it is done for experimental purposes relating to the subject-matter of the invention;

(c) it consists of the extemporaneous preparation in a pharmacy of a medicine for an individual in accordance with a prescription given by a registered medical or dental practitioner or consists of dealing with a medicine so prepared;

(d) it consists of the use, exclusively for the needs of a relevant ship, of a product or process in the body of such a ship or in its machinery, tackle, apparatus or other accessories, in a case where the ship has temporarily or accidentally entered the internal or territorial waters of the United Kingdom;

(e) it consists of the use of a product or process in the body or operation of a relevant aircraft, hovercraft or vehicle which has temporarily or accidentally entered or is crossing the United Kingdom (including the air space above it and its territorial waters) or the use of accessories for such a relevant aircraft, hovercraft or vehicle;

(f) it consists of the use of an exempted aircraft which has lawfully entered or is lawfully crossing the United Kingdom as aforesaid or of the importation into the United Kingdom, or the use or storage there, of any part or accessory for such an aircraft.

(6) For the purposes of subsection (2) above a person who does an act in relation to an invention which is prevented only by virtue of paragraph (a), (b) or (c) of subsection (5) above from constituting an infringement of a patent for the invention shall not be treated as a person entitled to work the invention, but –

(a) the reference in that subsection to a person entitled to work an invention includes a reference to a person so entitled by virtue of section 55 above, and

(b) a person who by virtue of section 28(6) above or section 64 below is entitled to do an act in relation to the invention without it constituting such an infringement shall, so far as concerns that act, be treated as a person entitled to work the invention.

(7) In this section –
"relevant ship" and "relevant aircraft, hovercraft or vehicle" mean respectively a ship and an aircraft, hovercraft or vehicle registered in, or belonging to, any country, other than the United Kingdom, which is a party to the Convention for the Protection of Industrial Property signed at Paris on 20th March 1883; and "exempted aircraft" means an aircraft to which [section 89 of the Civil Aviation Act 1982] (aircraft exempted from seizure in respect of patent claims) applies.

S.60(1) is derived from Community Patent Convention, Art. 29, s.60(2) and (4) from Art.30 and s.60(5)–(7) from Art.31; s.60(4) provides machinery for giving effect to the exhaustion principle prescribed in Arts.32 and 81.

1.3.2.2 *Smith Kline and French v Harbottle* [1980] R.P.C. 363 (Oliver J.)

The first defendant, Harbottle, ordered a drug, Cimetidine, patented by the plaintiff in the UK, from Italy. It arranged for its importation into England with the intention of re-exporting it. It was carried to Heathrow by British Airways and stored there in their bonded warehouse to the order of Harbottle. The plaintiff alleged that, under the Patents Act 1977, s 60(1), British Airways thereby infringed the patent as a person who "keeps" the product "whether for disposal or otherwise." It was argued on the plaintiff's behalf that this expression was deliberately meant to be wider than the equivalent provisions in the Community Patent Convention.

Oliver J.:

Article 29 of the Community Patent Convention is in these terms:

"A community patent shall confer on its proprietor the right to prevent all third parties not having his consent: (a) from making, offering, putting on the market, or using a product which is the subject matter of the patent, or importing or stocking the product for these purposes; (b) from using a process which is the subject-matter of the patent or when the third party knows or it is obvious in the circumstances that the use of the process is prohibited without the consent of the proprietor of the patent, from offering the process for use within the territories of the contracting states, and (c) from offering, putting on the market, using, importing or stocking for these purposes the product obtained directly by a process which is the subject-matter of the patent."

Article 31 is in terms which are very similar to those which appear in sub-section 5 of section 60. That article provides:

"The rights conferred by a community patent shall not extend to (a) acts done privately and for non-commercial purposes; (b) acts done for experimental purposes relating to the subject-matter of the patented invention," and then it goes on with similar provisions with regard to exempted aircraft and that sort of thing.

It is I think obvious from a comparison of the provisions of Article 31 and the provisions of section 60(5) that the intention of the framers of the statute was to give effect to the provisions of the Convention, and indeed, as I have pointed out, section 130(7) states not only that that was the intention but that it is indeed being achieved.

"Keep" is a word with many meanings. Indeed in its transitive sense the Shorter Oxford English Dictionary records no less than 26 different nuances. Literally an attendant in the left luggage office at Euston "keeps" a suitcase committed to his charge. If it contained a patented article I suppose he thus "keeps" the article. But it would be surprising if he thereby became an infringer and liable to an injunction. Mr Prescott does not — at least I do not think he does — so contend. But beyond this point at what point does a person "keep" property within the meaning of the section? In my judgment, clearly what the draftsman had in mind was "keeping" in the sense of "keeping in stock" so as to give effect to the words of the Convention "stocking the product for these purposes." Indeed it is worth noting that in the Shorter Oxford English Dictionary one of the meanings of the verb "to stock" is "(b) esp" — which I presume means "especially" — "to keep goods in stock for sale." Mr Gratwick therefore submits that, whatever else the word may mean in the section, the word "keep" in the context of this Act connotes a keeping in some capacity and for a purpose other than that of a mere custodian or warehouseman. He submits that there is at least an ambiguity here, and he referred me to the following passage from *Gartside v Inland Revenue Commissioners* [1968] A.C. 553, 612 where Lord Reid says: "It is always proper to construe an ambiguous word or phrase in light of the mischief which the provision is obviously designed to prevent, and in light of the reasonableness of the consequences which follow from giving it a particular construction.

I find this argument persuasive. If it had really been intended to effect a revolutionary change, such as Mr Prescott suggests, I would have expected it to be done by much stronger and more positive language than this. Indeed, as Mr Gratwick has pointed out, where the legislature did intend to make an alteration in the existing law or at least to clarify it, as in sub-section 2 of section 60, it did so quite expressly.

It is not, I think, necessary for me to seek to arrive at a definitive meaning of the statutory provision on this application, and I do not intend to do so. It is sufficient for the purposes of this case to say merely that I remain wholly unpersuaded that anything that British Airways have done in relation to the goods in carrying them or warehousing them in this case constitutes an infringement within the meaning of section 60. It follows from that, first, that the plaintiffs' motion for judgment against British Airways must fail and, secondly, that British Airways are entitled to succeed on their interpleader motion.

1.3.2.3 *Kalman v PCL Packaging* [1982] F.S.R. 406 (Falconer J.)

The plaintiffs owned a patent for filters that were used in processes for extruding plastics; the patent claimed both the filters and their use in plastics production. The first defendant, PCL, obtained two filters within the scope of the patent from the second defendant, Berlyn, a corporation which traded only in the US. These were consigned f.o.b. in Boston, Mass. to British Airways for shipment to PCL, the purchase price having been previously paid. Under the Uniform Commercial Code of the US, Art 2–401, Berlyn accordingly parted with all possession, actual and constructive, at this shipping point and the buyer assumed all risk of loss and liability for carriage charges. Shortly after delivery, PCL were notified by the plaintiffs of their patent, and Berlyn undertook to indemnify PCL against any consequent loss. In an action for infringement of the British patent, Berlyn sought to strike out the statement of claim and to set aside service upon them out of the jurisdiction on the ground that they had committed no tort in the jurisdiction.

Counsel for the plaintiff sought to make out his case against Berlyn upon a number of provisions of the Patents Act, 1977, s 60 and associated principles of common law.

Falconer J.:

(i) Offering to dispose within the jurisdiction and disposing within the jurisdiction (s 60(1)(a)).

It is convenient under this paragraph to deal with the second of the ways in which Mr Hobbs put his cause of action under this paragraph, first of all, that is to say the allegation that Berlyn Corporation had disposed of the apparatus, the filters in question, within the jurisdiction. This involves considering the meaning to be given to the phrase "dispose of" in paragraph (a) of the subsection. It is a term which is new to our patent jurisprudence, at least in relation to infringement. Referring to the long title to the Patents Act 1977, Mr Hobbs submitted that the Act had established a whole new system of law and in particular, so he submitted, the concept of vending as an infringing act had gone having been deliberately left out of the acts specified in paragraph (a) of the subsection, so that cases such as *Badische Anilin und Soda Fabrik v H Johnson & Co* (1897) 14 R.P.C. 919, were no longer good law. He submitted that if that case had had to be decided on the law as it is under section 60 of the 1977 Act it would have been decided differently and, so he submitted, on the lines of the dissenting judgment of Rigby L.J. in that case in the Court of Appeal, whose judgment is to be found in 14 R.P.C. at 416.

I do not accept this submission. In the first place, one way of disposing of an article is to sell it.

Falconer J. cites dictionary definitions in support and noted that s 60(1) was intended to correspond to the Community Patent Convention Art 29 (a):

"A Community patent shall confer on its proprietor the right to prevent all third parties not having his consent: (a) From making, offering, putting on the market or using a product which is the subject-matter of the patent, or importing or stocking the product for these purposes."

He continued:

Mr Hobbs agreed that the expression in that paragraph of that Article "putting on the market" is equivalent to the phrase "dispose of" in the statute. "Putting on the market," perhaps a somewhat colloquial expression, surely in its usually accepted sense connotes offering for sale and selling. Nowadays it may also I think embrace other forms of marketing a product, such as leasing, but I do not have to consider that possibility here. Certainly it seems to me that, bearing in mind the express provisions of section 130(7) and that wording of Article 29 of the Community Patent Convention, "dispose of" in paragraph (a) of section 60 must at least include selling, that a sale of an article must be a disposal of it within the meaning of paragraph (a) in the subsection.

It seems to me also that had the legislature intended to effect such a radical change in the law as to infringement as Mr Hobbs submits, one would have expected that to have been made clearer and stronger with more positive language, as was done for instance in section 60(2), which altered the previous law as to contributory infringement.

In the present case the sales of the two filters in question had been effected in the United States outside the jurisdiction, had been completed so that the property had passed to the buyer while the article was still in the United States and Berlyn Corporation had parted with possession, both actual and constructive, and had no further rights of any kind in either of the filters after delivery to the shipping point in the United States. Berlyn Corporation had disposed of the filters in the United States and, having no further property in them or possession of them or any right of any kind in them, could not effect any further disposal of them whatsoever.

Mr Hobbs submitted that the Berlyn Corporation had disposed of the filters in the United Kingdom by delivering them to PCL. He said the act of disposal by Berlyn Corporation was delivery into the possession of PCL and that act was completed, so he said, in the United Kingdom when the carrier delivered to PCL. He referred to the acts of the intervening parties, such as the forwarding agents and carriers as – and I quote – "mere ministerial acts," an expression I think he borrowed from the dissenting judgment of Rigby L.J. in the *Badische Anilin* case to which I have referred.

For the reasons I have already stated, I reject this argument. Once Berlyn Corporation delivered to the shipping point in the United States they had no further property in, possession of, or any rights in or any control of the goods, which were PCL's, and Berlyn Corporation could not effect any further act of disposing the goods.

Alternatively, still under this head of cause of action, Mr Hobbs submitted that Berlyn Corporation were liable for disposal of the goods in the United Kingdom on the footing that the carriers were agents of Berlyn Corporation and the carriers had disposed of the goods in the United Kingdom by delivery to PCL. I reject this argument also. It necessarily presupposes that the carriers in delivering to PCL in the United Kingdom had committed an act of infringement under section 60(1)(a) by so doing. As to that, I would refer to the judgment of Mr Justice Oliver, as he then was, in the case of *Smith, Kline & French Laboratories Limited v. R.D. Harbottle (Mercantile) Limited and Others* [1980] R.P.C. 363.

I now go back to consider Mr Hobbs' first way of putting the plaintiffs' case, namely, that Berlyn Corporation have infringed in that they have offered to dispose of within the jurisdiction apparatus within the claims of the patent in suit, namely, at least one of the two filters in question. In section 60(1)(a), which I have read, of the enumerated acts which if performed in the United Kingdom would be infringing, the one immediately preceding the words "offers to dispose of" is the one I have just considered, "disposes of". To be an infringement, that immediately preceding act, "disposes of" must of course be an act within the United Kingdom. In my view, the legislature was intending in the expression "offers to dispose of" to prohibit offering in the United Kingdom to do the immediately preceding prohibited act, that is, disposing of the product in the United Kingdom.

Falconer J. referred to a telex from Berlyn to PCL which stated "We can ship your machine on Monday via British Airways . . . Please advise the airport to ship to . . .". He continued:

Mr Hobbs says that that telex is an offer to dispose of the filter in question in the United Kingdom using British Airways as a carrier, as agents he says of Berlyn Corporation, to bring into the United Kingdom and hand over to PCL in this country, and that he says would be a disposal in the United Kingdom. He says that this telex, since it arrived in this country and was received in this country, is an offer in the jurisdiction, on the strength of the decision of the House of Lords in *Brinkibon Ltd v Stahag Stahl und Stahlwarenhandelgesellschaft mbH*, [1982] 1 All E.R. 239.

Assuming for present purposes without deciding, that it was an offer in the United Kingdom and assuming that British Airways as carrier were to be such as the agents of Berlyn Corporation, which I am not to be taken as deciding, I have already held that British Airways in carrying into and delivering the filters to PCL in this country did not dispose of the goods in the jurisdiction within the meaning of section 60(1)(a), so that there was no offer, whether made within or without the jurisdiction, of a disposal of the filters in the United Kingdom by reason of the action of British Airways in carrying in and handing over to PCL within the jurisdiction. So that, in my judgment, the plaintiffs have not shown a cause of action within the jurisdiction on this ground.

(ii) Offering a process for use within the jurisdiction (s 60(1)(b)).

With all respect to Mr Hobbs, it seems to me that this argument is a complete non-starter. Section 60(1)(b) requires the offer of a process for use in the United Kingdom. In my judgment, on no reasonable or sensible view of the facts in this case could Berlyn be said to have offered to PCL the use of a process in the United Kingdom. What was offered to PCL was the sale of the filters in question in the United States of America, to PCL in the case of the first filter and of course to the hire purchase company in the case of the second one, with delivery f.o.b. to the shipping point in the USA and I cannot see how either of those transactions could have amounted to an offer to PCL of the use of a process in the United Kingdom.

(iii) Supplying essential means for putting the invention into effect (s 60(2)).

This sub-section requires the supply in the United Kingdom, or the offer to supply in the United Kingdom, of the means in question for putting the patented invention into effect in the United Kingdom. There was no supply in the United Kingdom to PCL or offer to supply in the United Kingdom to PCL by Berlyn Corporation of the filters in question. They were supplied to PCL in the United States of America pursuant to sales in the United States of America, f.o.b. the shipping point in the United States of America and, in my judgment, the plaintiffs cannot have any cause of action against Berlyn Corporation under this head.

(iv) Joint tort committed by Berlyn and PCL.

As I understand the law, to be a joint tortfeasor a person must have acted in concert with another pursuant to a common design in the commission of the tort, that is to say, it has got to be a joint tort. . . .

What Mr Hobbs says is that Berlyn Corporation, with knowledge of the plaintiffs' British patent, have since at least 23 July 1981, which is the date of the indemnity, collaborated with PCL in an arrangement whereby PCL continued to use the filters in their process in the United Kingdom while Berlyn Corporation, to use Mr Hobbs' own expression, "have stood guard over the arrangement," which I understood to mean by reason of the indemnity and the submission is that all that amounts to a common design between Berlyn Corporation and PCL to infringe the plaintiffs' patent.

As I have said, I cannot accept that argument. On the facts as I have stated them, I do not consider that Berlyn Corporation were guilty of acting in concert to infringe the plaintiffs' patent at all. Moreover, it is quite clear that at common law, on the facts as I have stated them, Berlyn Corporation would not be infringers of the plaintiffs' patent either as joint tortfeasors or as procuring infringement by PCL.

The principle of law applicable was settled by the decisions of the Court of Appeal in *Townsend v Haworth* 48 L.J. (N.S.) 770, and in *Dunlop Pneumatic Tyre Co Ltd v D Moseley & Sons Limited* (1904) 21 R.P.C. 274. Those authorities were followed recently by the Court of Appeal in *Belegging- en Exploitatiemaatschappij Lavender B.V. v Witton Industrial Diamonds Limited* [1979] F.S.R. 59. Referring to those two old authorities Buckley L.J. with whose judgment the other lords justices agreed, Goff L.J. and Eveleigh, L.J. at p 64 after giving the references to the two cases, *Townsend v Haworth* and *Dunlop Pneumatic Tyre Co Ltd v D Moseley & Sons Limited*, said:

"In the former of these two cases" – that is *Townsend v Haworth* – "Mellish L.J. stated the principle tersely and forcefully as follows: 'Selling materials for the purpose of infringing a patent to the man who is going to infringe it, even although the party who sells it knows that he is going to infringe it and indemnifies him, does not by itself make the person who so sells an infringer. He must be a party with the man who so infringes and actually infringe'."

"In the latter case" – that is *Dunlop Pneumatic Tyre Co Ltd v D Moseley & Sons Ltd* – "Vaughan Williams L.J. said (at p 278):

'The real question which was intended to be raised by the plaintiffs was this – whether the selling of an article intended to be used for the purpose of infringing a patent is an infringement of the patent. In my judgment it is not.' In the same case Stirling C.J. said (at p 281) that *Townsend v Haworth* was authority that the sale of an article does not become an infringement merely because the vendor knows that the purchaser intends to use the article when sold for the purposes of infringing the patent, and Cozens Hardy L.J. said (at p 282) that *Townsend v Haworth* was a decision that there is no infringement by defendants, even though they sell to persons with the intent that those persons should afterwards use the article sold for infringing purposes, or even if they took an indemnity in the case of any infringement being made". . . .

"In *Dunlop v Moseley* Vaughan Williams L.J. *obiter* (at p 280) expressed the opinion that that action would have failed even though the plaintiffs were able to substantiate the proposition that the goods manufactured and sold by the defendants could not be used for any purpose other than an infringing purpose. I would agree with this, for goods which cannot be used otherwise than in an infringing manner may nevertheless be disposed of without any infringement. They may, for example, be exported."

No doubt the law so stated in those authorities has been altered by section 60(2) in the 1977 Act, to which provision I have already referred, but the alteration to the common law principle so effected, in my view, is strictly limited in that, as I have already pointed out, under section 60(2) a person who supplies any of the means relating to an essential element of the patented invention for putting the invention into effect only infringes within the subsection if he supplies in the United Kingdom.

Had it been the intention of the legislature to abrogate the principle of *Townsend v Haworth and Dunlop Pneumatic Tyre Co Ltd v D Moseley & Sons Ltd*, where the sale and supply was outside the United Kingdom, one would have expected clear language to that effect. On the contrary, the language restricts the alteration of the law to the case of supply in the United Kingdom. If that be right, so that the common law principle enunciated in those authorities still obtains in respect of supply outside the United Kingdom, as a matter of law Mr Hobbs' submission on joint tortfeasance must fail. But however that may be, in my judgment, on the facts there has been no common design between Berlyn Corporation and PCL to infringe the plaintiffs' patent in the United Kingdom.

Falconer J. proceeded to distinguish Morton-Norwich Products v Intercen *[1978] R.P.C. 501 as a case in which there had been a common design to infringe on the part of a foreign manufacturer and an English importer. He quoted from Graham J.'s judgment in that case:*

"If however I am wrong and the proper view is that Intercen have themselves done no acts here contributing to the actual commission of the tort, I still hold the view that by virtue of such common design they have no defence to the claim of joint tortfeasance. A person may be liable as a joint tortfeasor provided he has such common design although he has not himself done anything within the jurisdiction which taken by itself would amount to an actionable tort. See *The Koursk* [1924] p 140, and *Brook v Bool* [1928] 2 K.B. 578 at 586. I therefore hold here that the defendants are guilty of infringement of the English patent by reason of their acts of joint tortfeasance with the Easter companies, who in fact sold the material in question here."

I have read enough of that case to point the distinction on the facts of that case from the present one. There was in fact, as it was held, a common design to sell in this country and that was quite different to the facts in this case.

(v) Procuring commission of a tort within the jurisdiction.

Falconer J. quoted from Buckley L.J.'s judgment in Lavender v Witten *(above):*

"Facilitating the doing of an act is obviously different from procuring the doing of the act. In *Townsend v Haworth* the sale of an ingredient necessary for an infringing manufacture must have facilitated the infringement, but was held not to amount to an infringement, even though the vendor knew how the ingredient was to be used and indemnified the purchaser against any infringement claim. Mr Young says that this was because the purchaser approached the vendor and was not persuaded by the vendor to make the purchase or to infringe. But in the present case there is no allegation that the defendants persuaded Edel to make the purchase or even that they sought his custom in any way."

In this case there is no question of Berlyn Corporation persuading PCL to purchase the filters, less still to use them, or that Berlyn Corporation actually sought PCL's custom, that is to say, the United Kingdom PCL. The position was quite different. It was Mr Holmes of PCL who sought the filters from Berlyn Corporation, who persuaded both PCL Canada and PCL U.S. to release one of the two filters already destined for PCL U.S. that was only allowed by Berlyn Corporation on payment terms much more stringent than had been asked of PCL U.S. A filter was to be released, and was indeed released, only after payment of the whole of the purchase price in the United States prior to release to the shipping point. As to the second filter, it was again Mr Holmes who wrote to Berlyn Corporation and sought it. There was no question of persuading by Berlyn Corporation. That did not arise at all. I reject this contention of procuring as a possible cause of action against Berlyn Corporation on the facts.

1.3.3 Defence of Prior User

1.3.3.1 Patents Act 1977, s.64 (amended by CDPA 1988, Sch.5, para.17)

S.64(1) Where a patent is granted for an invention, a person who in the United Kingdom before the priority date of the invention –

- (a) does in good faith an act which would constitute an infringement of the patent if it were in force, or
- (b) makes in good faith effective and serious preparations to do such an act,

has the right to continue to do the act or, as the case may be, to do the act, notwithstanding the grant of the patent; but this right does not extend to granting a licence to another person to do the act.

(2) If the act was done, or the preparations were made, in the course of a business, the person entitled to the right conferred by subsection (1) may –

- (a) authorise the doing of that act by any partners of his for the time being in that business, and
- (b) assign that right, or transmit it on death (or in the case of a body corporate on its dissolution), to any person who acquires that part of the business in the course of which the act was done or the preparations were made.

(3) Where a product is disposed of to another in exercise of the rights conferred by subsection (1) or (2), that other and any person claiming through him may deal with the product in the same way as if it had been disposed of by the registered proprietor of the patent.

1.3.4   Procedure and Remedies

1.3.4.1   Patents Act 1977, s.61(1),(2): Proceedings for infringement of patent

S.61(1) Subject to the following provisions of this Part of this Act, civil proceedings may be brought in the court by the proprietor of a patent in respect of any act alleged to infringe the patent and (without prejudice to any other jurisdiction of the court) in those proceedings a claim may be made –

(a) for an injunction or interdict restraining the defendant or defender from any apprehended act of infringement;

(b) for an order for him to deliver up or destroy any patented product in relation to which the patent is infringed or any article in which that product is inextricably comprised;

(c) for damages in respect of the infringement;

(d) for an account of the profits derived by him from the infringement;

(e) for a declaration or declarator that the patent is valid and has been infringed by him.

(2) The court shall not, in respect of the same infringement, both award the proprietor of a patent damages and order that he shall be given an account of the profits.

1.3.4.2   *Watson Laidlaw v Potts Cassels and Williamson* [1914] 31 R.P.C. 104 (H.L.)

The plaintiff company's patent was for a device which reduced oscillation of the spindle in washing machines. The defendant was found to have infringed the patent by incorporating the invention in its washing machines. The plaintiff was awarded £1500 as a "jury estimate" by the Lord Ordinary, which was increased to £3000 by the Second Division of the Inner House. The number of machines sold by the defendant was 252, of which 130 were sold to the Java trade. There was evidence that the plaintiff would not have made these sales.

Lord Shaw:

In my opinion, the case does raise sharply an important question as to the assessment of damages in patent cases, and with that question I proceed to deal. It is probably a mistake in language to treat the methods usually adopted in ascertaining the measure of damages in patent cases as principles. They are the practical working rules which have seemed helpful to Judges in arriving at a true estimate of the compensation which ought to be awarded against an infringer to a patentee. In the case of damages in general, there is one principle which does underlie the assessment. It is what may be called that of restoration. The idea is to restore the person who has sustained injury and loss to the condition in which he would have been had he not so sustained it. In the cases of financial loss, injury to trade, and the like, caused either by breach of contract or by tort, the loss is capable of correct appreciation in stated figures. In a second class of cases, restoration being in point of fact difficult, as in the case of loss of reputation, or impossible, as in the case of loss of life, faculty, or limb, the task of restoration under the name of compensation calls into play inference, conjecture, and the like. This is necessarily accompanied by those deficiencies which attach to the conversion into money of certain elements which are very real, which go to make up the happiness and usefulness of life, but which were never so converted or measured. The restoration by way of compensation is therefore accomplished to a large extent by the exercise of a sound imagination and the practice of the broad axe. It is in such cases, my Lords, whether the result has been attained by the verdict of a jury or the finding of a single Judge, that the greatest weight attaches to the decision of the Court of first instance. The reasons for this are not far to seek – such as the value of testimony at first hand, down to even the nuances of its expression, and they include, of course, the attitude and demeanour of the witnesses themselves. In all these cases, however, the attempt which justice makes is to get back to the *status quo ante* in fact, or to reach imaginatively, by the process of compensation, a result in which the same principle is followed. In Patent cases the principle of restoration is in all instances to some extent, and in many instances to the entire extent dependent upon the same principle of restoration. The patentee may show that the trade done by the infringer would have been his (the patentee's) trade, and he is entitled in such cases to be restored against the action of the infringer; and he may adopt, in liquidating that principle in money, an alternative course. He may say, "I shall accept the profits which have been made by the infringer in this trade which ought to have been my trade;" or he may take the other head of the alternative and say, "The illicit opposition to, and interference with, my own trade caused me damage. I lost profit which I would have otherwise made in it; I lost business connexion; the development of my business on its natural lines was interrupted by my being driven by these acts of piracy out of sections of my own trade." These and other things may be heads of damage . . . In the course, however, of deciding cases, certain expressions have been used by learned Judges, which, according to the contention, are to the effect, or truly mean, that if the patentee chooses the latter course, namely, to reckon up his claim under heads of damage, he is limited, so to speak, by the principle of restoration. Phrases, for instance, have been used, which it is said imply that the entire measure of his damage is the loss which he has incurred of the trade done in the pirated articles. . . .

It is at this stage of the case, however, my Lords, that a second principle comes into play. It is not exactly the principle of restoration, either directly or expressed through compensation, but it is the principle underlying price or hire. It plainly extends – and I am inclined to think not infrequently extends to Patent cases. But, indeed, it is not confined to them. For wherever an abstraction or invasion of property has occurred, then, unless such abstraction or invasion were to be sanctioned by law, the law ought to yield a recompense under the category or principle, as I say, either of price or of hire. If A, being a liveryman, keeps his horse standing idle in the stable, and B, against his wish or without his knowledge, rides or drives it out, it is no answer to A for B to say: "Against what loss do you want to be restored? I restore the horse. There is no loss. The horse is none the worse; it is the better for the exercise." . . . [I will] assume that the Respondents would not have done the Java trade in the 130 machines sold in that island by the infringers, and containing the patented part. The argument is – for indeed this instance covers sufficiently the whole ground – the argument is: Here it is demonstrated that the Respondents have lost no trade which they could have obtained; and under the cover of certain judicial *dicta* the infringers are entitled to say that the entire measure of the Respondents' damage is exhausted when restoration of the *status quo ante* has been obtained . . . [S]uppose the Respondents had chosen to ask for an account of the profits made by the infringers upon the infringing machines, they would have been entitled to obtain it, and a decree for the amount, and it would have been no answer to say: "The account shall be given, but there shall be excluded from it places which we shall establish your trade would never have reached." . . .

[I]n such cases it appears to me that the correct and full measure is only reached by adding that a patentee is also entitled, on the principle of price or hire, to a royalty for the unauthorised sale or use of every one of the infringing machines in a market which the infringer, if left to himself, might not have reached. Otherwise, that property which consists in the monopoly of the patented articles granted to the patentee has been invaded, and indeed abstracted, and the law, when appealed to, would be standing by and allowing the invader or abstractor to go free. In such cases a royalty is an excellent key to unlock the difficulty, and I am in entire accord with the principle laid down by Lord Moulton in *Meters Ltd v Metropolitan Gas Meters Ltd* (1911) 28 R.P.C. 163. Each of the infringements was an actionable wrong, and although it may have been committed in a range of business or of territory which the patentee might not have reached, he is entitled to hire or royalty in respect of each unauthorised use of his property. Otherwise, the remedy might fall unjustly short of the wrong.

1.3.4.3   Patents Act 1977, s.62, 63: Remedies, Limitation upon Relief

S.62(1) In proceedings for infringement of a patent damages shall not be awarded, and no order shall be made for an account of profits, against a defendant or defender who proves that at the date of the infringement he was not aware, and had no reasonable grounds for supposing, that the patent existed; and a person shall not be taken to have been so aware or to have had reasonable grounds for so supposing by reason only of the application to a product of the word "patent" or "patented", or any word or words expressing or implying that a patent has been obtained for the product, unless the number of the patent accompanied the word or words in question.

(2) In proceedings for infringement of a patent the court or the comptroller may, if it or he thinks fit, refuse to award any damages or make any such order in respect of an infringement committed during any further period specified under section 25(4) above, but before the payment of the renewal fee and any additional fee prescribed for the purposes of that subsection.

(3) Where an amendment of the specification of a patent has been allowed under any of the provisions of this Act, no damages shall be awarded in proceedings for an infringement of the patent committed before the decision to allow the amendment unless the court or the comptroller is satisfied that the specification of the patent as published was framed in good faith and with reasonable skill and knowledge.

S.63(1) If the validity of a patent is put in issue in proceedings for infringement of the patent and it is found that the patent is only partially valid, the court or the comptroller may, subject to subsection (2) below, grant relief in respect of that part of the patent which is found to be valid and infringed.

(2) Where in any such proceedings it is found that a patent is only partially valid, the court or the comptroller shall not grant relief by way of damages, costs or expenses, except where the plaintiff or pursuer proves that the specification for the patent was framed in good faith and with reasonable skill and knowledge, and in that event the court or the comptroller may grant relief in respect of that part of the patent which is valid and infringed, subject to the discretion of the court or the comptroller as to costs or expenses and as to the date from which damages should be reckoned.

(3) As a condition of relief under this section the court or the comptroller may direct that the specification of the patent shall be amended to its or his satisfaction upon an application made for that purpose under section 75 below, and an application may be so made accordingly, whether or not all other issues in the proceedings have been determined.

Note also: s.65 – Certificate of contested validity; s.66,67 – Proceedings for infringement by a co-owner, and by an exclusive licensee; s.68 – Effect of non-registration of a transaction etc., on infringement proceedings; s.69 – Infringement of rights, conferred by publication of application; s.71 – Declaration of non-infringement. For threats proceedings under s.70, see below, 7.1.3.1.

1.4 Ownership and Dealership

1.4.1 Ownership: General

1.4.1.1 Patents Act 1977, s.7: Right to apply for and obtain a patent

S.7(1) Any person may make an application for a patent either alone or jointly with another.

(2) A patent for an invention may be granted –
  (a) primarily to the inventor or joint inventors;
  (b) in preference to the foregoing, to any person or persons who, by virtue of any enactment or rule of law, or any foreign law or treaty or international convention, or by virtue of an enforceable term of any agreement entered into with the inventor before the making of the invention, was or were at the time of the making of the invention entitled to the whole of the property in it (other than equitable interests) in the United Kingdom;
  (c) in any event, to the successor or successors in title of any person or persons mentioned in paragraph (a) or (b) above or any person so mentioned and the successor or successors in title of another person so mentioned;
and to no other person.

(3) In this Act "inventor" in relation to an invention means the actual deviser of the invention and "joint inventor" shall be construed accordingly.

(4) Except so far as the contrary is established, a person who makes an application for a patent shall be taken to be the person who is entitled under subsection (2) above to be granted a patent and two or more persons who make such an application jointly shall be taken to be the persons so entitled.

Note also: s.8 – Determination before grant of questions about entitlement; s.9 – Determination after grant of questions referred before grant; s.10 – Handling of application by joint applicants; s.11 – Effect of transfer of application under s.8 or 10; s.12 – Determination of questions about entitlements to foreign and convention patents, etc.; s.37 – Determination of right to patent after grant; s.38 – Effect of transfer under s.37.

1.4.2 Transactions

1.4.2.1 Patents Act 1977, s.30, 33: Transactions; Registration

S.30(1) Any patent or application for a patent is personal property (without being a thing in action), and any patent or any such application and rights in or under it may be transferred, created or granted in accordance with subsections (2) to (7) below.

(2) Subject to section 36(3) below, any patent or any such application, or any right in it, may be assigned or mortgaged.

(3) Any patent or any such application or right shall vest by operation of law in the same way as any other personal property and may be vested by an assent of personal representatives.

(4) Subject to section 36(3) below, a licence may be granted under any patent or any such application for working the invention which is the subject of the patent or the application; and –
- (a) to the extent that the licence so provides, a sub-licence may be granted under any such licence and any such licence or sub-licence may be assigned or mortgaged; and
- (b) any such licence or sub-licence shall vest by operation of law in the same way as any other personal property and may be vested by an assent of personal representatives.

(5) Subsections (2) to (4) above shall have effect subject to the following provisions of this Act.

(6) Any of the following transactions, that is to say –
- (a) any assignment or mortgage of a patent or any such application, or any right in a patent or any such application;
- (b) any assent relating to any patent or any such application or right;

shall be void unless it is in writing and is signed by or on behalf of the parties to the transaction (or, in the case of an assent or other transaction by a personal representative, by or on behalf of the personal representative) or in the case of a body corporate is so signed or is under the seal of that body.

(7) An assignment of a patent or any such application or a share in it, and an exclusive licence granted under any patent or any such application, may confer on the assignee or licensee the right of the assignor or licensor to bring proceedings by virtue of section 61 or 69 below for a previous infringement or to bring proceedings under section 58 below for a previous act.

Note: s.32 (amended 1986) creating Register of Patents.

S.33 Effect of registration, etc, on rights in patents
(1) Any person who claims to have acquired the property in a patent or application for a patent by virtue of any transaction, instrument or event to which this section applies shall be entitled as against any other person who claims to have acquired that property by virtue of an earlier transaction, instrument or event to which this section applies if, at the time of the later transaction, instrument or event –
- (a) the earlier transaction, instrument or event was not registered, or

(b) in the case of any application which has not been published, notice of the earlier transaction, instrument or event had not been given to the comptroller, and (c)in any case, the person claiming under the later transaction, instrument or event, did not know of the earlier transaction, instrument or event.

(2) Subsection (1) above shall apply equally to the case where any person claims to have acquired any right in or under a patent or application for a patent, by virtue of a transaction, instrument or event to which this section applies, and that right is incompatible with any such right acquired by virtue of an earlier transaction, instrument or event to which this section applies.

(3) This section applies to the following transactions, instruments and events:
  (a) The assignment or assignation of a patent or application for a patent, or a right in it;
  (b) the mortgage of a patent or application or the granting of security over it;
  (c) the grant, assignment or assignation of a licence or sub-licence, or mortgage of a licence or sub-licence, under a patent or application;
  (d) the death of the proprietor or one of the proprietors of any such patent or application of any person having a right in or under a patent or application and the vesting by an assent of personal representatives of a patent, application or any such right; and
  (e) any order or directions of a court or other competent authority –
      (i) transferring a patent or application or any right in or under it to any person; or
      (ii) that an application should proceed in the name of any person; and in either case the event by virtue of which the court or authority had power to make any such order or give any such directions.

(4) Where an application for the registration of a transaction, instrument or event has been made, but the transaction, instrument or event has not been registered, then, for the purposes of subsection (1)(a) above, registration of the application shall be treated as registration of the transaction, instrument or event.

1.4.3   Co-ownership

1.4.3.1   Patents Act 1977, s.36: Joint Ownership

S.36(1) Where a patent is granted to two or more persons, each of them shall, subject to any agreement to the contrary, be entitled to an equal undivided share in the patent.

(2) Where two or more persons are proprietors of a patent, then, subject to the provisions of this section and subject to any agreement to the contrary –
  (a) each of them shall be entitled, by himself or his agents, to do in respect of the invention concerned, for his own benefit and without the consent of or the need to account to the other or others, any act which would apart from this subsection and section 55 below, amount to an infringement of the patent concerned; and
  (b) any such act shall not amount to an infringement of the patent concerned.

(3) Subject to the provisions of section 8 and 12 above and section 37 below and to any agreement for the time being in force, where two or more persons are proprietors of a patent one of them shall not without the consent of the other or others grant a licence under the patent or assign or mortgage a share in the patent or in Scotland cause or permit security to be granted over it.

(4) Subject to the provisions of those sections, where two or more persons are proprietors of a patent, anyone else may supply one of those persons with the means, relating to an essential element of the invention, for putting the invention into effect, and the supply of those means by virtue of this subsection shall not amount to an infringement of the patent.

(5) Where a patented product is disposed of by any of two or more proprietors to any person, that person and any other person claiming through him shall be entitled to deal with the product in the same way as if it had been disposed of by a sole registered proprietor.

(6) Nothing in subsection (1) or (2) above shall affect the mutual rights or obligations of trustees or of the personal representatives of a deceased person, or their rights or obligations as such.

(7) The foregoing provisions of this section shall have effect in relation to an application for a patent which is filed as they have effect in relation to a patent and –
  (a) references to a patent and a patent being granted shall accordingly include references respectively to any such application and to the application being filed; and
  (b) the reference in subsection (5) above to a patented product shall be construed accordingly.

1.4.4   Employees' Inventions

1.4.4.1   European Patent Convention, Art. 60(1): Right to a European patent

Art.60(1) The right to a European patent shall belong to the inventor or his successor in title. If the inventor is an employee the right to the European patent shall be determined in accordance with the law of the State in which the employee is mainly employed; if the State in which the employee is mainly employed cannot be determined, the law to be applied shall be that of the State in which the employer has his place of business to which the employee is attached.

1.4.4.2   Patents Act 1977, s.39 (as amended by the Copyright, Designs and Patents Act 1988, Sch.5, para.11(1): Right to employees' inventions

S.39(1) Notwithstanding anything in any rule of law, an invention made by an employee shall, as between him and his employer, be taken to belong to his employer for the purposes of this Act and all other purposes if –

(a) it was made in the course of normal duties of the employee or in the course of duties falling outside his normal duties, but specifically assigned to him, and the circumstances in either case were such that an invention might reasonably be expected to result from the carrying out of his duties; or

(b) the invention was made in the course of the duties of the employee and, at the time of making the invention, because of the nature of his duties and the particular responsibilities arising from the nature of his duties he had a special obligation to further the interests of the employer's undertaking.

(2) Any other invention made by an employee shall, as between him and his employer, be taken for those purposes to belong to the employee.

(3) Where by virtue of this section an invention belongs, as between him and his employer, to an employee, nothing done –

(a) by or on behalf of the employee or any person claiming under him for the purposes of pursuing an application for a patent, or

(b) by any person for the purpose of performing or working the invention,

shall be taken to infringe any copyright or design right to which, as between him and his employer, his employer is entitled in any model or document relating to the invention.

1.4.4.3   *Worthington Pumping Engine v Moore* [1903] 20 R.P.C. 41 (Byrne J.)

Moore acted as general manager for the foreign business of the plaintiff, an American pump corporation. He was employed at a high salary and was in effect the alter ego of the plaintiff corporation outside the United States. He developed improvements in the plaintiff's pumps which resulted in his making two patent applications in his own name.

Byrne J.:

Both Patents were taken out by the Defendant without communication of his intention to do so to the Plaintiff Corporation, and they remained in ignorance of the fact that the Patents existed until a short time before the Defendant's dismissal, and the Defendant acted, during the whole of the time of his service subsequent to taking out the Patents by advertising, giving orders for pumps made in accordance with the Patents, and otherwise, in a manner only consistent with good faith if he recognised that the Plaintiff Corporation were entitled to treat the subject-matter of the Patents as their own. A great amount of evidence was adduced, and a large number of sketches, drawings, and copies of drawings called "blue prints", which are reproductions, by process, of drawings, were put in and dealt with in much detail in the course of the case.

In the result I think it is proved that everything in both Patents disclaimed, and also the cross-over ports and the independent passage in Patent No 4302 were represented in drawings belonging to the Plaintiff Corporation prior to instructions being given for taking out the Patents. There is no reasonable colour for any claim for a Patent on the part of the Defendant for anything in these Patents unless it be in respect of the piston valves having two heads at each end of the piston rod, and the concentric arrangement of valves in one plane. As to these, though I think that the idea of getting rid of stuffing boxes and of substituting the introduction of steam between two heads of the piston rod at each end were due to the Defendant, yet the realisation of the idea and bringing it to a practical result belongs, if the evidence adduced by the Defendant is to be relied on, to Marichal, another servant of the Plaintiff Corporation, working as a servant in the ordinary course of his employment, under the direction of the Defendant. As to the other matter, I think that the idea of the detail of construction so far as putting concentric rings in one plane is concerned, is probably due to the Defendant. It appears to me that every drawing supplied to Mr Marks, the Patent agent acting in the matter of preparing the Specifications, Provisional and Complete, were documents which were brought into existence for the purposes of the Corporation and by their servants, except such as are due to J Simpson & Co Ltd, in the ordinary course of their duty at the expense of the Corporation and without a notion of securing a Patent for the Defendant at the expense of the Corporation.

I propose now to deal with the principles of law applicable to the case; and, first, I desire to say that I recognise and quite appreciate the principle of those cases which have established that the mere existence of a contract of service does not *per se* disqualify a servant from taking out a Patent for an invention made by him during his term of service, even though the invention may relate to subject-matter germane to and useful for his employers in their business, and that, even though the servant may have made use of his employer's time and servants and materials in bringing his invention to completion, and may have allowed his employers to use the invention while in their employment; but, on the other hand, without repeating what has been so fully and admirably expressed by the Court of Appeal in the two cases of *Lamb v Evans* L.R. (1893) 1 Ch.218, and *Robb v Green*, L.R. (1895) 2 Q.B. 315 it is clear that all the circumstances must be considered in each case. I consider that, bearing in mind the principles laid down in the authorities to which I have referred, it is impossible to say in the present case that the Defendant has established the right he claims, having regard to the obligations to be implied arising from his contract of service, and I am of opinion that his case is inconsistent with an observance of that good faith which ought properly to be inferred or implied as an obligation arising from his contract.

Having regard to the nature and scope of the Defendant's employment, to the obligations and duties arising from such employment, to the trust reposed in him, to his own conduct in endeavouring to establish a trade for his employers in the very articles he, in the action brought by him against them, sought to preclude them from using, I think I should be wrong in holding that he is entitled to continue to hold his Patents as against the Plaintiff Corporation, even with the belated undertakings which his Counsel offered to give on his behalf.

1.4.4.4   *British Syphon v Homewood* [1956] R.P.C. 225 (Roxburgh J.)

The defendant was employed by the plaintiff company as chief technician, advising on all technical matters relating to their business and in charge of design and development. He invented a novel method of dispensing soda water that kept the remaining contents in better condition than any prior device. Shortly before leaving the plaintiff's employ for a rival firm, he applied to patent the device. The plaintiff sought an assignment of this application.

Roxburgh J. first considered whether the defendant made the invention only after a date on which his terms of employment were so changed as to leave him free to keep it. The judge concluded that the invention was made before this date and that the defendant had given false evidence on the matter.

Now that, to my mind, leads to the difficult and unexplored point of law. It is common ground that the Defendant had not been expressly asked to design any new method of dispensing soda water by a low-pressure system or any other system, and that he had not been asked to give any advice in relation to any such problem. This is the circumstance which, as far as I can see, differentiates this case from all that have gone before. I cannot find even an oblique discussion of this problem anywhere in the many authorities which the industry of Counsel has disclosed. I revert, then, to the Defendant's position. He was employed to give the Plaintiffs technical advice in relation to the design or development of anything connected with any part of the Plaintiffs' business. No particular problem had been put before him, but if, and as often has, any problem of that kind was put before him, it was his duty to be ready to tender his advice and to assist in any matter of design or development. He was, as I put it during the argument, standing by, and paid to stand by, in that respect. He had other functions, but those are not material to the present case.

Now, would it be consistent with good faith, as between master and servant, that he should in that position be entitled to make some invention in relation to a matter concerning a part of the Plaintiffs' business and either keep it from his employer, if and when asked about the problem, or even sell it to a rival and say: "Well, yes, I know the answer to your problem, but I have already sold it to your rival"?

In my judgment, that cannot be consistent with a relationship of good faith between a master and a technical adviser. It seems to me that he has a duty not to put himself in a position in which he may have personal reasons for not giving his employer the best advice which it is his duty to give if and when asked to give it. Of course, what I am saying only relates to matters concerning the business of his employer. That, of course, is quite clear; but, in matters of that type, it seems to me that he has a duty to be free from any personal reason for not giving his employer the best possible advice. *A fortiori*, it seems to me that he is not entitled to put himself into the position of being able to say: "Well, you retained me to advise you, and I will tell you what I advise you. Do it this way, but you will have to buy the method from your rival, because I have just sold it to him, having invented it yesterday".

That seems to me to be reasoning which, in the absence of authority, makes it right and proper for me to decide that this invention (which, in my judgment, plainly relates to and concerns the business of the Plaintiff Company, namely, the distribution of soda water to the public in containers of a satisfactory character), if made during a time during which the chief technician is standing by under the terms of his employment, must be held to be in equity the property of the employer. Accordingly, my decision is for the Plaintiffs.

The Plaintiffs were given relief as follows: An order that the Defendant assign to the Plaintiffs the patent when granted: an order that the Defendant execute any additional necessary documents relating to the invention; and an injunction against disclosure of the invention. The Defendant was ordered to pay the costs of the action.

1.4.4.5 *Harris' Patent* [1985] R.P.C. 19 (Falconer J.)

Wey valves are used to control the flow of coal dust and similar material through chutes and ducts. Reiss Engineering manufactured Wey valves under licence from a Swiss company, Sistag. Harris was employed (at a salary of £6900 in 1978) as manager of Reiss' Wey valve division. In August 1978 he was notified of redundancy and left in December 1978. In between he invented an improved valve which he subsequently applied to patent. Reiss Engineering sought, by reference under the Patents Act 1977, s 8 and 37, to establish its ownership of the right to apply and patent as Harris's employer.

Falconer J. referred to the 1977 Act, s 39 as the source of substantive principle concerning employees' inventions. He continued:

Mr Pumfrey, for the appellants, submitted that it was common ground that paragraphs (a) and (b) of section 39(1) reflected the prior law; and Miss Vitoria, for Mr Harris, submitted that section 39 was declaratory of the common law position. No doubt it is true that subsection (1) of section 39 reflects, at least to a considerable degree, the prior law developed in the authorities as to the rights, as between employer and employee, in inventions made by employees, but I wish to make it clear that I am not to be taken as holding that section 39 is declaratory of the previous common law position in that regard, for, as at present advised, I entertain some doubt as to whether section 39 is so declaratory of the common law position. It is not necessary to decide that point for the purposes of this appeal, and I leave it open.

However, it seems to me to be quite clear from the language of section 39 – see the opening six words and the wording of subsection(2) – that the intention of the legislature was that rights, as between employer and employee, in any employee's invention made after the appointed day are to be governed by, and only by, the provisions of section 39, and that is reinforced by the provisions of section 42(1) and (2), which render unenforceable against an employee any contractual provision which diminishes his rights under section 39.

I have referred to this aspect because I have had cited to me, as did the superintending examiner, a number of the well-known cases concerning employees' inventions decided under the law as developed in the earlier authorities. No doubt, guidance may be obtained from such previous cases as to how courts have assessed the duties of the employee in a particular case and particular circumstances; but, having regard to the clear opening words of section 39, it is the provisions of section 39 to which regard must be had for the law governing any employee's invention made after the appointed day.

Falconer J. noted the submission that this invention belonged to the employer, under s 39(1)(a), as (i) having been made in the course of normal duties and (ii) the circumstances were such that an invention might reasonably be expected to result from the carrying out of the duties. He continued:

As to the second requirement in the paragraph, that is to say, whether the circumstances were such that an invention might reasonably be expected to result from his carrying out those duties, Miss Vitoria submitted that the circumstances referred to in paragraph (a) must be the circumstances in which the invention was made: and it seems to me that submission must be right. Mr Pumfrey, in the course of his argument, pointed out that the wording of the paragraph was "an invention might reasonably be expected to result" and not "the invention might" and so on. But plainly, the wording "an invention" cannot mean any invention whatsoever; it is governed by the qualification that it has to be an invention that "might reasonably be expected to result from the carrying out of his duties" by the employee. That wording applies equally to the second alternative in paragraph (a), that of "specifically assigned" duties falling outside the employee's normal duties; and, therefore, in my judgment the wording "an invention might reasonably be expected to result from the carrying out of his duties" must be referring to an invention which achieves, or contributes to achieving, whatever was the aim or object to which the employee's efforts in carrying out his duties were directed, in the case of alternative (i) of paragraph (a) his normal duties being performed at the time; in the case of alternative (ii) of paragraph (a) the specifically assigned duties, that is to say, such an invention as that made, though not necessarily the precise invention actually made and in question. The circumstances to be taken into account for the purposes of paragraph (a) of section 39(1) will, of course, depend on the particular case, but clearly a circumstance which must always loom large will be the nature of the employee's duties, either his normal duties or the specifically assigned duties, as the case may be. The nature of Mr Harris's normal duties have to be examined, therefore, from this aspect also.

Falconer J. proceeded to find that Harris's duties as manager were confined to selling Wey valves and dealing in the first instance with the difficulties of customers. If these difficulties were technical he was expected to refer them to Sistag for solution. Reiss Engineering conducted no research and on one occasion when Harris suggested a technical improvement, Reiss's managing director indicated that he had no interest in it. In consequence, it was held to be no part of his employment to perform duties that might result in invention. Accordingly, the patent properly belonged to Harris under s 39(2).

1.4.4.6   *Electrolux v Hudson* [1977] F.S.R. 312 (Whitford J.)

The first defendant, Hudson, was employed as a senior storekeeper by the plaintiff company, which manufactured vacuum cleaners. In collaboration at home with his wife (second defendant), Hudson devised an adaptor for connecting a dust-bag to a vacuum cleaner. Together they applied to patent it, but the plaintiff claimed to be entitled to it by virtue of the terms, express and implied, of Hudson's employment. The plaintiff contended that the following standard term was a condition of that employment:

(a) If at any time during the period of your employment, you shall invent, discover or ascertain any process, invention or improvement (whether patentable or not) relating to any articles manufactured and/or marketed by the company or its associated companies or undertakings or firms in the United Kingdom or elsewhere, you shall forthwith, at the expense of the company, disclose to the company or any agent appointed by it, a full and complete description of the nature of the said process, invention, discovery or improvement and the mode of performing it, and the said process, invention, discovery or improvement shall remain the sole and absolute property of the company; and you shall, if and when required by the company, at the expense of the company, join with the company in applying for letters patent for the said process, invention, discovery or improvement (if patentable) and/or other similar protection in any part of the world and shall on the request by, and at the cost of, the company, execute and do all such instruments and things necessary to test the said process, invention, discovery or improvement, and any letters patent and/or other similar protection that may be obtained relating thereto, in the company or otherwise as the company may direct.

(b) Should the company consider the said process, discovery, invention, or improvement, to be of such importance that your usual remuneration is inadequate compensation for it, the company will make you an allowance and in fixing such allowance, special consideration will be given to the fact of whether the said process, discovery, invention or improvement is outside the scope of your normal duties and has not been invented, discovered, or ascertained as a result of the experience you have gained in the employment of the company. The company's decision as to making the said allowance and as to the amount thereof is final and is binding on you.

Whitford J. referred to Schroeder v Macaulay *[1974] 3 All E.R. 616):*

Lord Diplock says that what you have got to consider when you have to come to a conclusion as to whether a particular restraint is enforceable is whether the bargain in question was a fair bargain, whether the restrictions imposed were reasonably necessary for the protection of the legitimate interests of the person imposing the restrictions, and also whether they were commensurate with the benefit secured by the person on whom the restriction was imposed.

Of course, if you employ somebody to make inventions or do research you pay them at a rather different rate than the rate at which Mr Hudson was employed as a storeman. His salary in 1971 was £1,302 per annum. It may no doubt have been subsequently increased, though nobody bothered to lead any evidence about it. But one can take it that this was just the sort of salary that was paid to a storeman; it is not the sort of salary that is paid to a research worker. He was not employed to do research or to make inventions, and it is to my mind absurd to suggest that it could reasonably have been necessary in the protection of the interests of the plaintiffs to impose upon Mr Hudson a restraint in respect of any processes, inventions or improvements relating not only to articles manufactured by the plaintiffs, and which might be in store at the depot where he was a storeman, but also relating to articles manufactured or marketed by any of the associated undertakings, companies or firms, the diversity of whose activities I have already briefly made reference to. This clause is much too wide to be enforceable as against Mr Hudson.

His Lordship proceeded to find that there was no basis on which to separate out a more limited obligation to disclose any invention that the plaintiff had made. Nor could he find any implied undertaking upon Hudson to hold the invention for the plaintiff, since he was not employed to invent and he had made the invention outside working hours without using his employers' materials.

1.4.4.7 Patents Act 1977, s.40–43: Compensation of employees for certain inventions

S.40(1) Where it appears to the court or the comptroller on an application made by an employee within the prescribed period that the employee has made an invention belonging to the employer for which a patent has been

granted, that the patent is (having regard among other things to the size and nature of the employer's undertaking) of outstanding benefit to the employer and that by reason of those facts it is just that the employee should be awarded compensation to be paid by the employer, the court or the comptroller may award him such compensation of an amount determined under section 41 below.

(2) Where it appears to the court or the comptroller on an application made by an employee within the prescribed period that –

(a) a patent has been granted for an invention made by and belonging to the employee;

(b) his rights in the invention, or in any patent or application for a patent for the invention, have since the appointed day been assigned to the employer or an exclusive licence under the patent or application has since the appointed day been granted to the employer;

(c) the benefit derived by the employee from the contract of assignment assignation or grant or any ancillary contract ("the relevant contract") is inadequate in relation to the benefit derived by the employer from the patent and

(d) by reason of those facts it is just that the employee should be awarded compensation to be paid by the employer in addition to the benefit derived from the relevant contract;

the court or the comptroller may award him such compensation of an amount determined under section 41 below.

(3) Subsections (1) and (2) above shall not apply to the invention of an employee where a relevant collective agreement provides for the payment of compensation in respect of inventions of the same description as that invention to employees of the same description as that employee.

(4) Subsection (2) above shall have effect notwithstanding anything in the relevant contract or any agreement applicable to the invention (other than any such collective agreement).

(5) If it appears to the comptroller on an application under this section that the application involves matters which would more properly be determined by the court, he may decline to deal with it.

(6) In this section –

"the prescribed period", in relation to proceedings before the court, means the period prescribed by rules of court, and

"relevant collective agreement" means a collective agreement within the meaning of the Trade Union and Labour Relations Act 1974, made by or on behalf of a trade union to which the employee belongs, and by the employer or an employers' association to which the employer belongs which is in force at the time of the making of the invention.

(7) References in this section to an invention belonging to an employer or employee are references to it so belonging as between the employer and the employee.

S.41 Amount of compensation

(1) An award of compensation to an employee under section 41(1) or (2) above in relation to a patent for an invention shall be such as will secure for

the employee a fair share (having regard to all the circumstances) of the benefit which the employer has derived, or may reasonably be expected to derive, from the patent or from the assignment, assignation or grant to a person connected with the employer of the property or any right in the invention or the property in, or any right in or under, an application for that patent.

(2) For the purposes of subsection (1) above the amount of any benefit derived or expected to be derived by an employer from the assignment, assignation or grant of –

    (a) the property in, or any right in or under, a patent for the invention or an application for such a patent; or

    (b) the property or any right in the invention;

to a person connected with him shall be taken to be the amount which could reasonably be expected to be so derived by the employer if that person had not been connected with him.

(3) Where the Crown or a Research Council in its capacity as employer assigns or grants the property in, or any right in or under, an invention, patent or application for a patent to a body having among its functions that of developing or exploiting inventions resulting from public research and does so for no consideration or only a nominal consideration, any benefit derived from the invention, patent or application by that body shall be treated for the purposes of the foregoing provisions of this section as so derived by the Crown or, as the case may be, Research Council.

In this subsection "Research Council" means a body which is a Research Council for the purposes of the Science and Technology Act 1965.

(4) In determining the fair share of the benefit to be secured for an employee in respect of a patent for an invention which has always belonged to an employer, the court or the comptroller shall, among other things, take the following matters into account, that is to say –

    (a) the nature of the employee's duties, his remuneration and the other advantages he derives or has derived from his employment or has derived in relation to the invention under this Act;

    (b) the effort and skill which the employee has devoted to making the invention;

    (c) the effort and skill which any other person haas devoted to making the invention jointly with the employee concerned, and the advice and other assistance contributed by any other employee who is not a joint inventor of the invention; and

    (d) the contribution made by the employer to the making, developing and working of the invention by the provision of advice, facilities and other assistance, by the provision of opportunities and by his managerial and commercial skill and activities.

(5) In determining the fair share of the benefit to be secured for an employee in respect of a patent for an invention which originally belonged to him, the court or the comptroller shall, among other things, take the following matters into account, that is to say –

    (a) any conditions in a licence or licences granted under this Act or otherwise in respect of the invention or the patent;

(b) the extent to which the invention was made jointly by the employee with any other person; and

(c) the contribution made by the employer to the making, developing and working of the invention as mentioned in subsection (4)(d) above.

S.41(6) provides for lump sum or periodic payments, s.41(7) for further applications, s.41(8) for variation, discharge or suspension of orders and s.41(9)–(11) for execution.

S.42 Enforceability of contracts relating to employee's inventions

(1) This section applies to any contract (whenever made) relating to inventions made by an employee, being a contract entered into by him –

(a) with the employer (alone or with another); or

(b) with some other person at the request of the employer or in pursuance of the employee's contract of employment.

(2) Any term in a contract to which this section applies which diminishes the employee's rights in inventions of any description made by him after the appointed day and the date of the contract, or in or under patents for those inventions or applications for such patents, shall be unenforceable against him to the extent that it diminishes his rights in an invention of that description so made, or in or under a patent for such an invention or an application for any such patent.

(3) Subsection (2) above shall not be construed as derogating from any duty of confidentiality owed to his employer by an employee by virtue of any rule of law or otherwise.

(4) This section applies to any arrangement made with a Crown employee by or on behalf of the Crown as his employer as it applies to any contract made between an employee and an employer other than the Crown, and for the purposes of this section "Crown employee" means a person employed under or for the purposes of a government department or any officer or body exercising on behalf of the Crown functions conferred by any enactment [or a person serving in the naval, military or air forces of the Crown].

S.43 Supplementary

(1) Sections 39 to 42 above shall not apply to any invention made before the appointed day.

(2) Sections 39 to 42 above shall not apply to an invention made by an employee unless at the time he made the invention one of the following conditions was satisfied in his case, that is to say –

(a) he was mainly employed in the United Kingdom; or

(b) he was not mainly employed anywhere or his place of employment could not be determined, but his employer had a place of business in the United Kingdom to which the employee was attached, whether or not he was also attached elsewhere.

(3) In section 39 to 42 above and this section, except so far as the context otherwise requires, references to the making of an invention by an employee are references to his making it alone or jointly with any other person, but do not include references to his merely contributing advice or other assistance in the making of an invention by another employee.

(4) Any references in sections 40 to 42 above to a patent and to a patent being granted are respectively references to a patent or other protection and to its being granted whether under the law of the United Kingdom or the law in force in any other country or under any treaty or international convention.

(5) For the purposes of sections 40 and 41 above the benefit derived or expected to be derived by an employer from a patent shall, where he dies before any award is made under section 40 above in respect of the patent, include any benefit derived or expected to be derived from the patent by his personal representatives or by any person in whom it was vested by their assent.

(6) Where an employee dies before an award is made under section 40 above in respect of a patented invention made by him, his personal representatives or their successors in title may exercise his right to make or proceed with an application for compensation under section (1) or (2) of that section.

(7) In sections 40 and 41 above and this section "benefit" means benefit in money or money's worth.

(8) Section 533 of the Income and Corporation Taxes Act 1970 (definition of connected persons) shall apply for determining for the purposes of section 41(2) above whether one person is connected with another as it applies for determining that question for the purposes of the Tax Acts.

1.4.5   Abuse of Monopoly

1.4.5.1   Patents Act 1977, s.44: Avoidance of certain restrictive conditions

S.44(1) Subject to the provisions of this section, any condition or term of a contract for the supply of a patented product or of a licence to work a patented invention, or of a contract relating to any such supply or licence, shall be void in so far as it purports –

  (a) in the case of a contract for supply, to require the person supplied to acquire from the supplier, or his nominee, or prohibit him from acquiring from any specified person, or from acquiring except from the supplier or his nominee, anything other than the patented product;

  (b) in the case of a licence to work a patented invention, to require the licensee to acquire from the licensor or his nominee, or prohibit him from acquiring from any specified person, or from acquiring except from the licensor or his nominee, anything other than the product which is the patented invention or (if it is a process) other than any product obtained directly by means of the process or to which the process has been applied;

  (c) in either case, to prohibit the person supplied or licensee from using articles (whether patented products or not) which are not supplied by, or any patented process which does not belong to, the supplier or licensor, or his nominee, or to restrict the right of the person supplied or licensee to use any such articles or process.

(2) Subsection (1) above applies to contracts and licences whether made or granted before or after the appointed day, but not to those made or granted before 1st January 1950.

(3) In proceedings against any person for infringement of a patent it shall be a defence to prove that at the time of the infringement there was in force a contract relating to the patent made by or with the consent of the plaintiff or pursuer or a licence under the patent granted by him or with his consent and containing in either case a condition or term void by virtue of this section.

(4) A condition or term of a contract or licence shall not be void by virtue of this section if –

  (a) at the time of the making of the contract or granting of the licence the supplier or licensor was willing to supply the product, or grant a licence to work the invention, as the case may be, to the person supplied or licensee, on reasonable terms specified in the contract or licence and without any such condition or term as is mentioned in subsection (1) above; and

  (b) the person supplied or licensee is entitled under the contract or licence to relieve himself of his liability to observe the condition or term on giving to the other party three months' notice in writing and subject to payment to that other party of such compensation (being, in the case of a contract to supply, a lump sum or rent for the residue of the term of the contract and, in the case of a licence, a royalty for the residue of the term of the licence) as may be determined by an arbitrator or arbiter appointed by the Secretary of State.

(5) If in any proceeding it is alleged that any condition or term of a contract or licence is void by virtue of this section it shall lie on the supplier or licensor to prove the matters set out in paragraph (a) of subsection (4) above.

(6) A condition or term of a contract or licence shall not be void by virtue of this section by reason only that it prohibits any person from selling goods other than those supplied by a specific person or, in the case of a contract for the hiring of or licence to use a patented product, that it reserves to the bailor (or in Scotland, hirer) or licensor, or his nominee, the right to supply such new parts of the patented product as may be required to put or keep it in repair.

1.4.5.2 *Tool Metal v Tungsten Electric* (1955) 72 R.P.C. 209 (H.L.)

Tool Metal had patents for making hard tips for machine tools from tungsten carbide. These originally covered two grades of – "contract material" – the iron grade and the steel grade, but the patent for the iron grade expired in 1941. In a licence under both patents, Tungsten Electric agreed that for its use of contract material it would pay a 10 per cent royalty up to 50 Kgs per month and for any excess not obtained from Tool Metal or one of its licensees additional "compensation" at the rate of 30 per cent (Clause 5). The obligation to do so was resisted on a number of grounds, one of which was the Patents and Designs Act 1907, s 38 (precursor of the 1977 Act, s 44).

Lord Oaksey (reading for and agreeing with Lord Reid) referred to the inducement offered by Clause 5, and continued:

It will be seen that a number of contingencies were involved before this inducement could operate; TECO must want to buy iron grade material instead of making it and they must want to buy it for use and not for immediate resale; some independent manufacturer must have started making the material; and the material must be of suitable quality and must be available at a competitive price. If then the independent manufacturers' price were more than 30 per cent below T.M.M.C.'s price the 30 per cent compensation would not matter as it would still pay TECO to buy from the independent manufacturer, and if that manufacturer's price were above T.M.M.C.'s price the compensation would not matter as TECO would in any case buy from T.M.M.C. But if that manufacturers' price were below, but less than 30 per cent below, T.M.M.C.'s price, then the liability to pay compensation would probably induce TECO to buy from T.M.M.C. whereas, in the absence of Clause 5, they would probably have bought from the independent manufacturer. It is the possibility of that happening which, on the argument for TECO, makes it necessary to hold that the effect of Clause 5 "will be" to restrict TECO from using iron grade material supplied by any person other than T.M.M.C. and their licensees.

There appear to me to be four key words in the subsection – "the effect of which will be (a) to prohibit or restrict ... or (b) to require". To my mind, the natural meaning of the subsection is that the effect of the condition must be to limit the right of the licensee to make a choice, and I do not think that these words are appropriate to cover a case such as the present where the licensee remains free to choose but the presence of the condition will in some circumstances create an inducement to choose to buy from the licensor. I take first the word "require" in subsec (1)(b): the effect of a particular condition may be to offer so great an advantage to the licensee if he buys from the licensor that it would be extremely foolish of him not to do that, but I do not think that in the ordinary use of language it could properly be said that the effect of such a condition will be to "require" the licensee to do it. I feel bound to hold that subsec

(1)(b) only applies if the effect of the condition is that whenever certain circumstances occur the licensee, if he wishes to buy the article, is obliged to buy it from the licensor. Then I take the word "prohibit" in subsec (1)(a). It is true that the adjective "prohibitive" is frequently used when there is no legal prohibition, as in the phrase "a prohibitive price", and it may be that the verb "prohibit" is sometimes used in that way, but I would not expect the word "prohibit" to be used in this context to denote a state of affairs where the inducement not to buy the other person's goods is so great that no reasonable person would choose to do so, and I see nothing in the context pointing to such a meaning. I think that the meaning is that the effect of the condition will be such as to oblige the licensee in certain circumstances not to use the other person's goods. Then I come to the word "restrict". A person though not prohibited is restricted from using something if he is permitted to use it to a certain extent or subject to certain conditions but otherwise obliged not to use it, but I do not think that a person is properly said to be restricted from using something by a condition the effect of which is to offer him some inducement not to use it, or in some other way to influence his choice. To my mind, the more natural meaning here is restriction of the licensee's right to use the article and I am fortified in that opinion by two considerations.

If I am right in thinking that "require" and "prohibit" refer to legal obligations to buy or not to use, I see nothing to suggest that "restrict" is used in quite a different sense which has nothing to do with legal obligation but which relates to financial disadvantage. And, secondly, to say that the effect will be to restrict seems to me much more appropriate if restriction refers to restriction of the licensee's right to use than it would be if restriction refers to an inducement not to use. The legality of the condition has to be determined at the time when the licence is granted and if the terms of the conditions are such as to restrict the licensee's right to use an article in certain circumstances then it can properly be said that its effect will be to restrict him from using it. But if, as in the present case, all that can be said is that the effect of the condition in some circumstances will be to offer a financial advantage, which may be considerable or may be small, if the licensee uses the licensor's goods, I do not see how it can be said that its effect will be to restrict the licensee from using other goods. The licensee may be influenced by this financial advantage or he may, perhaps for good reason, choose to disregard it; it is impossible to say in advance what the effect will be.

I recognise that to give this meaning to the section leaves room for evasion. I do not think that the primary purpose of Clause 5 was to evade this section, and the absence of any reported case in a period of 48 years since the section was enacted would seem to show that evasion of this kind has not been common. But undoubtedly it would often be possible to achieve a preference for the licensor by coupling the licence with a condition, which, though not having the effect of limiting the licensee's freedom of choice, imposed some burden on the licensee if he bought certain articles in the open market. The question is whether it is legitimate to stretch the words of sec 38 to make them apply to such a case. Sec 38(1) is a highly penal provision. It not only makes the whole condition void, although the circumstances in which it would have the effect of restricting the licensee may be very unlikely to occur, but by subsec (4) it also makes the existence of the condition a defence to an action for infringement of the patent. At best the section is ambiguous, and if a penal provision is ambiguous it ought not, in my view, to be construed in a wider sense than the ordinary meaning of its terms requires. This section appears to have been enacted to deal with a definite and limited abuse, and if Parliament failed to take the opportunity to deal with the whole matter sufficiently comprehensively, then the remedy was an amending Act of Parliament.

Lord Tucker and Lord Cohen agreed; but Viscount Simonds dissented.

1.4.5.3 *Hunter's Patent* [1965] R.P.C. 416 (Irish S.C.)

Th. Hunter Ltd held a patent for sealing heads for fixing lids to jam jars. In the Irish Republic they hired out these heads to jam manufacturers, subject to a covenant that they remained the property of Hunter and bore no licence to use as sealers (Clause 5). Hunter imported and sold lids, on each package of which was printed a licence to use the heads with the enclosed lids. A rival lid manufacturer, Fox, claimed inter alia that the restrictive arrangement was void under the Irish Patents Act s 54 (equivalent to the UK Patents Act 1907, s 38 – precursor of the 1977 Act, s 44 and in suit in the Tool Metal *case, above, 1.4.5.2):*

Kingsmill Moore J. (for the Court):

It seems to me impossible to separate clause 5 from the licences subsequently issued. The patent heads are objects neither of adornment nor of intellectual interest. No lessee would pay money merely to keep them in his possession without being permitted to use them and I cannot conceive of any lessee signing the agreement unless on an understanding, tacit or expressed, that he was to be furnished with as many licences as he wanted for their use on Hunter's goods, though on Hunter's goods alone. Indeed, I am willing to read into the agreement an implied term that the hirer was to be furnished with a licence to use the head on any Hunter's goods that he might buy. The effect of the arrangement affected by the hiring agreement and licence was to force the hirer of a head to purchase his caps from Hunter's and so to transgress the prohibitions of section 54(1)(a) and (b).

I have used the neutral word "arrangement" because it is contended for Hunter's that even if this was the effect of the arrangement there was no "contract" containing a "condition" to this effect and that it is necessary to find a "condition" in a "contract" before the section operates. The section is drafted vaguely but I think it would be erroneous to confine the meaning of "condition" too strictly and it must be read as equivalent to "term". Moreover, the section does not merely make unlawful a condition directly prohibiting or restricting the licensee from doing or requiring him to do what is forbidden by the section. It makes unlawful any condition "the effect of which will be" to create such a prohibition restriction or requirement, and to consider what the effect of the term will be involves an examination of all the circumstances of the case. In the circumstances of this case the effect of clause 5 is to prohibit the licensee from using the head on the goods of any person other than Hunter's and to require him to purchase any goods which are to be used with the head, from Hunter's.

Mr O'Neill relied on the fact that in the *Tool Metal* case (above, 1.4.5.2), the majority of the court adopted Lord Oaksey's opinion that the provisions of the section had not been infringed. But the circumstances of that case were very different. There was no prohibition on using any person's goods. In the opinion of the majority there was also no restriction on using any person's goods though there was a monetary inducement to use the goods of the patentee. I think it is clear from the second paragraph of the passage I have cited from the judgment of Lord Oaksey that he would have held that there was a prohibition in the circumstances of the present case and Lord Simonds held that there was such a restriction even in the circumstances of the *Tool Metal* case.

I hold therefore that the existing agreement between Hunter's and the jam manufacturers is, in the circumstances of this case, illegal under section 54(1) because the effect of clause 5, taken in conjunction with the terms of the licence, is a condition which has the effect of transgressing (a) and (b) of that section. What then is the effect of this finding? The section gives the answer. The condition, by subsection 1, is null and void, and by subsection 4 its existence affords a good defence to an action for infringement of the patent. I read subsection 1 as having the effect of making the condition void *ab initio*. It stands as if it had never been inserted. The jam manufacturers are in the position of persons who have a lease of the head without any restriction as to its use on any particular lids and they may use it on lids manufactured by Fox's. Hunter's may determine the agreement by serving the requisite notice and may substitute an agreement different in terms, seeking to recoup themselves by charging larger royalties, or in any other way which is legal. The legality of any substituted agreement can be tested in subsequent proceedings.

1.4.5.4   Patents Act 1977, s.45: Determination of Parts of Certain Contracts

S.45(1) Any contract for the supply of a patented product or licence to work a patented invention, or contract relating to any such supply or licence, may at any time after the patent or all the patents by which the product or invention was protected at the time of the making of the contract or granting of the licence has or have ceased to be in force, and notwithstanding anything to the contrary in the contract or licence or in any other contract, be determined, to the extent (and only to the extent) that the contract or licence relates to the product or invention, by either party on giving three months' notice in writing to the other party.

(2) In subsection (1) above "patented product" and "patented invention" include respectively a product and an invention which is the subject of an application for a patent, and that subsection shall apply in relation to a patent by which any such product or invention was protected and which was granted after the time of the making of the contract or granting of the licence in question, on an application which had been filed before that time, as it applies to a patent in force at that time.

(3) If, on an application under this subsection made by either party to a contract or licence falling within subsection (1) above, the court is satisfied that, in consequence of the patent or patents concerned ceasing to be in force, it would be unjust to require the applicant to continue to comply with all the terms and conditions of the contract or licence, it may make such order varying those terms or conditions, as, having regard to all the circumstances of the case, it thinks just as between the parties.

(4) Without prejudice to any other right of recovery, nothing in sub-section (1) above shall be taken to entitle any person to recover property bailed under a hire-purchase agreement (within the meaning of the Consumer Credit Act 1974).

(5) The foregoing provisions of this section apply to contracts and licences whether made before or after the appointed day.

(6) The provisions of this section shall be without prejudice to any rule of law relating to the frustration of contracts and any right of determining a contract or licence exercisable apart from this section.

1.4.5.5   *Hansen v Magnavox* [1977] R.P.C. 301 (C.A.)

The plaintiff, an individual inventor, granted the defendant manufacturer of record players an exclusive licence to manufacture and sell the automatic record player protected by the plaintiff's patents and pending applications. These were in a number of countries including the UK (where the last patent expired in 1972) and the US (where the last patent would not expire until 1982). The licence was for all countries in the world save continental Europe and the royalties (including a minimum annual royalty) were calculated without reference to sales in particular countries. In 1974, the defendant gave notice of termination of the agreement under the Patents Act 1949, s 58 (this was in most respects equivalent to the Patents Act 1977, s 45, but contained no provision equivalent to s 45(3)). The effect of the termination would have been that liability to pay royalties ceased but that the defendant had no licence in those countries where patents continued.

The plaintiff argued that, on construction of the particular agreement, by its terms the royalties payable after 1972 included nothing for any licence under the British patents, so that there was no subject-matter to which s 58 could apply. Ormrod L.J. accepted this construction and Bridge L.J. (dissenting) rejected it. Lord Denning M.R. decided the case not on construction alone but upon a general interpretation of s 58 (Bridge L.J. dissented specifically from this, claiming that it "cuts clean across the agreed assumptions we were invited by both counsel to accept as the starting point of the argument)."

Lord Denning M.R.:

Can that section 58 be applied to a contract relating both to English patents and to foreign patents? The answer is: Yes, it can, at any rate in those cases where the provisions relating to the English patents can be severed from those relating to the foreign patents. Either party can then make use of section 58 so as to give three months' notice to determine the English part: but neither can make use of section 58 to determine the foreign part. This is, I think, all that was intended by Lloyd-Jacob J. in *Advance Industries Ltd v Paul Frankfurter* [1958] R.P.C. 392 at 394:

> "This provision (section 58) in my judgment is to be exercised in relation to the patent monopoly conferred by British letters patent and neither extends to nor can be defected by the existence of patent monopolies conferred by other powers".

But when the provisions are inseparably mixed up – the provisions relating to the English patent mixed up with the provisions relating to the foreign patent – so that they cannot be severed – I do not think that either party can make use of section 58 so as to bring the whole contract to an end – contrary to the very terms of the agreement itself.

In this case, seeing that the royalties are payable on a global basis (without division between the various countries) I think the provisions relating to the English patent are inseparably mixed up with the USA patent. So section 58 cannot be applied. Test it this way: We know that the English patents expired in 1972 but the USA patents continue until 1982. By the very terms of the agreement the company is licensed to manufacture and sell in the USA until 1982. Suppose that in 1974 the inventor were to give three months' notice to determine the agreement, relying on section 58, can it be supposed that the whole agreement comes to an end at that time? If this were so, it would mean that the company had no licence at all to manufacture and sell in the USA from 1974 to 1982 and could be prevented from doing so – despite the express terms of the agreement. That would be utterly unreasonable – so unreasonable that the courts should not interpret section 58 so as to produce that result.

Take now this very case. The company in 1974, relying on section 58, gave three months' notice to determine the whole agreement. Can it be supposed that the whole agreement comes to an end? If that were so, the company could deprive the inventor of the minimum royalty of £15,000 a year for all the years from 1974 to 1982. The company could continue to utilise the invention in the USA for those years: and, meanwhile, it could contest any action there for infringement, hoping perhaps that the inventor would be deterred by the cost and delay from pursuing it to the end. That seems to produce a very unreasonable result. Yet it was very much in their minds. An inter-office memorandum shows it.

In short, I think that section 58 is a piece of domestic legislation relating to English patents only. It can be sensibly applied to contracts which deal only with English patents, and to contracts where the provisions relating to the English patents are clearly severable from those relating to foreign patents. But I do not think it can be applied where the provisions are so mixed up as to be inseparable. Parliament cannot have intended adversely to affect those mixed contracts in a piece of legislation which, by its very wording, is confined to English patents.

On this ground, I think that the company were not entitled to invoke section 58 so as to determine the agreement. The notice of 1st April 1974 was of no effect. The agreement remains in force, accordingly.

1.4.6 Compulsory Licences and Crown Use

1.4.6.1 Patents Act 1977, s.48, 50: Compulsory licences

S.48(1) At any time after the expiration of three years, or of such other period as may be prescribed, from the date of the grant of a patent any person may apply to the comptroller on one or more of the grounds specified in subsection (3) below –

(a) for a licence under a patent,

(b) for an entry to be made in the register to the effect that licences under the patent are to be available as of right, or

(c) where the applicant is a government department, for the grant to any person specified in the application of a licence under the patent.

(2) A rule prescribing any such other period under subsection (1) above shall not be made unless a draft of the rule has been laid before, and approved by resolution of, each House of Parliament.

(3) The grounds are:

(a) where the patented invention is capable of being commercially worked in the United Kingdom, that it is not being so worked or is not being so worked to the fullest extent that is reasonably practicable;

(b) where the patented invention is a product, that a demand for the product in the United Kingdom –

(i) is not being met on reasonable terms, or

(ii) is being met to a substantial extent by importation;

(c) where the patented invention is capable of being commercially worked in the United Kingdom, that it is being prevented or hindered from being so worked –

(i) where the invention is a product, by the importation of the product,

(ii) where the invention is a process by the importation of a product obtained directly by means of the process or to which the process has been applied;

(d) that by reason of the refusal of the proprietor of the patent to grant a licence or licences on reasonable terms –

(i) a market for the export of any patented product made in the United Kingdom is not being supplied, or

(ii) the working or efficient working in the United Kingdom of any other patented invention which makes a substantial contribution to the art is prevented or hindered, or

(iii) the establishment or development of commercial or industrial activities in the United Kingdom is unfairly prejudiced;

(e) that by reason of conditions imposed by the proprietor of the patent on the grant of licences under the patent, or on the disposal or use of the patented product or on the use of the patented process, the manufacture, use or disposal of materials not protected by the patent, or the establishment or development of commercial or industrial activities in the United Kingdom, is unfairly prejudiced.

(4) Subject to the provisions of subsections (5) to (7) below, if he is satisfied that any of those grounds are established, the comptroller may –

(a)   where the application is under subsection (1)(a) above, order the grant of licence to the applicant, on such terms as the comptroller thinks fit;

(b)   where the application is under subsection (1)(b) above, make such an entry as is there mentioned;

(c)   where the application is under subsection (1)(c) above, order the grant of a licence to the person specified in the application on such terms as the comptroller thinks fit.

S.48(5)–(7) impose further conditions on the comptroller's discretion in relation to grounds (3)(a), (c) and d(i).

S.48(8) permits an existing licensee to apply for a compulsory licence, whereupon the Comptroller is given additional powers by s.49.

S.50(1) The powers of the comptroller on an application under section 48 above in respect of a patent shall be exercised with a view to securing the following general purposes: –

(a)   that inventions which can be worked on a commercial scale in the United Kingdom and which should in the public interest be so worked shall be worked there without undue delay and to the fullest extent that is reasonably practicable;

(b)   that the inventor or other person beneficially entitled to a patent shall receive reasonable remuneration having regard to the nature of the invention;

(c)   that the interests of any person for the time being working or developing an invention in the United Kingdom under the protection of a patent shall not be unfairly prejudiced.

(2) Subject to subsection (1) above, the comptroller shall, in determining whether to make an order or entry in pursuance of such an application, take account of the following matters, that is to say –

(a)   the nature of the invention, the time which has elapsed since the publication in the journal of a notice of the grant of the patent and the measures already taken by the proprietor of the patent or any licensee to make full use of the invention;

(b)   the ability of any person to whom a licence would be granted under the order concerned to work the invention to the public advantage; and

(c)   the risks to be undertaken by that person in providing capital and working the invention if the application for an order is granted.

but shall not be required to take account of matters subsequent to the making of the application.

S.51 gives government the power, after an unfavourable report from the Monopolies and Mergers Commission, to apply to the Comptroller for various forms of relief, including endorsement of the patent, "Licences of Right".

For licences of right in general, see s.46, 47.

S.52 provides for opposition, appeal and arbitration in respect of compulsory licences; and s.53 and 54 contain supplementary provisions.

1.4.6.2   Patents Act 1977, s.55, 56: Crown Use

S.55(1) Notwithstanding anything in this Act, any government department and any person authorised in writing by a government department may, for the services of the Crown and in accordance with this section, do any of the following acts in the United Kingdom in relation to a patented invention without the consent of the proprietor of the patent, that is to say –

    (a)   where the invention is a product, may –

        (i)   make, use, import or keep the product, or sell or offer to sell it whether to do so would be incidental or ancillary to making, using, importing or keeping it; or

        (ii)   in any event, sell or offer to sell it for foreign defence purposes or for the production or supply of specified drugs and medicines, or dispose or offer to dispose of it (otherwise than by selling it) for any purpose whatever;

    (b)   where the invention is a process, may use it or do in relation to any product obtained directly by means of the process anything mentioned in paragraph (a) above;

    (c)   without prejudice to the foregoing, where the invention or any product obtained directly by means of the invention is a specified drug or medicine, may sell or offer to sell the drug or medicine;

    (d)   may supply or offer to supply to any person any of the means, relating to an essential element of the invention, for putting the invention into effect;

    (e)   may dispose or offer to dispose of anything which was made, used, imported or kept in the exercise of the powers conferred by this section and which is no longer required for the purpose for which it was made, used, imported or kept (as the case may be),

and anything done by virtue of this subsection shall not amount to an infringement of the patent concerned.

(2) Any act done in relation to an invention by virtue of this section is in the following provisions of this section referred to as use of the invention; and "use", in relation to an invention, in sections 56 to 58 below shall be construed accordingly.

S.55(3) provides for royalty-free use of certain prior inventions, recorded and tried.

(4) So far as the invention has not been so recorded or tried, any use of it made by virtue of this section at any time either –

    (a)   after the publication of the application for the patent for the invention; or

    (b)   without prejudice to paragraph (a) above, in consequence of a relevant communication made after the priority date of the invention otherwise than in confidence;

shall be made on such terms as may be agreed either before or after the user by the government department and the proprietor of the patent with the approval of the Treasury or as may in default of agreement be determined by the court on a reference under section 58 below.

S.55(5)–(7) deal with royalties for use after publication of the patent application, the timing of the government department's authorisation and notification of use to the patentee.

(8) A person acquiring anything disposed of in the exercise of powers conferred by this section, and any person claiming through him, may deal with it in the same manner as if the patent were held on behalf of the Crown.

S.55(9) defines "relevant communication".

(10) Subsection (4) above is without prejudice to any rule of law relating to the confidentiality of information.

S.56(1) Any reference in section 55 above to a patented invention, in relation to any time, is a reference to an invention for which a patent has before that time been, or is subsequently, granted.

(2) In this Act, except so far as the context otherwise requires, "the services of the Crown" includes –

    (a) the supply of anything for foreign defence purposes;

    (b) the production or supply of specified drugs and medicines; and

    (c) such purposes relating to the production or use of atomic energy or research into matters connected therewith as the Secretary of State thinks necessary or expedient;

and "use for the services of the Crown" shall be construed accordingly.

S.56(3) further defines the case under s.56(2)(a).

(4) For the purposes of section 55(1)(a) and (c) above and subsection (2)(b) above, specified drugs and medicines are drugs and medicines which are both –

    (a) required for the provision of pharmaceutical services, general medical services or general dental services, that is to say, services of those respective kinds under Part II of the National Health Service Act 1977, Part II of the National Health Service (Scotland) Act 1978, or the corresponding provisions of the law in force in Northern Ireland or the Isle of Man, and

    (b) specified for the purposes of this subsection in regulations made by the Secretary of State.

S.57 relates to the position of exclusive and similar licensees under a patent where there is Crown use.

S.57A (added in 1988) reverses Patchett's Patent [1967] R.P.C. 237, by permitting compensation to be awarded in respect of lost production for which the patentee or exclusive licensee had spare capacity.

S.58 confers on the court jurisdiction to award compensation under these provisions. S.59 makes special provision for Crown use during a period of emergency.

2 CONFIDENTIAL INFORMATION

2.1 Nature of Obligation

2.1.1 *Prince Albert v Strange* (1849) 1 Mac & G 25 (L.C.)

Queen Victoria and her consort had executed a private collection of etchings of which impressions had been printed and carefully guarded. By his amended bill, the Prince asserted that Strange, together with two other defendants, both called Judge, and their confederates, had in some manner obtained impressions, which had been surreptitiously taken from the plates. The defendants were restrained by injunction from exhibiting, publishing, parting with or disposing of the etchings, and from printing a descriptive catalogue of the etchings.

The defendant, while protesting his loyalty as a subject, maintained that as a matter of strict right, he was free to publish both etchings and catalogue and would surrender the copies in his possession only if indemnified as to costs. He then applied to have the injunction dissolved so far as it related to the catalogue. The defendant appealed from Knight Bruce V.-C.'s refusal to grant this application.

Lord Cottenham L.C.:

The property of an author or composer of any work, whether of literature, art, or science, in such work unpublished and kept for his private use or pleasure, cannot be disputed, after the many decisions in which that proposition has been affirmed or assumed. I say assumed, because in most of the cases which have been decided, the question was not as to the original right of the author, but whether what had taken place did not amount to a waiver of such right; as in the case of letters, how far the sending the letter; in the case of dramatic compositions, how far the oral delivery of the lecture had deprived the author of any part of his original right and property; questions which could not have arisen if there had not been such original right of property. It would be a waste of time to refer in detail to the cases upon this subject. If, then, such right and property exist in the author of such works, it must so exist exclusively of all other persons: can any stranger have any right or title to, or interest in, that which belongs exclusively to another, and yet this is precisely what the Defendant claims, although by a strange inconsistency he does not dispute the general proposition as to the Plaintiff's right and property in the etchings in question, and as incident to it, the right to prevent the exhibition or publication of any copies of them, yet he insists that some person, having had access to certain copies, how obtained I will presently consider, and having from such copies composed a description and list of the originals, he, the Defendant, is entitled to publish such list and description; that is, that he is entitled, against the will of the owner, to make such use of his exclusive property. It being admitted that the Defendant does not publish a copy, that is an impression of the etching, how in principle does a catalogue, list, or description differ? A copy or impression of the etching would only be a means of communicating knowledge and information of the original, and does not a list and description do the same? The means are different, but the object and effect are similar; for, in both, the object and effect is to make known to the public more or less of the unpublished work and composition of the author, which he is entitled to keep wholly for his private use and pleasure, and to withhold altogether, or so far as he may please, from the knowledge of others. Cases upon abridgements, translations, extracts, and criticisms of published works, have no reference whatever to the present question; they all depend upon the extent of right under the acts respecting copyright, and have no analogy to the exclusive rights in the author of unpublished compositions, which depend entirely upon the common law right of property. A clerk of Sir John Strange having, whilst in his employ, made an abridgment of such of his MS cases as related to evidence, was restrained by Lord Hardwicke in 1754, from publishing it, the cases being then unpublished. Upon the first question, therefore, that of property, I am clearly of opinion that the exclusive right and interest of the Plaintiff in the composition or work in question being established, and there being no right or interest whatever in the Defendant, the Plaintiff is entitled to the injunction of this Court to protect him against the invasion of such right and interest by the Defendant, which the publication of any catalogue would undoubtedly be; but this case by no means depends solely upon the question of property, for a breach of trust, confidence, or contract, would of itself entitle the Plaintiff to an injunction. The Plaintiff's affidavits state the private character of the work or composition, and negative any licence or authority for publication, the gifts of some of the etchings to private friends certainly not implying any such licence or authority and state distinctly the belief of the Plaintiff, that the catalogue and the descriptive and other remarks therein contained, could not have been compiled or made, except by means of the possession of the several impressions of the said etchings surreptitiously and improperly obtained. To this case no answer is made, the Defendant saying only that he did not, at the time, believe that the etchings had been improperly obtained, but not suggesting any mode by which they could have been properly obtained, so as to entitle the possessor to use them for publication. If, then, these compositions were kept private, except as to some given to private friends, possession of the Defendant, or of his intended partner Judge, must have originated in a breach of trust, confidence, or contract, in Brown or some person in his employ taking more impressions than were ordered, and retaining the extra number, or in some person to whom copies were given, which is not to be supposed, but which, if the origin of the possession of the Defendant or Judge, *Duke of Queensberry v Shebbeare* ((1758) 2 Eden. 329); and upon the evidence on behalf of the Plaintiff, and in the absence of any explanation on the part of the Defendant, I am bound to assume that the possession of the etchings by the Defendant or Judge has its foundation in a breach of trust, confidence, or contract, as Lord Eldon did in the case of Mr Abernethy's lectures (3 Law J. Chanc. 209); and upon this ground also I think the Plaintiff's title to the injunction sought to be discharged, fully established. The observations of Vice-Chancellor Wigram in *Tipping v Clarke* ((1843) 2 Hare 393) are applicable to this part of the case. He says: "Every clerk employed in a merchant's counting-house is under an implied contract that he will not make public that which he learns in the execution of his duty as clerk. If the Defendant has obtained copies of books, it would very probably be by means of some clerk or agent of the Plaintiff; and if he availed himself surreptitiously of the information which he could not have had except from a person guilty of a breach of contract in communicating it, I think he could not be permitted to avail himself of that breach of contract." In this opinion, I fully concur, and think that the case supposed by Sir J Wigram has actually arisen, or must from the evidence be assumed to have arisen in the present, and that the consequences must be what Sir J Wigram thought would follow. Could it be contended that the clerk, though not justified in communicating copies of the accounts, might yet be permitted to publish the substance and effect of them? In that, as in this case, the matter or thing of which the party has obtained knowledge, being the exclusive property of the owner, he has a right to the interposition of this Court to prevent any use being made of it, that is to say, he is entitled to be protected in the exclusive use and enjoyment of that which is exclusively his. This was the opinion of Lord Eldon, expressed in the case of *Wyatt v Wilson* in 1820 (unreported), respecting an engraving of George the Third during his illness, in which, according to a note with which I have been favoured by Mr Cooper, he said, "If one of the late king's physicians had kept a diary of what he heard and saw, this Court would not, in the king's lifetime, have permitted him to print and publish it." The case of Sir J Strange's MSS is applicable upon this point also.

2.1.2 *Saltman Engineering v Campbell Engineering* (1948) 65 R.P.C. 203 (C.A.)

Saltmans or Ferotec, associated companies, owned copyright in drawings for a leather punch. On their behalf, a third plaintiff, Monarch, arranged for the defendant to manufacture punches for them. It was alleged that, in implied breach of confidence, the defendant used the designs to manufacture and sell its own punches (claims in copyright and contract were not the subject of the judgments given in the C.A.):

Lord Greene, M.R.:

Vaisey, J., dealt with the case in this way. He, first of all, declined to find that any contract was made between Monarch and the defendants. There was no question of any contractual relationship between the defendants and either of the other two plaintiffs and accordingly, so far as contract was concerned, it was essential to find a contract between Monarch and the defendants. That the learned judge refused to find.

The main part of the claim is based on breach of confidence, in respect of which a right may be infringed without the necessity of there being any contractual relationship. I will explain what I mean. If two parties make a contract, under which one of them obtains for the purpose of the contract or in connexion with it some confidential matter, then, even though the contract is silent on the matter of confidence, the law will imply an obligation to treat that confidential matter in a confidential way, as one of the implied terms of the contract: but the obligation to respect confidence is not limited to cases where the parties are in contractual relationship. The learned judge, having declined to find any contract between Monarch and the defendants, went on, if I understand his judgment correctly, to hold that for that reason there could be no relationship of confidence between any of the plaintiffs and the defendants. In my opinion, the learned judge erred in law in coming to that conclusion. He did not deal with the really substantial point in the case, namely, whether or not the defendants had committed a breach of confidence which infringed the rights of Saltmans, who owned the confidential matter. Into that question he did not go and the consequence is, from our point of view, that we have not the advantage of any findings of his own matters of fact which are relevant to the issue of breach of confidence as between Saltmans and the defendants.

Without going further into the matter it seems to me that the existence of a confidential obligation in relation to these drawings, as between Saltmans and the defendants, is abundantly proved; in fact it is not disputed.

His Lordship referred to certain passages in the evidence of the defendants' works manager and continued:

I need not go into the law, which I think is correctly stated in a formula which leading counsel for the defendants himself accepted. I will read it:

> "If a defendant is proved to have used confidential information, directly or indirectly obtained from a plaintiff, without the consent, express or implied of the plaintiff, he will be guilty of an infringement of the plaintiff's rights."

There are several cases which deal with this (*Morison v Moat* (1851) 8 Hare 241, is one of the better known of them) and I need not examine them further. The principle is established and is not disputed; and it is perfectly clear that an obligation, based on confidence, existed and bound the conscience of the defendants down to November 22, 1945. I think that I shall not be stating the principle wrongly, if I say this with regard to the use of confidential information. The information, to be confidential, must, I apprehend, apart from contract, have the necessary quality of confidence about it, namely, it must not be something which is public property and public knowledge. On the other hand, it is perfectly possible to have a confidential document, be it a formula, a plan, a sketch, or something of that kind, which is the result of work done by the maker on materials which may be available for the use of anybody; but what makes it confidential is the fact that the maker of the document has used his brain and this produced a result which can only be produced by somebody who goes through the same process.

What the defendants did in this case was to dispense in certain respects with the necessity of going through the process which had been gone through in compiling these drawings, and thereby to save themselves a great deal of labour and calculation and careful draughtsmanship. No doubt, if they had taken a finished article, namely, the leather punch, which they might have bought in a shop, and given it to an expert draughtsman, that draughtsman could have produced the necessary drawings for the manufacture of machine tools required for making that particular finished article. In at any rate a very material respect they saved themselves that trouble by obtaining the necessary information either from the original drawings or from the tools made in accordance with them. That, in my opinion, was a breach of confidence. In the view that I take this case is a simple one: there has been a breach of confidence, the duty of confidence owed in the circumstances of this case by the defendants to Saltmans. It is not necessary to go into the question whether there was an implied obligation of confidence as between the two contracting parties, Monarch and the defendants. I need say nothing about that, because quite obviously in the circumstances, if Monarch obtained any relief based on that, they could hold it only for the benefit of the Saltmans, who are the owners of this confidential matter.

Somervell and Cohen L. JJ. delivered concurring judgments.

2.1.3   *Seager v Copydex* (No. 1) [1967] 2 All E.R. 415 (C.A.)

The plaintiff invented and patented one carpet-grip, the "Klent", which he was seeking to exploit. While discussing with two of the defendant's managers the possibility of the defendant marketing the "Klent", the plaintiff revealed to them in confidence the crucial idea for another grip, whose characteristics were a V-tang and a strong point. The managers stated that they were not interested in the idea. However, after negotiations over the "Klent" came to nothing, the defendant developed their own carpet grip which turned out to embody the very idea of the plaintiff's alternative and to be called the "Invisigrip" – a name which the plaintiff said he had suggested. At the trial allegations of fraud against the defendant were rejected. On appeal, the CA found that the managers must have been responsible for unconsciously making use of the plaintiff's information, thus engaging in an honest breach of confidence.

Lord Denning M.R.:

The Law: I start with one sentence in the judgment of Lord Greene, M.R., in *Saltman Engineering Co Ltd v Campbell Engineering Co Ltd* [1963] 3 All E.R. 423n.) (1):

> "If a defendant is proved to have used confidential information, directly or indirectly obtained from the plaintiff, without the consent, express or implied, of the plaintiff, he will be guilty of an infringement of the plaintiff's rights."

To this I add a sentence from the judgment of Roxburgh, J. in *Terrapin Ltd v Builders' Supply Co (Hayes) Ltd, Taylor Woodrow Ltd & Swiftplan Ltd* [1960] R.P.C. 128) (2), which was quoted and adopted as correct by Roskill J. in *Cranleigh Precision Engineering Co Ltd v Bryant* [1966] R.P.C. 81) (3):

> "As I understand it, the essence of this branch of the law, whatever the origin of it may be, is that a person who has obtained information in confidence is not allowed to use it as a springboard for activities detrimental to the person who made the confidential communication, and springboard it remains even when all the features have been published or can be ascertained by actual inspection by any member of the public."

The law on this subject does not depend on any implied contract. It depends on the broad principle of equity that he who has received information in confidence shall not take unfair advantage of it. He must not make use of it to the prejudice of him who gave it without obtaining his consent. The principle is clear enough when the whole of the information is private. The difficulty arises when the information is in part public and in part private. As for instance in this case. A good deal of the information which the plaintiff gave to the defendant company was available to the public, such as the patent specification in the Patent Office, or the "Klent" grip, which he sold to anyone who asked. But there was a good deal of other information which was private, such as, the difficulties which had to be overcome in making a satisfactory grip; the necessity for a strong, sharp tooth; the alternative forms of tooth; and the like. When the information is mixed, being partly public and partly private, then the recipient must take special care to use only the material which is in the public domain. He should go to the public source and get it: or, at any rate, not be in a better position than if he had gone to the public source. He should not get a start over others by using the information which he received in confidence. At any rate, he should not get a start without paying for it. It may not be a case for injunction but only for damages, depending on the worth of the confidential information to him in saving him time and trouble.

Conclusion: Applying these principles, I think that the plaintiff should succeed. On the facts which I have stated, he told the defendant company a lot about the making of a satisfactory carpet grip which was not in the public domain. They would not have got going so quickly except for what they had learned in their discussions with him. They got to know in particular that it was possible to make an alternative grip in the form of a "V-tang", provided the tooth was sharp enough and strong enough, and they were told about the special shape required. The judge thought that the information was not significant. But I think it was. It was the springboard which enabled them to go on to devise the "Invisigrip" and to apply for a patent for it. They were quite innocent of any intention to take advantage of him. They thought that, as long as they did not infringe his patent, they were exempt. In this they were in error. They were not aware of the law as to confidential information.

I would allow the appeal and give judgment to the plaintiff for damages to be assessed.

Salmon L.J.:

... the germ of the idea and the broad principle of the domed v-shaped prong was I am certain implanted in their minds by the plaintiff at the interview of March 13, 1962, and afterwards subconsciously reproduced and used, if only as a springboard, to forestall the plaintiff with "Invisigrip". This is no reflection on their honesty, but it infringes the plaintiff's rights. I would accordingly allow the appeal.

Winn, L.J.:

To my own mind it appears that the proper conclusion to be drawn from all the material before the court, not by any means primarily from the direct evidence, is that the plaintiff did explain his "Invisigrip" idea to Mr Boon and Mr Preston; that they absorbed what he told them; and were able to recall enough from their memories to indicate to Mr Sudbury and Mr Turl what they wanted them to produce.

In doing so they did not, I think, realise that they were infringing a duty of confidence: I think that they did infringe it. In so holding I do not imply any condemnation of Mr Boon or Mr Preston as dishonest men. Mr Preston made a most revealing statement in evidence in the court below where he said "... action for breach of confidence. I did not know such a thing existed ... the only problem was that we might infringe his patent". In my view the appeal succeeds.

Lord Denning, M.R.:

The court grants neither an account of profits, nor an injunction, but only damages to be assessed by the master. Damages should be assessed on the basis of reasonable compensation for the use of the confidential information which was given to the defendant company.

For subsequent proceedings on the quantification of damages, see below, 2.4.1.

2.1.4   *Fraser v Evans* [1969] 1 All E.R. 8 (C.A.)

The plaintiff, a public relations consultant, was employed by the Greek Government to make a report. The plaintiff expressly agreed never to "reveal to any person or organisation any information related to the work in the areas where it was operating, or information which comes to the knowledge during the course of [the] contract"; but there was no corresponding undertaking by the Greek Government.

The report subsequently fell into the hands of a journalist for "The Sunday Times" (Defendant) who then obtained an interview with the plaintiff. At the interview the defendant's English translation of the report was compared with the plaintiff's original English version and some discrepancies were noted. Following the interview, the plaintiff became concerned that "The Sunday Times" might publish an article on the report which might be damaging to him. He succeeded in obtaining an injunction against "The Sunday Times" from which the newspaper appealed.

The plaintiff's claim alleged libel, breach of confidence and infringement of copyright. "The Sunday Times" admitted that the article would be defamatory of the plaintiff but argued that the facts alleged were true and that any comments on the extracts from the Report were fairly and honestly made on a matter of public interest.

Lord Denning M.R.:

First, *Libel*. Insofar as the article will be defamatory of the plaintiff, it is clear he cannot get an injunction. The court will not restrain the publication of an article, even though it is defamatory, when the defendant says that he intends to justify it or to make fair comment on a matter of public interest. That has been established for many years ever since *Bonnard v Perryman* ([1891] 2 Ch 269). The reason sometimes given is that the defences of justification and fair comment are for the jury, which is the constitutional tribunal, and not for a judge; but a better reason is the importance in the public interest that the truth should out. As the court said in that case (at p 284):

"The right of free speech is one which it is for the public interest that individuals should possess, and, indeed, that they should exercise without impediment, so long as no wrongful act is done."

There is no wrong act done if it is true, or if it is fair comment on a matter of public interest. The court will not prejudice the issue by granting an injunction in advance of publication.

Second, *Breach of confidence*. The plaintiff says that the report was a confidential document and that the publication of it should be restrained on the principles enunciated in the cases from *Prince Albert v Strange* ((1849) 1 Mac & G 25); to *Margaret Duchess of Argyll (Femme Sole) v Duke of Argyll* ([1967] Ch 302). These cases show that the court will, in a proper case, restrain the publication of confidential information. The jurisdiction is based, not so much on property or on contract, but rather on the duty to be of good faith. No person is permitted to divulge to the world information which he has received in confidence, unless he has just cause or excuse for doing so. Even if he comes by it innocently, nevertheless, once he gets to know that it was originally given in confidence, he can be restrained from breaking that confidence. For the party complaining must be the person who is entitled to the confidence and to have it respected. He must be a person to whom the duty of good faith is owed. It is at this point that I think that the plaintiff's claim breaks down. There is no doubt that the plaintiff himself was under an obligation of confidence to the Greek government. The contract says so in terms; but there is nothing in the contract which expressly puts the Greek government under any obligation of confidence. Nor, so far as I can see, is there any implied obligation. The Greek government entered into no contract with the plaintiff to keep it secret. We have seen affidavits – one of them as late as this morning – which say that it was not the policy of the Greek government to publish, or allow the publication of any documents prepared by the plaintiff or his firm, and that they would, as a matter of practice, keep them confidential. But that policy still leaves them free, in point of law, to circulate the documents or their contents to anyone whom they please. The information was obtained for them by the plaintiff under a contract with them. They paid for it. They were the people entitled to the information. They were the people to say aye or no whether it should be communicated elsewhere, or be published generally. It follows that they alone have any standing to complain if anyone obtains the information surreptitiously or proposes to publish it. And they did not complain of the publication now proposed. At any rate, they have not come to the court to complain. On this short point it seems to me that the plaintiff himself cannot proceed on breach of confidence in his own behalf, to prevent "The Sunday Times" publishing the article.

Even if the plaintiff had any standing to complain, "The Sunday Times" say that, in any event, they have just cause or excuse for publishing. They rely on the line of authority from *Gartside v Outram* ((1856) 26 L.J. Ch 113) to the latest case, *Initial Services Ltd v Putterill* ([1968] 1 Q.B. 396). They quote the words of Wood, V.-C. (in *Gartside v Outram* at p 114), that ". . . there is no confidence as to the disclosure of iniquity." I do not look on the word "iniquity" as expressing a principle. It is merely an instance of just cause or excuse for breaking confidence. There are some things which may be required to be disclosed in the public interest, in which event no confidence can be prayed in aid to keep them secret. I feel that it might be difficult for "The Sunday Times" to make out that case here. We have the plaintiff's report before us, and on a reading of it, I doubt whether it is such as to enable them to make out this ground for publication.

Third. *It was said*: Seeing that no injunction should be granted in respect of the defamatory aspect of the article, likewise no injunction should be granted in respect of the breach of confidence. The plaintiff should not be able to avoid the salutary rule of law in libel by framing the case in breach of confidence. Reliance was placed on *Sim v H.J. Heinz Co Ltd* ([1959] R.P.C. 75). I do not think it necessary to rule on this point today. I can well see that there may be cases where it would be wrong to grant an injunction on breach of confidence when it would not be granted on libel; but I can equally well see that there are some cases of breach of confidence which are defamatory, where the court might intervene, even though the defendant says that he intends to justify.

The final point is on *copyright*. There is no doubt that the plaintiff was the author of this report and is entitled to the literary copyright in it. But copyright does not subsist in the information contained in the report. It exists only in the literary form in which the information is dressed. If "The Sunday Times" were going to print this report in full, thus taking the entire literary form, it might well be a case for an injunction to restrain the infringement of copyright. But "The Sunday Times" say that they are going to do no such thing. They say that they are only going to print short extracts from it, followed up with some of the statements which the plaintiff made to them and their comments on it. They say that that would be a "fair dealing" such as is permitted by s 6 (3) (a) of the Copyright Act, 1956, which provides that:

> "No fair dealing with a literary . . . work shall constitute an infringement of the copyright in the work if it is for the purpose of reporting current events – (a) in a newspaper . . ."

We have not seen what is going to be published. We cannot pre-judge the matter. We cannot say that there is going to be an unfair dealing when "The Sunday Times" say that it is to be a fair dealing. So no injunction should be granted to prevent them publishing.

It all comes back to this. There are some things which are of such public concern that the newspapers, the Press, and, indeed, everyone is entitled to make known the truth and to make fair comment on it. This is an integral part of the right of free speech and expression. It must not be whittled away. "The Sunday Times" assert that, in this case, there is a matter of public concern. They admit that they are going to injure the plaintiff's reputation, but they say that they can justify it; that they are only making fair comment on a matter of public interest; and, therefore, that they ought not to be restrained. We cannot pre-judge this defence by granting an injunction against them. I think that the injunction which has been granted should be removed. "The Sunday Times" should be allowed to publish the article at their risk. If they are guilty of libel or breach of confidence, or breach of copyright, that can be determined by an action hereafter and damages awarded against them. But we should not grant an interim injunction in advance of an article when we do not know in the least what it will contain. I would allow the appeal accordingly and discharge the injunction.

Davies and Widgery L.JJ. concurred.

2.1.5 *Coco v A.N. Clark (Eng) Ltd* [1969] R.P.C. 41 (Megarry J.)

The plaintiff had developed the "Coco" moped which featured, inter alia, some special engine parts. He entered into negotiations with the defendants with a view to them ultimately manufacturing it. After approximately four months of discussions the defendants broke off negotiations, alleging difficulties with the transmission design. The defendants then wrote to the plaintiff offering him a royalty of 5/- per engine on the first 50,000 engines made, but this was not accepted.

The defendants subsequently manufactured and sold their own "Scamp" moped. They admitted that the piston and carburettor were of the same type as the plaintiff's.

The plaintiff sought an injunction against the manufacture and sale of any machines in which the defendants had made use, directly or indirectly, of any confidential information the property of the plaintiff.

Megarry J.:

The equitable jurisdiction in cases of breach of confidence is ancient: confidence is the cousin of trust. The Statute of Uses, 1535, is framed in terms of "use, confidence or trust;" and a couplet, attributed to Sir Thomas More, Lord Chancellor, avers that

> "Three things are to be helpt in Conscience;
> Fraud, Accident and things of Confidence."

(See 1 Rolle's Abridgement 374.) In the middle of the last century, the great case of *Prince Albert v Strange* (1849) 1 Mac & G 25 reasserted the doctrine. In the case before me, it is common ground that there is no question of any breach of contract, for no contract ever came into existence. Accordingly, what I have to consider is the pure equitable doctrine of confidence, unaffected by contract. Furthermore, I am here in the realms of commerce, and there is no question of any marital relationship such as arose in *Duchess of Argyll v Duke of Argyll* ([1967] Ch 302.) Thus limited, what are the essentials of the doctrine?

Of the various authorities cited to me, I have found *Saltman Engineering Co Ltd v Campbell Engineering Co Ltd* ([1948] 65 R.P.C. 203); *Terrapin Ltd v Builders' Supply Co (Hayes) Ltd* ([1960] R.P.C. 128) and *Seager v Copydex Ltd* ([1967] 1 W.L.R. 923; [1967] R.P.C. 349) of the most assistance. All are decisions of the Court of Appeal. I think it is quite plain from the *Saltman* case that the obligation of confidence may exist where, as in this case, there is no contractual relationship between the parties. In cases of contract, the primary question is no doubt that of construing the contract and any terms implied in it. Where there is no contract, however, the question must be one of what it is that suffices to bring the obligation into being; and there is the further question of what amounts to a breach of that obligation.

In my judgment, three elements are normally required if, apart from contract, a case of breach of confidence is to succeed. First, the information itself, in the words of Lord Greene, M.R. in the *Saltman* case on page 215, must "have the necessary quality of confidence about it." Secondly, that information must have been imparted in circumstances importing an obligation of confidence. Thirdly, there must be an unauthorised use of that information to the detriment of the party communicating it. I must briefly examine each of these requirements in turn.

First, the information must be of a confidential nature. As Lord Greene said in the *Saltman* case at page 215, "something which is public property and public knowledge" cannot *per se* provide any foundation for proceedings for breach of confidence. However confidential the circumstances of communication, there can be no breach of confidence in revealing to others something which is already common knowledge. But this must not be taken too far. Something that has been constructed solely from materials in the public domain may possess the necessary quality of confidentiality: for something new and confidential may have been brought into being by the application of the skill and ingenuity of the human being. Novelty depends on the thing itself, and not upon the quality of its component parts. Indeed, often the more striking the novelty, the more commonplace its components. Mr Mowbray demurs to the concept that some degree of originality is requisite. But whether it is described as originality or novelty or ingenuity or otherwise, I think there must be some product of the human brain which suffices to confer a confidential nature upon the information: and, expressed in those terms, I think that Mr Mowbray accepts the concept.

The difficulty comes, as Lord Denning, M.R. pointed out in the *Seager* case on page 931, when the information used is partly public and partly private; for then the recipient must somehow segregate the two and, although free to use the former, must take no advantage of the communication of the latter. To this subject I must in due course return. I must also return to a further point, namely, that where confidential information is communicated in circumstances of confidence the obligation thus created endures, perhaps in a modified form, even after all the information has been published or is ascertainable by the public; for the recipient must not use the communication as a springboard (see the *Seager* case, pages 931 and 933). I should add that, as shown by *Cranleigh Precision Engineering Ltd v Bryant* ([1965] 1 W.L.R. 1293; [1966] R.P.C. 81), the mere simplicity of an idea does not prevent it being confidential (see pages 1309 and 1310). Indeed, the simpler an idea, the more likely it is to need protection.

The second requirement is that the information must have been communicated in circumstances importing an obligation of confidence. However secret and confidential the information, there can be no binding obligation of confidence if that information is blurted out in public or is communicated in other circumstances which negative any duty of holding it confidential. From the authorities cited to me, I have not been able to derive any very precise idea of what test is to be applied in determining whether the circumstances import an obligation of confidence. In the *Argyll* case at page 330, Ungoed-Thomas, J. concluded his discussion of the circumstances in which the publication of marital communications should be restrained, as being confidential by saying, "If this was a well-developed jurisdiction doubtless there would be guides and tests to aid in exercising it." In the absence of such guides or tests he then in effect concluded that part of the communications there in question would on any reasonable test emerge as confidential. It may be that that hard-worked creature, the reasonable man, may be pressed into service once more: for I do not see why he should not labour in equity as well as at law. It seems to me that if the circumstances are such that any reasonable man standing in the shoes of the recipient of the information would have realised that upon reasonable grounds the information was being given to him in confidence, then this should suffice to impose upon him the equitable obligation of confidence. In particular, where information of commercial or industrial value is given on a business-like basis and with some avowed common object in mind, such as a joint venture or the manufacture of articles by one party for the other, I would regard the recipient as carrying a heavy burden if he seeks to repel a contention that he was bound by an obligation of confidence: see the *Saltman* case at page 216. On that footing, for reasons that will appear, I do not think I need explore this head further. I merely add that I doubt whether equity would intervene unless the circumstances are of sufficient gravity; equity ought not to be invoked merely to protect trivial tittle-tattle, however confidential.

Thirdly, there must be an unauthorised use of the information to the detriment of the person communicating it. Some of the statements of principle in the cases omit any mention of detriment; others include it. At first sight, it seems that detriment ought to be present if equity is to be induced to intervene; but I can conceive of cases where a plaintiff might have substantial motives for seeking the aid of equity and yet suffer nothing which could fairly be called detriment to him, as when the confidential information shows him in a favourable light but gravely injures some relation or friend of his whom he wishes to produce. The point does not arise for decision in this case, for detriment to the plaintiff plainly exists. I need therefore say no more than that although for the purposes of this case I have stated the proposition in the stricter form I wish to keep open the possibility of the true proposition being in the wider form.

Before I turn to the second main head, that of interlocutory relief, I should mention one point on the substantive law that caused me some difficulty during the argument. This is what may be called the "spring-board" doctrine. In the *Seager* case at page 931, Lord Denning quoted a sentence from the judgment of Roxburgh, J. in the *Terrapin* case, which was quoted and adopted as correct by Roskill, J. in the *Cranleigh* case. It runs as follows:

"As I understand it, the essence of this branch of the law, whatever the origin of it may be, is that a person who has obtained information in confidence is not allowed to use it as a spring-board for activities detrimental to the person who made the confidential communication, and spring-board it remains even when all the features have been published or can be ascertained by actual inspection by any member of the public."

Salmon, L.J. in the *Seager* case on page 933 also states:

"The law does not allow the use of such information even as a spring-board for activities detrimental to the plaintiff."

Quite apart from authority I would recognise the principle enshrined in those words as being salutary. Nevertheless, I am not entirely clear how it is to be put into practical effect in every case. Suppose a case where there is a confidential communication of information which is partly public and partly private; suppose that the recipient of the information adds in confidence ideas of his own, improving the initial scheme; and suppose that the parties then part, with no agreement concluded between them. How is a conscientious recipient of the ideas to comply with the requirements that equity lays upon him? For in the words of Lord Denning at page 931 in the *Seager case*, he

"must take special care to use only the material which is in the public domain. He should go to the public source and get it: or, at any rate, not be in a better position than if he had gone to the public source. He should not get a start over others by using the information which he received in confidence."

Suppose that the only confidential information communicated is that some important component should be made of aluminium instead of steel and with significant variations in its design and dimensions. The recipient knows that this change will transform a failure into success. He knows that, if he had persevered himself, he might have come upon the solution in a week or in a year. Yet he is under a duty not to use the confidential information as a spring-board or as giving him a start.

What puzzles me is how, as a law-abiding citizen, he is to perform that duty. He could, I suppose, commission someone else to make the discovery anew, carefully abstaining from saying anything to him about aluminium or the design and dimensions which will achieve success; but this seems to me to be artificial in the extreme. Yet until this step is taken and the discovery made anew, he cannot make use of his own added ideas for the further improvement of the design which he had already communicated in confidence to the original communicator, ideas which would perhaps make a success into a triumph. He cannot build his superstructure as long as he is forbidden to use the foundations. Nor is the original communicator in a much better case. He is free to use his own original idea, which converted failure into success; but he cannot take advantage of the original recipient's further ideas, of which he knows, until such time as he or someone commissioned by him would, unaided by any coincidence, have discovered them.

For those who are not law-abiding and conscientious citizens there is, I suppose, a simple answer; ignore the duty, use the information, and then pay damages. This may be the course which Lord Denning envisaged in the *Seager* case: for after stating that the recipient should not get a start over others by using the confidential information, he continued on page 932: "At any rate, he should not get a start without paying for it. It may not be a case for injunction or even for an account, but only for damages, depending on the worth of the confidential information to him in saving time and trouble." I also recognise that a conscientious and law-abiding citizen, having received confidential information in confidence, may accept that when negotiations break down the only honourable course is to withdraw altogether from the field in question until his informant or someone else has put the information into the public domain and he can no longer be said to have any start. Communication thus imposes upon him a unique disability. He alone of all men must for an uncertain time abjure this field of endeavour, however great his interest. I find this scarcely more reasonable than the artificiality and uncertainty of postponing the use of the information until others would have discovered it.

The relevance of the point, I think, is this. If the duty is a duty not to use the information without consent, then it may be the proper subject of an injunction restraining its use, even if there is an offer to pay a reasonable sum for that use. If, on the other hand, the duty is merely a duty not to use the information without paying a reasonable sum for it, then no such injunction should be granted. Despite the assistance of counsel, I feel far from assured that I have got to the bottom of this matter. But I do feel considerable hesitation in expressing a doctrine of equity in terms that include a duty which law-abiding citizens cannot reasonably be expected to perform. In other words, the essence of the duty seems more likely to be that of not using without paying, rather than of not using at all. It may be that in fields other than industry and commerce (and I have in mind the *Argyll* case) the duty may exist in the more stringent form; but in the circumstances present in this case I think that the less stringent form is the more reasonable. No doubt this matter may be canvassed and resolved at the trial; but on motion, in a case where both the probabilities and the evidence support the view that the fruits of any confidential communication were to sound in monetary compensation to the communicator, I should be slow to hold that it was right to enjoin the defendant company from making any use of the information.

Megarry J. then considered whether under the circumstances this was an appropriate case for granting an interlocutory injunction. Given the conflict between the defendant's letter offering a royalty and the plaintiff's allegation of fraud based on his conviction that the defendant was out to get his engine "without paying for it", and the fact that at this interlocutory stage no cross-examination had taken place, he refused the grant and adjourned the matter to trial. The Terrapin *case was distinguished on its facts. The defendants gave an undertaking to keep an account of a royalty of 5/- per "Scamp" engine manufactured. This was to be paid into a special trust account which would protect the plaintiff in the event of any financial disaster to the defendant pending the outcome of the trial.*

2.1.6   *Thomas Marshall v Guinle* [1979] 1 Ch 227 (Megarry V.-C.)

The defendant was appointed managing director of the plaintiff company for a period of ten years. His service agreement provided that he was not to engage in any other business without the company's consent while he was employed as managing director; that during and after his employment, he was not "to disclose" confidential information in relation to the affairs, customers or trade secrets of the company and its group; and that after ceasing to be managing director he was not, inter alia, "to use or disclose" confidential information about the suppliers and customers of the group. Without the company's knowledge, the defendant began to trade on his own account and on behalf of his two companies in competition with the company and, in doing so, he bought from the company's suppliers and sold to the company's customers. The defendant purported to resign as managing director at a time when his contract had another four and a half years to run. The company applied for interim injunctions to restrain the defendant, inter alia, from disclosing or using any confidential information or trade secret of the company during or after his employment.

Megarry V.-C., in granting the application held that in view of the contractual limitation of obligation concerning confidential information to "disclosing", the breaches of confidence could not themselves justify an injunction against using the information, but that the defendant's breaches of fiduciary duty did so. On the meaning of "confidential information" to be covered by the injunction, he said:

It is far from easy to state in general terms what is confidential information or a trade secret. Certain authorities were cited, but they did not carry matters very far. Plainly "something which is public property and public knowledge" is not confidential: see *Saltman Engineering Co Ltd v Campbell Engineering Co Ltd* ((1948) 65 R.P.C. 203, 215), per Lord Greene M.R. On the other hand, "something that has been constructed solely from materials in the public domain may possess the necessary quality of confidentiality: for something new and confidential may have been brought into being by the application of the skill and ingenuity of the human brain. Novelty depends on the thing itself, and not upon the quality of its constituent parts": *Coco v A.N. Clark (Engineers) Ltd* [1969] R.P.C. 41, 47, a case that was not cited, but in part draws on the *Saltman* case, which was. Costs and prices which are not generally known may well constitute trade secrets or confidential information: see *Herbert Morris Ltd v Saxelby* [1916] 1 A.C. 688, 705, referring to prices.

If one turns from the authorities and looks at the matter as a question of principle, I think (and I say this very tentatively, because the principle has not been argued out) that four elements may be discerned which may be of some assistance in identifying confidential information or trade secrets which the court will protect. I speak of such information or secrets only in an industrial or trade setting. First, I think that the information must be information the release of which the owner believes would be injurious to him or of advantage to his rivals or others. Second, I think the owner must believe that the information is confidential or secret, i.e., that it is not already in the public domain. It may be that some or all of his rivals already have the information: but as long as the owner believes it to be confidential I think he is entitled to try and protect it. Third, I think that the owner's belief under the two previous heads must be reasonable. Fourth, I think that the information must be judged in the light of the usage and practices of the particular industry or trade concerned. It may be that information which does not satisfy all these requirements may be entitled to protection as confidential information or trade secrets: but I think that any information which does satisfy them must be of a type which is entitled to protection.

2.2 Protectable Secrets

2.2.1 *Fraser v Thames Television* [1983] 2 All E.R. 101 (Hirst J.)

Three actresses and a composer (who acted as manager) conceived a television series concerned with the formation of a female rock group and its subsequent adventures. The events and personalities would be based upon the actual lives of the three actresses, who had already formed a rock group. These ideas were disclosed to the defendant television company, together with a script-writer and script-editor who were also defendants.

The four plaintiffs granted Thames an option on the ideas, it being held to be a term of this that Thames would, if it made the series, offer the three actresses first refusal of the three parts in the rock group. Thames decided to make the series. It subsequently had a dispute with the actresses over the availability of one of them for filming and it used this as a reason for engaging other actresses for the parts. This was held by Hirst J. to amount to an unreasonable repudiation of contractual obligations amounting to breach.

In addition the plaintiffs claimed damages for the breach of confidence involved in using the ideas for the series in the programme actually made (the series "Rock Follies") without permission. On this aspect Hirst J. said:

The basic principles of the law of confidence are conveniently set out in *Copinger and Skone James on Copyright* (12th edn, 1980) para 711 as follows:

> "There is broad and developing equitable doctrine that he who has received information in confidence shall not take unfair advantage of it or profit from the wrongful use or publication of it. He must not make any use of it to the prejudice of him who gave it, without paying him for it ... If, therefore, a defendant is proved to have used confidential information, directly or indirectly obtained from a plaintiff, without his consent, express or implied, he will be guilty of an infringement of the plaintiff's rights."

It is well settled that the obligation of confidence rests not only on the original recipient, but also on any person who received the information with knowledge acquired at the time or subsequently that it was originally given in confidence: see *Copinger and Skone James on Copyright*, para 731.

Counsel for the defendants accepted that as a matter of principle the law of confidence is capable of protecting the confidential communication of an idea. But he argued that a literary or dramatic idea cannot be protected unless it is fully developed in the form of a synopsis or treatment and embodied in permanent form (i.e. in writing or on film or tape). His argument relied substantially on analogies with the law of copyright.

He further submitted that considerations of legal policy require that anything so ephemeral and so subject to contradictory recollection as an oral idea should not be protected; that such protection would unduly stultify an author's freedom to develop ideas; and that such protection would be unfair to third parties confronted with rival claims to the origination of an idea, since he says it would be impossible for them to decide which claimant was right in the absence of any written formulation of the idea in question.

Counsel for the defendants further argued that where an idea is capable of development in more than one format (e.g. situation comedy or drama) it is not entitled to protection.

I consider first the argument by analogy with the law of copyright, which may be summarised as follows. (1) It is trite law that there is no copyright in an idea as such. How anomalous would it be, argued counsel for the defendants, if the originator of an idea was in a better position under the law of confidence than under the law of copyright with its strict time limits and carefully defended limitations. (2) The authorities on the law of copyright clearly establish that a plaintiff can only succeed if his work is in a developed written form. The same, argued counsel for the defendants, should apply in confidence. (3) Decided copyright cases in relation to dramatic works, with particular reference to s 1(2) of the Copyright Act 1911 (now incorporated in s 2 of the Copyright Act 1956) establish that mere reproduction of a plot (i.e. an idea) is not an infringement. Infringement only arises if there is substantial reproduction of actual dramatic incidents or situations (*Copinger and Skone James on Copyright*, paras 539–540).

On these issues, Hirst J. referred to a number of authorities and concluded:

It is therefore an essential ingredient of every copyright action that the plaintiff should start with a work in permanent form.

On the other hand, under the general law of confidence the confidential communication relied on may be either written or oral (see e.g. *Seager v Copydex Ltd* ([1967] 2 All E.R. 415, [1967] 1 W.L.R. 923)).

Copyright is good against the world generally, whereas confidence only protects against those who receive information or ideas in confidence. Although copyright has a fixed (albeit extensive) statutory time limit, and confidence, at all events in theory, no time limit, in practice the obligation in confidence ceases the moment information or idea becomes public knowledge.

Furthermore, although the law of copyright protects unpublished as well as published works, it is no part of its purpose to protect confidentiality as such. Indeed s 46(4) of the 1956 Act expressly provides that "nothing in this Act shall affect the operation of any rule of equity relating to breaches of . . . confidence".

Of much more assistance are the cases cited by counsel for the defendants which deal directly with breaches of confidence in the field under consideration. In *Gilbert v Star Newspapers Co Ltd* (1894) 11 T.L.R. 4 Chitty J. granted an *ex parte* injunction restraining the defendants from publishing the plot of Mr W.S. Gilbert's comic opera "His Excellency", which was due to open a few days later. It was argued that an actor or employee at the theatre must have communicated the information to the newspaper contrary to an established custom in the theatrical profession that such information was confidential. Chitty J. based his decision on the principles of the law of confidence as enunciated in *Prince Albert v Strange* ((1849) 1 Mac & G 25, 41 E.R. 1171). Counsel for the defendants submitted that this case supported his argument that there must be a written libretto in existence before the law of confidence can apply to such a situation; but there is no indication in the report that the libretto as such was ever passed to the newspaper, and Chitty J. did not base his decision on any such consideration. It is, however, noteworthy that the confidential information in *Gilbert's* case related to the plot of the opera, which (as the copyright authorities cited above show) would not be protected as such under the law of copyright. This case therefore seems to establish a wider protection under the law of confidence than under the law of copyright.

In *Fraser v Edwards* [1905–10] MacG Cop Cas 10 the defendant was held liable for breach of confidence by appropriation of the character, plot and idea from a scenario which had earlier been submitted by the plaintiff to the defendant's theatre manager. Counsel for the defendants pointed out that this case concerned a fully developed written scenario.

Finally in this group of cases, counsel for the defendants cited the very recent Australian decision of *Talbot v General Television Corp Pty Ltd* ([1981] R.P.C. 1), a case which on the facts has some remarkable similarities with the present case. The judgment reported is that of Harris J. at first instance in the Supreme Court of Victoria. The decision was affirmed by the Full Court, but the appellate decision is not reported, so I am informed, either here or in Australia. In this case the plaintiff, a film producer, developed an idea for a television series, which he submitted in the form of a written submission to the defendants. He heard no more about his proposal. The defendants subsequently broadcast the first segment of a series of programmes which they claimed were their own idea, but which the plaintiff claimed were derived from his. The plaintiff sought an injunction on the ground of breach of confidence, and the hearing of the application was treated as the trial of the action. The learned judge found in favour of the plaintiff. He said (at 8–9):

"It is clear that an obligation of confidence may exist where there is no contractual relationship between the parties. Where a plaintiff sues, relying upon breach of confidence, he must establish three elements. These are: (1) that the information was of a confidential nature; (2) that the information was communicated in circumstances importing an obligation of confidence; and (3) that there has been an unauthorised use of the information to the detriment of the person communicating it (i.e. the plaintiff). Those statements of law are taken from the judgment of Megarry J. in *Coco v A.N. Clark Engineers Ltd* ([1969] R.P.C. 41 at 47–48): see also *Ansell Rubber Co Pty Ltd v Allied Rubber Industries Pty Ltd* ([1967] V.R. 37); *Mense and Ampere Electrical Manufacturing Co Pty Ltd V Milenkovic* ([1973] V.R. 784 at 800–801); and *Deta Nominees Pty Ltd v Viscount Plastic Products Pty Ltd* ([1979] V.R. 167). Both counsel agreed that the three elements that I have referred to were the relevant principles to be applied in this case. Mr Gillard (counsel for the defendant) submitted that none of those elements had been established by the plaintiff, and further submitted that, even if they were, there were two other reasons why the plaintiff's claim should be dismissed. Mr Archibald (counsel for the plaintiff) submitted that the plaintiff had made out his case for relief and that none of the matters raised by Mr Gillard afforded any reason why relief should be denied to the plaintiff. Mr Gillard began by submitting that the information which the plaintiff alleged had been misused by the defendant did not have the necessary quality of confidence. He put it that the plaintiff was seeking to protect an idea for a programme about millionaires, how they succeeded and what viewers could learn from them, and that this was not original. He pointed to evidence that there had been programmes before on the careers of successful men and that it was a usual practice for interviewers to ask such people the secret of their success. He also put it that there was authority for the proposition that there is "no property in an idea" (or in knowledge) and that as all the plaintiff had conveyed to the network was an idea, it was not susceptible of protection. The authorities he referred to were *F.C. of T v United Aircraft Corp* ((1943) 68 C.L.R. 525 at 534 per Latham C.J.) and *Halsbury*, 4th ed, vol 9, para 829. But the passages referred to deal with the point in different contexts (those of the construction of the word "idea" in a statue and in copyright law) and do not support Mr Gillard's submission in this case. What Mr Archibald said was that this abstract proposition could only divert one from the real problem, and he referred to what Lord Upjohn said in *Boardman v Phipps* ([1966] 3 All E.R. 721 at 759, [1967] 2 A.C. 46 at 127) where his Lordship pointed out that "the real truth is that it [i.e. information] is not property in any normal sense but equity will restrain its transmission to another if in breach of some confidential relationship". The real problem, Mr Archibald said, was to decide whether the idea, or concept, had been sufficiently developed. Where it had been developed to the point of setting out a format in which it could be presented, so that it was apparent that the concept could be carried into effect, then, said Mr Archibald, it was something that was capable of being the subject of a confidence. Without deciding that it is always necessary for a plaintiff to go that far, I am satisfied that where a concept or idea has been developed to the stage where the plaintiff had developed his concept, it is capable of being the subject of a confidential communication. The plaintiff had developed his concept so that it would be seen to be a concept which had at least some attractiveness as a television programme and to be something which was capable of being realised as an actuality."

Counsel for the defendants accepted, indeed contended, that the case was rightly decided, and, though not binding on me, I find it of great assistance. He submitted that the decision rested essentially on the fact that the material submitted by the plaintiff included a substantial written submission (see [1981] R.P.C. 1 at 5). However, it is clear that the judge expressly refrained from deciding that any less elaborately worked idea would not qualify for protection.

Counsel for the plaintiffs also accepted the correctness of *Talbot's* case. He drew attention to the twist or slant which was held to be original (at 9); and he submitted that this twist or slant was the kernel of the idea to which, he submitted, the written submission added nothing of substance. He also drew attention to the fact that this kernel may have been communicated orally (at 10).

Counsel for the plaintiffs submitted that, as a matter of general principle, an obligation of confidence is implied in law if the communication is made in circumstances where the parties understand the recipient will treat it as confidential. He argued that this arises either (1) where the information or idea is given in a situation where both parties recognise an ethical obligation of confidence or (2) where information or an idea is communicated by one party to another with a view to a possible joint commercial venture or contractual relationship.

So far as ideas specifically are concerned, counsel for the plaintiffs submitted that there is no requirement that the idea must be developed to any particular degree, still less that it must be embodied in writing. He accepted that it must be specific in the sense that it must be clear and identifiable and that it must be original, at least to the extent that it is distinguishable from the ordinary run of ideas in common use. While he accepted it must have potential commercial merit, he argued that there is no requirement that it should have been developed to a state where it was ready for commercial exploitation.

On general principles of the law of confidence, Hirst J. quoted from Saltman v Campbell *(above, 2.1.2),* Seager v Copydex *(Nos 1 and 2) (above, 2.1.3; below 2.4.1),* Coco v Clark *(above, 2.1.5) and* Thomas Marshall v Guinle *(above, 2.1.6). He continued:*

In my judgment there is no reason in principle why an oral idea should not qualify for protection under the law of confidence, provided it meets the other criteria I discuss below. Neither the originality nor the quality of an idea is in any way affected by the form in which it is expressed. No doubt both the communication and the content of an oral idea may be more difficult to prove than in the case of a written idea, but difficulties of proof should not affect the principle any more than in any other branches of the law where similar problems arise (e.g. contract and defamation).

I do not accept counsel for the defendants' argument that this will cause unfairness to third parties, since it is clear that, in order to be fixed with an obligation of confidence, a third party must know that the information was confidential; knowledge of a mere assertion that a breach of confidence has been committed is not sufficient: see *Carl-Zeiss-Stiftung v Herbert Smith & Co (a firm) (No 2)* [1969] 2 All E.R. 367, [1969] 2 Ch 276.

Nor do I accept counsel for the defendants' argument that an idea which is capable of development in more than one format is not entitled to protection. In my judgment the precise format is a matter for the writer to decide, and the fact that it is developable in more than one format in no way diminishes its intrinsic value.

I accept that to be capable of protection the idea must be sufficiently developed, so that it would be seen to be a concept which has at least some attractiveness for a television programme and which is capable of being realised as an actuality (see per Harris J. in *Talbot's* case [1981] R.P.C. 1 at 9). But I do not think this requirement necessitates in every case a full synopsis. In some cases the nature of the idea may require extensive development of this kind in order to meet the criteria. But in others the criteria may be met by a short unelaborated statement of an idea. In *Talbot's* case itself I do not think the detailed submission (at 5) added very much of substance to the idea which is set out in one sentence (also at 5).

Unquestionably, of course, the idea must have some significant element of originality not already in the realm of public knowledge. The originality may consist in a significant twist or slant to a well-known concept (see *Talbot's* case). This is, I think, by analogy, consistent with the statements in *Saltman's* case and *Coco's* case that novelty in the industrial field can be derived from the application of human ingenuity to well-known concepts.

To the best of my recollection, every witness in the theatre or television business on both sides agreed that if he or she received an idea from another it would be wrong to make use of it without the consent of the communicator. They of course were expressing their views in the context of a moral usage in their profession rather than of a strict legal obligation. However, the authorities, and in particular *Saltman's* case per Somervell L.J. and *Marshall's* case, strongly support counsel for the plaintiff's argument that the existence of such a usage is a factor of considerable force in deciding whether a legal obligation exists. I think the law as laid down in the authorities I have cited clearly establishes that the obligation which the witnesses saw as moral is in fact also legal in character.

This of course does not mean that every stray mention of an idea by one person to another is protected. To succeed in his claim the plaintiff must establish not only that the occasion of communication was confidential, but also that the content of the idea was clearly identifiable, original, of potential commercial attractiveness and capable of being realised in actuality. With these limitations, I consider there is no basis for the fears of counsel for the defendants that authors' freedom to develop ideas will be unduly stultified.

Hirst J. concluded on the facts that there had been an actionable breach of confidence and ordered an inquiry as to damages on this and other issues.

2.2.2   *Mustad v Allcock and Dosen* (1928) [1963] 3 All E.R. 416n. (H.L.)

Dosen was employed by a Norwegian firm, Thoring & Co., as a foreman engaged in manufacturing fish-hooks, subject to an express undertaking not to reveal confidential information. Thoring became insolvent and the business was purchased by the plaintiff company. Dosen was advised that, under Norwegian law, he owed no further duty of confidence. He joined the defendant company, Allcock, and disclosed to them details of a fish-hook manufacturing machine developed by Thoring. The plaintiff began proceedings for this breach of confidence but then applied for and obtained a patent for the very idea at issue. Upon request, its solicitors twice stated that the patent covered precisely the machine referred to in the Statement of Claim and in the Court of Appeal counsel appeared to make a similar concession.

Lord Buckmaster:

The important point about the patent is not whether it was valid or invalid, but what it was that it disclosed, because, after the disclosure had been made by the appellants to the world, it was impossible for them to get an injunction restraining the respondents from disclosing what was common knowledge. The secret, as a secret, had ceased to exist. But the appellants say – and, I think, say with considerable force – that it might well have been that, in the course of the experience which the respondent Dosen had gained in their service, he had obtained knowledge of ancillary secrets connected with the patented invention which were not in fact included in the invention but which would be of very great service to any person who proceeded to make the machine to which the invention related. Junior counsel for the appellants in his admirable argument satisfied me that it was at least probable or possible that such a set of circumstances might have existed; but, having regard to what had taken place and to the express request on the part of the respondents that they should be informed if the patented machine did in fact cover the very matter the disclosure of which was made the subject of complaints, it appears to me that there was thrown on the appellants the burden of showing that there were in fact these outside matters which were not included in the specification, that they had been or there was reasonable ground for believing they might be disclosed, and that their disclosure would be a wrong against which they were entitled to be protected by injunction. Nothing of the kind occurred. There was no attempt whatever made at the trial to distinguish between those parts of the machine which were outside the patent and those which were within. At no time was evidence led for the purpose of showing the added matter which the respondent Dosen might have learned in his former master's service and which he might disclose to the detriment of the appellants.

My lords, in those circumstances it appears to me that the appellants failed to discharge their primary duty at the hearing of this dispute, and that the Court of Appeal were quite right in dissolving the injunction which had been granted, and that, in consequence, this appeal must fail.

Viscount Dunedin and Lords Phillimore, Blanesburgh and Warrington of Clyffe concurred.

2.2.3 *Cranleigh Precision Engineering v Bryant* [1964] 3 All E.R. 289 (Roskill J.)

The plaintiff company, Cranleigh, manufactured above-ground swimming pools to a design invented by Bryant, its managing director. He learned, from the company's patent agent, of a British patent owned by Bischoff which covered features of the Cranleigh design. Cranleigh accordingly needed a licence under it. Instead of informing Cranleigh of this, Bryant took steps to set up a rival business and for it he purchased the Bischoff patent.

Cranleigh sued, inter alia, for an injunction against making use of confidential information obtained by Bryant as an officer of Cranleigh. To this, Bryant pleaded that the relevant information, the existence of the Bischoff patent, was in the public domain and that, in accordance with Mustad v Dosen (above, 2.2.2), it could not be protected as confidential. On this question Roskill J. said:

The effect of that decision clearly is that if the master had published his secret to the whole world (as had the appellants in that case) the servant is no longer bound by his promise to the master not to publish that same secret, but it is important to observe that the publication in that case was publication by the master. In the present case the publication was by Bischoff, who was never the master of Bryant. Bryant's master was the plaintiffs and the plaintiffs have never published anything, even their own specification. Counsel for the defendants sought to extract from the decision in *Mustad's* case the wider proposition that no matter by whom the publication took place, all attributes of secrecy of any kind which otherwise might have attached to the information in Bryant's possession automatically disappeared, once publication had taken place.

Roskill J. then referred to support for this view in Lord Greene's judgment in Saltman v Campbell *(above, 2.1.2) and to counsel's invitation to treat Roxburgh J.'s judgment in the* Terrapin *case ([1960] R.P.C. 128) as accordingly not binding on him. He continued:*

It may be that, strictly speaking, counsel for the defendants is right in saying that in those circumstances it would be open for me to hold that the passage in Roxburgh J.'s judgment in the *Terrapin* case misstated the law. I apprehend that it would be my duty to do so if I were convinced that it conflicted with the decision in the *Mustad* case, but in my judgment there is no such conflict, because the two matters are separate and distinct. I would respectfully borrow and adopt the passage as correctly stating the law which I have to apply, and I respectfully agree with the learned judge in stating that the principle, as he stated it, is a logical consequence of the decision of the Court of Appeal in *Saltman's* case. *Mustad's* case was, as I have said, a case where the employer made the publication in question. In the present case, Bryant, as possessor of what I have held to be the plaintiffs' confidential information, is seeking to free himself from his obligations of confidence, not because of what the plaintiffs have published, for they have published nothing, but because of what Bischoff published − a publication of which Bryant only became aware because of his contractual and confidential relationship with the plaintiffs.

I have dealt with this question at length, for the matter was argued at length before me. Applying the law as I conceive it to be, I have no doubt that Bryant acted in grave dereliction of his duty to the plaintiffs in concealing from the plaintiffs' board the information which he received from the plaintiffs' patent agents, and in taking no steps whatsoever to protect the plaintiffs against the possible consequences of the existence and publication of the Bischoff patent. I also have no doubt that Bryant acted in breach of confidence in making use, as he did as soon as he left the plaintiffs, of the information regarding the Bischoff patent which he had acquired in confidence and about its various effects on the plaintiff's position, for his own advantage and for that of the defendant company. Any other conclusion would involve putting a premium on dishonesty by managing directors. In reaching this conclusion I have not lost sight of the fact that the heads of agreements, unlike the draft service agreement which Bryant refused to sign, contained no express obligation not to divulge confidential information, but this makes no difference, for, were it necessary, I would not hesitate to imply the contract of employment between Bryant and the plaintiffs the relevant obligation. It is both reasonable and necessary so to do. The plaintiffs relied on the decision of the Court of Appeal in *Swain v West (Butchers) Ltd* ([1936] 3 All E.R. 261) in support of their argument that Bryant was under a duty to report to the plaintiff's board that of which the plaintiff's patent agents had informed him. I need only say that my conclusion on that part of the case is, I think, consistent with that decision. I reject the argument that it was a mere error of judgment on Bryant's part not to report this. It is difficult to think that as Bryant was able to buy the Bischoff specification in October-November, 1963, for a relatively trivial sum, the plaintiffs could not have done so at least as cheaply, had Bryant given them the opportunity of so doing.

2.2.4 *Interfirm Comparison v Law Society of New South Wales* [1977] R.P.C. 137; (Bowen J., S.C., N.S.W.)

The plaintiff conducted comparisons of costs, productivity, profitability etc between firms in the same business or profession. The defendant, the solicitors' professional body of N.S.W., wanted to collect certain objective data and so approached the plaintiff for that purpose.

Following a meeting between the parties, the defendant received a document described as a proposal for the survey, together with copies of a questionnaire which had previously been used and developed in 1972. The defendant decided that the proposal was unsuitable. With the assistance of the University of New England, it prepared and issued its own survey and questionnaire.

The plaintiff sought (i) to restrain the defendants from making use of confidential information and copyright material belonging to it; and (ii) an inquiry as to damages.

The defendant, by making a photostat copy of the plaintiff's questionnaire and sending the copy to the university, was held to have infringed the plaintiff's copyright in it. There was also found to be a breach of confidence in sending the plaintiff's questionnaire to the university, even though this was done by error or oversight and even though there was no evidence that the university had made any use of it. On this issue, Bowen J. said:

In my opinion, having regard to the amount of skill, judgment and labour involved in the preparation of the proposal and the 1972 questionnaire, and to the limited purpose of the negotiation between the plaintiff and the defendant in furtherance of which the material was supplied, both documents were confidential, in the sense that they could be used by the Law Society only for the purpose for which they had been given to it, that is to say, for the purpose of considering and deciding whether it would engage the services of the plaintiff for its own survey and interfirm comparison; they could not, without the plaintiff's assent, be used for other unrelated purposes – for example, for the purpose of publishing a book of precedents of writing an article in the *Law Society's Journal.*

It was argued for the defendant that much, if not all, of the material in the proposal and the questionnaire was already well-known, and should, on this ground, be denied the protection of confidentiality.

Although it is true, as I have pointed out in relation to copyright, that much of the material in the proposal and questionnaire was generally known, the particular expression and arrangement of this material found in the proposal and questionnaire was new; it was not generally known.

Then it is argued for the defendant that disclosure to any member of the public will destroy the claim to confidentiality, and that the plaintiff itself had destroyed any confidentiality in the 1972 questionnaire by the manner in which it had distributed it. In this regard counsel for the defendant relied upon patent cases dealing with disclosure which would cause an invention to be regarded as part of public knowledge in that field of the law (*R v Patents Appeal Tribunal: Ex parte Lovens Kemiske Fabriks Handelsaktieselskab* [1968] 1 W.L.R. 1727 at 1734; [1968] 3 All E.R. 536 *Fomento Industrial SA and others v Mentmore Manufacturing Co Ltd* [1956] R.P.C. 87 at 99).

It appears to me that decisions relating to patents are not helpful in dealing with questions of confidentiality. The Patents Act itself by its provisions raises some points of difference. But apart from that, in the case of an invention the State offers to the inventor a monopoly in return for disclosure in his specification of his invention. If an inventor has already disclosed his invention, even to one member of the public, it may be held as a matter of principle that he has no consideration to offer in return for the grant of monopoly (see *Humpherson v Syer* (1887) 4 R.P.C. 407 at 413). The law relating to confidentiality of communications appears to me to be based upon different principles – the long-standing equitable principles relating to fair-dealing with the work of another. It is closer to the law relating to copyright in unpublished works than to the law of patents. The authorities indicate that even though secrecy may be imperfect in relation to communication which is given in confidence, that communication may still be protected by the principles of confidentiality.

2.2.5 *Potters-Ballotini v Weston-Baker* [1977] R.P.C. 202 (C.A.)

The plaintiff company was the only British manufacturer of ballotini (glass beads), though it had competitors in Germany and Austria. Its general manager and works manager gave notice and, while working out the notice period, formed Bishop Auckland Glass with a leading employee of the company which had installed the plaintiff's furnace. The new company was able to set up its production assembly and factory on lines very similar to the plaintiff's so as to be in a position to start manufacturing almost before the plaintiff learned of what had happened. It accordingly sought interlocutory relief on the wide terms referred to in Lord Denning M.R.'s judgment. After reviewing the facts, he said:

All this sounds as if these three men were guilty of much wrongdoing. But it must be remembered that it is only wrong if Potters have a right to be protected. It is clear that Potters have no patent for any part of their machines, their process or their products; and that they have no claim to any copyright in any sketch, design, or drawing which was used in making the plant or any part of it. Thus, having no industrial property vested in them, Potters have sought to rely on the protection which the courts give to information imparted in confidence. It is well settled that information imparted in confidence (especially information which is imparted in confidence to servants or agents) will be protected. The courts will restrain the use of it if it is in breach of good faith. I need only quote the sentence which I have used in *Seager v Copydex Ltd* [1967] 1 W.L.R. 931: "The law on this subject does not depend on any implied contract. It depends on the broad principle of equity that he who has received information in confidence shall not take unfair advantage of it. He must not make use of it to the prejudice of him who gave it without obtaining his consent." Potters rely here on breach of confidence, and particularly in regard to Mr Weston-Baker and Mr Cramphorn.

At the outset, however, there is this point to consider. Potters had made express agreements with Mr Weston-Baker and Mr Cramphorn by which each agreed not for one year to use for himself, confidential information. What is the effect of the "one year"? Does it mean that after the year has ended, then men can use the information freely? We have been referred to passages from Lord Greene's statements in *Vokes Ltd v Heather* (1945) 62 R.P.C. 135, and his later statement in *British Celanese Ltd v Moncrieff* [1948] Ch 578. I do not think it is necessary or desirable to give any final ruling, but I must say that these clauses seem to me designed to cover the period for which the company is seeking to protect confidential information. It can well be said that, after the men had left for one year, they were free from an obligation as to the use of confidential information. The dates are these: In February 1974 Mr Weston-Baker gave a year's notice. It was because of differences of policy. He was paid a year's salary, and worked a certain amount during the year. One year was the right period of notice. It would end in February or March 1975. In November 1974 Mr Cramphorn gave notice. He left in February 1975 and went to Messrs Boylin. So the employment of these two men certainly came to an end in March 1975. If the obligation as to confidence is governed by the contract – and was only for one year after the service ended – it would come to an end in March 1976, that is, next month. If either of them broke it in the past, there might be a remedy in damages, but there would not be a remedy by way of injunction for the future, seeing thaat they will soon be free to use it as they please.

The next point is: To what extent was this information to be regarded truly as confidential? Here we come up against another difficulty. As I have said, there is no patent and no copyright relied upon. There is no doubt whatever that a man, even in the course of his employment by others, may have quite a range of expertise and knowledge of his own which he is entitled to have for his own benefit. We know that Mr

Cramphorn worked on these plants. He knew, I should have thought, as much as anyone about them. As I ventured to say myself in *Stephenson Jordan & Harrison Ltd v MacDonald & Evans* [1952] 69 R.P.C. 23: "A servant cannot help acquiring a great deal of knowledge of his master's method of business and of the science which his master practises. The servant when he leaves cannot be restrained from using the knowledge so acquired, so long as he does not take away trade secrets or lists of customers". I added: "The claim for breach of confidence seemed to be an attempt to acquire a monopoly of a branch of human knowledge which the law does not permit except so far as Parliament has authorised it."

In this case it seems to me there would be great difficulty in determining to what extent the features of this plant or this process were confidential, especially when one remembers that there are other rival plants making ballotini in Germany and Austria, and have done for many years. There is a great deal of information which may be said to be in the public domain. But, apart from that, if not in the public domain, how far was it confidential to Potters – so as to belong to them – as distinct from the man's own knowledge and expertise, which he certainly is not to be prevented from using, as was pointed out, of course, in *Morris (Herbert) Ltd v Saxelby* [1916] 1 A.C. 688.

So there seems to me to be a great difficulty in defining what are the items of confidential information to which Potters would be entitled. We were given by Mr Leggatt a most useful table showing 13 items. Some of them he had to acknowledge could not be said to be confidential although they were items which had been copied. But he pointed to others which were confidential, particularly a part of the furnace and how it was made. He may succeed upon some items eventually, but it must be remembered that the injunction which is sought is in the most general terms. It is sought to restrain the defendants from using information, and so forth, obtained during their employments as to the working of any processes, as to know-how and the like. That is uncertain in the extreme. It is well established that an injunction ought to be such that the party affected can know with certainty what he is or is not allowed to do. There is no such certainty here.

Potters have even more difficulty in making a case against Mr Boylin. He was not a servant but only a contractor doing work on premises. He gave no pledge of secrecy. It would be even more difficult to find him guilty of a breach of confidential information.

Mr Leggatt said, and said forcibly, that the plaintiff's know-how and their process was such that in Japan and Australia there were firms and companies ready to pay for the information: and that the Japanese Government would not dream of paying 4 per cent royalty unless they were satisfied that they could not have found it out themselves. Mr Leggatt says that shows how important and confidential this information is. That is a telling point, but, nevertheless, it does not overcome to my mind, the difficulty of saying what is confidential and what is not.

Assuming that the point is overcome, there is the problem, which has been discussed, and much discussed of late, of what is called the "springboard" doctrine, whereby it is said that a servant or any other person who has got confidential information ought not to save himself the time of working it out for himself or getting it from some other people without paying for it. I need not go through all the cases. They are all well summarised by Megarry J. in his valuable judgment in *Coco v A.N. Clark (Engineers) Ltd* [1969] R.P.C. 41. Although a man must not use such information as a springboard to get a start over others, nevertheless that springboard does not last for ever. If he does use it, a time may come when so much has happened that he can no longer be restrained. That is another point of difficulty.

Accordingly, Lord Denning M.R. refused to grant the interlocutory injunction sought, applying American Cyanamid v Ethicon *[1975] A.C. 396. Scarman L.J. and Sir John Pennycuick delivered concurring judgments.*

2.2.6   *Dunsford & Elliott v Johnson and Firth Brown* [1978] F.S.R. 143 (C.A.)

*The plaintiff, a company in financial difficulties, decided to raise £3,000,000 by way of a rights issue to their shareholders. In order to induce institutional shareholders who held 43 per cent of the shares to underwrite the rights issue they had been shown a confidential report on the company's financial and technical prospects under an obligation of confidence. The institutional shareholders were of the view that £3,000,000 was inadequate to secure the company and therefore approached on their own initiative the defendant and one othe*r *company, suggesting that each should underwrite a further £500,000 without reference to the plaintiff. Representatives from both companies were permitted to study the confidential report in depth and make notes thereon. Soon afterwards the defendant announced that it was making a takeover bid for the plaintiffs. The plaintiffs sought an injunction to restrain the use of the confidential information in the report and to restrain the takeover bid itself. In the course of refusing interlocutory relief, Lord Denning M.R. referred to Megarry J.'s three requisites (Coco v Clark, above, 2.1.5) and said:*

Taking those three requisites. The first is satisfied. The information did have the quality of confidence. The second is satisfied. It was imparted in circumstances importing an obligation of confidence. That is shown by the letter which I have read by Morgan Grenfell to the consortium. It is said, also, that the third requisite is satisfied. D & E say that there was an unauthorised use of the information to their detriment; or, at any rate, to the detriment of their shareholders.

I do not think, however, that these three requisites cover the whole ground. Megarry J. drew attention to circumstances in which it would be unjust to enforce a stipulation for confidence, even though all three requisites are fulfilled. For instance when, in the course of negotiations, a confidential process is disclosed, and then the negotiations break down. His instances lead me to think there is a further principle applicable in these cases. If the stipulation for confidence was unreasonable at the time of making it; or if it was reasonable at the beginning, but afterwards, in the course of subsequent happenings, it becomes unreasonable that it should be enforced: then the courts will decline to enforce it: just as in the case of a covenant in restraint of trade.

It seems to me that that principle applies to this case. Although Dunsford and Elliott (through Morgan Grenfell) stipulated that this report was confidential, it seems to me that, as events turned out, it would be quite unreasonable that the courts should enforce it. For one thing, it has since been discovered that Dunsford and Elliott – or, at any rate, their directors – have made considerable use themselves of the forecasts contained in the report. We have been given figures showing that three of their directors, on 7 and 8 October, bought 55,000 of the shares of Dunsford and Elliott at a price of 14p – very nearly the lowest price they ever reached. I would imagine that they had some at least of the favourable forecasts – the confidential forecasts – before them at the time, and were better placed to buy the shares than outsiders. In addition, we know that Dunsford and Elliott disclosed this confidential information to 43 per cent of the shareholders in the company – that is, to all the institutional shareholders; and none of the others. This widespread use of the information drives a hole into the blanket of confidence: especially when that information is being used – or, shall I say misused – for the benefit of some potential shareholders, and not for the benefit of the others. So much so that it would not be reasonable that the stipulation for confidence should be enforced.

Roskill and Lawton L.JJ delivered concurring judgments.

2.2.7 *Hubbard v Vosper* [1972] 2 Q.B. 84 (C.A.)

The defendant had participated in a course of initiation into the cult of Scientology, undertaking at the time to use the knowledge gained only for Scientology purposes and not to reveal "Level VI" materials to outsiders. He became disillusioned and wrote a book criticising the cult and quoting from Level VI materials comprising the works of the cult's moving spirit, Lafayette Ronald Hubbard. In interlocutory proceedings to prevent its publication, allegations of copyright infringement and breach of confidence were made.

On the issue of copyright infringement, it was held that the defendant might have a defence of fair dealing for purposes of criticism or review even though the documents from which he was quoting had been kept private and confidential (on this issue see the summary of judgments in Beloff v Pressdram, *below, 3.5.5.3.*

On breach of confidence, Megaw L.J. said:

The law will, in a proper case, intervene to restrain a defendant from revealing information or other material obtained in confidence, such as trade secrets, and the like. This depends on the broad principle of equity that he who has received information in confidence shall not take unfair advantage of it: see *Seager v Copydex* (above, 2.1.3). But the information must be such that it is a proper subject for protection. As I said in *Fraser v Evans* (above, 2.1.4):

"There are some things which may be required to be disclosed in the public interest, in which event no confidence can be prayed in aid to keep them secret."

In this case counsel for the defendants has drawn our attention to the nature of these courses for which confidence is claimed. The plaintiffs themselves say that: "the material contained in these courses can be dangerous in untrained hands." Counsel for the defendants took us through the books and said that they indicate medical quackeries of a sort which may be dangerous if practised behind closed doors. They are so dangerous, he said, that it is in the public interest that these goings-on should be made known. The closed doors should be opened for all to see. We cannot decide on it today, as this is only an interlocutory application. But, I think that, even on what we have heard so far, there is good ground for thinking that these courses contain such dangerous material that it is in the public interest that it should be known.

I turn to the question of confidentiality. Lord Denning M.R. has referred to one passage which occurred in some of the documents put before us in relation to fair game. I think it is right, in fairness to the plaintiffs, that it should be said that it would seem that that particular provision has disappeared from the latest, or 1970, edition of the book "Introduction to Scientology Ethics". It is right in these circumstances that something should be said about the history of that provision. So far as the documents before us are concerned, it appears chronologically for the first time in what is described as the "Hubbard Communications Office Policy Letter of March 1, 1905", under the heading, "Justice, Suppressive Acts, Suppression of Scientology and Scientologists. The Fair Game Law". That document defined "Potential Trouble Sources. They were persons who were active in Scientology, or persons known as "preclears", who remained "connected to a person or group that is a suppressive person or group". A "suppressive person or group" is then defined in the document as "one that actively seeks to suppress or damage Scientology or a Scientologist by Suppressive Acts". "Suppressive acts" are then defined as "acts calculated to impede or destroy Scientology or a Scientologist and which are listed at length in this policy letter". I should refer to some of these "suppressive acts", the carrying out of which turns a person, for the purpose of this document, into a "suppressive person or group". "Suppressive acts" include "proposing, advising or voting for legislation or ordinances, rules or laws directed toward the Suppression of Scientology . . ." so that if a voter in this country were to have the temerity to cast a vote in a Parliamentary election for a candidate who had indicated that he was minded to propose legislation which would "suppress" Scientology, that person would be guilty in the eyes of this organisation of having committed "a suppressive act". Again, "testifying hostilely before state or public enquiries into Scientology to suppress it"; "reporting or threatening to report Scientology or Scientologists to civil authorities in an effort to suppress Scientology or Scientologists from practising or receiving standard Scientology"; "bringing civil suit against any Scientology organisation or Scientologist including the non-payment of bills or failure to refund without first calling the matter to the attention of the Chairman . . ."; "writing anti-Scientology letters to the press or giving anti-Scientology or anti-Scientologist evidence to the press"; "testifying as a hostile witness against Scientology in public". If words mean anything, that meant that in the eyes of this organisation a person became "a suppressive person" − "a suppressive person" guilty of a suppressive act − if, however truthful, however much compelled by process of law, he should give evidence in a court of law hostile to the organisation of Scientology. And this is the organisation which is seeking to have its documents treated as confidential by the order of the court. It went on to include among "suppressive acts": "1st degree murder, arson, disintegration of persons or belongings not guilty of suppressive acts". There can be no doubt that the last five words relate to the preceding word "persons". What does that mean? That it was, in the eyes of this organisation in 1965, "a suppressive act" to be guilty of "first degree murder", provided that the person you murdered had not been guilty of suppressive acts. The implication is obvious. Yet another "suppressive act" is, "delivering up the person of a Scientologist without defense or protest to the demands of civil or criminal law".

In the 1968 edition of "Scientology Ethics" those provisions remain substantially the same and they continue at that date to include the "fair game" provisions which I have mentioned as having been included in the "Justice policy" document of 1965. In this year's it was provided that suppressive persons or groups became "Fair Game":

"... by Fair Game is meant, without rights for self, possessions or position, and no Scientologist may be brought before a Committee of Evidence or punished for any action taken against a Suppressive Person or Group during the period that person or group is 'fair game'."

Well, it may be that there is or was some explanation of that general provision, as of the related "first degree murder" provision, which will take away from it the meaning which to any ordinary person it would carry; namely, that here was an organisation which had laid down a criminal code of its own and by that criminal code it treated and required its adherents to treat, persons as outlaws deprived of any protection or sanction so far as the Scientological organisation was concerned if they had been guilty of "suppressive acts", and no Scientologist was to be condemned, under the ethical code of Scientology, for any action − I repeat any action − which he might take against such "fair game". It is right that this should be mentioned: in the latest edition of the Scientology Ethics, which appears to have been published in the year 1970 the provisions as to "fair game" have been removed from its code of ethics.

Most of the matters which I have mentioned earlier, as being examples of "suppressive acts" will remain as "suppressive acts". They come under the heading "High Crimes (Suppressive Acts)"; but the provisions as to "fair game" have disappeared from the code. One other respect in which "suppressive acts" have changed since the original policy document is this: the last five words have disappeared from that extraordinary example of a "suppressive act": "1st degree murder, arson, disintegration of persons or belongings not guilty of suppressive acts". So that the Scientology organisation has now changed its provisions, from those that previously prevailed, in such a way that "first degree murder" may now apparently be regarded as a crime within this organisation, even though the murderer is a Scientologist, and even though the victim is one who, in the eyes of the organisation, has committed a "suppressive act", such as having written a letter to a newspaper adversely criticising Scientology.

In the circumstances, the Court was not prepared to grant interlocutory relief.

2.2.8   *Lion Laboratories v Evans* [1984] 2 All E.R. (C.A.)

The plaintiff company manufactured and sold the Lion Intoximeter, an instrument for measuring intoxication from alcohol, particularly in drivers. 60 per cent of sales of the device were in the UK, where it was one of two devices approved by the Home Office for police use in breathalysing. Despite an ex parte injunction, the Daily Express, one of the defendants, published a report alleging that the Intoximeter was liable to serious error which could lead to wrongful conviction. This information came from two former employees of the plaintiff, who were also defendants. The Court of Appeal discharged the interlocutory injunctions granted below, save in respect of specified documents.

Stephenson L.J.:

The problem before the judge and before this court is how best to resolve, before trial, a conflict of two competing public interests. The first public interest is the preservation of the right of organisations, as of individuals, to keep secret confidential information. The courts will restrain breaches of confidence, and breaches of copyright, unless there is just cause or excuse for breaking confidence or infringing copyright. The just cause or excuse with which this case is concerned is the public interest in admittedly confidential information. There is confidential information which the public may have a right to receive and others, in particular the press, now extended to the media, may have a right and even a duty to publish, even if the information has been unlawfully obtained in flagrant breach of confidence and irrespective of the motive of the informer. The duty of confidence, the public interest in maintaining it, is a restriction on the freedom of the press which is recognised by our law, as well as by Art.10(2) of the European Convention for the Protection of Human Rights and Fundamental Freedoms (Rome, 4 November 1950; TS 71 (1953); Cmd 8969); the duty to publish, the countervailing interest of the public in being kept informed of matters which are of real public concern, is an inroad on the privacy of confidential matters.

So much is settled by decisions of this court, and in particular by the illuminating judgments of Lord Denning M.R. in *Initial Services Ltd v Putterill* [1967] 3 All E.R. 145, [1968] 1 Q.B. 396, *Fraser v Evans* [1969] 1 All E.R. 8, [1969] 1 Q.B. 349, *Hubbard v Vosper* [1972] 1 All E.R. 1023, [1972] 2 Q.B. 84, *Woodward v Hutchins* [1977] 2 All E.R. 751 [1977] 1 WLR 760 and (dissenting) *Schering Chemicals Ltd v Falkman Ltd* [1981] 2 All E.R. 321, [1982] Q.B. 1. I add to those the speeches of Lord Wilberforce, Lord Salmon and Lord Fraser in *British Steel Corp v Granada Television Ltd* [1981] 1 All E.R. 417, [1981] A.C. 1096.

There are four further considerations. First, "There is a wide difference between what is interesting to the public and what it is in the public interest to make known": per Lord Wilberforce in *British Steel Corp v Granada Television Ltd* [1981] 1 All E.R. 417 at 455, [1981] A.C. 1096 at 1168. The public are interested in many private matters which are no real concern of theirs and which the public have no pressing need to know. Second, the media have a private interest of their own in publishing what appeals to the public and may increase their circulation or the numbers of their viewers or listeners; and (I quote from the judgment of Sir John Donaldson M.R. in *Francome v Mirror Group Newspapers Ltd* [1984] 2 All E.R. 408 at 413) "... they are peculiarly vulnerable to the error of confusing the public interest with their own interest". Third, there are cases in which the public interest is best served by an informer giving the confidential information not to the press but to the police or some other responsible body, as was suggested by Lord Denning M.R. in the *Initial Services* case and by Sir John Donaldson M.R. in the *Francome* case. Fourth, it was said by Page Wood V.-C. in *Gartside v Outram* (1856) 26 L.J. Ch 113 at 114, "there is no confidence as to the disclosure of iniquity";

and although counsel concedes on the plaintiffs' behalf that, as Salmon L.J. said in *Initial Services v Putterill* [1967] 3 All E.R. 145 at 151, [1968] 1 Q.B. 396 at 410, "what was iniquity in 1856 may be too narrow, or too wide, in 1967", and in 1984 extends to serious misdeeds or grave misconduct, he submits that misconduct of that kind is necessary to destroy the duty of confidence or excuse the breach of it, and nothing of that sort is alleged against the plaintiffs in the evidence now before the court.

Counsel for the third and fourth defendants and counsel for the first and second defendants have not been able to find any case where a defendant has been able to rely on public interest in defence of a claim for breach of confidence and the plaintiff has not also been guilty of such misconduct. And there are passages in the speeches of Lord Wilberforce and Lord Fraser in *British Steel Corp v Granada Television Ltd* in which they appear to be satisfied with describing the public interest rule as the "iniquity rule". But I nowhere find any authority for the proposition, except perhaps in the judgment of Ungoed-Thomas J. in *Beloff v Pressdram Ltd* [1973] 1 All E.R. 241 at 260, that some modern form of iniquity on the part of the plaintiffs is the only thing which can be disclosed in the public interest; and I agree with the judge in rejecting the "no iniquity, no public interest" rule and in respectfully adopting what Lord Denning M.R. said in *Fraser v Evans* [1969] 1 All E.R. 8 at 11, [1969] 1 Q.B. 349 at 362 that some things are required to be disclosed in the public interest, in which case no confidence can be prayed in aid to keep them secret, and [iniquity] is merely an instance of a just cause and excuse for breaking confidence.

Griffiths L.J. put this case in argument. Suppose the plaintiffs had informed the police that their Intoximeter was not working accurately or safe to use, and the police had replied that they were nevertheless going to continue using it as breath test evidence. Could there then be no defence of public interest if the defendants sought to publish that confidential information, simply because the plaintiffs themselves had done nothing wrong but the police had? There would be the same public interest in publication, whichever was guilty or misconduct, and I cannot think the right to break confidence would be lost, though the public interest remained the same.

Bearing this last consideration in mind, in my opinion we cannot say that the defendants must be restrained because what they want to publish does not show misconduct by the plaintiffs.

We have then, with the other three considerations in mind and remembering that confidentiality is admitted, to ask what the judge called the "sole question", namely:

"... whether the defendants have shown that they have an arguable defence to the plaintiffs' claims in respect of breach of confidentiality and breach of copyright"

and that means, as counsel for the third and fourth defendants ultimately expressed it, a serious defence of public interest which may succeed, not, of course, will succeed, at the trial. He had expressed it rather differently as a reasonable defence, taking the words from the judgment of Lord Denning M.R. in *Hubbard v Vosper* [1972] 1 All E.R. 1023, [1972] 2 Q.B. 84, where it was treated like a plea of justification or fair comment in a libel suit. And there are statements in the judgments of Lord Denning M.R. in *Fraser v Evans* [1969] 1 All E.R. 8, [1969] 1 Q.B. 349 and of Roskill L.J. in the unreported case of *Khashoggi v Smith* [1980] CA Transcript 58, which indicate that a plaintiff should not be better off if he claims for breach of confidence than if he claims for defamation. But I respectfully agree with Sir David Cairns in *Khashoggi's* case "that there is a fundamental distinction between the two types of action". To be allowed to publish confidential information, the defendants must do more than raise a plea of public interest: they must show "a legitimate ground for supposing it is in the public interest for it to be disclosed". The, as Lord Denning M.R. said in *Woodward v Hutchins* [1977] 2 All E.R. 751 at 755, [1977] 2 W.L.R. 760 at 764, "the courts should not restrain it by interlocutory injunction, but should leave the complainant to his remedy in damages", after (I will assume, though I am not sure that Lord Denning M.R. would have agreed) considering and weighing in the balance all relevant matters, such as whether damages would be an adequate remedy to compensate the plaintiffs if they succeeded at the trial.

We cannot of course at this stage decide whether the balance will come down on the side of confidentiality or of public interest. But, to see if there is serious defence of public interest which may succeed at the trial, we have to look at the evidence and if we decide that there is such a defence, to perform a balancing exercise, as indicated for instance in the judgment of Lord Denning M.R. in *Woodward v Hutchins* and in the speech of Lord Fraser in *British Steel Corp v Granada Television Ltd* [1981] 1 All E.R. 417 at 480, [1981] A.C. 1096 at 1202, which is so apt that I follow the judge in quoting it. In that case Lord Fraser said:

> "The answer to the question therefore seems to me to involve weighing up the public interest for and against publication. The balance does not in my opinion depend on the use made of the leaked information by the appellants in this particular case. Anyone who hands over to the press a bundle of confidential documents belonging to someone else must surely expect, and intend, that, if they contain information of topical interest, it will be published in some form. The informer's motives are, in my opinion, irrelevant. It is said, and I am willing to accept, that in this case the informant neither asked for nor received any money, or other reward, but that he acted out of a keen sense of indignation about the dealings between BSC and the government before and during the strike. No doubt there is a public interest in maintaining the free flow of information to the press, and therefore against obstructing informers. But there is also I think a very strong public interest in preserving confidentiality within any organisation, in order that it can operate efficiently, and also be free from suspicion that it is harbouring disloyal employees. There is no difference in this respect between a public corporation like BSC and an ordinary company."

Stephenson L.J. reviewed the evidence in detail and continued:

The judge never referred to the damage already done to the reputation of the plaintiffs and their Intoximeter by what had already been published and merely recorded the arguments of counsel for the plaintiffs on the damage which would be done by further publication without putting it in the scales, I think because he had already decided that they tipped in the plaintiff's favour for breach of confidence and also because the damage done by 14 March is not as great as the damage done by further publication since that date. It may be distasteful to let damage done by a newspaper weigh in support of its application to be allowed to do more damage by breaking confidence. Nevertheless, the existing damage is, in my view, a matter which the court must now take into account, and that is another factor which entitles us to differ from the judge.

...

Stephenson L.J.'s final conclusion was:

The issue raised by the defendants is a serious question concerning a matter which affects the life, and even the liberty, of an unascertainable number of Her Majesty's subjects, and though there is no proof that any of them has been wrongly convicted on the evidence of the plaintiffs' Intoximeter, and we certainly cannot decide that any has, we must not restrain the defendants from putting before the public this further information how the Lion Intoximeter 3000 has worked, and how the plaintiffs regard and discharge their responsibility for it, although the information is confidential and was unlawfully taken in breach of confidence.

O'Connor and Griffiths L.JJ. delivered concurring opinions.

2.2.9   *Stephens v Avery* [1988] 2 All E.R. 477 (Browne-Wilkinson V.-C.)

According to the plaintiff's pleading, she told her friend, Mrs Avery (first defendant), about a lesbian relationship with a Mrs Telling, who had been killed by her husband. This revelation was expressly upon terms that it was confidential. Despite this, Mrs Avery revealed the information to the Mail on Sunday, which published it. The plaintiff sued Mrs Avery, the paper and its editor for damages for the breach of confidence. The defendants sought to strike out the action as revealing no reasonable cause of action. The master refused to do so and an appeal did not succeed.

In giving judgment, Browne-Wilkinson V.-C. dealt with arguments arising under the first two requirements for liability prescribed by Megarry J. in Coco v Clark *(above, 2.1.5). As regards the requirement of confidential subject-matter, he referred to* Glyn v Weston Feature Film *[1916] 1 Ch 261 at 269, and continued:*

I entirely accept the principle stated in that case, the principle being that a court of equity will not enforce copyright, and presumably also will not enforce a duty of confidence, relating to matters which have a grossly immoral tendency. But at the present day the difficulty is to identify what sexual conduct is to be treated as grossly immoral. In 1915 there was a code of sexual morals accepted by the overwhelming majority of society. A judge could therefore stigmatise certain sexual conduct as offending that moral code. But at the present day no such general code exists. There is no common view that sexual conduct of any kind between consenting adults is grossly immoral. I suspect the works of Elinor Glyn if published today would be widely regarded as, at the highest, very soft pornography.

The sexual conduct of the plaintiff was not so morally shocking in this case as to prevent the third defendant, a major national Sunday newspaper, from spreading the story all over its front and inside pages. The submission on behalf of these defendants that the actions of the plaintiff in this case are so grossly immoral as to produce a tendency towards immoral conduct and thereby to be without the law lies ill in their mouths, since they have themselves spread the news of such conduct nationwide for their own personal profit.

If it is right that there is now no generally accepted code of sexual morality applying to this case, it would be quite wrong in my judgment for any judge to apply his own personal moral views, however strongly held, in deciding the legal rights of the parties. The court's function is to apply the law, not personal prejudice. Only in a case where there is still a generally accepted moral code can the court refuse to enforce rights in such a way as to offend that generally accepted code.

As to the submission that there is no confidentiality in tittle-tattle and gossip, counsel for the defendants relied on a passage in the *Coco* case [1969] RPC 41 at 48, where Megarry J. said:

> "... I doubt whether equity would intervene unless the circumstances are of sufficient gravity; equity ought not to be invoked merely to protect trivial tittle-tattle, however confidential".

Since the *Coco* case was exclusively concerned with information which was of industrial value, those remarks were plainly obiter dicta. Moreover, I have the greatest doubt whether wholesale revelation of the sexual conduct of an individual can properly be described as "trivial" tittle-tattle. Again, although it is true that the passage I have quoted occurs in that part of the judgment which deals with the nature of information which can be protected, it is to be noted that the judge appeared to be considering when equity would give a remedy, not dealing with the fundamental nature of the legal right. If, as I think he was, Megarry J. was saying that the discretion to grant an injunction or to award damages would not be exercised in a case which was merely trivial, I agree. But the exercise of such a discretion can only be decided in the light of all the circumstances. Those cannot be known until there has been a trial.

The Vice-Chancellor also rejected as misconceived an argument that information relating to any type of mutual sexual conduct could not be confidential since both parties to it must be aware of the facts.

As to the requirement that the information be communicated in circumstances giving rise to a duty of confidence, he stated:

Counsel for the defendants submits that in the absence of either a legally enforceable contract or a pre-existing relationship, such as that of employer and employee, doctor and patient, or priest and penitent, it is not possible to impose a legal duty of confidence on the recipient of the information merely by saying that the information is given in confidence. In my judgment that is wrong in law. The basis of equitable intervention to protect confidentiality is that it is unconscionable for a person who has received information on the basis that it is confidential subsequently to reveal that information. Although the relationship between the parties is often important in cases where it is said there is an implied as opposed to express obligation of confidence, the relationship between the parties is not the determining factor. It is the acceptance of the information on the basis that it will be kept secret that affects the conscience of the recipient of the information. I quote again from the judgment of Bingham L.J. in the *Spycatcher* case, where he said ([1988] 2 WLR 805 at 904):

> "The cases show that the duty of confidence does not depend on any contract, express or implied, between the parties. If it did, it would follow on ordinary principles that strangers to the contract would not be bound. But the duty 'depends on the broad principle of equity that he who has received information in confidence shall not take unfair advantage of it': *Seager v Copydex Ltd* ([1967] 2 All ER 415 at 417, [1967] 1 WLR 923 at 931), *per* Lord Denning M.R. 'The jurisdiction is based not so much on property or on contract as on the duty to be of good faith': *Fraser v Evans* ([1969] 1 All ER 8 at 11, [1969] 1 QB 349, 361), *per* Lord Denning M.R."

If, as is here alleged, the information was communicated and accepted expressly in confidence, the conscience of Mrs Avery is just as much affected as in any other case. In my judgment the express statement that the information is confidential is the clearest possible example of the imposition of a duty of confidence.

2.2.10   *A.G. v Guardian Newspapers (No. 2)* [1988] 3 All E.R. 545

The scandal surrounding the publication of Spycatcher – *the memoirs of former MI5 agent, Peter Wright – led to extensive litigation both in New South Wales and England. The former proceedings had a considerable impact on the latter. The book was, however, first published in the US on July 13, 1987. This the British government did not try to stop; there were Constitutional objections there to imposing any prior restraint on the publication of such material.*

The timetable of events can be set out thus:

Events outside UK

1. *1985: A.G. (UK) obtains undertaking in NSW from Wright and his publishers not to publish pending trial of actions there against them for breach of confidence.*

2. *November 1986 – March 1987. Powell J. tries and dismisses NSW action, but undertakings not to publish continue pending appeal.[2]*

3. *13 July 1987: publication of* Spycatcher *in US. Copies begin to appear in Britain without attempts by Customs to stop them.*

Events in UK

1.(a) *June 1986: after receiving a leak,* Observer *and* Guardian *some of revelations of MI5 publish accounts of forth-coming NSW trial and mention activity contained in the book.*

(b) *Millett J. grants injunctions restraining further similar reports by these newspapers, subject to exceptions including the reporting of things said in open court in Australia.*

2. *April 1986:* Independent, *Evening* Standard *and* London Daily News *publish articles repeating some of Wright's allegations. CA holds to be capable of constituting contempt of court by undermining the Millett injunctions against* Observer *and* Guardian.[1]

3. *12 July 1987: by secret arrangement with Wright's US publishers, an extract from* Spycatcher *appears in* Sunday Times. *More promised but (i)* Sunday Times *held by CA to be in contempt of the Millett injunctions.*

(ii) *HL (3–2) refuse to discharge those injunctions and even remove the exception concerning reports of Australian proceedings.[3]*

---

[1] *A.G. v Newspaper Publishing* [1988] Ch. 333. After this determination of the preliminary issue, the matter came to trial against several newspapers. Three were found to have committed the *actus reus* of a contempt and to have had the necessary *mens rea*, the contempt being "in respect of conduct intended to impede or prejudice the administration of justice" (Contempt of Court Act 1981, s.6(c)): *re A.G. v Observer et al, The Times*, May 9, 1989.

[2] (1987) 8 N.S.W.L.R. 341.

[3] [1987] 3 All E.R. 316; [1987] 1 W.L.R. 1248.

4. September 1987: NSW CA upholds dismissal of the action there and undertaking not to publish lapses.[4] Further appeal to HCA upholds judgments below: June 1988.[5]

4. November 1987 – October 1988: Trial of actions for permanent injunctions against Observer/Guardian *and* Sunday Times *commences. Injunctions refused by Scott J., CA and HL; but* Sunday Times *is held liable to account for profits of publication on 12 July 1987.*

Extracts given here are from H.L. speeches in the U.K. proceedings for permanent injunctions (4 above).

Lord Keith of Kinkel:

The Crown's case on all the issues which arise invokes the law about confidentiality. So it is convenient to start by considering the nature and scope of that law. The law has long recognised that an obligation of confidence can arise out of particular relationships. Examples are the relationships of doctor and patient, priest and penitent, solicitor and client, banker and customer. The obligation may be imposed by an express or implied term in a contract but it may also exist independently of any contract on the basis of an independent equitable principle of confidence: see *Saltman Engineering Co Ltd v Campbell Engineering Co Ltd* (1948) [1963] 3 All E.R. 413. It is worthy of some examination whether or not detriment to the confider of confidential information is an essential ingredient of his cause of action in seeking to restrain by injunction a breach of confidence. Presumably that may be so as regards an action for damages in respect of a past breach of confidence. If the confider has suffered no detriment thereby he can hardly be in a position to recover compensatory damages. However, the true view may be that he would be entitled to nominal damages. Most of the cases have arisen in circumstances where there has been a threatened or actual breach of confidence by an employee or ex-employee of the plaintiff, or where information about the plaintiff's business affairs has been given in confidence to someone who has proceeded to exploit it for his own benefit: an example of the latter type of case is *Seager v Copydex Ltd* [1967] 2 All E.R. 415, [1967] 1 WLR 923. In such cases the detriment to the confider is clear. In other cases there may be no financial detriment to the confider, since the breach of confidence involves no more than an invasion of personal privacy. Thus in *Margaret, Duchess of Argyll v Duke of Argyll* [1965] 1 All E.R. 611, [1967] Ch 302 an injunction was granted against the revelation of marital confidences. The right to personal privacy is clearly one which the law should in this field seek to protect. If a profit has been made through the revelation in breach of confidence of details of a person's private life it is appropriate that the profit should be accounted for to that person. Further, as a general rule it is in the public interest that confidences should be respected, and the encouragement of such respect may in itself constitute a sufficient ground for recognising and enforcing the obligation of confidence even where the confider can point to no specific detriment to himself. Information about a person's private and personal affairs may be of a nature which shows him up in a favourable light and would by no means expose him to criticism. The anonymous donor of a very large sum to a very worthy cause has his own reasons for wishing to remain anonymous, which are unlikely to be discreditable. He should surely be in a position to restrain disclosure in breach of confidence of his identity in connection with the donation. So I would think it a sufficient detriment to the confider that information given in confidence is to be disclosed to persons whom he would prefer not to know of it, even though the disclosure would not be harmful to him in any positive way.

[4] (1987) 75 A.L.R. 353.
[5] (1988) 78 A.L.R. 449.

The position of the Crown, as representing the continuing government of the country, may, however, be regarded as being special. In some instances disclosure of confidential information entrusted to a servant of the Crown may result in a financial loss to the public. In other instances such disclosure may tend to harm the public interest by impeding the efficient attainment of proper governmental ends, and the revelation of defence or intelligence secrets certainly falls into that category. The Crown, however, as representing the nation as a whole, has no private life or personal feelings capable of being hurt by the disclosure of confidential information. In so far as the Crown acts to prevent such disclosure or to seek redress for it on confidentiality grounds, it must necessarily, in my opinion, be in a position to show that the disclosure is likely to damage or has damaged the public interest. How far the Crown has to go in order to show this must depend on the circumstances of each case. . . .

There are two important cases in which the special position of a government in relation to the preservation of confidence has been considered. The first of them is *A-G v Jonathan Cape Ltd* [1975] 3 All E.R. 484, [1976] Q.B. 752. That was an action for injunctions to restrain publication of the political diaries of the late Richard Crossman, which contained details of Cabinet discussions held some ten years previously, and also of advice given to ministers by civil servants. Lord Widgery C.J. said ([1975] 3 All E.R. 484 at 495, [1976] Q.B. 752 at 770–771):

> "In these actions we are concerned with the publication of diaries at a time when 11 years have expired since the first recorded events. The Attorney-General must show (a) that such publication would be in breach of confidence, (b) that the public interest requires that the publication be restrained, and (c) that there are no other facets of the public interest contradictory to and more compelling than that relied on. Moreover, the court, when asked to restrain such a publication, must closely examine the extent to which relief is necessary to ensure that restrictions are not imposed beyond the strict requirement of public need".

Lord Widgery C.J. went on to say that, while the expression of individual opinions by Cabinet ministers in the course of Cabinet discussions were matters of confidence, the publication of which could be restrained by the court when clearly necessary in the public interest, there must be a limit in time after which the confidential character of the information would lapse. Having read the whole of volume one of the diaries he did not consider that publication of anything in them, ten years after the event, would inhibit full discussion in the Cabinet at the present time or thereafter, or damage the doctrine of joint Cabinet responsibility. He also dismissed the argument that publication of advice given by senior civil servants would be likely to inhibit the frankness of advice given by such civil servants in the future. So, in the result, Lord Widgery's decision turned on his view that it had not been shown that publication of the diaries would do any harm to the public interest.

The second case is *Commonwealth of Australia v John Fairfax & Sons Ltd* (1980) 32 A.L.R. 485. That was a decision of Mason J. in the High Court of Australia, dealing with an application by the Commonwealth for an interlocutory injunction to restrain publication of a book containing the texts of government documents concerned with its relations with other countries, in particular the government of Indonesia in connection with the "East Timor crisis". The documents appeared to have been leaked by a civil servant. Restraint of publication was claimed on the ground of breach of confidence and also on that of infringement of copyright. Mason J. granted an injunction on the latter ground but not on the former. Having mentioned an argument for the Commonwealth that the government was entitled to protect information which was not public property, even if no public interest is served by maintaining confidentiality, he continued (at 492–493):

"However the plaintiff must show, not only that the information is confidential in quality and that it was imparted so as to import an obligation of confidence, but also that there will be 'an unauthorized use of that information to the detriment of the party communicating it' (*Coco v A N Clark (Engineers) Ltd* ([1969] R.P.C. 41 at 47)). The question then, when the executive government seeks the protection given by Equity, is: What detriment does it need to show? The equitable principle has been fashioned to protect the personal, private and proprietary interests of the citizen, not to protect the very different interests of the executive government. It acts, or is supposed to act, not according to standards of private interest, but in the public interest. This is not to say that Equity will not protect information in the hands of the government, but it is to say that when Equity protects government information it will look at the matter through different spectacles. It may be a sufficient detriment to the citizen that disclosure of information relating to his affairs will expose his actions to public discussion and criticism. But it can scarcely be a relevant detriment to the government that publication of material concerning its actions will merely expose it to public discussion and criticism. It is unacceptable, in our democratic society, that there should be a restraint on the publication of information relating to government when the only vice of that information is that it enables the public to discuss, review and criticize government action. Accordingly, the court will determine the government's claim to confidentiality by reference to the public interest. Unless disclosure is likely to injure the public interest, it will not be protected. The court will not prevent the publication of information which merely throws light on the past workings of government, even if it be not public property, so long as it does not prejudice the community in other respects. Then disclosure will itself serve the public interest in keeping the community informed and in promoting discussion of public affairs. If, however, it appears that disclosure will be inimical to the public interest because national security, relations with foreign countries or the ordinary business of government will be prejudiced, disclosure will be restrained. There will be cases in which the conflicting considerations will be finely balanced, where it is difficult to decide whether the public's itnerest in knowing and in expressing its opinion, outweighs the need to protect confidentiality".

I find myself in broad agreement with this statement by Mason J. In particular I agree that a government is not in a position to win the assistance of the court in restraining the publication of information imparted in confidence by it or its predecessors unless it can show that publication would be harmful to the public interest.

Lord Keith then held (i) that, in view of the world-wide dissemination of Spycatcher, *injunctions against the* Guardian *and the* Observer *designed to prevent them from reporting and commenting on Wright's allegations could not be justified; nor could an injunction to prevent further serialisation in the* Sunday Times.

(ii) That an injunction should be granted against the newspaper in respect of future revelations from secret service members.

(iii) that if proceedings had been against Wright, an injunction against publication in England might have been justified "on the principle that he should not be permitted to take advantage of his own wrong-doing".

(iv) that The Sunday Times *were in breach of confidence in publishing extracts from* Spycatcher *on the day before U.S. publication.*

On the last issue he stated:

This leads on to consideration of the question whether the *Sunday Times* should be held liable to account to the Crown for profits made from past and future serialisation of *Spycatcher*. An account of profits made through breach of confidence is a recognised form of remedy available to a claimant: see *Peter Pan Manufacturing Corp v Corsets Silhouette Ltd* [1963] 3 All E.R. 402, [1964] 1 W.L.R. 96; cf *Reading v A-G* [1951] 1 All E.R. 617, [1951] A.C. 507. In cases where the information disclosed is of a commercial character an account of profits may provide some compensation to the claimant for loss which he has suffered through the disclosure, but damages are the main remedy for such loss. The remedy is, in my opinion, more satisfactorily to be attributed to the principle that no one should be permitted to gain from his own wrongdoing. Its availability may also, in general, serve a useful purpose in lessening the temptation for recipients of confidential information to misuse it for financial gain. In the present case the *Sunday Times* did misuse confidential information and it would be naive to suppose that the prospect of financial gain was not one of the reasons why it did so. I can perceive no good ground why the remedy should not be made available to the Crown in the circumstances of this case, and I would therefore hold the Crown entitled to an account of profits in respect of the publication on 12 July 1987. I would add that in my opinion the *Sunday Times*, in the taking of the account, is not entitled to deduct in computing any gain the sums paid to Mr Wright's publishers as consideration for the licence granted by the latter, since neither Mr Wright nor his publishers were or would in the future be in a position to maintain an action in England for recovery of such payments. Nor would the courts of this country enforce a claim by them to the copyright in a work the publication of which they had brought about contrary to the public interest: cf *Glyn v Weston Feature Film Co* [1916] 1 Ch 261 at 269. Mr Wright is powerless to prevent anyone who chooses to do so from publishing *Spycatcher* in whole or in part in this country, or to obtain any other remedy against them. There remains, of course, the question whether the Crown might successfully maintain a claim that it is in equity the owner of the copyright in the book. Such a claim has not yet been advanced, but might well succeed if it were to be.

In reaching the same conclusions, Lord Goff of Chieveley paid particular attention to one submission on behalf of the A.G.: that, although the effect of Wright's breach of confidence was to disseminate the information widely throughout the world, nevertheless he remained under his obligation of confidence, because he could not destroy it by his own wrongful act. Of this Lord Goff said:

As I have already indicated, it is well established that a duty of confidence can only apply in respect of information which is confidential: see *Saltman Engineering Co Ltd v Campbell Engineering Co Ltd* (1948) [1963] 3 All E.R. 413 at 415 per Lord Greene M.R. From this it should logically follow that, if confidential information which is the subject of a duty of confidence ceases to be confidential, then the duty of confidence should cease to bind the confidant. This was held to be so in *O Mustad & Son v S Allcock & Co Ltd* (1928) [1963] 3 All E.R. 416, [1964] 1 W.L.R. 109. That was however a case in which the confidential information was disclosed by the confider himself; and stress was placed on this point in a later case where the disclosure was not by the confider but by a third party and in which *Mustad's* case was distinguished (see *Cranleigh Precision Engineering Ltd v Bryant* [1964] 3 All E.R. 289, [1965] 1 W.L.R. 1293). It was later held, on the basis of the *Cranleigh Precision Engineering* case, that, if the confidant is not released when the publication is by a third party, then he cannot be released when it is he himself who has published the information (see *Speed Seal*

Products Ltd v Paddington [1986] 1 All E.R. 91, [1985] 1 W.L.R. 1327). I have to say however that, having studied the judgment of Roskill J. in the *Cranleigh Precision Engineering* case, it seems to me that the true basis of the decision was that, in reliance on the well-known judgment of Roxburgh J. in the "springboard" case, *Terrapin Ltd v Builders' Supply Co (Hayes) Ltd* (1959) [1967] R.P.C. 375, the defendant was in breach of confidence in taking advantage of his own confidential relationship with the plaintiff company to discover what a third party had published and in making use, as soon as he left the employment of the plaintiff company, of information regarding the third party's patent which he had acquired in confidence (see [1964] 3 All E.R. 289 at 302, [1965] 1 W.L.R. 1293 at 1319). The reasoning of Roskill J. in this case has itself been the subject of criticism (see e.g. Gurry *Breach of Confidence* (1984) pp 246–247); but in any event it should be regarded as no more than an extension of the springboard doctrine, and I do not consider that it can support any general principle that, if it is a third party who puts the confidential information into the public domain, as opposed to the confider, the confidant will not be released from his duty of confidence. It follows that, so far as concerns publication by the confidant himself, the reasoning in the *Speed Seal* case (founded as it is on the *Cranleigh Precision Engineering* case) cannot, in my mind, be supported. I recognise that a case where the confider himself publishes the information might be distinguished from other cases on the basis that the confider, by publishing the information, may have implicitly released the confidant from his obligation. But that was not how it was put in *Mustad's* case [1963] 3 All E.R. 416 at 418, [1964] 1 W.L.R. 109 at 111, in which Lord Buckmaster stated that, once the disclosure had been made by the confider to the world, "the secret, as a secret, had ceased to exist". For my part, I cannot see how the secret can continue to exist when the publication has been made not by the confider but by a third party.

Even so, it has been held by the judge, and by all members of the Court of Appeal in the present case, that Peter Wright cannot be released from his duty of confidence by his own publication of the confidential information, apparently on the basis that he cannot be allowed to profit from his own wrong. . . .

I have to say, however, that I know of no case (apart from the present) in which the maxim has been invoked in order to hold that a person under an obligation is not released from that obligation by the destruction of the subject matter of the obligation, on the ground that that destruction was the result of his own wrongful act. To take an obvious case, a bailee who by his own wrongful, even deliberately wrongful, act destroys the goods entrusted to him, is obviously relieved of his obligation as bailee, though he is of course liable in damages for his tort. Likewise, a nightwatchman who deliberately sets fire to and destroys the building he is employed to watch; and likewise also, the keeper at a zoo who turns out to be an animal rights campaigner and releases rare birds or animals which escape irretrievably into the countryside. On this approach, it is difficult to see how a confidant who publishes the relevant confidential information to the whole world can be under any further obligation not to disclose the information, simply because it was he who wrongfully destroyed its confidentiality. The information has, after all, already been so fully disclosed that it is in the public domain: how, therefore, can he thereafter be sensibly restrained from disclosing it? Is he not even to be permitted to mention in public what is now common knowledge? For his wrongful act, he may be held liable in damages, or may be required to make restitution; but, to adapt the words of Lord Buckmaster in *Mustad's* case, the confidential information, as confidential information, has ceased to exist, and with it should go, as a matter of principle, the obligation of confidence. In truth, when a person entrusts something to another, whether that thing be a physical thing such as a chattel or some intangible thing such as confidential information, he relies on that other to fulfil his obligation. If he discovers that the other is about to commit a breach, he may be able to impose an added sanction against his doing so by persuading the court to grant an injunction; but if the other simply commits a breach and destroys the thing, then the injured party is left with his remedy in damages or in restitution. The subject matter is gone; the obligation is therefore also gone; all that is left is the remedy or remedies for breach of the obligation. This approach appears to be consistent with the view expressed by the Law Commission in their Report on Breach of Confidence (Law Com no. 110 (1981)), para 4.30 (see also the Law Commission's working paper, Breach of Confidence (Working Paper no. 58 (1974)) paras 100–101). It is right to say, however, that they may have had commercial cases in mind, rather than a case such as the present. It is however also of interest that, in the *Fairfax* case (1980) 32 A.L.R. 485 at 494 Mason J. was not prepared to grant an injunction to restrain further publication of a book by the defendants on the ground of breach of confidence, because the limited publication which had taken place was sufficient to cause the detriment which the plaintiff, the Commonwealth of Australia, apprehended. If, however, the defendants had published the book in breach of confidence, it is difficult to see why, on the approach so far accepted in the present case, the defendants should not have remained under a duty of confidence despite the publication and so liable to be restrained by injunction. . . .

I have naturally been concerned by the fact that so far in this case it appears to have been accepted on all sides that Peter Wright should not be released from his obligation of confidence. I cannot help thinking that this assumption may have been induced, in part at least, by three factors: first, the fact that Peter Wright himself is not a party to the litigation, with the result that no representations have been made on his behalf; second, the wholly unacceptable nature of his conduct; and third, the fact that he appears now to be able, with impunity, to reap vast sums from his disloyalty. Certainly, the prospect of Peter Wright, safe in his Australian haven, reaping further profits form the sale of his book in this country is most unattractive. The purpose of perpetuating Peter Wright's duty of confidence appears to be, in part to deter others, and in part to ensure that a man who has committed so flagrant a breach of duty should not be enabled freely to exploit the formerly confidential information, placed by him in the public domain, with impunity. Yet the real reason why he is able to exploit it is because he has found a safe place to do so. If within the jurisdiction of the English courts, he would be held liable to account for any profits made by him fron his wrongful disclosure, which might properly include profits accruing to him from any subsequent exploitation of the confidential information after its disclosure: and, in cases where damages were regarded as the appropriate remedy, the confidant would be liable to compensate the confider for any damage, present or future, suffered by him by reason of his wrong. So far as I can see, the confider must be content with remedies such as these.

I have considered whether the confidant who, in breach of duty, places confidential information in the public domain, might remain at least under a duty thereafter not to exploit the information, so disclosed, for his own benefit. Suppose that the confidant in question was a man who, unwisely, has remained in this country, and has written a book containing confidential information and has disposed of the rights to publication to an American publishing house, whose publication results in the information in the book entering the public domain. The question might at least arise whether he is free thereafter to dispose of the film rights to the book. To me however, it is doubtful whether the answer to this question lies in artificially prolonging the duty of confidence in information which is no longer confidential. Indeed, there is some ground for saying that the true answer is that the copyright in the book, including the film rights, are held by him on constructive trust for the confider, so that the remedy lies not in breach of confidence, but in restitution or in property, whichever way you care to look at it.

Lord Goff concluded that, even if this view was not correct, he would hold it contrary to the public interest to restrain publication of a book which was freely circulating in the country already.

Lords Brightman and Jauncey of Tullichettle delivered concurring speeches. Lord Griffiths dissented on two points: he found the Guardian *and* Observer *to have been in breach of confidence in their reports; and he would have restrained the* Sunday Times *from further serialisation of* Spycatcher.

2.3 Extent of Obligation

2.3.1 Exployees

2.3.1.1 *Hivac v Park Royal* [1946] 1 All E.R. 350 (C.A.)

The plaintiff company manufactured small thermionic valves for use in hearing aids, being at the end of the war the only company in Britain to do so. Five of its skilled manual workers worked on Sundays for the defendant company, which had been established to make hearing aids with valves that competed with the plaintiff's. The plaintiff was subject to the Essential Work Order and so could not dismiss the five (who by contract were subject to 24 hours notice) without following a complex statutory procedure. It sought interlocutory relief enjoining the defendant from procuring breach by the workers of their employment contracts.

Lord Greene M.R. reviewed the facts and continued:

There is one matter which I think I can get out of the way at once. It is argued on behalf of the plaintiffs that on the evidence what may be called confidential information must have been disclosed or utilised by these five employees for the benefit of the defendant company. The judge took the view that no such case had been made out. I do not in any way differ from that view. It seems to me that, having regard particularly to the evidence of Mr Gill, confidential information has not down to the present, at any rate, been made use of by these five employees, if, indeed, they were in possession of any such information. Of course, when one gets into the area of confidential information the law is fortunately much more certain, but once that particular element is excluded, we are in an area which has not, as I have said, been sufficiently explored.

The argument on behalf of the plaintiffs with regard to confidential information was also to the effect that, even assuming no confidential information has as yet been disclosed, and assuming there is no threat to disclose it or use it for the benefit of the defendants, it will, nevertheless, be inevitable, if those employees continue to work for the defendants, that they will put at the disposal of the defendants any confidential information which, in the course of their work for the plaintiffs, they may obtain. It is said, and said with force, that employees engaged in this particular work are bound to become acquainted with any improvements or any experiments which the plaintiffs may make in the course of their business in relation to these midget valves because they would be given the task of constructing or assembling valves for the purpose of incorporating such improvements, and so forth. That is, I think, a matter which the court cannot ignore. After all, one has to be practical in these matters, and one has to consider what the practical result will be. It may very well be said that to say that people in these circumstances can, so to speak, make a division in their minds between what is confidential and what is not, and be quite careful while they are working for the defendants to keep the confidential information locked up in some secret compartment of their minds theoretically may be all very well, but from the practical point of view has a certain unreality.

Leaving that on one side for the moment, and looking at the question from another angle, it has been said on many occasions that an employee owes a duty of fidelity to his employer. As a general proposition that is indisputable. The practical difficulty in any given case is to find exactly how far that rather vague duty of fidelity extends. *Prima facie* it seems to me on considering the authorities and the arguments that it must be a question on the facts of each particular case. I can very well understand that the obligation of fidelity, which is an implied term of the contract, may extend very much further in the case of one class of employee than it does in others. For instance, when you are dealing, as we are dealing here, with mere manual workers whose job is to work five and a half days for their employer at a specific type of work and stop their work when the hour strikes, the obligation of fidelity may be one the operation of which will have a comparatively limited scope. The law would, I think, be jealous of attempting to impose on a manual worker restrictions the real effect of which would be to prevent him utilising his spare time. He is paid for five and a half days in the week. The rest of the week is his own, and to impose upon a man, in relation to the rest of the week, some kind of obligation which really would unreasonably tie his hands and prevent him adding to his weekly money during that time would, I think, be very undesirable. On the other hand, if you have employees of a different character, you may very well find that the obligation is of a different nature. A manual worker might say: "You pay me for five and a half days work. I do five and a half days work for you. What greater obligation have I taken upon myself? If you want in some way to limit my activities during the other day and a half of the week, you must pay me for it". In many cases that may be a very good answer. In other cases it may not be a good answer because the very nature of the work may be such as to make it quite clear that the duties of the employee to his employer cannot properly be performed if in his spare time the employee engages in certain classes of activity. One example was discussed in argument, that of a solicitor's clerk who on Sundays, it was assumed, went and worked for another firm in the same town. He might find himself embarrassed because the very client for whom he had done work while working for the other firm on the Sunday night might be a client against whom clients of his main employer were conducting litigation, or something of that kind. Obviously in a case of that kind, by working for another firm he is in effect, or may be, disabling himself from performing his duties to his real employer and placing himself in an embarrassing position. I can well understand it being said: "That is a breach of the duty of fidelity to your employer because as a result of what you have done you have disabled yourself from giving to your employer that undivided attention to their business which it is your duty to do". I merely put that forward, not for the purpose of laying down the law or expressing any concluded opinion, but merely as illustrating the danger of laying down any proposition and the necessity of considering each case on its facts.

His Lordship referred in particular to Robb v Green *[1895] 2 Q.B. 315 and* Wessex Dairies v Smith *[1935] 2 K.B. 80 and continued:*

The question here is not a question of getting the customers to leave the business but a question of building up a rival in business to the prejudice of the goodwill of the employer's business.

I am not ashamed to confess that in the course of the argument my mind has fluctuated considerably on this question. As I see it, the court stands in a sense between Scylla and Charybdis, because it would be most unfortunate if anything we said, or any other court said, should place an undue restriction on the right of the workman, particularly a manual workman, to make use of his leisure for his profit. On the other hand, it would be deplorable if it were laid down that a workman could consistently with his duty to his employer, knowingly deliberately and secretly set himself to do in his spare time something which would inflict great harm on his employer's business. I have endeavoured to raise the questions in the way that they appeal to me and, on the best consideration I can give to this matter, I think that the plaintiffs are *prima facie* right in this case.

That being so, what is the right course for this court to pursue? Counsel for the defendants took several points, on the assumption that a *prima facie* case was established, to suggest that it was not a case for an injunction. He said, for instance, that in the absence of the five workpeople in question the action was not properly constituted. There is no doubt that, in a way, it is unfortunate in an action complaining of procuring breach of contract, not to have before the court the contracting party whose breach of the contract, it is said, the defendants have procured, but the circumstances of the present case are peculiar. There is a very good practical reason why these workpeople should not be joined, and I can see no reason why the court should not be able to decide the question satisfactorily and in their absence.

Then counsel said there is no case for an injunction because if the plaintiffs are right the workpeople could be dismissed for serious misconduct. That is a much more difficult thing under the Essential Work Order than would appear from that bald statement, because the plaintiffs have not the last word in the matter. It would be unreasonable to expect them, in the circumstances of the shortage of labour and the difficult procedure they would have to go through, to take any such course. The times are peculiar, and it seems to me that the plaintiffs are entitled to have the position considered in the light of the circumstances as they in fact exist, and not in the light of some circumstances, which might have existed, in more normal times, and would have given them a remedy ready to their hand which would have made it unnecessary for them to invoke the assistance of the court.

Then counsel said, in any case there is no case for an interlocutory order. I do not think myself that any of those arguments ought to be allowed to prevail.

I conclude by saying that this is a case of deliberate and secret action by these employees, deliberate and secret action by the defendants in circumstances where both the employees and the defendants must have known the exact result of what they were doing and must have realised that what they were doing was wrong, even if they did not distinguish in their minds between the question of commercial morality and legal obligation. That being so, and there being in my opinion a *prima facie* case and the balance of convenience and fairness being in favour of an injunction, I think the Judge who took the other view came to the wrong conclusion. I should perhaps have mentioned that he did not think that, once the question of confidential information was excluded, there was sufficient left in the action of the plaintiffs' workpeople to constitute a breach of any implied obligation. It is on that point that I take a different *prima facie* view. The way the matter struck me was that *prima facie*, in the absence of direct authority on the point, he did not feel that he ought to say that the obligation of the servants in this case went as far as it was said it did. I have come to the opposite conclusion without expressing any final judgment on the matter, because we have not all the facts before us. I think that *prima facie* on the facts of this case, so far as they at present appear, the conclusion ought to be the opposite one. This is the extent of our difference. In my opinion, the injunction asked for should be granted.

Morton L.J. delivered a concurring judgment and Bucknill L.J. agreed.

2.3.1.2   *Stevenson Jordan & Harrison v MacDonald & Evans*
[1951] 68 R.P.C. 190 (Lloyd-Jacob J.)

The case concerned a firm of "management engineers" for whom a Mr Hemming worked as "chief of staff" to the managing director. Hemming prepared a book to be published under contract by the defendant. The extract given here is from the decision of Lloyd-

Jacob J. at first instance. Unlike the C.A., Lloyd-Jacob J. found that the proposed publication involved a breach of the confidence which Hemming owed to his employers, the plaintiffs. He continued:

The Defendants contend that at the time they agreed to publish this work they had no knowledge or notice of the Plaintiff's claims, nor were they aware that the work contained any secret or confidential information, and they claim that in consequence they cannot now be restrained. It is to be noted that the absence of any right to publish on Mr Hemming's part must safeguard the Defendants from any claim for breach of contract by his estate. It would appear, therefore, to be the position that the Defendants' insistence on disclosing the contents of this book to the world, and thereby causing irreparable damage to the business of the Plaintiffs, is due in part to unwillingness to bear the cost already incurred in preparing for publication (although the publishing agreement (D.10) specifically safeguards them against loss in this connection) and possibly in part to a public-spirited insistence upon a supposedly legal right. It is difficult to reconcile this attitude with the evidence of Mr J.D. MacDonald, but as the claim is made and persisted in it is necessary to examine the position so created.

Counsel for the Plaintiffs expressly disclaimed any suggestion that at the date of the execution of D.10 the Defendants were (or should have been) aware that Mr Hemming was acting in breach of his duty to the Plaintiffs. Does this circumstance frank their avowed intention to consummate Mr Hemming's wrongdoing? The original and independent jurisdiction of this court to prevent, by the grant of an injunction, any person availing himself of a title which arises out of a violation of a right or a breach of confidence, is so well established as a cardinal principle that only a binding authority to the contrary should prevent its application by this Court. None of the cases cited by Counsel for the Defendants appears to fetter in any way the freedom of this court to protect the Plaintiffs from the disclosure of their confidential information; and Lord Cottenham's judgment in *Prince Albert v Strange* (1849) 1 Mac & G 25, expressly supports the principle. The wrong to be restrained is not the entry into the contract to publish, but the act of publishing, and an innocent mind at the time of the former cannot overcome the consequences of full knowledge at or before the time of the latter.

The judgment of Kekewich J., in *Philip v Pennell* [1907] 2 Ch 577, which was strongly urged in argument by Counsel for the Defendants, does not, in my view, support his contention. The learned Judge there expressly excluded from the ambit of his judgment any consideration of letters obtained improperly.

Turner V.-C., in *Morison v Moat* (1851) 9 Hare 241, 263 expressed the view that a purchaser for value of a secret without notice of any obligation affecting it might be in a different position from a volunteer. Such a view is not inconsistent with the power of the Court to prevent disclosure by injunction if proceedings are commenced in time.

2.3.1.3 *Printers & Finishers v Holloway* [1965] 1 W.L.R. 1 (Cross J.)

Holloway, manager of the plaintiff company's flock printing plant, showed a director and employee of Vita-Tex around the plant. The plant had been set up under a confidential know-how agreement and Holloway was under instructions to keep the process involved secret. He removed some secret documents and copied others; he also ordered a machine part (a cyclone) for Vita-Tex from the know-how licensors. He then left his employ and the plaintiff began proceedings against him, two Vita-Tex directors and Vita-Tex itself for various injunctions relating to breach of confidence.

In the course of the litigation, the defendants obtained an order for a expert (nominated by the President of the Chartered Institute of Patent Agents) to inspect the plaintiff's process on their behalf in order to ascertain what parts were alleged to be secret. Of this order Cross J. stated:

The order (for inspection by the defendants' expert) is not a usual one and it does not prescribe the procedure to be followed. In fact, however, an order of this sort ought, in my judgment, to be regarded as a substitute for particulars. Consequently it is for the party whom the Court has relieved of the necessity of giving particulars on the terms of allowing inspection by an expert to take the initiative in explaining in detail to the expert precisely what elements in his process he claims to be secret and why he makes that claim. Insofar as he does not do so he ought not to be allowed to give evidence at the trial in support of the claim.

Cross J. was prepared to grant an injunction respecting the documentary material. He continued:

The second part of the injunction sought against Holloway is directed to the use or disclosure by him of information in his head, and the question whether or not it should be granted involves a consideration of the principles on which the court should act in a case of this kind. The wording of the proposed injunction is based on the description of each step in their process given by the plaintiffs in general terms in their particulars dated November 5, 1959, and in detail in the evidence of their managing director given "in camera" at the trial, with the omission of a few matters in regard to which the evidence at the trial showed clearly that the managing director was wrong in thinking that what the plaintiffs did was peculiar to them. The mere fact that the confidential information is not embodied in a document but is carried away by the employee in his head is not, of course, of itself a reason against the granting of an injunction to prevent its use or disclosure by him. If the information in question can fairly be regarded as a separate part of the employee's stock of knowledge which a man of ordinary honesty and intelligence would recognise to be the property of his old employer and not his own to do as he likes with, then the court, if it thinks that there is a danger of the information being used or disclosed by the ex-employee to the detriment of the old employer, will do what it can to prevent that result by granting an injunction. Thus an ex-employee will be restrained from using or disclosing a chemical formula or a list of customers which he has committed to memory. Again, in *Reid & Sigrist Ltd v Moss & Mechanism Ltd* (1932) 49 R.P.C. 461 the defendant was restrained from disclosing any methods of construction or features of design of turn indicators for use in aeroplanes evolved by the plaintiffs and made known to the defendant or evolved by him whilst in their employment. The salient point there was that in the course of the development of the instrument by the plaintiffs the defendant took part in confidential discussions with an outside expert called in to advise the plaintiffs as to the best method of dealing with certain problems which had arisen. It appears, indeed, that after the discussions and while he was still in the plaintiffs' employ the defendant made and later took away with him drawings embracing the various matters discussed. But even if he had not done so and relied simply on his memory of the confidential discussions I think that an injunction would still have been granted.

What is asked for here, however goes far beyond any relief granted in any case which was cited to me. The plaintiffs are saying, in effect: "True it is that other flock printers use print and machinery similar to ours and that as we did not trouble to exact any covenant from him not to do so Holloway was entitled to go and work for a trade competitor who uses such plant and machinery. Nevertheless we are entitled to prevent him from using for the benefit of his new employers his recollection of any features of our plant, machinery or process which are in fact peculiar to us".

If this is right then, as it seems to me, an ex-employee is placed in an impossible position. One naturally approaches the problem in this case with some bias in favour of the plaintiffs, because Holloway has shown himself unworthy of their trust; but to test their argument fairly one must take the case of an employee who has been guilty of no breach of contract. Suppose such a man to be told by his new employers that at this or that stage in the process they encounter this or that difficulty. He may say to himself: "Well, I remember that on the corresponding piece of machinery in the other factory such-and-such a part was set at a different angle or shaped in a different way"; or again, "When that happened we used to do this and it seemed to work", "this" being perhaps something which he had been taught when he first went to the other factory or possibly an expedient which he had found out for himself by trial and error during his previous employment.

Recalling matters of this sort is, to my mind, quite unlike memorising a formula or list of customers or what was said (obviously in confidence) at a particular meeting. The employee might well not realise that the feature or expedient in question was in fact peculiar to his late employer's process and factory; but even if he did such knowledge is not readily separable from his general knowledge of the flock printing process and his acquired skill in manipulating a flock printing plant, and I do not think that any man of average intelligence and honesty would think that there was anything improper in his putting his memory of particular features of his late employer's plant at the disposal of his new employer. The law will defeat its own object if it seeks to enforce in this field standards which would be rejected by the ordinary man. After all, this involves no hardship on the employer. Although this law will not enforce a covenant directed against competition by an ex-employee it will enforce a covenant reasonably necessary to protect trade secrets (see the recent case of *Commercial Plastics Ltd v Vincent* ([1964] 3 All E.R. 546), in which the plaintiff only failed because the covenant was too widely drawn as regards area). If the managing director is right in thinking that there are features in the plaintiffs' process which can fairly be regarded as trade secrets and which their employees will inevitably carry away with them in their heads, then the proper way for the plaintiffs to protect themselves would be by exacting covenants from their employees restricting their field of activity after they have left their employment, not by asking the court to extend the general equitable doctrine to prevent breaking confidence beyond all reasonable bounds.

Accordingly, Cross J. refused the injunction sought against Holloway and equivalent injunctions against the other defendants. However, regarding the visit of Vita-Tex's electrician, James, to the plaintiff's premises he said:

But Holloway showed him the inside of the electrical testing room because he thought that James, as Vita-Tex's electrician, would be interested in seeing how the plaintiffs coped with certain electrical problems incidental to their process, and I think that James may well have gleaned much more information from his visit than he would admit. Vita-Tex was no doubt innocent in the matter but *Prince Albert v Strange* (above, 2.1.1) shows that an injunction may be granted against someone who has acquired – or may acquire – information to which he was not entitled without notice of any breach of duty on the part of the man through whom he obtained it.

I am therefore prepared to grant an injunction restraining Vita-Tex from making any use of any information relating to the electrostatic machines or electrodes of the plaintiffs obtained by James on the occasion of his visit or visits to the plaintiffs' factory particularised in paragraph (8) of the statement of claim.

Though it is a very small matter I am also prepared to grant an injunction restraining Vita-Tex from making any use, for the purpose of flock printing, of the cyclone which Holloway improperly caused to be copied for them from the plaintiffs' cyclone.

2.3.1.4   *Faccenda Chicken v Fowler* [1986] 1 All E.R. 617 (C.A.)

The plaintiff company sold fresh chickens from refrigerated vans, which travelled around set routes visiting customers. Fowler was one of its van salesmen and he accordingly received information concerning customers, routes, goods sold and prices. He left the plaintiff after having been unsuccessfully prosecuted for stealing, and set up a competitive business using the same routes and visiting the same types of customer. In this he was joined by eight other former employees of the plaintiff. None of them were subject to any express covenant of restraint. The plaintiff sued them for damages of breach of implied contractual duty of fidelity and for conspiracy to injure its business. Goulding J. rejected the claims, holding that any information taken was not capable of protection in the absence of express covenants. In the course of doing so, he classified the information which an employee might receive during employment into three categories:

First there is information which, because of its trivial character or its easy accessibility from public sources of information, cannot be regarded by reasonable persons or by the law as confidential at all. The servant is at liberty to impart it during his service or afterwards to anyone he pleases, even his master's competitor. An example might be a published patent specification well known to people in the industry concerned ... Second, there is information which the servant must treat as confidential, either because he is expressly told it is confidential, or because from its character it obviously is so, but which once learned necessarily remains in the servant's head and becomes part of his own skill and knowledge applied in the course of his master's business. So long as the employment continues, he cannot otherwise use or disclose such information without infidelity and therefore breach of contract. But when he is no longer in the same service, the law allows him to use his full skill and knowledge for his own benefit in competition with his former master; and ... there seems to be no established distinction between the use of such information where its possessor trades as a principal, and where he enters the employment of a new master, even though the latter case involves disclosure and not mere personal use of the information. If an employer wants to protect information of this kind, he can do so by an express stipulation restraining the servant from competing with him (within reasonable limits of time and space after the termination of his employment). ...

Third, however, there are, to my mind, specific trade secrets so confidential that, even though they may necessarily have been learned by heart and even though the servant may have left the service, they cannot lawfully be used for anyone's benefit but the master's. An example is the secret process which was the subject matter of *Amber Size and Chemical Co Ltd v Menzel* [1913] 2 Ch 239.

On appeal, Neill L.J. (for the C.A.) defined the relevant law on breach of confidence by an employee as follows:

(1) Where the parties are, or have been, linked by a contract of employment, the obligations of the employee are to be determined by the contract between him and his employer: cf *Vokes Ltd v Heather* (1945) 62 RPC 135 at 141.

(2) In the absence of any express term, the obligations of the employee in respect of the use and disclosure of information are the subject of implied terms.

(3) While the employee remains in the employment of the employer the obligations are included in the implied term which imposes a duty of good faith or fidelity on the employee. For the purpose of the present appeal it is not necessary to consider the precise limits of this implied term, but it may be noted: (a) that the extent of the duty of good faith will vary according to the nature of the contract (see *Vokes Ltd v Heather*); (b) that the duty of good faith will be broken if an employee makes or copies a list of the customers of the employer for use after his employment ends or deliberately memorises such a list, even though, except in special circumstances, there is no general restriction on an ex-employee canvassing or doing business with customers of his former employer (see *Robb v Green* [1895] 2 Q.B. 315, [1895–9] All E.R. Rep 1053 and *Wessex Dairies Ltd v Smith* [1935] 2 K.B. 80, [1935] All E.R. Rep 75).

(4) The implied term which imposes an obligation on the employee as to his conduct after the determination of the employment is more restricted in its scope than that which imposes a general duty of good faith. It is clear that the obligation not to use or disclose information may cover secret processes of manufacture such as chemical formulae (see *Amber Size and Chemical Co Ltd v Menzel* [1913] 2 Ch 239), or designs or special methods of construction (see *Reid Sigrist Ltd v Moss Mechanism Ltd* (1932) 49 R.P.C. 461), and other information which is of a sufficiently high degree of confidentiality as to amount to a trade secret.

The obligation does not extend, however, to cover all information which is given to or acquired by the employee while in his employment, and in particular may not cover information which is only "confidential" in the sense that an unauthorised disclosure of such information to a third party while the employment subsisted would be a clear breach of the duty of good faith.

This distinction is clearly set out in the judgment of Cross J. in *Printers and Finishers Ltd v Holloway* [1964] 3 All E.R. 731, [1965] 1 W.L.R. 1, where he had to consider whether an ex-employee should be restrained by injunction from making use of his recollection of the contents of certain written printing instructions which had been made available to him when he was working in his former employers' flock printing factory. In his judgment, delivered on 29 April 1964 (not reported on this point in the Weekly Law Reports), Cross J. said ([1964] 3 All E.R. 731 at 738n):

> "In this connexion one must bear in mind that not all information which is given to a servant in confidence and which it would be a breach of his duty for him to disclose to another person during his employment is a trade secret which he can be prevented from using for his own advantage after the employment is over, even though he has entered into no express covenant without regard to the matter in hand. For example, the printing instructions were handed to [the first defendant] to be used by him during his employment exclusively for the plaintiffs' benefit. It would have been a breach of duty on his part to divulge any of the contents to a stranger while he was employed, but many of these instructions are not really 'trade secrets' at all. [The first defendant] was not, indeed, entitled to take a copy of the instructions away with him; but insofar as the instructions cannot be called 'trade secrets' and he carried them in his head, he is entitled to use them for his own benefit or the benefit of any future employer".

The same distinction is to be found in *E Worsley & Co Ltd v Cooper* [1939] 1 All E.R. 290, where it was held that the defendant was entitled, after he had ceased to be employed, to make use of his knowledge of the source of the paper supplied to his previous employer. In our view it is quite plain that this knowledge was nevertheless "confidential" in the sense that it would have been a breach of the duty of good faith for the employee, while the employment subsisted, to have used it for his own purposes or to have disclosed it to a competitor of his employer.

(5) In order to determine whether any particular item of information falls within the implied term so as to prevent its use or disclosure by an employee after his employment has ceased, it is necessary to consider all the circumstances of the case. We are satisfied that the following matters are among those to which attention must be paid. (a) The nature of the employment. Thus employment in a capacity where "confidential" material is habitually handled may impose a high obligation of confidentiality because the employee can be expected to realise its sensitive nature to a greater extent than if he were employed in a capacity where such material reaches him only occasionally or incidentally. (b) The nature of the information itself. In our judgment the information will only be protected if it can properly be classed as a trade secret or as material which, while not properly to be described as a trade secret, is in all the circumstances of such a highly confidential nature as to require the same protection as a trade secret *eo nomine*. The restrictive covenant cases demonstrate that a covenant will not be upheld on the basis of the status of the information which might be disclosed by the former employee if he is not restrained unless it can be regarded as a trade secret or the equivalent of a trade secret: see for example *Herbert Morris Ltd v Saxelby* [1916] 1 A.C. 688 at 710, [1916–17] All E.R. Rep 305 at 317 *per* Lord Parker and *Littlewoods Organisation Ltd v Harris* [1978] 1 All E.R. 1026 at 1037, [1977] 1 W.L.R. 1472 at 1484 *per* Megaw L.J.

We must therefore express our respectful disagreement with the passage in Goulding J.'s judgment where he suggested that an employer can protect the use of information in his second category, even though it does not include either a trade secret or its equivalent by means of a restrictive covenant (see [1985] 1 All E.R. 724 at 731). As Lord Parker made clear in *Herbert Morris Ltd v Saxelby* [1916] 1 A.C. 688 at 709, [1916–17] All E.R. Rep 305 at 317, in a passage to which counsel for Faccenda Chicken Ltd drew our attention, a restrictive covenant will not be enforced unless the protection sought is reasonably necessary to protect a trade secret or to prevent some personal influence over customers being abused in order to entice them away.

In our view the circumstances in which a restrictive covenant would be appropriate and could be successfully invoked emerge very clearly from the words used by Cross J. in *Printers and Finishers Ltd v Holloway* [1964] 3 All E.R. 731 at 736, [1965] 1 W.L.R. 1 at 6 (in a passage quoted later in his judgment by Goulding J. (see [1985] 1 All E.R. 724 at 732–733):

> "If [the managing director] is right in thinking that there are features in his process which can fairly be regarded as trade secrets and which his employees will inevitably carry away with them in their heads, then the proper way for the plaintiffs to protect themselves would be by exacting covenants from their employees restricting their field of activity after they have left their employment, not by asking the court to extend the general equitable doctrine to prevent breaking confidence beyond all reasonable bounds".

It is clearly impossible to provide a list of matters which will qualify as trade secrets or their equivalent. Secret processes of manufacture provide obvious examples, but innumerable other pieces of information are capable of being trade secrets, though the secrecy of some information may be only short-lived. In addition, the fact that the circulation of certain information is restricted to a limited number of individuals may throw light on the status of the information and its degree of confidentiality. (c) Whether the employer impressed on the employee the confidentiality of the information. Thus, though an employer cannot prevent the use or disclosure merely by telling the employee that certain information is confidential, the attitude of the employer towards the information provides evidence which may assist in determining whether or not the information can properly be regarded as a trade secret. It is to be observed that in *E Worsley & Co Ltd v Cooper* [1939] 1 All E.R. 290 at 307 Morton J. attached significance to the fact that no warning had been given to the defendant that "the source from which the paper came was to be treated as confidential". (d) Whether the relevant information can be easily isolated from other information which the employee is free to use or disclose. In *Printers and Finishers Ltd v Holloway* [1964] 3 All E.R. 731 at 736, [1965] 1 W.L.R. 1 at 6 Cross J. considered the protection which might be afforded to information which had been memorised by an ex-employee. He put on one side the memorising of a formula or a list of customers or what had been said (obviously in confidence) at a particular meeting, and continued:

> "The employee might well not realise that the feature or expedient in question was in fact peculiar to his late employer's process and factory; but even if he did such knowledge is not readily separable from his general knowledge of the flock printing process and his acquired skill in manipulating a flock printing plant, and I do not think that any man of average intelligence and honesty would think that there was anything improper in his putting his memory of particular features of his late employer's plant at the disposal of his new employer".

For our part we would not regard the separability of the information in question as being conclusive, but the fact that the alleged "confidential" information is part of a package and that the remainder of the package is not confidential is likely to throw light on whether the information in question is really a trade secret.

Neill L.J. proceeded to hold that the information at issue in the case was not capable of protection in confidence once the employees had left employment.

In Balston v Headline Filters, *[1987] F.S.R. 330, a case primarily concerned with an express covenant, Scott J. made the following observations upon point 5(b) in Neill L.J.'s judgment.*

Both counsel before me have expressed some reservations about that passage in so far as it suggests that confidential information cannot be protected by a suitably worded restrictive covenant binding on an ex-employee unless the information can be regarded as a trade secret in the third of the categories described by Goulding J. I am bound to say I share these reservations. I do not however think the Court of Appeal can have intended to exclude all information in Goulding J.'s second category from possible protection by a restrictive covenant.

After noting Neill L.J.'s references to Cross J.'s judgment in Printers & Finishers v Holloway, *Scott J. continued:*

Trade secrets falling in Goulding J.'s third category would, consequent upon the judgment of the Court of Appeal, be protected under an implied term of the contract. Cross J. in the *Holloway* case and Neill L.J. in the passage I have last cited, clearly had in mind an express restrictive covenant. An express restrictive convenant would not be needed to protect third category trade secrets; the implied term would do that. Neill L.J. must, therefore, in my view, have been contemplating the protection by an express restrictive covenant of confidential information in respect of which an obligation against use or disclosure after the determination of the employment could not be implied. Moreover, the criteria that determine whether or not an express covenant in a contract of employment restricting the use or disclosure of particular information after the determination of the employment is enforceable are very different from the criteria that determine whether or not an obligation restricting the use or disclosure of that information can be implied into the contract. The implied obligation will always, I think, be unlimited in time and probably in area as well. It is difficult to construct a case in which an obligation could be implied that restrained disclosure for, say, one year only or restrained use in, say, the Home Counties. If the information sought to be protected is not fit for protection, unlimited by time or area, it is very difficult to see how protection can be supplied by an implied term. On the other hand, an express covenant against use or disclosure is very likely to be limited both as to time and as to area. In short, express restricted covenant and implied term raise to my mind quite different considerations and I decline to read the *Faccenda* judgment as holding that confidential information that could not be protected by an implied term *ipso facto* could not be protected by a suitably limited express covenant.

2.3.1.5 *Triplex Safety Glass v Scorah* [1938] 55 R.P.C. 21 (Farwell J.)

The plaintiff glass manufacturer employed the defendant chemist under a written agreement which contained an undertaking to keep secret all records, knowledge or information of value in the manufacture of safety glass; an acknowledgement that all knowledge and information gleaned or discovered was to be the property of the plaintiffs; an obligation to communicate to the company any new application of such knowledge relating to safety glass that the defendant might conceive; an obligation to assign to the plaintiff any patent taken out by the defendant; and an undertaking, within one year, of leaving the plaintiff's employ, not to act as a chemist in the manufacture of safety glass.

During the course of his employment the defendant discovered a method of producing a particular acid which he communicated to the plaintiff together with various recommendations and suggestions. The plaintiff ignored these and did not pursue the invention.

The defendant subsequently left the plaintiff's employ and set up business on his own account manufacturing laboratory glass. The defendant carried out further experiments with the acid and found it to be useful for his own glass manufacturing. He applied for and was granted a patent. The plaintiff sought inter alia to compel the defendant to assign the patent to it in accordance with the earlier contract of employment.

Farwell J. held the express covenants of the contract to be in unreasonable restraint of trade and therefore unenforceable. However he continued:

That leaves me to deal with the question how far there may be an obligation on the Defendant to do that which the Plaintiffs asked him to do, apart from express contract altogether. With regard to that, the first ground on which the Defendant seeks to avoid that conclusion is by saying that, where there is an express contract containing terms which are not enforceable for any reason, the Court will not imply terms, because the Court will assume that all the terms were in the written document and that, therefore, there is no room for implication as to other terms and that, since this contract is not enforceable, there cannot be any implied term in the contract arising from the employment under which the Defendant is under any obligation to do that which he is asked to do here.

No doubt to some extent the contention that an express contract excludes any implication is true, but I do not think it can be taken to the length to which Mr Willes has invited me to go. As I suggested in argument, it cannot be that, because a servant covenants in his contract of service to behave properly and honestly towards his employer and that contract of service as a whole is too wide to be enforceable, he is thereby entitled to be as dishonest and to act as unfairly as he pleased towards his employer. That obviously cannot be so and that contention does not afford a good answer to the Plaintiff's claim.

In a case of this kind, in my judgment it is a term of the employment apart altogether from any express covenant, that any invention or discovery made in the course of the employment of the employee, in doing that which the employee was engaged and instructed to do during the time of his employment, during working hours and using the materials of his employers, is the property of the employers and not of the employee, and that, having made such a discovery or invention, the employee becomes a trustee for the employer of it, and he is, therefore, as a trustee, bound to give the benefit of it to his employer.

Then it is said: even if that be so, this employee was permitted, having communicated this discovery to his employers, to leave the employment of the Company at a time when the Company had made no kind of use of this invention or discovery or, rather, had made no attempt to patent or protect it in any way; that he was allowed to remain out of the employment of the Company on his own account for some two years and that, when he did patent it for his own purposes, it would be inequitable for the Company to be allowed to intervene and say: Now we want the benefit of this discovery; kindly assign your Patent to us.

That argument overlooks this: that it is well settled that, once a person is put into the position of a trustee, he cannot avoid the obligations attached thereto unless the beneficiaries release him either expressly or impliedly. It might be that in certain cases the Court might be able to imply a release from some special circumstances, but, in my judgment, the mere fact that nothing was done in this matter for some period is wholly insufficient to suggest that there was any such release in this case.

Under those circumstances, in my judgment, by reason of the fact that the Defendant made this discovery or invention while in the employ of the Company, during the Company's working hours, and in pursuance of the orders of the Company's servants, he became a trustee of it for the Company and he has not ceased and cannot have ceased to be a trustee. If that be so, the result must follow that, when the beneficiary calls upon him to assign to the beneficiary the property of which he is a trustee, he is bound to do so subject only to this: the trustee is entitled to be indemnified against the costs to which he has been put in connection with the property of the beneficiary. A trustee is not bound to spend money on the property of another and he is entitled to be protected against any expense which he has properly incurred in protecting that property; but, subject to that, the beneficiary is entitled to call upon the trustee to transfer the property to him. In this case it seems to me that, on that ground, the Plaintiffs are right in this action; that the Company is entitled now to call upon the Defendant to assign to them the Letters Patent in question and I will make a declaration to that effect and an Order upon the Defendant to assign to them the Letters Patent in question.

2.3.2   Indirect Recipients

2.3.2.1   *Morison v Moat* (1851) 9 Hare 492 (Turner V.-C.)

Morison senior and Moat senior entered a partnership to exploit Morison senior's "invention" (unpatented), which was sold as "Morison's Universal Medicine". Morison senior gave the recipe of the medicine to Moat senior under a bond not to reveal it to any other person. Shortly before Moat senior's death he appointed his son, the defendant, to succeed him in the partnership, as he had power to do. Morison senior and his sons were led to believe that Moat had not told the secret recipe to the defendant, but he had. The partnership eventually terminated and Moat junior began to manufacture in accordance with the recipe on his own account. The Morisons succeeded in obtaining an injunction to restrain him (though they failed to have him enjoined from using the name "Morison's Universal Medicine").

Turner V.-C.:

It was much pressed in argument, on the part of the Defendant, that the effect of granting an injunction in such a case as the present would be to give the Plaintiffs a better right than that of a patentee; and the case of *Canham v Jones* (2 V & B 218) was cited on the Defendant's behalf; but what we have to deal with here is, not the right of the Plaintiffs against the world, but their right against the Defendant. It may well be that the Plaintiffs have no title against the world in general, and may yet have a good title against this Defendant; and the case of *Canham v Jones* does not appear to me to touch the question.

The Defendant admits that the secret was communicated to him by Thomas Moat. His allegation that he acquired a knowledge of it by acting as partner in the concern is disproved; and it is shewn that, if he did acquire such knowledge, he did so surreptitiously. The question is whether there was an equity against him; and I am of the opinion that there was. It was clearly a breach of faith and of contract on the part of Thomas Moat to communicate the secret. The Defendant derives under that breach of faith and of contract, and I think he can gain no title by it. In *Green v Folgham* (1 Sim. & St. 398), upon a trust admitted, an account was decreed against the party to whom the secret had been divulged; and it cannot, I think, make any difference whether the trust is admitted or proved; and the cases of *Tipping v Clarke* (2 Hare 393) and *Prince Albert v Strange* (above, 2.1.1) show that the equity prevails against parties deriving under the breach of contract or duty.

It might indeed be different if the Defendant was a purchaser for value of the secret without notice of any obligation affecting it; and the defendant's case was attempted to be put upon this ground. It was said that, as appointee, he came in as purchaser under the deed of the 23rd of June 1830, and that he had no notice of the bond; but I do not think that this view of the case can avail him, for, in whatever character he may stand as appointee, he has no consequential right in the secret. So far as the secret is concerned he is a mere volunteer deriving under a breach of trust or of contract.

2.3.2.2   *Wheatley v Bell* [1984] F.S.R. 16 (Helsham J., S.C. N.S.W.)

The plaintiffs developed a "Teleguide" system of information concerning local businesses whose commercial value lay in its concentration upon a suburban area of appropriate size. They exploited their idea by dividing a city into such areas and then selling the "exclusive" franchise for each area to a franchisee, who would be supplied with information about how to attract business subscribers and market the operation gener-

ally. They tested the idea in Perth, Western Australia, where the first defendant learnt about the scheme by attending a session for intending franchisees. He did not take up any franchise but instead took the scheme himself to Sydney, New South Wales, where he and an associate began to market it to franchisees in advance of the plaintiffs' launch of their scheme there.

In proceedings for interlocutory injunctions against the defendants' activities, it was held by Helsham J. that these were prima facie *in breach of confidence and should therefore be restrained until trial. The question arose whether injunctions could also be granted against franchisees who had unwittingly purchased the scheme without any knowledge of the plaintiff's rights.*

Helsham J.:

There is a real question as to whether the injunction should go against the innocent defendants. One of them has not appeared, that is, Mr Smith, the fourth defendant, and no problem arises here because he has not established that he is innocent of any knowledge of the circumstances of the acquisition of the idea by the first defendant. Other defendants, in effect, claim that they are persons who should be likened to *bona fide* purchasers for value without notice. It is said that persons in that position are, in this field of confidentiality, free to make use of information which has come to them innocently; that they are in no way tainted with the breach of trust or *quasi* breach of trust that affects the person from whom they obtained the information, and that, therefore, there is no equity in the plaintiffs to obtain any relief of any sort against the innocent recipients of information, albeit that it comes through the hands of a person who is guilty of imparting it in breach of the duty of confidentiality that that imparter owes to the giver of the information.

I am satisfied that the analogy which has been drawn in some of the American cases and by some of the text writers, of the situation of the innocent defendants to a *bona fide* purchaser for value without notice, is not the correct way of approaching the question of whether the injunction should go in the present circumstances or not. The defence of *bona fide* purchaser for value is an equitable defence directed towards the resolution of priorities in relation to property rights. It is an attempt to sort out amongst the claimants interested in property the order in which their various interests should prevail. But I believe that there are not property rights associated with the type of equity involved here; it is equity to restrain a person from acting in breach of confidence which is owed to another, arising from all the circumstances, and I believe that this is the way in which the authorities, to which I should pay a great regard, have treated the matter. Thus the learned author of *Equity and the Law of Trusts*, Professor Pettit, in the 3rd ed. [1974] deals directly with this situation. I have been referred by senior counsel for the plaintiffs to a passage appearing in that edition at page 422, which reads:

> "In any case it is clear that an injunction can be obtained not only against the original guilty party, but against any third party who knowingly obtained the confidential information in breach of confidence or in any other fraudulent manner. Indeed, even if a man obtains the confidential information innocently, once he gets to know that it was originally given in confidence, he can be restrained from breaking that confidence".

At least two cases are referred to as authority for that proposition. One is the case of *Fraser v Evans* [1969] 1 Q.B. 349. Lord Denning M.R. said this (at page 361):

> "The jurisdiction is based not so much on property or on contract as on duty to be of good faith. No person is permitted to divulge to the world information which

he has received in confidence, unless he has just cause or excuse for doing so. Even if he comes by it innocently, nevertheless once he gets to know that it was originally given in confidence, he can be restrained from breaking that confidence".

A similar approach was taken by Goff J. in *Butler v Board of Trade* [1971] Ch. 680 at 690 where his Lordship refers to just cause and excuse for not being responsible for divulging confidential information. It may well be, as was suggested, again by learned counsel for the plaintiffs, that he is referring to a case where the confidential information has lost its aspect or character of confidence and has passed into the domain of public knowledge. There is no suggestion that this is the case here.

In those circumstances and in spite of the very interesting and well researched argument of counsel for the fifth defendant, I am of the view that it is proper for injunctions to be granted against all defendants and I propose to grant them in a form that can be settled in due course. I believe that the undertaking for damages, which I am instructed the plaintiffs are prepared to give, will provide adequate protection for the innocent defendants in the event that my approach to this problem turns out to be incorrect. For those reasons I propose to grant injunctions against all of the defendants.

2.3.3   No Relationship of Confidence

2.3.3.1   *Franklin v Giddings* [1978] Qd. R.72 (Dunn J., S.C. Queensland)

The plaintiffs bred a new form of nectarine, the Franklin Early White, and were the sole marketers of it. The male defendant stole budwood cuttings from the plaintiff's orchard and, by grafting them onto his own root stocks, developed an orchard of Franklin Early Whites in direct competition with the plaintiffs. The female defendant, his wife, did not learn how he had obtained the budwood until later. The plaintiffs claimed equitable relief, rather than damages for conversion of the budwood.

Dunn J. referred to textbooks on breach of confidence, and said:

What has been protected by equity has been "confidential information," that is defined by those authors as "facts, schemes or theories which the law regards as of sufficient value or importance to afford protection against use of them by the defendant otherwise than in accordance with the plaintiff's wishes".

Usually, the relevance of the plaintiff's wishes is that the protected "information" has been voluntarily imparted in confidence, often being imparted by an employer to a trusted employee. But it is clear that equity recognised a personal obligation to respect trust and confidence which did not arise consequently upon a contractual relationship. See Prince Albert v Strange 2 DeG & Sm 651 (64 E.R. 293), and 1 Mac and G 25 (41 E.R. 1171).

Dunn J. then referred to Caird v Sime, *(1887) 12 A.C. 326,* Saltman Engineering v Campbell *(above, 2.1.2) and* Argyll v Argyll *[1967] Ch 302. He continued:*

If I have laboured the point that the jurisdiction which I am asked to exercise exists independently of contract, it is because learned counsel for the defendants placed a good deal of reliance upon the circumstances that the male defendant was never employed by the plaintiffs at Pozieres, notwithstanding an allegation in the pleadings that that had been the case.

He also argued that the budwood twigs were not "information confidentially imparted" and that therefore no obligation of confidence deserving of protection had arisen, challenging the proposition that "it would be extraordinary if a defendant, who acquired by eavesdropping or other improper covert means the secrets of the plaintiff because he would not have been able to get them by consensual arrangement, could defend proceedings by the plaintiff on the ground that no obligation of confidence could arise without communication of the information by the plaintiff." (Meagher, Gummow and Lehane, *Equity – Doctrines and Remedies* at page 719.)

I find myself quite unable to accept that a thief who steals a trade secret, knowing it to be a trade secret, with the intention of using it in commercial competition with its owner, to the detriment of the latter, and so uses it, is less unconscionable than a traitorous servant. The thief is unconscionable because he plans to use and does use his own wrong conduct to better his position in competition with the owner, and also to place himself in a better position than that of a person who deals consensually with the owner.

I have already expressed the opinion that, when the male defendant stole budwood from the plaintiff's orchard, what he got was a trade secret. The secret was the technique of propagating Franklin Early White nectarines, using budwood from the plaintiff's orchard. The technique of budding was no secret, but the budwood existed only in the plaintiff's orchard, where the plaintiff guarded it by exercising general surveillance over fruit-pickers and visitors, and by bruiting it abroad that it was theirs and theirs alone. The "information" which the genetic structure of the wood represented was of substantial commercial value, much time and effort had been expended by the male plaintiff in evolving it and it could not be duplicated by anybody whatsoever.

I hold that the male defendant has been guilty of infringements of the plaintiff's rights since he stole and used the budwood: as for the female defendant, she has since at least the middle of last year known that the Franklin Early White nectarine trees in the orchard conducted by her husband and herself are the product of a stolen trade secret, and – this being so – it is unconscionable for her to derive any benefit from the trees, and she too infringes the plaintiff's rights.

Dunn J. treated the defendants as constructive trustees of the Franklin Early White Trees and fruit which they had produced and granted the order for delivery up of the trust property for destruction which the plaintiffs had sought.

2.3.3.2 *Malone v Metropolitan Police Commissioner* (No. 2) [1979] 1 Ch 344 (Megarry V.-C.)

The Metropolitan Police, following established procedure, arranged with the Post Office to tap the plaintiff's telephone. Partly as the result of this, the plaintiff was charged with handling stolen antiques but was acquitted. He then sought a declaration that the telephone tapping was wrongful on a number of grounds.

Megarry V. C. refused him any relief and held in particular:

(i) that there had been no breach of the European Convention on Human Rights, Art 8, since the matter was not justiciable in an English court (the plaintiff subsequently succeeded on the issue before the European Court of Human Rights);

(ii) that the plaintiff had no relevant right of property in his conversation;

(iii) that the plaintiff had no right of privacy protecting him;

(iv) that the plaintiff had no contractual right to confidentiality, since his relations with the Post Office were entirely statutory;

(v) that there was no general right to confidentiality in telephone conversations; or if there were, the tapping by the police had been justified. On the last issue Megarry V.-C. observed:

In the present case, the alleged misuse is not by the person to whom the information was intended to be communicated, but by someone to whom the plaintiff had no intention of communicating anything: and that, of course, introduces a somewhat different element, that of the unknown overhearer.

It seems to me that a person who utters confidential information must accept the risk of any unknown overhearing that is inherent in the circumstances of communication. Those who exchange confidences on a bus or a train run the risk of a nearby passenger with acute hearing or a more distant passenger who is adept at lip-reading. Those who speak over garden walls run the risk of the unseen neighbour in a tool-shed nearby. Office cleaners who discuss secrets in the office when they think everyone else has gone run the risk of speaking within earshot of an unseen member of the staff who is working late. Those who give confidential information over an office intercommunication system run the risk of some third party being connected to the conversation. I do not see why someone who has overheard some secret in such a way should be exposed to legal proceedings if he uses or divulges what he has heard. No doubt an honourable man would give some warning when he realises that what he is hearing is not intended for his ears; but I have to concern myself with the law, and not with moral standards. There are, of course, many moral precepts which are not legally enforceable.

When this is applied to telephone conversations, it appears to me that the speaker is taking such risks of being overheard as are inherent in the system. As I have mentioned, the Younger Report referred to users of the telephone being aware that there were several well-understood possibilities of being overheard, and stated that a realistic person would not rely on the telephone system to protect the confidence of what he says. That comment seems unanswerable. In addition, so much publicity in recent years has been given to instances (real or fictional) of the deliberate tapping of telephones that it is difficult to envisage telephone users who are genuinely unaware of this possibility. No doubt a person who uses a telephone to give confidential information to another may do so in such a way as to impose an obligation of confidence on that other: but I do not see how it could be said that any such obligation is imposed on those who overhear the conversation, whether by means of tapping or otherwise.

If certain requirements are satisfied, then I think that there will plainly be just cause or excuse for what is done by or on behalf of the police. These requirements are, first, that there should be grounds for suspecting that the tapping of the particular telephone will be of material assistance in detecting or preventing crime, or discovering the criminals, or otherwise assisting in the discharge of the functions of the police in relation to crime. Second, no use should be made of any material obtained except for these purposes. Third, any knowledge of information which is not relevant to those purposes should be confined to the minimum number of persons reasonably required to carry out the process of tapping. If those requirements are satisfied, then it seems to me that there will be just cause or excuse for carrying out the tapping, and using information obtained for those limited purposes. I am not, of course, saying that nothing else can constitute a just cause or excuse: what I am saying is that if these requirements are satisfied, then in my judgment there will be a just cause or excuse. I am not, for instance, saying anything about matters of national security: I speak only of what is before me in the present case, concerning tapping for police purposes in relation to crime.

So far as the evidence goes, it seems to me that the process of tapping, as carried out on behalf of the police in relation to crime, fully conforms with these requirements: indeed, there are restrictions on tapping and safeguards, which go beyond these requirements. The only possible difficulty is in relation to the "strict conditions" laid down by the Home Office which have to be satisfied before the warrant of the Home Office is sought; for I do not know what these conditions are. However, Mr Kelland's affidavit states in relation to the plaintiff that if a warrant had been sought by the Metropolitan Police (and he says nothing as to whether in fact it was) "the sole purpose in seeking such a warrant would have been to obtain information of value in the detection and prevention of serious crime." This, coupled with the other evidence, makes it clear enough, I think, that the first of the three requirements that I have stated would be satisfied. Accordingly, in my judgment, if, contrary to my opinion, telephone tapping on behalf of the police is a breach of any duty of confidentiality, there is just cause or excuse for that tapping in the circumstances of this case.

2.3.3.3   *Francome v Mirror Group* [1984] 2 All E.R. 408 (C.A.)

John Francome, a highly successful jockey, had his telephone tapped privately and illegally by an unrevealed person. The resulting tapes, which were said to show breaches by him of Jockey Club rules and possibly the commission of criminal offences, came into the defendant newspaper's hands and they proposed to publish an exposé.

In interlocutory proceedings for an injunction to restrain publication of material obtained in contravention of the Wireless Telegraphy Act 1949 s.5 and in breach of confidence, and to require disclosure of the source from which the tapes had been obtained, the plaintiff succeeded on the first but not the second ground.

Fox L.J., after referring to Megarry V.-C.'s view of the nature of telephone tapping in the Malone *case (above, 2.3.3.2), continued:*

The Vice-Chancellor went on to say ([1979] 2 All E.R. 620 at 645, [1979] Ch 344 at 376):

> "It seems to me that a person who utters confidential information must accept the risk of any unknown overhearing that is inherent in the circumstances of communication."

It is said that this statement negatives the existence of any right to confidentiality in the present case. I do not agree. The Vice-Chancellor was only dealing with a case of authorised tapping by the police and he makes that clear (see [1979] 2 All E.R. 620 at 651, [1979] Ch 344 at 384). Illegal tapping by private persons is quite another matter, since it must be questionable whether the user of a telephone can be regarded as accepting the risk of that in the same way as, for example, he accepts the risk that his conversation may be overheard in consequence of the accidents and imperfections of the telephone system itself. Accordingly, in my opinion, there is a serious issue to be tried on the matter of confidentiality.

The "Daily Mirror" states that it will rely on iniquity and public interest as a defence to any claim of confidentiality. The claim of confidentiality and the claim of iniquity raise questions of law and fact which cannot be determined on an interlocutory application. They require a full trial.

If the "Daily Mirror" is permitted to publish the tapes now, the consequent harm to Mr Francome might be such that he could not be adequately compensated in damages for any wrong thereby done to him whatever the result of subsequent proceedings. Unless Mr Francome is given protection until the trial, I think that a trial might be largely worthless from his point of view even though he succeeded.

Fox L.J. added by way of comment on an affidavit by the Editor of the Daily Mirror*:*

There is one further matter. Mr Molloy, in his affidavit, says that he would have to give careful consideration to the probability that publication of the tapes would be an offence under the 1949 Act. He goes on to say that he would not regard that fact as an absolute bar to publication if he considered that publication was justifiable in the public interest. This suggests that Mr Molloy has a choice in the matter even though publication would be unlawful. It must be said flatly that he has no choice. His duty is to obey the law. Parliament by s 5(b) of the 1949 Act created a criminal offence. The proposition that citizens are free to commit a criminal offence if they have formed the view that it will further what they believe to be the public interest is quite baseless in our law and inimical to parliamentary authority. I do not disregard the existence of what is called the moral imperative. But such cases are rare in the extreme. On the evidence before us, there is nothing in the present case which approaches such a situation.

I would make the orders which I have indicated.

Sir John Donaldson M.R. and Stephen Brown L.J. delivered judgments to similar effect.

2.4 Remedies

2.4.1 *Seager v Copydex* (No 2) [1969] 2 All E.R. 718 (C.A.)

The inquiry as to damages ordered in the first proceedings (above, 2.1.3) led to a second appeal.

Lord Denning M.R.:

Now a question has arisen as to the principles on which the damages are to be assessed. They are to be assessed, as we said, at the value of the information which the defendant company took. If I may use an analogy, it is like damages for conversion. Damages for conversion are the value of the goods. Once the damages are paid, the goods become the property of the defendant. A satisfied judgment in trover transfers the property in the goods. So, here, once the damages are assessed and paid, the confidential information belongs to the defendant company.

The difficulty is to assess the value of the information taken by the defendant company. We have had a most helpful discussion about it. The value of the confidential information depends upon the nature of it. If there was nothing very special about it, that is, if it involved no particular inventive step but was the sort of information which could be obtained by employing any competent consultant, then the value of it was the fee which a consultant would charge for it; because in that case the defendant company, by taking the information, would only have saved themselves the time and trouble of employing a consultant. But, on the other hand, if the information was something special, as, for instance, if it involved an inventive step or something so unusual that it could not be obtained by just going to a consultant, then the value of it is much higher. It is not merely a consultant's fee, but the price which a willing buyer – desirous of obtaining it – would pay for it. It is the value as between a willing seller and a willing buyer. In this case, the plaintiff says that the information was very special. People had been trying for years to get a carpet grip and then he hit on this idea of a dome-shaped prong. It was, he said, an inventive step. And he is supported in this issue by the fact that the defendant company themselves have applied for a patent for it. Furthermore, if he is to be regarded as a seller, it must be remembered that he had a patent for another carpet grip called "Klent": and, if he was selling the confidential information (which I will call the "Invisigrip" information) then the sales of the "Klent" might be adversely affected. The sales of the "Klent" would be reduced owing to the competition of the "Invisigrip". So he would ask for a higher price for the confidential information in order to compensate him for the reduction in the "Klent". In these circumstances, if the plaintiff is right in saying that the confidential information was very special indeed, then it may well be right for the value to be assessed on the footing that, in the usual way, it would be remunerated by a royalty. The courts, of course, cannot give a royalty by way of damages; but it could give an equivalent by a calculation based on a capitalisation of a royalty. Thus it could arrive at a lump sum. Once a lump sum is assessed and paid, then the confidential information would belong to the defendant company in the same way as if they had bought and paid for it by an agreement of sale. The property, so far as there is property in it, would vest in them. They would have the right to use that confidential information for the manufacture of carpet grips and selling of them. If it is patentable, they would be entitled to the benefit of the patent as if they had bought it. In other words, it would be regarded as a real outright purchase of the confidential information. The value should, therefore, be assessed on that basis; and damages awarded accordingly.

In these circumstances, I do not think that we should make any such declaration as the defendant company asks. It is sufficient for us to say that, on a satisfied judgment for damages, the confidential information belongs to the defendant. There is one thing more. We have been told that patent proceedings are pending by the defending company. They are applying for a patent and the plaintiff is opposing it. That cannot affect directly the matters which we have to decide today. But the matters are so linked together that I think that the damages should be assessed not by a master in the Chancery Division but by a patent judge. I hope that one patent judge will deal with the patent proceedings as well as these damages. The only order which I would make on the motion is simply to say that the damages are to be assessed in conformity with our judgments.

Salmon and Winn L. JJ. concurred.

2.4.2 *Peter Pan Manufacturing v Corsets Silhouette* [1963] 3 All E.R. 402 (Pennycuick J.)

The plaintiff established that in producing and marketing brassieres, the defendant had misused confidential information embodied in two of its own brassieres, U15 and U25. The plaintiff sought an account of profits. As to its form, Pennycuick J. quoted in particular from Lever v Goodwin *([1887] 36 Ch. D.1) per Cotton L.J.:*

"It is well known that, both in trade-mark cases and patent cases, the plaintiff is entitled, if he succeeds in getting an injunction, to take either of two forms of relief. He may either say 'I claim from you the damage I have sustained from your wrongful act', or 'I claim from you the profit which you have made by your wrongful act' ... The profit for which the defendants must account is the profit which they have made by the sale of soap in that fraudulent dress to the middlemen. It is immaterial how the middleman deal with it".

I have been referred to a number of forms of order in *Seton's Judgments and Orders* Vol 1, in which an account of profits has been ordered. They were patent cases, trade mark cases, or otherwise.

It seems to me that on the plain terms of those orders, what a plaintiff who elects in favour of an account of profits is entitled to, is simply an account of profits in the sense which I have indicated, that is, what has the plaintiff expended on manufacturing these goods? What is the price which he has received on their sale? And the difference is profit. That is what Peter Pan claims in the order for an account as formulated by it; that is simply an account of the profits made by Silhouette in the manufacture and sale of the brassieres U15 and U25.

Counsel for Silhouette has said that that is not the true meaning of the order for an account in the various cases to which I have referred, and that the true meaning of the order, if I understand him, is an account of the amount by which the profit made by the defendant from manufacturing articles with the aid of patents, trade-marks, confidential information, or whatever it may be, which he has in fact used exceeds the amount of the profit which he would have made if he had manufactured the same article without the aid of that material. It seems to me quite impossible to construe the orders made in the various cases as bearing that meaning, and further, so far as I can see, it is perfectly impossible to take as one factor in an account the amount of profit which Silhouette would have made by manufacturing brassieres in the styles U15 and U25 without the use of confidential information, since the manufacture of brassieres of those styles necessarily and inevitably involves the use of confidential information. Indeed, counsel very aptly said that an account in the only form which he says that Peter Pan is entitled to an account would be impracticable. I am quite unsatisfied by any authorities which have been cited to me that that is the only account to which Peter Pan is entitled, or that the account to which I have held it is entitled would present any serious difficulty in its working out.

I should, I think, mention that one of the cases cited to me by counsel for Silhouette was *Siddell v Vickers* ((1892) 9 R.P.C. 152). In that case on the particular facts of the case the Court of Appeal laid down that

> "The true test of comparison was with what the defendants would probably have used instead of the invention, looking at all the circumstances of the case".

That means only this, that the defendants could have manufactured the product in question by other means, but were able to manufacture more economically by making use of a particular appliance which they were not entitled to use. The position there seems to be wholly different from that in the present case, where the manufacture of the article in question of itself involved the use of the confidential information and Silhouette could not have manufactured that article at all without the use of confidential information. So again it seems to me that the proper order for an account is in the terms which Peter Pan have put forward, which is the time-honoured form, and I do not see myself any reason why that form should not be adopted.

3 COPYRIGHT

3.1 Copyright and Related Rights

3.1.1 Copyright Designs and Patent Act 1988, s.171, 172: General Provisions

S.171(1) Nothing in this Part affects –
  (a) any right or privilege of any person under any enactment (except where the enactment is expressly repealed, amended or modified by this Act);
  (b) any right or privilege of the Crown subsisting otherwise than under an enactment;
  (c) any right or privilege of either House of Parliament;
  (d) the right of the Crown or any person deriving title from the Crown to sell, use or otherwise deal with articles forfeited under the laws relating to customs and excise;
  (e) the operation of any rule of equity relating to breaches of trust or confidence.

(2) Subject to those savings, no copyright or right in the nature of copyright shall subsist otherwise than by virtue of this Part or some other enactment in that behalf.

(3) Nothing in this Part affects any rule of law preventing or restricting the enforcement of copyright, on grounds of public interest or otherwise.

(4) Nothing in this Part affects any right of action or other remedy, whether civil or criminal, available otherwise than under this Part in respect of acts infringing any of the rights conferred by Chapter IV (moral rights).

(5) The savings in subsection (1) have effect subject to section 164(4) and section 166(7) (copyright in Acts, Measures and Bills: exclusion of other rights in the nature of copyright).

S.172(1) This Part restates and amends the law of copyright, that is, the provisions of the Copyright Act 1956, as amended.

(2) A provisions of this Part which corresponds to a provision of the previous law shall not be construed as departing from the previous law merely because of a change of expression.

(3) Decisions under the previous law may be referred to for the purpose of establishing whether a provision of this Part departs from the previous law, or otherwise for establishing the true construction of this Part.

3.2 Categories of Protected Work

3.2.1 Basic Definitions

3.2.1.1 Copyright, Designs and Patents Act 1988, s.1, 3(1), 4–8: "Works" protected

S.1(1) Copyright is a property right which subsists in accordance with this Part in the following descriptions of work –
- (a) original literary, dramatic, musical or artistic works,
- (b) sound recordings, films, broadcasts or cable programmes, and
- (c) the typographical arrangement of published editions.

(2) In this Part "copyright work" means a work of any of those descriptions in which copyright subsists.

(3) Copyright does not subsist in a work unless the requirements of this Part with respect to qualification for copyright protection are met (see section 153 and the provisions referred to there).

S.3(1) In this Part –
"literary work" means any work, other than a dramatic or musical work, which is written, spoken or sung, and accordingly includes –
- (a) a table or compilation, and
- (b) a computer program;

"dramatic work" includes a work of dance or mime; and "musical work" means a work consisting of music, exclusive of any words or action intended to be sung, spoken or performed with the music.

For s.3(2), 3(3), see below, 3.3.1

S.4(1) In this Part "artistic work" means –
- (a) a graphic work, photograph, sculpture or collage, irrespective of artistic quality,
- (b) a work of architecture being a building or a model for a building, or
- (c) a work of artistic craftsmanship.

(2) In this Part –
"building" includes any fixed structure, and a part of a building or fixed structure; "graphic work" includes –
- (a) any painting, drawing, diagram, map, chart of plan, and
- (b) any engraving, etching, lithograph, woodcut or similar work;

"photograph" means a recording of light or other radiation on any medium on which an image is produced or from which an image may by any means be produced, and which is not part of a film; "sculpture" includes a cast or model made for purposes of sculpture.

S.5(1) In this Part –
"sound recording" means –
- (a) a recording of sounds, from which the sounds may be reproduced, or
- (b) a recording of the whole or any part of a literary, dramatic or

musical work, from which sounds reproducing the work or part may be produced, regardless of the medium on which the recording is made or the method by which the sounds are reproduced or produced; and

"film" means a recording on any medium from which a moving image may by any means be produced.

(2) Copyright does not subsist in a sound recording or film which is, or the extent that it is, a copy taken from a previous sound recording or film.

S.6(1) In this Part a "broadcast" means a transmission by wireless telegraphy of visual images, sounds or other information which –

    (a) is capable of being lawfully received by members of the public, or

    (b) is transmitted for presentation to members of the public; and references to broadcasting shall be construed accordingly.

(2) An encrypted transmission shall be regarded as capable of being lawfully received by members of the public only if decoding equipment has been made available to members of the public by or with the authority of the person making the transmission or the person providing the contents of the transmission.

(3) References in this Part to the person making a broadcast, broadcasting a work, or including a work in a broadcast are –

    (a) to the person transmitting the programme, if he has responsibility to any extent for its contents, and

    (b) to any person providing the programme who makes with the person transmitting it the arrangements necessary for its transmission;

and references in this Part to a programme, in the context of broadcasting, are to any item included in a broadcast.

(4) For the purposes of this Part the place from which a broadcast is made is, in the case of a satellite transmission, the place from which the signals carrying the broadcast are transmitted to the satellite.

(5) References in this Part to the reception of a broadcast include reception of a broadcast relayed by means of a telecommunications system.

(6) Copyright does not subsist in a broadcast which infringes, or to the extent that it infringes, the copyright in another broadcast or in a cable programme.

S.7(1) In this Part –

"cable programme" means any item included in a cable programme service; and "cable programme service" means a service which consists wholly or mainly in sending visual images, sounds or other information by means of a telecommunications system, otherwise than by wireless telegraphy, for reception –

    (a) at two or more places (whether for simultaneous reception or at different times in response to requests by different users), or

    (b) for presentation to members of the public, and which is not, or so far as it is not, excepted by or under the following provisions of this section.

S.7(2)–(4) introduce exceptions for inter-active systems, internal business systems and personal domestic systems.

(5) References in this Part to the inclusion of a cable programme or work in a cable programme service are to its transmission as part of the service; and references to the person including it are to the person providing the service.

(6) Copyright does not subsist in a cable programme –
- **(a) if it is included in a cable programme service by reception and immediate re-transmission of a broadcast, or**
- **(b) if it infringes, or to the extent that it infringes, the copyright in another cable programme or in a broadcast.**

S.8(1) In this part "published edition", in the context of copyright in the typographical arrangement of a published edition, means a published edition of the whole or any part of one or more literary, dramatic or musical works.

(2) Copyright does not subsist in the typographical arrangement of a published edition if, or to the extent that, it reproduces the typographical arrangement of a previous edition.

3.2.2 Original Literary, Dramatic and Musical Works

3.2.2.1 *University of London Press v University Tutorial Press* [1916] 2 Ch. 601 (Peterson J.)

The University of London assigned to the plaintiff publishers copyright in examination papers set by it for school matriculation examinations. The defendants published a number of these papers without licence, together with criticisms of them and model answers, including three on mathematics set by two co-plaintiffs, Professor Lodge and Mr Jackson. An action for copyright infringement raised the issue of the existence of copyright. Peterson J. said:

Section 1, sub-section 1, of the Copyright Act of 1911 provides for copyright in "every original literary dramatic musical and artistic work", subject to certain conditions which for this purpose are immaterial and the question is, therefore, whether these examination papers are, within the meaning of this Act, original literary works. Although a literary work is not defined in the Act, section 35 states what the phrase includes: the definition is not a completely comprehensive one, but the section is intended to show what, amongst other things, is included in the description "literary work", and the words are "'Literary work' includes maps, charts, plans, tables and compilations". It may be difficult to define "literary work" as used in this Act, but it seems to be plain that it is not confined to "literary work" in the sense in which the phrase is applied, for instance, to Meredith's novels and the writings of Robert Louis Stevenson. In speaking of such writings as literary works, one thinks of the quality, the style, and the literary finish which they exhibit. Under the Act of 1842, which protected "books", many things which had no pretensions to literary style acquired copyright; for example, a list of registered bills of sale, a list of foxhounds and hunting days, and trade catalogues; and I see no ground for coming to the conclusion that the present Act was intended to curtail the rights of authors. In my view the words "literary work" cover work which is expressed in print or writing, irrespective of the question whether the quality or style is high. The word "literary" seems to be used in a sense somewhat similar to the use of the word "literature" in political or electioneering literature and refers to written or printed matter. Papers set by examiners are, in my opinion, "literary work" within the meaning of the present Act.

Assuming that they are "literary work", the question then is whether they are original. The word "original" does not in this connection mean that the work must be the expression of original or inventive thought. Copyright Acts are not concerned with the originality of ideas, but with the expression of thought, and, in the case of "literary work", with the expression of thought in print or writing. The originality which is required relates to the expression of the thought. But the Act does not require that the expression must be in an original or novel form, but that the work must not be copied from another work – that it should originate from the author. In the present case it was not suggested that any of the papers were copies. Professor Lodge and Mr Jackson proved that they had thought out the questions which they set, and that they made notes or memoranda for future questions and drew on those notes for the purposes of the questions which they set. The papers which they prepared originated from themselves, and were, within the meaning of the Act, original. It was said, however, that they drew upon the stock of knowledge common to mathematicians, and that the time spent in producing the questions was small. These cannot be tests for determining whether copyright exists. If an author, for purposes of copyright, must not draw on the stock of knowledge which is common to himself and others who are students of the same branch of learning, only those historians who discovered fresh historical facts could acquire copyright for their works. If time expended is to be the test, the rapidity of an author like Lord Byron in producing a short poem might be an impediment in the way of acquiring copyright, and, the completer his mastery of his subject, the smaller would be the prospect of the author's success in maintaining his claim to copyright.

3.2.2.2 *Ladbroke (Football) v Wm. Hill* [1964] 1 All E.R. 465 (H.L.)

The plaintiff respondents ran a weekly football pool competition by sending out coupons for completion by participants. They alleged that the defendant-appellants had copied the standard forms of their coupon into a rival version. The defendants denied that the coupons were copyright works.

Lord Reid:

A coupon is a sheet of paper on which are printed various lists of forthcoming matches between well-known teams. One called "Nothing Barred" is a full list of some fifty matches. The others are shorter list of matches selected by the bookmaker from the full list. The bets offered in respect of these lists vary in character. From some the punter must pick a certain number of winners. From others he must pick so many home or away wins or draws or a combination of these. And there are other kinds of bets offered. The variety of bets offered is very great. The respondents' coupon contained sixteen lists each with an appropriate name, and we were told that no less than 148 different varieties of bet were offered if one adds up all those offered under each list. Naturally the odds offered differ widely from as low as 5–2 to as high as 20,000–1. And the respondents have one list of peculiar difficulty where they offer £100,000 for two pence. It is not disputed that a vast amount of skill, judgment, experience and work has gone into the building up of the respondents' coupon. There is keen competition in this field. If the bookmaker selects matches too easy to forecast, or offers too favourable odds, he may lose very large sums. If his selections of types of bet, matches and odds do not appeal to punters they will go to rival firms. It appears that the respondents have not altered the general form of their coupon since 1951. They only occasionally alter the odds offered for each type of bet. What is new each week is the selection of matches which are to go into the lists.

When the appellants decided to enter this field they had to devise a suitable form of coupon. Their manager who was given this task was formerly employed by the respondents, but it appears that he tried to devise a form of coupon substantially different from the respondents' coupon. The coupons of some twenty other firms in the business were produced at the trial, and, while they have a general similarity, they vary very much in the nature of their lists and the variety of bets offered in respect of many of the lists. Most of them were studied by the appellants' manager, but his proposals were rejected by the appellants' managing director, who adopted a form closely similar to the respondents' coupon. The respondents had sixteen lists: the appellants' coupon contains fifteen of these lists, all of which appear in the same order as in the respondents' coupon. Moreover, the varieties of bets offered by the appellants in each of these fifteen lists are almost identical with the offers by the respondents in their corresponding list. It is true that, with I think one exception, each of these lists is to be found in one or more of the other bookmakers' coupons and some are to be found in almost all of them. But the appellants do not suggest that the close resemblance between their coupon and the respondents' coupon is fortuitous. They admit that a good deal was simply copied from the respondents, and they say that they were entitled to do that. By no means everything was copied. For some of the lists they devised new names or headings, and the learned trial judge has found that they worked out for themselves the hundred or more different odds offered in respect of the various kinds of bets. It was impossible to copy the selections of matches: the selections must be from the matches to take place in the following week, so there would not be time for one bookmaker to copy from the coupon of another matter which alters every week.

The first question to be determined is whether or to what extent copyright attaches to these coupons. The respondents say that a coupon must be regarded as a single work and that as such it is protected by copyright. The appellants seek to dissect the coupon. They would not only dissect it into the sixteen lists, but they would further dissect each list into heading, selection of matches, and statement of odds offered for the various kinds of bets. They admit that there is copyright in the selection and in the statements of odds offered: they can safely do that because there they did not copy. But they deny any copyright as regards the rest of the coupon. The Copyright Act, 1956, provides, by section 2, that copyright shall subsist in every original literary work and, by section 48, that literary work includes any written table or compilation. I have no doubt that the coupon must be treated as a single compilation. The appellants' dissection theory is derived from some statements in infringement cases and I must, therefore, examine at this point the law regarding infringement. Copyright gives the exclusive right to do certain things including "reproducing the work in any material form", (section 2(5)(a)), and reproduction includes reproduction of a substantial part of the work (s.49(a)). Broadly, reproduction means copying, and does not include cases where an author or compiler produces a substantially similar result by independent work without copying. If he does copy, the question whether he has copied a substantial part depends more on the quality than on the quantity of what he has taken. One test may be whether the part which he has taken is novel or striking, or is merely a commonplace arrangement of ordinary words or well-known data. So it may sometimes be a convenient short cut to ask whether the part taken could itself be the subject of copyright. But, in my view, that is only a short cut, and the more correct approach is first to determine whether the plaintiff's work as a whole is "original" and protected by copyright, and then to inquire whether the part taken by the defendant is substantial. A wrong result can easily be reached if one begins by dissecting the plaintiff's work and asking, could section A be the subject of copyright if it stood by itself, could section B be protected if it stood by itself, and so on. To my mind, it does not follow that, because other fragments taken separately would not be copyright, therefore the whole cannot be. Indeed, it has often been recognised that if sufficient skill and judgment have been exercised in devising the arrangements of the whole work, that can be an important or even decisive element in deciding whether the work as a whole is protected by copyright.

The appellants relied on cases where it has been held that in general the title of a work is not copyright. Those cases are dealt with by Lord Wright in the judgment of the Privy Council in *Francis Day and Hunter Ltd v Twentieth Century Fox Corpn. Ltd*, [1940] A.C. 112) and I think that he rightly expressed the principle when he said (p. 123–124):

> "The copying which is complained of is the use of the title, and that is too unsubstantial on the facts of this case to constitute an infringement".

None of the decisions cited in argument appears to me to conflict with the view that one must first decide whether the part taken is a substantial part. The only apparent exception would seem to be a case such as *Leslie v Young & Sons* ([1894] A.C. 335) where a compilation was treated as consisting of severable parts, one of which was held to be original work and copyright while the rest was not. The appellants' main argument was based on quite a different ground. They deny that the respondents' coupon is an original compilation. There is no dispute about the meaning of the term "original":

His Lordship quoted from the University of London *case, (above, 3.2.2.1). He continued:*

In the present case, if it is permissible to take into account all the skill, judgment and labour expended in producing the respondents' coupon, there can be no doubt that it is "original". But the appellants say that the coupon must be regarded as having been produced in two stages: first, the respondents had to decide what kind of business they would do – what kinds of bets they would offer to their clients – and then they had to write these out on paper. The appellants say that it is only the skill, judgment and labour involved in the latter stage that can be considered and that that part of their operation involved so little skill, judgment or labour that it cannot qualify as "original". In fact the respondents did not proceed in that way. Their business was to devise a coupon which would appeal to the betting public, and its form and arrangement were not something dictated by previous decisions about the nature of the bets to be offered. The appellants likened the coupon to a trader's catalogue of his wares, and argued that in considering whether a catalogue is entitled to copyright one must disregard the maker's skill and work in deciding what wares he will stock for sale and only consider the skill and labour involved in the actual preparation of the catalogue. I do not think that that is a true analogy. Even in the case of a catalogue there may be a question whether the work in deciding what to sell and the work in deciding how to sell it are not so inter-connected as to be inseparable. Copyright in a catalogue in no way prevents honest competition – any other trader can decide to stock and sell any or all of the catalogued articles, and he can thereafter make a new catalogue of his own wares. What he must not do is simply to copy the other trader's catalogue.

The other members of the House delivered concurring speeches. The defendant was held to infringe.

3.2.2.3   *Cramp v Smythson* [1944] A.C. 329 (H.L.)

The plaintiffs asserted that a series of initial tables in the defendants' "Surrey Lightweight Diary, 1942" were copied from their "Liteblue Diary 1933" so as to constitute infringement of copyright.

Viscount Simon L.C.:

The respondents base their claim to copyright on the selection of these tables to form a combination of information, and the declaration made by the Court of Appeal is "that the collection of tables comprised in the plaintiffs' Liteblue Diary for 1933" (other than the calendar), "is a copyright work", and that the infringement by the plaintiffs consists in printing and publishing in "the Surrey Lightweight Diary, 1942" this collection of tables. Granted that the appellants copied the respondents' tables (and this is not only admitted but is indicated by the almost precise similarity of language), there seems to be nothing that can properly be described as an "original literary work" in grouping together this information. A summarized statement of the most important of the postal charges, inland, imperial and foreign, is part of the ordinary contents of any pocket diary. There would, indeed, as it seems to me, be considerable difficulty in successfully contending that ordinary tables which can be got from or checked by, the postal guide or the Nautical Almanac are a subject of copyright as being original literary work. One of the essential qualities of such tables is that they should be accurate, so that there is no question of variation in what is stated. The sun does in fact rise, and the moon set, at times which have been calculated, and the utmost that a table can do on such a subject is to state the result accurately. There is so far no room for taste or judgment. There remains, I agree, the element of choice as to what information should be given, and the respondents contend that the test of originality is satisfied by the choice of the tables inserted, but the bundle of information furnished in the respondents' diary is commonplace information which is ordinarily useful and is, at any rate to a large extent, commonly found prefixed to diaries, and, looking through the respondents' collection of tables, I have difficulty in seeing how such tables in the combination in which they appear in the respondents' 1933 diary, can reasonably claim to be "original work". There was no evidence that any of these tables was composed specially for the respondents' diary. There was no feature of them which could be pointed out as novel or specially meritorious or ingenious from the point of view of the judgment or skill of the compiler. It was not suggested that there was any element of originality or skill in the order in which the tables were arranged. My own conclusion is that the selection did not constitute an original literary work.

The other members of the House agreed.

3.2.2.4   *Byrne v Statist Co* [1914] 1 K.B. 622 (Bailhache J.)

The plaintiff alleged infringement of copyright in translations. On the existence of copyright, Bailhache J. said:

I think the words "original literary work" mean a literary work of which the person in whom the copyright is laid, or through whom the title to the copyright is traced, is the author. A translator of the literary work has for many years been held to be the author of his translation, and the House of Lords, in *Walter v Lane* ([1900] A.C. 539) went so far as to hold that a shorthand writer who reported a speech verbatim was the author of his report.

3.2.2.5   *Exxon Corp v Exxon Insurance Consultants* [1982] R.P.C. 69 (C.A.)

The plaintiffs, constituent companies of the Exxon petroleum group, (formerly Standard Oil of New Jersey) objected to the use by the defendants of "Exxon" as part of their corporate name. They secured relief against passing off; but on a claim for infringement of copyright in the word, they failed before Graham J. and the C.A. Stephenson L.J. delivered a substantial judgment, in concurring with which Oliver L.J. said:

But "original literary work" as used in the statute is a composite expression, and for my part I do not think that the right way to apply a composite expression is, or at any rate is necessarily, to ascertain whether a particular subject-matter falls within the meaning of each of the constituent parts, and then to say that the whole expression is merely the sum total of the constituent parts. In my judgment it is not necessary, in construing a statutory expression, to take leave of one's common-sense, and the result to which Mr Price seeks to drive us is one which, to my mind, involves doing just that.

We have been referred to a number of cases in which copyright has been successfully claimed in, for instance examination papers, football coupons and tables of ciphers; but all these – and I do not exclude the case of the telegraphic code in *Anderson v Lieber Code* ([1917] 2 K.B. 469) – seem to me to fall fairly within Davey L.J.'s commonsense formulation.*

But that for which protection is sought in the instant case does not appear to me to have any of the qualities which commonsense would demand. It conveys no information; it provides no instruction; it gives no pleasure that I can conceive; it is simply an artificial combination of four letters of the alphabet which serves a purpose only when it is used in juxtaposition with other English words, to identify one of other of the companies in the plaintiff group.

Sir David Cairns concurred in both judgments.

3.2.2.6   *Express Newspapers v Liverpool Daily Post* [1985] F.S.R. 306 (Whitford J.)

The plaintiff publisher organised a competition, "Millionaire of the Month", in which contestants received a free card containing a sequence of five letters and matched it against sequences published in the Sunday Express, Daily Express *and* Star. *Each day or week's paper would contain a grid of 5 x 5 letters and two additional lines of 5 letters. Matching these with an individual card gave a claim to various prizes and further opportunities.*

The defendants copied each day's or week's grid and lines into their own newspapers. On a motion for an interlocutory injunction to restrain infringement of copyright in the varying grids and lines, the main issue was whether they amounted to literary works.

Whitford J.:

If these grids and these sequences of five letters can be said to be copyright works, I do not understand it to be argued on the defendants' side that what they have done would not be an infringement. The defendants, however, say that there is here disclosed no copyright work. The Copyright Act 1956 provides for the giving of protection under the Act in respect of a variety of works. The only relevant heading so far as the present proceedings are concerned is "literary works". By the definition section, "literary work" includes tables; and it was not suggested by Mr Jeffs, on the defendant's side, that a table could not be the subject of protection. It is of course accepted, because it is easily established by reference to one of a number of well-known authorities, that mathematical tables can acquire copyright protection as "literary work". They do so because their compilation – and compilations in themselves are by definition "literary work" – involves the exercise of skill and labour, or possibly maybe only labour.

That a great deal of skill and, indeed, a good deal of labour went into the production of the grid and the two separate sequences of five letters is, to my mind, quite plainly established from the evidence of Mr Ertel, who is with an American corporation, Amphora Enterprises Inc., who were saddled with the task of preparing these grid patterns and sequences to be used in the plaintiffs' competition. Mr Ertel's affidavit sets out in detail what he has had to do and the steps that had to be taken. He describes how participants in the competition look at the grid and see if they can match certain patterns of letters and in the same way see if they can match the sequence of five letters. He describes the difficulties that are involved in preparing these grids and five-letter sequences if you are going to arrive at a situation in which you do not get so many winning lines that the whole thing is going to become hopelessly uneconomic from the point of view of the person running the competition. He describes the constraints with which he was necessarily faced in ensuring that a sufficient number of possible winning combinations emerged to make the game attractive, without producing such a number of combinations to make the whole thing hopelessly uneconomic. He goes to some length to point out the difficulties of achieving these results. He describes also how the effort had to be made to introduce a system of some sort of check codes to avoid frauds.

Whitford J. then described how Mr Ertel achieved his result by programming a computer and rejected an argument that in consequence Mr Ertel was not the author of the grid and lines. He proceeded to address an argument that they could not constitute a literary work by virtue of the Exxon *case (above, 3.2.2.5):*

Of course, the facts in that case were very different from the facts of the present case. The earlier decision upon which Graham J. and the Court of Appeal relied, which concerned a sleeve chart – a case very well known in this field of the law – was a case in relation to which Davey L.J., speaking of the sleeve chart, said:

"It does not add to the stock of human knowledge or give, and is not designed to give, any instruction by way of description or otherwise; and it certainly is not calculated to afford literary enjoyment or pleasure";

and he came to the conclusion that the sleeve chart in question was no more entitled to copyright as a literary work than the scale attached to a barometer in the case of *Davis v Comitti*. What the finding would be today if a claim to copyright in a sleeve chart were brought I do not need to consider.

Of this passage, Stephenson L.J. (in *Exxon Corporation v Exxon Insurance Consultants International Limited*) said:

"The words of the Lord Justice do, however, appeal to me as stating the ordinary meaning of the words 'literary work'. I would have thought, unaided or unhampered by authority, that unless there is something in the context of the Act which forbids it, a literary work would be something which was intended to afford either information and instruction, or pleasure in the form of literary enjoyment, whatever those last six words may add to the word 'pleasure'";

and counsel were unable to persuade their Lordships that this word did in fact provide information or instruction or give pleasure.

Of course, Mr Jeffs can well say that some tables – and he gave the instance of a table of logarithms – even if to some people they may give very little pleasure, do at least provide information. So, in my judgment, do the grids and the five-letter sequences. They are looked at by those who have had one of the Millionaire Club cards for the very purpose of acquiring information; they want to know whether they have won or lost. They might find out that they have won, or more probably that they have lost; but information is the whole purpose of the publication of these grids and five-letter sequences. Indeed, if they did not give information, I do not suppose the defendants would be troubling to include them in their newspapers.

3.2.2.7 *Green v Broadcasting Corpn. of New Zealand* [1989] R.P.C. 700 (J.C.)

In Britain, the plaintiff compered the popular television talent contest, "Opportunity Knocks". The defendant broadcast a similar show in New Zealand, using the same title. The plaintiff sued for infringement of copyright and passing off. The claims failed.

As to copyright, Lord Bridge stated:

The copyright alleged to have been infringed was claimed to subsist in the "scripts and dramatic format" of "Opportunity Knocks" as broadcast in England. The appellant's primary difficulty arises from the circumstances that no script was ever produced in evidence. Ongley J. concluded that:

> "There was really no evidence that any part of the show was reduced to a written text which could properly be called a script . . ."

He added later:

> "No writing has been produced in evidence in this action in which, in my view, copyright could subsist".

The Court of Appeal differed from the trial judge to the extent that they accepted that the evidence established the existence of scripts. But the evidence as to the nature of the scripts and what their text contained was exiguous in the extreme. It is to be found in two short passages from the evidence given by the appellant himself. He said in the course of examination-in-chief:

> "In the year 1956, I wrote the scripts of Opportunity Knocks shows, such as they were, because we would have what we would call the introductions, our stock phrases like 'For So-and-So, Opportunity Knocks', phrases such as 'This is your show, folks, and I do mean you'. The other part of the writing dealt with interviews with the people and one could not really call it writing because you were really only finding out what the artists wanted to talk about".

He said in cross-examination:

> "The script of Opportunity Knocks has continuously been the same for the catch phrases, the interviews each week with the artists has differed, the script for the past 17 years and long before 1975 contained particularly the end of the show beginning with the words 'make your mind up time' using the clapometer and bringing back the five people".

On the basis of this evidence Somers J. concluded that:

> ". . . the scripts as they are inferred to be from the description given in evidence did not themselves do more than express a general idea or concept for a talent quest and hence were not the subject of copyright".

In the absence of precise evidence as to what the scripts contained, their Lordships are quite unable to dissent from this view.

The alternative formulation of the appellant's claim relies upon the "dramatic format" of "Opportunity Knocks", by which their Lordships understand is meant those characteristic features of the show which were repeated in each performance. These features were, in addition to the title, the use of the catch phrases "for [name of competitor] opportunity knocks", "this is your show folks, and I do mean you", and "make up your mind time", the use of a device called a "clapometer" to measure audience reaction to competitors' performances and the use of sponsors to introduce competitors. It was this formulation which found favour with Gallen J.

It is stretching the original use of the word "format" a long way to use it metaphorically to describe the features of a television series such as a talent, quiz or game show which is presented in a particular way, with repeated but unconnected use of set phrases and with the aid of particular accessories. Alternative terms suggested in the course of argument were "structure" or "package". This difficulty in finding an appropriate term to describe the nature of the "work" in which the copyright subsists reflects the difficulty of the concept that a number of allegedly distinctive features of a television series can be isolated from the changing material presented in each separate performance (the acts of the performers in the talent show, the questions and answers in the quiz show etc.) and identified as an "original dramatic work". No case was cited to their Lordships in which copyright of the kind claimed had been established.

3.2.2.8 *Wiseman v George Wiedenfeld & Nicolson* [1985] F.S.R. 525 (Whitford J.)

The second defendant, Donaldson, turned his novel, The English Way of Doing Things, *into a play with the same title. He did so on the suggestion of the plaintiff, who at various stages of the adaptation made suggestions and criticisms. The Plaintiff subsequently claimed to be co-author of the play and so entitled to a share in the copyright.*

Whitford J.:

We are here concerned with a dramatic work. Both collaborators, Mr Wiseman and Mr Donaldson, must answer to the description of authors of the dramatic work. To be a joint author, a collaborator must make some contribution to the literary or dramatic form in which alone copyright can subsist.

In *Tate v Thomas* [1921] 1 Ch. 503, Eve J. said this of a Mr Peterman, who was contending that he was a joint author (at page 509):

"Mr Peterman contends that he was really the author or at least a joint author with the plaintiffs. It is not disputed that he suggested the name of the piece, and there is no doubt that in many parts of the work are introduced incidents suggested in his rough sketch or culled from works in which he has no copyright interest. One of the witnesses called for the defendants went so far as to say that the whole play was 'pinched' from other people's productions. I had the opportunity of seeing Mr Peterman in the witness box and I can well understand that he is speaking the truth when he states that he was frequently making suggestions to the authors and indicating to them how they were to do the work they had undertaken. He is a gentleman of a fertile imagination and possessed of a fluency and powers well qualifying him for communicating his views to the authors.

The plaintiffs do not deny that their work embodies some ideas and a few catch lines or words for which Mr Peterman may claim credit, but they dispute altogether his claim to a share in the authorship of the work and contend (and in my opinion rightly contend) that the sum total of his contribution does not amount to anything entitled to protection under the Act. His assistance, such as it was, was confined to accessorial matters such as scenic effects, or stage 'business' not the subject matter of copyright".

I should perhaps say at this stage that Mr Donaldson conceded that there may have been a line here or there and possibly even an idea which emanated from Mr Wiseman, but he too, as in this case, contends that he and he alone was the author of the work.

At page 511 of the report Eve J. said this;

"The question whether Mr Peterman's claim to be a joint author of this work, so far as it is subject matter for protection under the Act, is one of fact; and, having heard all the evidence, I have come to the conclusion that his contributions to the matter capable of being printed and published were so insignificant and negligible as to make it quite impossible for me to hold him to have been in any sense a joint author within the Act".

In *Evans v E Hulton & Co Ltd* [1923–28] MacG. C.C. 51 Tomlin J. put the question in relation to the alleged joint author in this way:

> "Did he take any part in producing the express matter which is the original literary work the subject matter of copyright?"

In *Bagge v Miller* [1917–23] MacG. C.C. 179 Russell J., speaking of the respective contributions of the plaintiff and the defendant, said this (at page 182):

> "As regards the plaintiff Milburn he can only succeed if he was a joint author of the sketch and so a co-owner of the copyright. He must establish that he is a joint author of the dramatic work *The Truth for an Hour*. If he does that then he would be a co-owner of the copyright which would subsist therein if it be an original dramatic work.
>
> Mr Milburn outlined the plot verbally to Mr Bagge and suggested to him that he should write a play. Mr Bagge did so. The written sketch was entirely his, Bagge's: the dialogue is entirely his. After the sketch was written by Mr Bagge, it was discussed and Mr Milburn said that he made certain suggestions which Mr Bagge adopted. What they were I was not told. They were not apparently of sufficient importance to be told in detail. Mr Milburn had no place in composing the dramatic work beyond suggesting the idea of the sketch. He had no share in the design or execution of the work, the whole of which, so far as any character of originality belongs to it, flowed from the mind of Mr Bagge. Certainly in ordinary parlance no one would describe Mr Milburn as the author or joint author of the dramatic work. Neither is he in law an author of joint author of the dramatic work. The mere suggestion of an idea which is then embodied by another in a dramatic work written by him does not, in my opinion, constitute the originator of the idea an author or a joint author of the dramatic work. For this proposition the case of *Shepherd v Conquest* 17 C.B. 427 is, in my opinion, a sufficient authority.
>
> On the printed copies of the sketch Mr Milburn's name appeared (by special arrangement with Mr Bagge) as one of the authors, and Mr MacGillivray relied upon the presumption raised by section 6(3)(a) of the Act: but in my opinion the statutory presumption is displaced by the facts proved in this case".

I found Mr Donaldson a thoroughly reliable witness, very careful, very fair, and in no way prepared to overstate his case, and in complete contrast to Mr Wiseman, who was neither careful nor fair, but quite prepared to make very extravagant and unjustified claims. I am sure that Mr Wiseman is under a sense of grievance. He has no doubt persuaded himself that his pretensions are justified, and that in fact he has made a contribution to the production of this work far in excess of that which he has in fact contributed. He has, however, wholly failed to persuade me.

A good many years ago, it would seem that Mr Wiseman was likely to achieve some success in the theatre as a director; and, indeed, he referred me to certain productions in which he was concerned. He has not had any great success as an author; his promise in the field of directorial activity has not apparently been realised – at least in recent years – so far.

Mr Donaldson, of course, has basically always been a writer. As I have said, he had started to achieve some success as an author at the time when the play first came to be written. He had never really had any great experience in the theatre, and did not pretend to such experience as Mr Wiseman has in fact had. Mr Wiseman thought that *Both the Ladies and the Gentlemen* could be a success as a play. He undoubtedly saw himself as a director of a stage version, if a stage version could be produced.

When what might be described as a strict adaptation of *Both the Ladies and the Gentlemen* proved impossible, Mr Donaldson formed the view that the characters from this work could be pressed into service in a play. He urged this upon Mr Donaldson; he eventually, as I have said, managed to persuade Mr Donaldson into writing the dramatic work in which he, Mr Wiseman, now claims joint authorship.

A dramatic work involves, of course, not only dialogue but a series of incidents – dramatic situations – which in a particular order or occurrence can form the backbone of the piece. Mr Wiseman, in his evidence-in-chief and in cross-examination, however made claims extending beyond this. He claimed that he had made a significant contribution to the dialogue. "Mr Donaldson", Mr Wiseman told me, "took the lead in the dialogue, but we went over every line together". In cross-examination, again, he said: "We went over every single line inch by inch in collaboration".

I cannot accept a word of this. It was the evidence of Mr Donaldson, which I accept without reservation, that he finds himself unable to write anything other than perhaps some very simple part of a work in somebody else's presence. It was Mr Donaldson's evidence that he effectively did all the writing before Mr Wiseman, who at this stage was living at a different address, arrived at the flat occupied by Mr Donaldson around 11 o'clock in the morning or at some later stage, possibly in the evening, and at weekends.

Mr Donaldson entirely accepted that he found Mr Wiseman a most valuable critic of the lines that he had written. He accepted, indeed, that he tore up two weeks of work written while Mr Wiseman was away, as a result of criticisms by Mr Wiseman, and he re-wrote the scenes in question. It was, however, his evidence that Mr Wiseman virtually took no part in writing any single line of the dialogue; and of this I am satisfied.

3.2.2.9 *Wood v Boosey* [1868] L.R. 3 Q.B. 223 (Exchequer Chamber)

Nicolai's opera, "Die lustigen Weiber von Windsor", was first performed in March, 1849, the composer dying two months later. Brissler then made a reduction for pianoforte of the orchestral score. Under the then existing arrangements (International Copyright Act 1844), in order for an author from a country with which there was a bi-lateral arrangement to acquire British copyright, he had to register his work giving the author's name. A registration for the Brissler arrangement of the opera was obtained in 1851, naming Nicolai as composer. The plaintiffs, claiming to be assignees of this copyright, sued the defendants for infringement. The defence denied that the registration had been properly made in Nicolai's name.

Bramwell B.:

The truth is, an opera is originally written for the voice and for different instruments. In this pianoforte score, as it is called, the parts written for the voice are identically preserved, and there can be no doubt that if a man had a copyright in the original opera, such a score would be an infringement of his copyright. But when we come to the part, not for the voices, but for the pianoforte, which is not an identical repetition of what the author wrote, it is the business of the adapter, the person who arranges it for the pianoforte, to preserve the harmony and, as far as he can, the notes and all the effects of the original composer, but he cannot produce upon the pianoforte everything that the author wrote, as he wrote it. . . .

Anybody who plays any musical instrument knows it is a very common expression to say, such a piece is very well arranged, such a piece is very ill arranged; this is a very difficult arrangement, that is an easy arrangement. Those who play the German arrangements know they are more difficult than the English, because the German, with great conscientiousness, endeavours to put into the arrangement every note that the composer has put into the score as far as he can; whereas the English composer endeavours in all arrangements to make them clear for the player, and an English arrangement is by no means so laborious as the German. It is manifest, therefore, that there is some judgment and taste required on the part of the arranger for the pianoforte; and it is also certain that if it should so happen that a man should compose an opera without being able to play on the pianoforte – which is, I believe, a perfectly possible thing – he could not arrange it himself for the pianoforte. . . .

It is clear, therefore, that there is something in the nature of authorship in Brissler, and his name not having been stated as the author in the register, it seems to me manifest the plaintiff has not a copyright of the pianoforte score, as it is called, and consequently cannot complain of this infringement.

Kelly C.B. delivered a judgment to the same effect; and Willes, Keating and Montague Smith JJ. and Channell B. concurred.

* For which see *Express Newspapers v Liverpool Daily Post* (below, 3.2.2.6).

3.2.3 Original Artistic Works

3.2.3.1 *Kenrick v Lawrence* (1890) 25 Q.B.D. 93 (Wills J.)

The plaintiffs claimed copyright in the representation of a hand pointing to a square on an electoral voting paper.

Wills J.:

It was in evidence that more than a million copies of the card of the plaintiffs have been sold since the year 1885, and that they have been used at nearly every election in the kingdom. It was urged, probably with truth, that such a card was practically the only mode of instructing the illiterate voter how to record his vote, and it is obvious that if the privilege of instructing the illiterate voter how to vote, by the only vehicle by which the act of voting can be represented to the eye, and the instructions how to vote and whom to vote for can be brought home to him, be vested in the plaintiffs for seven years beyond the termination of a life which may very well subsist for half a century longer – for Mr Jefferson is now only thirty-six years of age – and be their monopoly, it is difficult to put an adequate value upon their property in such a right. If that period should shortly arrive, which to many politicians appears to be a kind of constitutional millenium, when all the remaining ignorance, male and female, of the three kingdoms shall be swept into the electoral fold, the amount of political power which may become vested in the plaintiffs or their assignees will be greater than it is possible to estimate, and the destinies of the country may be placed in the hands of the fortunate owner of the talisman. The mere choice of subject can rarely, if ever, confer upon the author of the drawing an exclusive right to represent the subject, and certainly where the subject chosen is merely the representation to the eye of a simple operation which must be performed by every person who records a vote there cannot possibly be an exclusive right to represent in a picture that operation. It may well be that something special in the way of artistic treatment even of this simple operation, if it existed, might be the subject of copyright; but nothing of the kind has been suggested or exists in the present case, and if it does exist without being discovered it has not been imitated, for there is nothing which in any flight of imagination can be called artistic about either the plaintiffs' or the defendants' representation of a hand making the mark of a cross. It may be also that even the coarsest, or the most commonplace, or the most mechanical representation of the commonest object is so far protected on registration that an exact reproduction of it, such as photography for instance would produce, would be an infringement of copyright. But in such a case it must surely be nothing short of an exact literal reproduction of the drawing registered that can constitute the infringement, for there seems to me to be in such a case nothing else that is not the common property of all the world. It is possible that in this case the proprietors of the drawing registered may have a right to be protected from a reproduction of their picture of a hand drawing a cross in which every line, dot, measurement, and blank space shall be rendered exactly as in the original, or in which the variations from such minute agreement shall be microscopic. But I cannot see how they can possibly make a higher claim, or say that because they have registered a drawing of a hand pencilling a cross within a square that no other person in the United Kingdom is at liberty to draw a hand pencilling a cross within a square for perhaps the next half century.

3.2.3.2 *Interlego v Tyco Industries* [1988] R.P.C. 343 (J.C.)

The plaintiff and its associated companies made and marketed the "Lego" toy brick system internationally. The defendants intended to manufacture a competing system in Hong Kong which, the plaintiff alleged, constituted infringement of its copyright in designs for the bricks, since the defendants had reached their designs by "reverse engineering" of the plaintiff's products.

In part, the claims related to drawings made after 1972. These were virtual copies of earlier drawings, to which were added written instructions for modifying the dimensions of the joining knobs on the bricks. The defendants accordingly denied that they attracted copyright. In giving judgment for the J.C., Lord Oliver referred to Peterson J.'s remarks on the meaning of "originality" in copyright law (*University of London Press *case, above, 3.2.2.1). He proceeded:*

That statement is, of course, not complete in itself because there may clearly be original work which makes use of material obtained by the author from pre-existing sources. Perhaps the most useful exegesis is to be found in three passages from the opinion of the Board delivered by Lord Atkinson in the Privy Council case of *Macmillan & Co Ltd v Cooper* (1923) 40 T.L.R. 186, a case concerned with university textbooks consisting of abridgments of or excerpts from existing works with appropriate notes for students. Lord Atkinson observed (at 188):

"... it is the product of the labour, skill, and capital of one man which must not be appropriated by another, not the elements, the raw material, if one may use the expression, upon which the labour and skill and capital of the first have been expended. To secure copyright for this product it is necessary that labour, skill, and capital should be expended sufficiently to impart to the product some quality or character which the raw material did not possess, and which differentiates the product from the raw material".

A little later, he quoted with approval the following passage from the judgment of Story J. in *Emerson v Davies* (1845) 3 Story 768 at 778–779:

"The question is not, whether the materials which are used are entirely new, and have never been used before; or even that they have never been used before for the same purpose. The true question is, whether the same plan, arrangement, and combination of materials have been used before for the same purpose or for any other purpose. If they have not, then the plaintiff is entitled to a copyright, although he may have gathered hints for his plan and arrangement, or parts of his plan and arrangement, from existing and known sources. He may have borrowed much of his materials from others, but if they are combined in a different manner from what was in use before ... he is entitled to a copyright ... It is true, that he does not thereby acquire the right to appropriate to himself the materials which were common to all persons before, so as to exclude those persons from a future use of such materials; but then they have no right to use such materials with his improvements superadded, whether they consist in plan, arrangement or illustrations, or combinations; for these are strictly his own".

Lord Atkinson continued:

"This decision is, of course, not binding on this tribunal; but it is, in the opinion of

---

* From 1973, a Hong Kong Copyright Ordinance introduced the UK Copyright Act 1956 (as amended by the Design Copyright Act 1968) into the colony. The effect of this was that the post-1972 drawings were protected by artistic copyright and that copyright could be infringed by industrial reproduction (directly or indirectly) in three dimensions. In UK law this position is now changing, by virtue of the Copyright Designs and Patents Act 1988, s.51: for which see below, Part 4. For an aspect of this case concerning the pre-1972 drawings, see below, 4.2.6.

the Board, sound, able, convincing and helpful. It brings out clearly the distinction between the materials upon which one claiming copyright has worked and the product of the application of his skill, judgment, labour and learning to those materials; which product, though it may be neither novel or ingenious, is the claimant's original work in that it is originated by him, emanates from him, and is not copied".

Finally, he observed (at 190):

"What is the precise amount of the knowledge, labour, judgment or literary skill or taste which the author of any book or other compilation must bestow upon its composition in order to acquire copyright in it within the meaning of the Copyright Act of 1911 cannot be defined in precise terms. In every case it must depend largely on the special facts of that case, and must in each case be very much a question of degree".

In that context he cited with approval a passage from the judgment of Lord Kinloch in *Black v Murray* (1870) 9 M 341 at 355:

"I think it clear that it will not create copyright in a new edition of a work, of which the copyright has expired, merely to make a few emendations of the text, or to add a few unimportant notes. To create a copyright by alterations of the text, these must be extensive and substantial, practically making a new book. With regard to notes, in like manner, they must exhibit an addition to the work which is not superficial or colourable, but imparts to the book a true and real value, over and above that belonging to the text".

That case was, of course, concerned with literary copyright, but there is no distinction in principle in the case of artistic copyright, although obviously the opportunities for the creation of an original work by way of compilation of existing materials are here more limited. In *British Northrop Ltd v Texteam Blackburn Ltd* [1974] R.P.C. 57 at 68 the principle was conveniently summarised by Megarry J. as follows:

"Copyright is concerned not with any originality of ideas but with their form of expression, and it is in that expression that originality is requisite. That expression need not be original or novel in form, but it must originate with the author and not be copied from another work ... A drawing which is simply traced from another drawing is not an original artistic work: a drawing which is made without any copying from anything originates with the artist".

Lord Oliver referred to certain general remarks of Whitford J. at first instance in LB *(Plastics) v Swish [1979] R.P.C. 551. He proceeded:*

Originality in the context of literary copyright has been said in several well-known cases to depend on the degree of skill, labour and judgment involved in preparing a compilation. *Macmillan & Co Ltd v Cooper* (1923) 40 T.L.R. 186 was such a case. So was *G.A. Cramp & Son Ltd v F. Smythson Ltd* [1944] 2 All E.R. 92, [1944] A.C. 329. Similarly, in the speeches of Lord Reid and Lord Hodson in *Ladbroke (Football) Ltd v William Hill (Football) Ltd* [1964] 1 All E.R. 465 at 469, 475, 477, [1964] 1 W.L.R. 273 at 277, 285, 287 it is stressed that the amount of skill, judgment or labour is likely to be decisive in the case of compilations. To apply that, however, as a universal test of originality in all copyright cases is not only unwarranted by the context in which the observations were made but palpably erroneous. Take the simplest case of artistic copyright, a painting or a photograph. It takes great skill, judgment and labour to produce a good copy by painting or to produce an enlarged photograph from a positive print, but no one would reasonably contend that the copy painting or enlargement was an 'original' artistic work in which the copier is entitled to claim copyright. Skill, labour or judgment merely in the process of copying cannot confer originality. In this connection some reliance was placed on a passage from the judgment of Whitford J. in *LB (Plastics) Ltd v Swish Products Ltd* [1979] R.P.C. 551 at 568–569 where he expressed the opinion that a drawing of a three-dimensional prototype, not itself produced from the drawing and not being a work of artistic craftsmanship, would qualify as an original work. That may well be right, for there is no more reason for denying originality to the depiction of a three-dimensional prototype than there is for denying originality to the depiction in two-dimensional form of any other physical object. It by no means follows, however, that that which is an extract and literal reproduction in two-dimensional form of an existing two-dimensional work becomes an original work simply because the process of copying it involves the application of skill and labour. There must in addition be some element of material alteration or embellishment which suffices to make the totality of the work an original work. Of course, even a relatively small alteration or addition quantitatively may, if material, suffice to convert that which is substantially copied from an earlier work into an original work. Whether it does so or not is a question of degree having regard to the quality rather than the quantity of the addition. But copying, *per se*, however much skill or labour may be devoted to the process, cannot make an original work. A well-executed tracing is the result of much labour and skill but remains what it is, a tracing. Moreover, it must be borne in mind that the Copyright Act 1956 confers protection on an original work for a generous period. The prolongation of the period of statutory protection by periodic reproduction of the original work with minor alterations is an operation which requires to be scrutinised with some caution to ensure that that for which protection is claimed really is an original artistic work.

The other important consideration which has also to be borne in mind in any case of three-dimensional copying by reverse engineering is that the plaintiff's claim to protection in the case of a non-patented industrial article not registered under the Registered Designs Act 1949 rests solely on artistic copyright, that is to say on the visual image in the form of a drawing of the article from which that which is claimed to be an infringement is produced. It does not rest on the copyright owner's inventiveness or method of working, on the confidentiality of his instructions to his engineering or production staff or on his literary copyright in any written communication of those instructions. Essentially artistic copyright is concerned with visual image. This is of particular importance in the instant case, which has the unusual feature that the artistic copyright claimed stems in origin from drawings which are themselves out of copyright and therefore available for copying.

His Lordship then concluded (i) that the drawings by themselves involved alterations too insignificant to be original artistic works; but (ii) that the design information given was of technical significance and the result of considerable labour and expertise.

Reliance is . . . principally placed, in this context, on the decision of the Court of Appeal in *British Leyland Motor Corp v Armstrong Patents Co Ltd* [1984] F.S.R. 591 (reversed in the House of Lords on other grounds: see [1986] 1 All E.R. 850, [1986] 1 A.C. 577). There the argument was that what had been copied was not the artistic work but the co-ordinates shown on the drawing in the form of figures. That argument was rejected. Thus, it is argued, the explanatory legend forms part of the drawing and substantial alterations to the explanatory legend are substantial alterations to the drawing.

It has, however, to be borne in mind that all these cases were concerned with a very different question from that with which this appeal is concerned. It is one thing to say that the explanatory figures and legend, because they are of value (and, indeed, perhaps essential) to an informed understanding of the drawing, cannot be ignored in considering whether copyright in the drawing has been infringed by the making of a three-dimensional article or whether the article would appear to a non-expert to be a reproduction of the drawing. It is quite another to say that explanatory material, in the form of words or figures, which are clearly the subject of literary copyright, can confer on an artistic work an originality which it does not possess in its own right. It has always to be borne in mind that infringement of copyright by three-dimensional copying is restricted to artistic copyright (s 48(1)). To produce an article by following written instructions may be a breach of confidence or an infringement of patent, but it does not infringe the author's copyright in his instructions. This is a distinction of crucial importance and it is well brought out in the following passage from the judgment of Buckley L.J. in *Catnic Components Ltd v Hill & Smith Ltd* [1982] R.P.C. 183 at 223:

"I do not question the principle that in deciding whether what has been reproduced by an alleged infringer is a substantial part of the work allegedly infringed, one must regard the quality (that is to say the importance) rather than the quantity of the part reproduced (see *Ladbroke (Football) Ltd v William Hill (Football) Ltd* ([1964] 1 All E.R. 465 at 469, 481 [1964] 1 W.L.R. 273 at 276, 293) *per* Lord Reid and Lord Pearce; but what is protected is the plaintiffs' 'artistic work' as such, not any information which it may be designed to convey. If it is said that a substantial part of it has been reproduced, whether that part can properly be described as substantial may depend upon how important that part is to the recognition and appreciation of the 'artistic work'. If an 'artistic work' is designed to convey information, the importance of some part of it may fall to be judged by how far it contributes to conveying that information, but not, in my opinion, by how important the information may be which it conveys or helps to convey. What is protected is the skill and labour devoted to making the 'artistic work' itself, not the skill and labour devoted to developing some idea or invention communicated or depicted by the 'artistic work'. The protection afforded by copyright is not, in my judgment, any broader as counsel submitted, where the 'artistic work' embodies a novel or inventive idea than it is where it represents a commonplace object or theme".

The essence of an artistic work (to adopt the words of Whitford J. in *Rose Plastics GmbH v William Beckett & Co (Plastics) Ltd* (2 July 1987, unreported, of which their Lordships have seen only an approved transcript) is that which is "visually significant"; and counsel for Tyco asks, forensically, what is there in the 1976 drawings which is visually significant and which was not contained in and directly copied from the 1968 drawings? With deference to the Court of Appeal and accepting both the importance of and the skill involved in producing the design information transmitted to the mould makers by the revised figures substituted on the drawing, their Lordships can see no alteration of any visual significance such as to entitle the drawing, as a drawing, to be described as original.

3.2.3.3 *Merchandising Corp. of America v Harpbond* [1983] F.S.R. 32 (C.A.)

The plaintiffs were Adam (Mr Goddard), of the pop group Adam and the Ants, and various companies associated with him. In 1981 Adam Ant devised a new look for himself involving facial make-up and regency clothing. The make-up comprised two broad red lines in grease-paint with a light blue line between, running from nose to jaw on one cheek. Adam drew this in a sketch of his face, using red chalk for the red markings. Mr Ballard was commissioned to take various photographs of Adam in his "new look" and the plaintiff companies licensed the reproduction of these photographs. One of them appeared in the Sun *newspaper.*

The defendants, working from an old photograph of Adam (which they were entitled to use as they did) super-imposed his new look make-up upon it. The plaintiff sought relief for copyright infringement.

Lawton L.J.:

Mr Wilson on behalf of the plaintiffs, has asked us to say that there has been a breach of copyright in reproducing the characteristic make-up used by Mr Goddard in his "new look" and (it is said) indirectly copying the sketch which was wisely made, perhaps on advice, by Mr Goddard before he launched his "new look".

It is said, so far as the make-up aspect of the submission is concerned, that the make-up is covered by section 3 of the Copyright Act 1956. Subsection (1) of that section, for the purposes of this appeal, and I will only concern myself with the parts which are relevant to this appeal, provides as follows:

> "In this Act 'artistic work' means a work of any of the following descriptions, that is to say, (a) the following irrespective of artistic quality, namely, paintings, sculptures, drawings, engravings and photographs".

Mr Swift on behalf of the defendants, pointed out that there is a marked difference between the provisions of section 2 of that Act, which deal with copyright in literary, dramatic and musical works, and those in section 3, which deal with copyright in artistic works. The difference is that, under section 2 "the acts restricted by the copyright in a literary, dramatic or musical work are" and then a number are set out and the relevant one is in paragraph (f), "making any adaptation of the work". In section 3, subsection (5) the acts restricted by the copyright in the artistic work are set out and they do not include "adaptation of the work".

Mr Wilson's bold submission at the beginning of his presentation of his clients' case was that the marks on Mr Goddard's face by way of facial make-up were painting. That caused me very considerable surprise, because, although there are various statutory provisions in the Act defining various words used in it, there is no statutory definition of a painting. "Painting" is a word in the ordinary usage of the English language and it is a question of fact in any particular case whether that which is under discussion is or is not a painting. It seemed to me, right at the beginning of Mr Wilson's submissions (and I want to be restrained in my language), that it was fantastic to suggest that make-up on anyone's face could possibly be a painting.

Mr Swift, in his succinct and concise reply, pointed out what had occurred to me and I had mentioned to Mr Wilson in the course of argument, that a painting must be on a surface of some kind. The surface upon which the startling make-up was put was Mr Goddard's face and, if there were a painting, it must be the marks plus Mr Goddard's face. If the marks are taken off the face there cannot be a painting. A painting is not an idea: it is an object; and paint without a surface is not a painting. Make-up, as such, however idiosyncratic it may be as an idea, cannot possibly be a painting for the purposes of the Copyright Act 1956.

Lawton L.J. proceeded also to find that there were insufficient similarities to constitute infringement. Brightman and Oliver L.JJ. concurred.

3.3 Fixation

3.3.1 Copyright, Designs and Patents Act 1988, s.3, 178, 58

S.3 (2) Copyright does not subsist in a literary, dramatic or musical work unless and until it is recorded, in writing or otherwise; and references in this Part to the time at which such a work is made are to the time at which it is so recorded.

(3) It is immaterial for the purposes of subsection (2) whether the work is recorded by or with the permission of the author; and where it is not recorded by the author, nothing in that subsection affects the question whether copyright subsists in the record as distinct from the work recorded.

S.178 . . . "writing" includes any form of notation or code, whether by hand or otherwise and regardless of the method by which or the medium in or on which, it is recorded, and "written" shall be construed accordingly.

S.58 (1) Where a record of spoken words is made, in writing or otherwise, for the purpose –
  (a) of reporting current events, or
  (b) of broadcasting or including in a cable programme service the whole or part of the work,
it is not an infringement of any copyright in the words as a literary work to use the record or material taken from it (or to copy the record, or any such material, and use the copy) for that purpose, provided the following conditions are met.

(2) The conditions are that –
  (a) the record is a direct record of the spoken words and is not taken from a previous record or from a broadcast or cable programme;
  (b) the making of the record was not prohibited by the speaker and, where copyright already subsisted in the work, did not infringe copyright;
  (c) the use made of the record or material taken from it is not of a kind prohibited by or on behalf of the speaker or copyright owner before the record was made; and
  (d) the use is by or with the authority of a person who is lawfully in possession of the record.

3.3.2 *Walter v Lane* [1900] A.C. 539 (H.L.)

On five occasions in 1896 and 1899 the Earl of Rosebery delivered speeches on subjects of public interest to public audiences. Reporters attended on behalf of The Times and other newspapers. The reporters for The Times took down the speeches in shorthand, wrote out their notes, corrected, revised and punctuated their reports for publication, and the reports were published in The Times, the speeches being given verbatim as delivered by Lord Rosebery.

In 1899 the respondent published a book, incorporating these reports. Lord Rosebery made no claim, but The Times (as assignees of the reporters' copyright) sought inter alia an injunction, damages and costs. In the Court of Appeal the parties agreed that the appeal should be treated as the trial of the action.

Earl of Halsbury L.C.:

My Lords, I should very much regret it if I were compelled to come to the conclusion that the state of the law permitted one man to make profit and to appropriate to himself the labour, skill, and capital of another. The law which I think restrains it is to be found in the Copyright Act, and that Act confers what it calls copyright – which means the right to multiply copies – which it confers on the author of books first published in this country.

The sole ground, as I understand the judgment of the Court of Appeal, is, that in their judgment the producer of a written speech unless he is the original speaker cannot be an "author" within the meaning of the Act. My Lords, it seems to me that this argument is based upon a too narrow and misleading use of the word "author". In my view the statute was not meant so to confine it, and I do not understand the explanation the Court of Appeal gives of the application of the word "author" to such publications as directories, red books, maps, etc.

I observe the Court of Appeal uses the word "analogy" as applicable to such questions. To my mind it is no analogy at all. If the maker of a directory, red book, or a map is an "author", one has to analyze what in such cases is the distinction between the "author" as thus referred to and the author of a spoken speech. If the producer of such a book can be an author within the meaning of the Act, I am unable to understand why the labour of reproducing spoken words into writing or print and first publishing it as a book does not make the person who has so acted as much an author as the person who writes down the names and addresses of the persons who live in a particular street.

I observe that the Court of Appeal introduces the words "original composition" as if those were the words of the statute; and at another part of the judgment it is said that "the report and the speech reported are no doubt different things, but the printer or publisher of the report is not the 'author' of the speech reported, which is the only thing which gives any value or interest to the report". The sentence is a little difficult to construe, but, as I understand it, it means to convey that the thing to which the statute gives protection must be of some value or interest. Again, I am compelled to point out that such words are not to be found in the statute.

If the question here were whether there was the right to publish at all a speech made by someone who did not himself publish it, questions like those determined in this House in *Caird v Sime* ([1887] 12 App. Cas. 326) might arise. Whether the speech was delivered so as to give it to all the world and to prevent the original author of it from restricting its publication is a question with which your Lordships have here no concern. Lord Rosebery is not here complaining of the publication of it, nor claiming any proprietary right in the speeches delivered.

My Lords, I cannot help thinking that underlying the argument which has been addressed to us there is something of the contention which was boldly made nearly half a century ago in the case of *Maclean v Moody* ((1858) 20 J.C. Court Sess. Cas. 1154) in the Court of Session, where, relying on the preamble, the advocate argued that the object of the statute of Victoria was to encourage literary merit, that the intellectual labour constituting authorship was alone thereby protected, and that there could be no authorship without an author. Lord Deas refused to accept such an argument, and expressed the opinion that the Act did not confine the privilege to cases in which there was a known author. But it appears to me that, although it may be true that a preamble may be a guide to the general objects of the statute, it undoubtedly is unquestioned law that it can neither restrict nor limit express enactment. And though I think in these compositions there is literary merit and intellectual labour, yet the statute seems to me to require neither, nor originality either in thought or in language.

It is admitted apparently by the Court of Appeal (and indeed insisted on as part of the reasons for their judgment) that the owner of an unpublished manuscript, although not the author of it, acquires copyright in it by first publishing it. And I observe that it is said Lord Rosebery had no copyright in his speech, and although he could have acquired copyright in it by putting it into writing and printing and publishing it, he did not do so. Here, again, the implied proposition is that the only person who could gain copyright in his speech is the person who spoke it, and that the word "original" must by construction be read into the statute – that the true analogy is the true and first inventor of the patent laws.

I think the analogy is a false one. I do not find the word "original" in the statute, or any word which imports it, as a condition precedent, or makes originality of thought or idea necessary to the right. But if the analogy were strictly pursued, I think it would not be favourable to the defendant. An importer of a foreign invention is for the purpose of the patent laws an inventor, and, as Lord Brougham said in *Re Berry's Patent,* there were "two species of public benefactors – the one, those who benefit the public by their ingenuity, industry, and science and invention and personal capability; the other, those who benefit the public without any ingenuity or invention of their own, by the appropriation of the results of foreign inventions. Now the latter is a benefit to the public incontestably, and therefore they render themselves entitled to be put upon somewhat, if not entirely, the same footing as inventors".

My Lords, if I have not insisted upon the skill and accuracy of those who produce in writing or print spoken words, it is not because I think the less of those qualities, but because, as I have endeavoured to point out, neither the one nor the other are conditions precedent to the right created by the statute. That right, in my view, is given by the statute to the first producer of a book, whether that book be wise or foolish, accurate or inaccurate, of literary merit or of no merit whatever.

I must notice one supposed difficulty in this view very persistently urged at the bar. It is said that in the view I have suggested there would be as many copyrights as reporters. I do not see the difficulty. Each reporter is entitled to report, and each undoubtedly would have a copyright in his own published report; but where is the difficulty?

Lords Davey, James of Hereford, Brampton and Robertson delivered concurring speeches.

3.3.3 *Roberton v Lewis* (1960) [1976] R.P.C. 169 (Cross J.)

The plaintiffs asserted copyright in the tune of a Scottish folk-song, "Westering Home", as arranged by Sir Hugh Roberton. Of one argument put to him, Cross J. stated:

In view of the conclusion which I have reached with regard to the verse section of the song, it is clear that the plaintiffs are not entitled to any copyright in respect of any part of the tune of "Westering Home". They argue, however, in reliance on the case of *Walter v Lane* [1900] A.C. 539, that, even if Sir Hugh had no copyright in the time or any part of it, he nevertheless had copyright in the printed record of it which he made, and that the defendants have infringed that copyright.

Cross J. referred to the facts of Walter v Lane *(above) and continued:*

Sir Hugh's executors have this limited form of copyright which they claim but I am by no means satisfied that they have. In the first place, it is to be observed that Lord Halsbury in his speech laid considerable stress on the fact that the Copyright Act 1842, which was the Act then in force, did not provide that a work must be "original" in order to be entitled to copyright whereas the 1956 Act, reproducing in this respect the provisions of the 1911 Act, only gives copyright in "original works": see section 2(1). In view of this change it is I think at least arguable that *Walter v Lane* is no longer good law. Assuming, however, that the law is still as there laid down, the facts of this case differ very materially from those which existed in *Walter v Lane*. There the shorthand writers took down the words of speeches from the lips of a speaker who had not himself previously reduced his words into writing. In this case no one knows who the author of the tune was but in the long period of time which must have elapsed since it first came into existence it must have been sung or piped on innumerable occasions, and many of those who sung or piped it may have written down the notes, either to aid their own memories or to enable them to teach it to others. I am by no means clear that the decision in *Walter v Lane* has any application to a case where the speech or tune in question has already been accorded a material form before the record of it for which copyright is claimed came into existence. It is perhaps worth noting that counsel for the shorthandwriters in his argument in the Court of Appeal in the case of *Walter v Lane* expressly conceded that, if Lord Rosebery had written his speech out and had read it or repeated it from memory, the shorthandwriters would have no copyright in their reports of it: see [1899] 2 Ch. 766. It appears to me that this admission of counsel may well have been justified.

3.4 Qualification and Publication

3.4.1 Copyright, Design and Patents Act 1988, s.157(1)–(2), s.159(1), s.160(1): Qualification

S.157(1) This Part extends to England and Wales, Scotland and Northern Ireland.

(2) Her Majesty may by Order in Council direct that this Part shall extend, subject to such exceptions and modifications as may be specified in the Order, to –
  (a) **any of the Channel Islands,**
  (b) **the Isle of Man, or**
  (c) **any colony.**

S.157(3)–(5) add a number of ancillary powers. S.158 deals with countries which cease to be colonies.

S.159 (1) Her Majesty may by Order in Council make provision for applying in relation to a country to which this Part does not extend any of the provisions of this Part specified in the Order, so as to secure that those provisions –
  (a) **apply in relation to persons who are citizens or subjects of that country or are domiciled or resident there, as they apply to persons who are British citizens or are domiciled or resident in the United Kingdom, or**
  (b) **apply in relation to bodies incorporated under the law of that country as they apply in relation to bodies incorporated under the law of a part of the United Kingdom, or**
  (c) **apply in relation to works first published in that country as they apply in relation to works first published in the United Kingdom, or**
  (d) **apply in relation to broadcasts made from or cable programmes sent from that country as they apply in relation to broadcasts made from or cable programmes sent from the United Kingdom.**

S.159(2) gives ancillary power, inter alia, to apply the Part subject to exceptions; s.159(3) requires, save in respect of Convention and E.C. countries, reciprocity of provision as a precondition; s.159(4) defines convention country and s.159(4) allows for annulment of an Order by resolution of either House.

S.160 (1) If it appears to Her Majesty that the law of a country fails to give adequate protection to British works to which this section applies, or to one or more classes of such works, Her Majesty may make provision by Order in Council in accordance with this section restricting the rights conferred by this Part in relation to works of authors connected with that country.

S.160(2)–(4) introduce ancillary duties and definitions.

3.4.2 Copyright, Designs and Patents Act 1988, s.175: Publication

S.175 (1) In this Part "publication", in relation to a work
- (a) means the issue of copies to the public, and
- (b) includes, in the case of a literary, dramatic, musical or artistic work, making it available to the public by means of an electronic retrieval system;

and related expressions shall be construed accordingly.

(2) In this Part "commercial publication", in relation to a literary, dramatic, musical or artistic work means –
- (a) issuing copies of the work to the public at a time when copies made in advance of the receipt of orders are generally available to the public, or
- (b) making the work available to the public by means of an electronic retrieval system;

and related expressions shall be construed accordingly.

(3) In the case of a work of architecture in the form of a building, or an artistic work incorporated in a building, construction of the building shall be treated as equivalent to publication of the work.

(4) The following do not constitute publication for the purposes of this Part and references to commercial publication shall be construed accordingly –
- (a) in the case of a literary, dramatic or musical work
  - (i) the performance of the work, or
  - (ii) the broadcasting of the work or its inclusion in a cable programme service (otherwise than for the purposes of an electronic retrieval system);
- (b) in the case of an artistic work –
  - (i) the exhibition of the work,
  - (ii) the issue to the public of copies of a graphic work representing, or of photographs of, a work of architecture in the form of a building or a model for a building, a sculpture or a work of artistic craftsmanship,
  - (iii) the issue to the public of copies of a film including the work, or
  - (iv) the broadcasting of the work or its inclusion in a cable programme service (otherwise than for the purposes of an electronic retrieval system);
- (c) in the case of a sound recording or film –
  - (i) the work being played or shown in public, or
  - (ii) the broadcasting of the work or its inclusion in a cable programme service.

(5) References in this Part to publication or commercial publication do not include publication which is merely colourable and not intended to satisfy the reasonable requirements of the public.

(6) No account shall be taken for the purposes of this section of any unauthorised act.

3.4.3 *Francis Day & Hunter v Feldman* [1914] 2 Ch. 728; (Neville J., C.A.), 83 L.J. Ch. 906; 111 L.T. 521; 59 S.J. 41

The song, "You made me love you (I didn't want to do it)", was composed by an American in the US. It was published simultaneously in New York and London on May 5, 1913. The plaintiffs, acting for the American copyright owners, placed six copies for sale in their retail showroom in London on that date, sent one copy to the British Museum and next day four to the agent for the universities which held the deposit libraries. The song became a success the following July, whereupon the plaintiffs acquired the British Empire copyright and made large sales of the sheet music. Their action for infringement was against the publisher of a "reply song". The principal issue was whether there had been first publication in England.

Neville J.:

The first question that I have to decide is whether there has been publication in England within fourteen days after May 5, 1913, within the meaning of the statute. The material words are "unless the publication in such parts of His Majesty's Dominions as aforesaid is colourable only and is not intended to satisfy the reasonable requirements of the public". There you have really a definition of what "colourable only" means. It means a case where there is no intention to satisfy the reasonable requirements of the public. In the present case I find no evidence upon which I could come to such a conclusion. It is quite true that the demand anticipated was insignificant and the supply secured to satisfy the demand was also insignificant. A dozen copies were all that were sent at the time, and it was not until some time afterwards that further copies were applied for and forwarded from America. It seems to me that the intention from the first was to satisfy the public demand in this country. In this case I think that is what the publication in England was for. I hold therefore that there was a good publication in England.

The C.A. affirmed this judgment without giving reasons.

3.4.4   *British Northrop v Texteam Blackburn* [1974] R.P.C. 57 (Megarry J.)

The plaintiff's company manufactured looms and weaving machinery. The defendant's company, run by a former managing director of the plaintiff together with ex-employees, began marketing the most frequently requested of the many spare parts needed for the machines. The plaintiff alleged that all the defendant's spares infringed design copyright in drawings for the parts. In interlocutory procedures the defendants asserted inter alia *that copyright by first publication in the UK or a convention country had not been proved since publication only took place when and where members of the public who had ordered them received them.*

Megarry J.:

"Place of publication. In cases where the place of publication is material it would appear that it is the place where copies are received by the public, or at least capable of being so received, and not the place where copies are printed or produced".

The authority cited for this is *McFarlane v Hulton* [1899] 1 Ch. 884. That case concerned a clause in an agreement for the sale of the copyright in a sporting paper within a radius of 10 miles of the office in London. The vendors subsequently printed a sporting paper in Manchester, but in addition to offering copies for distribution or sale at their Manchester office, they sent copies to London which were offered for distribution or sale at an office within the 10 miles radius. Cozens-Hardy J. held that the paper was published both in Manchester and London; and he said at page 889:

"It seems to me that a paper is published when and where it is offered to the public by the proprietor".

I can find not a word in the case to support the proposition that publication occurs at "the place where copies are received by the public", a view which would suggest that a periodical which is offered to the public by postal subscription and has 10,000 subscribers would have 10,000 places of publication.

His Lordship derived support from Francis Day & Hunter v Feldman *(above, 3.4.3) and continued:*

Accordingly, in my judgment, under the Act of 1956 an artistic work is "issued to the public", and so published when reproductions of the work are put on offer to the public. Normally, no doubt, the reproduction will be offered for sale; but I do not see why an offer gratis should not be an offer. Again, no doubt there will usually be some process of advertisement or announcement to the public that the reproductions are on offer; but I agree with Neville J. in thinking that no such advertisement or announcement is requisite where the person concerned is prepared to supply on demand. I therefore reject Mr Mervyn Davies' contention that the plaintiffs must fail because they have not proved any positive acts of offer by the plaintiffs. Passive availability suffices, without active offering. In my judgment, subject to the 30 days' rule, the work is first published when it is first put on offer, and the place of first publication is where this occurs. In this case, it seems plain to me that, at any rate for the purposes of the motion, there is enough evidence to establish, directly or by inference, that the drawings in question were first published when parts made in accordance with the drawings were offered for sale by the plaintiffs in Blackburn. Accordingly, this ground for contending that no copyright exists in the drawings must fail. I may add that if, contrary to my opinion, the drawings are unpublished works, I should hold that it is sufficiently established for the purposes of the motion that the author was a "qualified person", when the work was made, within section 3(2), so that by this different route the defendants' attack on the subsistence of copyright in the drawings must fail. That conclusion also suffices to sustain copyright under section 3(3)(b) for drawings first published after May 1957 if the drawings, though published, were not first published in the United Kingdom or another country within the section, so that (contrary to my view) section 3(3)(a) is not satisfied.

3.4.5 *Bodley Head v Flegon* [1972] R.P.C. 587 (Brightman J.)

The Russian author, Alexander Solzhenitzyn, signed a Swiss power of attorney authoriz-
ing H to deal outside Russia with a novel ("August 1914"). H entered into a contract
whereby a Russian edition of the work was published by the YMCA press in France in
June 1971. In return for Royalties, the plaintiff obtained the exclusive right to translate the
work into English and publish and serialize it in (inter alia) the UK but not before August
1972. The defendant who had obtained a Russian copy of the work intended to publish his
own English translation in December 1971. On the plaintiff's motion for an interlocutory
injunction to restrain this, the defendant claimed that, since the author was a Russian (and
Russia was not at that date party to the UCC) UK copyright could be acquired only by first
publication in a convention country; but that first publication had taken place by
"samizdat" – clandestine circulation in typed form among educated people in Russia.

On this question, Brightman J. said:

I wish to make it absolutely clear that, so far as this court is concerned, the evidence of
any such publication of the novel is, at present, totally non-existent. This makes it
unnecessary for me to decide whether samizdat circulation could, in any event, be
treated as publication within the meaning of the Copyright Act 1956 so as to prevent
the YMCA Press publication being treated as first publication. Section 49 (2) of the
Copyright Act 1956 reads in part:

> "With regard to publication, the provisions of this subsection shall have effect for
> the purposes of this Act, that is to say … (b) except in so far as it may constitute
> an infringement of copyright, or a contravention of any restriction imposed by
> section 43 of this Act, a publication which is merely colourable, and not intended
> to satisfy the reasonable requirements of the public, shall be disregarded; (c)
> subject to the preceding paragraphs, a literary, dramatic or musical work, or an
> edition of such a work, or an artistic work, shall be taken to have been published if,
> but only if, reproductions of the work or edition have been issued to the public".

It appears from the judgment of Neville J. in *Francis Day & Hunter v Feldman & Co*
[1914] 2 Ch. 728, 732, that the words "not intended to satisfy the reasonable
requirements of the public" are in effect a definition of "colourable publication".
Although I do not so decide, because it is unnecessary, I would myself doubt whether
samizdat circulation could possibly be regarded as an effort to satisfy the reasonable
requirements of the Russian public. It is rather, as it seems to me, a clandestine
circulation which intentionally disregards the requirements of the Russian public
because such requirements cannot lawfully be voiced by potential readers or satisfied
by the author.

The learned judge then refused to hold that the international community of nations would
be jeopardised by granting relief, since neither publishing contract required the doing of
any illegal act within Russia. He upheld the validity of the power of attorney as governed
by Swiss and not by Russian law.

3.5 Infringement

3.5.1 Substantial Taking of Expression

3.5.1.1 *Plix Products v Frank M. Winstone* [1986] F.S.R. at 92–94 (Pritchard J., S.Ct., N.Z.)

The plaintiff company claimed copyright in drawings, moulds and models of "pocket packs" for transporting kiwi fruit. Under the New Zealand Copyright Act 1962 artistic copyright extends to industrial products in a number of ways (as to which, see Wham-O v Lincoln, *below, 4.1.4). Infringement occurred, according to the plaintiff, because the defendants gave the designer of their competing packs instructions to produce packs of the same standard dimensions as the plaintiff's. On the issue, Pritchard J. observed:*

This proposition touches on the question of the idea/expression dichotomy, which is probably the most difficult concept in the law of copyright. It is no longer universally accepted that there is "no copyright in ideas".

The learned authors of *Copinger and Skone James* (12th ed., paras. 2, 103, 179, 156) state unequivocally that the ideas and original thought of the author are not protected – that copyright is concerned only with the concrete forms in which ideas are expressed. There is an insistent line of authority to support this view, ranging from *Kenrick & Co v Lawrence & Co* (1890) 25 Q.B.D. 99 to *L.B. Plastics Ltd v Swish Products Ltd* [1979] R.P.C. 551, 619. In *Wham-O*, Mr Hillyer (as he then was) argued that a preliminary drawing in which the plaintiff asserted copyright was only a sketch which did no more than illustrate an idea and could not therefore be copyright material. That argument was rejected by the Court of Appeal – not on the basis that there is copyright in ideas but on the facts, because the drawing was no mere sketch but a working drawing.

The concept that copyright does not protect ideas is found unacceptable by the authors of several recent textbooks e.g. *Laddie, Prescott & Vitoria* at pages 31 to 33, and *Lahore* on *Intellectual Property in Australia*, paragraphs 1121, 1151.

I think the conflict between these two philosophies is more apparent than real, and that if there is any conflict it can be resolved by an analysis of the concept of "ideas".

There are in fact two kinds of "ideas" involved in the making of any work which is susceptible of being the subject of copyright. In the first place, there is the general idea or basic concept of the work. This idea is formed (or implanted) in the mind of the author. He sets out to write a poem or a novel about unrequited love or to draw a dog listening to a gramophone or to make a kiwi fruit pocket pack – or whatever project he has in mind. While this "idea" remains as a thought in the author's mind it is, of course, not copyright. It is accepted by the proponents of the "copyright in ideas" theory that the mere act of reducing a general or basic concept of this sort to a tangible form does not result in a monopoly in the concept (*Laddie, Prescott & Vitoria*, para. 3.27).

Then there is a second phase – a second kind of "idea". The author of the work will scarcely be able to transform the basic concept into a concrete form i.e. "express" the idea – without furnishing it with details of form and shape. The novelist will think of characters, dialogue, details of plot and so forth. The artist will think of a certain tilt to the dog's head, to the effect of perspective, colour, light and shade. The pocket pack maker will likewise design the shapes, forms, patterns whereby he believes he can most effectively express the basic idea of pocket packs. Each author will draw on his skill, his knowledge of the subject, the results of his own researches, his own imagination in forming his idea of how he will express the basic concept. All these modes of expression have their genesis in the author's mind – these too are "ideas". When these ideas (which are essentially constructive in character) are reduced to concrete form, the forms they take are where the copyright resides.

So it is true to say (with *Laddie, Prescott & Vitoria et al.*) that copyright does extend to the protection of ideas – not to basic concepts, but to the ideas which are applied in the exercise of giving expression to basic concepts. It is equally true to say with *Copinger & Skone James* (and a formidable line of authority) that copyright subsists only in the form of expression and that infringement occurs only when such forms are copied.

The difficulty, of course, is to determine just where the general concept ends and the exercise of expressing the concept begins. It is, as Professor Cornish observes in his recent work, *Intellectual Property*, an "ill-defined boundary". There can be no general formula by which to establish the line between the general idea and the author's expression of the idea. The basic idea (or concept) is not necessarily simple – it may be complex. It may be something innovative; or it may be commonplace, utilitarian or banal. The way the author treats the subject, the forms he uses to express the basic concept, may range from the crude and simplistic to the ornate, complicated – and involving the collation and application of a great number of constructive ideas.

It is in this area that the author expends the skill and industry which (even though they may be slight) give the work its originality and entitle him to copyright. Anyone is free to use the basic idea – unless, of course, it is a novel invention which is protected by the grant of a patent. But no one can appropriate the forms or shapes evolved by the author in the process of giving expression to the basic idea. So he who seeks to make a product of the same description as that in which another owns copyright must tread with care. If he copies the details which properly belong to the expression and not the basic concept, he will infringe the copyright. That is why, when the basic idea is expressed in a crude, or simplistic form, the potential plagiarist or business competitor can, without offending, come very close to an exact reproduction of the copyright work. But where the expression is ornate, complex or detailed, then he must keep his distance: the only product he can then make without infringing may bear little resemblance to the copyright work.

While it is true that copyright law does have the effect of preventing the appropriation by a copyist of the constructive ideas of the author as to the form in which an original work is produced, this is so only because the law provides that to reproduce a substantial part of the material form (i.e. the shape or pattern) of the work by process of "copying" is an infringement. To hold otherwise would be to disregard the explicit terms of the Copyright Act 1962. Section 7(3) defines the restricted act as "reproducing the work in any material form". There is no copyright except by virtue of the Act (s.5(1)): the Act says nothing about taking ideas. The position is stated in clear and unambiguous terms in the following *dicta* from speeches delivered in the House of Lords in *L.B. Plastics Ltd v Swish Products Ltd* (above).

Lord Wilberforce at p.619:

"There can be no copyright in a mere idea, so if all that the respondents had done was to take from the appellants the idea of external latching, or the 'unhanding' of components, or any other idea implicit in their work, the appellants could not complain. Nor is there infringement if a person arrives by independent work at a substantially similar result to that sought to be protected. The protection given by the law of copyright is against copying, the basis of the protection being that one man must not be permitted to appropriate the result of another's labour".

Lord Hailsham at p.629:

"Of course, it is trite law that there is no copyright in ideas, and it may be that if all the respondents were shown to have copied from the appellants was the idea of some sort of external latching of the moulded corner pieces and clips to the extrusions this would have been a sound enough conclusion. But, of course, as the late Professor Joad used to observe, it all depends on what you mean by 'ideas'. What the respondents in fact copied from the appellants was no mere general idea".

3.5.1.2 *Independent Television Publications v Time Out* [1984] F.S.R. 64 (Whitford J.)

The publishers of TV Times *and* Radio Times *asserted literary copyright in the schedules of television and radio programmes which they published each week.* Time Out, *the entertainment listings magazine, began to publish selections from these schedules without permission.*

Whitford J.:

The plaintiffs in both actions say that these are compilations qualifying for protection under section 2(1) of the Act of 1956 as literary works. By the definition section, section 48(1), "'literary work' includes any written table or compilation". The putting together of a number of items will, as I understand the meaning of the word, produce a compilation. In *British Broadcasting Company v Wireless League Gazette Publishing Company* [1926] Ch. 433, Astbury J. held that, whether or not there might be copyright in an individual item defining a programme, there would be "copyright in a compilation of several advance programmes" (see p.442). In my view the daily programme schedules are compilations. Mr Jacob (for the defendants) was prepared to accept that a sufficient degree of skill and labour goes into the production of these daily programme schedules to justify a claim to copyright were it not for the fact that what is being done, so he says, is no more than creating information – information as to forthcoming programmes. Mere information, Mr Jacob says, cannot be the subject of copyright protection and the plaintiffs' claim accordingly falls to the grounds, for the daily programme schedules are information and nothing else.

Now it is plain from the report of Mr Macgillivray's argument that it was argued before Astbury J. that there can be no copyright in a mere list. It is equally plain that Astbury J. did not accept this argument.

Mr Jacob referred me to quite a number of authorities in which it has been pointed out that there is no copyright in information as such. He started with a case way back in 1806 of *Matthewson v Stockdale* and he went on to somewhat more recent times, with *Leslie v Young* [1894] A.C. 335. In his speech in this latter case Lord Herschell observed at p.340 that:

"The mere publication in any particular order of the timetables which are to be found in railway guides and the publications of the different railway companies could not be claimed as a subject matter of copyright. Proceedings could not be taken against a person who merely published that information which it was open to all the world to publish and to obtain from the same source".

One question before the House was whether the plaintiffs' abridgment of certain railway timetables was a proper subject of copyright. The House held that it was. They further held that there was infringement.

While it is apparent from the opinions of their Lordships that they were of the view that a mere copy of timetables would not create a separate copyright in such copies, the question as to whether there was copyright in the original timetables was not before the House, and the case does not decide, as I think Mr Jacob sought to suggest, that there can be no copyright in, for example, a railway timetable. It must of course also be remembered that this case was heard before the Act of 1911, which for the first time (see section 35(1)) expressly brought compilations within the definition of "literary work".

Chilton v Progress Printing Company [1895] 2 Ch. 29 was a case in which it was decided that the plaintiffs' list of forecasted winners at a race meeting was not in the nature of a literary composition and that what the plaintiffs were seeking to do was to protect their opinion as to the likely winners. In cases subsequent to the Act of 1911, however, lists of brood mares and their sires and stallions and their daughters have been protected, as has, under a comparable statute in Australia, a list of weights and acceptances for horse races: *Winterbotham v Wintle* (1947) 50 W.A.L.R. 58.

The most recent citation by Mr Jacob on the question of "mere information" was from the judgment of Goff L.J. in *Elanco Products Ltd v Mandops (Agricultural Specialists) Ltd* [1980] R.P.C. 213. It was a case on motion in which Goff L.J. observed (see p.52) that the compilation cases are based essentially upon the plaintiffs being able to establish the requisite degree of skill and labour in making the compilation as distinct from ascertaining the information. This observation I think must be subject to some reservation in the light of a decision of Upjohn J. to which I shall be coming. *Elanco v Mandops* was a case in which Goff L.J. cited with approval a passage from the judgment of the Vice-Chancellor in *Scott v Stanford* (1867) L.R. 3 Eq. 723: "No man is entitled to avail himself of the previous labour of another for the purpose of conveying to the public the same information". It was a case in which Goff L.J. repeated the oft-cited words that there is no copyright in information or ideas. But again it was a case in which the existence of copyright in compilations as such or the possibility of such existence was reaffirmed.

Anyone reading a copyright work based upon publicly available information is of course free to go away and, starting with that public source and from that source, to produce his own work which may correspond very closely with the work of the earlier author. What he is not entitled to do is to take a short cut. I have spoken about "publicly available information". There is nothing in the Act which gives to the public at large the right to copy a compilation merely because the information contained in that compilation is not available from any other source. It would be strange if this were the case, for in the making of a compilation the generation of the relevant information may involve very much more of that skill and labour which is thought worthy of protection that any arrangement of the information once it becomes available. To apply this to the present case, it seems to me that, though the requisite degree of skill and labour went into both activities, more skill and labour was involved in getting out the daily programme schedules than in producing the listing in the *TV Times* and *Radio Times*.

Naturally enough reference on both sides was made to the judgment of Upjohn J. in *Football League Limited v Littlewoods Pools Limited* [1959] 1 Ch. 637. This was a case concerned with a football fixture lists produced by the plaintiffs and used by the defendants in the making up of their pool entry forms. As in the present case there were various stages in the production of the "chronological list" which was the compilation alleged to be infringed. Arguments in this case, which as I understood it were very similar to the arguments advanced before me by Mr Jacob, are dealt with by Upjohn J.

Whitford J. quoted extracts from Upjohn J.'s judgment and concluded with the following extract concerning Mr Sutcliffe, compiler of the fixtures list:

"Every case must depend on its own facts. It is perfectly true that Sutcliffe was not employed to produce a work of art *per se* nor even a work primarily as a book of reference, such as a directory or a railway guide, but he was employed the produce the best possible programme of fixtures. The League's duty is to arrange the best possible programme of games, to please the football public in general and the clubs' finances in particular, and they can only do that by producing a list or lists of those games. If, as a result of prolonged cogitations, Sutcliffe reaches the conclusion that it will be best if, for example, Arsenal plays Manchester City at Highbury on September 20, 1958 (as the programme provided) he is doing so no doubt primarily because that is best from the point of view of League football, but if, as a result of the whole of his prolonged and skilled cogitations, he produced in a particular form the season's list consisting of 2,028 matches or thereabouts, in my judgment, he or the League (who have, by direct assignment, any copyright which might otherwise vest in him) are entitled to claim that the chronological list is produced as a result of the entire skill, labour, time, judgment and ingenuity of the League, their servants and agents. In my judgment, on the facts of this case, it is not open to the defendants to try and dissect and break down the efforts of Sutcliffe in the way suggested. Accordingly, in my judgment, the plaintiffs are entitled to copyright in the chronological list".

Upjohn J. came to the conclusion that there was sufficient work in the production of the chronological list from the club to justify the separate claim to copyright and, indeed, that the work done was sufficient to justify a copyright claim at all relevant stages.

On this case again Mr Jacob submitted that there is a holding that there is no copyright in information but only in presentation, that is, in the particular arrangement of the information, and I understand him to be submitting that, as the daily programme schedules were mere information, they cannot be said to have a form and accordingly are not compilations, this upon the basis that the order of presentation hour by hour is part of the information.

Whitford J. proceeded to find that the defendant's selections amounted to substantial reproductions of the plaintiffs' schedules; and that what was being taken did not amount to fair dealing for purposes of criticism or review, or for reporting current events. Accordingly the cases of copyright infringement were made out.

3.5.1.3   *Ravenscroft v Herbert* [1980] R.P.C. 193 (Brightman J.)

The plaintiff's work was a book of non-fiction. It detailed the history of the spear which forms part of the Hapsburg treasure in the Hofburg Museum, Vienna. He had traced this spear back through time and had identified it as the spear which pierced the side of Christ at the crucifixion, the spear used by many legendary historical personages, and the source of inspiration for Hitler's Germany. He had researched the history of the spear by orthodox methods and by using mystical meditation through the medium of a Dr Stein. The first defendant wrote fiction. He had read the plaintiff's book and thought it would make a good basis for a novel. He wrote a work of fiction about the post-war fate of the spear. The prologues of each section of the book recounted the story of the Hofburg spear from the Crucifixion to the end of the 1939 war. The first defendant admitted using the plaintiff's work as a source but denied copying such a substantial part as to amount to infringement of copyright.

Brightman J.:

The question which I have to decide is a question of fact, whether there has been substantial copying of *"The Spear of Destiny"* amounting to an infringement of the plaintiff's rights. This raises two issues, first whether there has been copying, and, secondly, whether such copying is substantial within the meaning of section 49. I have read both books. The plaintiff gave evidence before me during a period over four days, and the defendant for almost three days. It is absolutely plain that in writing five of the prologues that I have mentioned the defendant copied from the plaintiff's book. The next issue, therefore, is whether such copying is in relation to a substantial part of the plaintiff's book and therefore in excess of what is a legitimate degree of copying.

Mr Laddie, for the defendants, rightly says that an author has no copyright in his facts, nor in his ideas, but only in his original expression of such facts or ideas. He submitted that in deciding whether copying is substantial there are four principal matters to be taken into account. First, the volume of the material taken, bearing in mind that quality is more important than quantity; secondly, how much of such material is the subject-matter of copyright and how much is not; thirdly, whether there has been an *animus furandi* on the part of the defendant; this was treated by Page-Wood V.-C. in *Jarrold v Houlston* ((1857) 3 K & J 708) as equivalent to an intention on the part of the defendant to take for the purpose of saving himself labour; fourthly, the extent to which the plaintiff's and the defendant's books are competing works.

Copyright protects the skill and labour employed by the plaintiff in production of his work. That skill and labour embraces not only language originated and used by the plaintiff, but also such skill and labour as he has employed in selection and compilation. The principles are clear from the cases. There is a helpful summary of the authorities in *Harman Pictures NV v Osborne* [1967] 1 W.L.R. 723. For my purposes it is sufficient to cite two passages from that case which are taken from earlier authority:

"... another person may originate another work in the same general form, provided he does so from his own resources and makes the work he so originates a work of his own by his own labour and industry bestowed upon it. In determining whether an injunction should be ordered, the question, where the matter of plaintiff's work is not original, is how far an unfair or undue use has been made of the work? If, instead of searching into the common sources and obtaining your subject-matter from thence, you avail yourself of the labour of your predecessor, adopt his arrangements and questions, or adopt them with a colourable variation, it is an illegitimate use".

This appears at page 730 of the report. There is also a passage:

"In the case of works not original in the proper sense of the term, but composed of, or compiled or prepared from materials which are open to all, the fact that one man has produced such a work does not take away from anyone else the right to produce another work of the same kind, and in doing so to use all the material open to him. But as the law has been precisely stated by Hall V.-C. in *Hogg v Scott* (1874) L.R. 18 Eq. 444 'the true principle in all these cases is that the defendant is not at liberty to use or avail himself of the labour which the plaintiff has been at for the purpose of producing his work, that is, in fact, merely to take away the result of another man's labour or, in other words, his property'": see page 732.

In this case the judge was confronted with the well-known book by Mrs Cecil Woodham Smith entitled *"The Reason Why"* and also the script for a motion picture written by John Osborne. The question which the judge posed was this (at page 736):

"... did John Osborne work independently and produce a script which, from the nature of things, has much in common with the book, or did he proceed the other way round and use the book as a basis, taking his selection of incidents and quotations therefrom, albeit omitting a number and making some alterations and additions, by reference to the common sources and by some reference to other sources?"

The main thrust of Mr Laddie's argument was that the plaintiff intended his book to be read as a factual account of historical events, that the defendant accepted it as fact and did no more than repeat certain of those facts. The plaintiff cannot claim a monopoly in historical facts. The law of copyright does not preclude another author from writing upon the same theme. It is perfectly legitimate for another person to contrive a novel about the Hofburg spear, even about its supposed ancestry and supernatural powers. Otherwise one would be driven to the conclusion that the plaintiff has a monopoly of the facts. Members of the public are entitled to use *"The Spear of Destiny"* as a historical work of reference.

I am inclined to accept that a historical work is not to be judged by precisely the same standards as a work of fiction. The purpose of a novel is usually to interest the reader and to contribute to his enjoyment of his leisure. A historical work may well have that purpose, but the author of a serious and original historical work may properly be assumed by his readers to have another purpose as well, namely to add to the knowledge possessed by the reader and perhaps in the process to increase the sum total of human experience and understanding. The author of a historical work must, I think, have attributed to him an intention that the information thereby imparted may be used by the reader, because knowledge would become sterile if it could not be applied. Therefore, it seems to me reasonable to suppose that the law of copyright will allow a wider use to be made of a historical work than of a novel so that knowledge can be built upon knowledge.

Having studied the two books and heard the evidence, I have no shadow of doubt that the defendant has copied from *"The Spear of Destiny"* to a substantial extent. In the prologues that I have mentioned he has deliberately copied the language of the plaintiff on many occasions. To a more significant extent he has adopted wholesale the identical incidents of documented and occult history which the plaintiff used in support of his theory of the ancestry and attributes of the spear, of Hitler's obsession with it and also General Patton's. He did this in order to give his novel a backbone of truth with the least possible labour to himself. In so doing he annexed for his own purposes the skill and labour of the plaintiff to an extent which is not permissible under the law of copyright. The defendant has clearly infringed the plaintiff's copyright. I am only sorry that so much time, effort and money has had to be spent on the trial of this action.

3.5.1.4 *Elanco Products v Mandops* [1980] R.P.C. 213 (C.A.)

The plaintiffs invented and patented a weed-killer, trifluralin. They marketed it with a leaflet giving extensive information on its proper use. This information was mostly also published in scientific journals.

After expiry of the patent, the defendants brought out the product, accompanied by a leaflet which, in its initial version, closely resembled the plaintiff's in format and language. On receiving objection, the defendants made a second, and then a third, version, which while still conveying the same data, were not so similar in detail.

The C.A. granted an interlocutory injunction, mainly by reference to the balance of convenience. But, in finding that an arguable case had been made out, Goff L.J.

considered that there was a sufficient basis for a claim that the plaintiff's leaflet constituted a literary work as a compilation; and, as to infringement, he stated:

It may well be that if the respondents had in fact at the start simply looked at the available information, including what appears in ACAS and, I think, what appears in the appellants' own literature, and from that decided what they would put in their literature and how they would express it, the appellants would at least have had considerable difficulty in bringing home any charge of infringement, even, having regard to the evidence, if the result had been extremely similar and the selection of items had been the same. But they chose, on the evidence as it stands at the moment, to proceed by making a simple and, as I think unauthorised, copy, and then they proceeded to revise it. It may well be that the result produced that way is an infringement. I say no more than that, because it will be for the trial judge to make up his mind upon all that when he has the whole of the evidence, when it has been sifted and the matter has been argued before him.

I refer again to the case of *Scott v Stamford*, where the Vice-Chancellor stated the principle thus at the end of his judgment:

"No man is entitled to avail himself of the previous labours of another for the purpose of conveying to the public the same information, although he may append additional information to that already published".

I would refer also to a passage in the judgment of the Master of the Rolls in *Moffatt & Paige Ltd v George Gill & Sons Ltd* (1902) 86 L.T. 465 at 471. This is a case having some similarity to the history in this case, since there was there a first edition to which objection was taken and which was then withdrawn, and a second edition which was compiled making use of the first, but altering it in such ways as it was thought would protect the second from any charge that it was an infringement. The learned Master of the Rolls said:

"No doubt he says: 'I am a very well-informed man; I have given, in fact, the greater part of my attention to these works, and I have no doubt I could have evolved the whole of these quotations from researches which I could have made: I know not only where those quotations come from but I know the authors and have named them as appropriate to the particular matters, and I could tell you who they were'. But, unfortunately, he did not go through the process himself; he has adopted the work of another man who may or may not have gone through it, but whether he did or did not, the defendant did not. He simply took what another man had done".

There again it seems to me plain that the appellants have an arguable case. The learned judge at the trial may decide that it was sufficient to make revisions to the offending first copy, or he may think otherwise; but in my view it plainly is an arguable case that the respondents having started off, if I may put it that way, on the wrong foot by making what I think will be found to be a deliberate copy, did not sufficiently cure the position by working from that copy instead of going to the whole of the publicly available information and starting from scratch.

3.5.1.5   *Geographia v Penguin Books* **[1985] F.S.R. 208 (Whitford J.)**

Middleditch, a cartographer, prepared The Daily Telegraph *map for the plaintiff company. After a period of stress, he left its employ, and on his own initiative produced another map which he persuaded Penguin to publish. The plaintiff claimed that this constituted an infringement of its copyright in* The Daily Telegraph *map.*

Whitford J., in refusing to find infringement at trial of the action, said:

Under the Copyright Act 1956 maps are by definition artistic works. Under the Act of 1911 (s.35(1)) they were classified as literary works. Prior to the Act of 1911 it would seem that a map was entitled to be treated as a literary work if the owner of any alleged copyright described it as a map (*Stannard v Lee* (1871) L.R. 6 Ch.340), or alternatively as an artistic work if the owner of the alleged copyright chose to describe it as an engraving (*Stannard v Harrison* (1871) 19 W.R. 811). A map might be considered as being entitled to protection under either head.

The plaintiffs' claim here, with the possible exception of colouring, to which I shall be coming, must rest upon the work done in selecting the features, lakes, rivers, mountains, railways and so on, and the towns – to be included in *The Daily Telegraph* map, the whole being something that can be regarded as a compilation of information which involved a good deal of time and effort in the making and which it was hoped would be of value to any user of the map. In point of general presentation *The Daily Telegraph* map and the allegedly infringing map, save for the fact that they are both maps of the world, on a cylindrical projection, differ considerably. It stands agreed that in the context of such a map as we have here any commercial map maker setting out to make a map is going to have to refer to and take materials from earlier maps as well as other relevant information sources. Whether in so doing there will be an infringement of copyright in the materials consulted and used must depend upon the facts of each particular case. If the outlines of the countries and the positions of islands were traced from some earlier map for which a claim to a copyright in these features could be established this no doubt might in itself constitute an infringement. The plaintiffs here make no claim to copyright in such features as I have just outlined, features which were in any event on the evidence not copied from *The Daily Telegraph* map in the making of the alleged infringing map.

After detailed review of the evidence, and reference to General Drafting v Andrew *(37 F.2d 54), a decision of Judge Mack in a U.S. map case, he concluded:*

On the question of selection of towns and physical features of minor importance having regard to the similarities in colouring, there may have been some ground for suspicion in the plaintiffs' minds, when their attention was first brought to the Penguin map. It was quite apparent from the manner in which he gave his evidence that it would require but little to trigger off the suspicions of Mr Moore, the plaintiffs' present head of cartographical services. Having heard the evidence of Mr Middleditch, I am entirely satisfied that so far as his selections of towns and physical features of minor significance are concerned, these were made from a variety of sources. The plaintiffs have wholly failed to establish – and of course they could only do it by asking me to draw inferences – that his selection was derived in any substantial part, or indeed that they derived at all from *The Daily Telegraph* map. The use of *The Daily Telegraph* map through the Geographia atlas in the placing of colours is admitted but it is not really of any great significance. Adapting slightly the words of Judge Mack, if you take the Penguin map and put it against *The Daily Telegraph* map there is no doubt – Mr Fullard very frankly admitted this – that as compared with *The Daily Telegraph* the Penguin map shows a great deal of originality and that the Penguin map is manifestly different from *The Daily Telegraph* map. It was also quite apparent from the evidence in the case that a very great deal of skill, labour and expense was involved in the production of the Penguin map, and Mr Middleditch's evidence as to the effort that was involved and the expense that was involved was not challenged in cross-examination. This cannot be said to be a case in which there could have been any real saving of time or money. In coming to the conclusion that copying was established in the case before him, Judge Mack, who plainly did not believe the only witness called by the defendants, relied to a not inconsiderable extent on errors appearing in both maps, which must plainly have been copied by the defendants from the plaintiffs' map. There are errors in *The Daily Telegraph* map. Mr Jacob pointed out none of these have been copied into the Penguin map. That this is so is not disputed, but of course it does not dispose of the matter at all. The fact that no errors were copied from one map to the other cannot prove that there was no copying, though if such errors had been taken from one map to the other that might indeed have required some very convincing explanation.

In a map case, even if, on a close examination, there be some apparent similarity in the finer features the question is always going to remain as to whether having regard to the quantity and quality of the information taken there has been any real prejudice to the interests of the copyright owner. As Lord Reid observed in *Ladbroke (Football) Limited v William Hill (Football) Limited* [1964] 1 W.L.R. 273 at 276: "The question whether he has copied a substantial part depends much more on the quality than on the quantity of what he has taken". All that can be said to have been proved to have been taken here is some relatively insignificant features of colouring. The plaintiffs' case fails and the action must stand dismissed.

3.5.1.6   *Bauman v Fussell* (1953) [1978] R.P.C. (C.A.)

The plaintiff photographed two cocks fighting. The defendant, impressed by the photo-graph, painted a picture in which the birds were in similar positions, though the colouring was much altered. The county court judge held that the effect was entirely different and refused to find infringement. An appeal was dismissed.

Somervell L.J.:

Prima facie, the question whether the alleged infringement is a copy or reproduction within the Act is a question of fact, and unless the learned judge had misdirected himself we should not interfere. Mr Skone-James for the appellant submits that he has, and puts his case as follows. Design is a substantial part of an artistic work. The position of the birds is the main part of the design of the photograph. It has been copied or reproduced.

I think the first proposition requires some examination in relation to photographs. A man takes a photograph of a procession or the laying of a foundation stone. He, of course, has chosen when and from where the photograph should be taken. The relative position of those in the procession, or their taking part in the ceremony is not, however, his work, or his design, in the sense in which the relative position of the figures on the ceiling of the Sistine chapel was the work and design of Michelangelo. The order and arrangement of the procession has been, no doubt, carefully planned and designed by someone else. It is an individual's work that the Act is intended to protect. I do not think that a painter who was minded to make a picture of the procession, in his own style, would be committing a breach of copyright if he used the photograph to enable him to get accurately the relative positions of those taking part. What he would be taking would not be a substantial portion of the plaintiff's work. At the other end of the photographic scale one can imagine a case where the photographer has made an original arrangement of the objects animate and inanimate which he photographs in order to create a harmonious design representing, for example, Spring. Here the design would be his work. The position of the birds here is betwixt and between. It is, I think, nearer to the former than the latter category.

There is another consideration which is, I think, relevant here. It is referred to by Romer, L.J. in *Brooks v Religious Tract Society* (1897) 45 W.R. 476. That was a case where part of the engraving had been copied, a collie dog, and part altered. Romer L.J. says "It was not only the dog which was taken, but also the feeling and artistic character of the plaintiff's work. They had taken the design whilst substituting cats and a tortoise for the child". This was under earlier Acts somewhat differently worded but clearly the question whether "the feeling and artistic character" have been taken is relevant to the question whether a substantial portion of the plaintiff's work has been copied or reproduced. Here the feeling and artistic character of the picture are the work of the defendant. I am not suggesting this is conclusive. I think there might well be a case where what was taken was part of the plaintiff's work in the fullest sense, there might yet be an infringement although the feeling and artistic character of the two works were different.

Birkett L.J. reached a similar conclusion; Romer L.J. dissented.

3.5.1.7 *Krisarts v Briarfine* [1977] F.S.R. 577 (Whitford J.)

Legendre painted a series of well-loved views of London, of which the plaintiff company owned the copyright. The defendant company first produced postcard versions of the paintings under a licence agreement with the plaintiff. On expiry of the agreement, the defendant had Mrs Gardner paint the same scenes after showing her copies of Legendre's paintings. Her versions were not slavish copies.

Whitford J. reviewed the evidence in detail and concluded:

I think it is established, indeed I think in the end it was accepted in this case, that both artists worked in some quite considerable measure at least from view cards and photographs as well as possibly, in part, from sketches which they make individually. There is of course nothing wrong in this. It is a commonplace for artists of distinction not to paint on the spot but to prefer to make sketches or impressions or notes from which they work up their paintings at home, and it is by no means uncommon for artists to reinforce their memory by photographic representations of works which are painted in the studio. Nonetheless, at the end of the day most artists produce some distinctive contribution to a scene which may be very well known indeed, and I think, looking at the works it can be said that M. Legendre has done this and I am of the opinion that there is undoubtedly an arguable case on the plaintiffs' side that in producing the work which she in fact produced, although as I have said, it was entirely accepted that a great deal of what she did was original, Mrs Gardner has in fact made a use of the work of M. Legendre in respect of all five paintings, the subject of dispute, sufficiently substantial to base a claim of infringement of copyright. Whether at the end of the day the case will be satisfactorily made out is another matter altogether but I cannot for one moment begin to accept the submission of counsel for the defendants that this application for an interlocutory injunction must fail because there is no arguable case on the issue of infringement.

On the balance of convenience, however, Whitford J. found damages to be an adequate remedy and refused interlocutory relief.

3.5.1.8   *MS Associates v Power* [1988] F.S.R. 242 (Falconer J.)

The defendant, Power, had been employed by the plaintiff company in writing detailed code for the Library (or dictionary) Section of its "C-Gen" computer program, a program which effected translation from the computer language "Basic" into the language, "C". Subsequently the defendant had been a licensed distributor of "C-Gen" and had adapted it to the needs of a particular customer. During this period he spent eight months writing a program, "B-tran", for the same purpose which allegedly infringed copyright in the Library section of "C-Gen". On motion for an interlocutory injunction, Falconer J. said:

As to whether, on the materials now before me on the motion, it appears that the plaintiffs have a real prospect of obtaining a permanent injunction at the trial, their case is that the library section in the defendants' B-tran translator program has been derived from the library of the plaintiffs, copied to an extent that constitutes infringement of copyright. In support of their case the plaintiffs rely on what Mr Wilson referred to as "many objective similarities in structure and in detail," coupled with the fact that there had been opportunity for the first defendant to copy from the plaintiffs' Microsoft BASIC to "C," "C-Gen", program when he had access to it, first as their employee engaged on work on it and, secondly, as their distributor of that program, and particularly when as their distributor he was concerned in adapting the library section of the C-Gen program purchased by Pegasus to the particular requirements of that purchaser.

It is the first defendants' evidence that the library in his B-tran program was not copied from the plaintiffs' program. The matters relied on as similarities are set out at some length by Mr Maskell in Part D of Exhibit KRM.2 to his first affidavit and they are commented on by the first defendant, again at some length, in his Exhibit JMP.1.

I should refer briefly to the particular matters which Mr Wilson relied upon especially. The library in the plaintiffs' program, as is the defendants', is a library of "C" functions which can be called upon; to most of the functions the plaintiffs have given names beginning with "m.s.", followed by letters related to the BASIC equivalent, where there is one. In the defendants' B-tran program many of the function names are the same without the "m.s." so that many resemble the BASIC equivalent. But there is a striking line similarity in the list of functions at the beginning of the plaintiffs' program, a list which is in random order – see paragraph 3.1.5 of section D of KRM.2. It is noteworthy that in the defendants' list, as in the plaintiffs', is the function "vptrs", and, it is Mr Maskell's evidence, not apparently disputed by the first defendant, that that function is not used in the defendants' program.

Mr Hammond, an independent expert who is a lecturer in computer science at the City University and has sworn on affidavit on behalf of the defendants, regards that function list similarity as one requiring explanation. Mr Wilson regarded that as one of the closest similarities, but there are also other line similarities in section D of KRM.2 – they are referred to collectively in paragraph 19 of the first defendant's affidavit and he points out that they amount to only 43 lines in a total program of 15,000 lines. (I think that total should be limited to 9,000 as that was the extent of the program made available on the second inspection).

Mr Wilson accepted that the plaintiffs have not been able to find a large number of line identities but he submitted that their case is based on similarities not just identities, although, so he argued, such identities as the lines containing the list of functions show that the similarities result from copying.

As to similarities in structure, Mr Wilson drew attention to: (i) In the defendants' program, as in the plaintiffs', the library section includes a MAP function, generating an internal reference number for an opened file – the defendants' MAP function is not identical to the plaintiffs' which includes two intermediate steps not present in the defendants' MAP function. But it is not in dispute that there is no equivalent function in BASIC – nor in BASTOC, the only competitive program for the translation of Microsoft BASIC into "C".

(ii) In the plaintiffs' program the "oct" function is arbitrarily grouped with the "hex" function following it. In the defendants' B-tran, the "oct" function similarly is grouped with the "hex" function in the source code file called "hex c". It is Mr Maskell's evidence that there is no obvious reason why it should be so grouped with the "hex" function, other than that the plaintiffs had so grouped them together, and indeed that it would have been better not to put it there but allocate it a separate source code file of its own. However, in commenting on this point, the first defendants' evidence is that the "hex" and "oct" functions are commonly grouped together and are so in Microsoft BASIC.

(iii) The plaintiffs say that the file structure itself on the library in the defendants' B-tran is logically equivalent and very similar and they point, in particular, to the "GET" function; however, Mr Power says the file structure is fundamentally different. In Exhibit JMP.2 to Mr Power's affidavit are printouts of the "GET" function and Mr Carr pointed out the defendants' takes 25 lines and the plaintiffs' takes 91. But reference to figure 4 in Exhibit JMP.3 together with the same printouts numbered and lettered as in Exhibit KRM.9 makes reasonably clear that in fact both "GET" functions follow the same routine – the only difference being that after the second stage in the routine (MAP) the plaintiffs "GET" routine offers an alternative facility (see right hand path in the left hand block diagram of figure 4 of Exhibit JMP.3). Following the routine of the left hand path in that diagram appears to show the same routine as that in the defendants' routine shown in figure 4, resulting in the same data in the same form.

Falconer J. referred to other allegations of similarity and concluded, on the materials before him, that an arguable case had been made out by the plaintiff under the first requirement of the American Cyanamid *judgment (below, 7.1.1.1). On the balance of convenience, however, he ordered a speedy trial, while refusing interlocutory relief.*

3.5.1.9 *Williamson Music v Pearson Partnership* [1987] F.S.R. 97 (Judge Paul Baker, QC)

An advertising agency produced a television advertisement for a bus company, which set out to parody the lyrics and music of "There's Nothing Like a Dame" from Rodgers and Hammerstein's musical, "South Pacific". The plaintiffs as owners of copyright in the latter sued for infringement and sought interlocutory relief.

Judge Baker:

The first issue to which I should address myself is the question as to how far a parody is an infringement of copyright. Mr Prescott observed in the course of his submissions that it is hard to see how a parody could ever be an infringement and this has been canvassed, to some extent, in the authorities. Before I look into them, I call attention to two features of parody or burlesque. First of all, it is to be observed that the parodist of the successful parody does himself do a lot of original work in parodying the first work and so can be said to create a new and original work. Of course it has necessarily to conjure up the old or it would fail as a parody, but it is commonplace in this branch of the law that copyright resides not in ideas, but in the expression of them. So the parodist may take an idea and from it a completely new and original work may be created. Another element of this is that the parodist may be indulging in literary criticism or a review of the original work. This latter point, however, does not arise in the present case, because that was not the purpose of the compilers of the advertisement, so I need not deal with any sort of defence under section 6 of the Copyright Act, that is, the fair dealing exception.

I said that there were a number of authorities and I was referred, among others, to an American authority, which I propose to take first. It is the case of *Irving Berlin v E.C. Publications Inc.*, which was heard by the United States Court of Appeals, Second Circuit, in 1964, 329 Fed. 2d 541. Irving Berlin is a well known composer of songs and it seems that in this case the defendants had created and published 25 parodies of his songs. The judgment was given by Judge Kaufman of the Court of Appeals. I propose just to read two passages from his judgment, where he dealt with two precedent cases where a parody was alleged, in one of which the copyright owners had succeeded and in the other of which they had failed. Of those two cases, and I need not refer to them further, Judge Kaufman says:

> "The distinction between the two situations, Judge Carter reasoned, turned on the relative significance or 'substantiality' – in terms of both quality and quantity – of the material taken from the original motion pictures. In both cases, the court recognised in painstaking and scholarly opinions the historic importance and social value of parody and burlesque; in both, it conceded that the parodist must be permitted sufficient latitude to cause his reader or viewer to 'recall or conjure up' the original work if the parody is to be successful. But in Benny's case, the court concluded this licence had been grossly exceeded".

I note from there the reference to quality and quantity of the material taken and in terms of substantiality.

Judge Kaufman concluded his judgment in which he rejected the claim for copyright in relation to all the 25 parodies in these terms:

> "For, as a general proposition, we believe that parody and satire are deserving of substantial freedom – both as entertainment and as a form of social and literary criticism".

He makes reference to *Don Quixote* and Swift's *Gulliver's Travels* and goes on:

> "At the very least, where, as here, it is clear that the parody has neither the intent nor the effect of fulfilling the demand for the original, and where the parodist does not appropriate a greater amount of the original work than is necessary to 'recall or conjure up' the object of his satire, a finding of infringement would be improper".

That is of great interest although the US law on copyright is in material respects different from that here but I notice that, although the parodist is treated generously in the proceedings in the United States, he does not in fact have a licence to appropriate the other person's work.

I suppose in England the high water mark of any liberty allowed to parodies was the judgment of Younger J., as he then was, in *Glyn v Weston Feature Film Company* [1916] 1 Ch. 261. A number of points came up in this case which are not relevant to the issues I have to decide, and I will not take time reading through the facts, beguiling as they are. The passage I had in mind came after the learned judge had concluded that there was no substantial taking by the film *Pimple's Three Weeks* of the work of Eleanor Glyn of her novel *Three Weeks*, so that the case was disposed of on that ground. What followed were some helpful observations although they are *obiter*. At page 268,

Younger J. says:

"Making all allowance for the fact that prior to the Act of 1911 literary copyright did not include the acting right, it certainly is remarkable that no case can be found in the books in which a burlesque even of a play has been treated as an infringement of copyright, although burlesque, frequently more distinguished than the thing burlesqued, is as old as Aristophanes, to take Mr Hartree's example".

Then he refers to certain authorities. He says why the older order had to go and then he says:

"Most probably, however, the reason is to be found involved in such observations as those of Lindley L.J. in *Hansfstaengl v Empire Palace*, or in such a decision as that of the Court of Appeal in *Francis, Day & Hunter v Feldman & Co*, or in the principle that no infringement of the plaintiff's rights takes place where a defendant has bestowed such mental labour upon what he has taken and has subjected it to such revision and alteration as to produce an original result".

He goes on to deal with another case, which perhaps qualifies that, later on in the same paragraph, because he says:

"If, in considering whether such a literary work as a novel has been infringed by such a thing as a cinematograph film, the true enquiry is, as I think it must be, whether, keeping in view the idea and general effect created by a perusal of the novel, such a degree of similarity is attained as would lead one to say that the film is a reproduction of incidents described in the novel or of a substantial part thereof, then in my opinion, the answer in the present case must be in the negative".

That case is perhaps the high water mark but there is something on the same lines in *Joy Music Limited v Sunday Pictorial Newspapers (1920) Limited* [1960] 2 Q.B. 60, a decision of McNair J. This had arisen out of a feature article in the *Sunday Pictorial* which was reported the activities of H.R.H. The Duke of Edinburgh, which activities had caused raised eyebrows in some quarters. At the time there was, and still is for all I know, a form of music known as rock-and-roll and one of the then popular songs had the line: "Rock-a-Billy, Rock-a-Billy, Rock-a-Billy, Rock". It went on with that three times and ended up with some slight variation. The *Sunday Pictorial* adapted that to: "Rock-a-Philip, Rock-a-Philip, Rock-a-Philip, Rock". That was the chorus. The verses were totally different.

The complaint was that the newspaper version was an infringement of the literary copyright in the original song. There was no question of music in this case – the infringers had not used music at all. It might be said that there was no copyright as it is difficult to see how the original lines were an original literary work. They are more gibberish than anything else, but that may be too fastidious a view. That, however, is not quite the way that the learned judge disposed of the case. He found against the claim for copyright and disposed of it on these lines (at page 70):

"If one had to direct a jury on this question"

– that is to say, whether a parody is an infringement

"one would clearly tell them of the various tests that have been suggested as guiding tests, and it would be proper to emphasise to them this test which Younger J. suggested as to whether the defendant had bestowed such mental labour on what he had taken and subjected it to such revision and alteration as to produce an original work. I cannot help thinking that a jury with that direction would have said that, although it is clear that the article in the *Sunday Pictorial* had its origin in 'Rock-a-Billy', it was produced by sufficient independent new work by Paul Boyle to be in itself, not a reproduction of the original 'Rock-a-Billy', but a new original work derived from 'Rock-a-Billy'. And, that being my conclusion of fact, quite shortly I say that I am not satisfied that the article in the *Sunday Pictorial* does reproduce a substantial part of the words of the 'Rock-a-Billy' song of which the plaintiffs have the copyright".

In a case of artistic copyright, Falconer J. made some comments on that decision of McNair J. The case is *Schweppes Limited and Others v Wellingtons Limited* [1984] F.S.R. 210, and the article in question was the bottle of Schweppes tonic water with a distinctive label. That is a soft drink. The defendants were manufacturers of something known as a tonic bubble bath, which they put in a similar bottle with a very similar label, except that it had the name "Schlurppes" on it instead of "Schweppes". The design was something very similar, but it being for a totally different market there was no question of passing off. One of the points in resisting the claim for copyright infringement which was made by the defendants was that it was a parody. The learned judge deals with that in this way:

"What is said, and it has been said forcibly by Mr Tager, is that this bottle is in the nature of a parody; the article itself is meant to be sold, no doubt, as a joke, and to have the characteristics of a caricature".

Then he goes on to point out that Mr Tager relied on the decision of McNair J. in *Joy Music Limited* and he referred especially to what the headnote in that case said, which was:

"that in considering whether a parody of a literary work constituted an infringement of the copyright in that work the main test to be applied was whether the writer had bestowed such mental labour upon the material he had taken and had subjected it to such revision and alteration as to produce an original work".

Falconer J. goes on:

"and of course it is on that proposition that Mr Tager argues that there is a defence in this particular case to infringement. Put in that form, with all due respect, I do not think that a correct statement of the law. The sole test is whether the defendant's work has reproduced a substantial part of the plaintiff's *ex hypothesi* copyright work. The fact that the defendant in reproducing his work may have himself employed labour and produced something original, or some part of his work which is original, is beside the point if none the less the resulting defendant's work reproduces without the licence of the plaintiff a substantial part of the plaintiff's work. The test every time in my judgment is, as the statute makes perfectly plain: 'Has there been a reproduction in the defendant's work of a substantial part of the plaintiff's work?'"

When considering any question of parody, I accept that test of Falconer J., that the test every time is, as the statute makes perfectly plain: "Has there been a reproduction in the defendant's work of a substantial part of the plaintiff's work?"

Judge Baker examined the facts and concluded that there was no serious question to be tried in respect of the lyrics, but that there was such an issue regarding the music.

3.5.2 Proof of Copying

3.5.2.1 *Francis, Day & Hunter v Bron* [1963] Ch. 587 (C.A.)

The plaintiffs claimed that a song, "Why", composed by Mr de Angelis and published by the defendants infringed copyright in their song, "In a Spanish Town". The trial judge, Wilberforce J., found that despite various points of effective similarity, the composer had not intentionally copied and this conclusion was accepted by the Court of Appeal.

Willmer L.J.:

The composer of "Why" was called as a witness, and not only denied copying, but denied that he had ever seen the music of "Spanish Town", or even consciously heard it. He was a man of thirty-three years of age and had lived most of his life in the United States. He stated that he had been composing music since he was eleven, and had played various instruments in dance bands. In cross examination he admitted that at a younger age he might have heard "Spanish Town", because he had heard a lot of music, but he adhered to his statement that he had never consciously studied it, and said that he did not recall ever playing it. The judge accepted his evidence, and I do not think that we in this court could properly interfere with that finding even if we were invited to do so, which we were not. But the plaintiffs say that that is by no means the end of the case, for Mr de Angelis could well have copied from "Spanish Town" subconsciously. The song having been extensively exploited in the United States, the overwhelming probability (it is said) is that he must have heard it; and the degree of similarity between "Spanish Town" and "Why" is such that an inference of, at any rate, subconscious copying should be drawn. That, it is contended, would be enough to constitute an infringement of the plaintiffs' copyright. The judge, however, decided that there was not sufficient material to justify the inference that Mr de Angelis copied the plaintiffs' work, even subconsciously; and he accordingly dismissed the action. It is to this point that the present appeal has been mainly directed.

Counsel, in presenting his argument on behalf of the defendants, drew attention to the fact that in relation to musical copyright, under section 2 of the Act of 1958, there are only three forbidden processes, viz., "reproduction", "arrangement" and "transcription". Arrangement and transcription, he submitted can be only the result of a conscious and deliberate process; a man cannot arrange or transcribe without knowing that he is doing so. The judge's acceptance of the evidence of Mr de Angelis, therefore, precludes the possibility of finding any infringement of the plaintiffs' copyright by arrangement or transcription. This submission must, I think, be accepted.

Counsel for the defendants conceded that reproduction could possibly be the result of a subconscious process. But he went on to submit that reproduction within the section could mean nothing short of identity. Reproduction, under section 49, may be of a substantial part; but there is no suggestion in the Act of 1956 of any such thing as a "substantial reproduction". In the present case it cannot be said that there is anything approaching identity between the plaintiffs' work and that of Mr de Angelis. Consequently, counsel submitted, there could be no infringement of the plaintiffs' copyright, whether conscious or unconscious, by way of reproduction.

I find myself quite unable to accept this submission, for I can find no warrant for the suggestion that reproduction, within the meaning of the section, occurs only when identity is achieved. This not only offends against common sense, but, I think, is contrary to authority. In *Austin v Columbia Gramophone Co Ltd* [1917–23] Mac. Cop. Cas. 398, the headnote reads:

"Infringement of copyright in music is not a question of note for note comparison, but of whether the substance of the original copyright work is taken or not".

In that case, Astbury J., quoted from the earlier case of *D'Alamaine v Boosey* ((1835) 1 Y & C Ex. 288) where it was laid down that "it must depend on whether the air taken is substantially the same with the original". I accept that as a correct statement of the principle.

On the other side, counsel for the plaintiffs submitted in the first place that Mr de Angelis's denial of copying was wholly irrelevant. For where, as was said to be the case here, a sufficient degree of similarity is shown, and it is further proved that the composer of the second work had access to the earlier work in the sense that he must probably have heard it, an irrebuttable presumption arises that the former has been copied from the latter. No authority was cited in support of this proposition, which, if well-founded, would eliminate the necessity for any further evidence once similarity coupled with access had been proved. In my judgment, the proposition contended for is quite untenable; the most that can be said, it seems to me, is that proof of similarity, coupled with access raises a *prima facie* case for the defendant to answer.

Counsel for the plaintiffs contended in the alternative that the degree of similarity found by the judge in the present case was such as to compel an inference of copying which, even if subconscious, was sufficient to give the plaintiffs a cause of action for infringement. I confess that I have found the notion of subconscious copying one of some difficulty, for at first sight it would seem to amount to a contradiction in terms, the word "copying" in its ordinary usage connoting what is essentially a conscious process. The text books on copyright make no reference to the subject, and English authority in relation to it is confined to a single dictum of Luxmoore J. in *G Ricordi & Co (London) Ltd v Clayton and Walter Ltd* ([1928–35] Mac.C.C. 91). Our attention, however, was called to a number of cases in the United States in which the subject has been discussed, and in some of which a decision in favour of the plaintiff has been based on a finding of subconscious copying. It appears to me that the question must be considered in two stages, viz, (i) whether subconscious copying is a psychological possibility; and (ii) if so, whether in a given case it is capable of amounting to an infringement of the plaintiff's copyright.

As to the first of these questions, it was suggested by counsel for the defendants that medical evidence should always be required before a finding of subconscious copying could be justified. I cannot think that this is necessary; for the psychological possibility of subconscious copying was clearly recognised by Luxmoore J. and in the various American decisions, which must be regarded as of high persuasive authority. What Luxmoore J. said in relation to the defendants before him in the *Ricordi* case [1928–35] Mac C.C. 154 was:

"If there has been any infringement it must have been subconsciously, because the persons responsible knew the air complained of so well that they have taken it because they knew it".

Similarly, in two American cases in which the plaintiff succeeded on the ground of subconscious copying, viz, *Fred Fisher Inc v Dillingham* ((1924) 298 Fed. 145) and *Edwards & Deutsch Lithographing Co v Boorman*, the decision was based on the finding of a high degree of familiarity with the plaintiffs' work. From this emerges the conclusion, which seems to me to be consonant with good sense, that, if subconscious copying is to be found, there must be proof (or at least a strong inference) of *de facto* familiarity with the work alleged to be copied. In the present case, on the findings of the judge, this element is conspicuously lacking.

On the second question, viz, whether any subconscious copying proved could amount to an infringement of the plaintiffs' copyright, it seems to me that all that can be said is that at least the *dictum* of Luxmoore J. envisages the possibility. On this point I do not think that much help is to be derived from the American decisions which have been cited, since the American statute under which they were decided is markedly different in its terms. No evidence of American law was adduced, and in its absence it is not for us to construe the American statute. However (as was pointed out by junior counsel for the plaintiffs) it may be observed that, in order to establish an infringement of copyright, it is not necessary to prove anything in the nature of *mens rea*. The printer, for instance, may be held guilty of infringement though he has no conscious intent.

The conclusion at which I arrive on his part of the case is that subconscious copying is a possibility which, if it occurs, may amount to an infringement of copyright. But in order to establish liability on this ground, it must be shown that the composer of the offending work was in fact familiar with the work alleged to have been copied. This view, I think, is not inconsistent with the submissions put forward by Mr Skone James. In the course of an argument which I found convincing, he submitted that, in considering whether there has been reproduction, so as to constitute an infringement within the Copyright Act, 1956, it is wholly irrelevant to inquire whether any copying has been conscious or subconscious. It is for this reason, he modestly suggested, that the text books are silent on the subject of subconscious copying. Mr Skone James presented his argument in four propositions which if I understood him correctly, may be summarised as follows: (i) in order to constitute reproduction, within the meaning of the Act, there must be (a) a sufficient degree of objective similarity between the two works; and (b) some causal connexion between the plaintiff's and the defendant's work. (ii) It is quite irrelevant to inquire whether the defendant was or was not consciously aware of such causal connexion. (iii) Where there is a substantial degree of objective similarity, this of itself will afford *prima facie* evidence to show that there is a causal connexion between the plaintiff's and the defendant's work; at least, it is a circumstance from which the inference may be drawn. (iv) The fact that the defendant denies that he consciously copied affords some evidence to rebut the inference of causal connexion arising from the objective similarity, but is in no way conclusive.

If this is the right approach (as I think it is), it becomes a simple question of fact to decide whether the degree of objective similarity proved is sufficient, in all the circumstances of the particular case, to warrant the inference that there is a causal connexion between the plaintiffs' and the defendants' work. This is the way in which, as it seems to me, the judge in the present case approached the question which he had to decide. He directed himself as follows:

> "The final question to be resolved is whether the plaintiffs' work has been copied or reproduced, and it seems to me that the answer can only be reached by a judgment of fact on a number of composite elements. The degree of familiarity (if proved at all, or properly inferred) with the plaintiffs' work, the character of the work, particularly its qualities of impressing the mind and memory, the objective similarity of the defendants' work, the inherent probability that such similarity as is found could be due to coincidence, the existence of other influences on the defendant composer, and not least the quality of the defendant composer's own evidence on the presence or otherwise in his mind of the plaintiffs' work".

In my judgment that was a proper direction, against which no criticism can fairly be brought.

Willmer L.J. proceeded to accept Wilberforce J.'s conclusion that there was no sufficient material from which to infer subconscious copying.

Upjohn and Diplock L.JJ. delivered concurring judgments.

3.5.3 Acts of Infringement

3.5.3.1   Copyright, Designs and Patents Act 1988, s.2, 16–27, 178

S.2(1) The owner of the copyright in a work of any description has the exclusive right to do the acts specified in Chapter II as the acts restricted by the copyright in a work of that description.

For S.2(2) (moral rights), see below, 3.6.

S.16(1) The owner of the copyright in a work has, in accordance with the following provisions of this Chapter, the exclusive right to do the following acts in the United Kingdom –
  - (a) to copy the work (see section 17);
  - (b) to issue copies of the work to the public (see section 18);
  - (c) to perform, show or play the work in public (see section 19);
  - (d) to broadcast the work or include it in a cable programme service (see section 20);
  - (e) to make an adaptation of the work to do any of the above in relation to an adaptation (see section 21);

and those acts are referred to in this Part as the "acts restricted by the copyright".

(2) Copyright in a work is infringed by a person who without the licence of the copyright owner does, or authorises another to do, any of the acts restricted by the copyright.

(3) References in this Part to the doing of an act restricted by the copyright in a work are to the doing of it –
  - (a) in relation to the work as a whole or any substantial part of it, and
  - (b) either directly or indirectly;

and it is immaterial whether any intervening acts themselves infringe copyright.

(4) This Chapter has effect subject to –
  - (a) the provisions of Chapter III (acts permitted in relation to copyright works), and
  - (b) the provisions of Chapter VII (provisions with respect to copyright licensing).

S.17(1) The copying of the work is an act restricted by the copyright in every description of copyright work; and references in this Part to copying and copies shall be construed as follows.

(2) Copying in relation to a literary, dramatic, musical or artistic work means reproducing the work in any material form.

This includes storing the work in any medium by electronic means.

(3) In relation to an artistic work copying includes the making of a copy in three dimensions of a two-dimensional work and the making of a copy in two dimensions of a three-dimensional work.

(4) Copying in relation to a film, television broadcast or cable programme includes making a photograph of the whole or any substantial part of any image forming part of the film, broadcast or cable programme.

(5) Copying in relation to the typographical arrangement of a published edition means making a facsimile copy of the arrangement.

(6) Copying in relation to any description of work includes the making of copies which are transient or are incidental to some other use of the work.

S.18(1) The issue to the public of copies of the work is an act restricted by the copyright in every description of copyright work.

(2) References in this Part to the issue to the public of copies of a work are to the act of putting into circulation copies not previously put into circulation, in the United Kingdom or elsewhere, and not to –

(a) any subsequent distribution, sale, hiring or loan of those copies, or
(b) any subsequent importation of those copies into the United Kingdom;

except that in relation to sound recordings, films and computer programs the restricted act of issuing copies to the public includes any rental of copies to the public.

S.19(1) The performance of the work in public is an act restricted by the copyright in a literary, dramatic or musical work.

(2) In this Part "performance", in relation to a work –

(a) includes delivery in the case of lectures, addresses, speeches and sermons, and
(b) in general, includes any mode of visual or acoustic presentation, including presentation by means of a sound recording, film, broadcast or cable programme of the work.

(3) The playing or showing of the work in public is an act restricted by the copyright in a sound recording, film, broadcast or cable programme.

(4) Where copyright in a work is infringed by its being performed, played or shown in public by means of apparatus for receiving visual images or sounds conveyed by electronic means, the person by whom the visual images or sounds are sent, and in the case of a performance the performers, shall not be regarded as responsible for the infringement.

S.20 The broadcasting of the work or its inclusion in a cable programme service is an act restricted by the copyright in –

(a) a literary, dramatic, musical or artistic work,
(b) a sound recording or film, or
(c) a broadcast or cable programme.

S.21(1) The making of an adaptation of the work is an act restricted by the copyright in a literary, dramatic or musical work. For this purpose an adaptation is made when it is recorded, in writing or otherwise.

(2) The doing of any of the acts specified in sections 17 to 20, or subsection (1) above, in relation to an adaptation of the work is also an act restricted by the copyright in a literary, dramatic or musical work. For this purpose it is immaterial whether the adaptation has been recorded, in writing or other-

wise, at the time the act is done.

(3) In this Part "adaptation" –
- (a) in relation to a literary or a dramatic work, means –
  - (i) a translation of work;
  - (ii) a version of a dramatic work in which it is converted into a non-dramatic work or, as the case may be, of a non-dramatic work in which it is converted into a dramatic work;
  - (iii) a version of the work in which the story or action is conveyed wholly or mainly by means of pictures in a form suitable for reproduction in a book, or in a newspaper, magazine or similar periodical;
- (b) in relation to a musical work, means an arrangement or transcription of the work.

(4) In relation to a computer program a "translation" includes a version of the program in which it is converted into or out of a computer language or code or into a different computer language or code, otherwise than incidentally in the course of running the program.

(5) No inference shall be drawn from this section as to what does or does not amount to copying a work.

Secondary infringement of copyright
S.22 The copyright in a work is infringed by a person who, without the licence of the copyright owner, imports into the United Kingdom, otherwise than for his private and domestic use, an article which is, and which he knows or has reason to believe is, an infringing copy of the work.

S.23 The copyright in a work is infringed by a person who, without the licence of the copyright owner –
- (a) possesses in the course of a business,
- (b) sells or lets for hire, or offers or exposes for sale or hire,
- (c) in the course of a business exhibits in public or distributes, or
- (d) distributes otherwise than in the course of a business to such an extent as to affect prejudicially the owner of the copyright,

an article which is, and which he knows or has reason to believe is, an infringing copy of the work.

S.24(1) Copyright in a work is infringed by a person who, without the licence of the copyright owner –
- (a) makes,
- (b) imports into the United Kingdom,
- (c) possesses in the course of a business, or
- (d) sells or lets for hire, or offers or exposes for sale or hire,

an article specifically designed or adapted for making copies of that work, knowing or having reason to believe that it is to be used to make infringing copies.

(2) Copyright in a work is infringed by a person who without the licence of the copyright owner transmits the work by means of a telecommunications system (otherwise than by broadcasting or inclusion in a cable programme service), knowing or having reason to believe that infringing copies of the

work will be made by means of the reception of the transmission in the United Kingdom or elsewhere.

S.25(1) Where the copyright in a literary, dramatic or musical work is infringed by a performance at a place of public entertainment, any person who gave permission for that place to be used for the performance is also liable for the infringement unless when he gave permission he believed on reasonable grounds that the performance would not infringe copyright.

(2) In this section "place of public entertainment" includes premises which are occupied mainly for other purposes but are from time to time made available for hire for the purposes of public entertainment.

S.26(1) Where copyright in a work is infringed by a public performance of the work, or by the playing or showing of the work in public, by means of apparatus for –

    (a) playing sound recordings,

    (b) showing films, or

    (c) receiving visual images or sounds conveyed by electronic means, the following persons are also liable for the infringement.

(2) A person who supplied the apparatus, or any substantial part of it, is liable for the infringement if when he supplied the apparatus or part –

    (a) he knew or had reason to believe that the apparatus was likely to be so used as to infringe copyright, or

    (b) in the case of apparatus whose normal use involves a public performance, playing or showing, he did not believe on reasonable grounds that it would not be so used as to infringe copyright.

(3) An occupier of premises who gave permission for the apparatus to be brought onto the premises is liable for the infringement if when he gave permission he knew or had reason to believe that the apparatus was likely to be so used as to infringe copyright.

(4) A person who supplied a copy of a sound recording or film used to infringe copyright is liable for the infringement if when he supplied it he knew or had reason to believe that what he supplied, or a copy made directly or indirectly from it, was likely to be so used as to infringe copyright.

Infringing copies
S.27(1) In this Part "infringing copy", in relation to a copyright work, shall be construed in accordance with this section.

(2) An article is an infringing copy if its making constituted an infringement of the copyright in the work in question.

(3) An article is also an infringing copy if –

    (a) it has been or is proposed to be imported into the United Kingdom, and

    (b) its making in the United Kingdom would have constituted an infringement of the copyright in the work in question, or a breach of an exclusive licence agreement relating to that work.

(4) Where in any proceedings the question arises whether an article is an infringing copy and it is shown –

(a) that the article is a copy of the work, and

(b) that copyright subsists in the work or has subsisted at any time,

it shall be presumed until the contrary is proved that the article was made at a time when copyright subsisted in the work.

(5) Nothing in subsection (3) shall be construed as applying to an article which may lawfully be imported into the United Kingdom by virtue of any enforceable Community right within the meaning of section 2(1) of the European Communities Act 1972.

S.178 . . . "electronic" means actuated by electric, magnetic, electromagnetic, electrochemical or electromechanical energy and "in electronic form" means in a form usable only by electronic means; "facsimile copy" includes a copy which is reduced or enlarged in scale;

"rental" means any arrangement under which a copy of a work is made available –

(a) for payment (in money or money's worth), or

(b) in the course of a business, as part of services or amenities for which payment is made, on terms that it will or may be returned;

"unauthorised", as regards anything done in relation to a work, means done otherwise than –

(a) by or with the licence of the copyright owner, or

(b) if copyright does not subsist in the work, by or with the licence of the author or, in a case where section 11(2) would have applied, the author's employer or, in either case, persons lawfully claiming under him, or

(c) in pursuance of section 48 (copying etc. of certain material by the Crown).

3.5.3.2 *Turner v Performing Right Society* [1943] Ch. 167 (C.A.)

Two companies performed music to their employees during working hours. The performing rights in works thus used was vested in the P.R.S. which sought to require the companies to take a licence for the performances. The companies claimed that the performances were not in public.

Lord Greene M.R.:

In the present case the nature of the audience, when properly understood in my opinion, puts the matter beyond doubt. In each case the audience constitutes a substantial part of the working population of the district. It is collected from different households in the district. From time to time groups of work-people or individual workmen or women asked for a particular song to be played by the gramophone record. It is quite obvious, therefore, that the whole object of these performances is to supply to the workpeople something which they like. So far as regards the music, the workpeople are an audience. The fact that it assists their work appears to me to be entirely irrelevant. While the performances are being given and the workpeople are doing their work, they are doing two things at once. They are working and they are enjoying music, which normally is a thing they would enjoy in their leisure hours. Instead of having the music in their leisure hours, they have it while they are working. None the less they are, so far as the music is concerned, an audience listening to music, and the fact that they are working at the same time does not alter that, any more than it alters the fact that a housewife who turns on her radio set while she is doing her housework is listening to the music at the same time as she is doing that work.

In the present case, having regard to the character of the audience and all the relevant facts which bear upon that matter, I have no doubt that these performances were performances in public. In *Jennings v Stephens* (1) ([1936] Ch. 469) to which I have referred, I ventured to suggest that in considering the character of the audience the primary matter to consider was the relationship of the audience to the owner of the copyright, rather than the relationship of the audience to the performers. I am confirmed in that view by a consideration of the present case. When the legislature under the Copyright Act conferred upon the owner of copyright a monopoly, it no doubt intended that that monopoly should be a real and not an illusory right of property, and it is, therefore, in my opinion, important to consider whether a particular performance, the character of which is in question, is of a kind calculated to whittle down that monopoly to any substantial extent. To take a case at one end of the scale, a purely domestic performance, or what is sometimes called a quasi-domestic perform-ance, is not a thing which is calculated to whittle down the value of the monopoly. It is a thing which can have no substantial effect in depriving the owner of the copyright of the public from whom he receives the value of the work of his brain and his imagination. If you take the other end of the scale, where there is a performance unquestionably in public, such as at a public theatre or a public concert hall, obviously if that were permitted that would whittle down the value of the monopoly. The monopoly is, of course, confined to performances in public, but in considering whether a performance is in public its effect upon the value to the owner of the copyright of his statutory monopoly is, I venture to think, a consideration to which at any rate great importance should be given.

In the present case counsel for the appellants in the second appeal invited us to pay regard not to any relationship of the audience to the owner of the copyright, but to the relationship of the audience to the performer in the present case. The performer, of course, is the proprietor of the factory who performs the music by turning on the broadcast or setting the gramophone in operation. Whatever may be the value of a consideration of the relationship of the performer to the audience in other cases, it seems to me that in the present case it affords an entirely misleading guide. It could make not the slightest difference, in my opinion, if in the present case the performances had been given not by diffusion through the factory by means of loudspeakers operated by the management, but by a neighbour who set up a system of diffusion with loudspeakers which could be heard through the factory. The relationship of the performer to the audience in such a case would not have been the same as the relationship of the performer to the audience in the present case. The difference in the relationship could not, it seems to me, affect in the slightest degree the question whether the performance was or was not a performance in public.

Counsel for the appellants in the second appeal said that the parties in this case were all members of a community organised for work. I have already dealt to a certain extent with the work element in this case, but it seems to me impossible to do what counsel for the appellants in the second appeal asks us to do and regard everything that takes place inside the factory in regard to this music as a purely domestic concern of those taking part in it, whether as performer or as audience. The test of the relationship of the audience to the performer seems to me to break down completely in this case, whereas the test which I venture to suggest would, at any rate in a great many cases, and certainly in the present, be the most helpful one, that is, the relationship of the audience to the composer and the effect that the performance has upon his monopoly, is a consideration which does seem to me in the present case to throw a good deal of light upon the situation.

It was said that it was not legitimate to consider what the effect would be of a decision in favour of the appellants having regard to the circumstance that there are thousands of factories in the country employing, no doubt, hundreds of thousands, indeed, millions of workpeople. If these performances can be given without infringement of copyright in these two cases, they can be given in every case. It is perfectly true, of course, to say that two rights do not make a wrong; but for the purpose of discovering the real nature of the audience and the effect on the monopoly of treating these performances as private performances, it does seem to me to be relevant to consider what the result would be if performances of this kind were given in all the other factories in the country. The result would be that the employers of millions of workpeople would be giving to their workpeople without payment the fruit of the brains, skill, imagination and taste of the author, if the author be the owner of the copyright, or the property of his successors in title, without any remuneration to him or them, and would be getting the advantage of that work, taste and skill, in obtaining increased or improved output.

Luxmoore and Goddard L.JJ. delivered concurring judgments.

3.5.3.3   *Sillitoe v McGraw Hill* [1983] F.S.R. 545 (Judge Mervyn Davies Q.C.)

The defendant company imported and distributed a series of study notes on texts which were set books for "O" level English literature papers. They included Sillitoe's Loneliness of the Long Distance Runner, *Lee's* Cider with Rosie *and Shaw's* St Joan. *The copyright owners of these works sued for secondary infringement by importing and selling within the Copyright Act 1956, s.5(2),(3). * The requirement of knowledge in those provisions was specified by the phrase, "if to his knowledge the making of the article constituted an infringement of that copyright, or (in the case of an imported article) would have constituted an infringement of that copyright if the article had been made in the place into which it was imported".*

Judge Mervyn Davies found in each case that the Notes took extracts and key phrases from the texts to a degree which amounted to substantial reproduction. He had accordingly to deal with two issues: (i) the knowledge requirement for secondary infringement; (ii) the defences of fair dealing for purposes of research or private study, or for purposes of criticism or review (Copyright Act 1956, s.6(1),(2)).

(i) The knowledge requirement. The defendant's principal argument was that it was acting on the advice of counsel that the Notes did not constitute infringement; and that accordingly it could not be acting with the requisite knowledge. As to this Judge Mervyn Davies said:

The onus of proving "knowledge" within section 5(2) and (3) is on the plaintiffs. The plaintiffs have to show that it was to the defendants' knowledge that the printing of the Notes would have constituted an infringement, had the Notes been printed in England. Mr Jeffs, for the defendants, said that the onus on the plaintiffs was heavy. I agree: see *Infabrics Ltd & Ors v Jaytex Shirt Co Ltd* [1978] F.S.R. 463. Mr Jeffs contrasted the wording of section 5(2) and (3) with sections 17(2)(b) and 18(2)(a) of the Act, and

---

* In the case of *St Joan*, it was also alleged that there was secondary infringement of an "adaptation" of a work from a dramatic into a non-dramatic form. Judge Mervyn Davies upheld this claim.

referred to *Secretary of State for Trade and Industry v Hart, The Times*, 30 November 1981 and *Laddie et al on Copyright*, at pp.385 and 386. The references to sections 17(2) and 18(2) show that the defendants having knowledge within section 5(2) is not to be read as meaning the defendants having "reasonable grounds for suspecting". . . .

Mr Mummery, for the plaintiffs, started from the basis that "knowledge" within section 5(2) means notice of fact such as would suggest to a reasonable man that a breach of copyright has been or is being committed. That submission is derived from some words of Harvey J. in the Australian case *Albert v Hoffnung & Co Ltd* [1921] S.R. (N.S.W.) 79 at 81, where the Australian equivalent of section 2(2) of the Copyright Act 1911 was under consideration. The Albert case was considered in *RCA Corporation v Custom Cleared Sales Pty Ltd* (1978) 19 A.L.R. 123, and also reported in [1978] F.S.R. 576. In that case the Court of Appeal were dealing with an Australian provision identical with section 5(3) of the Copyright Act 1956. The judgment of the court includes these words:

"In other words, the true position is that the court is not concerned with the knowledge of a reasonable man but is concerned with reasonable inferences to be drawn from a concrete situation as disclosed in the evidence as it affects the particular person whose knowledge is in issue".

It follows that one must consider the concrete situation disclosed by the evidence in this case and then decide what knowledge is to be attributed to the defendants, either in the way of express knowledge or knowledge that these particular defendants must have inferred.

Judge Mervyn Davies referred to authorities which did not address the question of belief in the legality of the actions. He continued:

My conclusion is that the question . . . is to be answered in the affirmative, that is that it was to the defendants' knowledge that a printing in England would constitute an infringement. I say that because in my opinion the knowledge mentioned in section 5(2) and (3) is a knowledge of the facts. Once a plaintiff fixes a defendant with notice of the facts relied on as constituting an infringement, the defendant cannot contend that he is without "knowledge" within section 5(2) because he has in good faith a belief that in law no infringement is being committed. There is here no ignorance of facts on which the defendants can rely. On the contrary, they well knew the facts, that is as to subsistence, ownership and the claim that there was a section 5(2) infringement. The defendants are in effect saying that if they are right in law, then there is no infringement and if they are wrong in law, there is no infringement either because they believed the law to be otherwise. What the defendants have done here, and knowing of the plaintiffs' complaints and the facts on which the complaints were based, was to take the risk of finding their legal advice wrong. If a person takes a deliberate risk as to whether what he is doing is wrong in law, I do not see that he can say later that he did not, at the time, know that what he was doing was wrong, if, in the event, his action is held to be wrong.

Following Van Dusen v Kritz [1936] 2 K.B. 176, Merchant Adventurers v Grew [1972] Ch. 242 and Infabrics v Jaytex [1978] F.S.R. 463, Judge Mervyn Davies held on the facts that the defendants were fixed with the requisite knowledge on receipt of the plaintiffs' letters before action and were liable once a grace period of 14 days from that date had elapsed.

(ii) Fair dealing. In regard to fair dealing for purposes of research or private study, Mervyn Davies J. stated:

The onus of showing that an exception applies is on the defendants. Mr Jeffs contended that section 6(1) is widely drawn and not limited to the actual student, so that if a dealing is fair and for the purposes of private study the subsection applies whether the private study in mind is one's own or that of somebody else. Here, he said, the dealing was for the purpose of private study by the examinees who would acquire the notes. I do not accept that argument. To my mind section 6(1) authorises what would otherwise be an infringement if one is engaged in private study or research. The authors of the Notes, when writing the Notes and thus "dealing" with the original work, were not engaged in private study or research. To my mind *University of London Press Ltd v University Tutorial Press Ltd* [1916] 2 Ch. 601 at 613, affords some support for this view.

In regard to fair dealing for purposes of criticism, Judge Mervyn Davies summarised the issue thus:

A reading of the Notes makes plain that there are passages of criticism in all three of them. The plaintiffs accepted that, but do the Notes, when reproduced in extract, show themselves to be written for the purposes of criticism only or so preponderantly for those purposes as to be regarded as works of criticism rather than anything else?

He reviewed each instance and concluded that in none did the passages of criticism justify the extensive use of extracts from the text and the summarising of storyline or plot.

In addition, he concluded that there had been no sufficient acknowledgement identifying the working in question, as required for the criticism defence. The defendants had contended that the absence of any express acknowledgement was of no consequence because the Notes immediately disclosed the title of the original and the identity of its author:

At first sight this argument appears strongly attractive. But then one sees in the *Shorter Oxford Dictionary* that the dictionary meaning of "acknowledgement" includes "the act of recognising the position or claims of". There is nothing in the Notes that suggests in any way that the author of the original work or anyone else has any position or claims in respect of the original work. The original work is treated, so far as appearances go, in the Notes, as though it was a non-copyright work. Accordingly, on this ground too I am of the view that the defendants, as to each of the Notes, failed to get within section 6(2).

3.5.3.4 *Interstate Parcel Express v Time-Life BV* (1978) 52 A.L.J.R. 9; (1977) 15 A.L.R. 35 (H.C. Australia)

Time Inc published a series of cookery books, (of which it was copyright owner) in the US and granted its Dutch subsidiary, Time-Life BV, an exclusive licence to publish them throughout the world save the US and Canada. The defendants purchased copies of the books from distributors (Raymar) in the US and imported them into Australia, where they substantially undercut the price of the Time-Life edition.

(Section 37 and 38 of the Australian Copyright Act 1968 are broadly equivalent to the Copyright, Designs and Patents Act 1988, s.22–27).

Gibbs J.:

It was very properly conceded by Mr Handley on behalf of the appellant that the only issue that arises under these sections in the present case is whether the appellant, when it imported the books into Australia for the purpose of selling them, or sold them in Australia, as the case may be, did so "without the licence of the owner of the copyright".

The word "licence" in sections 37 and 38, as in the more general provisions relating to infringement that are contained in section 35 of the Act, appears to mean no more than "consent", and a licence for the purpose of those sections need not result from a formal grant, but may be given orally or be implied by conduct: see *Copinger and Skone James on Copyright*, (11th ed 1971) para 404. There is no suggestion that the appellant had been formally granted a licence by either of the respondents, or had received from either of them any express consent, oral or written, to import the books into Australia or to sell them in Australia. The appellant's submission was that Time Inc had impliedly consented to the appellant doing these things. It was further submitted that the fact that this consent had been given would have constituted a defence to the action if it had been brought by Time Inc and was therefore available to the appellant in the action brought by Time-Life, by virtue of section 121 of the Act.

The implied consent of licence was said to have been given by Time Inc when that corporation, by itself or by Little, Brown and Co if that company was its agent first sold the books in the ordinary course of trade, without imposing any restriction upon their resale anywhere in the world. It was said that this sale impliedly gave to the buyer of the books, and to any person claiming title through him, the consent of Time Inc to use the books however and wherever he pleased, and therefore to import them into Australia and sell them there.

In support of the argument advanced on behalf of the appellant in favour of the view that the sale of books by or on behalf of the owner of the copyright imports a licence to sell them anywhere in the world, particular reliance was placed upon a line of cases decided in relation to patents. The effect of those cases is stated in *Blanco White: Patents for Inventions and the Protection of Industrial Designs* (11th ed 1974) at par. 3–219 as follows: "A sale of a patented article made by a patentee gives to the purchaser, in the absence of notice to the contrary, licence under the patent to exercise in relation to that article all the normal rights of an owner including the right to re-sell".

Again at par. 10–101, the same learned author says: "In the absence of any express term to the contrary, when a patented article is sold by or with the consent of a patentee (or the proprietor of a registered design) the purchaser will take it together with a full licence to deal with it as if it were not patented. Further, any person into whose hands it may later come is entitled to assume that such a full licence has been given with it; it makes no difference that he may later discover that this was not so, if he was ignorant of it at the time of purchase". It was submitted on behalf of the appellant that a similar principle is applicable to the case of copyright.

This principle of patent law finds its origin in *Betts v Willmott* [1871], LR 6 Ch. App. 239 where it was held that if the owner of a patent manufactures and sells the patented article in France, the sale imports a licence to use the article in England. Lord Hatherley L.C. said, at page 245 "When a man purchases an article he expects to have the control of it, and there must be some clear and explicit agreement to the contrary to justify the vendor in saying that he has not given the purchaser his licence to sell the article or to use it wherever he pleases as against himself. He cannot use it against a private assignee of the patent, but he can use it against a person who himself is proprietor of the patent, and has the power of conferring a complete right on him by the sale of the article".

The principle enunciated by Lord Hatherley L.C. is well established in patent law. However, it is not always stated by saying that the sale of the patented article confers a licence to use it. In *Société Anonyme des Manufactures de Glaces v Tilghman's Patent Sand Blast Co* [1883], 25 Ch. D.1 Cotton L.J. said, at page 9: "When an article is sold without any restriction on the buyer, whether it is manufactured under one or the other patent, that, in my opinion, as against the vendor gives the purchaser an absolute right to deal with that which he so buys in any way he thinks fit, and of course that includes selling in any country where there is a patent in the possession of and owned by the vendor".

In *National Phonograph Co of Australia Ltd v Menck* [1911] A.C. 336, Lord Shaw of Dunfermline, delivering the judgment of the Judicial Committee, said, at page 353 "In their Lordships' opinion, it is thus demonstrated by a clear course of authority, first, that it is open to a licensee, by virtue of his statutory monopoly, to make a sale *sub mode*, or accompanied by restrictive conditions which would not apply in the case of ordinary chattels; secondly that the imposition of these conditions in the case of a sale is not presumed, but, on the contrary, a sale having occurred, the presumption is that the full right of ownership was meant to be vested in the purchaser ..."

These statements seem to accord more with general principles than to say that a sale of an article imports a licence to use it. The sale of an article confers on the buyer all the rights of ownership including the right to use the article, but it seems a misuse of words to say that a person who sells an article consents to its being used in any way that the buyer wishes. However the statement that a patentee who sells a patented article gives the buyer his licence to use it has often been repeated by distinguished judges. In *Badische Anilin und Senda Fabrik v Isler* [1906] 1 Ch. 605 at page 610 Buckley J. said: "If a patentee sells the patented article to a purchaser and the purchaser uses it, he, of course, does not infringe. But why? By reason of the fact that the law implies from the sale a licence given by the patentee to the purchaser to use that which he has bought. In the absence of condition this implied licence is a licence to use or sell or deal with the goods as the purchaser pleases ..." And although in *National Phonograph Co of Australia Ltd v Menck* Lord Shaw of Dunfermline expressed his conclusion in the words I have quoted, other passages in his judgment suggest that he accepted that the consent or licence of the patentee to use the article might be implied from the sale: see at pages 349, 330. The words of Buckley J. in *Badische Anilin und Soda Fabrik v Isler* must be regarded as a correct statement of the patent law. The question is, does the same principle extend to the sale of a book the subject of copyright?

One obvious difference in form between the *Patents Act 1932* (Aust) (as amended) and the *Copyright Act* is that the former Act does not contain any provisions similar to those of sections 37 and 38 of the latter. Mr Handley submitted that this is not a valid point of distinction, because it is nevertheless an infringement of a patent to import and sell a patented article: *Pfizer Corporation v Ministry of Health* [1965] A.C. 512 at pages 557–558, 571. However there is another important difference between the law of patent and the law of copyright. By the grant of a patent in traditional form, a patentee is granted exclusive power to "make, use, exercise and vend" the invention. The sale of a patented article, by the patentee, would be quite futile, from the point of view of the buyer, if the buyer was not entitled either to use or to resell the article which he had bought. It therefore seems necessary, in order to give business efficacy to such a sale, to imply a term that the patentee consents to the use of the patented article by the buyer and those claiming under him. The law accordingly does ordinarily imply the consent of the patentee "to an undisturbed and unrestricted use" of the patented article: *National Phonograph Co of Australia Ltd v Menck* above, at page 349. To make such an implication, for the purpose only of avoiding the restrictions upon the use of the article that would otherwise be imposed by the patent, seems to be perfectly consistent with the ordinary rules governing the implication of terms in contracts. However no similar necessity exists to imply a term of this kind upon the sale of a book the subject of copyright. The owner of copyright has not the exclusive right to use or sell the work in which copyright subsists: see section 31 of the Act, and *Copinger and Skone James op. cit.* par. 1027. The buyer of a book in which copyright subsists does not need the consent of the owner of the copyright to read, or speaking generally to resell the book. The necessity to imply a term in the contract which exists when a patented article is sold does not arise on the sale of a book, the subject of copyright. It was not, and could not be, suggested that the sale of a copy of a book is a licence to do the acts comprised in the copyright and set out in section 31 of the Act.

An owner of copyright who sells a book in which copyright subsists passes to the buyer all the rights of ownership. He does not however consent to any particular use of the book – generally speaking his consent is irrelevant. For the reasons given, the cases on patent law are distinguishable. In some circumstances when the owner of copyright sells a book his consent to a particular use may be implied. For example if the owner of copyright sold in America a commercial quantity of books for delivery to a buyer in Australia, whom he knew to be a bookseller, his consent to the importation of those books into Australia and their sale there might well be implied. In the present case it might be possible to imply the consent of Raymar Inc to the importation of books into Australia and their resale, if the consent of Raymar Inc were necessary before such importation and sale could lawfully be effected. However the consent of Raymar Inc would not be material for the purposes of sections 37 and 38 of the Act. It was rightly conceded by Mr Handley that the transaction between Raymar Inc and the appellant is irrelevant to the question whether any licence had been given by Time Inc because Raymar Inc was not acting as the agent of Time Inc. There is no evidence that when the books were sold by Time Inc to Little, Brown and Co (if such a sale took place), or when they were sold by Little, Brown and Co to Raymar Inc there was anything to indicate that the books might subsequently be imported into Australia. It is not possible to imply in the contract between Time Inc and Little, Brown and Co, or in that between Little, Brown and Co and Raymar Inc the term that Time Inc consented to the importation of the books into Australia and their sale in Australia.

I have so far discussed the question with reference to the copyright law of Australia. There was no expert evidence as to the copyright law of the United States, except as to the effect of the Sherman Act. However we were referred to sections 1 and 27 of Title 17 (Copyright) of The United States Code, which are set out in *Copinger and Skone James op. cit.* at pp 839, 848. Although under section 1 a person is entitled to copyright has the exclusive right "to print, reprint, publish, copy and vend the copyrighted work". It is provided by section 27 that "nothing in this title shall be deemed to forbid, prevent, or restrict the transfer of any copy of a copyrighted work the possession of which has been lawfully obtained". It has been held that "Under this provision, where there is lawful ownership transferred to a first purchaser, the copyright holder's power of control in the sale of the copy ceases": *Independent News Co v Williams* (1961) 293 F 2d 510 at page 517. It would therefore appear that in the United States, as in Australia, it is not necessary, in order to give business efficacy to the sale of a book in which copyright subsists, to imply a term that the vendor consents to the purchaser reselling it.

The appellant submitted an alternative argument, that on the sale of the books there was an implied warranty that the buyer should have and enjoy quiet possession of them, and that this warranty would be broken if the appellant were prevented by the owner of the copyright, from importing the books into Australia and selling them there. I need not consider how such a warranty, if given by Time Inc to Little, Brown and Co or by Little, Brown and Co to Raymar Inc could be relied upon by the appellant. Nor need I consider how such a warranty, if given by Raymar Inc to the appellant could be set up by the appellant in an action brought by Time-Life. On any view, such a warranty would be irrelevant for the purposes of the provisions of sections 37 and 38. To warrant that the buyer shall have quiet possession of what he buys is not to warrant that the owner of the copyright consents to the importation of the purchases books into Australia and their sale there after importation, or to warrant that the buyer may import the books into Australia and resell them without the consent which these sections require.

If the arguments of the appellant were correct, sections 37 and 38 would apply only to the importation and sale of (1) articles which already infringed copyright (piratical copies) and (2) articles sold subject to an express restriction on subsequent importation and sale. To construe the sections in this way would limit their provisions in a manner which appears to be quite unwarranted by the words of the provisions themselves. The "licence of the owner of the copyright", of which the sections speak, means the consent of the owner to the importation of the articles into Australia for the purpose of selling them, or to their sale after importation, and such a licence cannot in my opinion be inferred from the mere fact that the owner of the copyright has sold the goods without any express restriction on their subsequent disposal. The provisions of section 135 of the Act, which empowers the owner of the copyright to give notice in writing to the Comptroller General of Customs, with the consequence that the importation of copies of the work in respect of which the notice was given, for the purpose of selling them is prohibited, and with the further consequence that such copies may be seized as forfeited to the Commonwealth, also appear quite inconsistent with the view that the sale of a book by itself implies a licence to import it into Australia for the purpose of resale.

For these reasons I conclude that the appellant did not have the licence of Time Inc to import the books in question or to resell them after importation. Infringements of the kind described in sections 37 and 38 were accordingly committed. It becomes unnecessary to consider the submission made by Mr Bannon, for the first respondent, that Time Inc could not validly have given a licence within sections 37 and 38 once it had give the exclusive licence to Time-Life and that in these circumstances section 121 would not assist the appellant, or allow the appellant to succeed, at least in relation to the second consignment of books, having regard to the knowledge with which it acted.

It seems apparent that sections 37 and 38 of the Act contemplate that the owner of copyright in a book may make regional arrangements for the distribution of copies, so as to prevent the importation into Australia for sale of books which have been sold elsewhere in the world. The appellant did not base any submission upon the provisions of the *Trade Practices Act 1974* (Aust) (as amended) and no argument was addressed to us as to the possible effect of that Act on such arrangements. I accordingly express no view, one way or the other, upon that question.

The conclusion reached by Bowen C.J. in Eq. was in my opinion correct.

I would dismiss the appeal.

3.5.4 Authorising Infringement

3.5.4.1   *Moorhouse v University of New South Wales* [1976] R.P.C. 151 (H.C. Australia); [1975] A.L.R. 193

B twice copied a story from the plaintiff's book, "The Americans, Baby" on a self-service coin-in-the-slot photocopying machine in the University's library. The proceedings were in the nature of a test case to determine whether the University was thereby liable for infringement of copyright in the story. The University was alleged to have authorised the act of unlicensed copying. (Section 40 of the Australian Copyright Act 1968 is broadly equivalent to section 29 of the 1988 Act, and section 49 to section 37ff).

Gibbs J.:

The word "Authorise", in legislation of similar intendment to section 36 of the Act, has been held judicially to have its dictionary meaning of "sanction, approve, countenance": *Falcon v Famous Players Film Co Ltd* [1926] 2 K.B. 474 at 491: *Adelaide Corporation v Australasian Performing Right Association Ltd* [1928] 40 C.L.R. 481 at 489, 497; [1928] A.L.R. 127. It can also mean "permit", as in *Adelaide Corporation v Australasian Performing Right Association Ltd* (40 C.L.R. at 497–8, 503). "Authorise" and "permit" appear to have been treated as synonymous. A person cannot be said to authorise an infringement of copyright unless he has some power to present it (40 C.L.R. at 497–8, 503). Express or formal permission or sanction, or active conduct indicating approval, is not essential to constitute an authorisation: "Inactivity or indifference, exhibited by acts of commission or omission, may reach a degree from which an authorisation or permission may be inferred": *Adelaide Corporation v Australasian Performing Right Association Ltd* at 504. However, the word "authorise" connotes a mental element and it could not be inferred that a person had, by mere inactivity, authorised something to be done if he neither knew nor had reason to suspect that the act might be done, Knox C.J. and Isaacs J. referred to this mental element in their dissenting judgments in *Adelaide Corporation v Australasian Performing Right Association Ltd*. Knox C.J. (at 487) held that indifference or omission is "permission" where the party charged (amongst other things) "knows or has reason to anticipate or suspect that the particular act is to be or is likely to be done". Isaacs J. apparently considered that it is enough if the person sought to be made liable "knows or has reason to know or believe" that the particular act of infringement "will or may" be done (see at 490–1). This latter statement may be too widely expressed: cf *Sweet v Parsley* [1970] A.C. 132 at 165; [1969] 1 All E.R. 347 at 363–4. It seems to me to follow from these statements of principle that a person who has under his control the means by which an infringement of copyright may be committed – such as a photocopying machine – and who makes it available to other persons, knowing, or having reason to suspect, that it is likely to be used for the purpose of committing an infringement and omitting to take reasonable steps to limit its use to legitimate purposes, would authorise any infringement that resulted from its use. Cases such as *Mellor v Australian Broadcasting Commission* [1940] A.C. 491; [1940] 2 All E.R. 20, and *Winstone v Wurlitzer Automatic Phonograph Co of Australia Pty Ltd* [1946] V.L.R. 338 are consistent with this view. Although in some of the authorities it is said that the person who authorises an infringement must have knowledge or reason to suspect that the particular act of infringement is likely to be done, it is clearly sufficient if there is knowledge or reason to suspect that any one of a number of particular acts is likely to be done, as for example, where the proprietor of a shop installs a gramophone and supplies a number of records any one of which may be played on it: *Winstone v Wurlitzer Automatic Phonograph Co of Australia Pty Ltd* above.

The University adopted a number of measures with a view to preventing the machines from being used to commit infringements. Each year it issued library guides and it was found by the learned trial judge that most, if not all, students commencing at the University would receive a library guide for the year of commencement and a lesser number of students would receive library guides later in their course. It thus appears that it was unlikely that all users of the library would have received any particular current library guide, and still less likely that all would have carefully read it. I find it unnecessary to consider the contents of the library guides issued in the years before 1973. The library guide for 1973 was published in a loose-leaf form and contained a bookmark on one side of which there appears, under the heading "Copyright" the following notice:

"Reader (sic) have a responsibility to obey the law under the Copyright Act 1968".

"A copy of the Act is available in the photocopying room and there is an extract of relevant sections on each machine".

"Photocopying may be done for the purpose of research or for private study and when a copy of the item to be copied has not previously been supplied to the person making the photocopy".

The notice did not mention that copying for the purpose of research or private study was only permissible if it amounted to a fair dealing with the work, although to have said that and no more would not have proved enlightening to most users of the library. In fact a copy of the Act was available in the photocopying room, but to provide a copy of a statute whose meaning would be obscure to the layman would not be an effective way of conveying to the users of the library advice as to how they should act to obey the law of copyright. There was, however, a notice on each machine. To place a clearly worded and accurate notice on each machine in a position where it could not be overlooked would be one measure which might be expected to have some value in informing users of the library of the limits which the University imposed on the permission which it gave them to use the machines. However, the notices in fact placed on the machines were ill adapted to that purpose. They merely set out the provisions of section 49 of the Act. Those provisions, as I have said, apply only where a copy is made by or on behalf of a librarian; they have no application where a person using the library makes a copy for himself. The notices placed on the machines were irrelevant to the position of those persons to whose attention they were intended to be directed. A further step taken by the University was to appoint attendants whose duties included the supervision of the use of the machines. The University Librarian was asked to tell the court what instructions he had given to these attendants, and he replied that he had circulated the relevant provisions of the Act to all members of the staff. He continued: "I had asked those people to supervise the machines, to within their competence, in which it was with the Act, see that it was observed. In particular I asked them to watch out for people who were using the machine for an excessive time or who appeared to be copying old books". No attendant was called to give evidence as to the manner in which these duties were carried out. However, Miss Stockman, a student who had been at the University for about three years, gave evidence of her own experience in making photocopies; the only functions which she had ever observed performed by an attendant related to the maintenance of the machines.

The fatal weakness in the case for the University is the fact that no adequate notice was placed on the machines for the purpose of informing users that the machines were not to be used in a manner that would constitute an infringement of copyright. It is unnecessary to consider what the position would have been in the present case if the notices on the machines had been sufficient. The fact is that the notices actually placed on the machines, which set out section 49, were completely ineffective for the purpose for which they were apparently intended.

Jacobs and McTiernan JJ. delivered concurring judgments.

3.5.4.2   *Performing Right Society v Harlequin Record Shops* [1979] F.S.R. 233 (Browne-Wilkinson J.)

The defendants played records continuously in their shops as a known means of encouraging purchases. The plaintiff society, which owned the performing right aspect of the copyright musical works thus played claimed for infringement by performance in public. The defendant denied this and relied, in the alternative, on an implied licence from the composer or publisher to use the work in this way in order to promote sales of the record, from which they would benefit.

Browne-Wilkinson J., after reviewing the facts, said:

On this factual basis the defendants mount their first argument as follows. They say that the authorities show that in considering whether a performance is or is not in public, a most important question is whether the performance injures the composer or interferes with his proprietary rights. Moreover the authorities show that it is also important to see whether the performance is given to an audience from whom the composer would expect to receive a fee: this is what I understand Greene L.J. to have meant by the "owner's public" in *Jennings v Stephens* [1936] 1 All E.R. 409 and *Performing Right Society v Gillette Industries Ltd* [1943] 1 All E.R. 228. Then the argument goes, since restraining performances in record shops would reduce the sale of records (causing a corresponding drop in recording royalties received by the composer) far from injuring the original owner of the copyright, performances in record shops positively benefit him. Moreover no composer would regard an audience of persons whose only common factor is that they are potential customers of records of his work as an audience for performances to which he would expect to receive a fee, i.e. they are not part of his public. Therefore, it is said, on the authorities the performance is not "in public".

In my judgment this first argument of the defendants is incorrect for a number of reasons. First, and to my mind decisively, its legal basis is defective. It is established that in deciding whether a performance is "in public" the character of the audience is the decisive factor. The authorities relied on by the defendants were cases in which the court had to decide whether a performance was properly called "public" when given to an audience which had certain features pointing to the performance being public and other features pointing to the performance being private: for example performances given to members of clubs and performances given by employers to employees. In such cases there is a relationship between the giver of the performance and the audience which raises the possibility of the performance being treated as being in private and the court has to decide whether the public or private features are to prevail. But in my judgment it is not a correct use of authority to lift passages from judgments dealing with performances capable of being described as being either public or private and to rely on them as authority for treating the words "in public" as not extending to a performance which on any normal meaning of the words could not be treated as anything but "public". In my judgment a performance given to an audience consisting of the persons present in a shop which the public at large are permitted, and indeed encouraged, to enter without payment or invitation with a view to increasing the shop owner's profit can only properly be described as a performance in public. I do not think the decisions relied on provide any authority for attaching to the words "in public" a special meaning which, in ordinary usage, they cannot bear.

I receive some support for this view from the decisions in *Performing Right Society v Hawthorns Hotel (Bournemouth) Ltd* [1933] Ch. 855 (in which music played in a hotel was held to be in public) and *Performing Right Society v Camelo* [1936] 3 All E.R. 557 (in which performances audible in a restaurant were treated as being "in public", though the point was not argued in that case). In this connection it was interesting that one of the witnesses, whose company runs a chain of record shops, drew a distinction between playing records to the staff of the shop (which he said was private) and to customers in the shop (which he said was public).

Even if I am wrong in this view I think there is another ground on which the defendants' first argument fails. It rests on the assumption that the court has to compare the position of the original copyright owner if records are played in record shops with his position if no records are played because the plaintiff Society obtains an injunction. I am not clear how this argument works when the original owner of the copyright no longer owns the performing rights. But even if it is right still to treat the matter as though all the rights are still in one hand, I do not think the argument is correct. Its legal basis is that one has to look to see if, by permitting the performance without a fee, the owner of the rights will be injured. If the position is that such owner can expect that the owners of record shops, rather than suffer the loss by not playing records at all, will agree to pay a fee to the Society, the composer will be getting the best of both worlds: not only will his records continue to be sold as heretofore but also via the Society he will get the benefit of the additional fee. I do not think it is for me to decide whether or not record shops in general will agree to pay the fee. But I am quite satisfied that the certainty of detriment by them refusing to do so has not been demonstrated in this case. Many record shop owners have already started to pay licence fees. The managing director of the defendant company and the managing director of another company running some 22 record shops (who was speaking for himself alone and not on behalf of his board) both said that rather than stop playing records in their shops, they would or would be likely to pay the fee, albeit reluctantly. The commercially prudent course would seem to be for the owner of a record shop to pay the fee rather than discontinue the playing of records. The only evidence of anyone acting against his commercial interest was from a gentleman who was acting on supposed principle. I think Mr Millett, for the Society, put the matter correctly when he said that it was for the owner of the performing rights to decide whether or not to try to get a fee for such performances: one of the rights which he possesses is the right to decide whether or not to charge a fee for performances to possible purchasers of records and that right is invaded by the defendant company's conduct. If a composer might take the view that a fee should be charged for performances to would-be purchasers of his work, such audiences form part of his public (in Greene L.J.'s sense) and by unauthorised performances the record shops are infringing his rights.

Browne-Wilkinson J. refused, on the evidence, to find that any licence could be implied such as was alleged to arise from the desirability of promotion.

3.5.4.3 *CBS Songs v Amstrad* [1988] R.P.C. 567 (H.L.)

Amstrad manufactured a twin-deck tape recorder. Sales literature encouraged home taping but warned that "The recording and playback of certain material may only be possible with permission. Please refer to the Copyright Act 1956, and the Performers' Protection Acts 1958–1972". The British Phonographic Industry asserted that this con- stituted infringement of copyright of its members, particularly in pop-song sound recordings. The litigation which was subject of consolidated appeal to the H.L. comprised an action for a declaration of non-infringement by Amstrad and an action to restrain sale of the recorders and other relief brought in representative form on behalf of BPI. It was argued that Amstrad were liable on a number of grounds: (i) authorising infringement under the Copyright Act 1956, s.1, either by marketing the recorder or by the form of advertisement used; (ii) joint infringement with purchasers who copied unlawfully; (iii) inciting commission of tort of infringement; (iv) inciting commission of criminal offences under the 1956 Act, s.21; (v) negligence through failure to prevent, discourage or warn against infringement.

Lord Templeman (for the H.L.):

BPI's initial submissions are that Amstrad "authorised" infringement and that Amstrad is a joint infringer together with any person who uses an Amstrad machine for the purpose of making an infringing reproduction of a recording in which copyright subsists. Section 1(1) of the 1956 Act confers on the copyright owners in a record the "exclusive right ... to authorise other persons" to copy the record. BPI submit that by selling a model which incorporates a double-speed twin-tape recorder Amstrad "authorise" the purchaser of the model to copy a record in which copyright subsists and therefore Amstrad infringe the exclusive right of the copyright owner. My Lords, twin- tape recorders, fast or slow, and single-tape recorders, in addition to their recording and playing functions, are capable of copying on to blank tape, directly or indirectly, records which are broadcast, records on discs and records on tape. Blank tapes are capable of being employed for recording or copying. Copying may be lawful or unlawful. Every tape recorder confers on the operator who acquires a blank tape the facility of copying; the double-speed twin-tape recorder provides a modern and efficient facility for continuous playing and continuous recording and for copying. No manufacturer and no machine confers on the purchaser authority to copy unlawfully. The purchaser or other operator of the recorder determines whether he shall copy and what he shall copy. By selling the recorder Amstrad may facilitate copying in breach of copyright but do not authorise it.

BPI's next submission is that Amstrad by their advertisement authorise the purchaser of an Amstrad model to copy records in which copyright subsists. Amstrad's advertise- ment drew attention to the advantages of their models and to the fact that the recorder incorporated in the model could be employed in the copying of modern records. But the advertisement did not authorise the unlawful copying of records; on the contrary, the footnote warned that some copying required permission and made it clear that Amstrad had no authority to grant that permission. If Amstrad had considered the interests of copyright owners, Amstrad could have declined to incorporate double-tape double-speed recorders in Amstrad's models or could have advertised the illegality of home copying. If Amstrad had deprived themselves of the advantages of offering improved recording facilities, other manufacturers would have reaped the benefit. The effect of double-tape double-speed recorders on the incidence of home copying is altogether speculative. If Amstrad had advertised the illegality of home copying the effect would have been minimal. Amstrad's advertisement was deplorable because Amstrad thereby flouted the rights of copyright owners. Amstrad's advertisement was cynical because Amstrad advertised the increased efficiency of a facility capable of being employed to break the law. But the operator of an Amstrad tape recording facility, like all other operators, can alone decide whether to record or play and what material is to be recorded. The Amstrad advertisement is open to severe criticism but no purchaser of an Amstrad model could reasonably deduce from the facilities incorporated in the model or from Amstrad's advertisement that Amstrad possessed or purported to possess the authority to grant any required permission for a record to be copied.

In *Monckton v Pathé Frères Pathephone Ltd* [1914] 1 K.B. 395 at 403 Buckley L.J. said: "The seller of a record authorizes, I conceive, the use of the record, and such use will be a performance of the musical work". In that case a performance of the musical work by the use of the record was bound to be an infringing use and the record was sold for that purpose. In *Evans v E Hulton & Co Ltd* (1924) 131 L.T. 534 at 535, [1924] All E.R. Rep 224 at 225–226 Tomlin J. said:

> "... where a man sold the rights in relation to a [manuscript] to another with a view to its production, and it was in fact produced, both the English language and common sense required him to hold that this man had 'authorised' the printing and publication".

The object of the sale, namely publication, was bound to infringe. In *Falcon v Famous Players Film Co* [1926] 2 K.B. 474 the defendants hired to a cinema a film based on the plaintiff's play. It was held that the defendants infringed the plaintiff's exclusive right conferred by the Copyright Act 1911 to authorise a performance of the play. Here again, the hirer sold the use which was only capable of being an infringing use. Bankes L.J. following *Monckton v Pathé Frères Pathephone Ltd and Evans v E Hulton & Co Ltd*, accepted that for the purpose of the 1911 Act the expression "authorise" meant "sanction, approve, and countenance" (at 491). Atkin L.J. said (at 499):

> "... to 'authorize' means to grant or purport to grant to a third person the right to do the act complained of, whether the intention is that the grantee shall do the act on his own account, or only on account of the grantor ..."

In the present case, Amstrad did not sanction, approve or countenance an infringing use of their model and I respectfully agree with Atkin L.J. and with Lawton L.J. in the present case that in the context of the Copyright Act an authorisation means a grant or purported grant, which may be express or implied, of the right to do the act complained of (see [1986] F.S.R. 159 at 207). Amstrad conferred on the purchaser the power to copy but did not grant or purport to grant the right to copy.

In *Moorhouse v University of New South Wales* [1976] R.P.C. 151 at 159, in the High Court of Australia, where the facilities of a library included a photocopying machine, Gibbs J. said:

> "... a person who has under his control the means by which an infringement of copyright may be committed – such as a photocopying machine – and who makes it available to other persons, knowing, or having reason to suspect, that it is likely to be used for the purpose of committing an infringement, and omitting to take reasonable steps to limit its use to legitimate purposes, would authorise any infringement that resulted from its use".

Whatever may be said about this proposition, Amstrad have no control over the use of their models once they are sold. In this country the duties of some libraries are defined by the Copyright (Libraries) Regulations 1957, SI 1957/868, made under s.15 of the 1956 Act.

In *CBS Inc v Ames Records and Tapes Ltd* [1981] 2 All E.R. 812, [1982] Ch. 91 Whitford J. held that a record library which lent out records and simultaneously offered blank tapes for sale at a discount did not authorise the infringement of copyright in the records. He said ([1981] 2 All E.R. 812 at 821, [1982] Ch. 91 at 106):

> "Any ordinary person would, I think, assume that an authorisation can only come from somebody having or purporting to have authority and that an act is not authorised by somebody who merely enables or possibly assists or even encourages another to do that act, but does not purport to have any authority which he can grant to justify the doing of the act".

This precisely describes Amstrad.

In *RCA Corp v John Fairfax & Sons Ltd* [1982] R.P.C. 91 at 100, in the Supreme Court of New South Wales, Kearney J. approved a passage in Laddie Prescott and Vitoria *The Modern Law of Copyright* (1980) para 12.9, p.403, in these terms:

> "... a person may be said to authorize another to commit an infringement if the one has some form of control over the other at the time of infringement or, if he has no such control, is responsible for placing in the other's hands materials which by their nature are almost inevitably to be used for the purpose of an infringement".

This proposition seems to me to be stated much too widely.

As Whitford J. pointed out in *CBS Inc v Ames Records and Tapes Ltd* [1981] 2 All E.R. 812 at 821, [1982] Ch. 91 at 107:

> "... you can home tape from bought records, borrowed records, borrowed from friends or public libraries, from the playing of records over the radio, and indeed, at no expense, from records which can be obtained for trial periods on introductory offers from many record clubs who advertise in the papers, who are prepared to let you have up to three or four records for a limited period of trial free of any charge whatsoever".

These borrowed records together with all recording machines and blank tapes could be said to be "materials which by their nature are almost inevitably to be used for the purpose of an infringement". But lenders and sellers do not authorise infringing use.

For these reasons, which are to be found also in the judgments of the Court of Appeal ([1986] F.S.R. 159 at 207, 210, 217), I am satisfied that Amstrad did not authorise infringement.

BPI next submitted that Amstrad were joint infringers; they became joint infringers if and as soon as a purchaser decided to copy a record in which copyright subsisted; Amstrad could become a joint infringer not only with the immediate purchaser of an Amstrad model but also with anyone else who at any time in the future used the model to copy records. My Lords, Amstrad sells models which include facilities for receiving and recording broadcasts, disc records and taped records. All these facilities are lawful although the recording device is capable of being used for unlawful purposes. Once a model is sold Amstrad has no control over or interest in its use. In these circumstances the allegation that Amstrad is a joint infringer is untenable. In *Townsend v Haworth* (1875) 48 L.J. Ch. 770 the defendant sold chemicals to be used by the purchaser in infringement of patent and agreed to indemnify the purchaser if the patent should prove to be valid. Mellish L.J. said (at 773):

> "Selling materials for the purposes of infringing a patent to the man who is going to infringe it, even although the party who sells it knows that he is going to infringe it and indemnifies him, does not by itself make the person who so sells an infringer. He must be a party with the man who so infringes, and actually infringe".

Counsel for BPI relied on the decision in *Innes v Short and Beal* (1898) 15 R.P.C. 449. In that case the defendant Short sold powdered zinc and gave instructions to a purchaser to enable the purchaser to infringe a process patent. Bingham J. said (at 452):

> "There is no reason whatever why Mr Short should not sell powdered zinc, and he will not be in the wrong, though he may know or expect that the people who buy it from him are going to use it in such a way it will amount to an infringement of Mr Innes' patent rights. But he must not ask the people to use it in that way, and he must not ask the people to use it in that way in order to induce them to buy his powdered zinc from him".

Assuming that decision to be correct, it does not assist BPI because in the present case Amstrad did not ask anyone to use an Amstrad model in a way which would amount to an infringement.

In *Dunlop Pneumatic Tyre Co Ltd v David Moseley & Sons Ltd* [1904] 1 Ch. 612 the defendant sold tyre covers which were an essential feature of a combination patent for tyres and rims. The tyre covers were adapted for use in the manner described in the patent but not necessarily solely for use in that manner. Swinfen Eady J. said that probably most of the "covers would ultimately form part of" one or other of the patented method but that –

> "those combinations do not exhaust the purposes to which the covers may be put, and that they would be useful for other purposes in connection with other tyres …"

(See [1904] 1 Ch. 164 at 171). Swinfen Eady J., upheld by the Court of Appeal (see [1904] 1 Ch. 612), decided that the defendants did not infringe.

In *The Koursk* [1924] P. 140 at 156, [1924] All E.R. Rep 168 at 175, where the question was whether the navigators of two ships had committed two separate torts or one tort in which they were both tortfeasors, Scrutton L.J. adopted the passage in *Clerk and Lindsell on Torts* (7th edn, 1921) p 59 to the effect that:

> "Persons are said to be joint tortfeasors when their respective shares in the commission of the tort are done in furtherance of a common design …"

In the present case there is no common design between Amstrad and anybody else to infringe copyright.

In *Rotocrop International Ltd v Genbourne Ltd* [1982] F.S.R. 241 Graham J. held, perhaps surprisingly, that there was novelty in a patent for a compost bin with removable panels and, less surprisingly, that a rival manufacturer who made and sold infringing bins in parts with assembly instructions was a joint tortfeasor with his customers. In that case, as in *Innes v Short and Beal* (1898) 15 R.P.C. 449, the vendor and the purchaser had a common design to carry out an infringing act.

In *Belegging- en Exploitatiemaatschappij Lavender BV v Witten Industrial Diamonds Ltd* [1979] F.S.R. 59 the defendants were alleged to have sold diamond grit for the sole purpose of making grinding tools in which it was to be embedded in a resin bond as part of a grinding material patented by the plaintiffs. Buckley L.J. held (at 66) that the defendants could not be infringers unless they –

> "sold the grits in circumstances which in some way made them participants in their subsequent embodiment in resin bonded grinding wheels, or that they induced someone so to embody them …"

My Lords, joint infringers are two or more persons who act in concert with one another pursuant to a common design in the infringement. In the present case there was no common design. Amstrad sold a machine and the purchaser or the operator of the machined decided the purpose for which the machine should from time to time be used. The machine was capable of being used for lawful or unlawful purposes. All recording machines and many other machines are capable of being used for unlawful purposes but manufacturers and retailers are not joint infringers if purchasers choose to break the law. Since Amstrad did not make or authorise other persons to make a record embodying a recording in which copyright subsisted, Amstrad did not entrench on the exclusive rights granted by the 1956 Act to copyright owners and Amstrad was not in breach of the duties imposed by the Act.

BPI submit, however, that, if the 1956 Act is defective to protect them, they are entitled to the protection of the common law. As a foundation for this submission BPI seek to elevate the quality of the rights granted by the Act. They point out that in s 17(1) of the Act the owner of copyright in any action for infringement is entitled to all such relief as is available in any corresponding proceedings in respect of infringements of other proprietary rights, that copyright is an example of intellectual property and that, in *Macmillan & Co Ltd v K & J Cooper* (1923) L.R. 51 Ind. App. 109 at 118, Lord Atkinson said that an infringer of copyright disobeyed the injunction, "Thou shalt not steal". My Lords, these considerations cannot enhance the rights of owners of copyright or extend the ambit of infringement. The rights of BPI are derived from statute and not from the Ten Commandments. Those rights are defined by Parliament, not by the clergy or the judiciary. The rights of BPI conferred by the 1956 Act are in no way superior or inferior to any other legal rights; if BPI prove that on the true construction of the Act Amstrad and Dixons have infringed the rights conferred on BPI by the Act, the court will grant appropriate and effective reliefs and remedies. But the court will not invent additional rights or impose fresh burdens.

On behalf of BPI it was submitted that even if Amstrad did not authorise infringement and were not themselves infringers, nevertheless the activities of Amstrad in the sale and advertisement of Amstrad's models constitute a common law tort. The suggested torts were three in number, namely incitement to commit a tort, incitement to commit a criminal offence and negligence.

BPI base their submission on incitement on a passage in *Lumley v Gye* (1853) 2 E & B 216 at 232, [1843–60] All E.R. Rep 208 at 214 where Erle J. said:

> "It is clear that the procurement of the violation of a right is a cause of action in all instances where the violation is an actionable wrong, as in violations of a right to property, whether real or personal, or to personal security: he who procures the wrong is a joint wrong-doer, and may be sued, either alone or jointly with the agent, in the appropriate action for the wrong complained of".

In *Lumley v Gye* an opera singer and the defendant theatre owner were joint wrongdoers. They had a common design that the opera singer should break her contract with the plaintiff theatre owner, refuse to sing in the plaintiff's theatre and instead sing in the defendant's theatre. The plaintiff's cause of action against the opera singer lay in contract, and the plaintiff's cause of action against the defendant lay in tort. But both the opera singer and the defendant were joint wrongdoers participating in an unlawful common design.

BPI referred to *Belegging- en Exploitatiemaatschappij Lavender BV v Witten Industrial Diamonds Ltd* [1979] F.S.R. 59 at 66, where Buckley L.J. said:

"The plaintiffs do not only assert infringement by the defendants. They also say that the defendants have procured, counselled and/or aided other persons to infringe. This may perhaps amount to an allegation of indirect infringement by the defendants themselves, but I am inclined to think that it is a claim in respect of a distinct suggested tort of procuring infringement by others (based upon the principle enunciated by Erle J. in *Lumley v Gye* ((1853) 2 E & B 216 at 231, [1843–60] All E.R. Rep 208 at 213) ..."

My Lords, I accept that a defendant who procures a breach of copyright is liable jointly and severally with the infringer for the damages suffered by the plaintiff as a result of the infringement. The defendant is a joint infringer; he intends and procures and shares a common design that infringement shall take place. A defendant may procure an infringement by inducement, incitement or persuasion. But in the present case Amstrad does not procure infringement by offering for sale a machine which may be used for lawful or unlawful copying and it does not procure infringement by advertising the attractions of its machine to any purchaser who may decide to copy unlawfully. Amstrad is not concerned to procure and cannot procure unlawful copying. The purchaser will not make unlawful copies because he has been induced or incited or persuaded to do so by Amstrad. The purchaser will make unlawful copies for his own use because he chooses to do so. Amstrad's advertisements may persuade the purchaser to buy an Amstrad machine but will not influence the purchaser's later decision to infringe copyright. Buckley L.J. observed in *Belegging- en Exploitatiemaatschappij Lavender BV v Witten Industrial Diamonds Ltd* (at 65): "Facilitating the doing of an act is obviously different from procuring the doing of an act". Sales and advertisements to the public generally of a machine which may be used for lawful or unlawful purposes, including infringement of copyright, cannot be said to "procure" all breaches of copyright thereafter by members of the public who use the machine. Generally speaking, inducement, incitement or persuasion to infringe must be by a defendant to an individual infringer and must identifiably procure a particular infringement in order to make the defendant liable as a joint infringer.

The next tort suggested by BPI was incitement to commit a criminal offence. In *Invicta Plastics Ltd v Clare* [1976] R.T.R. 251 the defendant company manufactured, advertised and sold a device to give warning of police radar speed traps. The device necessarily involved the unlawful use of apparatus for wireless telegraphy without a licence which would never have been granted. The defendants were convicted of incitement. In the present case it is submitted that Amstrad by the sale and advertisement of their models committed the tort of inciting the purchasers to commit a criminal offence. By s 21(3) of the 1956 Act it is an offence for any person to have in his possession a "plate" knowing that it is to be used for making infringing copies. By s 18(3) "plate" includes any stereotype, stone, block, mould, matrix, transfer negative or other appliance. It is said that when a purchaser of an Amstrad model has in his possession a record in which copyright subsists that record becomes a "plate" and the purchaser commits an offence under s 21(3) as soon as he forms the intention of copying that record.

There are two answers to this submission. First, as a matter of construction a record is not a plate but the product of the master recording which is a plate and from which the record is derived. Second, it is a mistake to compare crime and tort. If three persons are incited by a fourth to break into a house and cause damage each will be guilty of a crime and will receive separate punishment. The inciter will be guilty of the criminal offence of inciting others to commit crime. The other three will be guilty of the crime of breaking in. If the damage caused amounts to £5,000 then in a civil action the three who caused the damage will be jointly and severally liable for £5,000 and no more. The inciter will also be jointly and severally liable for the damage if he procures the commission of the tort and is a joint tortfeasor.

Finally, BPI submit that Amstrad committed the tort of negligence, that Amstrad owes to all owners of copyright a duty to take care not to cause or permit purchasers to infringe copyright or, alternatively, that Amstrad owes a duty to take care not to facilitate by the sale of their models or by their advertisement the infringement of copyright. My Lords, it is always easy to draft a proposition which is tailor-made to produce the desired result. Since *Anns v Merton London Borough* [1977] 2 All E.R. 492, [1978] A.C. 728 put the floodgates on the jar, a fashionable plaintiff alleges negligence. The pleading assumes that we are all neighbours now, Pharisees and Samaritans alike, that foreseeability is a reflection of hindsight and that for every mischance in an accident-prone world someone solvent must be liable in damages. In *Governors of the Peabody Donation Fund v Sir Lindsay Parkinson & Co Ltd* [1984] 3 All E.R. 529, [1985] A.C. 210 the plaintiffs were the authors of their own misfortune but sought to make the local authority liable for the consequences. In *Yuen Kun-yeu v A.-G. of Hong Kong* [1987] 2 All E.R. 705, [1988] A.C. 175 the plaintiff chose to invest in a deposit-taking company which went into liquidation; the plaintiff sought to recover his deposit from the commissioner charged with the public duty of registering deposit-taking companies. In *Rowling v Takaro Properties Ltd deposit-taking companies. In Rowling v Takaro Properties Ltd* 1 All E.R. 163, [1988] 2 W.L.R. 418 a claim for damages in negligence was made against a minister of the Crown for declining in good faith to exercise in favour of the plaintiff a statutory discretion vested in the minister in the public interest. In *Hill v Chief Constable of West Yorkshire* [1988] 2 All E.R. 238, [1988] 2 W.L.R. 1049 damages against a police force were sought on behalf of the victim of a criminal. In the present proceedings damages and an injunction for negligence are sought against Amstrad for a breach of statutory duty which Amstrad did not commit and in which Amstrad did not participate. The rights of BPI are to be found in the 1956 Act and nowhere else. Under and by virtue of that Act Amstrad owed a duty not to infringe copyright and not to authorise an infringement of copyright. They did not owe a duty to prevent or discourage or warn against infringement.

Lord Templeman ended by addressing the political difficulties posed by the new technical facilities for home taping. He regarded as "lamentable" the fact that the existing law often resulted in infringement at home but could not be enforced against those who copied privately. He also mentioned the blank tape levy as a possible solution and noted its varying fortunes in British policy-making.

3.5.5 Permitted Acts: General

3.5.5.1 Note on Material included on Permitted Acts

The 1988 Act, Part I, Chapter 3, comprises nearly 40 sections of exceptions to copyright infringement. Those of particular interest are set out in this and the ensuing sub-sections (3.5.5–3.5.9). Those concerned with public administration (s.45–50) have been omitted, as have the majority under the Miscellaneous heading (s.57 et seq.). S.51–53 (designs) are to be found at 4.1.1, s.58 (fixation) at 3.3.1.

3.5.5.2 Copyright, Designs and Patents Act 1988, s.28–31, 76, 178

S.28(1) The provisions of this Chapter specify acts which may be done in relation to copyright works notwithstanding the subsistence of copyright; they relate only to the question of infringement of copyright and do not affect any other right or obligation restricting the doing of any of the specified acts.

(2) Where it is provided by this Chapter that an act does not infringe copyright, or may be done without infringing copyright, and no particular description of copyright work is mentioned, the act in question does not infringe the copyright in a work of any description.

(3) No inference shall be drawn from the description of any act which may by virtue of this Chapter be done without infringing copyright as to the scope of the acts restricted by the copyright in any description of work.

(4) The provisions of this Chapter are to be construed independently of each other, so that the fact that an act does not fall within one provision does not mean that it is not covered by another provision.

S.29(1) Fair dealing with a literary, dramatic, musical or artistic work for the purposes of research or private study does not infringe any copyright in the work or, in the case of a published edition, in the typographical arrangement.

(2) Fair dealing with the typographical arrangement of a published edition for the purposes mentioned in subsection (1) does not infringe any copyright in the arrangement.

(3) Copying by a person other than the researcher or student himself is not fair dealing if –
  (a) in the case of a librarian, or a person acting on behalf of a librarian, he does anything which regulations under section 40 would not permit to be done under section 38 or 39 (articles or parts of published works: restriction on multiple copies of same material), or
  (b) in any other case, the person doing the copying knows or has reason to believe that it will result in copies of substantially the same material being provided to more than one person at substantially the same time and for substantially the same purpose.

S.30(1) Fair dealing with a work for the purpose of criticism or review, of that or another work or of a performance of a work, does not infringe any copyright in the work provided that it is accompanied by a sufficient acknowledgement.

(2) Fair dealing with a work (other than a photograph) for the purpose of reporting current events does not infringe any copyright in the work provided that (subject to subsection (3)) it is accompanied by a sufficient acknowledgement.

(3) No acknowledgement is required in connection with the reporting of current events by means of a sound recording, film broadcast or cable programme.

S.31(1) Copyright in a work is not infringed by its incidental inclusion in an artistic work, sound recording, film, broadcast or cable programme.

(2) Nor is the copyright infringed by the issue to the public of copies, or the playing, showing, broadcasting or inclusion in a cable programme service, of anything whose making was, by virtue of subsection (1), not an infringement of the copyright.

(3) A musical work, words spoken or sung with music, or so much of a sound recording, broadcast or cable programme as includes a musical work or such works, shall not be regarded as incidentally included in another work if it is deliberately included.

S.76 Adaptations – An act which by virtue of this Chapter may be done without infringing copyright in a literary, dramatic or musical work does not, where that work is an adaptation, infringe any copyright in the work from which the adaptation was made.

S.178 "sufficient acknowledgement" means an acknowledgement identifying the work in question by its title or other description, and identifying the author unless –

   (a) in the case of a published work, it is published anonymously;
   (b) in the case of an unpublished work, it is not possible for a person to ascertain the identity of the author by reasonable inquiry.

3.5.5.3   *Beloff v Pressdram* [1973] 1 All E.R. 241 (Ungoed Thomas J.)

The plaintiff, an Observer *journalist, wrote a memorandum to colleagues concerning Reginald Maudling in which she revealed William Whitelaw's confidential view that Maudling was the natural successor as Conservative leader to the then Prime Minister, Edward Heath. A copy of this was given surreptitiously to a* Private Eye *journalist, Paul Foot, that magazine being in the process of publishing exposes of Maudling's connections with an off-shore financing operator, Hoffmann.* Private Eye *published the memorandum in full as part of an attack on the plaintiff for her fostering of Maudling and her own aspersions on* Private Eye's *campaign against him.*

Her action for infringement of copyright failed because of her inability to prove ownership of the copyright. The learned judge also gave his views on other issues argued before him.

Ungoed Thomas J.:

Public interest and fair dealing

In the course of this case, the defence of public interest has been interwoven with fair dealing. They are, however, separate defences and have rightly been separately pleaded. They are governed by separate considerations. Fair dealing is a statutory defence limited to infringement of copyright only. But public interest is a defence outside and independent of statutes is not limited to copyright cases and is based on a general principle of common law. I will deal first with public interest and then with fair dealing.

Public interest

The most important recent cases referred to were the Court of Appeal cases, *Initial Services Ltd v Putterill* ([1967] 3 All E.R. 145) and *Hubbard v Vosper* ([1972] 1 All E.R. 1023) where the claims were for infringement of copyright and also for breach of confidence.

The *Initial Services* case was on appeal to strike out certain provisions in the defence relying, in justification of disclosure of confidential information on the exposure first of breach of statutory duty to register a restrictive trade agreement and secondly that a circular issued by the plaintiffs to their customers attributing increases in their charges to the selective employment tax was misleading to the public. Lord Denning M.R. said that the exception to the obligation not to disclose confidential information:

> "extends to any misconduct of such a nature that it ought in the public interest to be disclosed to others. Wood V.-C. put in a vivid phrase: 'There is no confidence as to the disclosure of iniquity'. In *Weld-Blundell v Stephens* ([1919] 1 K.B. 520) Bankes L.J. rather suggested that the exception was limited to the proposed or contemplated commission of a crime or a civil wrong; but I should have thought that that was too limited. The exception should extend to crimes, frauds and misdeeds, both those actually committed as well as those in contemplation, provided always – and this is essential – that the disclosure is justified in the public interest. The reason is because 'no private obligations can dispense with that universal one which lies on every member of the society to discover every design which may be formed, contrary to the laws of the society, to destroy the public welfare. See *Annesley v Earl of Anglesea* ((1743) 17 State Tr 1139".

And Salmon L.J. said:

> "I do not think that the law would lend assistance to anyone who is proposing to commit and to continue to commit a clear breach of a statutory duty imposed in the public interest".

In that case publication, justifiable in the public interest, was considered to extend beyond exposure of what appears, at first blush, to have been meant by "contrary to the laws of the society" as stated in *Annesley v Earl of Anglesea*, although not, as I see it, beyond "disclosure of iniquity" in Wood V.-C.'s phrase.

In *Hubbard v Vosper* Lord Denning M.R. treated material on scientology published in breach of confidence as susceptible to a defence of public interest on the ground that it was dangerous material, namely medical quackeries dangerous in untrained hands.

The defence of public interest clearly covers and, in the authorities does not extend beyond, disclosure, which as Lord Denning M.R. emphasised must be disclosure justified in the public interest, of matters carried out or contemplated. In breach of the country's security, or in breach of law, including statutory duty, fraud, or otherwise destructive of the country or its people, including matters medically dangerous to the public; and doubtless other misdeeds of similar gravity. Public interest, as a defence in law, operates to override the rights of the individual including copyright which would otherwise prevail and which the law is also concerned to protect. Such public interest, as now recognised by the law, does not extend beyond misdeeds of a serious nature and importance to the country and thus, in my view, clearly recognisable as such.

The learned judge proceeded to hold that the defence so conceived had not been made out.

Fair dealing

(1) the meaning of statutory "fair dealing". After referring to the Copyright Act 1956, section 6(2), 6(3) and 6(10) and to some of the evidence the learned judge continued:

I come now to the requirement, which I specified, of fair dealing with this memorandum. Fair dealing is not defined by the Act, although subject to the requirements which I have already stated including the purpose of criticism or review or reporting current events. The references to purposes, which I have just read, differ in their wording from the reference to purposes in section 6(1) which reads:

"No fair dealing with a literary ... work for purposes of research or private study shall constitute an infringement of the copyright in the work".

Thus "for the purpose" in sub-section (1) and "if it is for the purpose" in the other subsections fundamentally have the same meaning and effect; and the difference in wording is explained by the inclusion in sub-sections (2) and (3) of additional provisions and requirements without parallel in sub-section (1). It would, indeed, be whimsical if the relationship between fair dealing and the approved purposes were given a different significance in sub-sections (2) and (3) from sub-section (1), in the absence of obvious reasons for making such a difference. The relevant fair dealing is thus fair dealing with the memorandum for the approved purposes. It is fair dealing directed to and consequently limited to and to be judged in relation to the approved purposes. It is dealing which is fair for the approved purposes and not dealing which might be fair for some other purpose or fair in general. Mere dealing with the work for that purpose is not enough: it must also be dealing which is fair for that purpose; whose fairness, as I have indicated, must be judged in relation to that purpose.

Thus public interest as such is outside the purpose of the section and of fair dealing. It is not of itself justification for infringement of copyright, except insofar as recognised by common law as a separate defence irrespective of the section as already mentioned.

(2) Factors in the defence of fair dealing.

I come now to the relevant factors in determining fair dealing. A number of authorities were cited, but for present purposes, at any rate, the law is most conveniently stated in *Hubbard v Vosper* by Lord Denning M.R. and by Megaw L.J. To summarise the statements: fair dealing is a question of fact and of impression, to which factors that are relevant include the extent of the quotation and its proportion to comment (which may be justifiable although the quotation is of the whole work): whether the work is unpublished; and the extent to which the work has been circularised, although not published to the public within the meaning of the Copyright Act 1956.

In our case the memorandum was unpublished. Romer J. in *British Oxygen Co Ltd v Liquid Air Ltd* in dealing with a company's letter to a trade customer as a "literary work", said that publication without the author's consent would be "manifestly unfair" as it is not a "fair dealing" with the work. Romer J.'s observations were made when the relevant statute was section 2 of the Copyright Act 1911, the precursor of section 6 of the 1956 Act. It was in wide terms into which limitations were introduced by section 6, but the differences are not material for present purposes. However, unpublished as well as published works are within the fair dealing provisions of both Acts; and what would otherwise be infringement cannot of itself, without regard to any other circumstances, be outside the exception to infringement made by those sections, so that would be to exclude from the sections what the sections in terms include. So I doubt if Romer J. ever intended that his words should be read in the sense that an unpublished work should be automatically outside the provisions of the fair dealing defence rather than a factor, although doubtless an important factor, which with other factors have to be taken into consideration in considering fair dealing. And such a conclusion seems to be in accordance with the decision and observations of the Court of Appeal in *Hubbard v Vosper*.

But receiving and using leaked information, in the sense of confidential information, which someone who has it gives to someone not entitled to it appears to be common practice in the press, and occurs in such a reputable paper as the "Observer" itself. An instance was even given in evidence of the publication by the plaintiff of such a leak. Distinctions were sought to be drawn by or on behalf of the plaintiff between different ways in which leaks occur. It was sought to distinguish between a leak by theft as contrasted with breach of confidence, and it was strongly maintained, particularly by the plaintiff in the early stages of the hearing, that the memorandum was stolen from the "Observer's" offices by someone from "Private Eye"; but Mr Foot, who knew, said that the contents of the memorandum were disclosed by someone in the "Observer" who wanted the memorandum published; and I have no hesitation in accepting the evidence of Mr Foot. A distinction was also sought to be drawn between, on the one hand, receiving and using a leak of a rival's confidential information (for example, by "Private Eye" of the confidential information of another newspaper) and on the other hand, receiving and using confidential information of some other body not a rival (for example, by "Private Eye" from a government department, an industrial company or a private firm). Mr Foot disagreed and so do I. A distinction was also suggested between a leak of information never intended by its owner to be published and a pre-empting leak in anticipation of authorised publication. The pre-empting leak might well be substantially prejudicial; and although the later such a leak takes place before authorised publication the less is apt to be the ill-consequence, yet the less too is it apt to be in the public interest, which was mostly alone relied on to justify the publication of leaked information. On all these distinctions there may well be differences of responsible views sincerely held; but for my part I am unable to make any decisive distinction between the unsought voluntary leak in this case by a person who wanted the leaked information published and other press publications of leaks which were referred to in evidence.

The learned judge held the publication an unfair dealing.

3.5.5.4 *Commonwealth of Australia v Fairfax* [1981] 55 A.L.J.R. 45 (Mason J., H.C. Australia)

The Commonwealth sought to prevent the publication of a book, Documents on Australian Defence and Foreign Policy 1968–1975, *and newspaper extracts therefrom, asserting that it contained confidential government documents whose publication would prejudice Australia's foreign relations, particularly with Indonesia. In interlocutory proceedings, based* inter alia *on breach of confidence and copyright the defendants resisted the continuance of ex* parte *injunctions, asserting a public interest in publication and discussion of the information.*

Mason J.:

Disclosure of confidential information

The equitable principle has been fashioned to protect the personal, private and proprietary interests of the citizen, not to protect the very different interests of the executive Government. It acts, or is supposed to act, not according to standards of private interest, but in the public interest. This is not to say that Equity will not protect information in the hands of the Government, but it is to say that when Equity protects Government information it will look at the matter through different spectacles.

It may be a sufficient detriment to the citizen that disclosure of information relating to his affairs will expose his actions to public discussion and criticism. But it can scarcely be a relevant detriment to the Government that publication of material concerning its actions will merely expose it to public discussion and criticism. It is unacceptable in our democratic society that there should be a restraint on the publication of information relating to government when the only vice of that information is that it enables the public to discuss, review and criticize Government action.

Accordingly, the Court will determine the Government's claim to confidentiality by reference to the public interest. Unless disclosure is likely to injure the public interest, it will not be protected.

The Court will not prevent the publication of information which merely throws light on the past workings of government, even if it be not public property, so long as it does not prejudice the community in other respects. Then disclosure will itself serve the public interest in keeping the community informed and in promoting discussion of public affairs. If, however, it appears that disclosure will be inimical to the public interest because national security, relations with foreign countries or the ordinary business of government will be prejudiced, disclosure will be restrained. There will be cases in which the conflicting considerations will be finely balanced, where it is difficult to decide whether the public's interest in knowing and in expressing its opinion, outweighs the need to protect confidentiality.

Support for this approach is to be found in *Attorney-General v Jonathan Cape Ltd* [1976] Q.B. 752 where the Court refused to grant an injunction to restrain publication of the diaries of Richard Crossman. Widgery L.C.J. said (at pages 770–771):

"The Attorney-General must show (a) that such publication would be a breach of confidence; (b) that the public interest requires that the publication be restrained, and (c) that there are no other facets of the public interest contradictory of and more compelling than that relied upon. Moreover, the court, when asked to restrain such a publication, must closely examine the extent to which relief is necessary to ensure that restrictions are not imposed beyond the strict requirement of public need".

Although this statement has been criticized on the ground that it is contrary to principle and unduly restricts the right of Government to restrain disclosures (see M W Bryan, "The Crossman Diaries Developments in the Law of Breach of Confidence" (1976), 92 L.Q.R. 180), his Lordship was correctly elaborating the principle so as to take account of the *special character of the Government and defining the detriment which it needs to show.*

His Honour concluded that publication would not at that juncture prejudice national security nor cause such embarrassment to foreign relations as to warrant interim relief.

Infringement of copyright

But this is no answer to the claim in copyright. The plaintiff is the owner of the copyright in those documents which have been brought into existence by the relevant Departments and by public servants. Publication of the three instalments by the defendant will infringe the plaintiff's copyright unless the defendants can establish defences under sections 41 and 42 of the Copyright Act 1968 (Aust.), as amended, or the so-called common law defence of "public interest".

To bring themselves within section 41 the defendants must show that what they proposed to publish is "a fair dealing" with the plaintiff's documents "for the purpose of criticism or review" and that "a sufficient acknowledgement of the work" was made. It has been suggested that section 41 does not provide a defence in the case of unpublished literary works, as distinct from unpublished dramatic or musical work, on the ground that criticism or review of an unpublished literary work could never amount to "a fair dealing" (*Copinger and Skone James on Copyright* (11th ed, 1971 para 463). This suggestion is based on the remarks of Romer J. in *British Oxygen Company Ltd v Liquid Air Ltd* [1925] Ch. 383 at page 393, where his Lordship said that it would be unfair that an unpublished literary work should, without the consent of the author, be the subject of public criticism or review.

In *Hubbard v Vosper* [1972] 2 Q.B. 84, Lord Denning M.R. qualified these remarks by observing that a literary work not published to the world at large might be circulated to such a wide circle, for example, a circular sent by a company to its shareholders, as to make it "a fair dealing" to criticize or review it (pages 94–95). With this qualification I agree.

To my mind the absence of consent, express or implied, or such circulation by the author of an unpublished literary work as to justify criticism or review is ordinarily at least an important factor in deciding whether there has been "a fair dealing" under section 41.

However, there is another possible approach to the concept of "fair dealing" as applied to copyright in Government documents, an approach which was not spelled out in argument by the defendants. It is to say that a dealing with unpublished works which would be unfair as against an author who is a private individual may nevertheless be considered fair as against a government merely because that dealing promotes public knowledge and public discussion of government action. This would be to adopt a new approach to the construction of sections 41 and 42 and it would not be appropriate for me on an interlocutory application to proceed on the footing that it is a construction that will ultimately prevail. Situations such as the present case would scarcely have been within the contemplation of the draftsman when the two sections and their ancestors were introduced.

There is another obstacle in the way of a section 41 defence. The presentation to readers which the newspapers planned to publish was a presentation of hitherto unpublished documents from the secret files of the Government. The attraction offered to the reader was that, by courtesy of the newspapers he was able to read for the first time documents which were so important that the Government had maintained a secrecy blackout on them. The accompanying comment, which was significant only in the case of the first instalment, appears to have been designed to place the documents in their appropriate setting, to enable them to be understood and to highlight the more dramatic features. To speak of the publication of the three instalments as having been undertaken for the purpose of criticism or review is to add a new dimension to criticism and review. If there was criticism or review of the documents by the newspapers it was merely a veneer, setting off what is essentially a publication of the plaintiff's documents. The defendants did not propose to make any reference at all to the question raised on pages 2 and 3 of the Introduction to the book.

Similar problems surround the defendants' endeavour to mount a defence under section 42. The defendants seek to show that there has been "a fair dealing" with a literary work "for the purpose of, or . . . associated with, the reporting of news in a newspaper . . . and a sufficient acknowledgement of the work is made". The arguments advanced scarcely went beyond a bold assertion, and an equally stern denial, that what the defendants proposed to publish was "for the purpose of . . . the reporting of news".

I am inclined to allow that "news", despite its context of "the reporting of news" "in a newspaper, magazine or similar periodical" is not restricted to "current events". Even so, the concept of "a fair dealing" with a literary work in the circumstances mentioned in section 42(1)(a) again presents a difficulty for the defendants. As things presently stand, it will not be easy for the defendants to bring their use of the plaintiff's documents, particularly in the two unpublished instalments, within the sub-section. I refer to the East Timor cables and the "profiles".

It has been accepted that the so-called common law defence of public interest applies to disclosure of confidential information. Although copyright is regulated by statute, public interest may also be a defence to infringement of copyright. Lord Denning M.R. considered that it is; see *Fraser v Evans* [1969] 1 Q.B. 349 at pages 362–363, as did Ungoed Thomas J. in *Beloff v Pressdram Ltd* above, at page 260; cf *Hubbard v Vosper* above, at pages 96–97. Assuming the defence to be available in copyright cases, it is limited in scope. It makes legitimate the publication of confidential information or material in which copyright subsists so as to protect the community from destruction, damage or harm. It has been acknowledged that the defence applies to disclosures of things done in breach of national security, in breach of the law (including fraud) and to disclosure of matters which involve danger to the public. So far there is no recorded instance of the defence having been raised in a case such as this where the suggestion is that the advice given by Australia's public servants, particularly its diplomats, should be ventilated, with a view to exposing what is alleged to have been the cynical pursuit of expedient goals, especially in relation to East Timor. To apply the defence to such a situation would break new ground.

The defendants have not persuaded me that it is more likely than not that any of the suggested defences will prevail.

To say that the enforcement by injunction of the plaintiff's copyright in documents amounts indirectly to protection of the information contained in the documents is to confuse copyright with confidential information. Copyright is infringed by copying or reproducing the document; it is not infringed by publishing information or ideas contained in the document so long as the publication does not reproduce the form of the literary work.

3.5.6 Permitted Acts: Reprography

3.5.6.1 Copyright, Designs and Patents Act 1988, s.37(1)–(2), 38–40, 178

Libraries and archives

S.37(1) In sections 38 to 43 (copying by librarians and archivists) –
  (a) references in any provision to a prescribed library or archive are to a library or archive of a description prescribed for the purposes of that provision by regulations made by the Secretary of State: and
  (b) references in any provision to the prescribed conditions are to the conditions so prescribed.

(2) The regulations may provide that, where a librarian or archivist is required to be satisfied as to any matter before making or supplying a copy of a work –
  (a) he may rely on a signed declaration as to that matter by the person requesting the copy, unless he is aware that it is false in a material particular, and
  (b) in such cases as may be prescribed, he shall not make or supply a copy in the absence of a signed declaration in such form as may be prescribed.

S.37(3) deals with false declarations, s.37(4),(5) contain additional matter on the regulations; s.37(6) extends the exception to those acting on behalf of a librarian or archivist.

S.38(1) The librarian of a prescribed library may, if the prescribed conditions are compiled with, make and supply a copy of an article in a periodical without infringing any copyright in the text, in any illustrations accompanying the text or in the typographical arrangement.

(2) The prescribed conditions shall include the following –
  (a) that copies are supplied only to persons satisfying the librarian that they require them for purposes of research or private study and will not use them for any other purpose:
  (b) that no person is furnished with more than one copy of the same article or with copies of more than one article contained in the same issue of a periodical: and
  (c) that persons to whom copies are supplied are required to pay for them a sum not less than the cost (including a contribution to the general expenses of the library) attributable to their production.

S.39(1) The librarian of a prescribed library may, if the prescribed conditions are complied with, make and supply from a published edition a copy of part of a literary, dramatic or musical work (other than an article in a periodical) without infringing any copyright in the work, in any illustrations accompanying the work or in the typographical arrangement.

(2) The prescribed conditions shall include the following –
  (a) that copies are supplied only to persons satisfying the librarian that they require them for purposes of research or private study, and will not use them for any other purpose:

(b) that no person is furnished with more than one copy of the same material or with a copy of more than a reasonable proportion of any work; and

(c) that persons to whom copies are supplied are required to pay for them a sum not less than the cost (including a contribution to the general expenses of the library) attributable to their production.

S.40(1) Regulations for the purposes of sections 38 and 39 (copying by librarian of article or part of published work) shall contain provision to that effect that a copy shall be supplied only to a person satisfying the librarian that his requirement is not related to any similar requirement of another person.

(2) The regulations may provide –

(a) that requirements shall be regarded as similar if the requirements are for copies of substantially the same material at substantially the same time and for substantially the same purpose: and

(b) that requirements of persons shall be regarded as related if those persons receive instruction to which the material is relevant at the same time and place.

S.41 creates an exception for the supply of copies to other libraries; s.42 for replacement copies of works; s.43 for certain copying of some unpublished works in libraries and archives; and s.44 where copying is a condition of an export licence.

3.5.6.2   Copyright, Designs and Patents Act 1988, s.36, 130

S.36(1) Reprographic copies of passages from published literary, dramatic or musical works may, to the extent permitted by this section, be made by or on behalf of an educational establishment for the purposes of instruction without infringing any copyright in the work, or in the typographical arrangement.

(2) Not more than one per cent of any work may be copied by or on behalf of an establishment by virtue of this section in any quarter, that is, in any period 1 January to 31 March, 1 April to 30 June, 1 July to 30 September or 1 October to 31 December.

(3) Copying is not authorised by this section if, or to the extent that, licences are available authorising the copying in question and the person making the copies knew or ought to have been aware of that fact.

(4) The terms of a licence granted to an educational establishment authorising the reprographic copying for the purposes of instruction of passages from published literary, dramatic or musical works are of no effect so far as they purport to restrict the proportion of a work which may be copied (whether on payment or free of charge) to less than that which would be permitted under this section.

(5) Where a copy which would otherwise be an infringing copy is made in accordance with this section but is subsequently dealt with, it shall be treated as an infringing copy for the purposes of that dealing, as if that dealing infringes copyright for all subsequent purposes.

For this purpose "dealt with" means sold or let for hire, or offered or exposed for sale or hire.

S.130 Where a reference or application is made to the Copyright Tribunal under this Chapter relating to the licensing of reprographic copying of published literary, dramatic, musical or artistic works, or the typographical arrangement of published editions, the Tribunal shall have regard to –
  (a) the extent to which published editions of the works in question are otherwise available,
  (b) the proportion of the work to be copied, and
  (c) the nature of the use to which the copies are likely to be put.

S.136 imposes an implied indemnity in respect of schemes and licences for reprographic copying in respect of acts of infringement within the apparent scope of the permission granted.

S.137, in relation to reprographic copying in educational establishments, gives power to the Secretary of State to extend to works that copyright owners unreasonably refuse to allow within an appropriate scheme or licence (and see also s.138, 139). S.140 permits, in the same field, the Secretary of State to institute an inquiry into extension of a scheme or licence to fields not covered; s.141 prescribes consequential action.

3.5.7 Permitted Acts: Education

3.5.7.1   Copyright, Designs and Patents Act 1988, s.32(1), 34, 35(1)–(2)

S.32(1) Copyright in a literary, dramatic, musical or artistic work is not infringed by its being copied in the course of instruction or of preparation for instruction, provided the copying –

   (a) is done by a person giving or receiving instruction, and

   (b) is not by means of a reprographic process.

S.32(2) deals with instruction in film making; s.32(3), (4) with examinations; and s.32(5) with subsequent dealings.

S.33 creates an exception for anthologies of short passages from literary and dramatic works intended for educational use.

S.34(1) The performance of a literary, dramatic or musical work before an audience consisting of teachers and pupils at an educational establishment and other persons directly connected with the activities of the establishment –

   (a) by a teacher or pupil in the course of the activities of the establishment,

      or

   (b) at the establishment by any person for the purposes of instruction,

is not a public performance for the purposes of infringement of copyright.

(2) The playing or showing of a sound recording, film, broadcast or cable programme before such an audience at an educational establishment for the purposes of instruction is not a playing or showing of the work in public for the purposes of infringement of copyright.

(3) A person is not for this purpose directly connected with the activities of the educational establishment simply because he is the parent of a pupil at the establishment.

S.35(1) A recording of a broadcast or cable programme, or a copy of such a recording, may be made by or on behalf of an educational establishment for the educational purposes of that establishment without thereby infringing the copyright in the broadcast or cable programme, or in any work included in it.

(2) This section does not apply if or to the extent that there is a licensing scheme certified for the purposes of this section under section 143 providing for the grant of licences.

S.35(3) relates to subsequent dealings.

3.5.8 Permitted Acts: Rental Right and Home Taping

3.5.8.1 Copyright, Designs and Patents Act 1988, s.66, 70

S.66(1) The Secretary of State may by order provide that in such cases as may be specified in the order the rental to the public of copies of sound recordings, films or computer programs shall be treated as licensed by the copyright owner subject only to the payment of such reasonable royalty or other payment as may be agreed or determined in default of agreement by the Copyright Tribunal.

(2) No such order shall apply if, or to the extent that, there is a licensing scheme certified for the purposes of this section under section 143 providing for the grant of licences.

(3) An order may make different provision for different cases and may specify cases by reference to any factor relating to the work, the copies rented, the renter or the circumstances of the rental.

(4) An order shall be made by statutory instrument; and no order shall be made unless a draft of it has been laid before and approved by a resolution of each House of Parliament.

(5) Copyright in a computer program is not infringed by the rental of copies to the public after the end of the period of 50 years from the end of the calendar year in which copies of it were first issued to the public in electronic form.

(6) Nothing in this section affects any liability under section 23 (secondary infringement) in respect of the rental of infringing copies.

S.70 The making for private and domestic use of a recording of a broadcast or cable programme solely for the purpose of enabling it to be viewed or listened to at a more convenient time does not infringe any copyright in the broadcast or cable programme or in any work included in it.

3.5.8.2 Copyright, Designs and Patents Act 1988, s. 296(1), (2), (4), (5): Devices designed to circumvent copy-protection

S.296(1) This section applies where copies of a copyright work are issued to the public, by or with the licence of the copyright owner, in an electronic form which is copy-protected.

(2) The person issuing the copies to the public has the same rights against a person who, knowing or having reason to believe that it will be used to make infringing copies:
  (a) makes, imports, sells or lets for hire, offers or exposes for sale or hire, or advertises for sale or hire, any device or means specifically designed or adapted to circumvent the form of copy-protection employed, or
  (b) publishes information intended to enable or assist persons to circumvent that form of copy-protection,
as a copyright owner has in respect of an infringement of copyright . . . .

(4) References in this section to copy-protection include any device or

means intended to prevent or restrict copying of a work or to impair the quality of copies made.

(5) Expressions used in this section which are defined for the purposes of Part I of this Act (copyright) have the same meaning as in that Part.

S.296(3), (6) give remedial powers equivalent to those for copyright in respect of delivery up, seizure and disposal, presumptions and withdrawal of the privilege against self-incrimination.

3.5.9 Permitted Acts: Computer Material etc

3.5.9.1 Copyright, Designs and Patents Act 1988, s.56

S.56(1) This section applies where a copy of a work in electronic form has been purchased on terms which, expressly or impliedly or by virtue of any rule of law, allow the purchaser to copy the work, or to adapt it or make copies of an adaptation, in connection with his use of it.

(2) If there are no express terms –
    (a) prohibiting the transfer of the copy by the purchaser, imposing obligations which continue after a transfer, prohibiting the assignment of any licence or terminating any licence on a transfer, or
    (b) providing for the terms on which a transferee may do the things which the purchaser was permitted to do.

Anything which the purchaser was allowed to do may also be done without infringement of copyright by a transferee: but any copy, adaptation or copy of an adaptation made by the purchaser which is not also transferred shall be treated as an infringing copy for all purposes after the transfer.

(3) The same applies where the original purchased copy is no longer usable and what is transferred is a further copy used in its place.

(4) The above provisions also apply on a subsequent transfer, with the substitution for references in subsection (2) to the purchaser of references to the subsequent transferor.

3.5.10 Remedies

3.5.10.1   Copyright, Designs and Patents Act 1988, s.96, 97, 100, 104: Types of Remedy; Presumptions

S.96(1) An infringement of copyright is actionable by the copyright owner.

(2) In an action for infringement of copyright all such relief by way of damages, injunctions, accounts or otherwise is available to the plaintiff as is available in respect of the infringement of any other property right.

(3) This section has effect subject to the following provisions of this Chapter.

S.97(1) Where in an action for infringement of copyright it is shown that at the time of the infringement the defendant did not know, and had no reason to believe, that copyright subsisted in the work to which the action relates, the plaintiff is not entitled to damages against him, but without prejudice to any other remedy.

(2) The court may in an action for infringement of copyright having regard to all the circumstances, and in particular to –
> **(a) the flagrancy of the infringement, and**
> **(b) any benefit accruing to the defendant by reason of the infringement.**

award such additional damages as the justice of the case may require.

S.98 limits the amount of damages available against a person entitled to a licence of right in consequence of a Monopolies and Mergers Commission report.

S.99 gives the court power to order delivery up of infringing material, etc. (and see s.113, 114).

S.100(1) An infringing copy of a work which is found exposed or otherwise immediately available for sale or hire, and in respect of which the copyright owner would be entitled to apply for an order under section 99, may be seized and detained by him or a person authorised by him.

The right to seize and detain is exercisable subject to the following conditions and is subject to any decision of the court under section 114.

(2) Before anything is seized under this section notice of the time and place of the proposed seizure must be given to a local police station.

(3) A person may for the purpose of exercising the right conferred by this section enter premises to which the public have access but may not seize anything in the possession, custody or control of a person at a permanent or regular place of business of his, and may not use any force.

(4) At the time when anything is seized under this section there shall be left at the place where it was seized a notice in the prescribed form containing the prescribed particulars as to the person by whom or on whose authority the seizure is made and the grounds on which it is made.

(5) In this section –
> **"premises" includes land, buildings, movable structures, vehicles, vessels, aircraft and hovercraft; and**

"prescribed" means prescribed by order of the Secretary of State.

(7) An order of the Secretary of State under this section shall be made by statutory instrument which shall be subject to annulment in pursuance of a resolution of either House of Parliament.

S.101, 102 deal with the rights of action of an exclusive licensee. For s.103, see below, 3.6.5.1.

Presumptions relevant to literary, dramatic, musical and artistic works

S.104(1) The following presumptions apply in proceedings brought by virtue of this Chapter with respect to a literary, dramatic, musical or artistic work.

(2) Where a name purporting to be that of the author appeared on copies of the work as published or on the work when it was made, the person whose name appeared shall be presumed, until the contrary is proved –
   (a) to be the author of the work;
   (b) to have made it in circumstances not falling within section 11(2), 163, 165 or 158 (works produced in course of employment, Crown copyright, Parliamentary copyright or copyright of certain international organisations).

(3) In the case of a work alleged to be a work of joint authorship, subsection (2) applies in relation to each person alleged to be one of the authors.

(4) Where no name purporting to be that of the author appeared as mentioned in subsection (2) but –
   (a) the work qualifies for copyright protection by virtue of section 155 (qualification by reference to country of first publication), and
   (b) a name purporting to be that of the publisher appeared on copies of the work as first published,
the person whose name appeared shall be presumed, until the contrary is proved, to have been the owner of the copyright at the time of publication.

(5) If the author of the work is dead or the identity of the author cannot be ascertained by reasonable inquiry, it shall be presumed, in the absence of evidence to the contrary –
   (a) that the work is an original work, and
   (b) that the plaintiff's allegations as to what was the first publication of the work and as to the country of first publication are correct.

S.105 creates a series of presumptions relating to sound recordings and films; and s.106 in relation to Crown copyright.

S.107 creates a series of criminal offences relating to transactions in infringing copies. S.108 permits orders for delivery up in criminal proceedings (and see s.113, 114).

S.109 makes special provision for search warrants.

S.110 imposes criminal liability on certain corporate officers. For s.111, 112, see below, 7.3.1.

3.6 Moral Rights

3.6.1 Right to be Identified

3.6.1.1 Copyright, Designs and Patents Act 1988, s.77–79

S.77(1) The author of a copyright literary, dramatic, musical or artistic work, and the director of a copyright film, has the right to be identified as the author or director of the work in the circumstances mentioned in this section; but the right is not infringed unless it has been asserted in accordance with section 78.

(2) The author of a literary work (other than words intended to be sung or spoken with music) or a dramatic work has the right to be identified whenever –
   (a) the work is published commercially, performed in public, broadcast or included in a cable programme service; or
   (b) copies of a film or sound recording including the work are issued to the public;
and that right includes the right to be identified whenever any of those events occur in relation to an adaptation of the work as the author of the work from which the adaptation was made.

(3) The author of a musical work, or a literary work consisting of words intended to be sung or spoken with music, has the right to be identified whenever –
   (a) the work is published commercially;
   (b) copies of a sound recording of the work are issued to the public; or
   (c) a film of which the sound-track includes the work is shown in public or copies of such a film are issued to the public;
and that right includes the right to be identified whenever any of those events occur in relation to an adaptation of the work as the author of the work from which the adaptation was made.

(4) The author of an artistic work has the right to be identified whenever –
   (a) the work is published commercially or exhibited in public, or a visual image of it is broadcast or included in a cable programme service;
   (b) a film including a visual image of the work is shown in public or copies of such a film are issued to the public; or
   (c) in the case of a work of architecture in the form of a building or a model for a building, a sculpture or a work of artistic craftsmanship, copies of a graphic work representing it, or of a photograph of it, are issued to the public.

(5) The author of a work of architecture in the form of a building also has the right to be identified on the building as constructed or, where more than one building is constructed to the design, on the first to be constructed.

(6) The director of a film has the right to be identified whenever the film is shown in public, broadcast or included in a cable programme service or copies of the film are issued to the public.

(7) The right of the author or director under this section is –

(a) in the case of commercial publication or the issue to the public of copies of a film or sound recording, to be identified in or on each copy or, if that is not appropriate, in some other manner likely to bring his identity to the notice of a person acquiring a copy.

(b) in the case of identification on a building, to be identified by appropriate means visible to persons entering or approaching the building, and

(c) in any other case, to be identified in a manner likely to bring his identity to the attention of a person seeing or hearing the performance, exhibition, showing, broadcast or cable programme in question;

and the identification must in each case be clear and reasonably prominent.

(8) If the author or director in asserting his right to be identified specifies a pseudonym, initials or some other particular form of identification, that form shall be used; otherwise any reasonable form of identification may be used.

(9) This section has effect subject to section 79 (exceptions to right).

S.78(1) A person does not infringe the right conferred by section 77 (right to be identified as author or director) by doing any of the acts mentioned in that section unless the right has been asserted in accordance with the following provisions so as to bind him in relation to that act.

(2) The right may be asserted generally, or in relation to any specified act or description of acts –

(a) on an assignment of copyright in the work, by including in the instrument effecting the assignment a statement that the author or director asserts in relation to that work his right to be identified, or

(b) by instrument in writing signed by the author or director.

(3) The right may also be asserted in relation to the public exhibition of an artistic work –

(a) by securing that when the author or other first owner of copyright parts with possession of the original, or of a copy made by him or under his direction or control, the author is identified on the original or copy, or on a frame, mount or other thing to which it is attached, or

(b) by including in a licence by which the author or other first owner of copyright authorises the making of copies of the work a statement signed by or on behalf of the person granting the licence that the author asserts his right to be identified in the event of the public exhibition of a copy made in pursuance of the licence.

(4) The persons bound by an assertion of the right under subsection (2) or (3) are –

(a) in the case of an assertion under subsection (2)(a), the assignee and anyone claiming through him, whether or not he has notice of the assertion;

(b) in the case of an assertion under subsection (2)(b), anyone to whose notice the assertion is brought;

(c) in the case of an assertion under subsection (3)(a), anyone into whose hands that original or copy comes, whether or not the identification is still present or visible;

(d) in the case of an assertion under subsection (3)(b), the licensee and anyone into whose hands a copy made in pursuance of the licence comes, whether or not he has notice of the assertion.

(5) In an action for infringement of the right the court shall, in considering remedies, take into account any delay in asserting the right.

S.79(1) The right conferred by section 77 (right to be identified as author or director) is subject to the following exceptions.

(2) The right does not apply in relation to the following descriptions of work –

(a) a computer program;
(b) the design of a typeface;
(c) any computer-generated work.

(3) The right does not apply to anything done by or with the authority of the copyright owner where copyright in the work originally vested –

(a) in the author's employer by virtue of section 11(2) (works produced in course of employment), or
(b) in the director's employer by virtue of section 9(2)(a) (person to be treated as author of film).

(4) The right is not infringed by an act which by virtue of any of the following provisions would not infringe copyright in the work –

(a) section 30 (fair dealing for certain purposes), so far as it relates to the reporting of current events by means of a sound recording, film, broadcast or cable programme;
(b) section 31 (incidental inclusion of work in an artistic work, sound recording, film, broadcast or cable programme);
(c) section 32(3) (examination questions);
(d) section 45 (parliamentary and judicial proceedings);
(e) section 46(1) or (2) (Royal Commissions and statutory inquiries);
(f) section 51 (use of design documents and models);
(g) section 52 (effect of exploitation of design derived from artistic work);
(h) section 57 (anonymous or pseudonymous works: acts permitted on assumptions as to expiry of copyright or death of author).

(5) The right does not apply in relation to any work made for the purpose of reporting current events.

(6) The right does not apply in relation to the publication in –

(a) a newspaper, magazine or similar periodical, or
(b) an encyclopedia, dictionary, yearbook or other collective work of reference,

of a literary, dramatic, musical or artistic work made for the purposes of such publication or made available with the consent of the author for the purposes of such publication.

(7) The right does not apply in relation to –

(a) a work in which Crown copyright or Parliamentary copyright subsists, or

    (b) a work in which copyright originally vested in an international
        organisation by virtue of section 168,
unless the author or director has previously been identified as such in or on
published copies of the work.

3.6.2 Right against Derogatory Treatment

3.6.2.1   Copyright, Designs and Patents Act 1988, s.80–82, 178

S.80(1) The author of a copyright literary, dramatic, musical or artistic work, and the director of a copyright film, has the right in the circumstances mentioned in this section not to have his work subjected to derogatory treatment.

(2) For the purposes of this section –
  (a) "treatment" of a work means any addition to, deletion from or alteration to or adaptation of the work, other than –
    (i) a translation of a literary or dramatic work, or
    (ii) an arrangement or transcription of a musical work involving no more than a change of key or register; and
  (b) the treatment of a work is derogatory if it amounts to distortion or mutilation of the work or is otherwise prejudicial to the honour or reputation of the author or director;
and in the following provisions of this section references to a derogatory treatment of a work shall be construed accordingly.

(3) In the case of a literary, dramatic or musical work the right is infringed by a person who –
  (a) publishes commercially, performs in public, broadcasts or includes in a cable programme service a derogatory treatment of the work; or
  (b) issues to the public copies of a film or sound recording of, or including, a derogatory treatment of the work.

(4) In the case of an artistic work the right is infringed by a person who –
  (a) publishes commercially or exhibits in public a derogatory treatment of the work, or broadcasts or includes in a cable programme service a visual image of a derogatory treatment of the work,
  (b) shows in public a film including a visual image of a derogatory treatment of the work or issues to the public copies of such a film, or
  (c) in the case of –
    (i)   a work of architecture in the form of a model for a building,
    (ii) a sculpture, or
    (iii) a work of artistic craftsmanship,
    issues to the public copies of a graphic work representing, or of a photograph of, a derogatory treatment of the work.

(5) Subsection (4) does not apply to a work of architecture in the form of a building; but where the author of such a work is identified on the building and it is the subject of derogatory treatment he has the right to require the identification to be removed.

(6) In the case of a film, the right is infringed by a person who –
  (a) shows in public, broadcasts or includes in a cable programme service a derogatory treatment of the film; or
  (b) issues to the public copies of a derogatory treatment of the film,
or who, along with the film, plays in public, broadcasts or includes in a cable programme service, or issues to the public copies of, a derogatory treatment of the film sound-track.

(7) The right conferred by this section extends to the treatment of parts of a work resulting from a previous treatment by a person other than the author or director, if those parts are attributed to, or are likely to be regarded as the work of, the author or director.

(8) This section has effect subject to sections 81 and 82 (exceptions to and qualifications of right).

S.81(1) The right conferred by section 80 (right to object to derogatory treatment of work) is subject to the following exceptions.

(2) The right does not apply to a computer program or to any computer-generated work.

(3) The right does not apply in relation to any work made for the purpose of reporting current events.

(4) The right does not apply in relation to the publication in –
  (a) a newspaper, magazine or similar periodical, or
  (b) an encyclopedia, dictionary, yearbook or other collective work of reference,
of a literary, dramatic, musical or artistic work made for the purposes of such publication or made available with the consent of the author for the purposes of such publication.

Nor does the right apply in relation to any subsequent exploitation elsewhere of such a work without any modification of the published version.

(5) The right is not infringed by an act which by virtue of section 57 (anonymous or pseudonymous works: acts permitted on assumptions as to expiry of copyright or death of author) would not infringe copyright.

(6) The right is not infringed by anything done for the purpose of –
  (a) avoiding the commission of an offence,
  (b) complying with a duty imposed by or under an enactment, or
  (c) in the case of the British Broadcasting Corporation, avoiding the inclusion in a programme broadcast by them of anything which offends against good taste or decency or which is likely to encourage or incite to crime or to lead to disorder or to be offensive to public feeling,
provided, where the author or director is identified at the time of the relevant act or has previously been identified in or on published copies of the work, that there is a sufficient disclaimer.

S.82(1) This section applies to –
  (a) works in which copyright originally vested in the author's employer by virtue of section 11(2) (works produced in course of employment) or in the director's employer by virtue of section 9(2)(a) (person to be treated as author of film),
  (b) works in which Crown copyright or Parliamentary copyright subsists, and
  (c) works in which copyright originally vested in an international organisation by virtue of section 168.

(2) The right conferred by section 80 (right to object to derogatory treat-ment of work) does not apply to anything done in relation to such a work by or with the authority of the copyright owner unless the author or director –

    (a) is identified at the time of the relevant act, or

    (b) has previously been identified in or on published copies of the work;

and where in such a case the right does apply; it is not infringed if there is a sufficient disclaimer.

S.83 creates liability for secondary infringement of articles open to objection under s.80.

S.178 ... "sufficient disclaimer", in relation to an act capable of infringing the right conferred by section 80 (right to object to derogatory treatment of work), means a clear and reasonably prominent indication –

    (i)   given at the time of the act, and

    (ii) if the author or director is then identified, appearing along with the identification,

that the work has been subjected to treatment to which the author or director has not consented.

3.6.3 False Attribution

3.6.3.1 Copyright, Designs and Patents Act 1988, s.84

S.84(1) A person has the right in the circumstances mentioned in this section –
- (a) not to have a literary, dramatic, musical or artistic work falsely attributed to him as author, and
- (b) not to have a film falsely attributed to him as director;

and in this section an "attribution", in relation to such a work, means a statement (express or implied) as to who is the author or director.

(2) The right is infringed by a person who –
- (a) issues to the public copies of a work of any of those descriptions in or on which there is a false attribution, or
- (b) exhibits in public an artistic work, or a copy of an artistic work, in or on which there is a false attribution.

(3) The right is also infringed by a person who –
- (a) in the case of a literary, dramatic or musical work, performs the work in public, broadcasts it or includes it in a cable programme service as being the work of a person, or
- (b) in the case of a film, shows it in public, broadcasts it or includes it in a cable programme service as being directed by a person.

knowing or having reason to believe that the attribution is false.

(4) The right is also infringed by the issue to the public or public display of material containing a false attribution in connection with any of the acts mentioned in subsection (2) or (3).

(5) The right is also infringed by a person who in the course of a business –
- (a) possesses or deals with a copy of a work of any of the descriptions mentioned in subsection (1) in or on which there is a false attribution, or
- (b) in the case of an artistic work, possesses or deals with the work itself when there is a false attribution in or on it,

knowing or having reason to believe that there is such an attribution and that it is false.

(6) In the case of an artistic work the right is also infringed by a person who in the course of a business –
- (a) deals with a work which has been altered after the author parted with possession of it as being the unaltered work of the author, or
- (b) deals with a copy of such a work as being a copy of the unaltered work of the author,

knowing or having reason to believe that that is not the case.

(7) References in this section to dealing are to selling or letting for hire, offering or exposing for sale or hire, exhibiting in public, or distributing.

(8) This section applies where, contrary to the fact –
- (a) a literary, dramatic or musical work is falsely represented as being an adaptation of the work of a person, or
- (b) a copy of an artistic work is falsely represented as being a copy made by the author of the artistic work,

as it applies where the work is falsely attributed to a person as author.

3.6.4 Right of Privacy in Photographs and Films

3.6.4.1   Copyright, Designs and Patents Act 1988, s.85

S.85(1) A person who for private and domestic purposes commissions the taking of a photograph or the making of a film has, where copyright subsists in the resulting work, the right not to have –

    (a) copies of the work issued to the public,

    (b) the work exhibited or shown in public, or

    (c) the work broadcast or included in a cable programme service;

and, except as mentioned in subsection (2), a person who does or authorises the doing of any of those acts infringes that right.

(2) The right is not infringed by an act which by virtue of any of the following provisions would not infringe copyright in the work –

    (a) section 31 (incidental inclusion of work in an artistic work, film, broadcast or cable programme);

    (b) section 45 (parliamentary and judicial proceedings);

    (c) section 46 (Royal Commissions and statutory inquiries);

    (d) section 50 (acts done under statutory authority);

    (e) section 57 (anonymous or pseudonymous works: acts permitted on assumptions as to expiry of copyright or death of author).

3.6.5 General Provisions affecting Moral Rights

3.6.5.1 Copyright, Designs and Patents Act 1988, s.86, 87, 94, 95, 103

S.86(1) The rights conferred by section 77 (right to be identified as author or director), section 80 (right to object to derogatory treatment of work) and section 85 (right to privacy of certain photographs and films) continue to subsist so long as copyright subsists in the work.

(2) The right conferred by section 84 (false attribution) continues to subsist until 20 years after a person's death.

S.87(1) It is not an infringement of any of the rights conferred by this Chapter to do any act to which the person entitled to the right has consented.

(2) Any of those rights may be waived by instrument in writing signed by the person giving up the right.

(3) A waiver –
- (a) may relate to a specific work, to works of a specified description or to works generally, and may relate to existing or future works, and
- (b) may be conditional or unconditional and may be expressed to be subject to revocation;

and if made in favour of the owner or prospective owner of the copyright in the work or works to which it relates, it shall be presumed to extend to his licensees and successors in title unless a contrary intention is expressed.

(4) Nothing in this Chapter shall be construed as excluding the operation of the general law of contract or estoppel in relation to an informal waiver or other transaction in relation to any of the rights mentioned in subsection (1).

S.94 The rights conferred by Chapter IV (moral rights) are not assignable.

S.95(1) On the death of a person entitled to the right conferred by section 77 (right to identification of author or director), section 80 (right to object to derogatory treatment of work) or section 85 (right to privacy of certain photographs and films) –
- (a) the right passes to such person as he may by testamentary disposition specifically direct,
- (b) if there is no such direction but the copyright in the work in question forms part of his estate, the right passes to the person to whom the copyright passes, and
- (c) if or to the extent that the right does not pass under paragraph (a) or (b) it is exercisable by his personal representatives.

(5) Any infringement after a person's death of the right conferred by section 84 (false attribution) is actionable by his personal representatives.

S.95(2) deals with divided devolution of copyright, s.95(3) with multiple entitlement; s.95(4) with the continuing force of a consent or waiver; and s.95(6) with entitlement to damages recovered by personal representatives.

S.103(1) An infringement of a right conferred by Chapter IV (moral rights) is actionable as a breach of statutory duty owed to the person entitled to the right.

(2) In proceedings for infringement of the right conferred by section 80 (right to object to derogatory treatment of work) the court may, if it thinks it is an adequate remedy in the circumstances, grant an injunction on terms prohibiting the doing of any act unless a disclaimer is made, in such terms and in such manner as may be approved by the court, dissociating the author or director from the treatment of the work.

3.7 Authorship, Ownership and Dealings

3.7.1 Copyright, Designs and Patents Act 1988, s.9, 11: Authorship and ownership of copyright

S.9(1) In this Part "author", in relation to a work, means the person who creates it.

(2) That person shall be taken to be –
  (a) in the case of a sound recording or film, the person by whom the arrangements necessary for the making of the recording or film are
  (b) in the case of a broadcast, the person making the broadcast (see
  (b) in the case of a broadcast, the person making the broadcast (see broadcast by reception and immediate re-transmission, the person making that other broadcast;
  (c) in the case of a cable programme, the person providing the cable programme service in which the programme is included;
  (d) in the case of the typographical arrangement of a published edition, the publisher.

(3) In the case of a literary, dramatic, musical or artistic work which is computer-generated, the author shall be taken to be the person by whom the arrangements necessary for the creation of the work are undertaken.

(4) For the purposes of this Part a work is of "unknown authorship" if the identity of the author is unknown or, in the case of a work of joint authorship, if the identity of none of the authors is known.

(5) For the purposes of this Part the identity of an author shall be regarded as unknown if it is not possible for a person to ascertain his identity by reasonable inquiry; but if his identity is once known it shall not subsequently be regarded as unknown.

S.11(1) The author of a work is the first owner of any copyright in it, subject to the following provisions.

(2) Where a literary, dramatic, musical or artistic work is made by an employee in the course of his employment, his employer is the first owner of any copyright in the work subject to any agreement to the contrary.

(3) This section does not apply to Crown copyright or Parliamentary copyright (see sections 163 and 165) or to copyright which subsists by virtue of section 168 (copyright of certain international organisations).

S.178 . . . "computer-generated", in relation to a work, means that the work is generated by computer in circumstances such that there is no human author of the work: "employed", "employee", "employer" and "employment" refer to employment under a contract of service or of apprenticeship.

3.7.2   *Cummins v Bond* [1927] 1 Ch. 167; 76 L.J. Ch. 81; 136 L.T. 3; 70 S.J. 1003

During a seance, the plaintiff, a psychic medium, wrote down a text entitled "The Chronicles of Cleophas" about the acts and teachings of the apostles. It was in archaistic language without stops and was said to have been put down automatically by the plaintiff. The defendant took it away and edited it, then claimed the right to publish it.

Eve J.:

The issue in this action is reduced to the simple question, who, if any one, is the owner of the copyright in this work. *Prima facie* it is the author, and so far as this world is concerned there can be no doubt who is the author here, for it has been abundantly proved that the plaintiff is the writer of every word to be found in this bundle of original script. But the plaintiff and her witness and the defendant are all of opinion – and I do not doubt that the opinion is an honest one – that the true originator of all that is to be found in these documents is some being no longer inhabiting this world, and who has been out of it for a length of time sufficient to justify the hope that he has no reasons for wishing to return to it.

From this it would almost seem as though the individual who has been dead and buried for some 1900 odd years and the plaintiff ought to be regarded as the joint authors and owners of the copyright, but inasmuch as I do not feel myself competent to make any declaration in his favour, and recognizing as I do that I have no jurisdiction extending to the sphere in which he moves, I think I ought to confine myself when inquiring who is the author to individuals who were alive when the work first came into existence and to conditions which the legislature in 1911 may reasonably be presumed to have contemplated. So doing it would seem to be clear that the authorship rests with this lady, to whose gift of extremely rapid writing coupled with a peculiar ability to reproduce in archaic English matter communicated to her in some unknown tongue we owe the production of these documents.

The learned judge proceeded to find that there was no basis upon which the defendant could claim to be a co-author. He proceeded:

Alternatively, failing to establish any claim on his own behalf he submits that there is no copyright in the work at all, that it has come from a far off locality which I cannot specify, and that the plaintiff is the mere conduit pipe by which it has been conveyed to this world. I do not think that is a fair appreciation of the plaintiff's activities. They obviously involved a great deal more than mere repetition; but, apart altogether from these considerations, the conclusion which the defendant invites me to come to in this submission involves the expression of an opinion I am not prepared to make, that the authorship and copyright rest with some one already domiciled on the other side of the inevitable river. That is a matter I must leave for solution by others more competent to decide it than I am. I can only look upon the matter as a terrestrial one, of the earth earthy, and I propose to deal with it on that footing. In my opinion the plaintiff has made out her case, and the copyright rests with her.

3.7.3 Copyright, Designs and Patents Act 1988, s.90–93: Assignment, Licences, Prospective Ownership, Transmission on Death

S.90(1) Copyright is transmissible by assignment, by testamentary disposition or by operation of law, as personal or movable property.

(2) An assignment or other transmission of copyright may be partial, that is, limited so as to apply –
  (a) to one or more, but not all, of the things the copyright owner has the exclusive right to do;
  (b) to part, but not the whole, of the period for which the copyright is to subsist.

(3) An assignment of copyright is not effective unless it is in writing signed by or on behalf of the assignor.

(4) A licence granted by a copyright owner is binding on every successor in title to his interest in the copyright, except –
  (a) a purchaser in good faith for valuable consideration and without notice (actual or constructive) of the licence, or
  (b) a person deriving title from such a purchaser;
and references in this Part to doing anything with, or without, the licence of the copyright owner shall be construed accordingly.

S.91(1) Where by an agreement made in relation to future copyright, and signed by or on behalf of the prospective owner of the copyright, the prospective owner purports to assigning the future copyright (wholly or partially) to another person, then if, on the copyright coming into existence, the assignee or another person claiming under him would be entitled as against all other persons to require the copyright to be vested in him, the copyright shall vest in the assignee or his successor in title by virtue of this subsection.

(2) In this Part – "future copyright" means copyright which will or may come into existence in respect of a future work or class of works or on the occurrence of a future event; and "prospective owner" shall be construed accordingly, and includes a person who is prospectively entitled to copyright by virtue of such an agreement as is mentioned in subsection (1).

(3) A licence granted by a prospective owner of copyright is binding on every successor in title to his interest (or prospective interest) in the right, except a purchaser in good faith for valuable consideration and without notice (actual or constructive) of the licence or a person deriving title from such a purchaser; and references in this Part to doing anything with, or without, the licence of the copyright owner shall be construed accordingly.

S.92(1) In this Part an "exclusive licence" means a licence in writing signed by or on behalf of the copyright owner authorising the licensee to the exclusion of all other persons, including the person granting the licence, to exercise a right which would otherwise be exercisable exclusively by the copyright owner.

(2) The licensee under an exclusive licence has the same rights against a successor in title who is bound by the licence as he has against the person granting the licence.

S.93 Where under a bequest (whether specific or general) a person is entitled, beneficially or otherwise, to –
  (a) an original document or other material thing recording or embodying a literary, dramatic, musical or artistic work which was not published before the death of the testator, or
  (b) an original material thing containing a sound recording or film which was not published before the death of the testator.
The bequest shall, unless a contrary intention is indicated in the testator's will or a codicil to it, be construed as including the copyright in the work in so far as the testator was the owner of the copyright immediately before his death.

3.7.4   *Barker v Stickney* [1919] 1 K.B. 121 (C.A.)

The plaintiff, author of "The Theory and Practice of Heating and Ventilation" assigned copyright in it to J F Phillips & Sons Ltd in return for shares in the company and a royalty. The company undertook not to assign to a third party. A receiver was appointed for the company and the copyright was sold to the defendant, who had full notice of the terms of the original assignment. The plaintiff claimed from the defendant the royalty arising under that assignment.

Scrutton L.J.:

The case was considered in the court below on two lines. First, it was said the defendant has bought a copyright with notice of a contract affecting it, and, using the copyright, must perform the contract. Up to the year 1880 that argument might have prevailed. In *De Mattos v Gibson* ([1858] 4 De G. & J. 276) Knight Bruce L.J. laid down the following rule: "Reason and justice seem to prescribe that, at least as a general rule, where a man, by gift or purchase, acquires property from another, with knowledge of a previous contract, lawfully and for valuable consideration made by him with a third person, to use and employ the property for a particular purpose in a specified manner, the acquirer shall not, to the material damage of the third person, in opposition to the contract and inconsistently with it, use and employ the property in a manner not allowable to the giver or seller". Down to 1881 the cases where a purchaser of property was restricted in his use of it were based upon the doctrine of notice, and upon that alone. Those cases will be found in the judgment of the Court of Appeal in *London County Council v Allen* ([1914] 3 K.B. 642). About that time a change took place. In *Haywood v Brunswick Building Society* (8 Q.B.D. 403) the restriction was confined to cases where the covenant was negative. In 1882, the year after *Werderman's Case* (19 Ch.D. 246) was decided, Jessel M.R. himself further limited the restriction in cases of land to negative covenants for the benefit of land, treating them as analogous to covenants running with land which a plaintiff could not enforce unless he had land for the benefit of which the covenant could enure. This point was afterwards expressly decided by the Court of Appeal in *London County Council v Allen*. Thus the doctrine was evolved as to real property. But as to personal property it was found that the general rule of Knight Bruce L.J. was quite impracticable, and *Taddy & Co v Sterious & Co* ([1904] 1 Ch. 354) *McGruther v Pitcher* ([1904] 2 Ch. 306) and *Dunlop Pneumatic Tyre Co v Selfridge & Co* ([1915] A.C. 847) have settled the law that the purchaser of a chattel is not bound by mere notice of stipulations made by his vendor unless he was himself a party to the contract in which the stipulations were made. I see nothing to distinguish a chose in action such as copyright from chattels or land, and I think it is clear that a person acquiring a cause in action is not bound by mere notice of a personal covenant by his predecessor in title. That is the effect of *Bago Pneumatic Tyre Co v Clipper Pneumatic Tyre Co* ([1902] 1 Ch. 146) *Werderman's Case* was decided in the year before *London & South Western Ry Co v Gomm* ((1882) 20 Ch.D. 562) in which Jessel M.R. himself greatly restricted the effect of notice, and in my view *Werderman's Case* cannot be supported on the ground that notice of a contract relating to personal property will bind a purchaser who is not a party to that contract. So much for the first ground on which this appeal was based.

His Lordship proceeded to hold that the plaintiff could not assert a lien or charge as an unpaid vendor, since his entitlement to royalty did not put him in the position of seller. Bankes and Warrington L.JJ. delivered concurring judgments.

3.7.5   *Schroeder Music Publishing v Macaulay* [1974] 3 All E.R. 616 (H.L.)

When still an unknown 21-year-old song-writer the plaintiff agreed with the defendant music publishing company to give his services exclusively to the company for a period of five years, extending automatically to ten years, in circumstances which afterwards materialised. Under the agreement the plaintiff assigned copyright world-wide in the songs that he composed during its term and was to receive royalties in return. The company was not obliged to publish any of the plaintiff's work; it might terminate the agreement at any time on one month's notice, and it could assign its rights. The plaintiff had no equivalent rights of termination or assignment. In the fourth year, the plaintiff sought a declaration that the agreement was void as being contrary to public policy.

Lord Reid:

The public interest requires in the interests both of the public and of the individual that everyone should be free so far as practicable to earn a livelihood and to give to the public the fruits of his particular abilities. The main question to be considered is whether and how far the operation of the terms of this agreement is likely to conflict with this objective. The respondent is bound to assign to the appellants during a long period the fruits of his musical talent. But what are the appellants bound to do with those fruits? Under the contract nothing. If they do use the songs which the respondent composes they must pay in terms of the contract. But they need not do so. As has been said they may put them in a drawer and leave them there. No doubt the expectation was that if the songs were of value they would be published to the advantage of both parties. But if for any reason the appellants chose not to publish them the respondent would get no remuneration and he could not do anything. Inevitably the respondent must take the risk of misjudgment of the merits of his work by the appellants. But that is not the only reason which might cause the appellants not to publish. There is no evidence about this so we must do the best we can with common knowledge. It does not seem fanciful and it was not argued that it is fanciful to suppose that purely commercial consideration might cause a publisher to refrain from publishing and promoting promising material. He might think it likely to be more profitable to promote work by other composers with whom he had agreements and unwise or too expensive to try to publish and popularise the respondent's work in addition. And there is always the possibility that less legitimate reasons might influence a decision not to publish the respondent's work.

It was argued that there must be read into this agreement an obligation on the publisher to act in good faith. I take that to mean that he would be in breach of contract if by reason of some oblique or malicious motive he refrained from publishing work which he would otherwise have published. I very much doubt this but even if it were so it would make little difference. Such a case would seldom occur and then would be difficult to prove.

I agree with the appellants' argument to this extent. I do not think that a publisher could reasonably be expected to enter into any positive commitment to publish future work by an unknown composer. Possibly there might be some general undertaking to use his best endeavours to promote the composer's work. But that would probably have to be in such general terms as to be of little use to the composer. But if no satisfactory positive undertaking by the publisher can be devised, it appears to me to be an unreasonable restraint to tie the composer for this period of years so that his work will be sterilised and he can earn nothing from his abilities as a composer if the publisher chooses not to publish. If there had been in clause 9 any provision entitling the composer to terminate the agreement in such an event the case might have had a very different appearance. But as the agreement stands not only is the composer tied but he cannot recover the copyright of the work which the publisher refuses to publish.

It was strenuously argued that the agreement is in standard form, that it has stood the test of time, and that there is no indication that it ever causes injustice. Reference was made to passages in the speeches of Lord Pearce and Lord Wilberforce in the *Esso Case* ([1967] 1 All E.R. 699) with which I wholly agree. Lord Pearce said:

"It is important that the court, in weighing the question of reasonableness, should give full weight to commercial practices and to the generality of contracts made freely by parties bargaining on equal terms".

Later Lord Wilberforce said:

"The development of the law does seem to show, however, that judges have been able to dispense from the necessity of justification under a public policy test of reasonableness such contracts or provisions of contracts as, under contemporary conditions, may be found to have passed into the accepted and normal currency of commercial or contractual or conveyancing relations. That such contracts have done so may be taken to show with at least strong *prima* force that, moulded under the pressures of negotiation, competition and public opinion, they have assumed a form which satisfies the test of public policy as understood by the courts of the time, or, regarding the matter from the point of view of the trade, that the trade in question has assumed such a form that for its health or expansion it requires a degree of regulation".

But those passages refer to contracts "made freely by parties bargaining on equal terms" or "moulded under the pressures of negotiation, competition and public opinion". I do not find from any evidence in this case, nor does it seem probable, that this form of contract made between a publisher and an unknown composer has been moulded by any pressure of negotiation. Indeed, it appears that established composers who can bargain on equal terms can and do make their own contracts.

Any contract by which a person engages to give his exclusive services to another for a period necessarily involves extensive restriction during that period of the common law right to exercise any lawful activity he chooses in such manner as he thinks best. Normally the doctrine of restraint of trade has no application to such restrictions: they require no justification. But if contractual restrictions appear to be unnecessary or to be reasonably capable of enforcement in an oppressive manner, then they must be justified before they can be enforced.

In the present case the respondent assigned to the appellants "the full copyright for the whole world" in every musical composition "composed created or conceived" by him alone or in collaboration with any other person during a period of five or it might be ten years. He received no payment (apart from an initial £50) unless his work was published and the appellants need not publish unless they chose to do so. And if they did not publish he had no right to terminate the agreement or to have any copyrights re-assigned to him. I need not consider whether in any circumstances it would be possible to justify such a one-sided agreement. It is sufficient to say that such evidence as there is falls far short of justification. It must therefore follow that the agreement so far as unperformed is unenforceable.

Viscount Dilhorne concurred with Lord Reid.

Lord Diplock:

My Lords, the contract under consideration in this appeal is one whereby the respondent accepted restrictions on the way in which he would exploit his earning-power as a song-writer for the next ten years. Because this can be classified as a contract in restraint of trade the restrictions that the respondent accepted fell within one of those limited categories of contractual promises in respect of which the courts still retain the power to relieve the promisor of his legal duty to fulfil them. In order to determine whether this case is one in which that power ought to be exercised, what your Lordships have in fact been doing has been to assess the relative bargaining power of the publisher and the song-writer at the same time the contract was made and to decide whether the publisher had used his superior bargaining power to exact from the song-writer promises that were unfairly onerous to him. Your Lordships have not been concerned to enquire whether the public have in fact been deprived of the fruit of the song-writer's talents by reason of the restrictions, nor to assess the likelihood that they would be so deprived in the future if the contract were permitted to run its full course.

It is, in my view, salutary to acknowledge that in refusing to enforce provisions of a contract whereby one party agrees for the benefit of the other party to exploit or to refrain from exploiting his earning-power, the public policy which the court is implementing is not some 19th century economic theory about the benefit to the general public of freedom of trade, but the protection of those whose bargaining power is weak against being forced by those whose bargaining power is stronger to enter into bargains that are unconscionable. Under the influence of Bentham and of laissez-faire the courts in the 19th century abandoned the practice of applying the public policy against unconscionable bargains to contracts generally, as they had formerly done to any contract considered to be usurious; but the policy survived in its application to penalty clauses and to relief against forfeiture and also to the special category of contracts in restraint of trade. If one looks at the reasoning of 19th century judges in cases about contracts in restraint of trade one finds lip service paid to current economic theories but if one looks at what they said in the light of what they did, one finds that they did, one finds that they struck down a bargain if they thought it was unconscionable as between the parties to it, and upheld it if they thought that it was not.

So I would hold that the question to be answered as respects a contract in restraint of trade of the kind with which this appeal is concerned is: was the bargain fair? The test of fairness is, no doubt, whether the restrictions are both reasonably necessary for the protection of the legitimate interests of the promisee and commensurate with the benefits secured to the promisor under the contract. For the purpose of this test all the provisions of the contract must be taken into consideration.

My Lords, the provisions of the contract have already been sufficiently stated by my noble and learned friend, Lord Reid. I agree with his analysis of them and with his conclusion that the contract is unenforceable. It does not satisfy the test of fairness as I have endeavoured to state it. I will accordingly content myself with adding some observations directed to the argument that because the contract was in a "standard form" in common use between music publishers and song-writers, the restraints that it imposes on the song-writer's liberty to exploit his talents must be presumed to be fair and reasonable.

Standard forms of contracts are of two kinds. The first, of very ancient origin, are those which set out the terms on which mercantile transactions of common occurrence are to be carried out. Examples are bills of lading, charterparties, policies of insurance, contracts of sale in the commodity markets. The standard clauses in these contracts have been settled over the years by negotiations by representatives of the commercial interests involved and have been widely adopted because experience has shown that they facilitate the conduct of trade. Contracts of these kinds affect not only the actual parties to them but also others who may have a commercial interest in the transactions to which they relate, as buyers of sellers, charterers or shipowners, insurers or bankers. If fairness or reasonableness were relevant to their enforceability the fact that they are widely used by parties whose bargaining power is fairly matched would raise a strong presumption that their terms are fair and reasonable.

The same presumption, however, does not apply to the other kind of standard form of contract. This is of comparatively modern origin. It is the result of the concentration of particular kinds of business in relatively few hands. The ticket cases in the 19th century provide what are probably the first examples. The terms of this kind of standard form of contract have not been the subject of negotiation between the parties to it, or approved by any organisation representing the interests of the weaker party. They have been dictated by that party whose bargaining power, either exercised alone or in conjunction with other providing similar goods or services, enables him to say: "If you want these goods or services at all, these are the only terms on which they are obtainable. Take it or leave it".

To be in a position to adopt this attitude towards a party desirous of entering into a contract to obtain goods or service provides a classic instance of superior bargaining power. It is not without significance that on the evidence in the present case, music publishers in negotiating with song-writers whose success has been already established do not insist on adhering to a contract in the standard form they offered to the respondent. The fact that the appellants' bargaining power vis-à-vis the respondent was strong enough to enable them to adopt this take-it-or-leave-it attitude raises no presumption that they used it to drive an unconscionable bargain with him, but in the field of restraint of trade it calls for vigilance on the part of the court to see that they did not.

Lords Simon and Kilbrandon concurred in the speeches of Lords Reid and Diplock.

3.8   Copyright Tribunal

3.8.1 Copyright, Designs and Patents Act 1988, s.116–119, 121, 129: Licensing Schemes and Licensing Bodies: References and Applications to Copyright Tribunal

S.116(1) In this Part a "licensing scheme" means a scheme setting out –
  - (a) the classes of case in which the operator of the scheme, or the person on whose behalf he acts, is willing to grant copyright licences, and
  - (b) the terms on which licences would be granted in those classes of case: and for this purpose a "scheme" includes anything in the nature of a scheme, whether described as a scheme or as a tariff or by any other name.

(2) In this Chapter a "licensing body" means a society or other organisation which has as its main object, or one of its main objects, the negotiation or granting, either as owner or prospective owner of copyright or as agent for him, of copyright licences, and whose objects include the granting of licences covering works of more than one author.

(3) In this section "copyright licences" means licences to do, or authorise the doing of, any of the acts restricted by copyright.

(4) References in this Chapter to licences or licensing schemes covering works of more than one author do not include licences or schemes covering only –
  - (a) a single collective work or collective works of which the authors are the same, or
  - (b) works made by, or by employees of, or commissioned by, a single individual, firm, company or group of companies.

For this purpose a group of companies means a holding company and its subsidiaries, within the meaning of section 736 of the Companies Act 1985.

S.117 Sections 118 to 123 (references and applications with respect to licensing schemes) apply to –
  - (a) licensing schemes operated by licensing bodies in relation to the copyright in literary, dramatic, musical or artistic works or films (or film sound-tracks when accompanying a film) which cover works of more than one author, so far as they relate to licences for –
    - (i) copying the work,
    - (ii) performing, playing or showing the work in public, or
    - (iii) broadcasting the work or including it in a cable programme service;
  - (b) all licensing schemes in relation to the copyright in sound recordings (other than film sound-tracks when accompanying a film), broadcasts or cable programmes, or the typographical arrangement of published editions; and
  - (c) all licensing schemes in relation to the copyright in sound recordings, films or computer programs so far as they relate to licences for the rental of copies to the public;
and in those sections "licensing scheme" means a licensing scheme of any of those descriptions.

S.118(1) The terms of a licensing scheme proposed to be operated by a licensing body may be referred to the Copyright Tribunal by an organisation claiming to be representative of persons claiming that they require licences in cases of a description to which the scheme would apply, either generally or in relation to any description of case.

(2) The Tribunal shall first decide whether to entertain the reference, and may decline to do so on the ground that the reference is premature.

(3) If the Tribunal decides to entertain the reference it shall consider the matter referred and make such order, either confirming or varying the proposed scheme, either generally or so far as it relates to cases of the description to which the reference relates, as the Tribunal may determine to be reasonable in the circumstances.

(4) The order may be made so as to be in force indefinitely or for such period as the Tribunal may determine.

S.119(1) If while a licensing scheme is in operation a dispute arises between the operator of the scheme and –
  (a) a person claiming that he requires a licence in a case of description to which the scheme applies, or
  (b) an organisation claiming to be representative of such persons.
that person or organisation may refer the scheme to the Copyright Tribunal in so far as it relates to cases of that description.

(2) A scheme which has been referred to the Tribunal under this section shall remain in operation until proceedings on the reference are concluded.

(3) The Tribunal shall consider the matter in dispute and make such order, either confirming or varying the scheme so far as it relates to cases of the description to which the reference relates, as the Tribunal may determine to be reasonable in the circumstances.

(4) The order may be made so as to be in force indefinitely or for such period as the Tribunal may determine.

S.120 provides for further reference of a scheme to the Tribunal.

S.121(1) A person who claims, in a case covered by a licensing scheme, that the operator of the scheme has refused to grant him or procure the grant to him of a licence in accordance with the scheme, or has failed to do so within a reasonable time after being asked, may apply to the Copyright Tribunal.

(2) A person who claims, in a case excluded from a licensing scheme, that the operator of the scheme either –

  (a) has refused to grant him a licence or procure the grant to him of a licence, or has failed to do so within a reasonable time of being asked, and that in the circumstances it is unreasonable that a licence should not be granted, or
  (b) proposes terms for a licence which are unreasonable, may apply to the Copyright Tribunal.

(3) A case shall be regarded as excluded from a licensing scheme for the purposes of subsection (2) if –
  (a) the scheme provides for the grant of licences subject to terms

> excepting matters from the licence and the case falls within such an exception, or
>
> (b) the case is so similar to those in which licences are granted under the scheme that it is unreasonable that it should not be dealt with in the same way.

(4) If the Tribunal is satisfied that the claim is well-founded, it shall make an order declaring that, in respect of the matters specified in the order, the applicant is entitled to a licence on such terms as the Tribunal may determine to be applicable in accordance with the scheme or, as the case may be, to be reasonable in the circumstances.

(5) The order may be made so as to be in force indefinitely or for such period as the Tribunal may determine.

S.122 provides for review of an order made under S.121.

S.123 specifies the effect of an order as to a licensing scheme.

S.124–128 deal with references and applications to the Tribunal concerning licensing by licensing bodies, in cases not involving a licensing scheme. The sections follow an equivalent pattern to s.117–123, giving the Tribunal power, in the cases covered, to make orders reasonable in the circumstances.

S.129 In determining what is reasonable on a reference or application under this Chapter relating to a licensing scheme or licence, the Copyright Tribunal shall have regard to –

> **(a) the availability of other schemes, or the granting of other licences, to other persons in similar circumstances, and**
>
> **(b) the terms of those schemes or licences,**

and shall exercise its powers so as to secure that there is no unreasonable discrimination between licensees, or prospective licensees, under the scheme or licence to which the reference or application relates and licensees under other schemes operated by, or other licences granted by, the same person.

S.130 adds further considerations to be given account in relation to reprographic copying, and s.136–141 give special powers where such copying is in an educational establishment (see above, 3.5.6.2). S.131–135 deal with factors to be considered in a number of particular circumstances: educational recording of broadcasts and cable programmes (s.131), recordings etc of events which are subject to promoter's condition (s.132); licences of rental rights etc (s.133); licences concerning retransmissions (s.134). S.135 states the Tribunal's obligation always to have regard to all relevant circumstances.

3.9 Rights in Performances

3.9.1 Rights Granted

3.9.1.1 Copyright, Designs and Patents Act 1988, Part II, s.180, 181, 185

S.180(1) This Part confers rights –
- (a) on a performer, by requiring his consent to the exploitation of his performances (see sections 181 to 184), and
- (b) on a person having recording rights in relation to a performance, in relation to recordings made without his consent or that of the performer (see sections 185 to 188),

and creates offences in relation to dealing with or using illicit recordings and certain other related acts (see sections 198 and 201).

(2) In this Part –
"performance" means –
- (a) a dramatic performance (which includes dance and mime),
- (b) a musical performance,
- (c) a reading or recitation of a literary work, or
- (d) a performance of a variety act or any similar presentation,

which is, or so far as it is, a live performance given by one or more individuals; and

"recording", in relation to a performance, means a film or sound recording –
- (a) made directly from the live performance,
- (b) made from a broadcast of, or cable programme including, the performance, or
- (c) made, directly or indirectly, from another recording of the performance.

S.180(3) gives rights in "pre-commencement" performances, but only in relation to acts done after commencement which were not arranged before.

S.180(4) provides that the performance rights are independent of other intellectual property.

S.181 A performance is a qualifying performance for the purposes of the provisions of this Part relating to performers' rights if it is given by a qualifying individual (as defined in section 206) or takes place in a qualifying country (as so defined).

S.185(1) In this Part an "exclusive recording contract" means a contract between a performer and another person under which that person is entitled to the exclusion of all other persons (including the performer) to make recordings of one or more of his performances with a view to their commercial exploitation.

(2) References in this Part to a "person having recording rights", in relation to a performance, are (subject to subsection (3)) to a person –
- (a) who is party to and has the benefit of an exclusive recording contract to which the performance is subject, or
- (b) to whom the benefit of such a contract has been assigned, and who

is a qualifying person.

(3) If a performance is subject to an exclusive recording contract but the person mentioned in subsection (2) is not a qualifying person, references in this Part to a "person having recording rights" in relation to the performance are to any person –

    (a) who is licensed by such a person to make recordings of the performance with a view to their commercial exploitation, or

    (b) to whom the benefit of such a licence has been assigned,

and who is a qualifying person.

(4) In this section "with a view to commercial exploitation" means with a view to the recordings being sold or let for hire, or shown or played in public.

3.9.1.2   Copyright, Designs and Patents Act 1988, s.206, 208: Qualification for protection and extent

S.206(1) In this Part –

"qualifying country" means –

    (a) the United Kingdom,

    (b) another member State of the European Economic Community, or

    (c) to the extent that an Order under section 208 so provides, a country designated under that section as enjoying reciprocal protection;

"qualifying individual" means a citizen or subject of, or an individual resident in, a qualifying country; and

"qualifying person" means a qualifying individual or a body corporate or other body having legal personality which –

    (a) is formed under the law of a part of the United Kingdom or another qualifying country, and

    (b) has in any qualifying country a place of business at which substantial business activity is carried on.

(2) The reference in the definition of "qualifying individual" to a person's being a citizen or subject of a qualifying country shall be construed –

    (a) in relation to the United Kingdom, as a reference to his being a British citizen, and

    (b) in relation to a colony of the United Kingdom, as a reference to his being a British Dependent Territories' citizen by connection with that colony.

(3) In determining for the purpose of the definition of "qualifying person" whether substantial business activity is carried on at a place of business in any country, no account shall be taken of dealings in goods which are at all material times outside that country.

S.208(1) Her Majesty may by Order in Council designate as enjoying reciprocal protection under this Part –

    (a) a Convention country, or

    (b) a country as to which Her Majesty is satisfied that provision has been or will be made under its law giving adequate protection for British performances.

(2) A "Convention country" means a country which is a party to a Conven-

tion relating to performers' rights to which the United Kingdom is also a party.

(3) A "British performance" means a performance –

    (a) given by an individual who is a British citizen or resident in the United Kingdom,
        or
    (b) taking place in the United Kingdom.

S.207 applies the Part to England, Wales, Scotland and Northern Ireland. S.208(4) provides for designation under (1)(b) to be limited in scope; S.208(5) allows designation of the Channel Islands, Isle of Man and any British colony. S.209, 210 extend the art to British territorial waters and British ships, aircraft and hovercraft.

3.9.2 Duration and Transmission of Rights

3.9.2.1   Copyright, Designs and Patents Act 1988, s.191, 192

S.191 The rights conferred by this Part continue to subsist in relation to a performance until the end of the period of 50 years from the end of the calendar year in which the performance takes place.

S.192(1) The rights conferred by this Part are not assignable or transmissible, except to the extent that performers' rights are transmissible in accordance with the following provisions.

(2) On the death of a person entitled to performer's rights
- **(a) the rights pass to such person as he may by testamentary disposition specifically direct, and**
- **(b) if or to the extent that there is no such direction, the rights are exercisable by his personal representatives;**

and references in this Part to the performer, in the context of the person having performers' rights, shall be construed as references to the person for the time being entitled to exercise those rights.

S.192(3) makes multiple rights under (2)(a) independent of each other; s.102(4) exempts the rights of assignees under s.185(2)(b) and (3)(b) from the section; s.192(5) provides for any damages to devolve with the deceased's estate.

3.9.3 Infringement

3.9.3.1 Copyright, Designs and Patents Act 1988, s.194

S.194 An infringement of any of the rights conferred by this Part is actionable by the person entitled to the right as a breach of statutory duty.

S.193 defines the "consent" necessary if an act is not to constitute infringement of one of the rights.

S.182–184 define the acts which constitute infringement of performers' rights: making a recording (other than for private and domestic use); broadcasting live; cable-casting live; showing or playing in public, broadcasting or cable-casting a recording; importing, possessing or dealing with an illegal recording. All apply in relation to the whole or a substantial part of the performance. They do not apply in the absence of knowledge or reason to believe, e.g. that a recording was illicit.

S.186–188 define an equivalent set of acts constituting infringement of rights in exclusive recording contracts.

S.196–205 provide for delivery up and seizure of illicit recordings, and also for criminal proceedings, in terms equivalent to those affecting illicit copies of copyright material. See above, 3.5.10.1.

S.189 and Sch. 2 define a set of permitted acts in relation to rights in performances. These are mostly equivalent to defences applicable to copyright claims (for which see s.28–77; above, 3.5.5 et seq.). They include: fair dealing for criticism, review and news reporting; incidental inclusion; instruction and examination; playing or showing a sound recording, film, broadcast or cable-cast at an educational establishment; copying before export; various acts in public administration; copies in electronic form; recordings of spoken words in news reporting and broadcasting; recordings of folksongs; playing of sound recordings at clubs etc; incidental recording for broadcasts and cable-casts; supervision of broadcasts and cable-casts; free public showing of broadcasts and cable-casts immediate reception and re-transmission of broadcast in cable-cast; sub-titling for the handicapped; recording of broadcasts and cable-casts for archives.

4 INDUSTRIAL DESIGNS

4.1 Copyright

4.1.1 Copyright Designs and Patents Act 1988, s.51–53: Limitations on Copyright in Designs

S.51(1) It is not an infringement of any copyright in a design document or model recording or embodying a design for anything other than an artistic work or a typeface to make an article to the design or to copy an article made to the design.

(2) Nor is it an infringement of the copyright to issue to the public, or include in a film, broadcast or cable programme service, anything the making of which was, by virtue of subsection (1), not an infringement of that copyright.

(3) In this section –
> "design" means the design of any aspect of the shape or configuration (whether internal or external) of the whole or part of an article, other than surface decoration; and

> "design document" means any record of a design, whether in the form of a drawing, a written description, a photograph, data stored in a computer or otherwise.

Sch. 1, s.19 defers for ten years the application of s.51 to works existing at commencement, but subjects copyright in these works to the licence of right powers which apply to (unregistered) design right; for which, see below, 4.3.

S.52(1) This section applies where an artistic work has been exploited, by or with the licence of the copyright owner, by –

> (a) making by an industrial process articles falling to be treated for the purposes of this Part as copies of the work, and
> (b) marketing such articles, in the United Kingdom or elsewhere.

(2) After the end of the period of 25 years from the end of the calendar year in which such articles are first marketed, the work may be copied by making articles of any description, or doing anything for the purpose of making articles of any description, and anything may be done in relation to articles so made, without infringing copyright in the work.

(3) Where only part of an artistic work is exploited as mentioned in subsection (1), subsection (2) applies only in relation to that part.

(4) The Secretary of State may by order make provision –
> (a) as to the circumstances in which an article, or any description of

article, is to be regarded for the purposes of this section as made by an industrial process;

(b) excluding from the operation of this section such articles of a primarily literary or artistic character as he thinks fit.

(5) An order shall be made by statutory instrument which shall be subject to annulment in pursuance of a resolution of either House of Parliament.

(6) In this section –

(a) references to articles do not include films; and

(b) references to the marketing of an article are to its being sold or let for hire or offered or exposed for sale or hire.

S.53(1) The copyright in an artistic work is not infringed by anything done –

(a) in pursuance of an assignment or licence made or granted by a person registered under the Registered Designs Act 1949 as the proprietor of a corresponding design, and

(b) in good faith in reliance on the registration and without notice of any proceedings for the cancellation of the registration or for rectifying the relevant entry in the register of designs;

and this is so notwithstanding that the person registered as the proprietor was not the proprietor of the design for the purposes of the 1949 Act.

(2) In subsection (1) a "corresponding design", in relation to an artistic work, means a design within the meaning of the 1949 Act which if applied to an article would produce something which would be treated for the purposes of this Part as a copy of the artistic work.

The definition of "corresponding design" in the Registered Designs Act 1949, s.44, is in equivalent terms to those of s.53(2).

S.54 and 55 limit the scope of copyright in a typeface as an artistic work by excluding use of the typeface in the ordinary course of typing, printing etc., and associated acts from the scope of infringement.

4.1.2   *Hensher v Restawile* [1976] A.C. 64 (H.L.)

The appellant-plaintiffs, manufacturers of chairs and settees, produced a temporary "mock-up" for a newly-designed suite of furniture. This mock-up was used to produce suites of furniture which sold well under the mark "The Bronx", and were imitated by the defendants, among others. The plaintiffs registered no designs but relied upon copyright in the mock-up as a "work of artistic craftsmanship" (Copyright Act 1956, s.3(1)(c), equivalent to Copyright, Designs and Patents Act 1988, s.4(1)(c)).

Lord Reid:

It is common ground that we must consider the prototype and not the furniture put on the market by the appellants. Apparently this is because the articles put on the market were not works of craftsmanship. But if there was copyright in the prototype then the furniture put on the market by the appellants was copied from it, and the respondents' products were copied from the furniture which the appellants put on the market. The respondents do not deny that this would be infringement of that copyright.

The respondents have not taken the point that such a prototype however artistic could not be a "work of artistic craftsmanship", and the point was not argued. But I feel bound to say that I have great doubt about this matter. A work of craftsmanship suggests to me a durable, useful handmade object and a work of artistic craftsmanship suggests something, whether of practical utility or not, which its owner values because of its artistic character. It appears to me to be difficult to bring within the terms or the intention of the statute an object which, however artistic it might appear to be, is only intended to be used as a step in a commercial operation and has no value in itself. I express no concluded opinion on this matter on which the decision of this case can be of no authority. This case must I think be decided on the assumption that a real chair similar to those put on the market had been made by craftsmanship.

Section 3(1) is difficult to understand unless one takes account of its origin. The Copyright Act 1911 covered artistic works. Section 35 contains a definition: "Artistic work" includes works of painting, drawing, sculpture and artistic craftsmanship, and architectural works of art and engravings and photographs. "Architectural work of art" is defined as meaning any building or structure having an artistic character or design. This brought in artistic craftsmanship and buildings for the first time. It would seem that paintings, drawings, sculpture, engravings and photographs were protected whether they had any artistic character or not, but works of craftsmanship had to be of "artistic" craftsmanship and buildings must have an "artistic" character or design. There is no further explanation of what is meant by "artistic".

The 1956 Act in s.3(1)(a) makes explicit that the works to which it refers need have no artistic quality. Section 3(1)(b) removes the need for any artistic character or design in buildings. But s.3(1)(c) preserves the limitation that there must be "artistic" craftsmanship.

The word "artistic" is not an easy word to construe or apply not only because it may have different shades of meaning but also because different people have different views about what is artistic. One may have a word which substantially everyone understands in much the same way. Recently we had to consider such a word – "insulting" (*Brutus v Cozens* [1972] 2 All E.R. 1297). Then the matter can and, indeed, must be left to the judge or jury for further explanation will confuse rather than clarify.

But here two questions must be determined. What precisely is the meaning of "artistic" in this context and who is to judge of its application to the article in question? There is a trend of authority with which I agree that a court ought not to be called on to make an aesthetic judgment. Judges have to be experts in the use of the English language but they are not experts in art or aesthetics. In such a matter my opinion is of no more value than that of anyone else. But I can and must say what in my view is the meaning of the word "artistic".

I think we must avoid philosophic or metaphysical argument about the nature of beauty, not only because there does not seem to be any consensus about this but also because those who are ignorant of philosophy are entitled to have opinions about what is artistic. I think that by common usage it is proper for a person to say that in his opinion a thing has an artistic character if he gets pleasure or satisfaction or it may be uplift from contemplating it. No doubt it is necessary to beware of those who get pleasure from looking at something which has cost them a great deal of money. But if unsophisticated people get pleasure from seeing something which they admire I do not see why we must say that it is not artistic because those who profess to be art experts think differently. After all there are great differences of opinion among those who can properly be called experts.

It is I think of importance that the maker or designer of a thing should have intended that it should have an artistic appeal but I would not regard that as either necessary or conclusive. If any substantial section of the public genuinely admires and values a thing for its appearance and gets pleasure or satisfaction, whether emotional or intellectual, from looking at it, I would accept that it is artistic although many others may think it meaningless or common or vulgar.

I think that it may be misleading to equate artistic craftsmanship with a work of art. "Work of art" is generally associated more with the fine arts than with craftsmanship and may be setting too high a standard. During the last century there was a movement to bring art to the people. I doubt whether the craftsmen who set out with that intention would have regarded all their products as works of art, but they were certainly works of artistic craftsmanship whether or not they were useful as well as having an artistic appeal.

I am quite unable to agree with the view of the Court of Appeal that:

> "there must at least be expected in an object or work that its utilitarian or functional appeal should not be the primary inducement to its acquisition or retention".

The whole conception of artistic craftsmanship appears to me to be to produce things which are both useful and artistic in the belief that being artistic does not make them any less useful. A person who only wants, or has only room for, one of a particular kind of household object may be willing to pay more to get one which he regards as artistic; if a work of craftsmanship it is nonetheless of artistic craftsmanship because his primary purpose is to get something useful.

But on the other hand I cannot accept the appellants' submission or the view of Graham J. Many people – probably too many – buy things on eye appeal or because they are of a new or original design. But they would not claim that therefore they thought that their purchase had artistic merit. They might say that they were not interested in art, or that they would like to have bought an artistic object but that there was none to be had, at least at a price they could pay. It is notorious that manufacturers go to great expense in providing packaging which will catch the eye of customers. But the customer does not regard the packaging as artistic – he throws it away.

In the present case I find no evidence at all that anyone regarded the appellants' furniture as artistic. The appellants' object was to produce something which would sell. It was, as one witness said, "a winner" and they succeeded in their object. No doubt many customers bought the furniture because they thought it looked nice as well as being comfortable. But looking nice appears to me to fall considerably short of having artistic appeal. I can find no evidence that anyone felt or thought that the furniture was artistic in the sense which I have tried to explain. I am therefore of opinion that this appeal should be dismissed.

Lord Simon of Glaisdale:

The significant feature of this part of the law before 1911 was that the artistic works given copyright protection were works of fine art. This accorded with the almost universal concept current in 1862: a work of art was a product of the fine arts and primarily an easel painting. But almost from the moment of the Fine Arts Copyright Act 1862, there was a reaction, which came to be known as the Arts and Crafts movement. In 1862 itself William Morris founded "The Firm" producing a wide variety of work of decorative and applied art. In 1864 he produced his first wallpaper, hand-printed from wood blocks. In the 1880s at least five societies were founded to promote the guild ideal propagated by Ruskin and Morris. In 1883 the Arts and Crafts Exhibition Society began its work. In 1890 Morris set up the Kelmscott Press, to be followed by a number of other private presses within the decade. In 1893 came the Arts and Crafts Essays (of which eight were concerned with the design and decoration of furniture). In 1896 the Central School of Arts and Crafts was founded, with Lethaby and Frampton as joint principals. The tenth edition of the Encyclopaedia Britannica contained, for the first time, an article on "Arts and Crafts" – by Walter Crane. In 1905 Cobden-Sanderson published The Arts and Crafts Movement. In 1908 the Central School moved to its present purpose-built premises in Southampton Row. These are no more than a handful of key events: but they put beyond doubt what it was that prompted Parliament in 1911 to give copyright protection to "works of artistic craftsmanship" namely, the Arts and Crafts movement with its emphasis on the applied or decorative arts.

For the essence of the Arts and Crafts ideology was that "art" did not mean merely, or even primarily, the fine arts. Art was a way of life, standing in contrast to the prevailing life of industrialism and commercialism, which was seen as a threat to mankind's spiritual and physical well-being. "On every hand", Carlyle had written, "the living artisan is driven from his workshop, to make room for a speedier inanimate one". So the handicraftsman must be restored to his creative role in society. Moreover, his creation, wherever appropriate, should be a work of art – creation par excellence: and the artist must in turn be a craftsman. The aim of Mackmurdo's Century Guild (1882) was, on the one hand, to render all branches of art no longer "the sphere of the tradesman"; on the other, to "restore building, decoration, glass-painting, pottery, wood-carving and metal to their proper place beside painting and sculpture". The aesthetic of the movement was concerned with fitness and propriety, in contradistinction to irrelevant ornament (what Lethaby called "sham artistic twaddle"). Functional efficiency and respect for the worked material would impose its own appropriate form, showing, to quote Lethaby again, that it was "made for a human being by a human being".

But although, in my view, there can be no doubt that, when Parliament, in 1911, gave copyright protection to "works of artistic craftsmanship", it was extending to works of applied art the protection formerly restricted to works of the fine arts, and was doing so under the influence of the Arts and Crafts movement, and although the aesthetic of the

Arts and Crafts movement was a handicraft aesthetic, Parliament used the words "artistic craftsmanship", not "artistic handicraft". It seems likely that this was done advisedly: I have already indicated that s.22 of the 1911 Act envisaged that an industrial design might be an artistic work. Moreover, however ideologically opposed to current industrial and commercial society, at least some of the leaders of the Arts and Crafts movement recognised that they would have to come to terms with the machine. As early as 1850 Philip Webb designed table glassware for J Powell & Sons of Whitefriars. During the 1880s even Morris acknowledged that the machine could be useful in extinguishing all irksome and unintelligent labour, leaving us free to raise the standard of skill of hand and energy of mind of our workmen. The private presses may have used hand-made paper and designed their own typefaces, but they printed on machines. Ashbeec, who went to the United States in 1900 "to tilt at the great industrial windmill", by 1911, under the influence of Frank Lloyd Wright (who had lectured on "The Art and Craft of the Machine") could no longer deny to the unpretentious machine-made object an aesthetic value; and after the failure of his Guild and School of Handicraft he himself turned to industrial design. Much of Benson's metal-work was produced by machinery on a commercial scale. The Central School of Arts and Crafts, though foremost a school of handicrafts, had as a declared aim to encourage "the industrial application of decorative design". So, although "works of artistic craftsmanship" cannot be adequately construed without bearing in mind the aims and achievements of the Arts and Crafts movement, "craftsmanship" in the statutory phrase cannot be limited to handicraft; nor is the word "artistic" incompatible with machine production (see *Britain v Hanks Brothers and Co* (1902) 86 L.T. 764).

The concession that the prototype of the Bronx was a work of craftsmanship has tended to distort the argument by concentrating exclusively on the meaning of the word "artistic" in the statutory phrase. But "works of artistic craftsmanship" is a composite phrase which must be construed as a whole. There is nothing to suggest that any of the words is used in other than one of its ordinary senses. A work of craftsmanship, even though it cannot be confined to handicraft, at least presupposes special training, skill and knowledge for its production: see *Cuisenaire v Reed* ([1963] V.R. 719) and *Cuisenaire v South West Imports Ltd* ([1968] 1 Ex.C.R. 493). "Craftsmanship", particularly when considered in its historical context, implies a manifestation of pride in sound workmanship – a rejection of the shoddy, the meretricious, the facile. But the craftsmanship – not the work itself – must, in addition, be artistic. Before turning to the various criteria which have been propounded it may be helpful to consider some examples. A cobbler is a craftsman, and those in the Arts and Crafts movement would have valued his vocation as such. But neither they, nor anyone else using the words in their common acceptation, would describe his craftsmanship as artistic, or his products as "works of artistic craftsmanship". A dental mechanic is a similar example; so is a pattern-maker, a boiler-maker, a plumber, a wheelwright, a thatcher. At the other extreme is the maker of hand-painted tiles. He too is a craftsman; but his craftsmanship would properly be described as artistic and his products as "works of artistic craftsmanship". In between lie a host of crafts some of whose practitioners can claim artistic craftsmanship, much not – or whose practitioners sometimes exercise artistic craftsmanship, sometimes not. In the former class, for example, are glaziers. The ordinary glazier is a craftsman, but he could not properly claim that his craftsmanhip is artistic in the common acceptation. But the maker of stained glass windows could properly make such a claim; and indeed, the revival of stained glass work was one of the high achievements of the Arts and Crafts movement. In the latter class is the blacksmith – a craftsman in all his business, and exercising artistic craftsmanship perhaps in making wrought iron gates, but certainly not in shoeing a horse or repairing a ploughshare. In these intermediate – or rather, straddling – classes come, too, the woodworkers, ranging from carpenters to cabinet-makers: some of their work would be generally accepted as artistic craftsmanship, much not. Similarly, printers, book-binders, cutlers, needleworkers, weavers – and many others. In this straddling class also fall, in my judgment, the makers of furniture. Some of their products would be, I think, almost universally accepted as "works of artistic craftsmanship" but it would be a misuse of language to describe the bulk of their products as such. Where and how is the line to be drawn?

I think that the key passage of Graham J.'s judgment is the following:

> "My conclusion on this part of the case is therefore that these chairs and settees are 'works of artistic craftsmanship' in that they have, whether one admires them or not, distinctive characteristics of shape, form and finish, which were conceived and executed by Mr Hensher and those working with him so as to result in articles which are much more than purely utilitarian. They exhibit in my judgment distinctive features of design and skill in workmanship which the words of definition 'artistic craftsmanship' on their proper construction in their context connote."

Though this approach receives some support from *Blake v Warren*, ([1931] MacG. Cop. Cas. 268), a decision of an official referee on the "artistic character" of an "architectural work of art" under the 1911 Act, I respectfully agree with the comment of the Court of Appeal:

> "It seems to us that the judge has in effect come to the conclusion that in the field of furniture all that is needed to qualify as a work of artistic craftsmanship is a sufficient originality of design to qualify as a design under the Registered Designs Act 1949. Is this right in law? We do not think so. It seems to us to give no sufficient effect to the word 'artistic' in the definition in the 1956 Act. The phrase is not 'a work of craftsmanship of original design' ... Mere originality in points of design aimed at appealing to the eye as commercial selling points will not in our judgment suffice".

Although there is, as I have pointed out, an area of overlap between the Copyright Acts and the Registered Designs Acts, the two classes of statute do not give co-terminous protection as regards subject-matter: if that had been the intention, interpretative cross-reference would have been the appropriate drafting technique. Moreover, although true originality (in the way of a new sensibility or ideology or world view or technique) may be relevant aesthetically, mere novelty can hardly be so. A gimmick is almost the negation of a work of art. Its appeal, as Russell L.J. implied, is likely to be directed at satisfying other demands in the purchaser than the contemplation of beauty – desire for change, for modishness, for prestige, for example.

On the other hand, I cannot agree with the alternative criterion proposed by the Court of Appeal that:

> "... in order to qualify as a work of artistic craftsmanship, there must at least be expected in an object or work that its utilitarian or functional appeal should not be the primary inducement to its acquisition or retention".

Restawile's counsel did not attempt to support this test before your Lordships. It is, I fear, unworkable. One person may buy a chair because it is comfortable, another because it is beautiful, a third because it exactly fits the room, a fourth because it is the right price. Even without the third and fourth classes, which do not fit in the Court of

Appeal's categorisation, it would be impracticable to decide on the artistic quality of the craftsmanship by a show of hands or a card vote. And in one purchaser alone the motives may be so mixed that it is impossible to say what is the primary inducement to acquisition or retention. Even more important, the whole antithesis between utility and beauty, between function and art, is a false one – especially in the context of the Arts and Crafts movement. "I never begin to be satisfied", said Philip Webb, one of the founders, "until my work looks commonplace". Lethaby's object, declared towards the end, was "to create an efficiency style". Artistic form should, they all held, be an emanation of regard for materials on the one hand and for function on the other.

Hensher's counsel put forward an argument as follows. An object is artistic if it appeals to the eye of the beholder, giving him visual pleasure. The Bronx proved to be more appealing than the Denver. But, so far as utility or function was concerned, there was virtually nothing to choose between the two models. The greater appeal of the Bronx must, therefore, have been its "eye-appeal" – that it gave significantly greater visual pleasure. The prototype Bronx was admittedly a work of craftsmanship. It inevitably follows, it was argued, that it was a work of artistic craftsmanship.

With all respect, and admitting its ingenuity, there seems to me to be much that is unacceptable in this argument. First, it is based on a hedonistic aesthetic theory (the essence of art is that it gives pleasure) which, although it has had distinguished proponents, has also been strongly disputed. Secondly, it then proceeds to stand the theory on its head – the essence of art is that it gives (visual) pleasure, therefore what gives visual pleasure is artistic. This is not only illogical, but manifestly untrue – a pretty girl or a landscape give visual pleasure without being artistic. Thirdly, this argument to is based on a contradistinction between art and function which is unsound, and particularly unsound in the instant context. Fourthly, the argument proceeds on the basis that the Bronx must have been bought in preference to the Denver for its greater utility or for its great visual appeal – and, since it was not the former, it must have been the latter. But there were many other reasons why the Bronx might have been bought – because the Joneses next door had just acquired such a suite, for example, or because no one in the neighbourhood had such a novelty, or because it struck the purchaser as being in the "trend" of fashion (that word was actually used in evidence to explain the common appeal of these suites), or because it seemed to be the best general value for money of the available goods, or, no doubt, for a large variety of other reasons which have nothing to do with either function or eye-appeal.

Restawile's counsel, on the other hand, propounded two alternative criteria, both reflecting another theory of aesthetics – the idealistic. The first was: an article of craftsmanship is artistic if it can be seen from the article itself or from other evidence that the author is using a utilitarian article as a vehicle to carry an expression of his idea of beauty. Counsel defined neither "idea" nor "beauty" – wisely, since philosophers have been at odds over these concepts for millennia. But without some explanation the proffered criterion is virtually tautological; since art, both in the discipline of aesthetics and in popular usage, is generally understood to be the expression or impression of beauty.

Counsel's second criterion was a variant on the first: craftsmanship is artistic if the craftsman is using a utilitarian article to give expression to an idea unassociated with the utilitarian purpose. This avoids the tautology implicit in the use of the word "beauty", but at the cost of greater vagueness. Disregarding the metaphysical implications of the use of the word "idea" in this context, this criterion would extend to the expression of ideas which would seem to be irrelevant to art – for example, novelty and gimmickry (which I have already referred to), or modishness, or obscenity, or racial prejudice. The example given by counsel was an "archetypal" fork (a work of craftsmanship) with an ornament on the handle (making it a work of artistic craftsmanship). But, as I have ventured to point out, this whole contradistinction between art and utility, between function and ornament, is entirely alien to the concepts which lie behind s.3(1)(c) of the 1956 Act. An "archetypal" spoon (assuming such a metaphysical concept can materialise) may itself be a work of artistic craftsmanship; an apostle spoon is neither more nor less likely to be so.

It is, my Lords, I confess, easier to question the criteria put forward by others than to propound one's own. The attempt must nevertheless be made. I start by re-emphasising that the statutory phrase is not "artistic work of craftsmanship", but "work of artistic craftsmanship"; and that this distinction accords with the social situation in which Parliament was providing a remedy. It is therefore misleading to ask, first, is this a work produced by a craftsman, and secondly, is it a work of art? It is more pertinent to ask, is this the work of one who was in this respect an artist-craftsman? It follows that the artistic merit of the work is irrelevant. (It is, no doubt, because s.3(1)(a), "irrespective of artistic quality", which, as comparison with the words "artistic character" in the 1911 Act demonstrates, refer to artistic merit). Not only is artistic merit irrelevant as a matter of statutory construction, evaluation of artistic merit is not a task for which judges have any training or general aptitude. Words are the tools and subject-matter of lawyers; but even in matters of literary copyright the court will not concern itself with literary merit: *Walter v Lane* ([1900] A.C. 539). Since the tribunal will not attempt a personal aesthetic judgment (Stewart J. in *Hay v Sloan* (1957) 16 Fox P.C. 185) it follows again, that whether the subject-matter is or is not a work of artistic craftsmanship is a matter of evidence; and the most cogent evidence is likely to be either from those who are themselves acknowledged artist-craftsmen or from those who are concerned with the training of artist-craftsmen – in other words, expert evidence. In evaluating the evidence, the court will endeavour not to be tied to a particular metaphysics of art, partly because courts are not naturally fitted to weigh such matters, partly because Parliament can hardly have intended that the construction of its statutory phrase should turn on some recondite theory of aesthetics – though the court must, of course, in its task of statutory interpretation, take cognisance of the social-aesthetic situation which lies behind the enactment, nor can counsel be prevented from probing the reasons why a witness considers the subject-matter to be or not to be a work of artistic craftsmanship. It is probably enough that common experience tells us that artists have vocationally an aim and impact which differ from those of the ordinary run of humankind. Given the craftsmanship, it is the presence of such aim and impact – what Stewart J. called "the intent of the creator and its result" – which will determine that the work is one of artistic craftsmanship.

Against this construction of the statutory phrase, the result of the instant appeal cannot be in doubt: there was no, or certainly no adequate, evidence that the prototype of the Bronx chair was a work of artistic craftsmanship. A Mrs Watney, who had been the principal furniture buyer of the Times Furnishing Co gave evidence for Henshers: some passages were quoted in the judgment of the Court of Appeal. It is sufficient here to say that she nowhere stated that in her opinion any of the suites in question (or the prototype) was a work of artistic craftsmanship. Though she used the word "eye-appeal", it was in the context of commercial potentiality, selling points. Of the Bronx she said, "the shape ... was new. It was very flashy. It was horrible really". Of the Denver, in respect of its common features with the Bronx, she spoke of the "trend that was coming in". She used the word "winner" – appropriate enough in its commercial context, but hardly apt for anything more.

Mr Carter, a design consultant specialising in furniture, also gave evidence for Henshers. He did use the word "artistic"; but it was put into his mouth under the misapprehension that he had already used it. Again, the key passages are set out in the judgment of the Court of Appeal. Mr Carter agreed with Henshers' counsel that it was the intention of the designer to produce an article which appealed to the eye of the beholder: I have already ventured to indicate why this is an inadequate criterion of art or the artistic. He described the Bronx as "typical of the middle of the road commercial type of production furniture". He considered its design to be mediocre, although he could see that it had great appeal – slightly vulgar, though obviously quite a good commercial design, having "novelty . . . quite distinct individuality".

All this is very far from establishing the Bronx or its prototype as a work of artistic craftsmanship. I respectfully agree with the Court of Appeal that at the most it established originality in points of design aimed at appealing to the eye as commercial selling points. I also agree that this does not suffice. If it were permissible to express a personal view, I would agree with the Court of Appeal that Henshers' suites are perfectly ordinary pieces of furniture. It would be an entire misuse of language to describe them or their prototypes as works of artistic craftsmanship.

I would therefore dismiss the appeal.

Lord Morris of Borth-y-Gest, Viscount Dilhorne and Lord Kilbrandon delivered concurring speeches.

4.1.3   *Merlet v Mothercare* [1986] R.P.C. 115 (Walton J.)

The first plaintiff, a clothes designer and maker, designed a baby's cape – the "Raincosy" – originally for her own child. Later she arranged for its manufacture by the second plaintiff. The defendant copied the cape and sold its version in its chain-stores. One of the claims was against infringement of copyright in the prototype cape (P.1) as a "work of artistic craftsmanship". On this issue, Walton J. stated:

In the leading case on the relevant subsection in the House of Lords, *George Hensher Ltd v Restawile Upholstery (Lancs) Ltd* [1975] R.P.C. 31, the question of craftsmanship was not in issue, having been, as their Lordships thought, wrongly conceded at first instance. But from their varied observations on the point, craftsmanship requires a manifestation of pride in sound workmanship, or, alternatively, as Lord Reid put it, "a durable useful handmade object". There is no doubt that P.1 was a durable – it has survived the Highland weather – extremely useful handmade object. And I think, taking into account the function it was intended to perform, the garment was sound enough, but really no more than this. Can such workmanship be equated with craftsmanship? Unlike Hensher, the matter is not conceded and I think the case is one very much on the borderline. However, I do not think I would be justified in deciding this case simply on the basis that P.1 does not reach in its execution the standard required to amount to craftsmanship. However, "artistic craftsmanship" is a totally different matter.

The first question which arises on this point, and in many ways it is the most crucial question of all on this part of the case, is to what extent, when considering a work of artistic craftsmanship, it is permissible to consider notionally anything other than the precise work said to be a work of artistic craftsmanship itself. The reason why the matter is crucial is that Mr Fysh was in substance constrained to admit that, if regard was to be had only to the Raincosy itself, divorced from its use, it would be extremely difficult, if not totally impossible, to submit that any substantial section of the public would value the Raincosy for its appearance, or get pleasure or satisfaction, whether emotional or intellectual, from looking at it. This is the test which Lord Reid applied in the leading case already referred to of *George Hensher Ltd v Restawile Upholstery (Lancs) Ltd* at page 54, lines 41 to 44, and which is a test which is otherwise the most favourable one for the plaintiffs' case.

But, says Mr Fysh, if the complex of a mother, equipped with a Kangourou or equivalent baby sling, and baby, properly protected by a Raincosy, is observed by any mother (mothers doubtless being a substantial section of the public), they would derive immense aesthetic satisfaction from looking at the whole assemblage. Indeed, the plaintiffs' main witness on this point, Kathleen Linda Key-Scott, herself a mother, waxed lyrical, in an overtly Freudian manner, over the bundling of the baby with the mother thus effected in an alleged womb-like manner.

But how stands the law? I commence, as anybody dealing with the particular topic of garments of any nature must, with the doubts expressed by Clauson J., as he then was, in *Burke and Margot Burke Ltd v Spicers Dress Designs* [1936] Ch. 400 at 408–409. What he said was this:

> "I can conceive it possible that Mrs Burke might design a frock and make it all herself, and if she did that I can well understand she might be the author of an original work of artistic craftsmanship, but that is not what has happened in this case. I do not want it to be assumed that, even so, I should feel able to hold that a lady who designed a frock and made it all herself was necessarily entitled to copyright. The point is not one which it is necessary for me to decide. It must,

however, be borne in mind that the meaning of the term 'artistic' as indicated in the Oxford English Dictionary is that which pertains to an artist. An artist is defined in the same dictionary as: 'One who cultivates one of the fine arts in which the object is mainly to gratify the aesthetic emotions by perfection of execution whether in creation or representation'. Does a designer who herself designs and makes a frock cultivate one of the fine arts in which the object is mainly to gratify the aesthetic emotions by perfection of execution whether in creation or representation? A possible view is that what she does is merely to bring into being a garment as a mere article of commerce. If that is the right view there may be a difficulty in holding that even a lady who designs and executes a beautiful frock is necessarily the author of an original work of artistic craftsmanship. The frock when one looks at it, *qua* frock, as it might be held up on court, goes a very little way towards gratifying the aesthetic emotions. It is quite a different matter when the frock is placed upon a lady of the figure and colouring which it is designed to suit; then the frock in that connection may help to gratify the aesthetic emotions. The question whether a frock *per se* is the subject of copyright under the Act is one that can be determined only by forming a judgment upon the problem which I have thus indicated, but which in the present case it is not my duty to solve".

These observations were, of course, *obiter*; but it has been my experience, and, I think, the experience of anybody who has had anything to do with claims relating to the pirating of dress designs, that ever since that case the plaintiffs have never sought to rely upon any dress as itself being a work of artistic craftsmanship, but have always sought to rely instead upon the undoubted copyright in drawings related to the dress.

Walton J. referred to Bernstein v Sydney Murray *[1981] R.P.C. 303 and* Radley Gowns v Spirou *[1975] F.S.R. 455 and continued:*

I now return to *Hensher*. It appears to me quite clear that one thing upon which virtually all their Lordships were agreed was that the proper test was to consider whether the object under consideration had an artistic appeal in itself. Doubtless, the furniture in issue in that case was intended to be sat upon, conceivably by a united and happy family: but nobody there suggested that, as the contemplation of the furniture so filled by paterfamilias and materfamilias would give great aesthetic satisfaction, so that satisfaction could, as it were, be rubbed off on to the furniture itself.

Walton J. referred to passages in the speeches in Hensher. *He continued:*

Therefore, in my judgment I have to consider whether the Raincosy – or, I think, more accurately, the prototype thereof, P.1 – is in itself a work of artistic craftsmanship. What, then, is the true test by which a work of artistic craftsmanship is to be judged? At first sight, all their Lordships in *Hensher* were laying down different, and apparently irreconcilable, tests; but, after having, as I freely acknowledge, originally recoiled from the test propounded by Viscount Dilhorne, namely, is the object in question a work of art?, as propounding far too stringent a test (as indeed Lord Reid said), I have finally come to the reluctant conclusion that there exists a clear majority of voices in the House of Lords for that view.

Walton J. referred to passages from the speeches of Viscount Dilhorne, Lord Simon of Glaisdale and Lord Kilbrandon. He continued:

Thus there is a clear majority of their Lordships in favour of this approach to the question, and I think that I am therefore bound to accept it. However, on reflection, I have come to the conclusion that my – and Lord Reid's – initial reluctance to accept this test, as posing too stringent a criterion, is mistaken, being based upon an instinctive value judgment as to what might constitute a work of art. But this is to do precisely what I think their Lordships regarded as impermissible – namely, to make a value judgment. At any rate in the first instance, it is not for the court make a value judgment: the question is primarily the intention of the artist-craftsman. If his intention was to create a work of art and he has not manifestly failed in that intent, that is all that is required. It is not for the court to say that he has merely done the equivalent of flinging a paint pot in the face of the public. But, of course, he may have manifestly failed in his object, and his own *ipse dixit* cannot therefore be the sole, although it is the initial and predominant, test.

There is one further reflection. Although there must always come a first time when an artist-craftsman seeks to create a work of art, and the court may well look with just suspicion upon the first claim of this nature, it will be much easier to recognise the claim if the craftsman is already a recognised artist.

Finally, I say nothing as to the evidence which should be properly admitted as to whether the artist has succeeded in his aim of creating a work of art. There was a diversity of views in the House as to what evidence (apart of course from the intentions of the presumed artist-craftsman) was properly admissible, and especially in this last point. I do not think it would be right, since it is not required for the purposes of this case, to express any opinion thereon.

However, it appears to me clear beyond a peradventure that when creating the Raincosy Mme Merlet did not have in mind the creation of a work of art in any shape or form. What she had in mind, as appeared quite clearly from her evidence, was the utilitarian consideration of creating a barrier between the assumed rigours of a Highland summer and her baby in such a manner as to afford him complete protection, safely cocooned next to her warm body, in a stylish and attractive shape. It is, of course, I suppose conceivable that, although she did not set out to make a work of art, *per incuriam* she may have done so; but certainly nobody in court, whether the witnesses, counsel or the judge – or, indeed, anybody out of court who had written about the Raincosy and whose writing was in evidence – considered that she had done so, if one is to regard, as I have already decided, the Raincosy by itself. On this, the view of Mr Herbert, a witness of the greatest possible distinction in the field of designs of every nature, was terse and to the point: the Raincosy was, he said, a "basic commodity item". And I entirely agree.

The finding at first instance that the prototype cape did not constitute a work of artistic craftsmanship was not challenged in the proceedings before the C.A., which concerned infringement of design drawings for the cape.

4.1.4 *Wham-O Manufacturing v Lincoln* [1985] R.P.C. 127 (C.A., N.Z.)

The first plaintiff, an American corporation, developed the well-known flying disc, the "Frisbee". It was made from plastic and was distinguished from other similar products by the addition of one or more concentric rings or ribs. These improved its aerodynamic qualities. By surreptitious collusion with the first plaintiff's Australian licensee, the defendant company produced and marketed a very similar product in New Zealand, where legislative provisions equivalent to those of the UK Copyright Act 1956, s.3(1) and 48(1) (definitions) were in force. Inter alia, the plaintiffs succeeded in claims that the defendant's activities constituted infringement of their copyright in (i) preliminary working drawings; (ii) wooden models from which moulds were made (which were "sculptures"); (iii) moulds for production of the plastic articles (which were "engravings"); and (iv) the "Frisbees" produced by extruding liquid plastic into the moulds (which were "engravings", but not "sculptures").

On these associated issues, Davison C.J. (for the Court) stated:

Copyright protection which is statutory in nature is conferred by section 7 of the Act in any "artistic work" which is defined in section 2 as follows:

"Artistic work" means a work of any of the following descriptions, that is to say –
   (a) The following, irrespective of artistic quality, namely, paintings, sculptures, drawings, engravings and photographs;
   (b) Works of architecture, being either buildings of models for buildings;
   (c) Works of artistic craftsmanship, not falling within either of the preceding paragraphs of this definition.

"Engraving" is defined as including – "any etching, lithograph, woodcut, print, or similar work, not being a photograph".

"Sculpture" is defined as including – "any cast or model made for purposes of sculpture".

Moller J. held that the wooden models were "sculptures"; the moulds or dies were "engravings"; and that the plastic moulded products were also "engravings". Those findings are challenged by Mr Hillyer. The question whether the plastic moulded products were also "sculptures" was posed by Moller J. but not answered in his judgment.

Before Moller J. counsel for Wham-O, in contending that the wooden model was a "sculpture" and that the moulds or dies and the finished products were "engravings" and thus proper subjects of copyright, elected to rely solely upon that part of the definition of artistic work set out in section 2(1)(a) of the Copyright Act 1962. ...

A reading of the definition of "artistic work" in section 2(1)(a) of the Act indicates that the Act when it speaks of engraving primarily has in contemplation the final prints made from an engraved plate rather than the plate itself. That was the view expressed by Paul Baker Q.C. in *James Arnold & Co Ltd v Miafern Ltd* [1980] R.P.C. 397 at 403:

"'Engraving' can and usually does mean an image produced from an engraved plate. The first question here is whether the engraving can mean the actual engraved plate from which the copies are taken. Looking at the sections alone, particularly the association of the word in section 3 with sculptures, drawings and photographs, it would suggest that it must be the final picture, and of course it certainly includes that".

Davison C.J. analysed further the judgment in the Miafern *case and referred to dictionary definitions of "to engrave"; he continued:*

We agree with the conclusion reached by Paul Baker Q.C. that engraving embraces not only the image made from the engraved plate but the engraved plate itself, but we prefer to reach that result by giving the word "engraving" as used in the definition of "artistic work" in section 2(1)(a) of the Act its ordinary meaning as ascertained from the sources referred to earlier. It is the purpose of copyright to protect the original skill and labour of the author and there is a large degree of that skill and labour brought to bear in making the engraved plate. We do not believe that it was the intention of Parliament to deny copyright in the plate and yet allow it in the print taken from that plate.

At this point it is necessary to consider the nature of the moulds or dies and the finished products.

The manner in which the moulds were made has been described by Mr Gillespie. A cutting tool on a lathe was used to remove metal from the die block to create the desired shape. No doubt that is the way in which the ribs or rings appearing on the finished product were formed. We see no reason why the process involved in the production of the die or mould, particularly the creation of the cuts to produce the ribs or rings, should not be regarded as the act of engraving within the provisions of section 2(1)(a) of the Act, and the mould or die so created an "engraving" just as a "print" is an engraving in terms of the extended definition in section 2 of the Act.

Moller J. in his judgment came to the view that a die or mould of the kind in question is an engraving. We agree. The purpose of the Act is to protect original artistic works. The skill and labour of the craftsman is exercised in cutting and shaping the plate – engraving it – to produce the intended design. There appears to be no reason why skill and labour so applied should not be protected from copying equally as a print made from that plate is given protection if it can properly be described as an original artistic work.

Mr Hillyer submitted that an engraving in the form of a mould or die could not be an engraving as protected by the Act because it is not meant to be appreciated visually but rather is merely a device used to create an end product, namely, the finished plastic disc. This submission cannot be upheld, particularly in view of the developing nature of the law of copyright. The requirement for works to be of artistic quality has been removed from the definition of "artistic work" in section 2 of the Act so far as the items referred to in clause (a) of that definition are concerned, and so long as the die or mould falls within the words of the definition to which we have referred then it may be the subject of copyright protection.

We next consider whether the finished product – the plastic disc created from the mould or die – is an "engraving" or a "sculpture".

The process of creating the finished product was described by Mr Gillespie in these words:

"(Q) Describe the moulding operation in which those parts operate to form the disc?

(A) The injection mould is placed into a moulding machine and under very high pressure and heat plastic pellets which have been melted flow through a small opening in either the core of the cavity because it can be done from either side of the mould, that material flows into a void in between the core and the cavity. In this particular product the plastic then flows outward filling the entire cavity and then the material starts to harden. At the proper time which has been predetermined by prior testing of the mould, the moulding machine opens separating the core and the cavity from one another".

The word "print" although included in the definition "engraving" is not separately defined in the Act. The ordinary meaning of the word, however, can be readily ascertained.

Davison C.J. referred to dictionary definitions and continued:

The usual concept of a print is of something created by pressure of the plate upon a material. In the system of injection moulding used by Wham-O plastic material is forced upon the plate or into the mould. Does that method of operation prevent the finished disc so created being properly called a "print"? The result is the same although achieved by a somewhat different means. The shape of the mould is imprinted upon the plastic material forced into it.

Modern technology for creating reproductions has involved various new processes being devised and we doubt that the making of a "print" can any longer be identified with any one or more particular processes or procedures. There appears currently to be no good reason why an article produced by injection moulding from a mould which is an engraving should not be itself an engraving if it is produced from that mould.

Moller J. in his judgment after posing the question as to whether the final plastic moulded products could be brought within the definition of sculpture or engraving, simply noted that a consideration of *Arnold's* case (*James Arnold & Co Ltd v Miafern Ltd* [1980] R.P.C. 397) had brought him to the decision that each disc is an engraving in that it is "an image produced from an engraved plate" and comes within the category of a print.

We agree with Moller J. on this point.

Moller J. expressed no opinion as to whether or not the finished product was also a "sculpture". This is defined in section 2(1) of the Act simply as including: "Any cast or model made for purposes of sculpture". Being an inclusive definition, it is necessary to go to a dictionary to ascertain its comprehensive meaning. The Shorter Oxford English Dictionary defines "sculpture" as:

"Originally the process or art of carving or engraving a hard material so as to produce designs or figures in relief, in intaglio, or in the round. In modern use, that branch of fine art which is concerned with producing figures in the round or in relief, either by carving, by fashioning some plastic substance, or by making a mould for casting in metal".

Although that definition refers to sculpture as a branch of fine art, for the purposes of copyright, sculpture is classed as an artistic work, irrespective of artistic quality.

Davison C.J. considered further dictionary and other definitions and continued:

One must ask in the present case, what was the original work of the author which created the article sought to be classed as a sculpture? It was not directly the creation of the final disc. It was the creation variously of drawings, wooden models and finally dies or moulds from which the finished plastic product was formed.

It would seem that where a model which is a sculpture has been created and a cast or mould is later made form that model for the purposes of reproducing the model in metal and plastic or some other form then the articles so produced may be classified as sculptures.

But it appears to us to be straining the meaning of the word "sculpture" to apply it to the discs produced by the injection moulding process used in the present case where the moulds concerned have simply been created by a process of engraving and no original model has been created.

Copyright subsists in "original works" – see section 7 – but no original work in the nature of the finished disc has been created before the injection moulding process has created them. We do not overlook that the definition of sculpture in section 2 of the Act "includes any cast or model made for purposes of sculpture". But that is a different matter from a cast or model used to make the sculpture.

Furthermore it appears to be implicit in the definitions of sculpture to which we have already referred and from the article in the New Encyclopaedia Britannica, particularly the passage reading:

> "The art of sculpture is the branch of the visual arts that is especially concerned with the creation of expressive form in three dimensions"

that sculpture should in some way express in three-dimensional form an idea of the sculptor. It seems to us inappropriate to regard utilitarian objects such as plastic flying discs, manufactured as toys, by an injection moulding process, as items of sculpture for the purposes of the Copyright Act. They lack any expressive form of the creator and any idea which the creator seeks to convey.

In the result, we are unable to hold that the final plastic products – the discs – are sculptures in terms of the Act and entitled to copyright protection as sculptures.

Finally under this head of "sculpture" we pass to consider whether the wooden models created by Wham-O were sculptures. Moller J. held that they were sculptures within the meaning of section 2 of the Act.

We recall the definitions of "sculpture" referred to earlier in this judgment when considering whether the finished plastic products were sculptures and we note that whilst by virtue of section 7 of the Act copyright subsists in an "artistic work", an artistic work includes sculptures irrespective of artistic quality. All that is required therefore is that the work in question shall be a sculpture in the ordinary sense of that term or as included in the extended definition of sculpture contained in the Act.

We think that the wooden models of the Frisbees, which were prepared for the various models, do fall within the definition of sculptures and are thus properly the subject of copyright protection. We agree with Moller J. on this point.

The court found sufficient originality to attract copyright, and that the defendant had substantially reproduced the various works. In consequence, there was infringement and in respect of this the judgment contains a number of further rulings. It also held the defendant not entitled to retain its registered trade mark, "Frisbee", since the application for it had not been made in good faith.

4.1.5 *British Leyland v Armstrong Patents* [1986] F.S.R. 221 (H.L.)

BL claimed that Armstrong, by manufacturing exhaust pipes as replacements on BL cars, infringed BL's copyright in drawings for their exhaust pipes. Armstrong had necessarily reproduced the shape and configuration of these in making its own spares. The case arose under the Copyright Act 1956 and in the HL it was assumed that the drawings were the subject of artistic copyright which was not the subject of any special limit on its duration. In the House of Lords it was argued by Armstrong, first, that copyright in drawings whose sole purpose was as a blueprint for a three-dimensional, functional object was not capable of being infringed by copying in three dimensions. All members of the House save Lord Griffiths rejected this argument. Both Lord Bridge and Lord Templeman gave extensive surveys of the historical development of protection for industrial designs, the latter starting from the original prohibition of monopoly in the Statute of Monopolies 1623. Both speeches laid stress on the acceptance that reproduction by indirect copying in three dimensions was infringement in King Features v Kleeman *([1941] A.C. 417) and subsequent case-law, and that the special exception created by the Copyright Act 1956, s.9(8) bore the implication that Parliament in 1956 thought this to be so. The confirmation of this view in* LB (Plastics) v Swish *([1979] R.P.C. 551) could not now be reversed by the House, but only by legislation. From this view Lord Griffiths delivered a strong dissent.*

Secondly, it was argued (i) that the manufacturer of a car impliedly licensed the purchaser to repair it and that this licence extended to competing spare parts manufacturers; or, alternatively, (ii) that the manufacturer of a car was not entitled to derogate from his grant on sale to a purchaser by exercising his copyright so as to prevent the purchaser from effectively exercising his right to repair the car.

The extracts from the speeches of Lords Bridge, Templeman and Griffiths here given are concerned with this second line of argument.

Lord Bridge of Harwich:

The alternative argument in support of the appeal has been mainly canvassed on the basis of an implied licence. This terminology is primarily derived from the cases concerned with the repair of articles which are subject to patent protection. Letters patent, on their face, always granted to the patentee the exclusive right, "to make, use, exercise and vend" the invention. A literal application of this language would lead to the absurdity that a person who acquired the patented goods would infringe the patent if he used or resold them. To avoid this absurdity the courts had recourse to the doctrine of implied licence. In the field of repair it is clear that a person who acquires a patented article has an implied licence to keep it in repair, but must stop short of renewal: *Dunlop Pneumatic Tyre Co v Neal* [1899] 1 Ch. 807; of renewal: *Dunlop Pneumatic Tyre Co v Neal* [1899] 1 Ch. 807; *Co Ltd v Wallington Weston & Co* [1907] R.P.C. 539. In the latter case Lord Halsbury said at page 543:

> "The principle is quite clear although its application is sometimes difficult; you may prolong the life of a licensed article but you must not make a new one under the cover of repair".

His Lordship then referred to Solar Thompson v Barton *([1977] R.P.C. 537) and to Oliver L.J.'s refusal (in the C.A. in* British Leyland*) to accept that any licence of copyright to repair could extend from the purchaser to a spare parts manufacturer. He continued:*

It seems to me that when one is considering machinery which is not the subject of any patent protection, it is unnecessary and may be misleading to introduce the concept of an implied licence. The owner of a car must be entitled to do whatever is necessary to keep it in running order and to effect whatever repairs may be necessary in the most economical way possible. To derive this entitlement from an implied licence granted by the original manufacturer seems to me quite artificial. It is a right inherent in the ownership of the car itself. To curtail or restrict the owner's right to repair in any way may diminish the value of the car. In the field of patent law it may be right to start from the patentee's express monopoly and see how far it is limited by exceptions. In the field of law applied to machinery which enjoys no patent protection, it seems to me appropriate to start from a consideration of the rights of the owner of the machinery and then to see how far the law will permit some conflicting legal claim to impinge upon those rights.

I can see no reason to doubt that any owner of a BL car might exercise his right to repair the car, whenever the exhaust pipe needs replacement, by producing an exact copy of the original pipe in his own workshop or by instructing the local blacksmith to do the same. But in practical terms, of course, if the owner's right to repair is limited to these activities in a world of mass-produced goods, it is quite valueless. What the owner needs, if his right to repair is to be of value to him is the freedom to acquire a previously manufactured replacement exhaust system in an unrestricted market. Here then we come to the heart of the issue, where there appears to be a clear conflict of legal rights, the car owner's right to repair on the one hand, the copyright owner's right, on the other hand, to use his copyright in such a way as to maintain a monopoly in the supply of spare parts. It may be a novel, but seems to me to be an unavoidable, issue for the law to decide which of the two rights should prevail over the other.

It is, I think, conceded that in certain situations resort to copyright to starve the market of necessary spare parts for a car would be legally unacceptable. As it is put in one of the written summaries of counsel's submissions which have been such a helpful feature of the presentation of counsel's arguments in this appeal:

> "The respondents recognise that the owner of a vehicle or other apparatus must be able and free to deal with that article as he or she so wishes and must be able to buy spare parts lawfully on the market for that article".

Thus, to take an extreme example, suppose a car manufacturer, to encourage early obsolescence, decided to discontinue his own supply of spare parts for every model five years after it ceased production and sought to enforce his copyright in spare parts drawings to stifle any alternative source of supply. I cannot believe that in those circumstances the law would be prepared to sustain the copyright claim, nor did I understand counsel for BL to argue seriously to the contrary.

It follows that the starting point for the resolution of the conflict of competing rights to which I have referred is to recognise that in some circumstances the enforcement of the manufacturer's copyright in spare parts drawings must yield to the maintenance of a supply of spare parts to sustain the owner's right to repair. This immediately poses a problem as to where, if at all, and if so by what criteria, the law can draw a line to discriminate between acceptable and unacceptable claims to enforce copyright, which restrict the market in spare parts available to car owners for the purpose of effecting necessary repairs. The answer propounded to this problem on behalf of BL is two-fold. First, it is submitted that the problem has to be resolved by reference to other legislation directed to the control of anti-competitive practices, in particular the Fair Trading Act 1973, the Competition Act 1980, and the relevant provisions of the EEC Treaty (Cmnd. 5179–11). This answer is, to my mind, unacceptable, if only for the simple reason that to accept it would imply that, had the problem arisen before 1973, no answer could have been found to it in the combined operation of the Copyright Acts and the common law. BL's second answer is that the criterion for the maintenance of a supply of spare parts sufficient to meet the demands of car owners for the purposes of repair is one of necessity and that, so long as the manufacturer and his licensees are maintaining an adequate supply at reasonable prices, and more particularly if the manufacturer is willing to offer licences to all who wish to take them on reasonable terms, there can be no such necessity as to justify the subordination of the right of the copyright owner in spare parts drawings to the interest of the car owner in a free market in parts available for repair. This suggested answer to the problem seems to me both impracticable and unrealistic for two reasons. First, it would impose an impossible task on the court, whenever asked to decide whether a claim to copyright in spare parts drawings should be enforced, to have to determine without the aid of any defined criteria whether at the date of trial the manufacturer and his licensees were maintaining a supply on reasonable terms. Secondly, once the copyright owner had succeeded in his claim, he would be at liberty to vary his terms of trade to the detriment of owners of cars of his manufacture.

These considerations drive me to the conclusion that there is no such half-way house solution to the problem as has been urged upon us for BL. Either the court must allow the enforcement of the copyright claim to maintain a monopoly in the supply of spare parts for the copyright owner and his licensees, regardless of any adverse effect of the monopoly on car owners; or the right of car owners to a free market in spare parts necessary for economical repair should prevail and the court should accordingly decline to enforce copyright claims as against the manufacturer of spare parts intended exclusively as are Armstrong's exhaust systems, to be available as replacement parts for cars in need of repair. As I have already indicated, the first alternative would be unacceptable at one end of the spectrum of possible consequences. But, apart from this, it seems to me that there are sound reasons in principle why the second alternative should be preferred. By selling cars fitted with exhausts based on their copyright drawings BL have already enjoyed the primary benefit which their copyright protects. By selling those same cars BL have also created a large community of car owners who, quite independent of any contractual rights derived from BL, enjoy the inherent right as owners to repair their cars by replacing the exhaust whenever necessary in the most economical way possible. To allow BL to enforce their copyright to maintain a monopoly for themselves and their licensees in the supply and replacement exhausts is, to a greater or lesser extent, to detract from the owner's rights and, at least potentially, the value of their cars. There is an inconsistency between marketing cars and thereby creating whatever rights attach to their ownership on the one hand and acting to restrain the free exercise of those rights on the other. The law does not countenance such inconsistencies. It may be a novel application of the principle to preclude a plaintiff from enforcing a statutory right to which he is *prima facie* entitled. But, as my noble and learned friend Lord Templeman demonstrates, the application of the principle to the relationship between the mass car manufacturer and those who at any time acquire cars of his manufacture is no more than an extension to a non-contractual relationship of the considerations which underlie the classical doctrine of the law that a grantor may not derogate from his grant. Subject to two further grounds of objection canvassed on behalf of BL, which I have yet to consider, it seems to me within the capacity of the common law to adapt to changing social and economic conditions to counter the belated emergence of the car manufacturer's attempt to monopolise the spare parts market in reliance on copyright in technical drawings by invoking the necessity to safeguard the position of the car owner.

A recurrent theme in the argument for BL has been that they are not effectively claiming any true monopoly in exhaust pipes, since it is open to a rival manufacturer to take a BL car, throw away the original exhaust system, examine the features of the underside of the car, and design a new exhaust system suitable to be fitted to it. I find no substance in this argument for two reasons. First, the evidence stops far short of establishing that a new system designed in the way suggested, which must take full account of the shape and configuration of the underside of the frame, various other parts located beneath it, and of the fixing points provided for the exhaust system, would, even if marginally different in shape from the original pipe escape the charge of reproduction by copying of a substantial part of BL's drawings. Secondly, we are concerned with economic reality, and, if the BL car owner is to enjoy the freedom to have his car repaired in the most economical way possible when the exhaust needs replacing, that will undoubtedly only be achieved by straight copying.

BL's final objection on this aspect of the case is based on a comparison of the position under the Copyright Acts, on the one hand, and the Patents Act 1977 and the Registered Designs Act 1949 on the other. If the arguments advanced for Armstrong are permitted to defeat BL's claim under the Act of 1956, then it is said, there will be nothing to prevent similar arguments being invoked to defeat the statutory monopolies conferred by the other Acts when articles protected by patents or registered designs are incorporated as parts of cars. I do not accept that this follows. The rights conferred by the Acts of 1977 and 1949 are clearly distinguishable, in that they are truly and expressly monopolistic. Moreover each Act embodies its own conditions for the grant of compulsory licences which must be taken to provide such safeguards as Parliament considered necessary against the possibility of abuse of the monopoly granted. The position seems to me to be this. Where a specific part of a car which is the subject of a patent or registered design needs repair not amounting to replacement, it will be repairable under the well-established doctrine of implied licence. Where the part requires complete replacement, it can, if practicable, be replaced by any alternative part, which will not infringe the patent or registered design. If only a new part made in accordance with the patent or registered design will provide a satisfactory replacement, the express statutory monopoly of the patentee or design proprietor will prevail. In contrast with the copyright in drawings, the monopoly conferred by the patent or registered design could be invoked not only against other manufacturers making infringing parts and offering them for sale, but also against the car owner, to prevent him making in his own workshop or commissioning from a third party a replacement part which infringed the monopoly.

Having reached a conclusion in favour of allowing the appeal, for the reasons indicated, I would find it unnecessary to hear further argument on the provisions of the EEC Treaty on which Armstrong also rely. I would allow the appeal.

Lord Templeman:

As between landlord and tenant and as between the vendor and purchaser of land, the law has long recognised that "a grantor having given a thing with one hand is not to take away the means of enjoying it with the other" *per* Bowen L.J. in *Birmingham, Dudley and District Banking Co v Ross* (1888) 38 Ch.D 295 at 313.

In *Brown v Flower* [1911] 1 Ch. 219, 225 Parker J. said that:

> "... The implications usually explained by the maxim that no one can derogate from his own grant do not stop short with easements. Under certain circumstances there will be implied on the part of the grantor a lessor obligations which restrict the user of the land retained by him further than can be explained by the

implication of any easement known to the law. Thus, if the grant or demise be made for a particular purpose, the grantor or lessor comes under an obligation not to use the land retained by him in such a way as to render the land granted or demised unfit or materially less fit for the particular purpose for which the grant or demise was made".

These principles were followed in *Harmer v Jumbil (Nigeria) Tin Areas Ltd* [1921] 1 Ch. 200, *O'Cedar Ltd v Slough Trading Co Ltd* [1927] 2 K.B. 123, *Matania v The National Provincial Bank Ltd* [1936] 2 All E.R. 633 and *Kirkland* [1967] Ch. 194.

I see no reason why the principle that a grantor will not be allowed to derogate from his grant by using property retained by him in such a way as to render property granted by him unfit or materially unfit for the purpose for which the grant was made should not apply to the sale of a car. In relation to land, the principle has been said to apply

"beyond cases in which the purpose of the grant is frustrated to cases in which that purpose can still be achieved albeit at a greater expense or with less convenience";

per Branson J. in *O'Cedar Ltd v Slough Trading Co Ltd* [1927] 2 K.B. 123 at 127. The principle applied to a motor car manufactured in accordance with engineering drawings and sold with components which are bound to fail during the life of the car prohibits the copyright owner of the drawings from exercising his powers in such a way as to prevent the car from functioning unless the owner of the car buys replacement parts from the copyright owner or his licensee.

BL own the car and the copyright in a drawing of an exhaust pipe fitted to the car. BL sell the car and retain the copyright. The exercise by BL of their copyright in the drawing will render the car unfit for the purpose for which the car is held. BL cannot exercise their copyright so as to prevent the car being repaired by replacement of the exhaust pipe.

With this view of the second argument, Lords Scarman and Edmund-Davies agreed (the latter, after considerable doubt). Lord Griffiths dissented. On the second argument, he observed:

If, as I must for the purpose of this argument, I assume that Parliament has, through copyright, given a monopolistic right to the manufacturer in the shape of his spare parts, upon what principle is the court free to refuse to enforce that right given by Parliament to the manufacturer? It is said that the manufacturer would be derogating from his grant if he enforced his copyright against another manufacturer because it would interfere with the right of the user of the car to have it repaired. The interference is said to flow from the fact that the spare parts market might be smaller if spare parts could only be produced with the licence of the original manufacturer. This is obviously a possibility but it applies equally to patented items and items protected by design copyright and is an obvious consequence of the grant of a right in the nature of monopoly.

It seems to me highly improbable that a motor car manufacturer would exploit his copyright either to starve the spare parts market or to increase the fair price for his spare parts for I can think of nothing more damaging to his prospects of selling the car in the first place. However, if it did prove that the right Parliament had given was being abused it is, I think, for Parliament to correct the abuse and not for the courts to refuse to enforce a right that Parliament has given, particularly when it is quite obvious that the exercise of the right must impinge, to some extent, upon the rights of others.

One way in which Parliament could guard against possible abuse in the spare parts market would be to make provision for compulsory licensing as is done in the case of patents and design copyright. The fact that Parliament has not done so is, of course, yet another reason that convinces me that it never intended copyright to be used to protect the spare parts market.

Lord Griffiths was, however, prepared to hold that the Copyright Act 1956 did not give protection to the indirect copying in three dimensions of a drawing for a purely functional object.

4.2 Registered Designs

4.2.1 Registered Designs Act 1949 (as amended), s.1, 44: Registrable designs and proceedings for registration

S.1(1) In this Act "design" means features of shape, configuration, pattern or ornament applied to an article by any industrial process, being features which in the finished article appeal to and are judged by the eye, but does not include –

(a) a method or principle of construction, or

(b) features of shape or configuration of an article which –

    (i) are dictated solely by the function which the article has to perform, or

    (ii) are dependent upon the appearance of another article of which the article is intended by the author of the design to form an integral part.

(2) A design which is new may, upon application by the person claiming to be the proprietor, be registered under this Act in respect of any article, or set of articles, specified in the application.

(3) A design shall not be registered in respect of an article if the appearance of the article is not material, that is, if aesthetic considerations are not normally taken into account to a material extent by persons acquiring or using articles of that description, and would not be so taken into account if the design were to be applied to the article.

(4) A design shall not be regarded as new for the purposes of this Act if it is the same as a design –

(a) registered in respect of the same or any other article in pursuance of a prior application, or

(b) published in the United Kingdom in respect of the same or any other article before the date of the application,

or if it differs from such a design only in immaterial details or in features which are variants commonly used in the trade.

This subsection has effect subject to the provisions of sections 4, 6 and 16 of this Act.

(5) The Secretary of State may by rules provide for excluding from registration under this Act designs for such articles of a primarily literary or artistic character as the Secretary of State thinks fit.

S.44 "article" means any article of manufacture and includes any part of an article if that part is made and sold separately.

4.2.2 Registered Designs Act 1949, s.2: Ownership, Dealings

S.2(1) The author of a design shall be treated for the purposes of this Act as the original proprietor of the design, subject to the following provisions.

(1A) Where a design is created in pursuance of a commission for money or money's worth, the person commissioning the design shall be treated as the original proprietor of the design.

(1B) Where, in a case not falling within subsection (1A), a design is created by an employee in the course of his employment, his employer shall be treated as the original proprietor of the design.

(2) Where a design, or the right to apply a design to any article, becomes vested, whether by assignment, transmission or operation of law, in any person other than the original proprietor, either alone or jointly with the original proprietor, that other person, or as the case may be the original proprietor and that other person, shall be treated for the purposes of this Act as the proprietor of the design or as the proprietor of the design in relation to that article.

(3) In this Act the "author" of a design means the person who creates it.

(4) In the case of a design generated by computer in circumstances such that there is no human author, the person by whom the arrangements necessary for the creation of the design are made shall be taken to be the author.

S.19 provides for the registration of assignments, etc., of registered designs. In particular, an interest is not to be registered unless the Registrar is satisfied that the person entitled is also entitled to the corresponding (unregistered) design right (s.19(3A)). Assignment of the (unregistered) design right is presumed also to be an assignment of the registered design (s.19(3B)).

4.2.3 Registered Designs Act 1949, s.3, 4, 6: Registration, Priority, Factors Affecting Novelty

S.3(1) An application for the registration of a design shall be made in the prescribed form and shall be filed at the Patent Office in the prescribed manner.

(2) An application for the registration of a design in which design right subsists shall not be entertained unless made by the person claiming to be the design right owner.

(3) For the purpose of deciding whether a design is new, the registrar may make such searches, if any, as he thinks fit.

(4) The registrar may, in such cases as may be prescribed, direct that for the purpose of deciding whether a design is new an application shall be treated as made on a date earlier or later than that on which it was in fact made.

(5) The registrar may refuse an application for the registration of a design or may register the design in pursuance of the application subject to such modifications, if any, as he thinks fit; and a design when registered shall be registered as of the date on which the application was made or is treated as having been made.

(6) An application, which owing to any default or neglect on the part of the applicant, has not been completed so as to enable registration to be effected within such time as may be prescribed shall be deemed to be abandoned.

(7) An appeal lies from any decision of the registrar under this section.

S.13–15 provide for a priority period of six months (unless extended by reciprocal agreement) to operate in respect of design applications in Paris Convention countries.

S.17–23, 29–30, 39–43, define powers and duties of the Registrar of Designs in maintaining the Register. The Designs Appeal Tribunal is constituted under s.27, 28.

S.4(1) Where the registered proprietor of a design registered in respect of any article makes an application –
  (a) for registration in respect of one or more other articles, of the registered design, or
  (b) for registration in respect of the same or one or more other articles, of a design consisting of the registered design with modifications or variations not sufficient to alter the character or substantially to affect the identity thereof,
the application shall not be refused and the registration made on that application shall not be invalidated by reason only of the previous registration or publication of the registered design:

provided that the right in a design registered by virtue of this section shall not extend beyond the end of the period, and any extended period, for which the right subsists in the original registered design.

(2) Where any person makes an application for the registration of a design in respect of any article and either –
  (a) that design has been previously registered by another person in respect of some other article; or

(b) the design to which the application relates consists of a design previously registered by another person in respect of the same or some other article with modifications or variations not sufficient to alter the character or substantially to affect the identity thereof,

then if at any time while the application is pending the applicant becomes the registered proprietor of the design previously registered, the foregoing provisions of this section shall apply as if at the time of making the application the applicant had been the registered proprietor of that design.

S.5 makes secrecy provisions for defence purposes.

S.6(1) An application for the registration of a design shall not be refused, and the registration of a design shall not be invalidated by reason only of

(a) the disclosure of the design by the proprietor to any other person in such circumstances as would make it contrary to good faith for that other person to use or publish the design:

(b) the disclosure of the design in breach of good faith by any person other than the proprietor of the design: or

(c) in the case of a new or original textile design intended for registration, the acceptance of a first and confidential order for goods bearing the design.

(2) An application for the registration of a design shall not be refused and the registration of a design shall not be invalidated by reason only

(a) that a representation of the design, or any article to which the design has been applied, has been displayed, with the consent of the proprietor of the design, at an exhibition certified by the Secretary of State for the purposes of this subsection:

(b) that after any such display as aforesaid, and during the period of the exhibition, a representation of the design or any such article as aforesaid has been displayed by any person without the consent of the proprietor: or

(c) that a representation of the design has been published in consequence of any such display as is mentioned in paragraph (a) of this subsection,

if the application for registration of the design is made not later than six months after the opening of the exhibition.

(3) An application for the registration of a design shall not be refused, and the registration of a design shall not be invalidated, by reason only of the communication of the design by the proprietor thereof to a government department or to any person authorised by a government department to consider the merits of the design, or of anything done in consequence of such a communication.

(4) Where an application is made by or with the consent of the owner of copyright in an artistic work for the registration of a corresponding design, the design shall not be treated for the purposes of this Act as being other than new by reason only of any use previously made of the artistic work, subject to subsection (5).

(5) Subsection (4) does not apply if the previous use consisted of or included the sale, letting for hire or offer or exposure for sale or hire of

articles to which had been applied industrially –
  (a) the design in question, or
  (b) a design differing from it only in immaterial details or in features
        which are variants commonly used in the trade,
and that previous use was made by or with the consent of the copyright
owner.

(6) The Secretary of State may make provision by rules as to the circumstances in which a design is to be regarded for the purposes of this section as
"applied industrially" to articles, or any description of articles.

4.2.4 Registered Designs Act 1949, s.8: Duration

S.8(1) The right in a registered design subsists in the first instance for a period of five years from the date of the registration of the design.

(2) The period for which the right subsists may be extended for a second, third, fourth and fifth period of five years, by applying to the registrar for an extension and paying the prescribed renewal fee.

S.8(3), (4) make consequential provisions concerning renewals.

(5) Where it is shown that a registered design –
   (a) was at the time it was registered a corresponding design in relation to an artistic work in which copyright subsists, and
   (b) by reason of a previous use of that work would not have been registrable but for section 6(4) of this Act (registration despite certain prior applications of design),
the right in the registered design expires when the copyright in that work expires, if that is earlier than the time at which it would otherwise expire, and it may not thereafter be renewed.

(6) The above provisions have effect subject to the proviso to section 4(1) (registration of same design in respect of other articles, etc).

S.8A provides for restoration of a lapsed design and s.8B for the effect of an order to restore. S.11 permits cancellation.

4.2.5 Registered Designs Act 1949, s.7: Infringement, Compulsory Licences, Crown Use

S.7(1) The registration of a design under this Act gives the registered proprietor the exclusive right –
- (a) to make or import –
    - (i)   for sale or hire, or
    - (ii) for use for the purposes of a trade or business, or
- (b) to sell, hire or offer or expose for sale or hire, an article in respect of which the design is registered and to which that design or a design not substantially different from it has been applied.

(2) The right in the registered design is infringed by a person who without the licence of the registered proprietor does anything which by virtue of subsection (1) is the exclusive right of the proprietor.

(3) The right in the registered design is also infringed by a person who, without the licence of the registered proprietor makes anything for enabling any such article to be made, in the United Kingdom or elsewhere, as mentioned in subsection (1).

(4) The right in the registered design is also infringed by a person who without the licence of the registered proprietor –
- (a) does anything in relation to a kit that would be an infringement if done in relation to the assembled article (see subsection (1)), or
- (b) makes anything for enabling a kit to be made or assembled, in the United Kingdom or elsewhere, if the assembled article would be such an article as is mentioned in subsection (1);

and for this purpose a "kit" means a complete or substantially complete set of components intended to be assembled into an article.

(5) No proceedings shall be taken in respect of any infringement committed before the date on which the certificate of registration of the design under this Act is granted.

(6) The right in a registered design is not infringed by the reproduction of a feature of the design which, by virtue of section 1(1)(b), is left out of account in determining whether the design is registrable.

S.9 exempts a reasonably innocent infringer from liability for damages. S.10 gives a power to grant a compulsory licence of a registered design on the ground that it is not applied in the UK by an industrial process or means to the article in respect of which it is registered as is reasonable. S.11A and 11B give consequential powers upon an unfavourable report of the Monopolies and Mergers Commission. S.12 and Sch. 1 provide for Crown use of registered designs.

4.2.6 *Interlego v Tyco Industries* [1988] R.P.C. 343 (J.C.)

An extract from this case, concerning the originality of artistic works in copyright law, has already been given: see above, 3.2.3.2.

The claim in Hong Kong that Tyco's reverse engineering of "Lego" toy bricks involved infringement of artistic copyright in Lego production drawings turned partly on the question whether copyright existed in certain pre-1972 drawings. The relevant law was the UK Copyright Act 1911, as extended to the colony. Accordingly, the drawings would not be the subject of copyright if they were "capable of being registered" under the Registered Designs Act 1949 and were used or intended to be used as a model or pattern to be multiplied by an industrial process. This in turn raised the questions whether they were precluded from being registered designs (despite the fact that they had actually been registered) (i) because they were dictated solely by function; or (ii) because they lacked novelty, in being derived from earlier drawings that had previously been published (see Registered Designs Act 1949, s.1(3) and 1(2), above, 4.2.1).

On these issues, Lord Oliver (for the J.C.) said:

Nothing is to qualify as a design at all unless it has "features ... which appeal to and are judged solely by the eye", a requirement conveniently paraphrased by saying that the finished article must have "eye-appeal". That much is clear from the definition. What is less clear is the ambit of the exclusion. There are, apart from authority, three possible constructions of the definition taken as a whole, as was pointed out by Megaw L.J. in the Court of Appeal in *Amp Inc v Utilux Pty Ltd* [1970] R.P.C. 397 at 433. It could mean that all that is registrable or is to be considered in connection with an application for registration is that part of the shape or configuration which has eye-appeal, any purely functional feature being excluded from registration. Alternatively, it could mean that any design which includes any feature which is dictated solely by function is to be excluded from registration. Or, finally, it could mean that a design which, *ex hypothesi*, has eye-appeal will be excluded from registration only if every feature of it is one which is dictated solely by function.

No one has contended for the first of these possibilities and such a construction would, indeed, make very little sense. In approaching the definition it is always to be borne in mind what is to be registered. It is a shape, configuration or pattern to be applied to a particular specified article and it is the shape or configuration of the whole article in respect of which there is to be a commercial monopoly. That necessarily involves taking the design and the article as a whole. Thus, the effective choice must be between excluding the whole shape or configuration from registration because there is a part of it that is purely functional or treating the whole shape or configuration as registrable (assuming that it has eye-appeal) unless the whole of it is dictated solely by functional considerations.

In their Lordships' view the latter construction is the one which makes better sense and it is in fact the construction which is supported by the authorities. Harking back to the 1919 Act, the evident intention is to exclude a "mere" mechanical device, that is to say an article fulfilling a mechanical function and nothing more, and that is reflected in the words "the function which the article to be made in that shape or configuration has to perform" (see s.1(3) of the 1949 Act). What is contemplated here is that an article (and that must mean the whole of the article and not simply a part of it) is to be made in a particular shape or configuration. Thus, the shape or configuration as a whole is being "applied to" the article as a whole. It then has to be asked: is that shape or configuration (i.e. the shape or configuration of the whole article) dictated solely by the functional purpose? Moreover, it makes no sense to exclude from registration designs for articles which have, and, indeed, may be intended to have as their principal attraction, a distinctive and novel appearance merely because they contain also features, perhaps even very minor ones, which are dictated by functional requirements.

This construction accords with the original paraphrase by Luxmoore J., in *Kestos Ltd v Kempak Ltd* (1939) 53 R.P.C. 139 at 151, of the expression "mere mechanical device" as a "shape in which all the features are dictated solely by the function". He added:

"... the particular form must possess some features beyond those necessary to enable the article to fulfil the particular purpose, but the fact that some advantage is derived from the adoption of a particular shape does not exclude it from registration as a design".

It accords also with the views expressed in the House of Lords in *Stenor Ltd v Whitesides (Clitheroe) Ltd* [1947] 2 All E.R. 241, [1948] A.C. 107. There Viscount Simon (with whom Lord Macmillan agreed) expressed his concurrence with the views of Morton L.J. in the Court of Appeal that the design there in issue was excluded from registration because it possessed "no features beyond those necessary to enable the article to fulfil its function" (see [1947] 2 All E.R. 241 at 245, [1948] A.C. 107 at 122). Lord Porter expressed broadly the same view (see [1947] 2 All E.R. 241 at 249, [1948] A.C. 107 at 128). Lord Uthwatt observed ([1947] 2 All E.R. 241 at 255, [1948] A.C. 107 at 139):

"Every feature in the design was apt to serve a mechanical object and no feature had any other substantial quality. In the sum of the qualities of the design there was a mechanical device and nothing else".

Finally, it accords, on analysis, with the views expressed by the House of Lords in *Amp Inc v Utilux Pty Ltd* [1972] R.P.C. 103. That is a decision which has given rise to a little difficulty because the views expressed by the Lords who composed the committee in that case do not altogether coincide, with the result that both parties seek to avail themselves of the decision as support for different propositions. Counsel for Tyco derives from it the proposition that the mere co-existence of eye-appeal and functional efficiency is sufficient to entitle a design to registration, a proposition which appears to have been accepted in the instant case at least by Huggins V.-P. in the Court of Appeal in Hong Kong. Counsel for Lego derives from it, first, the proposition that eye-appeal involves something more than mere distinctiveness of shape and, second, that, given that there are features of shape which are dictated solely by function, the fact that there is also present in the shape, whether intentionally or not, an element of eye-appeal is not sufficient to confer on the shape the essential quality requisite for registrability as a design. To put it another way, a shape has to be tested by two criteria, one positive and one negative, and both must be satisfied in full before it can qualify as a design within the definition of the Act.

Accepting that there are differences of emphasis in the speeches of the various members of the committee in the *Amp* case, their Lordships are nevertheless of the view that the principles to be deduced from it are tolerably clear. First, the primary essential before a shape can be registered as a design is that it should have eye-appeal and in this context (a) the eye is that of the prospective customer and (b) the appeal is that created by a distinctiveness of shape, pattern or ornamentation calculated to influence the customer's choice. This, at least, emerges from the speeches of Lord Reid (with whom Lord Donovan agreed), Lord Morris and Viscount Dilhorne (see [1972] R.P.C. 103 at 108, 112, 118). Second, the negative part of the definition does not involve, in order to demonstrate that a particular shape is "dictated solely" by function, showing that that function could not have been performed by an article in some other shape. All that has to be shown is that the relevant features of the shape were brought about only by, or are attributable only to, the function which the article in that shape is to perform, even if the same function could equally well be performed by an article of a different shape. Third, if every feature of the shape is one which is attributable solely to the function which the finished article is to perform, then the exclusion operates even though the shape may also have eye-appeal.

His Lordship considered a somewhat unclear passage in Lord Reid's speech in Amp v Utilux *and concluded that:*

Their Lordships are clearly of the opinion that the mere coincidence of eye-appeal with functional efficiency will not confer the right to protection if, in fact, every feature of the design is dictated by the function which the article is to perform. But what is the position where the shape has eye-appeal but where some only of its features are dictated solely by functional considerations? If the interpretation placed on Lord Reid's remarks is correct, then he and Lord Donovan would clearly have contemplated that in these circumstances the exclusion would not operate to deprive the shape of protection as a design. Lord Morris clearly contemplated that it would not (at 113) and Viscount Dilhorne too appears to have contemplated that any feature which went beyond those dictated solely by function and provided eye-appeal would entitle the shape as a whole to protection (at 118). This is, in their Lordships' view, clearly right in principle. The incorporation into design was evolved, at least in part, with visual appeal in mind. Exactly the same consideration applied equally to the Duplo brick, which was, as Mr Christiansen observed, evolved with the intention "to look exactly the same way as the original eight knob brick". In another part of his evidence he stressed the importance of the appearance of a toy and asserted that he had always paid particular attention to the appearance of the Lego bricks.

It has already been mentioned that, in registering their designs, Lego had to overcome objections by the registrar that there were no features of ornament on the designs. Reliance had, at that time, been placed on the knobs as ornamental features and Mr Christiansen in his evidence asserted that they fulfilled both functional and ornamental purposes. Again in relation to the tubes, which in earlier versions of the brick were castellated and were equal to the length of the skirt, Mr Christiansen's evidence was that these were replaced by an amended design in which the tubes were circular and did not go to the level of the bottom of the skirt because the castellated version was "messier" and the new version looked nicer. Thus, although the presence of knobs and tubes is no doubt attributable simply and solely to the functional purpose of providing clutch-power, the actual shape and dimensions of the particular knobs and tubes employed for that purpose were not dictated solely by their function but, in part at least, with a view to the appearance of the article as a whole. This evidence cannot be ignored and in their Lordships' view it necessarily negatives any conclusion that the shape or configuration of the Lego brick is dictated solely by the function which it has to perform. It is a shape which, in their Lordships' opinion, not only clearly has eye-appeal but has also significant features, both of outline and proportion, which are not dictated by any mechanical function which the article has to perform as part of a construction set.

It is, however, Lego's submission that, even on this hypothesis, the pre-1973 drawings are not excluded from copyright by the operation of para 8(2) of Sch 7 to the 1956 Act, because they are not designs "capable of registration under the Registered Designs Act 1949". Section 1(2) of the 1949 Act, it is argued, authorises the registration only of a design which is "new or original". These drawings reproduced, with modifications, the

Page designs which had been previously published and used as the basis for manufactured articles. Thus, at the time when they were made, they ought not to have been registered and reliance is placed on a decision of the Eve J. in *Stephenson Blake & Co v Grant Legros & Co Ltd* (1916) 33 R.P.C. 406, a decision based on s.22(1) of the Copyright Act 1911, which provided that the Act should not apply to designs "capable of being registered" under the 1907 Act. In that case it had been held, on agreed preliminary issues, that the plaintiffs had, when the 1911 Act came into operation, a subsisting copyright under the Copyright Act 1842 in what was assumed to be a design which could have been registered under the Patents, Designs and Trade Marks Act 1883. One question raised was whether the effect of s.22 was to deprive them of all protection, since they could then no longer register under the 1907 Act for want of novelty. Eve J. held that, since, at the coming into operation of the 1911 Act, the plaintiffs' design was no longer new, it was then not "capable of registration" and thus was not excluded from copyright under the 1911 Act. That decision has been criticised as leading to the absurd conclusion that a person who had a design registrable under the 1907 Act but had not troubled to protect himself by registration retained his artistic copyright and was thus put in a better position than a person who had registered and who would so be deprived of his artistic copyright. Moreover, the status of the decision as an authority is open to doubt because, when the case went to the Court of Appeal, that court discharged the order on the ground that the questions raised were entirely hypothetical at the stage at which they were decided, Lord Cozens-Hardy M.R. observing that the discharge was "without prejudice to any question so that it cannot be used as a precedent" (see (1917) 34 R.P.C. 192 at 195).

The contrary conclusion was reached in the Canadian case of *Bayliner Marine Corp v Doral Boats Ltd* [1987] F.S.R. 497, where the Federal Court of Appeal of Canada, construing s.46(1) of the Canadian Copyright Act 1970 (which was in substantially the same terms as s.22(1) of the 1911 Act) held that a "design capable of being registered" did not mean "registrable" but meant only a design which complied with the criteria necessary to qualify as a "design" within the meaning of the Act. To hold the contrary would, it was pointed out, involve the absurdity that a design sufficiently novel to be entitled to registration would be excluded from copyright protection whilst one lacking novelty would be entitled to copyright for the full period of the life of the author plus 50 years. The reasoning of the Canadian court was followed by Whitford J. in *Interlego AG v Alex Folley (Vic) Pty Ltd* [1987] F.S.R. 283 at 302 and by the Court of Appeal in Hong Kong in the instant case.

Lord Oliver considered Usher v Barlow *[1952] Ch. 255 (C.A.) to lend only oblique support to Eve J.'s judgments in the* Stephenson Blake *case. Moreover, he accepted a number of contrary arguments concerning logical construction of the relevant statutory provision. He concluded:*

In their Lordships' opinion, the Court of Appeal correctly concluded that the only sensible construction of the words "constituted a design capable of registration" in para 8, having regard to the evident purpose of the statute, is that it refers to designs possessing, when they were made, those essential characteristics which qualify them as "designs". If such designs are, at that time, used or intended to be used for the purpose of industrial reproduction, they are not to qualify for copyright under the Copyright Act 1956. It follows that no copyright now subsists in Lego's pre-1973 drawings.

4.3 (Unregistered) Design Right

4.3.1 Copyright Designs and Patents Act 1988, s.213, 258–260: Right granted, Interpretation

S.213(1) Design right is a property right which subsists in accordance with this Part in an original design.

(2) In this Part "design" means the design of any aspect of the shape or configuration (whether internal or external) of the whole or part of an article.

(3) Design right does not subsist in –
- (a) a method or principle of construction.
- (b) features of shape or configuration of an article which –
  - (i) enable the article to be connected to, or placed in, around or against, another article so that either article may perform its function, or
  - (ii) are dependent upon the appearance of another article of which the article is intended by the designer to form an integral part, or
- (c) surface decoration.

(4) A design is not "original" for the purposes of this Part if it is commonplace in the design field in question at the time of its creation.

(5) Design right subsists in a design only if the design qualifies for design right protection by reference to –
- (a) the designer or the person by whom the design was commissioned or the designer employed (see sections 218 and 219), or
- (b) the person by whom and country in which articles made to the design were first marketed (see section 220),

or in accordance with any Order under section 221 (power to make further provision with respect to qualification).

(6) Design right does not subsist unless and until the design has been recorded in a design document or an article has been made to the design.

(7) Design right does not subsist in a design which was so recorded, or to which an article was made, before the commencement of this Part.

S.258(1) Where different persons are (whether in consequence of a partial assignment or otherwise) entitled to different aspects of design right in a work, the design right owner for any purpose of this Part is the person who is entitled to the right in the respect relevant for that purpose.

(2) Where design right (or any aspect of design right) is owned by more than one person jointly, references in this Part to the design right owner are to all the owners, so that, in particular, any requirement of the licence of the design right owner requires the licence of all of them.

S.259(1) In this Part a "joint design" means a design produced by the collaboration of two or more designers in which the contribution of each is not distinct from that of the other or others.

(2) References in this Part to the designer of a design shall, except as otherwise provided, be construed in relation to a joint design as references to all the designers of the design.

S.260(1) The provisions of this Part apply in relation to a kit, that is, a complete or substantially complete set of components intended to be assembled into an article, as they apply in relation to the assembled article.

(2) Subsection (1) does not affect the question whether design right subsists in any aspect of the design of the components of a kit as opposed to the design of the assembled article.

4.3.2 Copyright, Designs and Patents Act 1988, s.214, 215: Ownership, Dealings

S.214(1) In this Part the "designer", in relation to a design, means the person who creates it.

(2) In the case of a computer-generated design the person by whom the arrangements necessary for the creation of the design are undertaken shall be taken to be the designer.

S.215(1) The designer is the first owner of any design right in a design which is not created in pursuance of a commission or in the course of employment.

(2) Where a design is created in pursuance of a commission, the person commissioning the design is the first owner of any design right in it.

(3) Where, in a case not falling within subsection (2) a design is created by an employee in the course of his employment, his employer is the first owner of any design right in the design.

(4) If a design qualifies for design right protection by virtue of section 220 (qualification by reference to first marketing of articles made to the design), the above rules do not apply and the person by whom the articles in question are marketed is the first owner of the design right.

S.222 provides for assignment, licensing, etc of design right in equivalent terms to s.90 (above, 3.7.3) for copyright. So equally s.223 (prospective ownership) and s.225 (exclusive licences) are equivalent to s.91 and 92. S.224 provides that an assignment of registered design right is presumed to carry with it the (unregistered) design right.

4.3.3 Copyright, Designs and Patents Act 1988, s.216: Duration

4.3.3   Copyright Designs and Patents Act 1988, s.216: Duration

S.216(1) Design right expires –
  (a) fifteen years from the end of the calendar year in which the design was first recorded in a design document or an article was first made to the design, whichever first occurred, or
  (b) if articles made to the design are made available for sale or hire within five years from the end of that calendar year, ten years from the end of the calendar year in which that first occurred.

(2) The reference in subsection (1) to articles being made available for sale or hire is to their being made so available anywhere in the world by or with the licence of the design right owner.

4.3.4 Copyright, Designs and Patents Act 1988, s.217: Qualification

S.217(1) In this Part –

"qualifying individual" means a citizen or subject of, or an individual habitually resident in, a qualifying country; and

"qualifying person" means a qualifying individual or a body corporate or other body having legal personality which –

    (a) is formed under the law of a part of the United Kingdom or another qualifying country, and

    (b) has in any qualifying country a place of business at which substantial business activity is carried on.

(2) References in this Part to a qualifying person include the Crown and the government of any other qualifying country.

(3) In this section "qualifying country" means –

    (a) the United Kingdom,

    (b) a country to which this Part extends by virtue of an Order under section 255,

    (c) another member State of the European Economic Community, or

    (d) to the extent that an Order under section 256 so provides, a country designated under that section as enjoying reciprocal protection.

S.217(4) further defines "qualifying individual" in respect of UK and British colonial citizens; s.217(5) limits "substantial business activity". S.255 provides for the extension by Order to the Channel Islands, Isle of Man and British Colonies. S.256 makes provision for reciprocal protection. S.257 extends protection to British Territorial waters and continental shelf. Qualification is then secured on three bases:

    (i) S.218: where the design is not created under commission or employment, by virtue of the designer being a qualified person;

    (ii) S.219: where the design is created under commission or employment, by virtue of the commissioner or designer being a qualified person;

    (iii) S.220: where neither of these gives qualifications, then by virtue of first marketing in the UK (as extended) or an EC country by an exclusive licensee for the UK who is a qualified person. S.221 allows for further provision, with a view to fulfilling an international obligation of the UK, by Order-in-Council.

4.3.5 Copyright, Designs and Patents Act 1988, s.237, 246, 247: Licences of Right, Crown Use

S.237(1) Any person is entitled as of right to a licence to do in the last five years of the design right term anything which would otherwise infringe the design right.

(2) The terms of the licence shall, in default of agreement, be settled by the comptroller.

(3) The Secretary of State may if it appears to him necessary in order to –
    (a) comply with an international obligation of the United Kingdom, or
    (b) secure or maintain reciprocal protection for British designs in other countries,
by order exclude from the operation of subsection (1) designs of a description specified in the order or designs to articles of a description so specified.

(4) An order shall be made by statutory instrument; and no order shall be made unless a draft of it has been laid before and approved by a resolution of each House of Parliament.

S.238, 239 give consequential powers upon an unfavourable report of the Monopolies and Mergers Commission. S.240–244 provides for the Crown use of (unregistered) designs; and s.252 for reference of disputes over Crown use to the Court. S.245 gives a similar power to that under s.237(3), in this case to exclude specified acts from the scope of infringement.

S.246(1) A party to a dispute as to any of the following matters may refer the dispute to the comptroller for his decision
    (a) the subsistence of design right,
    (b) the term of design right, or
    (c) the identity of the person in whom design right first vested;
and the comptroller's decision on the reference is binding on the parties to the dispute.

(2) No other court or tribunal shall decide any such matter except
    (a) on a reference or appeal from the comptroller,
    (b) in infringement or other proceedings in which the issue arises incidentally, or
    (c) in proceedings brought with the agreement of the parties or the leave of the comptroller

(3) The comptroller has jurisdiction to decide any incidental question of fact or law arising in the course of a reference under this section.

S.247(1) A person requiring a licence which is available as of right by virtue of
    (a) section 237 (licences available in last five years of design right), or
    (b) an order under section 238 (licences made available in the public interest)
may apply to the comptroller to settle the terms of the licence.

(2) No application for the settlement of the terms of a licence available by virtue of section 237 may be made earlier than one year before the earliest date on which the licence may take effect under that section.

(3) The terms of a licence settled by the comptroller shall authorise the licensee to do

    (a) in the case of a licence available by virtue of section 237, everything which would be an infringement of the design right in the absence of a licence;

    (b) in the case of a licence available by virtue of section 238, everything in respect of which a licence is so available.

(4) In settling the terms of a licence the comptroller shall have regard to such factors as may be prescribed by the Secretary of State by order made by statutory instrument.

(5) No such order shall be made unless a draft of it has been laid before and approved by a resolution of each House of Parliament.

(6) Where the terms of a licence are settled by the comptroller, the licence has effect

    (a) in the case of an application in respect of a licence available by virtue of section 237 made before the earliest date on which the licence may take effect under that section, from that date:

    (b) in any other case, from the date on which the application to the comptroller was made.

4.3.6 Copyright, Designs and Patents Act 1988, s.226, 236, 229: Infringement

S.226 (*Primary infringement*) (1) The owner of design right in a design has the exclusive right to reproduce the design for commercial purposes –
- (a) by making articles to that design, or
- (b) by making a design document recording the design for the purpose of enabling such articles to be made.

(2) Reproduction of a design by making articles to the design means copying the design so as to produce articles exactly or substantially to that design, and references in this Part to making articles to a design shall be construed accordingly.

(3) Design right is infringed by a person who without the licence of the design right owner does, or authorises another to do, anything which by virtue of this section is the exclusive right of the design right owner.

(4) For the purposes of this section reproduction may be direct or indirect, and it is immaterial whether any intervening acts themselves infringe the design right.

(5) This section has effect subject to the provisions of Chapter III (exceptions to rights of design right owner).

S.227 defines acts of secondary infringement equivalent to those affecting copyright under s.22, 23(a)–(c) (above, 3.5.3.1) but in slightly different terms. S.228 defines "infringing article" in terms equivalent to those defining "infringing copy" in relation to copyright (see s.27, above, 3.5.3.1). A design document is not an infringing article: s.228(6).

S.236 Where copyright subsists in a work which consists of or includes a design in which design right subsists, it is not an infringement of design right in the design to do anything which is an infringement of the copyright in that work.

S.229(1) An infringement of design right is actionable by the design right owner.

(2) In an action for infringement of design right all such relief by way of damages, injunctions, accounts or otherwise is available to the plaintiff as is available in respect of the infringement of any other property right.

(3) The court may in an action for infringement of design right, having regard to all the circumstances and in particular to –
- (a) the flagrancy of the infringement, and
- (b) any benefit accruing to the defendant by reason of the infringement,

award such additional damages as the justice of the case may require.

(4) This section has effect subject to section 233 (innocent infringement).

S.230, 231 give power to make orders for delivery up of infringing articles and for their disposal. S.233 exempts a reasonably innocent primary infringer from damages and limits the remedies against such a secondary infringer to damages not exceeding a reasonable royalty. S.234 confers a right of action on an exclusive licensee. S.235 provides for the exercise of concurrent rights.

4.4 Design Right (Semiconductor Topographies) Regulations 1989

4.4.1 Definitions

These Regulations introduce modifications of (unregistered) design right under the Copyright, Designs and Patents Act 1988, Part III in relation to semi-conductors. They were initially made under the European Communities Act 1972 in implementation of Council Directive 87/54/EEC. The Regulations apply to products and designs defined as follows (para 2(1)):

"semiconductor product" means an article the purpose, or one of the purposes, of which is the performance of an electronic function and which consists of two or more layers, at least one of which is composed of semiconducting material and in or upon one or more of which is fixed a pattern appertaining to that or another function; and "semiconductor topography" means a design within the meaning of section 213(2) of the Act which is a design of either of the following:

(a) the pattern fixed, or intended to be fixed, in or upon –
  (i) a layer of a semiconductor product, or
  (ii) a layer of material in the course of and for the purpose of the manufacture of a semiconductor product, or
(b) the arrangement of the patterns fixed, or intended to be fixed, in or upon the layers of a semiconductor product in relation to one another.

For semiconductors, the 1988 Act is modified as indicated in 4.4.2–4.4.6.

4.4.2 Qualification

S.217 is altered in particular so as to allow the listing of countries with which reciprocal arrangements are established in pursuance of EC Council Directives on the matter (para 4(2)).

S.219 (qualification by reference to commissioner or employer) does not apply and instead s.218(2)–(4) (qualification by reference to designer) have effect (para 4(3)).

S.220 (qualification by reference to exclusive licensee) is altered so as to apply where the exclusive licensee for the whole EEC is a qualifying person and first marketing takes places anywhere in the EEC (para 4(4)).

4.4.3 Ownership

S.215, giving initial ownership to a commissioner or employer, is modified in each case by the addition, "subject to any agreement in writing to the contrary" (para 5).

4.4.4 Duration

S.216 is modified as follows (para 6):

"216. The design right in a semiconductor topography expires –
    (a) ten years from the end of the calendar year in which the topography or articles made to the topography were first made available for sale or hire anywhere in the world by or with the licence of the design right owner, or
    (b) if neither the topography nor articles made to the topography are so made available within a period of fifteen years commencing with the earlier of the time when the topography was first recorded in a design document or the time when an article was first made to the topography, at the end of that period".

4.4.5 Confidence

In relation qualification, initial ownership and duration, para 7 applies:

7. In determining, for the purposes of section 215(4), 216 or 220 of the Act (as modified by these Regulations), whether there has been any marketing, or anything has been made available for sale or hire, no account shall be taken of any sale or hire, or any offer or exposure for sale or hire, which is subject to an obligation of confidence in respect of information about the semiconductor topography in question unless either –

   (a) the article or semiconductor topography sold or hired or offered or exposed for sale or hire has been sold or hired on a previous occasion (whether or not subject to an obligation of confidence), or

   (b) the obligation is imposed at the behest of the Crown, or of the government of any country outside the United Kingdom, for the protection of security in connection with the production of arms, munitions or war material.

4.4.6 Infringement

S.226 is modified as follows (para 8(1)):

"226. – (1) Subject to subsection (1A), the owner of design right in a design has the exclusive right to reproduce the design –
- (a) by making articles to that design, or
- (b) by making a design document recording the design for the purpose of enabling such articles to be made.

(1A) Subsection (1) does not apply to –
- (a) the reproduction of a design privately for non-commercial aims; or
- (b) the reproduction of a design for the purpose of analysing or evaluating the design or analysing, evaluating or teaching the concepts, processes, systems or techniques embodied in it".

Para. 8(2)–(5) provide:

(2) Section 227 of the Act does not apply if the article in question has previously been sold or hired within –
- (a) the United Kingdom by or with the licence of the owner of design right in the semiconductor topography in question, or
- (b) the territory of any other member State of the European Economic Community or the territory of Gibraltar by or with the consent of the person for the time being entitled to import it into or sell or hire it within that territory.

(3) Section 228(6) of the Act does not apply.

(4) It is not an infringement of design right in a semiconductor topography to –
- (a) create another original semiconductor topography as a result of an analysis or evaluation of the first topography or of the concepts, processes, systems or techniques embodied in it, or
- (b) reproduce that other topography.

(5) Anything which would be an infringement of the design right in a semiconductor topography if done in relation to the topography as a whole is an infringement of the design right in the topography if done in relation to a substantial part of the topography.

5 TRADE MARKS AND NAMES

5.1 Liability at Common Law: Passing Off and Injurious Falsehood

5.1.1 Passing Off: General Principles

5.1.1.1 *Reddaway v Banham* [1896] A.C. 199 (H.L.)

The appellant (plaintiff) manufactured belting which, for the purpose of distinguishing it from similar products, he called "Camel-hair Belting". The yarn used was chiefly of camel hair though few people realised this. The respondent, a former employee of the appellant, began making similar belting, which he first called "Arabian" and then, in response to particular orders, "Camel-hair". Other manufacturers used almost identical yarn to make belts and sold them as "Yale", "Buffalo", etc.

The trial judge, after the jury's verdict for the plaintiff, granted an injunction restraining the defendant from continuing to use the word "Camel-hair" in such a manner as to lead purchasers into the belief that they were purchasing belting of the plaintiff's manufacture and yarn thereby passing off their belting as and for the belting of the plaintiff's manufacture. The C.A. reversed this but it was restored by the H.L.

Lord Herschell:

The principle which is applicable to this class of cases was, in my judgment, well laid down by Lord Kingsdown in *The Leather Cloth Company v The American Cloth Company*, 11 House of Lords, 538. It had been previously enunciated in much the same way by Lord Langdale in the case of *Croft v Day* (7 Beav. 84). Lord Kingsdown's words were as follows:

> "The fundamental rule is that one man has no right to put off his goods for sale as the goods of a rival trader, and he cannot therefore (in the language of Lord Langdale in the case of *Perry v Truefitt* (6 Beav. 66)) be allowed to use names, marks, letters, or other indicia, by which he may induce purchasers to believe that the goods which he is selling are the manufacture of another person".

It is, in my opinion, this fundamental rule which governs all cases, whatever be the particular mode adopted by any man for putting off his goods as those of a rival trader, whether it is done by the use of a mark which has become his Trade Mark, or in any other way. The word "property" has been sometimes applied to what has been termed a Trade Mark at common law. I doubt myself whether it is accurate to speak of there being property in such a Trade Mark, though, no doubt, some of the rights which are incident to property may attach to it. Where the Trade Mark is a word or device never in use before, and meaningless, except as indicating by whom the goods in connection with which it is used were made, there could be no conceivable legitimate use of it by another person. His only object in employing it in connection with goods of his manufacture must be to deceive. In circumstances such as those, the mere proof that the Trade Mark of one manufacturer had been thus appropriated by another, would be enough to bring the case within the rule as laid down by Lord Kingsdown, and to entitle the person aggrieved to an injunction to restrain its use. In the case of a Trade Mark thus identified with a particular manufacturer, the rights of the person whose Trade Mark it was would not, it may be, differ substantially from those which would exist if it were, strictly speaking, his property. But there are other cases which equally come within the rule that a man may not pass off his goods as those of his rival, which are not of this simple character – cases where the mere use of the particular mark or device which had been employed by another manufacturer would not of itself necessarily indicate that the person who employed it was thereby inducing purchasers to believe that the goods he was selling were the goods of another manufacturer.

The name of a person, or words forming part of the common stock of language, may become so far associated with the goods of a particular maker that it is capable of proof that the use of them by themselves, without explanation or qualification by another manufacturer, would deceive a purchaser into the belief that he was getting the goods of A, when he was really getting the goods of B. In a case of this description, the mere proof by the Plaintiff that the Defendant was using a name, word, or device which he had adopted to distinguish his goods would not entitle him to any relief. He could only obtain it by proving further, that the Defendant was using it under such circumstances or in such manner as to put off his goods as the goods of the Plaintiff. If he could succeed in proving this, I think he would, on well-established principles, be entitled to an injunction.

In my opinion, the doctrine on which the judgment of the Court of Appeal was based, that where a manufacturer has used as his Trade Mark a descriptive word, he is never entitled to relief against a person who so uses it as to induce in purchasers the belief that they are getting the goods of the manufacturer who has theretofore employed it as his Trade Mark, is not supported by authority and cannot be defended on principle. I am unable to see why a man should be allowed in this way more than in any other to deceive purchasers into the belief that they are getting what they are not, and thus to filch the business of a rival.

Lord Halsbury L.C., Lord Macnaghten and Lord Morris delivered concurring speeches.

5.1.1.2 *Spalding v Gamage* [1915] 32 R.P.C. 273 (H.L.)

The plaintiffs sold footballs. In 1910 and 1911 they used the mark "Orb" for a moulded ball calling it in some instances the "Improved Orb". In 1912, after discovering faults in some of these moulded balls, they produced a sewn ball under the mark "Improved Sewn Orb" and sold off old stock to waste rubber merchants. The defendant store, however, bought up these faulty moulded balls and advertised them in a manner imitating the announcement of the sewn balls in the plaintiffs' 1912 catalogue.

Lord Parker of Waddington:

My Lords, the action in which the Appeal arises is what is known as a passing-off action, and having regard to the arguments which have been addressed to your Lordships, I think it well to say a few words as to the principle on which such actions are founded. This principle is stated by Lord Justice Turner in *Burgess v Burgess* (14 Ch.D. at 748), and by Lord Halsbury in *Reddaway v Banham* ([1906] A.C. at 204), in the proposition that nobody has any right to represent his goods as the goods of somebody else. It is also sometimes stated in the proposition that nobody has the right to pass off his goods as the goods of somebody else. I prefer the former statement, for whatever doubts may be suggested in the earlier authorities, it has long been settled that actual passing-off of a defendant's goods for the plaintiff's need not be proved as a condition precedent to relief in Equity either by way of an injunction or of an inquiry as to profits or damages (*Edelsten v Edelsten* 1 De G., J & S 185, and *Iron-Ox Remedy Company Ltd v Co-operative Wholesale Society Ltd*, 24 R.P.C. 425). Nor need the representation be fraudulently made. It is enough that it has in fact been made, whether fraudulently or otherwise, and that damages may probably ensue, though the complete innocence of the party making it may be a reason for limiting the account of profits to the period subsequent to the date at which he becomes aware of the true facts. The representation is in fact treated as the invasion of a right giving rise at any rate to nominal damages, the inquiry being granted at the plaintiff's risk if he might probably have suffered more than nominal damages.

The view taken by the Common Law Courts was somewhat different. The plaintiff's remedy was said to have been in the nature of an action for deceit, but it only resembled the action for deceit in the fact that the misrepresentation relied on must have been fraudulently made. In all other respects it differed from an action for deceit. For example, the plaintiff was not the party deceived, and even if it were necessary to prove that someone had been deceived, nominal damage could be obtained though no actual damage was proved. Thus in *Blofield v Payne* (4 B. & Ad. 410) the defendants had sold their own hones in the plaintiff's wrappers as and for the plaintiff's, but there was no evidence that any purchasers had been actually deceived. Further, though special damage was alleged in the declaration, no actual damage was proved. On motion for a non-suit it was held in the King's Bench that the plaintiff was entitled to nominal damages. The action was, in fact, treated as one founded on the invasion of a right.

My Lords, the proposition that no one has a right to represent his goods as the goods of somebody else must, I think, as has been assumed in this case, involve as a corollary the further proposition, that no one, who has in his hands the goods of another of a particular class or quality, has a right to represent these goods to be the goods of that other of a different quality or belonging to a different class. Possibly, therefore, the principle ought to be re-stated as follows: A cannot, without infringing the rights of B, represent goods which are not B's goods or B's goods of a particular class or quality to be B's goods or B's goods of that particular class or quality. The wrong for which relief is sought in a passing-off action consists in every case of a representation of this nature.

My Lords, the basis of a passing-off action being a false representation by the defendant, it must be proved in each case as a fact that the false representation was made. It may, of course, have been made in express words, but cases of express misrepresentation of this sort are rare. The more common case is, where the representation is implied in the use or imitation of a mark, trade name, or get-up with which the goods of another are associated in the minds of the public, or of a particular class of the public. In such cases the point to be decided is whether, having regard to all the circumstances of the case, the use by the defendant, in connection with the goods of the mark name, or get-up in question impliedly represents such goods to be the goods of the plaintiff, or the goods of the plaintiff of a particular class or quality, or, as it is sometimes put, whether the defendant's use of such mark, name, or get-up is calculated to deceive. It would, however, be impossible to enumerate or classify all the possible ways in which a man may make the false representation relied on.

There appears to be considerable diversity of opinion as to the nature of the right, the invasion of which is the subject of what are known as passing-off actions. The more general opinion appears to be that the right is a right of property. This view naturally demands an answer to the question – property in what? Some authorities say property in the mark, name, or get-up improperly used by the defendant. Others say, property in the business or goodwill likely to be injured by the misrepresentation. Lord Herschell in *Reddaway v Banham* ([1896] A.C. 139) expressly dissents from the former view; and if the right invaded is a right of property at all, there are, I think, strong reasons for preferring the latter view. In the first place, cases of misrepresentation by the use of a mark, name, or get-up do not exhaust all possible cases of misrepresentation. If A says falsely, "These goods I am selling are B's goods", there is no mark, name or get-up infringed unless it be B's name, and if he falsely says, "These are B's goods of a particular quality", where the goods are in fact B's goods, there is no name that is infringed at all. Further, it is extremely difficult to see how a man can be said to have property in descriptive words, such as "Camel-hair" in the case of *Reddaway v Banham* ([1896] A.C. 199) where every trader is entitled to use the words, provided only he uses them in such a way as not to be calculated to deceive. Even in the case of what are sometimes referred to as Common Law Trade Marks the property, if any, of the so-called owner is in its nature transitory, and only exists so long as the mark is distinctive of his goods in the eyes of the public or a class of the public. Indeed, the necessity of proving this distinctiveness in each case as a step in the proof of the false representation relied on was one of the evils sought to be remedied by the Trade Marks Act 1875, which conferred a real right of property on the owner of a registered mark. I had to consider the matter in the case of *Burberrys v Cording* (26 R.P.C. 693) and I came to the same conclusion.

His Lordship then reviewed the evidence and concluded that there had been misrepresentation about the quality of the "Orb" balls sold by the defendant such as was likely to occasion actual damage to the plaintiffs. In particular, retailers who had purchased new "Orbs" at a price above that being charged to the public by the defendant thought that they were being unfairly treated and were likely to withdraw custom.

Lord Atkinson concurred and Lords Sumner and Parmoor gave concurring speeches.

5.1.1.3 *Samuelson v Producers Distributing* [1932] 1 Ch. 201 (C.A.)

The plaintiff wrote a revue sketch, "The New Car" which achieved fame particularly by its inclusion in a Royal Command Performance. The defendant made a film of a different sketch, "His First Car", and advertised it in a way suggesting that it was the sketch seen at the Performance.

The C.A. held this to constitute a form of passing off. Romer L.J. observed:

It is said that there has been no passing-off. It is true there has been no passing-off in fact, or indeed, perhaps, threatened, in the sense in which the word "passing-off" is used in what are popularly known as passing-off actions; that is to say, the defendants have never contended that the film which they were producing or going to produce was a film prepared or made by or on behalf of the plaintiff. But the cases in which the Court has restrained passing-off in the popular and usual sense, are merely instances of the application by the Court of a much wider principle, the principle being that the Court will always interfere by injunction to restrain irreparable injury being done to the plaintiff's property. In the present case, if, as we hold to be the case, the plaintiff was entitled to his copyright in "The New Car", he was, by virtue of the Copyright Act, entitled to the sole right of producing the sketch in film form. That was an item of his property, and how it can be said that these advertisements might not cause irreparable damage to that property of the plaintiff passes my comprehension.

5.1.1.4   *Warnink v Townend* [1979] A.C. 731 (H.L.)

The first plaintiff, a Dutch company, held 75 per cent of the English market for advocaat, a drink made of egg and spirits, and had increased it popularity by heavy advertising campaigns. Egg flip, which was also available on the English market, comprised egg and fortified wine and accordingly attracted a lower rate of excise. It was sold at a substantially cheaper price. The defendants changed the name of their egg flip to "Keeling's Old English Advocaat". Thereafter they captured an appreciable share of the advocaat market from the plaintiff and others.

Lord Diplock:

True it is that it could not be shown that any purchaser of Keeling's Old English Advocaat supposed or would be likely to suppose it to be goods supplied by Warnink or to be Dutch advocaat of any make. So Warnink had no cause of action for passing off in its classic form. Nevertheless, the learned judge was satisfied: (1) that the name "Advocaat" was understood by the public in England to denote a distinct and recognisable species of beverage; (2) that Warnink's product is genuinely indicated by that name and has gained reputation and goodwill under it; (3) that Keeling's product has no natural association with the word "Advocaat": it is an egg and wine drink properly described as an "Egg Flip", whereas Advocaat is an egg and spirit drink; these are different beverages and known as different to the public; (4) that members of the public believe and have been deliberately induced by Keeling to believe in buying their "Old English Advocaat" they are in fact buying advocaat; (5) that Keeling's deception of the public has caused and, unless prevented, will continue to cause, damage to Warnink in the trade and the goodwill of their business both directly in the loss of sales and indirectly in the debasement of the reputation attaching to the name "Advocaat" if it is permitted to be used of alcoholic egg drinks generally and not confined to those that are spirit based.

These findings, he considered, brought the case within the principle of law laid down in the *Champagne* ([1961] R.P.C. 116) case by Danckwerts J. and applied in the *Sherry* and *Scotch Whisky* ([1969] R.P.C. 1 (below, 5.1.3.3); [1970] 1 W.L.R. 917) cases. He granted Warnink an injunction restraining Keeling from selling or distributing under the name or description "Advocaat" any product which does not basically consist of eggs and spirit without any admixture of wine.

My Lords, these findings of fact were accepted by the Court of Appeal and have not been challenged in the Lordships' House. They seem to me to disclose a case of unfair, not to say dishonest, trading of a kind for which a rational system of law ought to provide a remedy to other traders whose business or goodwill is injured by it.

Unfair trading as a wrong actionable at the suit of other traders who thereby suffer loss of business or goodwill may take a variety of forms, to some of which separate labels have become attached in English law. Conspiracy to injure a person in his trade or business is one, slander of goods another, but most protean is that which is generally and nowadays, perhaps misleadingly, described as "passing off". The forms that unfair trading takes will alter with the ways in which trade is carried on and business reputation and goodwill acquired. Emerson's maker of the better mousetrap if secluded in his house built in the woods would today be unlikely to find a path beaten to his door in the absence of a costly advertising campaign to acquaint the public with the excellence of his wares.

After reviewing Reddaway v Banham *and* Spalding v Gamage *(above, 5.1.1.1, 5.1.1.2),*
Lord Diplock continued:

Lord Parker's explanation of the nature of the proprietary right protected by a passing
off action also supplied a new and rational basis for the two nineteenth-century
decisions of Page Wood V.-C. in *Dent v Turpin* (1861) 2 J & H 139, and *Southorn v*
Reynolds (1865) 12 L.T. (N.S.) 75, in which one of two traders, each of whom had by
inheritance acquired goodwill in the use of a particular trade name, was held entitled,
without joining the other, to obtain an injunction restraining a third trader from making
use of the name, despite the fact that the plaintiff's right of user was not exclusive. The
goodwill of his business would be damaged by the misrepresentation that the
defendant's goods were the goods of a limited class of traders entitled to make use of it,
of whom the plaintiff was one and the defendant was not.

My Lords, *Spalding v Gamage* and the later cases make it possible to identify five
characteristics which must be present in order to create a valid cause of action for
passing off: (1) a misrepresentation (2) made by a trader in the course of trade, (3) to
prospective customers of his or ultimate consumers of goods or services supplied by
him, (4) which is calculated to injure the business or goodwill of another trader (in the
sense that this is a reasonably foreseeable consequence) and (5) which causes actual
damage to a business or goodwill of the trader by whom the action is brought or (in a
quia timet action) will probably do so.

In seeking to formulate general propositions of English law, however, one must be
particularly careful to beware of the logical fallacy of the undistributed middle. It does
not follow that because all passing off actions can be shown to present these
characteristics, all factual situations which present these characteristics give rise to a
cause of action for passing off. True it is that their presence indicates what a moral code
would censure as dishonest trading, based as it is upon deception of customers and
consumers of a trader's wares but in an economic system which has relied on
competition to keep down prices and to improve products there may be practical
reasons why it should have been the policy of the common law not to run the risk of
hampering competition by providing civil remedies to every one competing in the
market who has suffered damage to his business or goodwill in consequence of
inaccurate statements of whatever kind that may be made by rival traders about their
own wares. The market in which the action for passing off originated was no place for
the mealy mouthed; advertisements are not on affidavit; exaggerated claims by a trader
about the quality of his wares, assertions that they are better than those of his rivals,
even though he knows this to be untrue, have been permitted by the common law as
venial "puffing" which gives no cause of action to a competitor even though he can
show he has suffered actual damage in his business as a result.

Parliament, however, beginning in the nineteenth century has progressively intervened
in the interests of consumers to impose on traders a higher standard of commercial
candour than the legal maxim *caveat emptor* calls for, by prohibiting under penal
sanctions misleading descriptions of the character of quality of goods; but since the
class of persons for whose protection the Merchandise Marks Acts 1887 to 1953 and
even more rigorous later statutes are designed, are not competing traders but those
consumers who are likely to be deceived, the Acts do not themselves give rise to any
civil action for breach of statutory duty on the part of a competing trader even though
he sustains actual damage as a result. *Cutler v Wandsworth Stadium* [1949] A.C. 398

and see *London Armoury Co Ltd v Ever Ready Co Ltd* [1941] 1 K.B. 742. Nevertheless the increasing recognition by Parliament of the need for more rigorous standards of commercial honesty is a factor which should not be overlooked by a judge confronted by the choice whether or not to extend by analogy to circumstances in which it has not previously been applied a principle which has been applied in previous cases where the circumstances although different had some features in common with those of the case which he has to decide. Where over a period of years there can be discerned a steady trend in legislation which reflects the view of successive Parliaments as to what the public interest demands in a particular field of law, development of the common law in that part of the same field which has been left to it ought to proceed upon a parallel rather than a diverging course.

The *Champagne* case came before Danckwerts J. in two stages: the first (reported at [1960] R.P.C. 16) on a preliminary point of law, the second (reported at [1961] R.P.C. 116) on the trial of the action. The assumptions of fact on which the legal argument at the first stage was based were stated by the judge to be:

"(1) The plaintiffs carry on business in a geographical area in France known as Champagne; (2) the Plaintiffs' wine is produced in Champagne and from grapes grown in Champagne; (3) the plaintiffs' wine has been known in the trade for a long time as Champagne with a high reputation; (4) members of the public or in the trade ordering or seeing wine advertised as Champagne would expect to get wine produced in Champagne from grapes grown there and (5) the defendants are producing a wine not produced in that geographical area and are selling it under the name of 'Spanish Champagne'".

These findings disclose a factual situation (assuming that damage was thereby caused to the plaintiffs' business) which contains each of the five characteristics which I have suggested must be present in order to create a valid cause of action for passing off. The features that distinguished it from all previous cases were (a) that the element in the goodwill of each of the individual plaintiffs that was represented by his ability to use without deception (in addition to his individual house mark) the word "Champagne" to distinguish his wines from sparkling wines not made by the champenois process from grapes produced in the Champagne district of France, was not exclusive to himself but was shared with every other shipper of sparkling wine to England whose wines could satisfy the same condition and (b) that the class of traders entitled to a proprietary right in "the attractive force that brings in custom" represented by the ability without deception to call one's wines "Champagne" was capable of continuing expansion, since it might be joined by any future shipper of wine who was able to satisfy that condition.

My Lords, in the *Champagne* case the class of traders between whom the goodwill attaching to the ability to use the word "Champagne" as descriptive of their wines was shared was a large one, 150 at least and probably considerably more, whereas in the previous English cases of shared goodwill the number of traders between whom the goodwill protected by a passing off action was shared had been two, although in the United States in 1893 there had been a case, *Pilsbury Washburn Flour Mills v Eagle* 86 Fed. Rep. 608 in which the successful complainants to the number of seven established their several proprietary rights in the goodwill attaching to the use of a particular geographical description to distinguish their wares from those of other manufacturers.

It seems to me, however, as it seemed to Danckwerts J., that the principle must be the same whether the class of which each member is severally entitled to the goodwill which attaches to a particular term as descriptive of his goods, is large or small. The larger it is the broader must be the range and quality of products to which the descriptive term used by the members of the class has been applied, and the more difficult it must be to show that the term has acquired a public reputation and goodwill as denoting a product endowed with recognisable qualities which distinguish it from others of inferior reputation that compete with it in the same market. The larger the class the more difficult it must also be for an individual member of it to show that the goodwill of his own business has sustained more than minimal damage as a result of deceptive use by another trader of the widely shared descriptive term. As respects subsequent additions to the class, mere entry into the market would not give any right of action for passing off; the new entrant must have himself used the descriptive term long enough on the market in connection with his own goods and have traded successfully enough to have built up a goodwill for his business.

For these reasons the familiar argument that to extend the ambit of an actionable wrong beyond that to which effect has demonstrably been given in the previous cases would open the floodgates or, more ominously, a Pandora's box of litigation leaves me unmoved when it is sought to be applied to the actionable wrong of passing off.

I would hold the *Champagne* case to have been rightly decided and in doing so would adopt the words of Danckwerts J. where he said (at [1960] R.P.C. 31):

> "There seems to be no reason why such licence (s.c. to do a deliberate act which causes damage to the property of another person) should be given to a person competing in trade, who seeks to attach to his product a name or description with which it has no natural association, so as to make use of the reputation and goodwill which has been gained by a product genuinely indicated by the name or description. In my view, it ought not to matter that the persons truly entitled to describe their goods by the name and description are a class producing goods in a certain locality, and not merely one individual. The description is part of their goodwill and a right of property. I do not believe that the law of passing off, which arose to prevent unfair trading, is so limited in scope".

In the *Champagne* case the descriptive term referred to the geographical provenance of the goods, and the class entitled to the goodwill in the term was accordingly restricted to those supplying on the English market goods produced in the locality indicated by it. Something similar was true in the *Sherry* case where the word "Sherry" as descriptive of a type of wine unless it was accompanied by some qualifying geographical adjective was held to denote wine produced by the solera method in the province of Jerez de la Frontera in Spain and the class entitled to the goodwill in the word was restricted to suppliers on the English market of wine produced in that province. In the *Scotch Whisky* case the product with which the case was primarily concerned was blended whisky and the class entitled to the goodwill in the descriptive term "Scotch Whisky" was not restricted to traders who dealt in whisky that had been blended in Scotland but extended to suppliers of blended whisky wherever the blending process took place provided that the ingredients of their product consisted exclusively of whiskies that had been distilled in Scotland. But the fact that in each of these first three cases the descriptive name under which goods of a particular type or composition were marketed by the plaintiffs among others happened to have geographical connotations is in my view without significance. If a product of a particular character or composition has been marketed under a descriptive name and under that name has gained a public reputation which distinguishes it from competing products of different composition, I can see no reason in principle or logic why the goodwill in the name of those entitled to make use of it should be protected by the law against deceptive use of the name by competitors, if it denotes a product of which the ingredients come from a particular locality, but should lose that protection if the ingredients of the product, however narrowly identified, are not restricted as to their geographic provenance. Yet in view of the findings of fact by Goulding J. to which I have already referred, this is the only way in which the instant case can be distinguished from the *Champagne*, *Sherry* and *Scotch Whisky* cases.

His Lordship then considered Native Guano v Sewage Manure *(1891) 8 R.P.C. 125 (H.L.) in which the plaintiff failed to prevent a competitor from calling his product "native guano" (a fertilizer made from human excreta). On this, the C.A. had relied in refusing to accord protection to "advocaat". Lord Diplock considered that the case did not involve proof of a relevant misrepresentation and that certain wider dicta, if still acceptable, would be in conflict with the* Champagne *case. In his view, that case could not be confined to the name of a product made by a particular class of producers. He continued:*

My Lords, the class of producers who could make "champagne" and whose right to use that word to describe their product on the English market formed a valuable part of their goodwill was a large one, much larger than the class with which the instant case is concerned, for it embraced everyone who engaged in the business of producing in the Champagne district, which is extensive, by the champenois method from grapes grown in the district and the class was capable of enlargement by the inclusion of anyone who chose to set up a new wine-producing business of that kind there. It is true that the whole process for making the finished product would have to be undertaken in the Champagne district; but this as I have already pointed out, was not so in the *Sherry* case where bottling of the wine produced from grapes grown in the province of Jerez de la Frontera and blended by the solera method there need not take place in Spain: nor was it so in the *Scotch Whisky* case where even the blending of malt and grain whiskies provided they were distilled in Scotland need not take place in that country.

Of course it is necessary to be able to identify with reasonable precision the members of the class of traders of whose products a particular word or name has become so distinctive as to make their right to use it truthfully as descriptive of their product a valuable part of the goodwill of each of them; but it is the reputation that that type of product itself has gained in the market by reason of its recognisable and distinctive qualities that has generated the relevant goodwill. So if one can define with reasonable precision the type of product that has acquired the reputation, one can identify the members of the class entitled to share in the goodwill as being all those traders who have supplied and still supply to the English market a product which possesses those recognisable and distinctive qualities.

It cannot make any difference in principle whether the recognisable and distinctive qualities by which the reputation of the type of product has been gained are the result of its having been made in, or from ingredients produced in, a particular locality or are the result of its having been made from particular ingredients regardless of their provenance: though a geographical limitation may make it easier (a) to define the type of product; (b) to establish that it has qualities which are recognisable and distinguish it from every other type of product that competes with it in the market and which have gained for it in that market a reputation and goodwill; and (c) to establish that the plaintiff's own business will suffer more than minimal damage to its goodwill by the defendant's misrepresenting his product as being of that type.

In the instant case it is true that all but a very small portion of the alcoholic egg drink which gained for the name "Advocaat" a reputation and goodwill upon the English market, was imported from the Netherlands where, in order to bear that name, the ingredients from which it was made had to conform to the requirements of official regulations applicable to it in that country; but that is merely coincidental, for it is not suggested that an egg and spirit drink made in broad conformity with the Dutch official recipe for "Advocaat", wherever it is made or its ingredients produced, is not endowed with the same recognisable and distinctive qualities as have gained for "Advocaat" its reputation and goodwill in the English market.

So, on the findings of fact by Goulding J. to which I referred at the beginning of this speech, the type of product that has gained for the name "Advocaat" on the English market the reputation and goodwill of which Keeling's are seeking to take advantage by misrepresenting that their own product is of that type, is defined by reference to the nature of its ingredients irrespective of their origin. The class of traders of whose respective businesses the right to describe their products as Advocaat forms a valuable part of their goodwill are those who have supplied and are supplying on the English market an egg and spirit drink in broad conformity with an identifiable recipe. The members of that class are easily identified and very much fewer in number than in the *Champagne*, *Sherry* or *Scotch Whisky* cases. Warnink with 75 per cent, of the trade have a very substantial stake in the goodwill of the name "Advocaat" and their business has been shown to have suffered serious injury as a result of Keeling's putting on the English market in competition with Warnink and at a cheaper price an egg and wine based drink which they miscall "Advocaat" instead of Egg Flip which is its proper name.

My Lords, all the five characteristics that I have earlier suggested must be present to create a valid cause of action in passing off today were present in the instant case. *Prima facie*, as the law stands today, I think the presence of those characteristics is enough, unless there is also present in the case some exceptional feature which justifies, on grounds of public policy, withholding from a person who has suffered injury in consequence of the deception practised on prospective customers or consumers of his product a remedy in law against the deceiver. On the facts found by the judge, and I stress their importance, I can find no such exceptional feature in the instant case.

I would allow this appeal and restore the injunction granted by Goulding J.

In a concurring speech, Lord Fraser of Tullybelton stated:

It is essential for the plaintiff in a passing off action to show at least the following facts:

(1) that his business consists of, or includes, selling in England a class of goods to which the particular trade name applies;

(2) that the class of goods is clearly defined, and that in the minds of the public, or a section of the public, in England, the trade name distinguishes that class from other similar goods;

(3) that because of the reputation of the goods, there is goodwill attached to the name;

(4) that he, the plaintiff, as a member of the class of those who sell the goods, is the owner of goodwill in England which is of substantial value;

(5) that he has suffered, or is really likely to suffer, substantial damage to his property in the goodwill by reason of the defendants selling goods which are falsely described by the trade name to which the goodwill is attached.

Lords Dilhorne, Salmon and Scarman concurred in both speeches.

5.1.1.5   *Cadbury Schweppes v Pub Squash* [1981] R.P.C. 429 (J.C.)

The plaintiffs launched a lemon squash under the name "Solo" in yellow cans with a medallion that bore a general resemblance to many beer-cans. Intensive and successful television advertising suggested (i) that it resembled squash sold in pubs in former times and (ii) that it was thoroughly masculine to have as a drink. Some months later the defendant brought out a similar drink, also in yellow cans, under the name "Pub Squash" and it conducted a similar, though smaller publicity campaign. Soon afterwards, the plaintiffs' market slumped by 16 per cent. This conduct was alleged to constitute passing off.

Lord Scarman (for the J.C.):

It is unnecessary to explore the law in any depth, because it is now accepted by both sides that the issue in the case is whether in promoting its product the respondent so confused or deceived the market that it passed its product off as the product of the appellants. Nevertheless the case presents one feature which is not to be found in the earlier case law. The passing off of which the appellants complain depends to a large extent on the deliberate adoption by the respondent of an advertising campaign based on themes and slogans closely related to those which the appellants had developed and made familiar to the market in the radio and television advertising of their product. Does confusion or deception, if it be shown to arise from such an advertising campaign, amount to a passing off? To answer the question it is necessary to consider the modern character of tort.

After referring to the "Advocaat" (above, 5.1.1.4) case and Hornsby Building v Sydney Building [1978] 52 A.L.J.R. 392 (H.C. Aust.) at 396–97 (per Stephen J.) he continued:

The width of the principle now authoritatively recognised by the High Court of Australia and the House of Lords is, therefore, such that the tort is no longer anchored, as in its early nineteenth century formulation, to the name or trade mark of a product or business. It is wide enough to encompass other descriptive material, such as slogans or visual images, which radio, television or newspaper advertising campaigns can lead the market to associate with a plaintiff's product, provided always that such descriptive material has become part of the goodwill of the product. And the test is whether the product has derived from the advertising a distinctive character which the market recognises.

But competition must remain free; and competition is safeguarded by the necessity for the plaintiff to prove that he has built up an "intangible property right" in the advertised descriptions of his product, or, in other words, that he has succeeded by such methods in giving his product a distinctive character accepted by the market. A defendant, however, does no wrong by entering a market created by another and there competing with its creator. The line may be difficult to draw; but, unless it is drawn, competition will be stifled. The test applied by Powell J. in the instant case was to inquire whether the consuming public was confused or misled by the get-up, the formula or the advertising of the respondent's product into thinking that it was the appellants' product. And he held on the facts that the public was not deceived. Their Lordships do not think that his approach in law (save in one respect, as will later appear) to the central problem of the case can be faulted. The real question in the appeal is, therefore, one of fact, whether the judge erred in the inferences he drew from the admitted primary facts.

The appellants' alternative case of unfair trading irrespective of whether the market was deceived or confused into mistaking the respondent's product for that of the appellants' need not be considered by the Board, since the appellants now restrict themselves to a case based on such confusion. For such a case to succeed it would be necessary to show that the law of Australia has developed a tort of unfair competition along the lines suggested in the well-known decision of the United States Supreme Court, *International News Service v Associated Press* [1918] 248 U.S. 215 at 241–242.

His Lordship quoted from the principal judgment of Pitney J. (see below, 5.1.1.6). He reviewed the trial judge's findings on the evidence and refused to depart from them: there had been no significant confusion or deception at the point of sale which was not immediately corrected; it was not established that the public associated yellow cans only with "Solo", and the themes in the television advertising had not become distinctive of the plaintiff's product.

5.1.1.6 *Moorgate Tobacco v Philip Morris* [1985] R.P.C. 219 (H.C. Australia)

In 1977, the plaintiff, a subsidiary company of British-American Tobacco, purchased a business in Australia which owned the trade mark "Kent" cigarettes. The "Kent" mark had been licensed to the defendant, Philip Morris, by the plaintiff's predecessor in title. Philip Morris had produced a successful brand under it. But that licence was coming to an end and was not going to be renewed.

In 1975–76 the plaintiff's predecessor had negotiated with Philip Morris over the production of a new low-tar cigarette perhaps to be called "Kent Golden Lights". At the time of the plaintiff's acquisition, Philip Morris applied to register "Golden Lights" as a mark for cigarettes. This action led to a number of claims, since it had the effect of blocking BAT's plan to launch a "Kent Golden Lights" cigarette.

Claims for breach of contract, breach of fiduciary duty and breach of contract all failed on the facts. A claim based upon unfair competition failed in that it disclosed no known cause of action. As to this Deane J. said:

The phrase "unfair competition" has been used in judgments and learned writings in at least three distinct ways, namely: (i) as a synonym of the doctrine of passing off; (ii) as a generic name to cover the range of legal and equitable causes of action available to protect a trader against the unlawful trading activities of a competitor: and (iii) to describe what is claimed to be a new and general cause of action which protects a trader against damage caused either by "unfair competition" generally or, more particularly, by the "misappropriation" of knowledge or information in which he has a "quasi-proprietary" right. The first and second of the above uses of the phrase are liable to be misleading in that they may wrongly imply that the relevant action or actions are restricted to proceedings against a competitor. The second use is also liable to imply that there exists a unity of underlying principle between different actions when, in truth, there is none. The third use of the phrase is, in an Australian context, simply mistaken in that "unfair competition" does not, in itself, provide a sufficient basis for relief under law of this country. It is in that third and mistaken sense that "unfair competition" was called in aid of Moorgate's case in the present appeal.

The genesis of the notion of a general cause of action for "unfair competition" is to be found in the majority judgment of the Unites States Supreme Court in *International News Service v Associated Press* (1918) 248 U.S. 215; 63 Law Ed. 211. As the name would indicate, that case was concerned with published news or information. The complainant, a co-operative association of newspaper publishers, gathered news which it telegraphed to its member publishers throughout the United States. The defendant was a corporation which was engaged in the business of gathering news for other publishers. The defendant made a practice of obtaining news from the early publications of the complainant's members and sending it by telegraph to its own customers thus enabling them in some parts of the United States, to publish news gathered by the complainant for its members as soon as or even earlier than it was published in the newspapers published by those members. The majority judgment, delivered by Pitney J., denounced (248 U.S. at 240; 63 Law Ed. at 221) the actions of the defendant as

> "an unauthorized interference with the normal operation of complainant's legitimate business precisely at the point where the profit is to be reaped, in order to divert a material portion of the profit from those who have earned it to those who have not; with special advantage to defendant in the competition because of the fact that it is not burdened with any part of the expense of gathering the news".

That fulsome description of the defendant's actions was immediately followed by the conclusion that the

> "transaction speaks for itself and a court of equity ought not to hesitate long in characterising it as unfair competition in business."

The majority judgment in *International News Service* assumed, rather than sought to establish, that such "unfair competition in business" was, in itself, an actionable wrong.

Deane J. further criticised the majority judgment, and continued:

It is difficult to know whether "misappropriation" of "news material" should be regarded as a separate basis of the decision or as but one instance of the general wrong of "unfair competition in business" to which the judgment had earlier referred. Either way, one searches in vain in the majority judgment for any identification of the ingredients of that general wrong.

Not surprisingly in a court of which Holmes and Brandeis JJ. were members, the muddled birth of the new action was not an occasion for unanimity. Holmes J., in what was essentially a dissenting judgment, held that the complainant was entitled to but limited relief on the basis of inverse passing off and that any entitlement to wider relief on the basis of inverse passing off and that any entitlement to wider relief was a matter for the legislature and not for the court. Brandeis J. filed a strong dissent in which he considered relevant United States and English authorities and concluded that the law did not recognize any general proprietary right in knowledge or information or any general action for unfair competition.

Subsequent decisions of United States courts have tended to isolate rather than develop the doctrine of a general action for unfair competition enunciated in the *International News Service* case. In *Kellogg Co v National Biscuit Co* (1938) 305 U.S. 111 at 123; 83 Law Ed. 73 at 81, the Supreme Court reversed decrees of the Third Circuit Court of Appeals which, *inter alia*, restrained Kellogg Co from using the term "shredded wheat" in relation to biscuits, on the ground that its use constituted "unfair competition". The Supreme Court, in a majority judgment delivered by Brandeis J., implicitly refuted any general doctrine of unfair competition and restricted the relevance of "fairness" to a passing off context: "Fairness requires that it be done in a manner which reasonably distinguishes its product from that of the plaintiff" (305 U.S. at 120; 83 Law Ed. at 79). In words reminiscent of Brandeis J.'s previous dissent, the majority commented (305 U.S. at 122; 83 Law Ed. at 80):

"Kellogg Co is undoubtedly sharing in the goodwill of the article known as 'Shredded Wheat'; and thus is sharing in a market which was created by the skill and judgment of plaintiff's predecessor and has been widely extended by vast expenditures in advertising persistently made. But that is not unfair. Sharing in the goodwill of an article unprotected by patent or trade mark is the exercise of a right possessed by all – and in the free exercise of which the consuming public is deeply interested."

In *Sears Roebuck & Co v Stiffel Co* (1964) 376 U.S. 225; 11 Law Ed. (2d) 661 and *Compco Corp v Day Brite Lighting Inc* (1964) 376 U.S. 234; 11 Law Ed. (2d) 669, the Supreme Court reaffirmed the approach which it had adopted in the Kellogg case.

Nor has the doctrine of a general action for unfair competition enunciated in *International News Service* evoked general enthusiasm in subordinate United States courts. In cases where the broad concept of "unfair competition" has been applied, as distinct from cases where the phrase has been used as a synonym of passing off, the attempts to define it have tended to involve resort to high-sounding and uninformative generalizations such as "fundamental rules of honesty and fair dealing" and "acts that shock judicial sensibilities" (see V.L. Knight, "Unfair Competition: A Comparative Study of Its Role in Common and Civil Law Systems": *Tulane Law Review*, vol. 53 (1978) 164 at 168–9). The general, though by no means universal, trend in lower courts has been to follow the approach adopted by the Second Circuit Court of Appeals and to restrict the decision in *International News Service* to its particular facts. That approach was most strongly expressed in *Cheney Bros v Doris Silk Corporation* (1929) 35 F. (2d) 279 at 280, in a judgment delivered by Learned Hand J.:

"... we think no more was covered than situations substantially similar to those then at bar. The difficulties of understanding it otherwise are insuperable. We are to suppose that the court meant to create a sort of common-law patent or copyright for reasons of justice. Either would flagrantly conflict with the scheme which Congress has for more than a century devised to cover the subject-matter".

As Professor Morison has remarked ("Unfair Competition at Common Law", *University of Western Australia Law Review*, vol. 2 (1951–53) 34 at 37), the decision in *International News Service*, which was hailed in the United States as a "landmark" in the law of unfair competition, has been seen even in that country to be more properly described as an island. Indeed, in a recent United States case (*Jacobs v Robitaille* (1976) 406 F. Supp. 1145 at 1151), the "legal concept" of unfair competition was described as a "child of confusion" which has "spawned a body of law that lacks in judicial definition and scope".

The notion of a general action for "unfair trading" or "unfair competition" has received little encouragement in either the House of Lords or this court. In so far as the House of Lords is concerned, it suffices to refer to the recent decision in *Warnink v Townend & Sons* (Hull) [1979] A.C. 731 (above, 5.1.1.4).

Deane J. referred to Lord Diplock's five characteristics of passing off to be found in that case, and continued:

In so far as this court is concerned, one need go no further than the decision in *Victoria Park Racing and Recreation Grounds Co Ltd v Taylor* (1937) 58 C.L.R. 479; [1937] A.L.R. 597. In that case, a majority of the court, in confirming the dismissal of an action to restrain a radio station broadcasting descriptions of horse races conducted on the plaintiff's land made from a platform erected on adjoining land for that purpose, expressed conclusions which correspond closely with those of Brandeis J. in the *International News Service* case. Dixon J. (at (C.L.R.) 509; (A.L.R.) 606) commented that the reasons of Brandeis J. substantially represented "the English view" which he described (at (C.L.R.) 508–9; (A.L.R.) 605–6) in terms which involved a rejection of the reasoning underlying the majority judgment in *International News Service*:

> "The fact is that the substance of the plaintiff's complaint goes to interference, not with its enjoyment of the land, but with the profitable conduct of its business. If English law had followed the course of development that has recently taken place in the United States, the 'broadcasting rights' in respect of the races might have been protected as part of the quasi-property created by the enterprise, organization and labour of the plaintiff in establishing and equipping a racecourse and doing all that is necessary to conduct race meetings. But courts of equity have not in British jurisdictions thrown the protection of an injunction around all the intangible elements of value, that is, value in exchange, which may flow from the exercise by an individual of his powers or resources whether in the organization of a business or undertaking or the use of ingenuity, knowledge, skill or labour. This is sufficiently evidenced by the history of the law of copyright and by the fact that the exclusive right to invention, trade marks, designs, trade name and reputation are dealt with in English law as special heads of protected interests and not under a wide generalization".

His Honour added (at (C.L.R.) 509; (A.L.R.) 606) that the judgment of Brandeis J. contained

> "an adequate answer both upon principle and authority to the suggestion that the defendants are misappropriating or abstracting something which the plaintiff has created and alone is entitled to turn to value".

Dixon J. identified that answer as being that

> "it is not because the individual has by his efforts put himself in a position to obtain value for what he can give that his right to give it becomes protected by law and so assumes the exclusiveness of property, but because the intangible or incorporeal right he claims falls within a recognized category to which legal or equitable protection attaches".

The rejection of a general action for "unfair competition" or "unfair trading" does not involve a denial of the desirability of adopting a flexible approach to traditional forms of action when such an approach is necessary to adapt them to meet new situations and circumstances. It has not, for example, prevented the adaptation of the traditional doctrine of passing off to meet new circumstances involving the deceptive or confusing use of names, descriptive terms or other indicia to persuade purchasers or customers to believe that goods or services have an association, quality or endorsement which belongs or would belong to goods or services of, or associated with, another or others (see eg *Warnink v Townend & Sons*, above at 739ff: *Henderson v Radio Corporation Pty Ltd* (1960) 60 S.R. (N.S.W.) 576). The rejection of a general action for "unfair competition" involves no more than a recognition of the fact that the existence of such an action is inconsistent with the established limits of the traditional and statutory causes of action which are available to a trader in respect of damage caused or threatened by a competitor. Those limits, which define the boundary between the area of legal or equitable restraint and protection and the area of untrammelled competition, increasingly reflect what the responsible Parliament or Parliaments have determined to be the appropriate balance between competing claims and policies. Neither legal principle nor social utility requires or warrants the obliteration of that boundary by the importation of a cause of action whose main characteristic is the scope it allows, under high-sounding generalizations, for judicial indulgence of idiosyncratic notions of what is fair in the market place.

5.1.2 Passing Off: Plaintiff's Reputation

5.1.2.1 *Star Industrial v Yap Kwee Kor* [1975] F.S.R. 256 (J.C.)

The appellant-plaintiff, a Hong Kong company, manufactured toothbrushes which it sold in Singapore under the mark "Ace Brand" with accompanying device. This mark was not registered in Singapore. In October 1965, the Singapore government imposed an import duty which rendered the appellant's trade unprofitable. In 1968, the respondent, a Singapore toothbrush manufacturer, changed its name to the New Star Industrial Co and adopted the appellants's mark for its brushes. These proceedings for an injunction against passing-off did not commence until 1971.

In 1968, the appellant formed a jointly-owned subsidiary in Singapore and granted it exclusive use of the mark.

Lord Diplock:

At common law this right of user of the mark or get-up in Singapore was incapable of being assigned except with the goodwill of that part of the business of the Hong Kong Company in connection with which it had previously been used. So, if despite the temporary cesser of the Hong Kong Company's business in Singapore after the import duty on toothbrushes had been imposed in 1965, it still retained – as well it might (cf *Mouson & Co v Boehm* [1884] 26 Ch. D 398) – a residue of goodwill capable of being revived in 1968, any right of property in that goodwill would have passed to the Singapore Company under the agreement. The Singapore Company is not a party to these proceedings and their Lordships express no view as to what rights, if any, it would have been entitled to enforce against the respondent if it had been the plaintiff in a passing-off action brought against him.

Their Lordships mention this, however, because the burden of the appellant's argument before the Board has been that the common law ought to provide the Hong Kong Company itself with a remedy against the respondent for the financial loss which it will sustain in the form of reduced dividends and royalties receivable from the Singapore Company, as a result of the respondent's piracy of the mark or get-up. The argument has been put in an alternative way.

The first is that the case of *Warwick Tyre Company Ltd v New Motor and General Rubber Co Ltd* [1910] 1 Ch. 248; (1910) 27 R.P.C. 161; 101 L.T. 889) is authority for the proposition that at common law a person who, in a business carried on by him, has used an unregistered mark or get-up to which goodwill has become attached, thereby requires a property in the mark or get-up which he may exploit by conferring for reward upon some other person the right to use the mark or get-up in his own business: and that this method of exploitation of the mark or get-up is entitled to protection at common law in an action at his suit for passing-off, notwithstanding that he himself has ceased to carry on the case the business in which the mark or get-up is used. In the *Warwick* case the mark "Warwick" had originally been used by the plaintiff company upon tyres which it manufactured and sold itself. At the time when it brought a passing-off action to restrain the use of the mark by a third party it had entered into an agreement with another company ("The Dunlop Company") under which tyres bearing the mark "Warwick" were manufactured and sold for it by the Dunlop Company. It is not possible from any of the three reports of the case to discover what were the terms of the agreement between the plaintiff company and the Dunlop Company, but from the language used by Neville J. in his judgment the inference is that the Dunlop Company had been appointed to act as selling agent for the plaintiff company for an agreed period. Whether upon the particular, but unknown, facts of the case the judge's decision in favour of the plaintiff company was right in law it is not now possible to say; but, in any event, the judge's reasoning is vitiated by the fact that it is based upon the assumption, later rejected by the House of Lords in the *Gamage* case, that what was entitled to protection by a passing-off action was a right of property in the mark itself – not a right of property in the business or goodwill in connection with which the mark was being used. In their Lordships' view the *Warwick* case cannot now be treated as authority in support of the appellant's argument.

5.1.2.2   *Ad-Lib Club v Granville* [1972] R.P.C. 673 (Pennycuick V.-C.)

In a passing off action the plaintiff company, which had run a successful night club called the "Ad-Lib Club" from 1964 to 1966 sought an interlocutory injunction to restrain the defendant from carrying on business as proprietor of a discotheque night club under the name or style "Ad-Lib". The plaintiff company's evidence was that it had been forced to discontinue running its own club due to noise emitting from the club's premises to those of neighbours, which had resulted in the grant of an injunction against it. Since 1966 the plaintiff company had been seeking alternative premises in order to re-open its club, but without success. The defendant, who did not file evidence or appear on the motion, had announced that a club called the "Ad-Lib Club" was opening on 11th December. The plaintiff company claimed that it still possessed goodwill to which the name "Ad-Lib" attached, that members of the public would be likely to regard the new club as a continuation of the plaintiff's club, and that an interlocutory injunction should be granted.

Pennycuick V.-C.:

The basis of the present action, to quote the words of Lord Parker in the case of *Spalding (A.G.) & Brothers v A.W. Gamage Limited* (above, 5.1.1.2), is a proprietory right not so much in the name itself but in the goodwill established through use of the name in connection with the plaintiff's, here, establishment. I have no doubt that on the evidence the plaintiff company had by the end of 1965 established a substantial goodwill to which the name "Ad-Lib Club" was attached and that that name had become distinctive of the plaintiff company's establishment. It follows beyond a doubt that if at the end of 1965 any other person had sought to use the name "Ad-Lib" in connection with a club of this character that would have been a plain invasion of the plaintiff company's goodwill. The question which is raised by the present action is simply whether by the interval of some five years which has passed since the plaintiff company's club was closed the plaintiff company must be regarded as having ceased to have any goodwill to which this name could fairly be said to be attached.

The matter is put in Halsbury's Laws of England, third edition, volume 38, page 59, in these terms:

> "Since the right of action for passing off is based on injury to goodwill, a person who has ceased to carry on the business in which a mark or name was used, or has discontinued the use of the name or mark in his business, cannot maintain an action for passing off in respect of the name or mark, unless, it seems, he can prove that the name or mark retains a residual renown as denoting his goods".

In support of that statement there is cited the case of *Norman Kark Publications Ltd v Odhams Press Ltd* [1962] 1 All E.R. 636, [1962] R.P.C. 163 in which the first paragraph of the headnote reads:

> "In an action to restrain the use of a magazine or newspaper title on the ground of passing off the plaintiff must establish that, at the date of the user by the defendant

of which the plaintiff complains, he has a proprietory right in the goodwill of the name, viz, that the name remains distinctive of some product of his, so that the use of the name by the defendant is calculated to deceive: but a mere intention on the part of the plaintiff not to abandon a name is not enough".

Wilberforce J. went at length into the principles underlying proprietory right in goodwill and annexation of a name to goodwill and the laws of the right to protection of a name and on the facts of that particular case he held that the plaintiff company had lost its right in respect of the name Today as part of the title of a magazine.

It seems to me clear on principle and on authority that where a trader ceases to carry on his business he may none the less retain for at any rate some period of time the goodwill attached to that business. Indeed it is obvious. He may wish to reopen the business or he may wish to sell it. It further seems to me clear in principle and on authority that so long as he does retain the goodwill in connection with his business he must also be able to enforce his rights in respect of any name which is attached to that goodwill. It must be a question of fact and degree at what point in time a trader who has either temporarily or permanently closed down his business should be treated as no longer having any goodwill in that business or in any name attached to it which he is entitled to have protected by law.

In the present case, it is quite true that the plaintiff company has no longer carried on the business of a club, so far as I know, for five years. On the other hand, it is said that the plaintiff company on the evidence continues to be regarded as still possessing goodwill to which this name "Ad-Lib Club" is attached. It does, indeed, appear firstly that the defendant must have chosen the name "Ad-Lib Club" by reason of the reputation which the plaintiff company's "Ad-Lib" acquired. He has not filed any evidence giving any other reason for the selection of that name and the inference is overwhelming that he has only selected that name because it has a reputation. In the second place, it appears from the newspaper cuttings which have been exhibited that members of the public are likely to regard the new club as a continuation of the plaintiff company's club. The two things are linked up. That is no doubt the reason why the defendant has selected this name.

It will be observed that there is no question here of a name referring to a locality, type of activity or anything of that kind, unless one considers "Ad-Lib" as a form of activity.

I think that the proper inference to be drawn from the evidence is that the plaintiff company has indeed a residual goodwill to which this name is attached and that that goodwill is an asset of value in the hands of the plaintiff company which it is entitled to exploit, if it is so minded, in future and which it cannot be said to have abandoned. That being the position, the name is something which it is entitled to have protected by injunction.

When one comes to the balance of convenience, there is a balance which, as far as I can see – and I have only the plaintiff company's evidence before me – is wholly in favour of granting immediate interlocutory relief. It is pointed out and it is plainly right that if the defendant once opens his club under the name of "Ad-Lib Club" the plaintiff company's goodwill in that name will be gone and gone for good. On the other hand, apart from, I suppose, such promotion expenditure as has been incurred it cannot be any hardship to the defendant to be restrained from carrying on his new club under a name which he can only have selected because of the reputation in that name which resulted from the successful activities of the plaintiff company.

5.1.2.3 *Anheuser-Busch v Budejovicky Budvar* [1984] F.S.R. 413 (C.A.)

The plaintiffs had brewed and sold "Budweiser" beer in the US for more than a century, taking its inspiration from the brewing techniques of the Czech town Budweis (now Ceske Budejovice). The defendants were successors to a brewing business in that town started in 1895. From 1960 they used "Budweiser" as a mark for their beer when exported from Czechoslovakia with labels in English, French and German. By a compromise agreement in 1911 between the plaintiffs and the defendants' predecessors (and with them the other brewing company of Budweis), the plaintiffs acquired exclusive rights in the mark outside Europe.

The plaintiffs had sold no significant quantity of their beer to the general public in the UK before 1974 and until 1980 sold only small quantities (thereafter it began to build a regular export trade). Well before this their beer had however been regularly supplied in the UK to US diplomatic and military personnel through US embassy and PX (military base) outlets. At the end of 1973, the defendants began a successful export business in the Czech beer to the UK. There was considerable evidence that as a result the public had become confused about the source of "Budweiser" beer in the UK. The plaintiffs sued the defendants for passing off.

Oliver L.J.:

The critical question, Mr Kentridge [for the plaintiffs] submits – and this must, in my judgment, be right – is what was the position when the defendants first entered the English market with their Budweiser beer in 1973/4? The learned judge's own findings establish that the plaintiffs already had by then a reputation with a substantial number of people in this country, but he regarded the plaintiffs as not themselves being in the market, and he attributed no significance to any goodwill attached to the sales of the plaintiffs' beer through the PX as a property which might be affected by the defendants' activities and which the plaintiffs might be entitled to protect. In this, Mr Kentridge submits, he was wrong, and it is the significance to be attached to these sales which forms the real bone of contention between the parties and which is, to my mind, the only really substantial point in the case. The question, in its simplest form, may be expressed thus: how far is it an essential ingredient of a successful claim in passing off that the plaintiff should have established in this country a business in which his goods or services are sold to the general public on the open market?

Oliver L.J. then referred to the characteristics of passing off listed by Lord Diplock and Lord Fraser in the "Advocaat" case (above, 5.1.1.4). He continued:

The substantial submission made on behalf of the defendants, however, is that the plaintiffs in this case do not satisfy Lord Fraser's first, third, fourth and fifth requirements. When the defendants first started to trade here, it is submitted, the plaintiffs had no business here and accordingly no goodwill in any relevant sense, and they could not thus suffer any damage from the defendants' activities which would ground an action here.

As mentioned above, Whitford J. found as a fact that the plaintiffs' name Budweiser was well known to a substantial number of people in this country (leaving aside for the moment US servicemen temporarily resident here) as a name associated with the beer brewed by the plaintiffs in the United States. The plaintiffs can thus legitimately claim that before the defendants' entry into the market here, they had a reputation as the brewers of a beer, Budweiser, with a substantial section of the public. The question is whether this reputation associated with a beer which, for practical purposes, nobody could buy here, constituted a goodwill in any relevant sense.

In the *Advocaat* case, Lord Diplock, at page 744, adverted to the fact that for a trader to establish his right as plaintiff he "must have himself used the descriptive term long enough *on the market* in connection with his own goods and have traded successfully enough to have built up a goodwill for his business" (emphasis supplied). This was, of course, said in the context of a claim by a group of traders all engaged in selling goods under a particular descriptive term, but it emphasises the point that goodwill (as opposed to mere reputation) does not exist here apart from a business carried on here.

This emerges with even greater clarity from the decision of the Privy Council in *Star Industrial Company Limited v Yap Kwee Kor* (above, 5.1.2.1). In that case it was quite clear that the defendant in Singapore had quite deliberately adopted the market and get-up formerly used there by the plaintiffs in connection with their goods. But the facts were that the plaintiffs had discontinued their trade in Singapore three years before, and had no intention of resuming it. They had in fact assigned any residual goodwill that they had, and their rights, in the mark formerly used on their goods to a subsidiary company which was not a party to the action. Thus the action failed. Lord Diplock, in delivering the judgment of the Board, said:

> "A passing off action is a remedy for the invasion of a right of property not in the mark, name or get-up improperly used, but in the business or goodwill likely to be injured by the misrepresentation made by passing off one person's goods as the goods of another. Goodwill, as the subject of proprietory rights, is incapable of subsisting by itself. It has no independent existence apart from the business to which it is attached. It is local in character and divisible; if the business is carried on in several countries a separate goodwill attaches to it in each. So when the business is abandoned in one country in which it has acquired a goodwill, the goodwill in that country perishes with it although the business may continue to be carried on in other countries".

The principle here enunciated by Lord Diplock is not, and indeed cannot very well be, disputed, but the question, to which no very clear answer emerges from the authorities, is what form of activity on the part of the plaintiff is required before it can be said that he has a "business" here to which goodwill can attach?

That the mere existence of a trading reputation in this country is insufficient in the absence of customers here is well exemplified by *The Athletes' Foot Marketing Associates Inc v Cobra Sports Ltd* [1980] R.P.C. 343, where Walton J. helpfully reviewed all the earlier cases. That case bears some similarity to the present in this respect that although the plaintiffs (these like the plaintiffs in the instant case) had expended considerable sums in advertising, all their advertising had been in the United States and was directed to the American market. There, as here, there was an awareness of the plaintiff's trade name and trading activities in a substantial section of the public in England, as a result of over-spill publicity through American journals circulating here. There were, however, no customers in England, because the plaintiffs' activities had got no further than the taking of preparatory steps for setting up business here.

The principle was expressed by Walton J. at page 350 as follows:

> "... as a matter of principle, no trader can complain of passing off as against him in any territory – and it will usually be defined by national boundaries, although it is well conceivable in the modern world that it will not – in which he has no customers, nobody who is in a trade relation with him. This will normally shortly be expressed by saying that he does not carry on any trade in that particular country ... but the inwardness of it will be that he has no customers in that country: no people who buy his goods or make use of his services (as the case may

be) there".

This is, I think, a helpful statement, but needs, in the light of the authorities, to be approached with the caveat that "customers" must not be read restrictively as confined to persons who are in a direct contractual relationship with the plaintiff, but includes persons who buy his goods in the market.

In *Société Anonyme des Anciens Etablissements Panhard et Levassor v Panhard Levassor Motor Company Limited* (1901) 18 R.P.C. 405, the plaintiffs obtained an injunction against passing off. They had no business in England nor any agency here. Indeed their cars could not lawfully be imported into England without the licence of certain English patentees. There was, however, an English market for their cars in the sense that there was an importer (presumably with the appropriate licences) in England who bought their cars for re-sale and there were individuals who from time to time bought their cars in Paris and imported them into England. Farwell J. observed that "England was one of their markets". Thus here the sale of the plaintiffs' goods by a third party and purchase and importation by English residents was regarded as a sufficient business to support the action.

Poiret v Jules Poiret Ltd (1920) 37 R.P.C. 177 was another case in which the successful foreign plaintiff had no actual place of business in England, but he exhibited his goods here and sold to customers here either directly or through an agent.

The case of *Sheraton Corporation of America v Sheraton Motels Limited* [1964] R.P.C. 202 may perhaps be said to represent the highwatermark, for there the successful plaintiffs carried on no business in the United Kingdom save that bookings for their hotels abroad were effected through an office which they maintained in London and through travel agents in this country. The case is, however, a somewhat slender authority, for it was a motion for an interlocutory injunction, and the decision really proceeded on the footing that the plaintiffs might succeed at the trial in establishing a goodwill which was entitled to protection and that the balance of convenience dictated that they should be protected in the meantime.

It is, however, clear that it is not every activity in this country which might loosely be called a "business" activity that qualifies as the carry on of a business here. *Alain Bernardin et Cie v Pavilion Properties* [1967] R.P.C. 581 is a case in point. There the plaintiffs, who carried on a restaurant business in Paris under the title "The Crazy Horse Saloon" had for many years publicised their establishment by publicity material distributed to tourist organisations and hotels in the United Kingdom. They failed to restrain the carrying on by the defendants of a restaurant in London under the same name. Pennycuick J. referred to the classic statement of Lord Macnaghten in *C.I.R. v Muller & Co's Margarine Ltd* [1901] A.C. 217:

"Goodwill has no independent existence. It cannot subsist by itself. It must be attached to a business. Destroy the business and the goodwill perishes with it, though elements remain which may perhaps be gathered up and be revived again".

He also referred to the judgment of Jenkins L.J. in *Oertli A.G. v Bowman (London) Ltd* [1957] R.P.C. 388, in which he said:

"It is of course essential to the success of any claim in respect of passing off based on the use of a given mark or get-up that the plaintiff should be able to show that the disputed mark or get-up has become by user in this country distinctive of the plaintiff's goods so that the use in relation to any goods of the kind dealt in by the plaintiff of that mark or get-up will be understood by the trade and public in this country as meaning that the goods are the plaintiffs' goods".

Pennycuick J. observed (at page 584):

> "The statement in the judgment of Jenkins L.J. which I have just read une-quivocally requires user to be in this country. That it seems to me is what one would expect: that the trader cannot acquire goodwill in this country without some sort of user in this country. His user may take many forms and in certain cases very slight activities have been held to suffice. On the other hand, I do not think that the mere sending to this country by a foreign trader of advertisements advertising his establishment abroad could fairly be treated as user in this country ... He may acquire a reputation in a wide sense in the sense of returning travellers speaking highly of that establishment, but it seems to me that those matters, although they may represent reputation in some wide sense, fall far short of user in this country and are not sufficient to establish reputation in the sense material for the purpose of a passing off action".

That case was followed by Brightman J., as he then was, in *Amway Corporation v Eurway International Ltd* [1974] R.P.C. 82, where the only activity relied on by the plaintiffs apart from preliminary steps for commencing business were what were referred to as "minor trading activities". Reliance was also placed on advertisements appearing in American journals circulating in England, such as the National Geographic Magazine. Brightman J. held that this activity was entirely inadequate to support a passing off action based on goodwill in this country.

On the other hand, in *Globelegance B.V. v Sarkissian* [1974] R.P.C. 603, where an internationally known fashion designer had exhibited in England, had sold patterns here which were made up into dresses sold under his trade name, and had supplied a modest, though not insubstantial, number of ties for resale here by retailers, Temple-man J. (as he then was) was prepared to hold that these activities were sufficient to constitute the carrying on of business here.

The plaintiffs in the instant case submit that they are not in any difficulty. They have proved, they submit, the existence here of a reputation with a substantial section of the public, and they have adduced evidence of sales here to such members of the public as have been admitted to bases and Embassy canteens and bars and as have attended from time to time those open days and air displays which have been organised at United States Air Force bases.

I confess that for my part I am quite unable to treat these sporadic and occasional sales as constituting in any real sense the carrying on by the plaintiffs of a business in this country. The fact is that no ordinary member of the public, whether he be indigenous or a foreign tourist, could consider himself a customer in this country for the plaintiffs' beer.

That, however, is not the end of the matter. If it is right, as I believe that it is, to regard the occasional and limited availability of the plaintiffs' beer to members of the British public in the United Kingdom as no more than a fortuitous overspill from the main area of supply, there remains the fact that the plaintiffs were in fact supplying to the PX for consumption in this country a rough average of 5,000,000 cans of beer every year – a supply which had begun well before the defendants' appearance and was continuing in 1973 when the defendants first started marketing in Great Britain under the name "Budweiser". The critical question upon which this appeal hinges seems to me to be whether this supply can properly be considered as the carrying on of a business in England creating a goodwill in this country which requires to be protected from the defendants' activities. If it does, then the occasional supply to non-Service personnel adds nothing. If it does not, then it cannot, as it seems to me, be elevated by such occasional outside supply into something which it was not.

Now Mr Kentridge has, throughout his clear and helpful address to the court, repeatedly referred to goodwill in the words of Lord Macnaghten in the *Muller's Margarine* ([1901] A.C. 217) case as "the attractive force which brings in custom". But one asks oneself "what custom in this country in 1973 was brought in by the knowledge of members of the indigenous British public of the plaintiffs' Budweiser beer?" And the answer must be that there was none, because however attractive they may have found the idea of drinking the plaintiffs' beer, they could not get it. In so far, therefore, as anyone was misled by the defendants' use of the name "Budweiser", the plaintiffs could suffer no damage either by loss of sales, for there were none at that time and none were contemplated, nor by loss of reputation, because if there was any such loss (which seems highly improbable) the reputation was quite unconnected with either an ability or a willingness to supply.

It may perhaps be tested in this way. Suppose an American product which is well known in America, but is and remains totally unknown to the general public in this country. It is, however, sold in the PX stores on American bases here but nowhere else. Is it credibly arguable that this could create a business goodwill in this country which would entitled the American manufacturer to a nationwide injunction against selling under a similar name in a market in which he does not sell and in which the name has never previously been used or heard of? It is, of course, true that some of the cases to which reference has been made above indicate that a business may be established by relatively modest acts. Nevertheless, all those cases have this feature in common, that the sales relied on were sales on the open market to the public generally. None was concerned with what we have here, namely, sales on a closed and separate market to a particular section of the public only, having the qualification of belonging to or being employed by the United States Services.

In my judgment, although for rather different reasons, the judge was right in the conclusion that he reached that both the defendants and the plaintiffs were entitled to use the name Budweiser in this country, and I would therefore dismiss the appeal.

O'Connor and Dillon L.JJ. delivered concurring judgments.

5.1.3 Passing Off: Defendant's Misrepresentation

5.1.3.1   *Reckitt & Colman v Borden* [1990] 1 W.L.R. 491 (H.L.)

The plaintiff sold lemon juice in a yellow plastic lemon-shaped container. "Jif" was embossed on the side and printed on a neck-label. There was strong evidence that the purchasing public would think that they were buying a "Jif lemon" if confronted with the defendants' lemon juice in similar packaging. Walton J. and the C.A. found the defendants' proposed get-up to amount to a threat of passing off against which a qua timet injunction should be granted. The H.L. agreed, Lord Oliver of Aylmerton dealing with the defendants' arguments thus:

The argument, so attractively put by Lord Alexander of Weedon, starts from a principle which is common to both parties and which is neatly expressed in the following short passage from the judgment of Lord Cranworth L.C. in *Farina v Silverlock* (1856) 6 De G.M. & G. 214, 218:

"... I apprehend that the law is perfectly clear, that anyone, who has adopted a particular mode of designating his particular manufacture, has a right to say, not that other persons shall not sell exactly the same article, better or worse, or an article looking exactly like it, but that they shall not sell it in such a way as to steal (so to call it) his trade mark, and make purchasers believe that it is the manufacture to which that trade mark was originally applied."

So, it is said, the distinction between the manufactured article itself, which anyone is free to copy in the absence of patent protection, and the special trade insignia used to designate its trade origin, which the courts will protect, is clearly brought out in the speech of Lord Macnaghten in *Weingarten Bros v Charles Bayer & Co* (1905) 22 R.P.C. 341, 349. The article itself cannot, it is submitted, constitute the special insignia of its own origin. All that the law will protect are such capricious additions or features as may be attached to the article for the purpose of indicating origin – for instance, the embossed word "Jif" or the respondents' containers in the instant case, which serves no functional purpose.

Whether in fact the particular shape or configuration of the very object sold by a trader is incapable as a matter of law of protection in a case where it has become associated exclusively with his business is a proposition which is at least open to doubt. The decision of Buckley J. in *R.J. Elliott & Co Ltd v Hodgson* (1902) 19 R.P.C. 518 suggests the contrary, although it has been doubted: see *Cadbury Ltd v Ulmer GmbH* [1988] F.S.R. 385. It is clear at least from the decision of this House in *William Edge & Sons Ltd v William Niccolls & Sons Ltd* [1911] A.C. 693 that where the article sold is conjoined with an object which, whilst serving the functional purpose of enabling the article to be more effectively employed, is of a shape or configuration which has become specifically identified with a particular manufacturer, the latter may be entitled to protection against the deceptive use in conjunction with similar articles of objects fashioned in the same or a closely similar shape.

I find it, however, unnecessary to pursue the question further for there is, to my mind, a fallacy in the argument which begins by identifying the contents with the container and is summarised in the central proposition that "you cannot claim a monopoly in selling plastic lemons." Well, of course you cannot any more than you can claim a monopoly in the sale of dimpled bottles. The deception alleged lies not in the sale of the plastic lemons or the dimpled bottles, but in the sale of lemon juice or whisky, as the case may be, in containers so fashioned as to suggest that the juice or the whisky emanates from the source with which the containers of those particular configurations have become associated in the public mind: see *John Haig & Co Ltd v Forth Blending Co Ltd* (1953) 70 R.P.C. 259. It is, no doubt, true that the plastic lemon-shaped container serves, as indeed does a bottle of any design, a functional purpose in the sale of lemon juice. Apart from being a container simpliciter, it is a convenient size; it is capable of convenient use by squeezing; and it is so designed as conveniently to suggest the nature of its contents without the necessity for further labelling or other identification. But those purposes are capable of being and indeed are served by a variety of distinctive containers of configurations other than those of a lemon-sized lemon. Neither the appellants nor the respondents are in the business of selling plastic lemons. Both are makers and vendors of lemon juice and the only question is whether the respondents, having acquired a public reputation for Jif juice by selling it for many years in containers of a particular shape and design which, on the evidence, has become associated with their produce, can legitimately complain of the sale by the appellants of similar produce in containers of similar, though not identical, size, shape and colouring.

So I, for my part, would reject the suggestion that the plastic lemon container is an object in itself rather than part of the get-up under which the respondents' produce is sold. But it is argued that that is not the end of the matter, for the get-up which is protected is not just a plastic lemon-shaped container, but the container plus the respondents' labelling, and it is not open to the respondents to argue that, though the labels themselves could not, fairly regarded, possibly be confused, a part, albeit perhaps a dominant part, of the get-up can, as it were, be separated and made the subject matter of protection in its own right. I confess that I do not see why not, given that the respondents establish a right to the protection of their get-up as a whole. The question is whether what the appellants are doing constitutes a misrepresentation that their juice is Jif juice, and whether that results from the similarity of their get-up to the whole of the respondents' get-up or to only the most striking part of it is wholly immaterial if – and of course this is critical – it is once established as a matter of fact that what they are doing constitutes a misrepresentation which effectively deceives the public into an erroneous belief regarding the source of the product.

Then it is said – and again there is no disagreement as to this – that the mere fact that the produce of the appellants and that of the respondents may be confused by members of the public is not of itself sufficient. There is no "property" in the accepted sense of the word in a get-up. Confusion resulting from the lawful right of another trader to employ as indicative of the nature of his goods terms which are common to the trade gives rise to no cause of action. The application by a trader to his goods of an accepted trade description or of ordinary English terms may give rise to confusion. It probably will do so where previously another trader was the only person in the market dealing in those goods, for a public which knows only of A will be prone to assume that any similar goods emanate from A. But there can be no cause of action in passing off simply because there will have been no misrepresentation. So the application to the defendants' goods of ordinary English terms such as "cellular clothing" (*Cellular Clothing Co Ltd v Maxton and Murray* (1899) 16 R.P.C. 397), or "Office Cleaning" (*Office Cleaning Services Ltd v Westminster Window and General Cleaners Ltd* (1946) 63 R.P.C. 39) or the use of descriptive expressions or slogans in general use such as "Chicago Pizza" (*My Kinda Town Ltd v Soll* [1983] R.P.C. 407) cannot entitle a plaintiff to relief simply because he has used the same or similar terms as descriptive of his own goods and has been the only person previously to employ that description.

All this is accepted by the respondents. The appellants, however, starting from this undoubted base, argue that what the respondents are asking the court to protect is no more than the use by them of a descriptive term, embodied in a plastic lemon instead of expressed verbally, which is common to the trade. They pray in aid a whole host of previously decided cases by way of analogy. *J.B. Williams Co v H Bronnley & Co Ltd* (1909) 26 R.P.C. 765, for instance, was a case where the plaintiffs had adopted a type of container for shaving soap which closely resembled in shape, size and colouring other containers whose salient features were widely used and already familiar in the trade. Not surprisingly, they failed in their claim for passing off. But these cases establish no fresh principle of law, and are really of very little assistance.

Every case depends upon its own peculiar facts. For instance, even a purely descriptive term consisting of perfectly ordinary English words may, by a course of dealing over many years, become so associated with a particular trader that it acquires a secondary meaning such that it may properly be said to be descriptive of that trader's goods and of his goods alone, as in *Reddaway v Banham* [1896] A.C. 199. In the instant case, what is said is that there was nothing particularly original in marketing lemon juice in plastic containers made to resemble lemons. The respondents were not the first to think of it even though they have managed over the past 30 years to establish a virtual monopoly in the United Kingdom. It is, in fact, a selling device widely employed outside the United Kingdom. It is a natural, convenient and familiar technique – familiar at least to those acquainted with retail marketing methods in Europe and the United States. If and so far as this particular selling device has become associated in the mind of the purchasing public with the respondents' Jif lemon juice, that is simply because the respondents have been the only people in the market selling lemon juice in this particular format. Because there has been in fact a monopoly of this sale of this particular article, the public is led to make erroneous assumption that a similar article brought to the market for the first time must emanate from the same source. This has been referred to in the argument as "the monopoly assumption". The likelihood of confusion was admitted by the appellants themselves in the course of their evidence, but it is argued that the erroneous public belief which causes the product to be confused arises simply from the existing monopoly and not from any deception by the appellants in making use of what they claim to be a normal, ordinary and generally available selling technique.

The difficulty about this argument is that it starts by assuming the only basis upon which it can succeed, that is to say, that the selling device which the appellants wish to adopt is ordinary and generally available or, as it is expressed in some of the cases, "common to the trade:" see e.g. *Payton & Co Ltd v Snelling, Lampard & Co Ltd* (1899) 17 R.P.C. 48. In one sense, the monopoly assumption is the basis of every passing off action. The deceit practised on the public when one trader adopts a get-up associated with another succeeds only because the latter has previously been the only trader using that particular get-up. But the so called "monopoly assumption" demonstrates nothing in itself. As a defence to a passing off claim it can succeed only if that which is claimed by the plaintiff as distinctive of his goods and his goods alone consists of something either so ordinary or in such common use that it would be unreasonable that he should claim it as applicable solely to his goods, as for instance where it consists simply of a description of the goods sold. Here the mere fact that he has previously been the only trader dealing in goods of that type and so described may lead members to the public to believe that all such goods must emanate from him simply because they know of no other. To succeed in such a case he must demonstrate more than simply the sole use of the descriptive term. He must demonstrate that it has become so closely associated with his goods as to acquire the secondary meaning not simply of goods of that description but specifically of goods of which and he alone is the source . . .

The trial judge here has found as a fact that the natural size squeeze pack in the form of a lemon has become so associated with Jif lemon juice that the introduction of the appellants' juice in any of the proposed get-ups will be bound to result in many housewives purchasing that juice in the belief that they are obtaining Jif juice. I cannot interpret that as anything other than a finding that the plastic lemon-shaped container has acquired, as it were, a secondary significance. It indicates not merely lemon juice but specifically Jif lemon juice.

Lord Oliver rejected the proposition that likelihood of deception should be judged only in relation to the literate and careful purchaser. He concluded overall:

It is pointed out that recent decisions of this House in, for instance, *British Leyland Motor Corporation Ltd v Armstrong Patents Co Ltd* [1986] A.C. 577 and *In re Coca Cola Co* [1986] 1 W.L.R. 695 have stressed the suspicion with which this House regards any attempt to extend or perpetuate a monopoly and it is suggested again that, because it is not easy in the circumstances of this market effectively to distinguish the appellants' products from the respondents' except at considerable expense, the respondents are achieving, in effect, a perpetual monopoly in the sale of lemon juice in lemon-shaped squeeze packs. I do not accept at all that this is so, but in any event the principle that no man is entitled to steal another's trade by deceit is one of at least equal importance. The facts as found here establish that, unless the injunction is continued, that is what the appellants will be doing and it is not necessary for them to do so in order to establish their own competing business for there is nothing in the nature of the product sold which inherently requires it to be sold in the particular format which the appellants have chosen to adopt. I would dismiss the appeal.

Lord Bridge and Lord Jauncey delivered concurring speeches; Lord Brandon and Lord Goff concurred.

5.1.3.2 *Parker Knoll v Knoll International* [1962] R.P.C. 265 (H.L.)

Parker Knoll, the English furniture makers, acquired their name and mark when in the 1930s Frederick Parker & Sons adopted a form of springing for chairs invented by Wilhelm Knoll of Stuttgart. A nephew of Wilhelm, Hans, went to the US and with his wife developed the modern furniture firm, Knoll International, which built up an international business. In 1957, the latter sought to enter the British market marking their own furniture "Knoll International". Parker Knoll sought an injunction to restrain the American company from passing off their goods as those of the plaintiffs.

Lord Morris of Borth-y-Gest:

My Lords, in the interests of fair trading and in the interests of all who may wish to buy or to sell goods the law recognises that certain limitations upon freedom of action are necessary and desirable. In some situations the law has had to resolve what might at first appear to be conflicts between competing rights. In solving the problems which have arisen there has been no need to resort to any abstruse principles but rather, I think, to the straightforward principle that trading must not only be honest but must not even unintentionally be unfair.

The present case is concerned with the selling of goods under a mark or name. The respondents fear that if the appellants, whose honesty is not in any way impugned, are allowed to sell furniture in the way that they desire to do, a great many people would buy furniture in the belief that they were buying the respondents' furniture whereas they would in reality be buying the appellants' furniture.

In approaching the facts of the case I propose to state a few propositions, which, though they are by no means exhaustive, seem to me to apply to such a case as the present.

1. No one has any right to represent his goods as being the goods of someone else (*Reddaway v Banham* [1896] A.C. 199; *Joseph Rodgers & Sons Limited v W.N. Rodgers & Company* (1924) 41 R.P.C. 2771).

2. The court will restrain the making of any such representation even though it is not made fraudulently (see *John Brinsmead & Sons Ltd v Brinsmead* (1913) 30 R.P.C. 493). If A represents his goods as being the goods of B, then B is likely to suffer and is entitled to be protected whether A makes the representation innocently or fraudulently. If there is room for doubt as to whether A has represented his goods as the goods of B, then if there is evidence that A deliberately intended to and set out to make such a representation that evidence will in some cases assist to prove that there was in fact such a representation.

3. A name may be used as a mark under which a person's goods are sold so that the name comes to denote goods made by that person and not the goods made by anyone else or even made by anyone else who has the same name. So also a mark under which a person's goods are sold may come to denote goods made by that person. The name or the mark will have acquired a secondary meaning (see *Chivers v Chivers* (1900) 17 R.P.C. 420).

4. It follows that someone may, even by using his own name and using it innocently, make a representation that is untrue, that is a representation that goods which in fact are his are the goods of someone else (see *Reddaway v Banham* [1896] A.C. 199).

   In *Joseph Rodgers & Sons Limited v W.N. Rodgers & Company* (1924) 41 R.P.C. 277, Romer J. (at page 29) said that no man is entitled so to describe or mark his goods as to represent that the goods are the goods of another, and further said at page 292 that to the rule as so stated there is no exception at all (see also *Baume v Moore* [1958] Ch. 137). In *Marengo v Daily Sketch and Sunday Graphic Limited* (1948) 65 R.P.C. 242, Lord Simonds said at page 251: "It is an unassailable general proposition that the interests alike of honest traders and of the public require that the goods of A should not be confused with the goods of B. But that proposition is subject to the qualification that a man must be allowed to trade in his own name and, if some confusion results, that is a lesser evil than that a man should be deprived of what would appear to be a natural and inherent right. But ... it is a fantastic gloss upon this well-established qualification to say that it justifies a trader in placing upon his goods a mark which, however much he may intend it to signify his name, is yet liable to suggest to reasonable men the name of another". Having regard to this passage, I think that some observations made by Lord Greene, M.R., in *Wright, Layman & Umney Ltd v Wright* (1949) 66 R.P.C. 149 at 152, must be regarded as incomplete.

5. It is a question of fact, to be decided on the evidence, whether it is proved that a name or a mark has acquired a secondary meaning so that it denotes or has come to mean goods made by a particular person and not goods made by any other person even though such other person may have the same name.

6. If it is proved on behalf of a plaintiff that a name or a mark has acquired such a secondary meaning, then it is a question for the court whether a defendant, whatever may be his intention, is so describing his goods that there is a likelihood that a substantial section of the purchasing public will be misled into believing that

his goods are the goods of the plaintiff (see *Chivers & Sons v S Chivers & Co Ltd* (1900) 17 R.P.C. 420). In arriving at a decision the court must not surrender in favour of any witness its own independent judgment (see per Lord Macnaghten in *Payton & Company Limited v Snelling, Lampard & Company Limited* [1901] A.C. 308 at page 311: *Spalding v Gamage* (1915) 32 R.P.C. 273, at page 286; *George Ballantine & Son Limited v Ballantyne Stewart & Company Limited* [1959] R.P.C. 273 at page 280).

Deriving such assistance as the evidence afforded, Lord Morris concluded that marketing of the defendant's furniture as "Knoll International" would not avoid passing off; and that accordingly the plaintiff was entitled an injunction qualified by the phrase, "without clearly distinguishing from the goods of the plaintiff's". Lords Hodson and Devlin delivered concurring speeches. Lord Denning dissented, applying Lord Greene's dictum without qualification.

5.1.3.3   *Vine Products v Mackenzie* [1969] R.P.C. 1 (Cross J.)

This action – the "Sherry" case – was initially brought by the producers of "British Sherry", "South African Sherry" etc for a declaration that they were entitled to describe their wines by these geographical-cum-descriptive names.

The case was an outcome of the "Spanish Champagne" case [1961] R.P.C. 116. Both are referred to in "Advocaat" (above, 5.1.1.4) on the question of the title of a group of producers to exclusive rights in a word descriptive of their product. In "Champagne" and "Sherry" a further point arose out of the addition of a national adjective by the initiator to the descriptive word.

Cross J. said of the earlier "Champagne" case [1961] R.P.C. 116:

The evidence established that the word "champagne" meant in England wine produced in the Champagne district of France by the plaintiffs and the other growers and shippers of that district. The defendants argued that nevertheless the addition of the word "Spanish" showed that their produce was not a wine produced in France, and that accordingly the description "Spanish Champagne" could mislead no-one. The judge described this as "a fairly specious argument" (see page 120, line 41) but he rejected it. In doing so he drew a distinction between those who were knowledgeable and those who were ignorant in matters of wine. The former would know that Champagne came exclusively from France, and so would realise if they bought a bottle labelled "Spanish Champagne" that they were not buying real Champagne but a Spanish sparkling wine. But according to the evidence given in that case – which was to the same effect as that given in this case – many people in this country are today drinking wine who were not brought up to this habit and know little or nothing of the various types of wine and their countries of origin. Such people, the judge thought, might well be deceived by a bottle labelled "Spanish Champagne". But how would they be deceived? Counsel for the plaintiffs, if I understand his argument correctly, suggested that Danckwerts J. meant that they would think that the wine which they were buying came from France in the same way as those who purchased from the defendants in the *Pilsbury Washburn* case ((1898) 86 Fed. R. 608) would have thought that the flour which they were buying came from Minnesota. That I am sure does far less than justice to the judge's reasoning. A man who does not know where Champagne comes from can have not the slightest reason for thinking that a bottle labelled "Spanish Champagne" contains a wine produced in France. But what he may very well think is that he is buying the genuine article – real Champagne – and that, I have no doubt, was the sort of deception which the judge had in mind. He thought, as I read his judgment, that if people were allowed to call sparkling wine not produced in Champagne "Champagne" even though preceded by an adjective denoting the country of origin, the distinction between genuine Champagne and "champagne type" wines produced elsewhere would become blurred; that the word "Champagne" would come gradually to mean no more than "sparkling wine" and that the part of the plaintiffs' goodwill which consisted in the name would be diluted and gradually destroyed. If I may say so without impertinence I agree entirely with the decision in the *Spanish Champagne* case – but as I see it it uncovered a piece of common law or equity which had till then escaped notice – for in such a case there is not, in any ordinary sense, any representation that the goods of the defendant are the goods of the plaintiffs, and evidence that no-one has been confused or deceived in that way is quite beside the mark. In truth the decision went beyond the well-trodden paths of passing off into the unmapped area of "unfair trading" or "unlawful competition".

Cross J. proceeded to find on the evidence that "Sherry" did properly mean a wine from Jerez district of Spain, and not a type of wine that may be produced anywhere and in any way. He also held that failure to object to the use of "British Sherry", "South African Sherry", etc. over a very long period raised a defence of acquiescence in those usages. On this see also Bulmer v Bollinger *[1978] R.P.C. 79.*

5.1.4 Passing Off: Likely Damage

5.1.4.1 *Henderson v Radio Corporation* (1960) [1969] R.P.C. 218
(S.C., N.S.W.)

The plaintiffs, well-known professional ballroom dancers, commenced proceedings against the defendant record company for the unauthorised use of photographs of them on a record cover. The trial judge granted an injunction but refused an inquiry as to damages.

Evatt C.J. and Myers J.:

The respondents have contended that the acts of the appellant were likely to lead to the belief that the business of the appellant was connected with the business of the respondents because, it was said, the picture of the respondents on the record cover would lead buyers of the record to believe that the respondents recommended the record as providing good music for ballroom dancing.

Four witnesses were called on this issue on behalf of the respondents. They were the president of an association of dancing teachers, the secretary of another such association, a theatrical agent and the assistant secretary of the trade union to which the professional dancers belong. Each said in substance that when he saw the record he recognised either Henderson or Henderson and his wife and gathered from the fact that their pictures were on the cover, that they had sponsored, that is recommended or approved, the record, or were associated in some way with it. The appellant called no evidence on this aspect. His Honour did not express any adverse view of these witnesses but he did not accept the view that buyers of the record would come to the same conclusion as the witnesses.

However, the facts relevant to this issue, including the evidence to which we have referred, are not in dispute. The only question is the proper inference to be drawn from them, and in those circumstances we are entitled to form our own opinion, *Benmax v Austin Motor Co Ltd* [1955] A.C. 370.

Unaided by evidence, one might consider that the dancing figures merely indicate the type of music on the record and that it is not possible to come to the conclusion for which the respondents contend. But one is not unaided by evidence and, having regard to the fact that the record was primarily intended for professional dancing teachers, and to the uncontradicted evidence of four experts in that field, we are of opinion that the proper finding is that the class of persons for whom the record was primarily intended would probably believe that the picture of the respondents on the cover indicated their recommendation or approval of the record. The only rational purpose of the wrongful use of the respondents' photograph on the disc container was to assist the sale of the disc it contained.

This false representation was not only made by the appellant, but would almost inevitably lead to a similar false representation on the part of every shopkeeper who might buy the records from the appellant and sell them or display them for sale. It still remains to be considered whether that finding established the necessary element of deception, namely, that the business of the appellant was connected with the business of the respondents. In our opinion it does.

The representation that the respondents recommended the record is an inducement to buy it. The recommendation can only be attributed to the respondents in their capacity of professional dancers, that is, a recommendation made in the course of their professional activities, and means that as professional dancers they have associated themselves with the appellant in promoting sales of the record, and that amounts to a connection, in respect of the marketing of the record, between the business of the respondents and the business of the appellant.

The point is not without authority. In *British Medical Association v Marsh* (1931) 48 R.P.C. 565 at 574, Maugham J. referring to the professional cases on passing off, said that they did not establish the proposition that if a tradesman puts forward a remedy as having been prescribed by, or sold for the benefit, or with the approval of a medical man, the latter would have no remedy. "What it is necessary in such a case to prove is, either positive injury, or in a *quia timet* action, a reasonable probability of injury, and if that is done, I, for my part, see no reason why such an action should not succeed".

In our opinion the evidence established a passing off by the appellant and, subject to proof of injury, as to which we will have something to say later, the respondents were entitled to relief by way of injunction.

It has been contended, however, that the court has no jurisdiction to grant an injunction unless there is what has been called a common field of activity and in the case, it is said, there is none. The argument is based on a statement by Wynn Parry J. in *McCulloch v Lewis A May (Produce Distributors) Ltd* 65 R.P.C. 58 at 66, 67.

> "I am satisfied", he said, "that there is discoverable in all those (cases) in which the Court has intervened this factor, namely, that there was a common field of activity in which,, however remotely, both the plaintiff and the defendant were engaged and that it was the presence of that factor that accounted for the jurisdiction of the court".

This principle was accepted by Sugerman J., who found a common field of activity in the capacity of the respondents to place their approval upon a record of ballroom dance music, which, he said, might be regarded as appurtenant or potentially appurtenant to the profession or business of ballroom dancing.

We have some difficulty in accepting the proposition stated in *McCulloch's* case. If deception and damages are proved, it is not easy to see the justification for introducing another factor as a condition of the court's power to intervene.

The physician whose name is attached by the maker to a quack remedy has no business in publicly recommending any remedy at all. It would be improper on his part if he had. The British Medical Association in *British Medical Association v Marsh* (1931) 48 R.P.C. 565 had no business in approving proprietary medicines and it was contrary to the principles of the association to do so. It seems to us to be quite unreal to say that there is a common field of activity in such cases because, whether self-imposed or not, there is an actual restraint on the injured person entering the common field at all. In our opinion, the representation in such cases that the plaintiff recommended or approved the product is, having regard to the nature of his business, equivalent to a representation that he did so in the course of it. It associates both businesses with the sale of the product, the manufacturer in making and selling it and the plaintiff in assisting in its sale by making it attractive by his professional recommendation.

In *McCulloch's* case, the plaintiff had been widely and favourably known as a broadcaster for many years in the "Children's Hour" programme of the British Broadcasting Corporation. He used the name "Uncle Mac" and was well-known by that name. He had written books for children, delivered lectures to them and given away prizes at prizegivings and was clearly a popular and well-known figure.

The defendant placed on the market a cereal which it called "Uncle Mac's Puffed Wheat". It was packed in cartons containing a number of references to "Uncle Mac", associating him with children. One was in these words, "Uncle Mac loves children – and children love Uncle Mac". There was evidence that some witnesses believed that the plaintiff had put his name to a poor or low venture and a well-known broadcaster thought that the plaintiff had been forced to lend his name to the venture through financial difficulties.

An injunction was refused because, there being no "common field of activity", there was no passing off. "Upon the postulate that the plaintiff is not engaged in any degree in producing or marketing puffed wheat, how can the defendant, in using the fancy name used by the plaintiff, be said to be passing off the goods or the business of the plaintiff? I am utterly unable to see any element of passing off in this case" per Wynn-Parry J. at page 69.

We find it impossible to accept this view without some qualification. The remedy in passing off is necessarily only available where the parties are engaged in business, using that expression in its widest sense to include professions and callings. If they do there does not seem to be any reason why it should also be necessary that there be an area, actual or potential, in which their activities conflict. If it were so, then, object only to the law of defamation, any businessman might falsely represent that his goods were produced by another provided that other was not engaged, or not reasonably likely to be engaged, in producing similar goods. This does not seem to be a sound general principle.

The present case provides an illustration of the unjust consequences of such a principle. For the purposes of this part of its argument, the appellant concedes that it is falsely representing that the respondents recommend, favour or support its dance music record, but it claims that because the respondents are not engaged or likely to be engaged in making or selling gramophone records, it is entitled to appropriate their names and reputations for its own commercial advantage and that the court has no power to prevent it doing so. It would be a grave defect in the law if this were so.

In our view, once it is proved that A is falsely representing his goods as the goods of B, or his business to be the same as or connected with the business of B, the wrong of passing off has been established and B is entitled to relief.

While *McCulloch's* case is open to strong criticism, in actual fact the respondents here are in a real sense competing in the special area of providing gramophone records specially adapted to dancing and dancing teaching. Their activities are competitive in a broad sense. If so, *McCulloch's* case provides no obstacle to the plaintiff's success in the suit.

We now turn to the question of damage and, in view of certain submissions by counsel for the respondents, desire to make a few general remarks on the subject.

Passing off is a wrong and is actionable at law. In such an action damage is presumed on proof of passing off and therefore a nominal sum by way of damages follows as a matter of course. General damages may, however, only be awarded if there is evidence of damage. Instead of proceeding at law a plaintiff may sue in equity for an injunction, as may be done in respect of other wrongful acts of a different nature. If he sees in equity, he takes advantage of the equitable principle that the court will interfere by injunction to restrain irreparable injury to property: per Romer L.J. in *Samuel v Producers Distributing Company Limited* (above, 5.1.1.3) and therefore he must go further than he need at law. He must show irreparable injury, that is that he has suffered injury which cannot be properly compensated by damages, or that he will probably suffer such injury.

If a plaintiff in equity succeeds in having the defendant enjoined, he may also have an account of profits or an inquiry as to damages. Formerly, he could only have had an account, because that was equity's only remedy, but since Lord Cairns' Act, he may have damages. If he elects to take an inquiry as to damages, he takes a common law remedy and his damages will be ascertained in the same way as they would have been ascertained at law.

In a judgment to the same effect, Manning J. said:

Today we find leading amateur sportsmen lending their names for reward to recommendations for a variety of goods and articles, and not merely those which, in the course of their amateur sporting activities, they come to know and appreciate. Indeed, from what I have myself read and observed I believe it to be the fact that at least one prominent amateur sportsman has formed a proprietary company for the exploitation of his name and reputation so that he may sell his recommendations in the advertising market and yet, so I assume, attract a minimum of taxes. In making this comment I do not wish it to be thought that I desire for one moment to criticise amateur sportsmen who have indulged in this activity. The new and altered standards must be accepted by the courts once it is apparent that they have been accepted by the community.

The point which seems to emerge with clarity is that one's conception of the status of an amateur sportsman thirty years ago is quite different to what is accepted today. The development in the advertising of products to which I have referred has opened up a new field of gainful employment for many persons who, by reason not only of their sporting, but of their social, artistic or other activities, which have attracted notoriety, have found themselves in a position to earn substantial sums of money by lending their recommendation or sponsorship to an almost infinite variety of commodities.

To meet changes in the manner of conducting commercial enterprises, I would prefer in considering cases of this kind to propound as the test the one to which I have referred above, namely, whether the plaintiff has suffered a financial detriment and such detriment flows from or arises as a result of the defendant's act, rather than to ask whether the defendant's act caused financial loss to the plaintiff.

The plaintiffs in this case had acquired a reputation which doubtless placed them in a position to earn a fee for any recommendation which they might be disposed to give to aid the sale of recorded dance music of the type in question. I have referred to those engaged in sporting activities because of the facts in *Tolley's* case [1931] A.C. 333, but the position of the plaintiffs is better compared with that of a well-known actress or model. I can see no distinction in any such cases provided, as has been established in this case, that the activity of the party concerned has resulted in their recommendation becoming a saleable commodity.

The result of the defendant's action was to give the defendant the benefit of the plaintiffs' recommendation and the value of such recommendation and to deprive the plaintiffs of the fee or remuneration they would have earned if they had been asked for their authority to do what was done. The publication of the cover amounted to a misrepresentation of the type which will give rise to the tort of passing off, as there was implied in the acts of the defendant an assertion that the plaintiffs had "sponsored" the record.

No evidence was given as to what fee or remuneration would have been payable in circumstances such as these and the major part of the argument was directed rather so the submission that damage would flow because the plaintiffs would be less likely to secure some reward for "sponsoring" some other record or records. In my view damage of the latter type is too remote.

However, I am satisfied that the unauthorised use by the defendant of the commercially valuable reputation of the plaintiffs justifies the intervention of the court. I would have thought that the relief to which the plaintiffs were entitled was an inquiry as to damages, an injunction to restrain the defendant from disposing of any further record covers bearing a visual representation of the plaintiffs and an order for delivery up for destruction of the unsold covers, but the only order made was for an injunction and there is no cross-appeal. I am therefore of opinion that this appeal should be dismissed with costs.

5.1.4.2 *Hogan v Pacific Dunlop* (1989) 12 I.P.R. 225 (F.Ct.Aust.)

Pacific Dunlop marketed shoes by using the ideas of the famous "knife scene" from the film "Crocodile Dundee", of which the applicants were copyright owners and distributors. The latter accordingly sued for passing off and under sections 52 and 53(c) of the Australian Trade Practices Act 1974. They alleged that the defendant had created an erroneous association between their rights in the image and character of Mick "Crocodile" Dundee in the film and the images portrayed by the respondent in advertising its shoes.

Gummow J. (1st Instance):

Within the action for passing off as presently understood in Australia, there are accommodated and adjusted *inter se* three sets of interests. There is the plaintiff's interest in protecting his skill, effort and investment, the interest of the defendant in freedom to attract purchasers for his goods and services, and the interest of consumers in having available a range of competitive goods and services for selection by consumers without the practice upon them of misrepresentations. Any monopoly right so created is limited in duration to the persistence of the plaintiff's reputation and goodwill; if that evaporates, the cause of action in passing off goes with it (the authorities are collected in *10th Cantanae Pty Ltd v Shoshana Pty Ltd* (1987) 79 A.L.R. 299 at 317; 11 I.P.R. 249.

Further, the ability of the plaintiff to take unto himself exclusively striking images otherwise part of the general fund referred to by Mr Pendleton is limited by the nature of the passing off action. As I have stated earlier in these reasons, the action is concerned with misrepresentation, and with a particular type of misrepresentation involving use of the image or indicium in question to convey a representation of a commercial connection between the plaintiff and the goods or services of the defendant, which connection does not exist. This case, like *10th Cantanae Pty Ltd v Shoshana Pty Ltd*, above, is concerned with what will satisfy the requirement of commercial connection. Again, it is not all representations made in commerce, as to connection between the plaintiff and the goods of services of the defendant which will suffice.

These concerns are drawn together in the following passage from the judgment of Goff L.J. in *HP Bulmer Ltd & Showerings Ltd v J Bollinger SA* [1978] R.P.C. 79 at 117:

"Not every kind of connection claimed will amount to passing off; for example if one says that one's goods are very suitable to be used in connection with the plaintiff's. On the other hand in my view there can be a passing off of goods without representing that they are actually the well-known goods which the plaintiff produces or a new line which he is supposed to have started. It is sufficient in my view if what is done represents the defendant's goods to be connected with the plaintiff's in such a way as would lead people to accept them on the faith of the plaintiff's reputation. Thus for example it would be sufficient if they were taken to be made under licence, or under some trading arrangement which would give the plaintiff some control over them. . . ."

The misrepresentation may be actionable as passing off even though the effect thereof is not to divert sales to the public of goods or services from the defendant to the plaintiff. This is because the effect of the misrepresentation complained of may be to misappropriate the plaintiff's business goodwill. (Examples are given in *10th Cantanae Pty Ltd v Shoshana Pty Ltd* (1987) 79 A.L.R. at 318). However, in each case, the damage to the goodwill of the plaintiff is actionable only because of apprehended or actual deception of the relevant section of the public by the defendant's conduct.

Gummow J. proceeded to find a case of passing off to have been made out. This judgment was upheld by a majority of the Full Federal Court. On the general issue of misrepresentation Burchett J. said:

To ask whether the consumer reasons that Mr Hogan authorised the advertisement is therefore to ask a question which is a mere side issue, and far from the full impact of the advertisement. The consumer is moved by a desire to wear something belonging in some sense to Crocodile Dundee (who is perceived as a persona, almost an avatar, of Mr Hogan). The arousal of that feeling by Mr Hogan himself could not be regarded as misleading, for then the value he promises the product will have is not in its leather, but in its association with himself. When, however, an advertisement he did not authorise makes the same suggestion, it is misleading; for the product sold by that advertisement really lacks the one feature the advertisement attributes to it.

On the argument that the respondent's advertisement was merely a parody of the film, Beaumont J. commented:

As in *Tolley v Fry*, there is a real distinction to be drawn between a "mere" caricature on the one hand and a caricature "embedded" in an advertisement on the other. The former is innocent because viewers would receive the impression that the person caricatured would not have agreed. The latter carries with it a different impression, favourable to the subject of the caricature, in which he or she is perceived as endorsing the object of the advertising. The distinction between the "mere" caricature and one "embedded" in the advertising is of critical significance. If it were appropriate to divide the advertisement into two discrete parts, one part devoted to a parody of the Dundee figure and the other a sales promotion, it may be that no relevant misrepresentation could be made out. But such a division of the advertising is not possible. The Dundee figure, albeit a variant of the original image, is seen as sponsoring the appellant's shoes. The advertising is not a "mere" caricature.

5.1.4.3 *Tavener Rutledge v Trexapalm* [1977] R.P.C. 275 (Walton J.)

"Kojak" was the title of a well-known television series in which the eponymous detective-hero sucked lollipops. The plaintiff, without any licence from the promoters of the series, Universal City Studios, launched a "Kojakpop" lolly on the British market with considerable success. The defendant, claiming to be licensed by the promoters, then began selling "Kojak Lollies", which were found to be poor value for money in comparison with the plaintiff's product.

In granting the plaintiff an interlocutory injunction against passing off, Walton J. said:

When one is dealing, as one would here be dealing, in the field of passing off it is not sufficient undoubtedly to refer only to the actual fields of activities of the two parties concerned, one has to look and see what ordinary, reasonable people, the man in the street, would consider to be within the relevant fields of activities.

Walton J. quoted from Annabel's v Shock *[1972] R.P.C. 838 at 844, per Russell L.J. and continued:*

Applying those principles to the present case, as I say, the first step is that there is no risk of confusion or possibility of confusion between the actual lines of activity of the licensors and the plaintiffs; but, says Mr Morcom, that is too simple a view. The business of what he calls character merchandising has become very well known in our present times and everybody who has a character, whether real or fictional, to exploit, does so by the grant of licences to people who wish to use the name of the real or fictional character. I think one must leave real persons out of it because, when one deals with a real person, one has a real person with real qualities and, therefore, his endorsement or the use of his name undoubtedly suggest, or may suggest in proper circumstances, an endorsement which may or may not exist; but, when one has a fictional character such as Kojak, obviously Kojak in that sense does not exist and nobody would imagine that the lollipops put out by the plaintiff company have been actually endorsed by Kojak, still less by the actor who plays the fictional character.

What Mr Morcom says is that, because of this growth of merchandising, what now happens is that the owner of the rights in a series, such as "Kojak" here, licenses a large number of people to use the name "Kojak" in connection with products and members of the public would take it that, if one uses the word "Kojakpops", the right to use that name has been licensed by whoever are the owners of the rights in the series "Kojak", that moreover they have insisted upon a certain standard of quality and that, therefore, anybody who uses the word "Kojakpops" is to some extent taking advantage of the good name of the owner of the copyright.

I regret to say that I am wholly unimpressed by any such argument. Certainly it is not established by the evidence that it has yet arisen and I think that it is a good long way off, if in fact it ever does arise, but there may come a time when the system of character merchandising will have become so well known to the man in the street that immediately he sees "Kojakpops" he will say to himself: "They must have a licence from the person who owns the rights in the television series"; but that, by itself, so far as I can see would not be of any assistance to Mr Morcom at all, because that does not carry him home at all. What he would have to go on to show is that it had also become so well known that people in the situation of licensors of these names exercised quality control over any product bearing their name, so that as soon as anybody in the street came to the conclusion that a product was licensed by the owners of some series, such as the "Kojak" series, he would say to himself not only, "This must have been licensed by them", but also: "and that is a guarantee of its quality". That point we are miles away from reaching and there is not really a shred of evidence in front of me to that effect.

5.1.4.4 *Lego System v Lego M Lemelstrich* [1983] F.S.R. 155 (Falconer J.)

The Lego Group (of which the parent company and British subsidiary were plaintiffs) manufactured and distributed the well-known construction-kit toys in the UK and much of the world under the mark "Lego". The defendant Israeli company had manufactured irrigation equipment under the mark "Lego" since 1927. Its business had expanded to cover 40 countries and it was about to launch sales in the UK.

Falconer J. found that the plaintiff's mark was a household word with such a reputation that the public would be likely to think, despite the difference in character, that the defendant's products were the goods of the plaintiffs or connected with them. On this he accepted evidence collected by a properly conducted opinion survey.

After reviewing the principles of passing off stated by Lords Diplock and Fraser in the Advocaat *case (above, 5.1.1.4) he continued:*

However, as I have indicated, the defendants' case is essentially that the parties are in very different fields and the respective goods of the plaintiffs (toys such as construction sets and building bricks) and those of the defendants (irrigation equipment, particularly for gardens) are so far apart that there could be no misrepresentation ie actionable misrepresentation, or any damage or likelihood of damage by the defendants' use of Lego on their goods.

Mr Morcom, for the Defendants submitted that, if the plaintiffs were to succeed in this case, then such a decision would be breaking new ground in extending passing off further than it has ever been extended on the cases in a situation where, as here, there is no evidence of fraudulent intention. I am not impressed with that submission – as the recent *Advocaat* case, extending further the striking development in the *Champagne* case of passing off as a cause of action, clearly demonstrates, the law as to passing off, which is concerned with unfair trading, is constantly being developed to meet changing conditions and practices in trade. Moreover, all those earlier cases now have to be seen in the light of the authoritative statement of the law as to passing off enunciated by the House of Lords in the *Advocaat* case.

After referring to McCullough v May *and the criticisms of it in* Henderson v Radio Corporation *(above, 5.1.4.1), he concluded:*

However, I respectfully agree with the observation of Oliver J. in the *Abba* case: *Lyngstad & Others v Anabas Products Ltd* [1977] F.S.R. 62

"I think, if I may say so with respect, that the Australian case to which I have referred is to some extent based on a misconception of what Wynn-Parry J. was saying in *McCulloch v May*. The expression 'common field of activity' is not, I think, a term of art, but merely a convenient shorthand term for indicating what the High Court of New South Wales itself recognised, that is to say, the need for a real possibility of confusion, which is the basis of the action".

That observation is justified by a reference to an earlier part of the judgment of Wynn-Parry J. in 65 R.P.C. at page 64, lines 19–35.

Although Mr Morcom contended strongly that the respective fields of the plaintiffs and the defendants, toys such as construction sets and building bricks on the one hand, and irrigation equipment, particularly for gardens, on the other, are too far apart from the defendants' use of LEGO to amount to misrepresentation and, indeed, as I have indicated, went so far as to submit that a decision in this case in favour of the plaintiffs would be extending passing off further than it has hitherto been extended in the absence of fraudulent intention, nevertheless he conceded that, in the light of all the cases including the *Advocaat* case, he could not submit that as a matter of law (my emphasis) passing off could never be established when the respective activities of the plaintiff and the defendant were completely unrelated. In my judgment, he was right in making that concession. Of course, that is not to say that the proximity of a defendant's field of activity to that of the plaintiff will not be relevant to whether the defendant's acts complained of amount to a misrepresentation in any particular case – plainly it will, at least in most cases. But, in my judgment, there is much force in Mr Aldous's submission, based on the extent of the plaintiffs' reputation in their mark LEGO, that if, as he contended was this case, the plaintiffs' mark has become part of the English language in the sense that everybody associates LEGO with a particular company, namely, the manufacturers of the LEGO toy construction sets and building bricks, then the misrepresentation by the defendants' use of the mark is easier to assume and to prove; on the other hand, if the mark or name concerned has only a limited field of recognition it is obviously more difficult to establish its understanding as denoting the plaintiff's goods in a field which is not directly comparable with the field of that plaintiff's goods.

Whether or not the acts of a defendant complained of in a passing off action amount to a misrepresentation must be a question of fact and, in the end, that was common ground between Mr Aldous and Mr Morcom. I think Mr Morcom expressed it correctly when, at the conclusion of that part of his argument dealing with misrepresentation, he submitted that what has to be established by a plaintiff is that there is a real risk that a substantial number of persons among the relevant section of the public will in fact believe that there is a business connection between the plaintiff and the defendant. That, as I have found, has been established by the plaintiffs in this case.

On the question of likelihood of damage to the plaintiff, Falconer J. said:

However, Mr Morcom's main submission, as I understood his argument, was that the plaintiffs' and the defendants' respective good are so far apart that the plaintiffs have not established that injury to the business or goodwill they have built up is a reasonably foreseeable consequence of the defendants' use of the mark, as required by characteristic (4) in Lord Diplock's formulation in the *Advocaat* case. Developing that submission he argued that the plaintiffs are and always have been in a very specific field which, so he argued, is where their goodwill lies and the plaintiffs had not given any evidence of any intention to diversify or franchise. It is the fact that the plaintiffs' business has been in the toy and construction kit field, with some diversification into promotional goods such as I have mentioned earlier, and that they have not up to now operated in the area of garden equipment. It is also correct that there was no evidence of a present intention on their part to enter the garden equipment field, although Mr Skovmose, a member of the Danish bar, who is secretary to the management of the Lego Group and a co-director, *inter alia*, of the second plaintiffs, stated in evidence that "there is no reason why that should not come at a later stage". But, as to the plaintiffs' goodwill being only in a very specific field, I do not accept that submission – their reputation in their mark LEGO, to which their goodwill is attached, is such that it extends beyond the field in which they have hitherto been engaged and, as I have held, has been demonstrated to be so extensive that its used by the defendants on goods such as their coloured plastic garden sprinklers would mislead a very substantial number of persons who would think such use denoted the plaintiffs' goods or some association or connection with the plaintiffs. Mr Morcom further argued, in support of his main submission on damage, that, in the absence of any common field of activity, actual or potential, ie potential, as he explained, in the sense of a natural extension of the field of the plaintiffs' existing trade, there is no basis on which any injury to the business or goodwill of the plaintiff can be foreseen, apart from exceptional cases where some dishonest activity facilitates the finding that such injury is reasonably foreseeable. It seems to me that that argument cannot be right; as I have already pointed out, in Lord Diplock's formulation of the necessary characteristics to found a cause of action in passing off, there is no limitation as to the relation of the field of activity of the defendant to that of the plaintiff and, indeed, as I have also mentioned, Mr Morcom conceded, rightly in my view, that he could not submit that, as a matter of law, passing off could never be established when the respective activities of the plaintiff and the defendant were completely unrelated. If passing off can be established in a case where the respective activities of plaintiff and defendant are completely unrelated, it must follow that in such a case injury to the plaintiffs' business or goodwill must be reasonably foreseeable, notwithstanding the absence of any common field of activity, actual or potential, in Mr Morcom's narrow sense.

In the result, in my judgment, the plaintiffs have established their case of passing off against the defendants and the action succeeds.

5.1.4.5   *Stringfellow v McCain Foods* [1984] R.P.C. 501 (C.A.)

The first plaintiff set up a nightclub, "Stringfellows", in St Martins Lane, London in 1980. It soon established considerable éclat as a haunt of the young and trendy. The defendant company, having built a considerable business in oven chips – frozen chips needing to be heated only under the grill or in the oven – decided to launch a new line of long and thin oven chips using the name "Stringfellows". The name was found to have been honestly chosen without the least expectation that any benefit could be derived from any association with the plaintiff's club. The first television advertising for the chips, however, gave the appearance of a disco to a domestic kitchen and involved disco dancing by a boy and his two sisters. It was this advertisement in particular which caused the plaintiff to seek relief against passing off, alleging that damage to his reputation would flow from a supposed association between the chips and his club. The plaintiffs had a public opinion survey conducted upon understandings of the word "Stringfellows", which was subject to a degree of criticism but not rejected out of hand as evidence by the C.A. Neither this evidence nor that of other witnesses served to convince the C.A. that there had been any misrepresentation of the relevant kind up to the appearance of the television advertisement.

On the question of overlap of fields which formed part of this discussion, Slade L.J. remarked:

The only tenuous overlap between the respective fields of activities of the plaintiff and of McCain is that McCain market foodstuffs while the plaintiffs sell food in the restaurant at their night club. But frozen foods and potato chips are some of the last kinds of food which would be readily associated in the minds of the public with a high-class, "up-market" restaurant, so that the relevant overlap is very small. The answers to R.S.G.B.'s questionnaires show that a fair proportion of the public (22% of the sample) associate the word "Stringfellows" with a club, night-club or discotheque. But, as Walton J. pointed out in his judgment on the motion, the word is far from being a household word as was, for example, the word "Lego" which fell to be considered by Falconer J. in *Lego Systems A/S v Lego M Lemelstrick Limited* [1983] F.S.R. 155. The word "Stringfellow" unlike Lego, is an ordinary surname which, at least in certain parts of the country, is not uncommon. McCain, on the other hand, have a national reputation as purveyors of frozen foods, with their products bought and consumed by very large numbers of the population, as I have already indicated. A member of the public (albeit one already acquainted with the name of the Club), on simply seeing a packet of frozen potato chips clearly marked with the words "McCain Stringfellows Long Thin Oven

Ready Fries" (not just "Stringfellows Long Thin Oven Ready Fries") would, in my opinion, be most unlikely to draw the inference that there was any connection at all between the chips and Mr Peter Stringfellow or the Club. If he were to draw that inference, it would in my opinion to be an unreasonable one, which was not justified by the form in which the product had been presented to him. The reasonable inference would be that this was another frozen food product put on the market by McCain, to which they had chosen to attach the name Stringfellows because the chips in question were "long and thin".

The advertisement was, however, found unwittingly to involve a degree of misrepresenta-tion. Even so, following Lord Diplock's speech in the "Advocaat" case, it was necessary to establish damage or a likelihood of damage ensuing to the plaintiffs. After rejecting the one piece of evidence proffered to show actual refusal to deal with the plaintiff because of his supposed connection with the chips, the court considered whether there was sufficient likelihood of damage. It rejected as "little more than speculation based on no solid evidence" the trial judge's view that there would be a likely loss of bookings at the club. Slade J. proceeded:

I now turn to the remaining suggested head of likely damage. Mr Jones, Mr Patrick and Mr Townley, in what in the course of the proceedings have been referred to as "expert reports", gave evidence in regard to modern practices in relation to intellectual property licences. Mr Jones, for example, described in a little detail how licensing of such right can take the form of (*inter alia*) "franchising", "merchandising", "sponsor-ship" and "endorsement". All these three witnesses expressed the opinion, albeit in rather different words, that any association of the club with an oven-baked chip product would be likely to damage the image of the Club and to prejudice the plaintiffs' chances of valuable exploitation of the goodwill attached to the name "Stringfellows".

The status of the evidence of these three witnesses is by no means clear to me, but no objection has been taken to its admissibility. The Judge, having referred to this evidence, said (at page 24) that it established that:

> "the grant of merchandising rights of this character is now a matter of frequent occurrence, although with the exception of a possible inference that might be drawn from the registration of a trade mark by a club and the example of the Playboy Club backed up of course by the Playboy magazine, they could point to no other cases concerned with the grant of merchandising rights by an organiz-ation such as the plaintiffs".

He went on to say (ibid):

> "It does plainly emerge that this was thought to be an activity in which the plaintiffs might reasonably want to indulge and that if the impression got around that rights of this character were being granted by the plaintiffs to manufacturers of frozen chips, then it was unlikely to prove attractive to persons who might want to use the name in the luxury goods field".

Much later in his judgment, having referred to the possible loss of customers for special functions, he said (at pp. 38–39):

> "The same reasoning may apply so far as other potential sponsors are concerned, at least other potential sponsors selling products in what might be described as the high quality trade or at least expensive products ... Experience in these Courts alone has shown that in recent years there has been a vast extension in the field of franchising. The grant of rights of user by the owners of well known names in connection with products other than the original owners' products or business,

is a commonplace of today".

Mr Jacob, while not disputing that the practice of licensing merchandising rights is a common one and has indeed existed for many years, pointed out that the plaintiffs have not achieved a registration of the name "Stringfellows" under the Trade Marks Act 1938. He submitted that they could not grant a licence for the use of this name which would have any legal validity; he referred us to *Star Industrial Co Ltd v Yap Kwee Kor* [1976] F.S.R. 256.

For the purposes of this present appeal, I do not find it necessary to explore any of the niceties of the law relating to the grant of merchandising rights in respect of a name which has not been registered as a trade mark. For such purposes I am quite prepared to assume, without deciding that in many instances a person carrying on a business under a particular name (albeit not registered as a trade mark) to which a valuable goodwill is attached, may be able in practice to exploit that name to great profit in one or more of the ways suggested by Mr Jones, Mr Patrick or Mr Townley.

I do not, however, regard the evidence of these witnesses or any other witnesses in this case as having established either:

(i) that, but for the television advertisement, the plaintiffs would have been able profitably to exploit merchandising rights in the name "Stringfellows"; or

(ii) that the showing of the television advertisement has prejudiced or is really likely to prejudice such chances of profitable exploitation of this nature as they may possess.

(If I am right, it is only the television advertisement which has involved any misrepresentation). As to (i), presumably in view of their fears of tarnishing their image, the plaintiffs would only wish to grant licences (if at all) in connection with goods of a luxury or "up-market" variety, such as clothes or jewellery. But how many, if any, persons marketing goods of this nature would expect to derive any potential benefit from the use of the name of a night club, albeit a celebrated night club? The name "Stringfellows" is not a fancy name. It is a surname which, at least in some parts of the country, is not an uncommon one. Nor is it a name connected with a person, such as a sportsman who has a particular expertise and for the purpose of his job requires particular equipment, the quality of which he can endorse by lending his name. So far as the evidence shows, the plaintiffs possess no relevant copyright (save perhaps their logo) in connection with which they can grant licences. In all the circumstances I do not think it surprising that Mr Stringfellow for all his business acumen, had never contemplated the exploitation of the name in this manner until the present dispute arose. When it was put to him in cross-examination that he had never done anything about franchising the use of his name, he replied with characteristic frankness: "No, sir. The honest truth of that is that McCain's advert has woken me up that I should have been making moves. They jumped the gun on me". But, since the evidence does not show that McCain itself has derived, or is likely to derive, any benefit at all from any association of its product with the Club, McCain itself presumably would not have been in the market as a potential franchise. In my opinion, the evidence as a whole gives no solid basis for inferring that, but for the television advertisement, the plaintiffs would have been in a position profitably to exploit merchandising rights in the name Stringfellows.

5.1.5 Injurious Falsehood

5.1.5.1 *Wilts United Dairies v Robinson* [1957] R.P.C. 220; [1958] R.P.C. 94; (Stable J.)

The plaintiffs were well-known manufacturers of condensed milk under the brand "British Maid". The Ministry of Food acquired a stock of it. When it became too old for ordinary use, it was sold off on condition that it be used only in manufacturing, for animal feed or for export. The defendant company indirectly purchased large quantities of this, in circumstances where (it was held) it must have known that milk was old stock purchased from the Ministry. It resold at considerable profit. It was found that this conduct amounted to passing off.

On the issue of injurious falsehood, the question arose whether the defendant had been shown to have acted maliciously, given that it did not intend to injure the plaintiff.

Stable J.:

When the Court rose I was passing to consider the question of malice in relation to injurious falsehood. There are three authorities I should like to refer to. The first is *Mogul Steamship Coy Ltd v MacGregor, Gow & Coy & Ors*, the well-known case reported at [1892] A.C. 25, and more particularly the passage from Lord Field's speech at page 52. He says: "It follows therefore from this authority, and is undoubted law not only that it is not every act causing damage to another in his trade, nor even every intentional act of such damage, which is actionable, but also that acts done by a trader in the lawful way of his business, although by the necessary results of effective competition interfering injuriously with the trade of another, are not the subject of any action. Of course it is otherwise, as pointed out by Lord Holt, if the acts complained of, although done in the way and under the guise of competition or other lawful right, are in themselves violent or purely malicious, or have for their ultimate object injury to another from ill-will to him, and not the pursuit of lawful rights".

Pausing there, Lord Field says, "It follows ... and is undoubted law not only that it is not every act causing damage to another actionable, but also that acts done by a trader in the lawful way of his business, although by the necessary results of effective competition interfering injuriously with the trade of another are not the subject of any action". It seems to me that the difficulty there is to decide whether the acts done by the trader in the way of his business were lawful or not.

Then Lord Field goes on: "No doubt, also, there have been cases in which agreements to do acts injurious to others have been held to be indictable as amounting to conspiracy, the ultimate object or the means being unlawful, although if done by an individual no such consequence would have followed". Then this is the important part in relation to the present case: "... but I think that in all such cases it will be found that there existed either an ultimate object of malice, or wrong, or wrongful means of execution involving elements of injury to the public, or, at least, negativing the pursuit of a lawful object". He is saying: "... in all such cases it will be found that there existed either an ultimate object of malice, or wrong, or wrongful means of execution involving elements of injury".

The next case which I think has a very strong bearing on the problem is that of *Greers Ltd v Pearman & Corder Ltd* (1922) 39 R.P.C. 406 at pp. 412 and 417. That is an interesting case, because that was an appeal to the Court of Appeal from a decision arrived at the trial of the case before Bray J. and a jury. It is quite obvious, from reading the report and Bray J.'s summing-up, that in the Judge's view the action should have failed: but the matter was left to the jury, the jury found malice, and the Court of Appeal refused to interfere with that finding because they said that there was evidence from which the jury did infer malice, although I think they pretty clearly indicated, as did the learned Judge, that if it had been left to them or him no such inference would have been drawn.

The assistance to be derived from that case in the present one is partly in the direction in the summing-up which tacitly was approved by the Court of Appeal, and the observations, in particular, of Scrutton L.J. What Bray J. said to the jury at page 412 was this: "Members of the jury, it is a question for you, only I impress upon you that it is for the Plaintiffs to satisfy you that this man knew he had no right, in which case undoubtedly he would be actuated by malice, but if he acted *bona fide*, fairly believing, though wrongly believing, that they had the right to the protection of this name, having used it ever since 1905 – if you think he *bona fide* believed that – and it is not for the Defendants to prove it, but for the Plaintiffs to prove the contrary, then I do not see what evidence of malice there is about it". The Judge is directing the jury there that if a man says something that he knows to be untrue, it is malicious *ipso facto*, because he has said something that is false and something that he knows to be false, regardless of whether his object in making the false statement was his own advantage or the detriment of someone else.

Lord Justice Scrutton, at page 417, says: "The action is one for a form of what is called slander of title – for slander of goods, for making defamatory statements about a man's goods which are actionable if they are untrue, and cause him special damage and are made maliciously". We can eliminate the special damage now because the law has changed. "The only question in this case is – is there evidence on which the jury could find that the statements were made maliciously? 'Maliciously', not in the sense of illegally, but in the sense of being made with some indirect or dishonest motive. Honest belief in an unfounded claim is not malice: but the nature of the unfounded claim may be evidence that there was not an honest belief in it. It may be so unfounded that the particular fact that is put forward may be evidence that it is not honestly believed".

The Lord Justice there apparently is agreeing with the direction that the Judge gave the jury, namely, that quite apart from what object you had in mind, if you state something which is defamatory of somebody else's goods and you know what you say is untrue then (although your object and your only object may be your own benefit, although you have no intentional wish or desire to harm) the mere uttering of the untrue statement with knowledge that it is untrue is malice.

Balden v Shorter [1933] 1 Ch. 427 was an action for injurious falsehood. It was a case in which what the defendant had said was wholly inaccurate: it was injurious to the plaintiff. Lord Maugham – Maugham J. as he then was – decided that the man acted in good faith and honestly believed the truth of what he had said. What Lord Maugham said, at page 429 was this: "If I could properly conclude that the story told in the witness box by Mr Bensted was untrue and that he knew that the plaintiff was not employed by the defendants, I should have little difficulty in determining the action in the plaintiff's favour because, if Mr Bensted said that knowing it to be untrue, I should draw the inference that he did it from a dishonest motive and maliciously. But I cannot come to that conclusion". Of course, it may be that the learned Judge meant this: "If I come to the conclusion that what Mr Bensted said was untrue and that he knew it was untrue, it would be a fair inference that he did that with the object of harming the plaintiff". That passage taken literally means no more than this – that knowledge of the falsity is evidence of improper motive, therefore of malice, which is very different from saying that to utter a statement known to be false in such a context is malice irrespective of the motive with which the falsehood is uttered. Looking at the judgment as a whole I do not think the learned Judge intended to give such a restricted meaning to malice.

Then at page 430 Lord Maugham says this: "The meaning of 'malice' in connection with injurious falsehood is dealt with in Salmond on Torts, 7th edition, pages 582–583, in the following passage, which I accept as correct". Then, quoting from "Salmond": "What is meant by malice in this connection? Lord Davey, in the passage already cited – *Royal Baking Powder Coy v Wright, Crossley & Coy* (1901) 18 R.P.C. 95, at page 99 – defines it as meaning the absence of just cause or excuse. It is to be observed, however, that this is not one of the recognised meanings of the term malice in other connections; an act done without just cause or excuse is wrongful but not necessarily malicious: for example, a trespass by mistake on another man's land, or the conversion of his chattels under an erroneous claim of right. Notwithstanding Lord Davey's *dictum*, it is now apparently settled that malice in the law of slander of title and other forms of injurious falsehood means some dishonest or otherwise improper motive". Then these are the words that I think are important: "A *bona fide* assertion of title, however mistaken, if made for the protection of one's own interest or for some other proper purpose, is not 'malicious'". I emphasise the words "*bona fide*".

Lord Maugham proceeds: "In *Greers Ltd v Pearman & Corder Ltd* (1922) 39 R.P.C. 406 Lord Justice Bankes said that 'maliciously' for the purpose which the Court was considering meant 'with some indirect object', and Lord Justice Scrutton remarked that the only question in the case was whether there was evidence on which the jury could find that the statements were made maliciously 'in the sense of being made with some indirect or dishonest motive'".

So much for the authorities. As I understand the law it is this, that if you publish a defamatory statement about a man's goods which is injurious to him, honestly believing that it is true, your object being your own advantage and no detriment to him, you obviously are not liable. If you publish a statement which turns out to be false but which you honestly believe to be true, but you publish that statement not for the purpose of protecting your own interests and achieving some advantage to yourself but for the purpose of doing him harm, and it transpires, contrary to your belief, that the statement that you believed to be true has turned out to be false, notwithstanding the *bona fides* of your belief because the object that you had in mind was to injure him and not to advantage yourself, you would be liable for an injurious falsehood.

The third proposition which I derive from the cases is this, that if you publish an injurious falsehood which you know to be false, albeit that your only object is your own advantage and with no intention or desire to injure the person in relation to whose goods the falsehood is published then provided that it is clear from the nature of the falsehood that it is intrinsically injurious – I say "intrinsically", meaning not deliberately aimed with intent to injure but as being inherent in the statement itself, the defendant is responsible, the malice consisting in the fact that what he published he knew to be false.

To summarise that, I have come to the conclusion here that the representation was that this was what I may call the Plaintiffs' current milk, which the Defendants knew perfectly well that it was not: that their intention or object in selling the milk, making the representations and all the rest of it, was their own advantage and nothing else and own advantage, profit or gain; but the fact that they knew what they were saying was intrinsically injurious and they knew it was not true constitutes malice and therefore they are liable at the suit of the Plaintiff under the heading of injurious falsehood.

5.1.5.2 *White v Mellin* [1895] A.C. 156 (H.L.)

The defendant, Timothy White, the retail chemist, sold Mellin's infant food, attaching to it a label proclaiming the virtues of Vance's infant food. Mellin sought an injunction to prevent this practice on the ground of injurious falsehood.

Lord Herschell:

Now, my Lords, the only statement made by the defendant by means of the advertisement is this: that Vance's food was the most healthful and nutritious for infants and invalids that had been offered to the public. The statement was perfectly general, and would apply in its terms not only to the respondent's infants' food but to all others that were offered to the public. I will take it as sufficiently pointed at the plaintiff's food by reason of its being affixed to a bottle of the plaintiff's food when sold, and that it does disparage the plaintiff's goods by asserting that they are not as healthful and as nutritious as those recommended by the defendant. The question then arises, has it been proved on the plaintiff's own evidence that that was a false disparagement of the plaintiff's goods?

I will state what I understand to be the result of the plaintiff's evidence. Mellin's food for infants and invalids is a preparation of such a nature that the food is said to be predigested, and therefore not to make that call upon the digestion which food ordinarily does; that as regards children under six months of age Mellin's food is the only one which could be suitably used in the place of the ordinary means of nourishment, the mother's milk, and that any farinaceous food would at that age be not only not nutritious but prejudicial. And so far, accepting the plaintiff's evidence for this purpose, there being no evidence to the contrary, the plaintiff, I think, establishes that his food was specially meritorious for that class of cases, and that it would not be correct to say that as regards these children of very tender age Vance's food or any other farinaceous food would be not only more healthful and nutritious, but as healthful and nutritious. But then it appears that when a child has passed the age up to which nutrition at the breast may ordinarily be said to continue, the use of some farinaceous food is not only not prejudicial but desirable, and that if the child were to be always brought up upon a food which would be suitable during the very earliest weeks or months, its digestion would be likely to suffer rather than benefit, and there would be not more, but less nourishment. After twelve months, as I understand the evidence, the farinaceous food would be distinctly better for the purposes of nutrition and health than this pre-digested food.

Why is it to be supposed that any one buying this bottle at the chemist's would be led to believe that Mellin's food which he has bought was not a good article or not as good an article as another, merely because a person who obviously was seeking to push a rival article said that his article was better? My Lords, why should people give such a special weight to this anonymous puff of Vance's food, obviously the work of someone who wanted to sell it, as that it should lead him to determine to buy it instead of Mellin's foods, which was said to be recommended by the faculty as the best for infants and invalids? I confess I do not wonder that the plaintiff did not insist that he had sustained injury by what the defendant had done. There is an entire absence of any evidence that the statement complained of either had injured or was calculated to injure the plaintiff. If so, then the case is not brought even within the definition of the law which Lindley L.J. gives.

Lopes L.J. adds the word "maliciously", that "it is actionable to publish maliciously without lawful occasion a false statement disparaging the goods of another person". By that it may be intended to indicate that the object of the publication must be to injure another person, and that the advertisement is not published *bona fide* merely to sell the advertiser's own goods, or at all events, that he published it with a knowledge of its falsity. One or other of those elements, it seems to me must be intended by the addition of the word "maliciously". Both those are certainly absent here. There is nothing to show that the object of the defendant was other than to puff his own goods and so sell them, nor is there anything to show that he did not believe that his food was better than any other.

Lord Herschell then reviewed Western Counties v Lawes Chemical *(L.R. 9 Ex. 218);* Evans v Harlow *(5 Q.B. 624);* Canham v Jones *(2 V. & B. 218). He continued:*

But, My Lords, I cannot help saying that I entertain very grave doubts whether any action could be maintained for an alleged disparagement of another's goods, merely on the allegation that the goods sold by the party who is alleged to have disparaged his competitor's goods are better either generally or in this or that particular respect than his competitor's are. Of course, I put aside the question (it is not necessary to consider it) whether where a person intending to injure another, and not in the exercise of his own trade and vaunting his own goods, has maliciously and falsely disparaged the goods of another, an action will lie; I am dealing with the class of cases which is now before us where the only disparagement consists in vaunting the superiority of the defendant's own goods. In *Evans v Harlow* Lord Denman expressed himself thus: "The gist of the complaint is the defendant's telling the world that the lubricators sold by the plaintiff were not good for their purpose, but wasted the tallow. A tradesman offering goods for sale exposes himself to observations of this kind, and it is not by averring them to be 'false, scandalous, malicious and defamatory' that the plaintiff can found a charge of libel upon them. To decide so would open a very wide door to litigation, and might expose every man who said his goods were better than another's to the risk of an action". My Lords, those observations seem to me to be replete with good sense. It is to be observed that *Evans v Harlow* does not appear to have been decided on the ground merely that there was no allegation of special damage. The only judge who alludes to the absence of such an allegation is Patteson J. No reference to it is to be found either in the judgment of Lord Denman or in the judgment of Wightman J., the other two judges who took part in that decision; and I think it is impossible not to see that, as Lord Denman says, a very wide door indeed would be opened to litigation and that the Courts might be constantly employed in trying the relative merits of rival productions, if an action of this kind were allowed.

Mr Moulton sought to distinguish the present case by saying that all that Lord Denman referred to was one tradesman saying that his goods were better than his rival's. That, he said, is a matter of opinion, but whether they are more healthful and more nutritious is a question of fact. My Lords, I do not think it is possible to draw such a distinction. The allegation of a tradesman that his goods are better than his neighbour's very often involves only the consideration whether they possess one or two qualities superior to the other. Of course "better" means better as regards the purpose for which they are intended, and the question of better or worse in many cases depends simply upon one or two or three issues of fact. If an action will not lie because a man says that his goods are better than his neighbour's, it seems to me impossible to say that it will lie because he says that they are better in this or that or the other respect. Just consider what a door would be opened if this were permitted. That this sort of puffing advertisement is in use is notorious; and we see rival cures advertised for particular ailments. The Court would then be bound to inquire, in an action brought, whether this ointment or this pill better cured the disease which it was alleged to cure – whether a particular article of food was in this respect or that better than another. Indeed, the Courts of law would be turned into a machinery for advertising rival productions by obtaining a judicial determination which of the two was the better. As I said, advertisements and announcements of that description have been common enough; but the case of *Evans v Harlow* was decided in the year 1844, somewhat over half a century ago, and the fact that no such action – unless it be *Western Counties Manure Co v Lawes Chemical Manure Co* – has ever been maintained in the Courts of Justice is very strong indeed to show that it is not maintainable. It is, indeed, unnecessary to decide the point in order to dispose of the present appeal.

For the reasons which I have given I have come to the conclusion that the judgment of the Court below cannot be sustained, even assuming the law to be as stated by the learned judges; but inasmuch as the case is one of the great importance and some additional colour would be lent to the idea that an action of this description was maintainable by the observations in the Court below, I have thought it only right to express my grave doubts whether any such action could be maintained even if the facts brought the case within the law there laid down.

Upon the whole, therefore, I think that the judgment of Romer J. was right and ought to be restored and that this appeal should be allowed, with the usual result as to costs; and I so move your Lordships.

5.1.5.3 *De Beers v International General Electric* [1975] F.S.R. 323 (Walton J.)

Both plaintiffs and defendants manufactured and distributed abrasives made from diamonds. The plaintiffs' abrasives were made from natural diamonds, whereas those of the defendants' were made from synthetic diamonds. The second defendant caused to be circulated among prospective purchasers of such abrasives, a pamphlet which purported to show the results of comparative scientific tests on the products of the plaintiffs and defendants, carried out by the "Application Laboratory". This comparison purported to show that the plaintiffs' abrasives were distinctly inferior to those of the defendants. The plaintiffs, alleging that the pamphlet contained a number of mis-statements and was misleading, issued a writ claiming damages and an injunction restraining the defendants from publishing this pamphlet or any document containing mis-statements reflecting adversely on the plaintiffs' abrasives. Their claim was put on the two alternative bases of defamation of goods, and of unlawful inference and/or unfair competition in trade. The defendants applied for the statement of claim to be struck out on the ground, inter alia, *that it disclosed no reasonable cause of action.*

Walton J.:

What precisely is the law on this point? It is a blinding glimpse of the obvious to say that there must be a dividing line between statements that are actionable and those which are not; and the sole question of a dry point of law such as we are discussing there is: where does that line lie? On the one hand, it appears to me that the law is that any trader is entitled to puff his own goods, even though such puff must, as a matter of pure logic, involve the denigration of his rival's goods. Thus in the well-known case of the three adjoining tailors who put notices in their respective windows reading: "The best tailor in the world", "The best tailor in this town", and "The best tailor in this street" none of the three committed an actionable offence.

This is, I think, a proposition which extends to a much wider field than the slander of goods; for example, I think it extends to other vague commendatory statements about goods or services on offer. Principal among its application has been the case of auctioneers, who, within limits, have always been allowed to use language which is strictly perhaps not literally true; thus, for example, to take note of one instance, in *Hope v Walter* [1900] 1 Ch. D. 257 Lindley L.J., as he then was, stated "I do not attach any importance to the word 'eligible': it is the ordinary auctioneer's language". In other words, in the kind of situation when one expects, as a matter of ordinary common experience, a person to use a certain amount of hyperbole in the description of goods, property or services, the courts will do what any ordinary reasonable man would do, namely, take it with a large pinch of salt.

Where, however, the situation is not that the trader is puffing his own goods, but turns to denigrate those of his rival, then, in my opinion, the situation is not so clear cut. Obviously the statement: "My goods are better than X's" is only a more dramatic presentation of what is implicit in the statement: "My goods are the best in the world". Accordingly, I do not think such a statement would be actionable. At the other end of the scale, if what is said is: "My goods are better than X's, because X's are absolute rubbish", then it is established by *dicta* of Lord Shand in the House of Lords in *White v Mellin* (above, 5.1.5.2) which were accepted by Mr Walton as stating the law, the statement would be actionable.

Between these two kinds of statements there is obviously still an extremely wide field; and it appears to me that, in order to draw the line, one must apply this test, namely, whether a reasonable man would take the claim being made as being a serious claim or not.

There then followed *White v Mellin*. This was a case where one product was wrapped in a wrapper advertising another's goods as being superior, but without any direct disparagement of the goods of the first. There was, I think, a considerable diversity of opinion in the House upon that case, and it is very hard to find a completely satisfactory short statement of the law; the speeches cover a very great deal of ground. But I think that what has emerged as being the general approach of the courts is to be found in the speech of Lord Watson at page 167, where he said: "In order to constitute disparagement which is, in the sense of law, injurious, it must be shown that the defendant's representations were made of and concerning the plaintiff's goods; that they were in disparagement of his goods and untrue; and that they have occasioned special damage to the plaintiff. Unless each and all of these three things be established, it must be held that the defendant has acted within his rights and that the plaintiff has not suffered any legal injuria". Of course, the third matter – that they have occasioned special damage to the plaintiff – is now no longer required.

The next case is *Linotype Company Limited v British Empire Type-Setting Machine Company Limited* (1899) 81 L.T. 331 which went to the House of Lords; but that was a case of libel beyond any question, where the attack shifted from the goods purveyed to the purveyor of the goods; and, in my view, the headnote correctly reflects the decision. It says: "If the only meaning which can be reasonably attached to a writing is that it is a criticism upon the goods or manufacture of a trader, it cannot be the subject of an action for libel, but an imputation upon a man in the way of his trade is properly the subject of an action without proof of special damage ... Whether in any particular case the words complained of are susceptible of a defamatory meaning, or are simply a disparagement of goods, is for the jury".

In a sense, that case was the converse of the case of *Evans v Harlow* (5 Q.B. 624). It is true that the Lord Chancellor therein uses some language which might be thought, if taken at face value, to endorse the proposition that no reflection upon the plaintiffs' goods or machines could ever form the subject matter of an action; but, as it stands, it is obviously far too wide and I do not think he intended it to be taken in that sense in any event.

The next case was *Hubbuck & Sons Limited v Wilkinson, Heywood & Clark Limited* [1899] 1 Q.B. 86. In this case, the defendant bruited abroad what purported to be the results of a comparison test of some description between his paint and the plaintiffs' paint. If, however, one first gets rid of a certain flavour – and the Court of Appeal got rid of the flavour – which was imparted to the case by the use of the word "genuine" as applied to the defendants' paint as not in fact meaning that the plaintiffs' paint was other than genuine, the test became a rather simple one; and, so far as I can see, of a purely subjective nature. The conclusion of it was that, for all practical purposes, the two paints could be regarded as equal. The sting, of course, was that the defendants' paint was much cheaper.

The facts of this case bear some faint similarity to the facts of the present case, in that there was or purported to be a test of some description; but I do not think that a test ending up with such a statement (that is, that the two paints can be regarded as equal) can really be regarded as something which any reasonable man can be expected to take very seriously. There was in any event no real disparagement or untrue statement made about the plaintiffs' paint. It is hard to distinguish the whole affair from the statement "Our paint is as good as anybody else's", when a stronger statement still could obviously have been made with impunity.

The next case was *Alcott v Millar's Karri and Jarrah Forests Limited* [1904] 91 L.T. 722. Here a letter was written to a third party in terms which that third party must have taken seriously, to the effect that the plaintiff's wooden road blocks would only last 18 months. I think that was an extreme case, and I do not think that anybody would be surprised that the action laid there accordingly.

The next case is *Lyne v Nicholls* (1906) 23 T.L.R. 86. Unfortunately, there was no plea of special damage, so that this action failed; but it was in substance held by Swinfen-Eady J. that the statement that the circulation of a particular newspaper was "twenty to one of any other weekly paper in the district", and that, "where others count by the dozen, we count by the hundred", were not merely puffs, but were to be taken seriously. Mr Walton submitted that this case was plainly at variance with the earlier cases. On the contrary, I find it fully in line with them, properly understood.

The last case is *London Ferro-Concrete Company Limited v Justicz* (1951) 68 R.P.C. 65. In this case the defendant did not content himself with saying that his methods were better than the plaintiffs'; he said that the plaintiffs' methods were inadequate. Again, that was a statement which any outside third party would be likely to take seriously.

After this brief review of the relevant authorities I see no inconsistency between any of them; and I therefore now proceed to ask the question: can I be so certain that nobody would have taken the results of Tech-Data/1 seriously that I should grant the relief sought by the defendants and strike out the statement of claim? I do not feel able to do so in any way at all. It appears to me that, where the interested parties are presented with what purports to be a proper scientific test, properly carried out by the "Application Laboratory" (whatever that is) they must be intended by the persons who furnished them with this information to take it all very seriously indeed. Such a report framed as the present report is so framed cannot be dismissed in any way as a mere idle puff. It may well of course be that that is all in fact it is; but, if so, then the defendants have only themselves to blame for having dressed up a stupid old moke as a thoroughbred Arabian stallion.

If traders take the time and trouble to dress up their advertising material in this manner, then I think they must stand by it; and, if it contains, as in the case here, statements in disparagement of the plaintiffs' goods and if, further, on investigation those statements prove to be false and the plaintiff can show malice, the precise constituents of which for present purposes I think it is better not to investigate, it appears to me that they must answer for it.

Mr Walton in substance submitted that such a conclusion would mean that the courts would be used as a forum for advertising the plaintiffs' wares by means of a judicial decision that their goods were better than the defendants'. Nothing, I think, is further from the truth. All the courts will decide is whether a specific statement, which may of course be express or implied, made concerning the plaintiffs' goods or services is or is not untrue. This appears to me to be a task which the courts are well fitted to perform; which they have on numerous occasions in the past performed; and which they will continue to perform as and when necessary.

This conclusion renders it strictly unnecessary for me to deal with Mr Dillon's second point on the question of unlawful interference and/or unfair competition; and in fact I do not propose to deal with it. Whilst I am indebted to both Mr Dillon and Mr Walton for very interesting arguments on these branches of the law, it must be recognised that there are now very rapidly developing branches of it; and, that being so, I think it is unwise for any judge before whom the suggestion that there is unlawful interference or unfair competition comes to express any views on the matter unless it becomes absolutely necessary. Therefore, I am not going to deal with those questions at all, but I wish to make it perfectly plain that I intend thereby no disrespect whatsoever to the respective arguments which on both sides were very compelling indeed.

5.1.5.4 *Customglass Boats v Salthouse Brothers* [1976] R.P.C. 589 (Mahon J., S.C.N.Z.)

The plaintiff had previously manufactured "Cavalier" boats designed by Salthouses, one of the defendants. The defendants parted company from the plaintiff in circumstances leading to successful proceedings for passing off. In those proceedings Salthouse counterclaimed that the plaintiff's repeated statement that it designed the "Cavaliers" amounted to injurious falsehood. In finding in his favour on this issue, Mahon J. said:

The first ingredient of slander of title is malicious publication. The initial publication in this case arose from negligence, no doubt vicarious, but the repetition of the false statement after due warning from the second defendant was not excusable through inability to amend the advertisements and thus from the date of objection by the second defendant the further publications have been in my opinion malicious, using that term not colloquially but in the special sense attaching to it in the area of injurious falsehood. That sense includes an intent to injure the true owner of the property or, alternatively, publication with an indirect or dishonest motive: *Balden v Shorter* [1933] Ch. 427. The formulation preferred in *Joyce v Motor Surveys Ltd* [1948] Ch. 252 was "an intent to injure without just cause or excuse". This case is near the borderline between mere negligence and reckless disregard of the consequences of a known mis-statement, but I think it falls within the latter category and is thus a case of malicious publication.

The elements of the tort are, therefore, proved by the second defendant except special damage, but on the latter point Mr Gault relies upon section 5(1) of the Defamation Act 1954* which reads:

---

* Equivalent to Defamation Act 1952 (UK), section 3.

"In an action for slander of title, slander of goods, or other malicious falsehood, it shall not be necessary to allege or prove special damage if the words upon which the action is founded are calculated to cause pecuniary damage to the plaintiff".

The word "calculated" in this context is equivalent to "likely". The second defendant, Mr Robert Salthouse, has an established reputation as a designer of yachts and other craft. Yachting experts would not be deceived by the advertisements but potential purchasers of yachts might be deceived. There may be people who wish to have built a yacht designed to their own general specifications by the designer of the successful Cavalier 32 which is built by the Customglass company. Such people might go to either of the plaintiffs with a request that a yacht be built by them to a special design to be agreed upon. Perhaps the plaintiffs would answer that they only build production line yachts. But even so, the risk of loss of trade to the second defendant would exist. He might in such a case lose the royalty or fee otherwise receivable by him for a design to be used by the Salthouse company, or another company in building a yacht to the order of a specific client. I think, therefore, that the slander of title here established is within section 5(1) of the Defamation Act 1954, and that actual damage need not be proved.

5.2 Registered Trade and Service Marks

5.2.1 Basic Matters

5.2.1.1 Note on Trade Marks Act 1938 as amended

The Act was amended by the Trade Marks (Amendment) Act 1984 and the Patents, Designs and Marks Act 1986, so as to introduce the registration of marks for services alongside marks for goods. In effect two parallel statutes emerged, one for goods (i.e. trade) marks and the other for service marks. These can be found separately set out in Kerly's Law of Trade Marks and Names (12th ed., 1986) App.I (in parallel) and in C. Morcom, Service Marks (1987) App.3, 4 (seriatim). Both these presentations deal fully with minor difficulties relating to the texts. Here, for the sake of brevity, the separate versions will not be given in the text. Mostly the necessary variations will be indicated by an italicised alternative, e.g. "trade/service mark", "in relation to goods/services", etc. Where the differences are more complex, the alternative version for service marks is given in italics after the version for trade marks. In a few instances, sections of the Act are given only in their trade mark version.

5.2.1.2 Trade Marks Act 1938, s.2: Relation to Common Law Rights

S.2. No person shall be entitled to institute any proceeding to prevent, or to recover damages for, the infringement of an unregistered trade/*service* mark, but nothing in this Act shall be deemed to affect rights of action against any person for passing off or the remedies in respect thereof.

5.2.1.3 Trade Marks Act 1938, s.68: Definitions

S.68(1) In this Act, unless the context otherwise requires, the following expressions have the meanings hereby assigned to them respectively, that is to say:– ... "mark" includes a device, name, signature, word, letter, numeral, or any combination thereof. "Trade mark" means, except in relation to a certification trade mark, a mark used or proposed to be used in relation to goods for the purpose of indicating, or so as to indicate, a connection in the course of trade between the goods and some person having the right either as proprietor or as registered user to use. "Service mark" means "a mark ... used or proposed to be used in relation to services for the purpose of indicating, or so as to indicate, that a particular person is connected, in the course of business, with the provision of those services, whether with or without any indication of the identity of that person".

(2) References in this Act to the use of a mark shall be construed as references to the use of a printed or other visual representation of the mark, and references therein to the use of a mark in relation to goods shall be construed as references to the use thereof upon, or in physical or other relation to, goods.

(2B) References in this Act to a near resemblance of marks are references to a resemblance so near as to be likely to deceive or cause confusion.

5.2.1.4 *Aristoc v Rysta* [1945] A.C. 68 (H.L.)

The appellant, who manufactured stockings under the mark "Aristoc", opposed the registration of "Rysta" for stockings by the respondent. Of the three main grounds of opposition, the third arose from the respondent's proposed use of the mark to indicate that it had repaired second-hand stockings by an invisible mending process. This, it was argued, was not a proposed use of the mark as a trade mark (TMA 1938, s.68(1)). (The other grounds are dealt with below, 5.2.4.4). Of the third ground, Viscount Maugham said:

I now come to the third question, which is concerned with the true construction of the definition of a trade mark in Section 68(1) of the Trade Marks Act, 1938. This definition takes the place of the definition in Section 3 of the Trade Marks Act of 1905 which ran as follows: "A 'trade mark' shall mean a mark used or proposed to be used upon or in connection with goods for the purpose of indicating that they are the goods of the proprietor of such trade mark by virtue of manufacture, selection, certification, dealing with, or offering for sale".

The main difference between this section and the definition in the Act of 1938 (which I shall cite later) is in the words relating to the purpose of the mark. In the one case, the purpose is stated to be that of "indicating that they are the goods of the proprietor of such trade mark by virtue of manufacture, selection, certification, dealing with, or offering for sale". In the other, a much vaguer phrase is used, namely, indicating or so as to indicate "a connection in the course of trade" between the goods and the proprietor of the mark. I need not refer to the use by a registered user, which means the user under Section 28. It is not in dispute that the definition in Section 68(1) is wider than the older definition. The question is as to the extent of the alteration effected by the use of the words "in the course of trade".

My Lords, it seems to me beyond doubt that hitherto a registered trade mark has been understood as being used in relation to goods for the purpose of indicating the origin of the goods, in other words, for the purpose of indicating either manufacture or some other dealing with the goods in the process of manufacture or in the course of business before they are offered for sale to the public.

It must be remembered that in the early days when Trade Mark law was being slowly laid down, chiefly in Chancery Courts (where alone an injunction could be obtained), a trade mark was inevitably taken as indicating the origin of the goods. It was used for the purpose of indicating that the goods were those of the manufacturer or the merchant of the goods. It was closely connected with the goodwill of his business, of which it was often a valuable item, for the mark represented a quality or character on which the purchaser could place reliance.

The cases mentioned in the Introductory Chapters of Sebastian on Trade Marks (5th Edition) and Kerly on Trade Marks (6th Edition), which are too numerous to be cited here, are conclusive in my opinion to show that, until at any rate the recent Act, trade marks were always taken as indicative of the origin of the goods. The actual phrase is often used, and in other cases the same view is implicit. Bowen L.J. was not laying down any new law when he said: "It seems to me the answer is to be given by the simplest consideration of what is really the function of a trade mark. The function of a trade mark is to give an indication to the purchaser or possible purchaser as to the manufacture or quality of the goods – to give an indication to his eye of the trade source from which the goods come, or the trade hands through which they pass on their way to the market". (*In re Powell's Trade Mark* [1893] 2 Ch. 388, at pp. 403–4). This passage was not *obiter dictum*, but the reason for that part of the judgment. It has not infrequently been cited and so far as I know it has never been adversely criticised. I think it was undeniably correct in 1893.

In my opinion the same view was taken by the legislature when the Trade Marks Act,

1905, was passed, including for the first time a definition of a trade mark for the purpose of that Act. The purpose of a mark was said to be that of indicating that they (the goods) are the goods of the proprietor of such trade mark by virtue of manufacture, selection, certification, dealing with or offering for sale. It is argued that the words "dealing with" are sufficiently wide to cover any operation on the goods by a trader or workman after the goods have come into the hands of a member of the public, however slight the effect of the operation may be, and however little it indicates the origin of the goods or their character or quality. Having regard to the repeated statements in the authorities that a registrable mark must be an indication of origin and to the fact that the words "dealing with" (not, be it observed, "dealing in") are found in the midst of other words which have that general meaning, I am quite unable to take the view that the function of a trade mark was being so radically altered.

It is admitted by the Respondents, and it was indeed pointed out by the Assistant-Comptroller, that a trade mark could not be registered for a process or an operation; but the Assistant-Comptroller was of opinion that it could have the benefit of registration if the mark was for goods to which the process or the operation had been applied. The distinction can readily be understood by lawyers, but I doubt whether traders and the public will appreciate it. In a commercial sense and in substance it tends to give a trade mark for the process or operation; for it merely indicates that the process or operation has been applied. And there would seem to be nothing in the Act, if the Respondents are right, to require them to indicate by the mark the precise extent of the operation. It might be only for a single strand of the stocking or for the repair of one toe; yet the mark would be given for the stocking, a surprising result.

That a trade mark must still be related to origin was the view taken by my Lord Macmillan in this House in the case of *Bass Ratcliff & Gretton Ltd v Nicholson and Sons Ltd* ([1932] A.C. 130, at p.155) where he observed that a trade mark "must have been used for the purpose of indicating the origin of the goods in connection with which it is used".

The well known text books I have already referred to have taken the same view (see Sebastian on Trade Marks, 5th Edition, pp. 4 and 5; Kerly on Trade Marks 6th Edition at pp.27, 31, 35). A number of other cases might be cited, but I will add only one more, and that one of high authority.

In the case of *Irving's Yeast Vite v Horsenail* (51 R.P.C. 110 at p.111) the question was whether the word "Yeast-Vite" had been used as a trade mark. Lord Tomlin, in deciding that it had not been so used, said at p.115: "it is not a use of the word as a trade mark, that is, to indicate the origin of the goods in the Respondent by virtue of "manufacture, selection, certification, dealing with or offering for sale" and again, at p.116: "The phrase 'the exclusive right to the use of such trade mark' carries, in my opinion, the implication of use of the mark for the purpose of indicating in relation to the goods upon or in connection with which the use takes place, the origin of such goods the user of the mark by virtue of the matters indicated in the definition of 'trade mark' contained in Section 3".

These observations had reference to the definition of "trade mark" contained in Section 3 of the Trade Marks Act, 1905, as amended by the Act of 1919. The history of the matter affords further ground for the same view of the essential nature of a trade mark. It must be observed that there is a very striking difference between a mark intended to indicate origin and one intended to signify repair, cleaning, or some analogous process after, and it may be long after, the goods have come upon the market. The former will indicate a character or quality which will ordinarily remain so long as the goods remain recognisable. The latter may indicate a purely temporary connection with the goods such as repairing, washing, cleaning or adjusting them, and I am not able to see why the principle should not extend to the connection by warehousing or carrying the goods. Not only may the effect of such operation be quite ephemeral, but such operations may be repeated many times by different persons, and only one or some of these persons may desire to affix a trade marks to the goods. A washing mark or a cleaner's tab is usually affixed only to indicate that the articles are the property of a certain customer, that is, to prevent loss; but if the Respondents' view is right such persons may obtain a trade mark for the goods when washed or cleaned. In the course of a few years there may be, on the same hypothesis, half a dozen different marks attached to the goods each indicating that a laundryman or a cleaner has washed or cleaned the articles at some generally unknown time in the past – a matter of no interest to the owner of the goods and giving no information as to their character or quality. The usual phrase that the mark should be distinctive, meaning "adapted to distinguish the goods from those of other persons" (Sec. 9 of the Act of 1905) would seem to be curiously inappropriate if (to take an example) a number of piano-tuners or painters or overhaulers of motor cars or other mechanical instruments were to affix their respective marks from time to time. And it is clear that the value of the mark of origin, whether used by the maker or the merchant, would in some cases be rendered of little value. It is not clear to me that the purchaser of the article second-hand would be able to tell who was the maker or merchant on whose reputation he was disposed to rely. Many other and perhaps better illustrations might be given. My opinion is that until at any rate the recent Act there was no ground at all for the view that the basic meaning of the trade mark as a mark signifying origin had been altered by the Legislature.

Viscount Maugham set out the then current definition of "trade mark" in the 1938 Act, s.68 (above, 5.2.1.3), and continued:

There is also an amendment (as, contrasted with the Act of 1905) in Sec. 9 as to the distinctiveness requisite for registration in Part A. There is there a reference to the quality of distinguishing "goods with which the proprietor of the trade mark is or may be connected in the course of trade from goods in the case of which no such connection subsists". The present tense should be noted. Have these amendments or has anything else in the Act altered the essential nature of a trade mark as being generally limited to an indication of origin?

My Lords, I am unable to take the view that so vital an alteration could have been intended by the words used without much clearer language. There was, as far as your Lordships are aware, no demand among commercial men for any such an alteration, and certainly there was no custom in the Registrar's office to accept trade marks in substance intended to indicate a process or any mere operation on goods. If the new definition had been meant to extend to a mere temporary connection with goods after they have come into the hands of the public, I should have expected some qualification as to the nature of the right conferred. In such a case as this I think the remark in Maxwell on the Interpretation of Statutes (6th Edition), p. 148, ought to have weight, namely, that no substantial alteration of the law is to be anticipated in an amending Act unless that is clearly indicated. There is no such indication here. It is to be observed that under Sec. 4 of the new Act the proprietor of the repair mark (if I may so describe it) would have the exclusive right to the use of that mark in relation to the goods repaired. Why a person who has performed an operation of repair for his customer should be given a permanently exclusive right to a mark used to indicate that at some past date he repaired the article I do not understand. And I do not think the language of

Sec. 9, which I have quoted, is apt to describe a temporary connection such as is now in question. The last words in that section seem to contemplate a continuing connection.

Authority is also against the contention that the new definition has the effect in question. In *Bismag v Amblins* [1940] (below 5.2.7.3) my noble friend Lord Clauson (then Clauson L.J.) had to deal with the point. After referring to the old definition (in the Act of 1905) and the change in the modern Act, he said this: "That definition still, as I read it, treats a trade mark as something which indicates origin, but whereas the old definition contemplates that the trade mark is to be used upon or in connection with goods as an indication of origin, the new definition contemplates that the trade mark may be used not only upon or in connection with goods, but 'in relation to goods'". And in other passages of his judgment he emphasised the essential function of a trade mark, namely, that it indicates the origin of the goods.

The decision may perhaps be criticised; but that observation is, I doubt not, correct.

In *Saville Perfumery Ltd v June Perfect Ltd* (below, 5.2.7.2), it was observed by the Master of the Rolls: "In an infringement action, once it is found that the Defendant's mark is used as a trade mark, the fact that he makes it clear that the commercial origin of the goods indicated by the trade mark is some business other than that of the Plaintiff avails him nothing, since infringement consists in using the mark as a trade mark, that is, as indicating origin".

This passage was approved by your Lordships when the case came before this House (58 R.P.C. at p. 174). It fell to my duty to write the leading judgment; but it was approved in all respects by my noble friends Lord Atkin and Lord Russell of Killowen. I am therefore justified in saying that the statement of the Master of the Rolls was adopted as being correct by this House; and it is impossible to reconcile it with the view on behalf of the Respondents with which I am now dealing.

My conclusion upon a careful consideration of the Act of 1938 and of the authorities is that the repair of stockings undertaken or proposed to be undertaken by the Respondents does not constitute "a connection in the course of trade" within the meaning of the Trade Marks Act, 1938, and that a trade mark for stockings intended merely to indicate that they have been repaired by the person claiming to register such a mark cannot be accepted for registration. The claim is not improved in this case by the statement that they also intend to use the mark "Rysta" on stockings of their own manufacture in order to get the benefit of the goodwill they have acquired in the repair of stockings in connection with the same word.

I should add that it is not necessary in my opinion to determine the precise effect of Sec. 11 of the Act. The reasons I have given above, if correct, are sufficient to show that whether under that section or under the general discretion of the Registrar the mark cannot be accepted.

The result is that in my opinion this appeal should be allowed with costs and the judgment of Farwell J. should be restored. I move your Lordships accordingly.

The other members of the House delivered concurring speeches. Lord Macmillan said of the effect of the 1938 Act:

I was merely repeating a commonplace when on a former occasion I said in this House that it is "of the essence of a trade mark that it should indicate origin and be used as indicative of origin" (*Bass Ratcliff and Gretton Ltd v Nicholson and Sons Ltd* [1932] A.C. 130 at pp. 154–5). It is true that these pronouncements were made before the passing of the Act of 1938 and that this Statute enacted a new definition of a trade mark in the words which I have quoted and also in Section 4, when defining the right given by registration, used new language, namely, that registration of a person as the proprietor of a trade mark in respect of any goods should give that person "the exclusive right to the use of the trade mark in relation to those goods". But I do not agree that thereby "a radical alteration in the law relating to trade marks" has been effected or that there has thereby been conferred "a right crucially different in principle from the rights heretofore enjoyed by the owners of trade marks", as the Master of the Rolls and Clauson L.J. held in *Bismag Ltd v Amblins (Chemists) Ltd.* I do not think that the widened language of the 1938 Act has inferentially altered the essential conception of a trade mark in law and in this I agree with and prefer the judgments in the *Bismag* case of my noble and learned friend then Simonds J. ([1940] 1 Ch. 225) and MacKinnon L.J. whose reasoning I need not repeat.

5.2.1.5   *Smith Kline & French v Sterling Winthrop Group* [1976] R.P.C. 511 (H.L.)

The respondent opposed the appellant's application to register ten colour combinations which it used on various drug capsules to distinguish the sustained release drugs in them, most of which were available only on prescription. Evidence had shown that widespread sales and advertising had made the colouring distinctive of the appellant's products; copying by others for sale would have amounted to passing off.

Lord Diplock:

The colour combinations have thus been shown by undisputed evidence to serve the business purpose of a trade mark. They do precisely what a trade mark is meant to do: they indicate to potential buyers that the goods were made by SKF and not by any other manufacturer. To the ordinary business man it would, I think, appear a strange anomaly in the law of trade marks if these colour combinations applied to the capsules and their pellets were disentitled to the protection conferred by registration.

The main ground upon which the respondents relied in justification of this apparent anomaly was that what SKF claimed to be their trade mark was the mere external appearance of the goods in respect of which its registration was sought, and that upon the true construction of the Trade Marks Act 1938 this was incapable of being a "mark" registrable as a "trade mark". This argument failed before the Assistant Registrar. On the appeal from his decision to the High Court it also failed before Graham J., but it succeeded in the Court of Appeal from whose decision this appeal comes to your Lordships' House.

Lord Diplock referred to the then current definitions of "trade mark" and "mark" (1938 Act, s.68(1), and to s.68(2), above, 5.2.1.3). He continued:

So, if it is to be a trade mark, a "mark" must be something that can be represented visually and may be something that can be applied to the surface of the goods ("use upon") or incorporated in the structure of the goods ("use in physical relation to"). The inclusion of "heading" (viz. coloured threads woven into the selvedge of textile goods) in the meaning of "mark" also confirms that a mark, provided that it can be seen upon visual examination of the goods, may be incorporated in their structure.

My Lords, I see nothing in this context that requires one to exclude from the definition of "trade mark" a mark which covers the whole of the visible surface of the goods to which it is applied. Such a mark is as capable of indicating a connection in the course of trade between the goods and the proprietor of the mark as it would have been if it had only covered half or three-quarters of the visible surface. No one has been able to point to any business purpose that would be served by drawing a distinction between marks that cover the whole and those which cover part of the surface. For my part I should be loath to ascribe to Parliament an intention to do anything so irrational.

However, a mark may fall within the definition of trade mark but may still not be registrable. So it is necessary to see whether there is anything in the provisions of the Act dealing with registration that would exclude from registration a mark which covers the whole of the visible surface of the goods to which it is applied. Section 9 states what a trade mark must consist of in order to be registrable in Part A of the register. The colour combinations used on the capsules and their pellets for which registration is sought by SKF come under the heading "any other distinctive mark" in section 9 (1) (e). I shall have to revert to the meaning of "distinctive" when I come to deal with the second ground of the respondents' attack upon the registration of the marks; but for the purpose of dealing with the main point in this appeal I will assume that the requirement of distinctiveness is satisfied.

The provisions relating to registration are supplemented by rules made by the Board of Trade under section 40 of the Act. By subsection (2) these are of the same effect as if they were contained in the Act. The Trade Marks Rules 1938 do not in terms require the application for registration of a trade mark to contain a "representation" of the mark. In the ordinary way the representation would be a drawing or other pictorial representation of the mark, but rule 28 authorises the Registrar to accept instead a specimen or copy of the trade mark in such form as he thinks most convenient, and to deposit in the office a specimen or copy of any trade mark which cannot conveniently be shown by a representation. This is what happened in the instant case. In the case of a trade mark which is intended to be used upon the actual goods in respect of which it is to be registered, I see nothing in these rules to require a trade mark to be two-dimensional only or to exclude from registration a mark which covers the whole of the visible surface of the goods.

I turn from the statute to the cases. There is no English authority that is directly in point; but the registrability of what are substantially identical trade marks under the Australian Trade Marks Act was considered by Windeyer J. in *Smith Kline and French Laboratories (Australia) Ltd v Registrar of Trade Marks* [1972] R.P.C. 519. The terms of the Australian Act are close enough to those of the Trade Marks Act 1938 to make this judgment one of persuasive authority.

Windeyer J. held the marks not to be registrable. His *ratio decidendi* is stated in two sentences:

"But the test is not – Can the goods be described or depicted without reference to their markings? As I see it, a mark for the purposes of the Act must be capable of being described and depicted as something apart from the goods to which it is to be applied, or in relation to which it is to be used."

My Lords, I find the dichotomy between these tests elusive. Trade marks in their origin were marks that were applied to goods by their maker so that a buyer by visual examination of the goods could tell who made them. Makers' marks on silver and gold plate afford some of the earliest examples. With the growth of advertising, representations of trade marks have become widely used in advertisements so as to familiarise buyers with the mark, but the application of trade marks to the actual goods or to the packages containing them still constitutes their basic function. The mark may be applied by the maker to whatever visible part of the goods he chooses as suitable. If he habitually places it in a particular position on the goods, its distinctiveness in fact as indicating that the goods are of his manufacture may be associated with the position in which it appears upon the goods and in the case of markings of a kind which are not intrinsically uncommon their distinctiveness as a trade mark may depend upon the position in which the markings appear upon the goods; as, for example, bands of colour or a raised moulded pattern round the neck of a bottle containing the manufacturer's product.

If the test propounded by Windeyer J. means that in order to be registrable a trade mark must be capable of being described without referring to the part of the goods to which it is to be applied, a mark whose distinctiveness depended upon the position in which it appeared on the goods would not be registrable. In my view, however, there is clear and long-established English authority to the contrary in *Reddaway (F) & Co Ltd's Application* (1914) 31 R.P.C. 147. That was an application to register as a trade mark for hose, two blue lines with a red line in between them of about half an inch in width. The applicants had adopted the practice of weaving these lines of colour through the whole length of hose manufactured by them and when used in this way but not otherwise the three coloured lines had become distinctive of hose of their manufacture. In the course of his judgment Warrington J. said "I see no reason why three lines of colour woven into a fabric should not be a mark." He went on to consider whether the mark in that form would be adapted to distinguish the goods of Reddaway & Co from the goods of other persons. He concluded on the evidence that it would, and ordered the application to proceed in modified form by "limiting the mark to the colours blue and red in stripes ... extending throughout the whole length of the hose."

The correctness of this authority has never been questioned. In the later *Reddaway* case (1925) 42 R.P.C. 397 it was expressly followed by the Court of Appeal, and although their decision was reversed by the House of Lords (1927) 44 R.P.C. 27 upon the ground that the particular stripes extending throughout the whole length of the hose which formed the subject of that application, in contradistinction to those with which the earlier case had been concerned, were not adapted to distinguish Reddaway's hose, in the United Kingdom, Viscount Dunedin, with whose speech the other members of this House agreed, referred to Warrington J.'s decision in the earlier case in terms which clearly indicated that he accepted it as correct.

The respondents seek to explain away the decision of Warrington J. in the first *Reddaway* case as being one in which the registrable trade mark was the blue and red stripes and the reference to their extending throughout the whole length of the hose as a limitation upon the use of the mark. But this is in flat contradiction to the order actually made by Warrington J. and to the interpretation put upon it by this House in the second *Reddaway* case, where Viscount Dunedin said that the trade mark whose registration was granted by Warrington J. "consists of two blue lines with a red one between them, parallel and running the whole length of the hose."

My Lords, I can see no sensible distinction between the actual mark registered in the first *Reddaway* case and one which, in addition to the blue and red stripes, involved the application of some other colour to the remaining external surface of the hose throughout its length; nor can I see any sensible distinction between such a mark and the marks sought to be registered in the instant case. Nevertheless Windeyer J. in the Australian case and the Court of Appeal in the instant case considered that support for this distinction was to be found in an observation made by Lindley L.J. in *In re James's Trade Mark* (1886) 33 Ch. D. 392. "We must be careful to avoid confusion of ideas. A mark must be something distinct from the thing marked. A thing itself cannot be a mark of itself."

The *James* case was one which involved the validity of the registration of a mark in the shape of a dome as a trade mark for black lead. James had sold dome-shaped blocks of black lead and had, some 25 years before, registered that shape as a design under the Designs Act then in force. On the expiration of that registration in 1875 other manufacturers also began to make black lead in dome-shaped blocks and James, though he too continued to do so, also manufactured black lead in blocks of other shapes. At the hearing before Pearson J. that judge appeared to have taken the erroneous view that the effect of the registration of a trade mark in the shape of a dome would be to make it an infringement of that trade mark for anyone other than the proprietor of the trade mark to make blocks of black lead in that shape. At the hearing in the Court of Appeal it was made clear that no monopoly was or, indeed, could be claimed in the right to manufacture blocks of black lead of that shape, and that the mark in the shape of a dome was intended to be affixed to or impressed upon black lead of James's manufacture in whatever shape the actual block of black lead might be made. It was in that context that Lindley L.J. started his judgment with the observation that I have cited. The Court of Appeal upon evidence of distinctiveness of the mark upheld the validity of its registration.

James's case does not, in my view, throw any light upon the question involved in the instant appeal; but even if Lindley L.J.'s apothegm were treated as being of general application, the "thing marked" in the instant case is the pharmaceutical substance in pellet form within capsules and the "mark" is the colour applied to one half of the capsule and the various colours applied to the individual pellets within the capsule.

Windeyer J. in the Australian case also relied upon a dictum of Sargant L.J. in *Charles Goodall & Son Ltd v John Waddington Ltd* (1924) 41 R.P.C. 658, though the Court of Appeal in the instant case did not attach importance to it. In stating what he conceived to be the difference between a registrable design and a registrable trade mark, Sargant L.J. said:

"A design forms part of the goods themselves. A trade mark is something which is extra, which is added to the goods for the purpose of denoting the origin of the goods, and, speaking generally of trade mark and design, the same thing is not a trade mark and design."

It is conceded that if this is to be understood as meaning that what is capable of being registered as a design is *ipso facto* incapable of being registered as a trade mark, it does not correctly state the law. If this latter part of the *dictum* is omitted, the preceding words would not rule out the trade marks claimed by SKF in the instant case. The "extra" added to the goods is the colour applied to one half of the capsule and the various colours applied to the individual pellets within the capsules.

In the instant case the ground upon which all three members of the Court of Appeal overruled Graham J. and rejected SKF's applications was that the description of the mark was merely a description of the whole external appearance of the goods in respect of which it was intended to be registered, viz. the capsules and their pellets. This is another ways of saying that if the mark when applied to the goods will cover the whole visible surface of the goods it cannot be registered as a trade mark. For my part, as I have said, I cannot see any business reason why this should be so, and I can find nothing in the Act or in the authorities to justify such a conclusion. Upon this, which is the main point in the appeal, I would uphold the judgment of Graham J.

Lord Diplock refused to accept a separate objection – that the mark was not inherently adapted to distinguish the goods (s.9(1), (3)). This is reported below, 5.2.3.4. The other members of the House agreed with both aspects of Lord Diplock's speech.

5.2.1.6 *Coca-Cola Trade Marks* [1986] R.P.C. 421 (H.L.)

The Coca-Cola Company sought to register the well-known shape of its bottles for non-alcoholic beverages in Class 32. The Registrar contested the registrability of two forms in which this was sought to be done, viz., (i) "the distinctive shape and appearance applied to a bottle when used as a container for the goods and as shown in the accompanying representation"; (ii) three perspective drawings of a bottle, accompanied by the words "The mark consists of a bottle of the shape shown in the representation". (An application for a line drawing of the bottle was allowed at an earlier stage). All judgments below refused to allow the two applications.

Lord Templeman:

This is another attempt to expand the boundaries of intellectual property and to convert a protective law into a source of monopoly. The attempt to use the Copyright Act 1956 for this purpose failed recently in *British Leyland Motor Corporation v Armstrong Patents Co Ltd* [1986] 2 W.L.R. 400. The present attempt is based on the Trade Marks Act 1938.

It is not sufficient for the Coca-Cola bottle to be distinctive. The Coca-Cola Co must succeed in the startling proposition that a bottle is a trade mark. If so, then any other container or any article of a distinctive shape is capable of being a trade mark. This raises the spectre of a total and perpetual monopoly in containers and articles achieved by means of the Act of 1938. Once the container or article has become associated with the manufacturer and distinctiveness has been established, with or without the help of the monopolies created by the Patents Act, the Registered Designs Act or the Copyright Act, the perpetual trade mark monopoly in the container or article can be achieved. In my opinion the Act of 1938 was not intended to confer on the manufacturer of a container or on the manufacturer of an article a statutory monopoly on the ground that the manufacturer has in the eyes of the public established a connection between the shape of the container or article and the manufacturer. A rival manufacturer must be free to sell any container or article of similar shape provided the container or article is labelled or packaged in a manner which avoids confusion as to the origin of the goods in the container or the origin of the article. The respondent registrar of trade marks has always taken the view that the function of trade mark legislation is to protect the mark but not the article which is marked. I agree. By section 68(1) of the Act of 1938:

> "... 'mark' includes a device, brand, heading, label, ticket, name, signature, word, letter, numeral, or any combination thereof; ... 'trade mark' means ... a mark used or proposed to be used in relation to goods for the purpose of indicating, or so as to indicate, a connection in the course of trade between the goods and some person having the right either as proprietor or as registered user to use the mark, whether with or without any indication of the identity of that person ...".

The word "mark" in its normal meaning and in its statutory definition is apt only to describe something which distinguishes goods rather than the goods themselves. A bottle is a container not a mark. The distinction between a mark and the thing which is marked is supported by authority. In *In re James's Trade Mark* (1886) L.R. 33 Ch.D. 392, the plaintiffs sold black lead in the form of a dome and in other shapes. Their products were impressed with the representation of a dome and their labels carried a picture of a black dome. The plaintiffs were allowed to register the representation or picture of a black dome as their trade mark. Similarly, the Coca-Cola Co has been allowed to register a line drawing of a Coca-Cola bottle as a trade mark. But, dealing with the article itself, in *In re James's Trade Mark*, Lindley L.J. said at page 395:

"A mark must be something distinct from the thing marked. The thing itself cannot be a mark of itself, but here we have got the thing and we have got a mark on the thing, and the question is, whether that mark on the thing is or is not a distinctive mark within the meaning of that Act. Of course the plaintiffs in this case have no monopoly in black lead of this shape. Anybody may make black lead of this shape provided he does not mark it as the plaintiffs mark theirs, and provided he does not pass it off as the plaintiffs' black lead. There is no monopoly in the shape, and I cannot help thinking that that has not been sufficiently kept in mind. What the plaintiffs have registered is a brand, a mark like a dome intended to represent a dome".

In the course of argument counsel for the Coca-Cola Company relied on the decision of this House in *Smith, Kline and French Laboratories Ltd v Sterling-Winthrop Group Ltd* [1976] R.P.C. 511 ("the *SKF* case"). In that case the plaintiffs were allowed to register 10 distinctive colour combinations as trade marks for drugs sold in pellet form within capsules. One typical example was at page 533:

"The trade mark consists of a maroon colour applied to one half of the capsule at one end, and the other half being colourless and transparent, and yellow, blue and white colours being each applied, to a substantial number of pellets so that each pellet is of one colour only".

Lord Diplock, at page 536, rejected the argument that a mark could not cover the whole of the visible surface of the goods to which it was applied. The *SKF* case only related to the colour of goods and has no application to the goods themselves or to a container for goods. A colour combination may tend to an undesirable monopoly in colours but does not create an undesirable monopoly in goods or containers. I do not consider that the *SKF* case is of assistance to the Coca-Cola Co. I would accordingly dismiss this appeal.

Lords Keith of Kinkel, Brandon of Oakbrook, Griffiths and Oliver of Aylmerton concurred.

5.2.2 Registration

5.2.2.1 Trade Marks Act 1938, s.3, 14, 17(1)–(2), 18(1)–(2), 19(1), 20(1)–(2), 29(1), 46: Registration, Disclaimer, Application, Opposition, Duration

S.1 establishes the Trade Marks Register, with the Comptroller-General of Patents, Designs and Trade Marks as Registrar.

S.3 A trade/*service* mark must be registered in respect of particular goods/*services* or classes of goods/*services*, and any question arising as to the class within which any goods/*services* fall shall be determined by the Registrar, whose decision shall be final.

S.14 If a trade/*service* mark –
  (a) contains any part not separately registered by the proprietor as a trade/*service* mark; or
  (b) contains matter common to the trade/*common to the provision of services of that description* or otherwise of a non-distinctive character;
the Registrar or the Board of Trade or the Court, in deciding whether the trade/*service* mark shall be entered or shall remain on the register, may require, as a condition of its being on the register,–
  (i)   that the proprietor shall disclaim any right to the exclusive use of any part of the trade/*service* mark, or to the exclusive use of all or any portion of any such matter as aforesaid, to the exclusive use of which the tribunal holds him not to be entitled; or
  (ii) that the proprietor shall make such other disclaimer as the tribunal may consider necessary for the purpose of defining his rights under his registration:
Provided that no disclaimer on the register shall affect any rights of the proprietor of a trade/*service* mark except such as arise out of the registration of the trade/*service* mark in respect of which the disclaimer is made.

S.16 provides for a registration to be limited to specified colours, and for the effect of this.

S.17 (1) Any person claiming to be the proprietor of a trade/*service* mark used or proposed to be used by him who is desirous of registering it must apply in writing to the Registrar in the prescribed manner for registration either in Part A or in Part B of the register.

(2) Subject to the provisions of this Act, the Registrar may refuse the application, or may accept it absolutely or subject to such amendments, modifications, conditions or limitations, if any, as he may think right.

S.17(3)–(7) give power to treat as an application for Part B, require reasons to be given on request and provide for appeal to the Department of Trade and Industry or the High Court.

S.18(1) When an application for registration of a trade/*service* mark has been accepted, whether absolutely or subject to conditions or limitations, the Registrar shall, as soon as may be after acceptance, cause the application as accepted to be advertised in the prescribed manner, and the advertisement shall set forth all conditions and limitations subject to which the application has been accepted:

Provided that the Registrar may cause an application to be advertised before acceptance if it is made under paragraph (e) of subsection (1) of section nine of this Act, or in any other case where it appears to him that it is expedient by reason of any exceptional circumstances so to do, and where an application has been so advertised the Registrar may, if he thinks fit, advertise it again when it has been accepted but shall not be bound so to do.

(2) Any person may, within the prescribed time from the date of the advertisement of an application, give notice to the Registrar of opposition to the registration.

S.18(3)–(11) prescribe procedures for oppositions and appeal to the High Court from decisions thereon.

S.19(1) When an application for registration of a trade/*service* mark in Part A or Part B of the register has been accepted and either –
  (a) the application has not been opposed and the time for notice of opposition has expired, or
  (b) the application has been opposed and the opposition has been decided in favour of the applicant,
the Registrar shall, unless the application has been accepted in error or unless the Board of Trade otherwise direct, register the trade/*service* mark in Part A or Part B, as the case may be, and the trade/*service* mark, when registered, shall be registered, subject to section 39A(2) below, as of the date of the application for registration, and that date shall be deemed for the purposes of this Act to be the date of registration.

S.19(2)–(3) deal with registration formalities.

S.20(1) The registration of a trade/service mark shall be for a period of seven years, but may be renewed from time to time in accordance with the provisions of this section. . . .

(2) The Registrar shall, on application made by the registered proprietor of a trade/service mark in the prescribed manner and within the prescribed period, renew the registration of the original trade/service mark for a period of fourteen years from the date of expiration of the original registration or of the last renewal of registration . . .

S.20(3), (4) concern the formalities of renewal.

S.29(1) No application for the registration of a service mark in respect of any services shall be refused, nor shall permission for such registration be withheld, on the ground only that it appears that the applicant does not use or propose to use the service mark –
  (a) if the tribunal is satisfied that a body corporate is about to be constituted, and that the applicant intends to assign the service mark to the corporation with a view to the use thereof in relation to those services by the corporation; or
  (b) if the application is accompanied by an application for the registration of a person as a registered user of the service mark, and the

tribunal is satisfied that the proprietor intends it to be used by that person in relation to those services and the tribunal is also satisfied that that person will be registered as a registered user thereof immediately after the registration of the service mark.

S.29(2) allows the intended use under s.29(1)(a) to be brought into account under s.26 (non-use); s.29(3) permits security for costs to be required; s.29(4) imposes time-limits in respect of s.29(1)(a) applications.

S.46 In all legal proceedings relating to a registered trade/*service* mark (including applications under section thirty-two of this Act) the fact that a person is registered as proprietor of the trade/*service* mark shall be *prima facie* evidence of the validity of the original registration of the trade/*service* mark and of all subsequent assignments and transmissions thereof.

5.2.2.2   *"Genette" Trade Mark* [1968] R.P.C. 148; (Cross J.) [1969] R.P.C. 189 (C.A.)

In 1959 a Mr Johnson had the idea that the mark GINETTE would be suitable for a gin based drink, and he applied to register as a trade mark a device comprising a girl skater, a legend, and the word GINETTE. The word GINETTE was subject to official objection as being descriptive, and the mark was registered subject to disclaimer of any exclusive right in the word. In 1960 two individuals G and C had a similar idea. They too applied to register GINETTE, but abandoned their application when Mr Johnson's prior registration was cited. In 1963 G and C applied to register the marks GENETE and GENETTE for the same goods, and the applications were granted.

Mr Johnson applied for rectification of the register inter alia *on the ground that G and C had wrongfully claimed proprietorship of the marks. The Registrar found in his favour and rectified the registrations, finding that the case resembled and was indeed stronger than the* Vitamins *and* Brown Shoe *cases in which registrations had been refused on this ground where applicants had sought to register marks with the knowledge that someone else had originated a similar mark. On appeal to the High Court, Cross J. stated:*

I now proceed to consider what I understand to be the issue in this appeal, namely, whether Messrs Gibbs and Connett when they applied for registration of the marks GENETE and GENETTE could honestly claim that they were "proprietors" of those marks as they were required to by Section 17 (1) of the Act of 1938, or whether the claim to proprietorship which they made was false. Strictly speaking no one can be called "the proprietor" of an unregistered trade mark which has not in fact yet been used, but no doubt in the case of a mark which is only proposed to be used the section must be referring to someone who claims that he is entitled to be registered as proprietor of the trade mark which he proposes to use. Was that a claim which Messrs Gibbs and Connett could honestly make with regard to GENETE and GENETTE? In deciding that they could not the Assistant Registrar relied on *Vitamins Ltd's Application* [1956] R.P.C. 1 and *Brown Shoe Co Inc's Application* [1959] R.P.C. 29, to both of which I must refer.

The facts in the first case are that on 24 January 1952, an American company had applied for registration of the mark PABALATE in respect of pharmaceutical goods. That application was successfully opposed by Vitamins Limited, who were the registered proprietors of the mark PABAVEL and various other marks beginning PABA. In view of the opposition the American company withdrew its application and a week or so later Vitamins Limited themselves applied to be registered as proprietors of the mark

PABALATE. That application in its turn was opposed by the American company and Lloyd-Jacob J. in the exercise of his discretion decided that it should not be allowed to proceed. He held on the evidence that the American company had not abandoned all interest in the mark in this country and he remarked that Vitamins Limited had given no explanation of their choice of the word PABALATE. He considered that in the circumstances the claim of Vitamins Limited to be the proprietors of the mark was one which they could not properly make.

The facts in the *Brown Shoe* case were as follows. An American company applied in 1952 for registration of the mark NATURALIZER, which was a registered mark of theirs in the United States of America, in respect of ladies' shoes. The Registrar raised an objection under Section 9 and the American company did not then proceed with its application. Then in 1953 an English company applied for and obtained registration of the mark NATURALIZET in respect of footwear, and later the American company applied for the rectification of the register. Wynn-Parry J., in the exercise of his discretion, held that the mark NATURALIZET should be expunged from the register. Having regard to the similarity between the two words NATURALIZER and NATURAL-IZET and the fact that the chairman of the English company who had made a statutory declaration withdrew it when the American company expressed a wish to cross-examine him on it, the judge found as a fact that the English company had copied the American company's mark with the change of one letter. He also held that the American company had never abandoned their interest in their mark in this country. Consequently he regarded the case as covered by the decision in the *Vitamins* case, the principle of which he enunciated in the following words [1959] R.P.C. 29 at 33, line 22:

> "It is incumbent on an applicant for registration of a trade mark which has not yet been used in trade to assert that it is proposed to be used by him and that he claims to be the proprietor thereof. If there is an owner of a similar trade mark who has made an earlier assertion of proprietorship and who has not abandoned that claim, then the claim of the applicant is not well founded and the application should not be allowed to go forward."

The facts of this case plainly differ from those in the *Vitamins* case and the *Brown Shoe* case. In those cases the person whose claim to be the proprietor of the mark in question was in issue had copied the mark from someone else who had previously asserted his proprietorship of it. In this case, on the other hand, though Messrs Gibbs and Connett knew when they made their application in 1963 to register GENETE and GENETTE that Mr Johnson had previously asserted a claim to the proprietorship of the mark GINETTE, on which the marks GENETE and GENETTE were based, they had not copied Mr Johnson's mark. They had themselves thought of the mark GINETTE. They had thought of it later than Mr Johnson had thought of it, but before they knew that he had thought of it or asserted proprietorship of it. One cannot fairly say that the modifications of the word GINETTE which they thought of in order to overcome the difficulties raised with regard to GINETTE by the Excise authorities and the Trade Marks Registry were modifications of Mr Johnson's idea and not of their own idea.

Ought that difference in the facts to lead to a different result in this case? Although counsel for Mr Johnson argued strenuously to the contrary, I cannot myself see that the fact that his client obtained registration of his device mark strengthens his position in any way. As a condition of that registration of the device Mr Johnson was forced to disclaim any exclusive use of the word GINETTE. The effect of that was, as I understand it, that although he retained such rights in the name GINETTE as he would have had if the device mark had not been registered at all, he gained no additional rights in that word by reason of the registration of the device mark with the disclaimer. (See Trade

Marks Act, 1938, s. 14).

The result of that, as I see it, must be that Mr Johnson was not in any stronger position vis-à-vis Messrs Gibbs and Connett than he would have been had he applied in 1959 to register GINETTE as a trade mark and his application had been rejected on the ground that GINETTE was descriptive. When Messrs Gibbs and Connett applied in 1963 to register GENETE and GENETTE they knew that Mr Johnson had thought of GINETTE as a mark before they did and they had no reason to think that he had abandoned any interest in it. It would be reasonable to suppose that he might have been doing what they had been doing, namely, thinking of some modification of this mark which would be sufficiently near it to give the flavour of gin and sufficiently far from it to satisfy the Excise authorities and the Trade Mark Registry. But when they had hit on the words GENETE and GENETTE I cannot say that there was anything underhand or improper in their using those words as the name of a gin-based drink to be made by them or stating to the Trade Marks Registry that they claimed to be the proprietors of those marks. They had themselves thought of this word GINETTE of which GENETE and GENETTE were modifications. It is true that the passage from the judgment of Wynn-Parry J., in the *Brown Shoe* case, which I have quoted and which the Assistant Registrar relied on in his decision, does as a matter of words cover the facts of this case. But the judge used those words in relation to a case in which, as he held, the English company had stolen the American company's mark, and I do not suppose for a moment that he had a case of this sort in mind.

For those reasons I propose to allow the appeal.

On further appeal, the C.A. affirmed Cross J.'s judgment briefly.

5.2.2.3   *"Rawhide" Trade Mark* [1962] R.P.C. 133 (Cross J.)

Cheryl Playthings Ltd applied to register "Rawhide" for games, toys, toyhats, playsuits, pistols and plastic holsters. The name was the title of a CBS series, shown on US television in September 1959. CBS granted the Granada Group the right to show "Rawhide" in Britain and gave a Granada subsidiary the British "merchandising rights". Its applications for trade mark registrations were however later in time than Cheryl Playthings, which made a practice of procuring such registrations for series names likely to be broadcast in Britain.

Two grounds of objection were pressed by the Granada subsidiary: (1) that Cheryl was not entitled to claim to be the proprietor of the mark; and (2) that the application should be refused in the Registrar's discretion. Cross J. stated:

In the course of the argument, the question was raised whether there was any limit to the matters which the Registrar could properly take into account in exercising his discretion, and I was referred to the following sentence in Kerly on Trade Marks, 8th Edn., p 38: "The discretion, however, is not to be exercised arbitrarily, capriciously, or unreasonably, and a refusal must be based on some consideration the nature of which is clear and can be justified as founded upon principles to be deduced from the Act". The authority given for the last part of that statement is an alleged *dictum* of Fletcher Moulton, L.J., in the *National Cash Register Co's Application* (1917) 34 R.P.C. 273. In fact, however, Fletcher Moulton, L.J., was not a member of the Court which heard that case, and it appears likely that the reference intended was to the following words which the Lord Justice used in the case of *W & G Du Cros Limited* [1912] 1 Ch. 644 at 657: "Counsel for the respondent attempted to defend the action of the Comptroller-General by saying that the registration of a trade mark is not *ex debito justitiae*, basing their arguments on the *dicta* of Lord Herschell in the case of *Eno v Dunn*. That is true but it does not mean that the Comptroller-General has a discretion to register a trade mark or not according as he thinks it is a desirable form of trade mark or not. Such limitations must be found in the Act if they are to be enforced by the office". But that *dictum* was not approved by Lord Shaw and Lord Parker when the *Du Cros* case reached the House of Lords [1913] A.C. 624, and in the later case of *Garrett's Application* [1916] 1 Ch. 436 all three members of the Court of Appeal held that the Registrar had a general discretion to refuse to register a trade mark which satisfied all the positive conditions laid down by the Act. But, though the Registrar in exercising his discretion is not, I think, limited to any particular type of consideration, he must exercise it judicially on reasonable grounds which are capable of being clearly stated. A vague feeling of distaste for the applicant or his methods of business cannot justify a refusal to register a mark which satisfies the conditions laid down in the Act.

There is no doubt that Cheryl chose the name RAWHIDE as a trade mark because they hoped thereby to get some benefit from the publicity to be given to the name through the television broadcasts of the film, and it is natural enough that Granada, who were going to provide the publicity, should feel aggrieved at Cheryl's action in forestalling them. But Granada, as the Registrar held and it is admitted rightly held, were not themselves the proprietors of the mark at the date of Cheryl's application. Cheryl was not taking a name to which Granada had any legal title, and I do not think that the fact that the reason why a manufacturer chooses as a trade mark a name which it is open to him to choose is that he hopes thereby to gain the benefit of a publicity for which he will not have to pay can of itself be a good ground for refusing his application. It may be said, of course, that Mr Wolfin should have recognised that whoever broadcast RAWHIDE in this country would have some moral claim to be registered as proprietors of the mark consisting of the name, if they so wished, and that he should not have applied for registration himself until those persons had had a reasonable opportunity to secure registration and had failed to avail themselves of it. But different people might take very different views as to the strength of Granada's moral claims in this case and as to what constituted a reasonable opportunity for them to secure registration them-selves. For example, Counsel for the applicants submitted that Columbia and Granada could easily have precluded any prior registration by Cheryl by means of a "conven-tion" application by Columbia. It is not necessary for me to decide whether or not this is so. It is enough to say that this sort of argument illustrates the difficulty of founding an exercise of the discretion on such vague and disputable considerations as this.

Again it was suggested in argument that the fact that this was not the first application of this sort that Cheryl had made but that they were in the habit of applying to register similar marks should make some difference. This reasoning, if well founded, would presumably apply not only to numerous applications by a producer of films ac-companied by applications for the registration of some manufacturer as registered user. I cannot see why the fact that the application is one of a number should make any difference. I can well understand that the Registrar may think it undesirable that the Register should be cluttered up with numbers of marks, each of which will probably only be used during the relatively short period during which the title of the film in question stays in the memory of the public. Such a state of affairs can hardly have been contemplated by Parliament when the Act was passed, and it may well be that the Act needs to be amended in the light of recent developments. But, as things stand, I should hesitate to say that the Registrar could properly refuse to register a mark which is not itself open to objection simply because the applicant has previously registered what he considers to be an excessive number of the same kind of marks for use on the same kind of goods. But the applicants have still another hurdle to get over. When they applied for the registration of RAWHIDE as a trade mark in June, 1959, it was at least doubtful whether they would ever use the mark. Their user of it was contingent – or, at all events, was probably contingent – on the film being shown over here. In these circumstances, I should have thought that it was open to question whether they had brought themselves within section 17 (1) of the Act, which provides that the only person entitled to apply for registration is someone who claims to be the proprietor of a trade mark used or proposed to be used by him. The sub-section is not very happily worded, for it is not easy to see how anyone can be or claim to be the proprietor of a trade mark which no-one has yet used. Presumably, all that is needed in such a case is that the applicant should claim in good faith to be entitled to be registered as proprietor of the mark. Even so, however, I should have thought that it was arguable that the applicants had not in June, 1959, a sufficiently present and unconditional intention to use the mark to bring themselves within the section.

The Registrar does not expressly deal with this point in the reasons given for his decision; but, since he rested his refusal to register on an exercise of his discretion and not on ground (1) of the notice of opposition, I assume that he considered that the applicants had brought themselves within section 17 (1). Possibly this was because of the passage in the evidence of Mr Wolfin to which I have referred. Assuming, however that he was right in thinking that at the date of their application the applicants proposed to use the mark within the meaning of section 17, the fact that it was not clear that they meant to use it unless and until the film was shown here was, in my judgment, a circumstance which the Registrar was entitled to take into account in exercising his discretion. It is one thing to say that a man who is using or proposes here and now to use a mark on his goods is entitled to be registered notwithstanding that his reason for choosing that mark is the hope of getting the benefit of publicity for which he has not paid, but it is quite another thing to say that a man can put himself in the position of reaping the advantage of any publicity which may subsequently attach to the name though he has no intention of making any substantial use of the mark unless and until it is clear that publicity will attach to it. It would, I think, be altogether wrong that a manufacturer should be allowed to use the machinery of the Trade Marks Act for the purpose of staking out claims of this sort. Assuming, therefore, that the applicants brought themselves in all respects within the terms of the Act, I think that the Registrar exercised his discretion rightly in refusing registration in this case.

5.2.2.4   *"Holly Hobbie" Trade Mark* [1984] R.P.C. 329 (H.L.)

"Holly Hobbie" was the name given to a girl drawn in a pinafore and first exploited by American Greetings Corporation on their own products, greetings cards and similar goods. Subsequently the corporation successfully licensed the use of this sweet figure and her name, so that "Now over 412 products manufactured by some 66 companies bear Holly's name". As a basis for a similar "merchandising" operation in the UK, it sought to register the name in twelve classes of goods. In each case the application was accompanied by a user agreement with a licensee which related to goods within the particular class. This was done in order to bring the applicant's right to apply within the 1938 Act, section 29 (1)(b). Each licence agreement gave the corporation as licensor the right to inspect the finished goods and their method of manufacture, to receive samples and to receive for approval all packages, labels, advertising and other material bearing the trade mark.

The applications were rejected, and this rejection was upheld on appeal by Whitford J., the Court of Appeal and the House of Lords, by virtue of section 28 (6): "The Registrar should refuse an application under the fore-going provisions of this section if it appears to him that the grant thereof would tend to facilitate trafficking in a trade mark".

Lord Brightman:

There is no definition of trafficking in the Act. It is a word with several shades of meaning, ranging from ordinary reputable buying and selling to unlawful or improper commerce. When one seeks to discover the sense in which the word is used in a trade mark context, the clues are sparse. The starting point is, I think, *J Batt and Co's Trade Marks* (1898) 15 R.P.C. 262, decided at the close of the last century. In that case Romer J. directed that certain marks should be expunged from the Register on the ground that there had been no *bona fide* intention to use them. The learned judge said this (page 266):

> "... one cannot help seeing the evils that may result from allowing Trade Marks to be registered broadcast, if I may use the expression, there being no real intention of using them, or only an intention possibly of using them in respect of a few articles. The inconvenience it occasions, and the costs it occasions, are very large, and beyond that, I cannot help seeing that it would lead, in some cases, to absolute oppression, and to persons using the position they have got as registered owners of Trade Marks, which are not really *bona fide* Trade Marks, for the purpose of trafficking in them, and using them as a weapon to obtain money from subsequent persons who may want to use *bona fide* Trade Marks in respect of some classes, in respect of which they find these bogus Trade Marks registered".

There was an unsuccessful appeal to the Court of Appeal, and ultimately to your Lordships' House (1899) 16 R.P.C. 11, where the Lord Chancellor, Lord Halsbury, picked up the same notion of trafficking when he said

> "Here is a gentleman who, for seventeen years, has been in possession of a trade mark. There are a variety of circumstances which can be suggested – that it was needed for the purpose of trading under a particular form of mark, and so protecting the trade which he had either begun or intended to begin; or that he was disposed to register any number of trade marks for the purpose of vending them to others to whom they might appear as pleasant and attractive trade marks"

adding that there were

> "circumstances which certainly would suggest he was a dealer in trade marks ...".

The law clearly did not recognise the entitlement of the owner of a trade mark to deal with it, like a patent, as a commodity in its own right. The same point was highlighted 15 years later in your Lordships' House in *Bowden Wire Ltd v Bowden Brake Co Ltd* (1914) 31 R.P.C. 385, where Lord Loreburn said this (page 392):

> "The object of the law is to preserve for a trader the reputation he has made for himself, not to help him in disposing of that reputation as of itself a marketable commodity, independent of his goodwill, to some other trader. If that were allowed, the public would be misled, because they might buy something in the belief that it was the make of a man whose reputation they knew, whereas it was the make of someone else ... In this case the appellants parcelled out the right to use their trade mark as if they had been dealing with a patent".

The committee appointed in 1933 under the chairmanship of Viscount Goschen, to report whether any and if so what changes in the existing law and practice relating to trade marks was desirable, had this point in mind. The committee, reporting in the following year, recommended a relaxation of some of the restrictions on the assignment of trade marks, and in particular, a facility for a person to register a trade mark to be used only by others under the "registered user" provisions proposed by the committee.

This recommendation was, however, subject to the proviso (page 8) that "trafficking in registered trade marks is not thereby facilitated".

It was against this background that Parliament enacted section 8 of the Trade Marks (Amendment) Act 1937, which (with an immaterial exception) became section 28 of the consolidating Trade Marks Act 1938.

The crucial question, then, is what is meant by trafficking in a trade mark, a tendency to facilitate which is fatal to an application by the proprietor and the proposed registered user? Or, to put the question more bluntly, if a commercial activity such as that falling to be considered by your Lordships in the instant case is not trafficking in a trade mark, what is?

It is fair to say that the *Batt* case, at first instance, is the only pre-1938 reported case discovered by counsel in which the word "trafficking" has been used judicially in a trade mark context.

Counsel for the appellants has deployed formidable arguments in support of the appellants' case that subsection (6) is not fatal to them. It is said, correctly, that a number of famous trade marks are to be found on the Register in relation to classes of goods which have no conceivable connection with the goods responsible for the fame of the mark; the use of the name "Coca-Cola" on T-shirts, for example. But your Lordships do not know the circumstances in which such registrations were allowed, and in particular what weight may have been given to any advantage accruing to the licensor of a free advertisement for his products.

The appellants accept that in the case of the grant of a licence by the proprietor of a mark to another trader to use that mark on the licensee's own goods, there must always be some connection in the course of trade between the proprietor of the mark and the goods to which the mark is to be applied by the licensee, if registration is to be granted, but, the appellants submit, this connection is sufficiently established if the proprietor controls or is able to control the nature and quality of the goods put on the market under the mark; see paragraph 13(b) and (c) of the appellants' case. Put shortly, quality control is said to be enough. "Trafficking", it is submitted, is confined to the sort of situation described by Romer J. in Batt, where the mark is sought to be registered merely to enable the proprietor to use it as a means of extorting money from another who, on a later occasion, wishes to make *bona fide* use of the mark. No doubt a number of cases, e.g. *BOSTITCH Trade Mark* [1963] R.P.C. 183, a provision for quality control by the licensor over the goods of the licensee has been relevant in establishing a connection in the course of trade between the licensor and such goods. Such decisions are confined to their own factual circumstances, and I can discern no general rule that the mere ability to control quality is always to be sufficient to establish the required connection. In fact, the quality control exercisable in the cases before us, so far as we have seen examples of the license agreements, is slight. In the *Oneida* case it is confined to a right to inspect and to approve if the appellants so wish. In the *General Mills (Chad Valley)* case, the licensee must submit samples for written approval prior to use or sale.

For my part, I am quite prepared to accept that character merchandising, in the sense of the exploitation of the reputation of famous marks by making them available to a wide variety of products, has become a widespread trading practice on both sides of the Atlantic. It may well be that it is perfectly harmless and in most cases probably deceives nobody. These considerations do not, however help to decide what Parliament intended by trafficking in trade marks or justify placing a gloss on the meaning to be attributed to that expression. I do not feel able to agree with the appellants' submission that the purpose of subsection (6) was confined to the prevention of trafficking in the

Batt sense. Trafficking as stigmatised by Romer J. in that case was in effect the stockpiling of trade marks, without any use or intended use in relation to the goods of the proprietor, with the intention of turning them to account when other traders wished to make use of the marks on their own goods. I see no reason for thinking that subsection (6) was solely directed against trafficking in that very narrow sense.

My Lords, although as a matter of ordinary English, trafficking in trade marks might mean the buying and selling of trade marks, it seems obvious that it is to have a more specialised meaning in a trade mark context. I have no quarrel with the definitions suggested by the Assistant Registrar and by Sir Denys Buckley, but perhaps one further attempt on my part may not be out of place. The courts have to grope for some means of delineating the forbidden territory, and different modes of expression may help to indicate boundaries which are not and cannot be marked out with absolute precision. To my mind, trafficking in a trade mark context conveys the notion of dealing in a trade mark primarily as a commodity in its own right and not primarily for the purpose of identifying or promoting merchandise in which the proprietor of the mark is interested. If there is no real trade connection between the proprietor of the mark and the licensee or his goods, there is room for the conclusion that the grant of the licence is a trafficking in the mark. It is a question of fact and degree in every case whether a sufficient trade connection exists. In my opinion, on the facts of these particular applications, the Assistant Registrar and the High Court were entitled to take the view that the registration of the licensee as a registered user, pursuant to section 28, would tend to facilitate trafficking in a trade mark.

I would dismiss this appeal.

Lord Bridge (discussing "character merchandising"):

Many marks will, of course, be protected by copyright. But when a mark consists simply in a name, it will be unprotected. It would seem from examples shown to your Lordships in the course of the argument that not a few marks in the character merchandising field have already been accepted by the registrar under section 28 before the present very large group of applications thrust the trafficking issue to the forefront. I do not pause to consider whether marks already registered which ought not to have been will be open to challenge. It will be bad enough, in my view, that the whole field of character merchandising will now be wide open to piracy. The protection, if any, of the original inventor of the character will lie in the uncertain remedy of a passing off action. This situation seems likely to generate a mass of difficult and expensive litigation which cannot be in the public interest.

In short, though I find no escape from section 28(6) of the Act of 1938, I do not hesitate to express my opinion that it has become a complete anachronism and that the sooner it is repealed the better.

5.2.3 Distinctiveness for Parts A and B

5.2.3.1   Trade Marks Act 1938, s.9, 10

S.9(1) In order for a trade mark (other than a certification trade mark)/*service mark* to be registrable in Part A of the register, it must contain or consist of at least one of the following essential particulars:–

   (a) the name of a company, individual, or firm, represented in a special or particular manner;
   (b) the signature of the applicant for registration or some predecessor in his business;
   (c) an invented word or invented words;
   (d) a word or words having no direct reference to the character or quality of the goods, and not being according to its ordinary signification a geographical name or a surname;
   (e) any other distinctive mark, but a name, signature, or word or words, other than such as fall within the descriptions in the foregoing paragraphs (a), (b), (c) and (d), shall not be registrable under the provisions of this paragraph except upon evidence of its distinctiveness.

(2) For the purposes of this section "distinctive" means adapted, in relation to the goods/*services* in respect of which a trade/*service* mark is registered or proposed to be registered, to distinguish goods/*services* with which the proprietor of the trade/*service* mark is or may be connected in the course of trade/*business* from goods/*services* in the case of which no connection subsists, either generally or, where the trade/*service* mark is registered or proposed to be registered subject to limitations, in relation to use within the extent of the registration.

(3) In determining whether a trade/*service* mark is adapted to distinguish as aforesaid the tribunal may have regard to the extent to which –

   (a) the trade/*service* mark is inherently adapted to distinguish as aforesaid; and
   (b) by reason of the use of the trade/*service* mark or of any other circumstances, the trade/*service* mark is in fact adapted to distinguish as aforesaid.

S.10(1) In order for a trade/*service* mark to be registrable in Part B of the register it must be capable, in relation to the goods/*services* in respect of which it is registered or proposed to be registered, of distinguishing goods with which the proprietor of the trade/*service* mark is or may be connected in the course of trade/*business* from goods/*services* in the case of which no such connection subsists, either generally or, where the trade/*service* mark is registered or proposed to be registered subject to limitations, in relation to use within the extent of the registration.

(2) In determining whether a trade/*service* mark is capable of distinguishing as aforesaid the tribunal may have regard to the extent to which –

   (a) the trade/*service* mark is inherently capable of distinguishing as aforesaid; and
   (b) by reason of the use of the trade/*service* mark or of any other

circumstances, the trade/*service* mark is in fact capable of distinguishing as aforesaid.

(3) A trade/*service* mark may be registered in Part B notwithstanding any registration in Part A in the name of the same proprietor of the same trade/*service* mark or any part or parts thereof.

5.2.3.2 *Eastman Photographic's Application* [1898] A.C. 571 (H.L.)

An application to register "Solio" for photographic paper was refused at all levels before appeal to the H.L.

Lord Herschell:

The ground upon which the court proceeded was that the word "Solio" had reference to the character or quality of the goods, and was therefore incapable of registration. The Court of Appeal held itself bound by a previous decision of the same Court in the case of *In re Farbenfabriken Application*, [1894] 1 Ch. 645, to hold that an invented word could not be registered if it had any reference to the character or quality of the goods. The question turns upon the construction of the section which, by Section 10 of the Act of 1888, is substituted for Section 64 of the Patents, Designs, and Trade Marks Act of 1883.

The section to be construed provides that a Trade Mark "must consist of or contain at least one of the following essential particulars". Then follow seven particulars distinguished by the letters (a) to (e). The last two of these are as follows: "(d) An invented word or invented words, or (e) A word or words having no reference to the character or quality of the goods and not being a geographical name". ...

In considering the case of an application to register a Trade Mark under (d), the only question which in my opinion has to be determined is whether the word sought to be registered is an invented word. In one of the cases on this subject, Lord Justice Kay said: "There is extremely little invention in the matter". It may be that the word "Satinine", which was there in question, was objectionable on other grounds; but if the word be an "invented" one, I do not think the quantum of invention is at all material. An invented word is allowed to be registered as a Trade Mark, not as a reward of merit, but because its registration deprives no member of the community of the rights which he possesses to use the existing vocabulary as he pleases. It may no doubt sometimes be difficult to determine whether a word is an invented word or not. I do not think the combination of two English words is an invented word, even although the combination may not have been in use before, nor do I think that a mere variation of the orthography or termination of a word would be sufficient to constitute an invented word, if to the eye or ear the same idea would be conveyed as by the word in its ordinary form. Again, I do not think that a foreign word is an invented word, simply because it has not been current in our language. At the same time, I am not prepared to go so far as to say that a combination of words from foreign languages so little known in this country, that it would suggest no meaning except to a few scholars, might not be regarded as an invented word. It is in this respect that I desire to qualify my assent to Lord Justice A L Smith's proposition that an invented word can never have a meaning.

Coming now to the particular case under discussion, I cannot doubt that the word Solio is an invented word, unless it is to be regarded as the Italian word solio, which means a throne, in which case it certainly has no reference to the character or quality of photographic paper. If it is not to be so regarded, it has of itself no meaning. As I have said, I think it unimportant, if it be an invented word, whether it has reference to the character or quality of the goods or not; but if this were the test of validity of the word as a Trade Mark, I must say that I think there is no such reference. I daresay that it might occur to some minds given to etymology that *sol*, the Latin word for sun, was a component part of it when they found it connected with photographic paper, but the same minds would equally find other root bases for the word if they found it connected with boots or agricultural implements. It seems to me to have no reference to the character or quality of the goods in the sense in which those words must have been used by the Legislature. I think the judgments appealed from ought to be reversed.

5.2.3.3   *Crosfield's and other Applications* [1910] 1 Ch. 130 (C.A.)

The Court of Appeal dealt with applications to register several word marks with a descriptive content.

Fletcher Moulton L.J.:

In these cases the Court of Appeal is, for the first time, asked to interpret and apply the provisions of the Trade Marks Act 1905, relating to the registrability of words as Trade Marks. These provisions make a change in Trade Mark legislation which may in some respects be regarded as a new departure. Under previous Acts registrability, if granted at all, was confined to certain classes of words, and no word outside those specified classes would obtain registration as a Trade Mark. The questions which, under those Acts, came to the Courts for decision were purely legal questions, as to whether the particular words came within the classes thus privileged. But under the present Act – though it retains these privileged classes in a somewhat extended form – the fact that a word is not within any of the privileged classes is not decisive as to its registrability. If the permission of the Board of Trade, or the Court, can be obtained, words become capable of registration as Trade Marks which do not belong to these classes. In the cases before us that permission has, in effect, been asked and refused, and it is from those refusals that these appeals are brought.

The new provisions are to be found in paragraph 5 of Section 9 of the Trade Marks Act 1905. To my mind they were chiefly directed to remedy two well-known defects in the working of the previous legislation. In the first place the exclusion of words under that legislation was by whole classes. But though it might be desirable in general to exclude from registration words of a particular class, it by no means follows that every individual word in that class would be objectionable as a Trade Mark in the case of every kind of goods. For example, few would doubt the desirability of excluding geographical terms as a class; but if, as suggested during the argument, a trader desired to register Monte Rosa for cigarettes, or Teneriffe for boiler plates, no practical inconvenience could arise from his doing so. The second defect was more difficult to remedy but, on the other hand, it affected cases that had strong claims on their merits. It often occurs in trade that by continued use words get recognised as denoting the goods of a particular firm. These words may, in themselves, be unsuitable to be chosen as Trade Marks, but they have, in fact, become so. The oft-quoted case of "Yorkshire Relish" is one example of this, and the words "Worcester Sauce" would almost certainly have been another example had the original makers of the article exercised due vigilance in protecting their rights. Apart from the Trade Marks Acts there would be nothing to prevent such words becoming Trade Marks in the eyes of the law, and it was an obvious defect in the earlier legislation that it failed to give the benefits of registration to such marks when they had become duly established. The present Act seeks to remedy these defects by abandoning the policy of absolute exclusion of all the members of specified classes of words, and substituting therefore a judicial examination of the merits of each individual case, and leaving the Court free to pronounce the word or words to be eligible for registration, if, on such an examination, it holds it proper to do so. Paragraph 5 of Section 9 of the [1905] Act authorises the registration of: "Any other distinctive mark" – that is, a mark not included in the preceding classes – "but a name, signature, word or words other than such as fall within the descriptions in the above paragraphs 1, 2, 3 and 4 shall not, except by order of the Board of Trade, or the Court, be deemed a distinctive mark".

Much of the argument before us on the part of the Opponents and the Board of Trade was based on an assumption that there is a natural and innate antagonism between distinctive and descriptive as applied to words, and that if you can show that a word is descriptive you have proved that it cannot be distinctive. To my mind this is a fallacy. Descriptive names may be distinctive, and vice versa. No class of words are more directly and intentionally distinctive than proper names, and yet originally they were usually, if not invariably, descriptive in all languages. They still are so among savage people, and although among civilised nations the original significations of proper names are not remembered, or regarded, we see that the natural tendency to use descriptive words as names still exists since nick-names – the only names that are now invented – are usually descriptive. There is therefore no natural or necessary incompatibility between distinctiveness and descriptiveness in the case of words used as Trade Marks. The notion that there is such an incompatibility is confined to lawyers, and is, in my opinion, due to the influence of the earlier Trade Mark Acts. By those Acts, which are now repealed, the fact that words were descriptive of the goods was fatal to their registration as Trade Marks, and thus becoming in the eye of the law distinctive of the goods of a particular maker. But the question whether a word is or is capable of becoming distinctive of the goods of a particular maker is a question of fact, and is not determined by its being or not being descriptive. The law has never refused to recognise that this is the case, or to give protection to descriptive Trade Marks when once duly established in fact, although – except in the case of old marks – they refused registration, and left the owners to obtain protection in another form of action. This is now changed, and under the provisions of the present Act the Court clearly has power to allow descriptive words to be registered, if a case on its merits is proved before it is sufficiently strong to induce it to do so. The language of Section 9, paragraph 5, puts this beyond doubt, but if any doubt upon the point could remain it would be set at rest by the language of Section 44 which provides that: "No registration under this Act shall interfere with . . . the use by any person of any *bona fide* description of the character or quality of his goods"; clearly indicating that a registered Trade Mark may have as its essential part words capable of being used descriptively.

Having thus established the jurisdiction of the Court to permit the registration of words having a direct reference to the character and quality of the goods as well as geographical terms it remains to consider the principles on which this jurisdiction should be exercised. Nothing that I have said must be taken to imply that I consider the effect of paragraph 5 to be to leave the matter at large so that it is indifferent for the purposes of registration whether a word is within the classes specified in 3 and 4 or not. On the contrary, I am of opinion that the fact, that the legislature has required in these cases a preliminary permission to proceed, evidences that it intends the excepted cases to be carefully considered on their merits before they are pronounced to be eligible to obtain the privileges of registration. The tribunal before whom is brought an application to register a word under paragraph 5 is entitled to regard the word as *prima facie* unsuitable by reason of its being outside the specified classes, and it is for the applicant to show that it is proper to be registered. This he may do by arguments based on the word itself and the nature of the goods with respect to which it is sought to be registered, as I have already indicated in the case of geographical terms. The exact issue is formulated in the paragraph, and if the tribunal is of opinion that the nature of the word is such that it is adapted to distinguish those particular goods of the trader from those of other persons it will be its duty – in the absence of special circumstances – to allow the registration to proceed. But the applicant is not confined to arguments drawn from the word itself. He may support his application, in the case of a mark already in use, by showing that by user the mark has, in fact, become more or less completely identified with the goods by having been continuously used in connection therewith, and the Statute expressly provides that the Court may take this into consideration for the purposes of its decision. To my mind this provision can bear but one interpretation. It recognises that distinctiveness – that is, being adapted to distinguish the goods from those of other traders – is not necessarily an innate quality of the word. It may be acquired. There may be cases in which the Court might say: "The word is descriptive of the goods, and cannot be distinctive solely of your make of those goods". The Applicant may (if he can) reply thereto: "I will show that it can become distinctive of my make of those goods by showing that it has actually become so either generally or in a particular market". To use a phrase suggested by Lord Justice Farwell during the argument, the reply is of the type of *"Solvitur ambulando"*: "It can denote my goods because it actually does so". The extent to which the Court will require the proof of this acquired distinctiveness to go will depend on the nature of the case. If the objections to the word itself are not very strong it will act on less proof of acquired distinctiveness than it would require in the case of a word which in itself was open to grave objection. I do not think, for instance, that any amount of evidence of use would induce a Court to permit the registration of ordinary laudatory epithets, such as "best", "perfect", etc. On the other hand, in the case of a peculiar collocation of words it might be satisfied with reasonable proof of acquired distinctiveness even though the words taken separately might be descriptive words in common use. In this connection the provisions of Section 44 afford in my opinion useful guidance. The registration is not to affect the use of the words by other traders in any *bona fide* description of the goods. The Court will, therefore, do well to ask itself the question: Will the registration of the Trade Mark cause substantial difficulty or confusion in view of these rights of user by other traders? If the answer is in the affirmative the Court will probably hesitate to allow the word to be registered. But if the answer be in the negative, either by reason of the nature of the words, or because past use has limited the possibility of other traders safely or honestly so using the words the Court may well grant the desired permission.

In conclusion I desire to say that I have no doubt that the permission required by paragraph 5 is of the nature of a permission to proceed with the application for registration. Its sole effect is to enable the word or words to act as the essential particular of a Trade Mark. Whether it will ultimately be registered will depend on the facts brought to light by the opposition and the searches that may be made during that application. The decision of the Court in granting the permission in no way prejudices the rights of opposing parties. It only prevents it being alleged that the registration would be *ultra vires* because the word or words do not belong to any of the classes specified in paragraphs 3 and 4. It now remains to apply these conclusions of law to the special facts of the three cases before us.

"Perfection"

This is an application to register "Perfection", or "Perfection Soap" as a Trade Mark for household soap. The evidence, which is very voluminous, establishes the following facts: It has for many years past been the custom for large manufacturers of household soap in this country to put their soap on the market under special names or brands. Thus Messrs Lever Bros sell the largest part of their output under the name of "Sunlight Soap", Messrs Watsons of "Matchless Cleanser" and Messrs Crosfield, the Applicants, of "Perfection". These names or brands are well known to the makers of soap, and many of them are so widely known to the public that it may well be that no maker could honestly put out soap for sale in the general market under one of these well-known names. But that by itself is not sufficient to establish the case of the Applicants. The name they have selected is the ordinary laudatory term "Perfection". Speaking only for myself I am not much impressed by the argument that such a word ought not to be allowed to become a Trade Mark because a more perfect method of making soap might be invented, and that in such case the use of the Trade Mark would tend to deceive the public. The use of inordinate laudation of his goods by a trader is too deeply rooted, and too ineradicable not to be well known to all the public, and I do not believe that any person buying soap would suppose that it was perfection merely because the maker calls it so. But to my mind this tells against the Applicants. It shows that the word is one that probably, and I might almost say naturally, would be used by others in the description of their soap. To me there is not much difference in this respect between the noun "Perfection" and the adjective "perfect". Therefore I think we ought not to allow it to become a Trade Mark. I regret to have so to decide because I feel that there has grown up a vast trade round the word which cannot be protected by the agency of the Trade Marks Act, but must be defended, so far as it can, by other and less efficient methods. But it is the consequence of the Applicants having been so unwise as to choose a mere laudatory word for their brand. Had the word been less objectionable in its nature the case that has been proved before us would have influenced me greatly, for it shows, to my mind, that throughout about half of England the past user of the word has identified it in the eyes of the public with the goods of the Applicants.

"California Syrup of Figs"

These words collectively form the commercial name of a well known aperient medicine. The evidence is ample to establish a *prima facie* case of these words being identified by long use with the goods of the Applicants. There is no inherent difficulty in accepting such a conclusion in the case of a compound appellation such as this, nor is there, in my opinion, any likelihood of other traders being placed in difficulties by having to avoid it. They can easily find adequate descriptions of any goods they may wish to sell without adopting this compound name even if they could honestly make us of it at all. I am therefore of opinion that the evidence before us justifies us in allowing the registration to proceed.

"Orlwoola"

This case presents no difficulty. It is in substance a case of registration of the words "All wool", grotesquely mis-spelt, as a Trade Mark for textile fabrics. When a Trade Mark consists solely of words it will be used orally as well as in writing, and to be proper to constitute a Trade Mark such words must be suitable, whether spoken or written. The mis-spelling does not affect the words when spoken, so that we have only to decide whether the words "All wool" are proper for registration in respect of such goods. To this there can be but one answer. If the goods are wholly made of wool the words are the natural and almost necessary description of them. If they are not wholly made of wool it is a misdescription which is so certain to deceive that its use can hardly be otherwise than fraudulent. In either case the words are utterly unfit for registration as a Trade Mark.

Cozens Hardy M.R. and Farwell L.J. delivered concurring judgments.

5.2.3.4   *Smith Kline & French v Sterling Winthrop (II)* (above 5.2.1.5)

In respect of an argument against registration based on s.9(3), Lord Diplock stated:

My Lords, in the instant case it is not disputed that SKF colour combinations applied to the capsules and their pellets are in fact adapted to distinguish SKF goods from those of other manufacturers. They have served that purpose successfully for years. The reference to inherent adaptability would at first sight appear more apt where the mark has not already been used by the applicant in the course of his trade before the date of the application. However, long before the reference to inherent adaptability had been incorporated in the current statutes dealing with trade marks, it had been held upon grounds of public policy that a trader ought not to be allowed to obtain by registration under the Trade Marks Act a monopoly in what other traders may legitimately desire to use. The classic statement of this doctrine is to be found in the speech of Lord Parker in the *W & G* case (1913) 30 R.P.C. 660 at p. 672 where he said that the right to registration should

> "largely depend on whether other traders are likely, in the ordinary course of their business and without any improper motive, to desire to use the same mark, or some mark nearly resembling it, upon or in connection with their own goods."

The reference to "inherently adapted" in section 9(3) of the Consolidation Act of 1938, which was first enacted in 1937, has always been treated as giving statutory expression to the doctrine as previously stated by Lord Parker.

The Assistant Registrar held upon the evidence that there was no reason why any other manufacturers would be likely to desire to use, unless with an improper motive, precisely the same colour marks as those applied for by the applicants. He went on to say, however, that Lord Parker's test extends to "some mark nearly resembling it" and appears to have regarded this phrase as applying in the instant case to any marking of capsules or pellets with colours, whatever colour or combination of colours was used. I think, with respect, that the Assistant Registrar treated the phrase as having a wider connotation than was intended by Lord Parker, who clearly meant it to be limited to marks so nearly resembling the applicant's mark as to be likely to deceive or cause confusion; for it is only to such marks, additionally to identical marks, that the monopoly of the registered proprietor extends. Once it is conceded, as it has been, that the use of marks so nearly resembling the SKF marks as to be deceptive would amount to a passing off at common law which could be restrained by injunction, it cannot plausibly be argued that any other trader could have a legitimate reason for using them which could be justified upon grounds of public policy.

The Assistant Registrar's decision on this point was reversed on appeal by Graham J. It was not dealt with by the Court of Appeal. As was held by this House in the second *Reddaway* case the Trade Marks Acts leave to the Registrar a residue of discretion as to whether a particular trade mark should be registered, but by section 52 of the Act of 1938, on an appeal from a decision of the Registrar, the judge has the same discretion as the Registrar. Upon a matter such as this an appellate court would not in any event lightly interfere with the exercise by the judge of the discretion expressly conferred upon him by the statute; but in the instant case for the reasons that I have given I have no doubt that Graham J.'s decision was right.

One final point remains. For reasons which do not appear in his judgment Graham J.

limited the registration of each combination of colours in the first instance to use upon the individual drug for which that particular colour combination had been used by SKF, leaving them to apply for an extension of the registration if they wished to use the same combination upon another drug as well. It is common ground between the parties that if registration is permissible at all there is no necessity to impose this limitation and no useful purpose would be served by doing so.

I would allow the appeal and order that the Registrar do proceed with the registration of the marks as described in the applications advertised in the Trade Marks Journal for 11th January 1967.

5.2.3.5   *Electrix Ltd's Application* [1959] R.P.C. 283 (H.L.)

An application to register "Electrix" for electrical goods was rejected by the Court of Appeal. On further appeal Viscount Simonds spoke for the House:

My Lords, I can conveniently state the problem to be solved by the citation of a single sentence from the judgment of the Court of Appeal: "The doctrine", they said, "as we understand it, is that, if a given word is for any reason unregistrable in its proper spelling, then inasmuch as Trade Marks appeal to the ear as well as to the eye, the objection (whatever it may be) to the registration of the properly spelt word applies equally to a word which is merely its phonetic equivalent". Applying that view of the law to the facts of the present case the Court of Appeal held that "electrix" being the phonetic equivalent of "electrics" and that word being unregistrable, "electrix" also was unregistrable.

In my opinion the proposition or doctrine of law, upon which the Court of Appeal founded, is accurately stated and supported by authority and reason, and it was correctly applied. The more important of the cases which establish it are cited in the exhaustive judgment of the Court of Appeal. At the risk of repetition I must refer to some of them. In re *Edward Ripley & Son's Application* (1898) 15 R.P.C. 151, the question was whether the word "Pirle" should be registered for goods in Class 34, namely cloths and stuffs of wool, worsted and hair, the word "Pirle" being formed from the name "Ripley" with the omission of the "y". The application was refused on the ground that the word was identical in sound with "Pearl" and that "Pearl" itself was not eligible for registration, being a term of commendation. Kekewich, J., upheld the refusal, and so did the Court of Appeal in words which I quote because they are directly apposite: "We do not see our way", said Sir Nathaniel Lindley, M.R., "to accede to this application. We cannot do it, unless we are prepared to lay down a proposition that I do not think any Court should. We cannot say that a man may register, in any class of goods, a word which sounds exactly like a word that could not be registered. The reason is obvious: it would be putting a monopoly upon the public which would be utterly unjustifiable. That is the short reason". My Lords, the reason was short and was obvious. The judgment too was short: I have cited the whole of it. There is not a word in it to suggest that it matters why the word is unregistrable which the word proposed to be registered sounds exactly like. And in the 70 years which have passed since those very learned Judges gave that clear and emphatic judgment, there has never been a suggestion that it is material why the unregistrable word is unregistrable, nor any attempt to qualify the generality of its language. That case was decided under the Acts of 1883 and 1888. The next cases that I cite were heard after the passing of the Trade Marks Act, 1905.

Viscount Simonds referred to "Perfection" and "Orlwoola" and continued:

But I cannot refrain from citing a short passage from the judgment of Moulton, L.J., at p 860. With regard to "Orlwoola" he said: "The misspelling does not affect the words when spoken, so that we have only to decide whether the words 'All wool' are proper for registration in respect of such goods". That was for him the sole question, just as for your Lordships the sole question is whether the word, of which "Electrix" is the phonetic equivalent, is registrable – a question that in this case admits of only one answer. So also in the *Ogee* case (*Garrett's Application* (1916) 33 R.P.C. 117) Lord Cozens Hardy, M.R. reiterating that a trade mark appeals to the ear as well as to the eye, said: "If the letters 'O.G.' could not be registered, it seems to me that the word 'Ogee' ought not to be registered. . . . The applicant may or may not have the right to 'Ogee' as a common law mark, but it is not a registrable mark". It would be difficult to find words more directly applicable than these to the present case. Rather surprisingly, learned counsel for the Appellants sought to rely on the speech of Lord Parker in the *W & G* case *W & G Du Cros Ltd's Applications* (1913), 30 R.P.C. 660. In that speech there is much that is valuable. The noble and learned Lord had been Counsel to the Board of Trade at the passing of the 1905 Act and knew well the problem which led to its enactment. He pointed out that the definition of "distinctive" as meaning "adapted to distinguish" made no change in the law, for the word "distinctive" had been used in that sense in the earlier Acts. He emphasised that in order to determine whether a mark is distinctive it must be considered apart from the effects of registration, and (what is more important to the present case) that present distinctiveness in fact is not conclusive that a mark is adapted to distinguish. But neither in his speech nor in those of the other learned Lords was there suggested any qualification of the general principle that the phonetic equivalent of an unregistrable word is itself unregistrable. That was not in fact the question which had to be decided. The question was whether "W & G", not its phonetic equivalent, was registrable. The same may be said of the *Glastonbury* case (*Bailey & Co Ltd v Clark, Son & Morland Ltd* (1938) 55 R.P.C. 253) and of the *Yorkshire Copper Works Ltd's Application* (1953) 70 R.P.C. 1 which recently came before the House, and to the "*Trakgrip*" case (1942) 59 R.P.C. 134 which it fell to me to decide. In these and other cases that were cited it was the question of distinctiveness that was elaborately discussed. It is obvious that in observing the prescription of Section 9 (3) of the 1938 Act, viz that "in determining whether a trade mark is adapted to distinguish as aforesaid, the tribunal may have regard to the extent to which (a) the trade mark is inherently adapted to distinguish as aforesaid; and (b) by reason of the use of the trade mark or of any other circumstances, the trade mark is in fact adapted to distinguish as aforesaid" there is room for wide difference of opinion. It has nevertheless been consistently laid down that the discretion of the Registrar is not to be lightly overruled and the general excellence of the judgment of the Assistant-Comptroller in this case predisposes me to uphold it. But it appears to me that he has erred in principle. For, though he does not say in so many words that "electrics", of which "electrix" is the phonetic equivalent, could or could not be registered, saying merely "this does not mean that I necessarily regard "Electrics" as a word which could properly be registered", it is clear that he would not regard it as decisive of the unregistrability of "Electrix" that "Electrics" is unregistrable. Here he was, in my opinion, clearly wrong and, if I read his judgment aright, the learned Judge fell into the same error. So also the Appellants have sought to ignore the unregistrability of "Electrics" and claimed nevertheless that "Electrix" was registrable. Thus in their formal case they say "The Appellants do not contend that the word 'Electrics' would be registrable", and they did not resile from this position in argument before the House. Let it not be thought that I criticise them for making the admission. It appears to me that, whether or not distinctiveness in fact was or could be acquired by "Electrics" of which there was of course no evidence, it would be a hopeless task to persuade the tribunal that it was not inherently unregistrable. From this it follows that the word "Electrix" cannot be registered.

5.2.3.6 *"York" Trade Mark* [1982] F.S.R. 111 (H.L.)

An application to register "York" with pictorial additions for trailers and other goods was allowed but was then subject to a "leap frog" appeal to the House of Lords.

Lord Wilberforce (for the House):

The mark in question consists of the word "YORK" in block capital letters in white with a leaf, similar to a maple leaf, drawn inside the letter O, the whole being on a black rectilinear background. The parent company of the respondents is a Canadian company of York, Ontario; neither the parent company nor the subsidiary has any connection with the English City of York. There are three applications relating to various classes of goods in connection with which the mark is claimed to be used: these can broadly be described as trailers and containers for the transportation of freight; they are no doubt familiar to many frustrated motorists. Nothing turns upon the particular classes of trade marks within which these goods are specified.

The Assistant Registrar, acting for the Registrar of Trade Marks, based his decision essentially upon the ground that it should not be right to allow the respondents to monopolise, for use in connection with their goods, the name of an important city. There was evidence called as to the use of the mark by the respondents; this was shown to have been on a substantial scale and for a long period. It is not now disputed that the word "YORK" used as a trade mark for the relevant goods is distinctive of the proprietor and denotes his goods and those of no-one else – a situation commonly described as one of "100 per cent factual distinctiveness". The question of law upon this appeal is whether such 100 per cent factual distinctiveness entitles the applicant to registration in Part B of the Register of trade marks or whether the Registrar has a discretion whether or not in the interests of the public to allow or to disallow applications for the mark to proceed.

His Lordship set out section 9 and 10 of the Trade Marks Act 1938 and referred to the expressions "adapted to distinguish" and "capable of distinguishing" in the two sections. He continued:

I do not think that further analysis of the two expressions is necessary on this occasion, because it is not this that is the critical distinction in the present case. Indeed reliance upon it, and upon the supposed greater liberality of the word "capable" as opposed to "adapted" by the learned judge constitutes, to my mind, the essential fallacy in his judgment and in the respondents' argument in this House. Even if section 10 indicated a greater liberality of approach than section 9, it is liberality in a direction which is irrelevant for present purposes.

The second distinction (between "inherently adapted [or capable]", and "adapted [or capable] in fact") though verbally new in the Acts of 1937–8, is, on the other hand, relevant and crucial. It was not new in the law. In relation to adaptability it is sufficient to quote from a recent opinion of Lord Diplock in this House. In *Smith Kline and French Laboratories Ltd v Sterling Winthrop Group Ltd* [1976] R.P.C. 511 (above, 5.2.1.5), he said:

> "Long before the reference to inherent adaptability had been incorporated in the current statutes dealing with trade marks, it had been held upon grounds of public

policy that a trader ought not to be allowed to obtain by registration under the Trade Marks Act a monopoly in what other traders may legitimately desire to use. The classic statement of this doctrine is to be found in the speech of Lord Parker in the *W & G* case (1913) 30 R.P.C. 660 at page 672 where he said that the right to registration 'should largely depend on whether other traders are likely, in the ordinary course of their business and without any improper motive, to desire to use the same mark, or some mark nearly resembling it, upon or in connection with their own goods'."

and there can be no doubt that exactly similar reasoning must be applied to the words "inherently capable of distinguishing" in section 10 (2) (a) of the Act. They mean, in effect "capable in law of distinguishing", the relevant law being the accepted principle that, in relation to certain words, of which laudatory epithets and some geographical names were established examples, traders could not obtain a monopoly in the use of such words (however distinctive) to the detriment of members of the public who, in the future, and in connection with other goods, might desire to use them. That this principle has been firmly laid down in relation, in particular, to geographical words, by a strong current of authority, I shall now demonstrate.

I refer first to an authoritative pronouncement, to the judgment of Fletcher Moulton L.J. in a case concerned with both a laudatory word ("Perfection") and a geographical word ("California Syrup of Figs"). In an extended passage, the whole of which repays study, and which has been accepted as a classic statement of the law, he described the policy of the Act as substituting for an absolute exclusion, from use as trade marks, of geographical names, a judicial examination on the merits of each individual case. This was followed in *W & G du Cros Ltd* (1913) 30 R.P.C. 660, concerned with the use of initials in which Lord Parker said that the right to registration should

"largely depend upon whether other traders are likely, in the ordinary course of their business and without any improper motive, to desire to use the same mark, or some mark nearly resembling it, upon or in connection with their own goods".

These cases were prior to the introduction in 1919 of the Part B section of the register. However, it was not long before a case concerned with both Part A and Part B came before the courts. This was *Liverpool Electric Cable Co Ltd's Application* (1929) 46 R.P.C. 99, where what was sought was to register "Liverpool Cables" for electric cables, this mark being accepted as distinctive of the applicants' goods. The position as regards both Part A and Part B was considered. At first instance, Romer J. allowed the application holding that proof of distinctiveness established that the words were "capable of distinguishing" – essentially the respondents' argument here. But this decision was reversed by the Court of Appeal. All three members of the court dealt explicitly and at length with the position regarding Part B of the Register. As regards "capability" Lord Hanworth used these words:

"... when you come to regard the rights of the public at large, the traders at Liverpool and the like, it appears to me that the Registrar would be quite right in holding that a word of that importance and significance ought not to be used or allowed to be treated as a word capable of distinguishing, because it has not merely to be capable in fact, but it must be capable in law". (*loc. cit.* p 118)

Similar passages are to be found in the judgments of Lawrence and Russell L.JJ. This decision, if accepted, must conclude this appeal against the respondents and one would think would have so concluded it at first instance. What has been its subsequent history?

In 1938 it was referred to, without any sign of disapprobation, in this House, in *A Bailey*

& Co Ltd v Clark, Son & Morland Ltd (1938) 55 R.P.C. 253, concerned with the geographical mark "Glastonburys". Lord Russell of Killowen said this:

"It appears to me to be, from one aspect, a stronger case for refusing registration than the case of *Liverpool Cables*. That decision laid down no new law. It was based upon the view, well established by previous authority, that distinctiveness in fact is not conclusive upon the questions whether a Mark is 'distinctive' as defined in section 9, and whether it ought to be registered". (*loc. cit.* p 262).

This case was concerned with Part A but the reasoning is equally applicable to Part B: distinctiveness in fact is not conclusive.

In 1954 (i.e. after the passing of the Act of 1938) the correctness of the *Liverpool* case came directly in issue in *Yorkshire Copper Works Ltd's Application*, 71 R.P.C. 150, where again, 100 per cent distinctiveness in fact was shown. Registration was refused in both Part A and Part B. The *Liverpool* case was expressly approved by this House. It is sought to escape from the authority of this case on the basis that, as reported, counsel for the applicants conceded that registration under Part B could not be granted if the application under Part A were to fail. But this is desperate advocacy. Quite apart from the question whether the learned counsel concerned, whose determination is well known, would have conceded the point unless he had thought it unarguable, it cannot be supposed that the members of this House, with the two adjacent sections (9 and 10) before them, would have let it pass, and given unqualified approval to the *Liverpool* case, unless they had been of the clear opinion that the argument applied to both parts of the Register. And the reasoning of Lord Simonds shows that he must have thought so. I quote two passages:

"Just as a manufacturer is not entitled to a monopoly of a laudatory or descriptive epithet, so he is not to claim for his own a territory, whether country, county or town, which may be in the future, if it is not now, the seat of manufacture of goods similar to his own.

There will probably be border-line cases, but there is, in my opinion, no doubt on which side of the border lies Yorkshire, a county not only of broad acres but of great manufacturing cities. If the *Liverpool Cables* case was rightly decided, as I think it clearly was, *a fortiori* the Registrar was right in refusing registration to 'Yorkshire'. And if it were a border-line case, which it is not, I think that a court, to which an appeal is brought from the Registrar, though, no doubt, it must exercise its own discretion in the matter, should be slow to differ from the experienced official whose constant duty it is to protect the interests of the public not only of today but of tomorrow and the day after". (*loc. cit.* p 154).

What then is there to set against the authority of a decision of the Court of Appeal, twice approved by this House? In *Tijuana Smalls Trade Mark* [1973] R.P.C. 453, Graham J. appeared to follow its reasoning, though admitting registration in Part B, as I understand the decision, in the exercise of his discretion. In the present case he departed from it, founding in the main upon two arguments. First he drew support from some observations by members of the Court of Appeal in *Weldmesh Trade Mark* [1966] R.P.C. 220. There can indeed be found in the judgments of Wilmer L.J. and Harman L.J. (though not in that of the third member of the court) passages suggesting that distinctiveness in fact is enough to establish inherent capability to distinguish. The case was not directly concerned with registration in Part B, which has been accepted, so that these observations cannot have been intended as an analysis of the words of section 10 of the Act. If they were, they are inconsistent with the *Liverpool* case (cited in argument and judgment) and, in my opinion, wrong. Secondly, the learned judge argued that registration in Part B could be accepted because it could be removed at any time after registration so that other potential traders would not be prejudiced. In this he fell into error. There is no provision in the Act of 1938 whether as regards Part A or as regards Part B for removal of a mark for the reason that, through a change of circumstances, it no longer qualifies for registration under Section 9 or under Section 10. The difference between Part A and Part B registrations is that, as regards the latter, the original registration can, even after seven years be attacked, a difference which does not support the learned judge's argument. A related argument appears to be based on Section 8, which provides a defence to infringement proceedings in cases of *bona fide* use. But this is no argument in favour of allowing registration to the detriment of other possible users. It was used without success in the *Glastonburys* and *Yorkshire* cases (see above).

In my opinion, therefore, the Registrar's decision against allowing the application to proceed was based upon a correct application of authority, with which, though it is perhaps superfluous to say so, I am wholly in agreement. It should be restored and the appeal allowed with costs.

5.2.3.7   Trade Marks Act 1938, s.27(1): Defensive registration of well-known trade marks

S.27(1) Where a trade mark consisting of an invented word or invented words has become so well known as respects any goods in respect of which it is registered and in relation to which it has been used that the use thereof in relation to other goods would be likely to be taken as indicating a connection in the course of trade between those goods and a person entitled to use the trade mark in relation to the first-mentioned goods, then, notwithstanding that the proprietor registered in respect of the first-mentioned goods does not use or propose to use the trade mark in relation to those other goods and notwithstanding anything in the last foregoing section, the trade mark may, on the application in the prescribed manner of the proprietor registered in respect of the first-mentioned goods, be registered in his name in respect of those other goods as a defensive trade mark and, while so registered, shall not be liable to be taken off the register in respect of those goods under the last foregoing section.

S.27(2) permits defensive registration where the same proprietor has registered non-defensively for other goods, and allows transfer from a defensive to a non-defensive registration.

S.27(3) deems defensive and non-defensive registrations of a mark to be as associated marks.

S.27(4),(5) provide grounds and procedure for cancellation of a defensive mark.

S.27(6) applies the general provisions of the Act to defensive marks. Defensive registration does not apply to service marks.

5.2.3.8   *Ferodo's Application* [1945] Ch. 334 (Evershed J.)

Application was made under Section 27 to register the invented word mark "Ferodo" as a defensive trade mark for all goods in classes 5 (Pharmaceutical articles) and 34 (Tobacco, smokers' articles and matches). The mark was already registered in several classes but it was principally used for brake linings and clutches. The Applicants filed evidence showing that their turnover and advertising were on a very large scale, and that they had some 60,000 customers. They contended that this evidence sufficiently established the notoriety of their mark for the purpose of Section 27 and that no other evidence was needed.

The Assistant Comptroller refused the application, but gave the Applicants an opportunity to supplement their evidence. The Applicants appealed to the Court. After setting out section 27, Evershed J. continued:

As I have already stated, the word "Ferodo" is beyond doubt an "invented" word, having been invented by the Appellants' predecessors, owners of the Appellants' business, about the year 1906. Being an invented word, the goodwill attached to its use has been wholly built up by the work and energies of the Appellants and their predecessors. It is accordingly urged on the part of the Appellants that there is at least a strong moral case for justifying the grant of monopolistic rights in regard to that which is the exclusive creation of the Applicants or, conversely, that the Court should not be slow to prevent other persons obtaining for themselves the advantages attaching to a well established trade word in respect of goods however different in kind from those marketed by the inventor of the word. And no doubt on grounds such as these the new section has been enacted and its scope confined to the case of invented words.

But however cogent may be the moral argument, my duty is to construe the words used in the sub-section. The Appellants invite me to hold that if the invented word is sufficiently well known it does not matter that the persons who know the word should not also know the goods or the kind of goods with which it has been associated by the inventor, or should not know who are the persons entitled to use the word as a trade mark; or, at least, to hold that the reference to a likelihood of an indication of a connection in the course of trade between the goods in respect of which a defensive registration is sought and a person entitled to use the trade mark means no more than that the Court should infer a likelihood that persons seeing the word used in relation to such goods will identify the word as a trade mark already well known to them.

In my judgment these contentions fail to do justice to the limitations imposed by the phrase "as respects any goods etc" which immediately follow the words "so well known"; or to give proper weight to the latter requirement that the assumed use of the word would be likely to be taken as indicating a trade connection with a person entitled to use the trade mark. In my judgment the earlier phrase which I have mentioned requires that the knowledge of the word should be knowledge of it in its application to goods of a specific kind; and the conclusion to be reached by the Court or the Comptroller-General must be the inference, in the light of all the known facts, including the general knowledge of the word in its application to the specific goods mentioned, that persons seeing the mark attached to the new class of goods would assume that they originate from the proprietor of the mark or a registered user. Thus in the present case it is in my opinion necessary to show that the word "Ferodo" has become so well known in its application to goods of a specific kind, that is brake and clutch linings and the like (originating in fact from the Appellants), that is use in relation to "other goods" in clauses 5 and 34 for example, when applied to a bottle of aspirin tablets or a packet of cigarettes – would be likely to lead persons buying or observing those "other goods" – for example the aspirin tablets or the cigarettes – to suppose that they too originated from the same persons who made and marketed "Ferodo" brake or clutch linings, namely, the Appellants.

In reaching a conclusion on this matter it is obvious that the nature of the goods "in respect of which" the trade mark "is registered . . . and used" is an important factor, for generally speaking the more special in character those goods are and the more limited their market, the less likely will be the inference required by the sub-section to be drawn in relation to goods of a very different kind. If "Ferodo" were a mark which had achieved notoriety in connection, say, with a paint or a dye-stuff used by the domestic householder, the required inference would as it seems to me be much more easily drawn from its application to pharmaceutical products.

In this connection reference was made in the course of the arguments to an observation of a former Registrar of Trade Marks to the effect that some trade marks ("Bovril" and "Kodak" being given as examples) are so well known in one particular field that their use by any person other than the proprietor in respect of any goods whatsoever would *prima facie* suggest an association of such goods with the proprietors of the marks. For myself I am not persuaded of the soundness of this proposition. Words do not become known as words without any significance or without appreciation of the things which they indicate. And so far as trade marks are concerned it may well be that the better known the words become the more closely are they associated in the public mind with the class of articles to which they are in the course of trade applied. I do not intend to pass judgment on any case not now before the Court, but if, for example, "Bovril" is well known to the great majority of the population of this island, and if it is so known as indicating a particular kind of foodstuff then, on that very ground, the application of the word to, say, a typewriting machine might well be held not to be in the least degree likely to lead to the indication referred to in the sub-section. To take as another illustration a word which does not happen to be an invented word (for the principle seems to me to be the same); the events of the past five and a half years have, for the whole British people save to very small infants and a few idiots, made the word "Spitfire" familiar in their mouths as a household word, but familiar as a description of an aeroplane. If a manufacturer of toothpaste were to describe one of his products as "Spitfire toothpaste" I should find it difficult to suppose that to any purchaser of the toothpaste the name would indicate a connection in the course of trade between the toothpaste and the aircraft manufacturers.

On the other hand if the mark has been registered and used in respect of a wide variety of goods required by the common man, its application to other goods even of a very different kind might fairly lead to the inference of trade connection; and the example of "Kodak" may well illustrate the latter kind of case.

Each case will indeed be decided upon its own facts. It will suffice for me to say in regard to the word "Ferodo" that I agree with the Assistant Comptroller that the somewhat narrow and special field of manufacture to which the mark has been applied and become known increases the difficulty of establishing as a matter of fact that the adoption of the word "in relation to" goods of a widely different character would be likely, according to the standard of common sense, to lead to an inference of common origin.

In the last sentence I have intimated my answer to another point stressed by Mr Lloyd-Jacob in his argument for the Appellants. The reference in the sub-section to an indication of "a connection in the course of trade" is a reflection of the definition of a trade mark in s.68(1) of the Act. This language, according to the argument, imports a conception distinct from the conception implicit in the well-known phrase, "likely to deceive or cause confusion" which is used in Sections 11 and 12. It is therefore urged that the obligation imposed upon an applicant under s.27(1) is satisfied by something less than proof of likelihood of deception or confusion between the goods in respect of which defensive registration is sought and the goods in respect of which the mark has been registered and used. The argument adds that the reference to "a person entitled to use the trade mark in relation to the first mentioned goods" instead of to the proprietor of the trade mark supports the view that knowledge of the origin of the goods to which the mark has been applied is unnecessary; in other words that it is sufficient that persons assumed to see the word in its application to the new class of goods should identify it with a trade mark already observed and known to them, even though they are ignorant of the nature and origin of the goods to which it had been applied.

The argument in my judgment involves too great a nicety of language. Since *ex hypothesi* the Applicant's trade mark has not been and may never be used in respect of the goods for which registration under the sub-section is sought, it may well have been thought that the test of confusion would be inappropriate. But if an inference were drawn, and falsely drawn, of a connection in the course of trade, the result would nevertheless have been a form of deception. I do not therefore think that any great significance can be attached to the distinction in this respect between the wording of Section 27 on the one hand and that of Sections 11 and 12 on the other. Moreover the decision of the House of Lords in *Aristoc Ltd v Rysta Ltd* (above, 5.2.1.4) has made it clear that the langauge of the present definition section referring to "a connection in the course of trade etc" which has been incorporated also in Section 27 sub-section (1) involved no departure from the old-established conception of indication of origin. The use of the phrase "person entitled to use the trade mark" instead of "proprietor" is no doubt attributable to the introduction contemporaneously with Section 27 of Section 28 providing for the registration of users as well as proprietors. But though I do not say that the notoriety required by s.27(1) must involve exact knowledge of the identity of the registered proprietor or registered user, I think it does require knowledge of the kind of goods to which the mark has been applied by their manufacturers and distributors as an indication of origin.

It is not uncommon today for manufacturers of or traders in goods of a specific class to advertise their wares by the distribution as gifts of goods, eg, pencils or matches, bearing their name or trade mark though such last mentioned goods are wholly different in character from their own goods; and it is in evidence in the present case that the Appellants, Ferodo Limited have in fact adopted this practice in regard *inter alia* to matches. A member of the public seeing goods of the character of those comprised in classes 5 or 34 bearing the name "Ferodo" might suppose that such goods were being distributed as part of an advertising campaign. He would not, however, suppose that, being so distributed, the manufacture or distribution of the goods formed any part, save for advertising purposes, of the business of Ferodo Limited. In my judgment it follows from the *Aristoc* case that the phrase "connection in the course of trade etc" does not cover advertising media of this kind. In other words I think that by a connection in the course of trade is meant (as regards the present case) that the production and marketing of the goods in question is a part of the Appellants' business or trading enterprise.

In my judgment the conclusion I have reached upon the construction of the sub-section does not so confine its scope as to render unsubstantial any advantage given by the sub-section to the proprietor of the trade mark additional to the advantages conferred by older sections of the Act. I am content, without further analysis, to not the real and obvious benefit attached to the position of being first in the field.

I add finally before leaving this part of the case that I agree with the Assistant-Comptroller that the "other goods" mentioned in s.27(1) cannot be confined to goods of the same description (as that phrase is used in s.12(1) of the Act) as the goods in respect of which the mark has been registered and used. No doubt and for obvious reasons an applicant under s.27(1) would be able more easily to establish a claim to defensive registration in respect of a class of goods which were of the same description as goods in relation to which his mark had been registered and used. But it is to my mind reasonably plain (and Mr Danckwerts has not argued to the contrary) that there is no reason for construing the phrase "other goods" in a limited sense or otherwise than in accordance with its ordinary meaning.

There remains the question of the character of the evidence to be tendered in support of an application under s.27(1) sub-section (1) of the Act. This matter I approach with considerable caution since it cannot be the function of the Court to advise applicants under the sub-section generally, or the present Appellants in particular, on the evidence properly to be given in support of an application; nor would it be right for me in reference to the particular circumstances of the present case to lay down rules applicable to other cases the determination of which would depend upon their own particular facts.

Subject, however, to these qualifications and in deference to the arguments addressed to me, I make the following two observations:

(1) In addition to the evidence of the Appellants themselves in the present case it seems to me desirable that there should be available for the assistance of the Court at least some evidence from persons concerned and experienced in the trades affecting the classes of goods in respect of which defensive registration is sought. In the first place it should as it seems to me to be proved that the word "Ferodo" has not in fact already been used and applied to any goods falling within those classes. Secondly it might well, I think, be important for the Court to be informed of the significance within those trades of the use of brand names. Thus as regards, for example, aspirin tablets, purchasers of such goods may, by reason of the multiplicity of brand names applied to goods which are in quality substantially identical or for other reasons pay little or no regard to the proprietary name but be content when they ask for and obtain "aspirin" of whatever origin or manufacture. On the other hand it may equally be that a buyer of a packet of cigarettes will attach great importance to the brand or source of manufacture and will therefore pay particular regard to the name on the packet. Thirdly I think it would be both legitimate and useful for witnesses of the kind I have mentioned to state what, having regard to their own business experience, would be the effect on their own minds of seeing, say "Ferodo" aspirins or "Ferodo" cigarettes. These witnesses could not properly give in evidence their opinion upon what others might think on the hypothesis that the brand name were applied to aspirins or cigarettes; for the conclusion of that matter is the function of the Court or the Comptroller-General. But there would in my judgment be some value in statements by these trade witnesses themselves of what would be their assumptions on the hypothesis mentioned and what would be their reasons. On the other hand the production of a sheaf of affidavits sworn by members of the public each stating what he or she would think on seeing a bottle of "Ferodo" aspirins or a packet of "Ferodo" cigarettes and why, would in my judgment be of negligible value. Twenty-five such statements might appear impressive in weight of paper but would represent so slight a fraction of the whole population as to be no guide to popular opinion and no reliable measure of the notoriety of the mark.

The result therefore is that the appeal fails and must be dismissed with costs.

5.2.4 Deceptiveness and Conflicting Registrations

5.2.4.1 Trade Marks Act 1938, s.11–13: Prohibition of Registration of Deceptive Matter; and of Identical and Resembling Marks; Conclusiveness

S.11 It shall not be lawful to register as a trade/*service* mark or part of a trade/*service* mark any matter the use of which would, by reason of its being likely to deceive or cause confusion or otherwise, be disentitled to protection in a court of justice, or would be contrary to law or morality, or any scandalous design.

S.12(1) Subject to the provisions of subsection (2) of this section, no trade/*service* mark shall be registered in respect of any goods or description of goods that is identical with or nearly resembles a mark belonging to a different proprietor and already on the register in respect of –
   (a) the same goods/*services*,
   (b) the same description of goods/*services*, or
   (c) goods or a description of goods which are associated with those services or services of that description.

(2) In case of honest concurrent use, or of other special circumstances which in the opinion of the Court or the Registrar make it proper so to do, the Court or the Registrar may permit the registration by more than one proprietor, in respect of –
   (a) the same goods/*services*
   (b) the same description of goods/*services*, or
   (c) goods and services or descriptions of goods and services which are associated with each other,
of marks that are identical or nearly resemble each other, subject to such conditions and limitations, if any, as the Court or the Registrar, as the case may be, may think it right to impose.

(3) Where separate applications are made by different persons to be registered as proprietors respectively of marks that are identical or nearly resemble each other, in respect of –
   (a) the same goods/*services*,
   (b) the same description of goods/*services*, or
   (c) goods and services or descriptions of goods and services which are associated with each other,
the Registrar may refuse to register any of them until their rights have been determined by the Court, or have been settled by agreement in a manner approved by him or on an appeal (which may be brought either to the Board of Trade or to the Court at the option of the appellant) by the Board or the Court, as the case may be.

S.13(1) In all legal proceedings relating to a trade/*service* mark registered in Part A of the register (including applications under section thirty-two of this Act) the original registration in Part A of the register of the trade/*service* mark shall, after the expiration of seven years from the date of that registration, be taken to be valid in all respects, unless –
   (a) that registration was obtained by fraud, or

(b) the trade/*service* mark offends against the provisions of section eleven of this Act.

(2) Nothing in subsection (1) of section five of this Act shall be construed as making applicable to a trade/*service* mark, as being a trade/*service* mark registered in Part B of the register, the foregoing provisions of this section relating to a trade/*service* mark registered in Part A of the register.

5.2.4.2   *"Bali" Trade Mark (No.1)* [1969] R.P.C. 472 (H.L.)

The appellants registered "Berlei" for corsets and brassieres in 1924. In 1938 the respondents, a U.S. business, registered "Bali" in a device for much the same goods; and now sought to register the word by itself. The appellants resisted the new application under Sections 11 and 12; and sought to expunge the old "Bali" mark under s.11, since otherwise the registration would be valid under s.13.

Lord Upjohn considered section 11 and its predecessors from the 1875 Act onwards and the common law before 1875 in order to refute Bali's argument that before establishing that the mark was "disentitled to protection in a court of justice" the objector must show something akin to passing off of his mark.
He concluded:

So it seems to me impossible to give to the construction of the section that which is sought for by Bali. Section 11 and its forebears were designed not so much for the protection of other traders in the use of their marks or their reputation but for the protection of the public. This was made quite plain by the majority opinions in your Lordships' House in *Eno v Dunn* (1890) 7 R.P.C. 311.

With all respect to the recent judgment of Buckley J. in TRANSFERMATIC *Trade Mark* [1966] R.P.C. 568, I cannot agree with him if he meant to hold that the applicant seeking to have the mark expunged would have to discharge the burden of establishing a real and substantial likelihood of success in an action to obtain an injunction on the ground of passing off. The fact that in most cases the person seeking to expunge another's mark is himself the owner of a mark for which he could sue for infringement, or that he could establish such a reputation among the public, that he might succeed in an action against the owner of the mark for passing off the latter's goods as and for his goods, is, under the section, irrelevant.

Eno v Dunn (1890) 7 R.P.C. 311 itself also illustrates this point. During the course of the proceedings Mr Eno felt constrained to consent to the removal of his mark FRUIT SALT from the register, yet he was held entitled to object as a member of the public to the registration of the applicant's mark which contained the words "Fruit Salt". Lord Herschell (at page 318, line 27) concluded his speech with the words:

"To prevent misapprehension, I desire to add that your Lordships have not now to determine whether the appellant could in any, and, if so, in what cases, restrain the use of the words 'Fruit Salt'. I have already indicated my opinion that the appellant has no private property in them. The sole point for decision is, whether the Comptroller ought to be directed to proceed with the registration of a particular trade mark of which they form an element".

My Lords, I think the presence of these words "disentitled to protection in a court of justice" whether in their original form or in their phraseology of today are explained by the fact that in order to prevent the registration of a mark or to secure its removal it must be established (here, of course, I am not dealing with questions of onus) not merely that there is likelihood of deception or confusion between two marks judged upon the well-known tests laid down in *Piantotist Co's Application* (below, 5.2.4.3) and *Aristoc Limited v Rysta Limited* (below, 5.2.4.4) but something more, that is user at the relevant time by the owner of the existing mark which under the old common law the court, as Sir John Romilly said, would protect. The whole emphasis is upon the question whether the owner of the mark in suit, assuming him to bring some action against another trader, would be disentitled from succeeding for any of the reasons set out in Section 11; not whether anyone would succeed against him. This is the chief distinction between Section 11 and Section 12. Section 12 is principally a weapon in the hands of a registered proprietor though it is not necessary that he personally should object. Here no user by the registered proprietor need be shown; it is purely a question of similarity. Section 11 is, as I have said, for the protection of the public and anyone may object, but if he relies only on similarity he must prove the practical likelihood of confusion to the public and this he can only do, for the purposes of the section, by proving the existing user by another, not necessarily by himself, which is likely to cause deception or confusion; but if he does not establish likelihood of confusion by some present user of a similar mark likely to cause deception or confusion the court would not treat that as sufficient to disentitle the mark in suit to protection. Thus it came about that Evershed J. in *Smith Hayden & Co's Application* (1945) 63 R.P.C. 97 formulated the test under Section 11 in these terms (at page 101 line 40):

> "(a) (Under Section 11) 'Having regard to the reputation acquired by the name HOVIS, is the court satisfied that the mark applied for, if used in a normal and fair manner in connection with any goods covered by the registration proposed, will not be reasonably likely to cause deception and confusion amongst a substantial number of persons?'"

My Lords, I think the learned judge was wrong to use the words "reputation acquired by"; it should have been "the user of". Of course, in that case there was no difference between those two expressions, as the household word of HOVIS was involved; but in many cases, such as TRANSFERMATIC, the difference might be vital.

It may also be said that the desiderata that the deception and confusion (in Evershed J.'s statement) must be among a substantial number of persons is a matter of judicial gloss. I do not object to this provided it is properly and sensibly applied. Here again, the TRANSFERMATIC case is a good illustration of the application of this condition to special circumstances: I think Buckley J. was quite right to overrule the Assistant Comptroller and to reach a different conclusion on the facts of that case (see [1966] R.P.C. 577 and 578).

What then is the test? This must necessarily be a question of fact and degree in every case. I am content in amplification of the test laid down by Evershed J. to take the test as in effect laid down by Romer J. in *Jellinek's Trade Mark* (1946) 63 R.P.C. 59 at page 78.

It is not necessary in order to find that a mark offends against Section 11 to prove that there is an actual probability of deception leading to a passing off or (I add) an infringement action. It is sufficient if the result of the registration of the mark will be that a number of persons will be caused to wonder whether it might not be the case that the two products come from the same source. It is enough if the ordinary person entertains a reasonable doubt, but the court has to be satisfied not merely that there is a possibility of confusion; it must be satisfied that there is a real tangible danger of confusion if the mark which it is sought to register is put on the register. And so *mutatis mutandis* when it is sought to expunge a mark.

*His Lordship proceeded to find an inherent likelihood of confusion between the marks,
particularly in verbal use. Lords Morris of Borth-y-Gest, Guest, Wilberforce and Pearson
delivered concurring speeches.*

5.2.4.3   *Pianotist Co's Application* (1906) 23 R.P.C. 774 (Parker J.)

*An application to register "Neola" for player pianos was opposed by the proprietor of the
registered mark "Pianola" for musical instruments.*

Parker J.:

This is just one of those cases where it is perfectly possible that another mind, if
brought to bear on the subject, might take another view. It always is so in cases of this
sort where you cannot really test whether a confusion has arisen, but only have to judge
from the general appearance or sound of the words whether confusion is likely to arise.
With regard to the law upon the point, it seems to me quite settled and quite clear. In
this case the Comptroller has passed the mark for registration and there is opposition.
That opposition goes by way of appeal first to the Board of Trade, and the Board of
Trade refers it to the Court, and the Court then gets seisin of the matter, and has to
determine, in the words of the Act, whether the registration is to proceed, and if so,
under what conditions, if any. The only point at issue here is whether the limitation put
on the power of the Comptroller by Section 72 of the Act of 1883 is applicable. That
limitation is, reading it shortly and generally, that he is not allowed to register any
goods having such resemblance to a Trade Mark already on the Register as to be
calculated to deceive. That section has been the subject of judicial decision on many
occasions, and I think, without going into the details of the cases, it may be taken that
the law is as follows: You must take the two words. You must judge of them, both by
their look and by their sound. You must consider the goods to which they are to be
applied. You must consider the nature and kind of customer who would be likely to buy
those goods. In fact, you must consider all the surrounding circumstances; and you
must further consider what is likely to happen if each of those trade marks is used in a
normal way as a trade mark for the goods of the respective owners of the marks. If,
considering all those circumstances, you come to the conclusion that there will be a
confusion – that is to say, not necessarily that one man will be injured and the other will
gain illicit benefit, but that there will be a confusion in the mind of the public which will
lead to confusion in the goods – then you may refuse the registration, or rather you
must refuse the registration in that case. In this particular case we have this state of
circumstances, that the Opponents have on the Register the word "Pianola". The word
"Pianola" was undoubtedly invented by them and has been registered, and is a perfectly
good Trade Mark. There is some sort of evidence that it has become associated in the
mind of the public with the instrument and not with the maker of the instrument – that
is to say, that it has lost its primary signification of denoting an instrument made by a
particular manufacturer, and has come to mean a particular class of instrument. That
may be so, or may not be so. There is not any clear evidence on the subject, but some
suggestion has been made with regard to it. Now the mark which is proposed to be
registered, and which the Registrar has passed, is "Neola", and the argument before me
has taken two lines. In the first place, it is suggested that the importance of the Trade
Mark "Pianola" lies in its termination, and that anybody who takes a word with a similar
termination may cause confusion in the mind of the public. The second way it is put to
me is, that the sounds of the words, although the look of the words may be different, are
likely to be so similar that a person asking for a "Pianola" might have a "Neola" passed off
on him, or vice versa. Of course, one knows that the persons who buy these articles are

generally persons of some education (it is not quite the same as somebody going and asking for washing soap in a grocer's shop) and some consideration is likely to attend the purchase of any instrument of the cost of either of these instruments, whether it be a "Pianola" or a "Neola". Now, my opinion is that having regard to the nature of the customer, the article in question, and the price at which it is likely to be sold, and all the surrounding circumstances, no man of ordinary intelligence is likely to be deceived. If he wants a "Pianola" he will ask for a "Pianola", and I cannot imagine that anybody hearing the word "Pianola" if pronounced in the ordinary way in the shop, and knowing the instruments as all shopmen do would be likely to be led to pass off upon that customer a "Neola" instead of a "Pianola".

5.2.4.4 *Aristoc v Rysta* [1945] A.C. 68 (H.L.)

See above 5.2.1.4 for facts and the third issue in the case. The first two issues were:

1. Whether the word "Rysta", if used as a trade mark for stockings, so nearly resembles the word "Aristoc" already on the register in respect of the same class of goods as to be likely to deceive or cause confusion within the meaning of Section 12 of the Trade Marks Act, 1938.

2. Whether the use by the Respondents of "Rysta" as a trade mark both upon stockings of the Respondents' merchandise concurrently with use by them of the same mark upon stockings which are not their merchandise, but are only repaired by them, is likely to lead to confusion or deception and is therefore unlawful by virtue of the provisions of Section 11 of the Trade Marks Act, 1938, or for other reasons should be rejected by the Registrar.

On the first point, Viscount Maugham said:

Luxmoore L.J., however, preferred to dispose of the appeal on the simple ground that the word "Rysta" was likely to cause confusion having regard to the existence of the Appellants' Trade Mark "Aristoc". His grounds for differing from his colleagues and the Assistant-Comptroller seem to me to be clear and cogent, and I agree with his view as to how the word "Rysta" on the evidence must be taken to be pronounced and as to how a considerable number of persons pronounce the word "Aristoc", namely, with the emphasis on the middle syllable. He also stated, what is not in dispute, that it is well settled that the onus of proving that there is no reasonable probability of deception is cast on an applicant for registration of a mark. (*Eno v Dunn*, (1890) 15 A.C. 252 at pp. 257–261). There follows a passage which I completely accept as a fair statement of the duty cast upon the Court in such a case: "The answer to the question whether the sound of one word resembles too nearly the sound of another so as to bring the former within the limits of Section 12 of the Trade Marks Act, 1938, must nearly always depend on first impression, for obviously a person who is familiar with both words will neither be deceived nor confused. It is the person who only knows the one word and has perhaps an imperfect recollection of it who is likely to be deceived or confused. Little assistance, therefore, is to be obtained from a meticulous comparison of the two words, letter by letter and syllable by syllable, pronounced with the clarity to be expected from a teacher of elocution. The Court must be careful to make allowance for imperfect recollection and the effect of careless pronunciation and speech on the part not only of the person seeking to buy under the trade description, but also of the shop assistant ministering to that person's wants". And then he adds a little later "The tendency to slur a word beginning with 'a' is, generally speaking, very common, and the similarity between 'Rysta' and 'Ristoc' would, I think, be fairly obvious. It would not be surprising to learn that a person asking for 'Aristoc' stockings from a shop assistant who only knew of 'Rysta' stockings had been supplied with the latter and vice versa". He also said that he thought the Assistant Comptroller had failed to take into full account the effect of careless and slurred pronunciation, imperfect recollection, and the limitation of the knowledge of the customer and the shop assistant to one only of the marks, that being the one of which the other is ignorant. He felt strongly that the two words were likely to deceive and also to cause confusion, and that being so, he thought the Applicants had not discharged the onus which was on them of proving that there was no likelihood of deception or of confusion.

Viscount Maugham accepted this view. On the second point, he said:

The Court of Appeal decided this point on the rather special ground above stated, namely, that the circumstances in which ladies' stockings are sold and repaired are such that deception or confusion are most unlikely to occur. My Lords, I do not think reliance in a question of registration should be placed on the practice which has heretofore existed and been followed by the Respondents in their repair of stockings. In the first place it should be remembered that the mark for which the statutory monopoly is sought is for "stockings", and this will include those used by men and boys; and obviously a quite different method of getting stockings repaired might be adopted. Nor need the present system be followed in relation to women's stockings; and the laundry proprietors or cleaners may cease to have any part in the system. It seems to me that if the Respondents put upon the market stockings of their own manufacture with a "Rysta" mark consisting of the word alone, and continue also the business of repairing stockings of other makes, adding a "Rysta" mark to them, there may come into existence large quantities of stockings of both categories; and the question is whether there may not be a fair number of people who will have, or who may have, no means of knowing whether the word "Rysta" used as a mark is intended to indicate that the stockings have been made, or that they have only been repaired by the Respondents. I am not prepared to answer this question in the negative. It is, I think, a matter of general knowledge that stockings are constantly provided by persons for their children or given as presents to friends. Nor do I see anything unlikely in stockings both for men and children as well as women being dealt with, or in the future being largely dealt with, by purchasers and vendors of second-hand stockings. In this connection it is to be remembered that stockings are largely dealt in all over the country and are bought by rich and poor alike. Moreover, in my opinion, we have to bear in mind the reputation gained by a word mark if it becomes generally known. Women, for instance, may hear the word "Rysta" as denoting a quality in stockings and at other times may hear the word spoken of as denoting merely a repair, and this may lead to confusion. The Respondents themselves have in paragraph 3 of their counter-statement (quoted above) suggested that their goodwill as stocking repairers will help them to sell stockings which they will manufacture in the future if they can obtain a trade mark for the word "Rysta", which has hitherto merely indicated repair.

My conclusion, therefore, is that there is no sufficient reason for holding that in the ordinary course of business a number of persons to whose notice the mark "Rysta" will come in connection with stockings will not be in doubt as to whether the mark indicates that the stockings have been made by or have merely been repaired by the owners of the mark.

5.2.4.5 *Pirie's Application* (1933) 50 R.P.C. 147 (H.L.)

An application was made to register "Abermill Bond Made in Great Britain" in Part B in respect of writing paper. The application was opposed by the owners of "Hammermill" registered for writing paper. They had used that mark in Britain since 1920. The Applicants had used their mark for about six years prior to the date of application and their British trade under their mark was much greater than that of the Opponents under their mark.

Eventually, the opponents appealed to the House of Lords where Lord Tomlin delivered the leading speech on the proper interpretation of the Trade Marks Act 1905, Section 21 (the precursor of Trade Marks Act 1938, Section 12 (2):

There is little authority on the Section. A passage from the judgment of Mr Justice Sargant in *Re Joseph Emil Maeder*, [1916] 33 R.P.C. 77, was cited by the Master of the Rolls. I agree with the Master of the Rolls that the adjective "slight" appearing in that passage would have been better omitted, but that otherwise the passage is unexceptionable. The existence of the possibility of deception or confusion seems to me to be one of the conditions contemplated by the Section as giving rise to the power to exercise the discretion.

The user and its honesty is not in question in this case and I cannot doubt that the Section applies. Should the discretion be exercised in the Respondents' favour? The Appellants say no and they put their case, as I understand it, in two ways.

First, the Appellants say that where, as here, the Opponents are already on the Register they have a vested right of property which ought not to be cut down, at any rate except in circumstances of an exceptional kind, and certainly not in the circumstances of this case. The answer to this point seems to be that the right conferred by registration is only a right subject to the provisions of the Acts which confer upon the Registrar the power to register another mark under Section 21, and that logically there is no distinction between the case where the opponents have already a mark on the Register and the case where they are themselves applying to register.

Secondly, the Appellants say, and this is their main line of attack upon the conclusion of the Court of Appeal, that though the Respondents were honest in their user in the sense that they never intended to cause confusion or to pass off their goods as the goods of the Appellants, yet inasmuch as they knew of the Appellants' mark when they adopted their own and that the marks have been used on the same goods in the same market, the user of the Respondents' mark cannot be treated as honest within the meaning of the Section and that in any case by refusal of registration there would not in these circumstances be the hardship to the Respondents which the Section is intended to prevent.

My Lords, it has never been suggested throughout this case that the conduct of the Respondents has in the slightest respect been open to criticism, and I should be sorry to place upon this Statute a construction which would brand as statutory dishonesty conduct justified in the eyes of honourable men. There is in fact no ground for doing so. Knowledge of the registration of the opponent's mark may be an important factor where the honesty of the user of the mark sought to be registered is impugned, but when once the honesty of the user has been established the fact of knowledge loses much of its significance, though it may be a matter not to be wholly overlooked in balancing the considerations for and against registration.

In the course of his judgment Clauson J. said: "Above all I should deem it my duty so to weigh the competing factors as to avoid giving any colour to the idea that a trader, who knows of a competing trade mark and knows that he can get his trade mark registered only if he can show within Section 19 that it is not calculated to deceive, can put himself in a more advantageous position by taking the risk of building up commercial claims on his doubtful mark and, after due time, coming to the Court to claim indulgence under Section 21".

With all respect to the learned Judge, I think in that passage he is attributing to the factor of knowledge an importance which it had lost the moment the honesty of the user was recognised and that it is this mal-attribution which has coloured his ultimate conclusion.

In my opinion, when once the two factors, viz, the previous registration of the Appellants' mark and the Respondents' knowledge of the Appellants' mark have fallen into their right perspective, the case becomes easy of decision and should in my opinion be determined in favour of registration for the following reasons: (1) While recognising the possibility in certain, perhaps somewhat remote, contingencies of confusion from phonetic similarity between the two words and giving due weight to the possibility of mistake arising from inaccurate or ill-remembered impression on the mind of one or other of the marks, I am of opinion that the possibility of confusion is slender. (2) The choice of the word "Abermill" was honestly made. (3) Five years' honest concurrent user has been proved. (4) It is the user and not the registration which is liable to cause confusion, and the commercial user has not produced any proof of confusion. This fact cannot be regarded as unimportant even though allowance be made for difficulty of proof; and (5) the Appellants' trade is small, and for some years has remained more or less stationary. The Respondents, on the other hand, have built up with their trade mark a large and increasing business.

Bearing these matters in mind, the hardship to the Respondents of refusing registration appears to be out of all proportion to any hardship to the Appellants or inconvenience to the public which can possibly result from granting it.

I may add that I think, differing in this respect from Clauson J., that it is open to the Respondents to set up hardship and that there is nothing in the evidence to justify the learned judge's finding that the Respondents had taken the risk of building up their commercial claims on a mark for which they did not venture, when they began using it, to claim registration.

I do not think that the Respondents, though aware of the Appellants' mark, had it in mind at all when they adopted their own mark.

Further, I desire to say that without further consideration I am not prepared to accept the view that regard should be had under Section 21 to the effect in foreign countries of registration here. In the present case, even if I were satisfied that the Respondents, by registration here, were placed in a better position for registering in foreign countries where the Appellants' mark is already registered and that that matter was proper to be taken into account, I should reach the same ultimate conclusion.

5.2.4.6 *"Bali" Trade Mark (No.2)* [1978]) F.S.R. 193 (Fox J.)

After Bali had lost the registration of its mark (see above, 5.2.4.2), it applied to re-register its mark, relying principally on honest concurrent use during the period 1962–69.

Fox J. held that this use was honest in the sense defined in Pirie's Application *(above, 5.2.4.5). But in his discretion he refused to allow the registration under Section 12 (2):*

In essence the position appears to me to be as follows:

(i) There is a substantial risk that, phonetically, the two marks may be confused. That has been decided by the House of Lords and is, in my view, confirmed by the later trap orders. Whilst the trap orders do not suggest that in existing circumstances Berlei suffers as a result of confusion, the existence of confusion is contrary to the public interest.

(ii) Apart from the trap orders, there has been no reported instance of confusion. The Assistant Registrar took the view that this weighed heavily in Bali's favour. With respect, I do not feel able to agree with that. I think it overstates the position to a considerable degree. During the whole of the relevant period, the two marks were operating in quite different price and quality ranges. That difference would disappear if Bali commenced to operate in the field of mass-produced goods. It is only then that one would have a truly reliable test of the conditions most likely to give to the greatest confusion in relation to marks which the House of Lords have held are, phonetically, likely to lead to confusion.

(iii) Bali's sales in the United Kingdom, while not insignificant, are, I think, very much smaller than the, admittedly, "substantial" Berlei sales. One would, indeed, expect that, since Berlei operate in the mass-produced market and Bali do not.

(iv) Bali's advertising in the United Kingdom has always been on a very small scale indeed and does not suggest that Bali has had any very serious financial commitment to the mark in this country.

(v) There is no very sure basis for attributing Bali's sales in this country to the use of the Bali mark, since Bali has continued to effect sales on a not very dissimilar scale, without using the mark at all. Bali has not used the mark here since 1969.

(vi) Whilst Bali could always sell in the United Kingdom under a different mark or, as at present, without a mark, there is inconvenience to Bali in having to provide separate packaging and labelling for the United Kingdom market.

(vii) So far as Berlei is concerned, the inconvenience which it would suffer if the BALI mark was registered are (a) the risk of confusion which could have serious consequences for Berlei if Bali entered the mass market and (b) the dilution of Berlei's long-established rights to the mark BERLEI.

(viii) Bali is only able to mount this application at all by relying on use, between the years 1962 and 1969, carried on with knowledge of Berlei's mark, with knowledge that Berlei opposed the user, and which, having regard to the decision of the House of Lords, was an infringing use, because the BALI mark should never have been registered.

I differ from an opinion of the Assistant Registrar with hesitation, but, looking at the whole matter, it seems to me that the balance is against permitting this registration.

Berlei is a long-established mark; Bali has only been used in the United Kingdom, to any significant extent, between 1962 and 1969, and then only against the plainly demonstrated opposition of Berlei – an opposition upheld by the House of Lords. Bali's sales in the United Kingdom, while not unsubstantial, have never been very large and were not supported by advertising of any significant size at all. There is, as the House of Lords has held, a risk of confusion between the two marks – confusion which could have very serious results if Bali entered the market for mass-produced goods, as it would be perfectly entitled to do. Against these considerations, there is, it is quite true, the inconvenience and expense of separate labelling of Bali products in the United Kingdom; but Bali is able to sell here, and does so without a mark.

In all the circumstances of the case, I do not think that the inconvenience arising from the need for separate labelling and packaging is sufficient to justify an encroachment upon Berlei's long-established rights in the United Kingdom. In my judgment, registration should be refused. I therefore allow the appeal.

5.2.5   Removal of Registered Marks

5.2.5.1   Trade Marks Act 1938, s.26, 30: Removal for Non-Use; Use of Associated and Substantially Identical Marks

S.26(1) Subject to the provisions of the next succeeding section, a registered trade/*service* mark may be taken off the register in respect of any of the goods/*services* in respect of which it is registered on application by an person aggrieved to the Court or, at the option of the applicant and subject to the provisions of section fifty-four of this Act, to the Registrar, on the ground either –

  (a) that the trade/*service* mark was registered without any *bona fide* intention on the part of the applicant for registration that it should be used in relation to those goods/*services* by him, and that there has in fact been no *bona fide* use of the trade/*service* mark in relation to those goods by any proprietor thereof for the time being up to the date one month before the date of the application; or

  (b) that up to the date one month before the date of the application a continuous period of five years or longer elapsed during which the trade/*service* mark was a registered trade/*service* mark and during which there was no *bona fide* use thereof in relation to those goods/*services* by any proprietor thereof for the time being:

Provided that (except where the applicant has been permitted under subsection (2) of section twelve of this Act to register an identical or nearly resembling trade/*service* mark in respect of the goods/*service* in question or where the tribunal is of opinion that he might properly be permitted so to register such a trade/*service* mark) the tribunal may refuse an application made under paragraph (a) or (b) of this subsection in relation to any goods/*services*, if it is shown that there has been, before the relevant date or during the relevant period, as the case may be, *bona fide* use of the mark by the proprietor thereof for the time being in relation to –

  (i)   goods/*services* of the same description; or

  (ii) goods associated with those services or services of that description, being services or, as the case may be, goods in respect of which the mark is registered.

(2) Where in relation to any goods/*services* in respect of which a trade/*service* mark is registered –

  (a) the matters referred to in paragraph (b) of the foregoing subsection are shown so far as regards non-use of the trade mark in relation to goods to be sold, or otherwise traded in, in a particular place in the United Kingdom (otherwise than for export from the United Kingdom), or in relation to goods to be exported to a particular market outside the United Kingdom; and

  (b) a person has been permitted under subsection (2) of section twelve of this Act to register an identical or nearly resembling trade mark, in respect of those goods under a registration extending to use in relation to goods to be sold, or otherwise traded in, in that place (otherwise than for export from the United Kingdom), or in relation to goods to be exported to that market, or the tribunal is of opinion that he might properly be permitted so to register such a trade mark;

on application by that person to the Court or, at the option of the applicant and subject to the provisions of section fifty-four of this Act, to the Registrar, the tribunal may impose on the registration of the first-mentioned trade/*service* mark such limitations as the tribunal thinks proper for securing that that registration shall cease to extend to such use as last aforesaid.

(3) An applicant shall not be entitled to rely for the purposes of paragraph (b) of subsection (1), or for the purposes of subsection (2), of this section on any non-use of a trade mark that is shown to have been due to special circumstances in the trade and not to any intention not to use or to abandon the trade mark in relation to the goods to which the application relates.

S.30(1) Where under the provisions of this Act use of a registered trade/*service* mark is required to be proved for any purpose, the tribunal may, if and in so far as the tribunal thinks right, accept use of an associated registered trade/*service* mark, or of the trade/*service* mark with additions or alterations not substantially affecting its identity, as an equivalent for the use required to be proved.

(2) The use of the whole of a registered trade/*service* mark shall for the purposes of this Act be deemed to be also a use of any registered trade/*service* mark, being a part thereof, registered in the name of the same proprietor by virtue of subsection (1) of section twenty-one of this Act.

5.2.5.2 *J Lyons' Application* [1959] R.P.C. 120 (C.A.)

Angus Watson & Co Limited owned the registered mark "Hostess" for food, excluding drinks. They had used it principally on soups, peas and beans, to a minor extent on biscuits and jellies. Lyons applied for its removal so far as it related to ice cream and goods of the same description on the ground of non-use (section 26). They were already using the mark "Hostess de Luxe" for that product and Watson's registration was the basis of proceedings for infringement against them.

Evershed M.R. set out section 26 (1) and proceeded:

It is agreed that nothing in the present appeal turns on the opening words of the subsection, "Subject to the provisions of the next succeeding section"; and it is also agreed that Messrs J Lyons & Co Ltd, the Appellants (to whom I will hereafter refer as "Lyons") are "aggrieved persons" within the meaning of the sub-section.

Two questions of some general importance have arisen upon the sub-section with which I shall deal later in this judgment. The two questions are these. First, the Trade Marks Act, 1938, was a consolidating Act; but the proviso to the sub-section which I have read did not appear in the earlier legislation. The question then arises: having regard to the proviso, what is the nature of the discretion in the proviso, and what is the extent of the discretion (if any) now allowed to the tribunal or the court by the use of the word "may" in the second line of the sub-section? Secondly: On whom, in such cases as the present, does the onus of proof lie? . . .

It was not contended before us that any of the goods other than jellies are goods the sales of which, under the mark, as recorded, are of goods of the same description as ice cream, within the meaning of section 26 (1). But it is one of the two questions most debated before us on appeal whether ice creams and jellies are or are not "goods of the same description", within the meaning of the sub-section. . . .

On the question of the onus of proof, his Lordship concluded:

The language of the proviso appears to me to indicate that the onus of showing that the mark has been used by any proprietor in relation to goods of the same description as ice cream does (as I have already intimated) *prima facie* lie on him who seeks to show it. But however that may be – and in cases of this kind I venture to doubt whether the question of onus should be given quite the same strict significance as in a pleading in a Common Law action – the problem, upon all the evidence before us, may now be shortly stated thus: Are jellies, or jelly tablets, goods of the same description as ice cream? If they are, then the question at once claims an answer – What is the description? What form of words will properly describe ice cream and jellies, but without also comprehending categories of other goods which might fairly in common sense be said not to be of the same description as either?

The answer to the question propounded by Mr Levy was, "sweets", using that word as signifying the sweet course in a menu, "dessert" in French, rather than sweetmeats – that is, chocolates, and the like – what, according to Mr Levy is known in popular modern jargon as "afters". My difficulty about this simple solution lies in the fact that it would apparently comprehend an extremely wide variety of foodstuffs, ranging from fruit salad to a steamed suet pudding; and I am not satisfied, for my part, that, whatever may be said of jellies, a suet pudding could, by any sensible standard (other than its use as a sweet course) be regarded as goods "of the same description" as ice cream. A solution may, however, be provided by limiting the class of sweets somewhat thus – a light sweet course or refreshment also commonly provided at buffets, garden parties, and similar festivities.

A number of cases was cited to us, though they were, for the most part, decisions not under section 26 of the Act but under section 12 or its predecessors in which is also found the formula "goods of the same description". Thus, in *McDowell's* case (1926) 43 R.P.C. 334 (C.A.); (1927) 44 R.P.C. 342 (H.L.), it was held that paraffin oil intended to be used for machine lubrication constituted goods of the same description as paraffin oil used medicinally for human consumption, on the ground that both were chemically the same substance, the difference between them depending on the degree of refinement. As Sargant L.J. observed in the Court of Appeal, the qualitative difference between medicinal oil and a refined lubricating machine oil would appear to be appreciably less than the corresponding difference between machine lubricating oils of widely divergent refinement.

Another case much canvassed before us was the *Australian Wine* case, reported (in this Court) (1899) 6 R.P.C. 311. In that case, the claim for registration of the mark and device of the Golden Fleece in respect of wines was rejected, having regard to the existing registration of an identical device in respect of spirits, particularly rum and whisky. Cotton L.J. was of opinion that wines and spirits were goods of the same description, both being alcoholic liquid refreshment which would probably be bought for consumption from the same shop; and in one sentence of his judgment he appears to have based himself, partly at any rate, on the view that the manufacturing processes for both were similar – a view which might not, I venture to think, be universally accepted. He said: 'Well, it is not confined to the same goods, but it is the same goods 'or description of goods'; and if it were necessary to decide it absolutely on that point, my opinion would be that there was an application for registration with respect to the same description of goods; because although wine and whisky, and wines and spirits are in a great many ways considered as different goods, yet we are not considering here how chemists would describe them, but whether manufacturers would describe them as being the same description 'of goods or not'".

Lindley L.J., did not go so far. He said that if wine and whisky were not goods of the same description they were at least very nearly so: the result was the same, since the matter must be judged (he said) by business standards.

Lopes L.J., appears to have based himself rather on the view that the applicants were plainly trying to filch a part of the goodwill of the existing registered proprietor of the mark.

On the other side, we were referred to *Jellinek's Application* (1946) 63 R.P.C. 59 in which my Brother Romer, at first instance, after a careful review of all the cases and the grounds upon which they had been decided, held that shoe polish was not "goods of the same description" as shoes, though commonly sold in the same retail establishments. In *J & J Colman Ltd's Application* (1929) 46 R.P.C. 126, Eve J. held that mustard and semolina, though commonly sold in the same establishment over the counter, were not goods of the same description, having regard particularly to the divergence in use and method of preparation when they respectively reached the kitchen of the housewife.

To all these cases the oft-quoted proposition that each was decided on its own particular facts is, to my mind, peculiarly applicable. In all cases of this kind regard will be had to such matters as the nature and composition of the goods, to their respective uses and functions, and to the trade channels through which respectively they are marketed or sold; and in different cases (as Mr Levy observed) one (but not always the same one) of these characteristics may have greater significance or emphasis than the others. The matter falls to be judged, as Lindley L.J., observed in the case already quoted, "in a business sense"; and this is to my mind made clear by considering the legislative background against which the problem has to be judged. By the Trade Marks legislation Parliament has provided that a registered proprietor of a mark, to be used by him in the course of his trade, has a monopoly right to that mark as an indication of the trade source or origin of the goods, and the restriction contemplated by section 26 is an incident of the general legislative purpose. The question whether goods are or are not goods of the same description must therefore (I think) be one to be answered in the context of that purpose; and having regard to that context, the cases cited, and particularly *McDowells's* case and the *Australian Wine* case, lend some support to the view that the phrase "goods of the same description" ought not to be given too restrictive a construction – not, at all events, so as to be limited to goods substantially analogous in kind, or commonly used as mere substitutes or alternative the one for the other.

Evershed M.R. considered the case before him to be "very near the line" and was inclined to agree with the Assistant Comptroller and Lloyd-Jacob J. that the case had been made out. He expressed no concluded view because he decided the case on the discretion contained in the sub-section:

In my judgment, the terms of the proviso (to the effect that if use of the mark is shown as there specified, the tribunal "may refuse the application") carry with them the unavoidable implication that, if such use is not shown, then *prima facie* the tribunal ought not to refuse the application. This is not to say that no discretion whatever is left by the use of the word "may" in the second line of the sub-section. Exceptional circumstances may arise, for example from the special nature of the mark, which would make it just to refuse the application even though the proviso were not at all called into play. But no such exceptional circumstances arise here. In the present case, indeed, it was stated on behalf of the Respondents that, had there been no use of the mark by them in relation to jellies in 1953 (so that the proviso would not have come into play), the tribunal should have granted the application of Lyons – limited, of course, to ice cream.

Further, the discretion in the proviso should, in my judgment, be exercised as a matter of common sense – "in a business sense" (to cite again Lindley L.J.'s phrase) – in the light of all the circumstances of the case, which will, of course, include the nature of the mark itself and the relevant business history of the applicants and the registered proprietor respectively. Again, however, regard must in my view be had to the legislative purpose of the Act, as I have earlier attempted to define it. In other words, the tribunal, bearing in mind all the circumstances of the case, will have to ask itself the question, whether the grant of the application would unfairly or unjustly restrict or invade the statutory monopoly acquired for its trade by the registered proprietor? Bearing all these considerations in mind and giving, I hope, due weight to all, I conclude in the present case that Lyons' application ought not to be refused. I mention among those to be considered and those presented to us in argument two considerations which have influenced my mind. The first is this: the question whether the proviso can be invoked by the Respondents at all has seemed very difficult: and though I have expressed my view upon this point in favour of the Respondents and now assume that ice cream and jellies are goods of the same description, it cannot by any means be suggested that they are manifestly so. Yet, as I have many times said, it has been conceded that had it not been for the Respondents' excursion into table jellies in 1953 not since repeated – the Respondents could not have invoked the proviso at all. To hold, therefore, that the Respondents' trade in jellies was fatal to the application would in the circumstances be to give to it, in my view, too great a significance. But let me repeat that this is not to suggest any kind of want of good faith on the Respondents' part in regard to their business history which would disqualify them from having the discretion exercised in their favour.

The second matter relates to the nature of the mark. The word "Hostess" as applied to peas, soups and beans, over a long period, has no doubt acquired a significance as indicating the Respondents' goods: but it cannot be said that the word "Hostess" has acquired a reputation exclusively referable to the Respondents having regard particularly to its use upon their teas by the Maypole Dairy Coy. In further support of this view is the evidence concerning the sales by Lyons since the beginning of 1956 under the name of "Hostess de Luxe" of their ice creams. I do not, of course, suggest that such sales give to Lyons any kind of claim or right to such use on the lines suggested in "Bray and Underhay". But what is, I think – in the light particularly of what I have referred to as the legislative purpose of the Act – of some significance, is that, according to the evidence, these sales have never given rise to any case or suggestion of confusion with the Respondents' goods.

In the circumstances, therefore, I conclude that the application (limited to ice cream) ought not to be refused; and I would allow the appeal.

Romer and Ormerod L.JJ. delivered concurring judgments.

5.2.5.3 *Imperial Group v Philip Morris* [1982] F.S.R.72 (C.A.)

In 1974 the plaintiff tobacco company considered introducing a king-size cigarette with the mark "Merit". Although they did not immediately go ahead with the plan, they decided that they should seek to protect the mark, itself unregistrable because descriptive, by registering "Nerit" as a "ghost mark". This was allowed in Part B. In 1975, it learned of the defendant company's launch of a "Merit" cigarette in the United States. The plaintiff thereupon sold some 20,000 cigarettes under the mark "Nerit". In 1976, the defendant announced its intention of putting their "Merit" brand on the British market and the plaintiff thereupon organised the distribution (through 2600) outlets of a further 1,000,000 "Nerit" cigarettes. They did not, however, accompany this with the usual extensive advertising and in the event many of the packets were returned by retailers. Subsequently the plaintiff sued the defendant for infringement of its registered mark and was met with a counterclaim for expunction from the register on three grounds:

Ground 1: That the entry on the register had been made without sufficient cause (s.32) because the applicant did not intend to use it, nor did it use it as a trade mark within s.68(1), i.e., "for the purpose of indicating, or so as to indicate, a connection in the course of trade between the goods and some person having the right either as proprietor or as registered user to use the mark. . . ."

Lawton L.J.:

At the date of registration the plaintiffs were not using the mark "Nerit". They propose to use it, and did use it, in order to stop their rivals from using the mark "Merit". They did not propose to use the mark "Nerit" so as to indicate a connection in the course of their trade between the cigarettes and themselves. They did not want any trade in Nerit cigarettes, save as a means to an end. Their use of the mark did show such a connection between them and the cigarettes but that was incidental to the purpose for which they did propose to use the mark. They wanted to treat the word "Merit" as if they had a copyright interest in it. That the law will not allow. It follows, in my judgment, that "Nerit" was not a trade mark for the purposes of the Act and should not have been registered. The entry in the Register was made without sufficient cause. Pursuant to section 32 of the Act any person aggrieved by that entry could apply to the court for it to be expunged, which is what the defendants by their counterclaim did. On the hearing of such an application the Court has jurisdiction to expunge or vary the entry as it sees fit. This jurisdiction is discretionary. A mark which the registered proprietor at the date of registration had not proposed to use for the statutory purposes set out in the definition of trade mark, but which later he claimed successfully he had used for the statutory purposes, might not be ordered to be expunged. Thereafter any aggrieved party, on getting evidence that there had been neither *bona fide* intention to use, nor *bona fide* use for the statutory purposes, could apply for relief under section 26 of the act. I am not of the opinion, as Balcombe J. was, that section 26 constitutes a comprehensive code for the removal of a registered trade mark for non-use. Section 32 is available when there is no intention to use: see *Re Batts' Trade Mark* (1898) 15 R.P.C. 534; *Re Ducker's Trade Mark* (1928) 45 R.P.C. 397 and *Re Huggars Trade Mark* [1979] F.S.R. 310. Section 26 provides relief when there has been an intention but it has not been a *bona fide* one. If the court is entitled to consider the purpose for which a trade mark is used, and I adjudge it is, then the plaintiffs' use of the mark "Nerit" was not a use at all. It had the unreal qualities of the ghost mark which the plaintiffs always intended it to be. For these reasons I find myself in disagreement with Balcombe J., who adjudged that "Nerit" was a trade mark within the meaning of the Act.

Shaw and Brightman L.JJ. agreed.

Ground 2: That, because of its phonetic similarity to "Merit", "Nerit" was not capable of distinguishing the plaintiffs' goods from those of others (s.10).

Lawton L.J.:

If properly articulated, "Nerit" has a different sound from "Merit". As already stated, the visual impact is different. When either spoken properly or seen, "Nerit" has no laudatory connotations and is unlikely to set up any association of ideas with "Merit". Whether it would be capable in use of distinguishing the plaintiffs' cigarettes was a question of fact for the trial judge to decide. The likelihood of confusion when the word was spoken was a factor which had to be considered by Balcombe J., and it was. If "Nerit" was a trade mark within the meaning of the 1938 Act, I can see no good reason for differing from Balcombe J. that it was capable of being registered in Part B of the Register.

Shaw L.J. agreed, but Brightman L.J. considered the similarity to Merit, and the likely confusion between the two when spoken, rendered the registration incorrect on this ground.

Ground 3: *That the mark was expungeable under s.26(1)(a) on that ground that it had been registered without any* bona fide *intention to use it and without any* bona fide *use on cigarettes up to one month before delivery of the counterclaim.*

Lawton L.J.:

For the purpose of considering this part of the defendants' counterclaim I will assume, contrary to what I have adjudged above, that the use of the mark "Nerit" by the plaintiffs in 1976, and between 1977 and 1979, was enough to make it a trade mark within the meaning of the Act. I have already set out what led to this use during these years and what I infer from the evidence, which was not in dispute, were the plaintiffs' intentions in using the mark in the way they did. The use was limited in size, time and area. It was not accompanied, nor did the plaintiffs want it to be, by what they call "Press Support" and the advertising was small in amount. Compared with the ordinary way in which the plaintiffs marketed new brands of cigarettes, the effort they put into introducing the "Nerit" brand was tiny, but not so tiny as to be *de minimis*.

Could such a use be *bona fide*? When considering whether it was, it is irrelevant that the plaintiffs had a motive for the use which was to protect their use of the unregistrable mark "Merit": see *Electrolux Ltd v Electrix Ltd* (1954) 71 R.P.C. 23, *per* Lord Evershed M.R. and Jenkins L.J. at p.41. According to the judgments given in this court in that case a *bona fide* use should be "ordinary and genuine" (*per* Lord Evershed M.R.), "perfectly genuine", "substantial in amount", "a real commercial use on a substantial scale" (*per* Jenkins L.J.) and not "some fictitious or colourable use but a real or genuine use" (*per* Morris L.J. at p.42). The plaintiffs never intended to use the mark "Nerit" in the ordinary course of their business; their use of it was not substantial; it was not a real use in any commercial sense; it was a colourable stratagem for making their trade rivals think that they were using the mark "Nerit" in a way which gave it the protection of the Act. If the *Electrolux* case is an authority which binds this court – and seemingly it does – and I have applied it correctly to the evidence, then the defendants succeed on their section 26(1) claim.

Mr Walton submitted, however, that there is a conflict of authority as to the meaning of "*bona fide*" in section 26(1)(a). If there is such a conflict, this court must choose which decision to follow: see *Young v Bristol Aeroplane Co Ltd* [1944] K.B. 718 at p.726. The conflicting authority was said to be *Baume and Co Ltd v Moore (A.H.) Ltd* [1958] R.P.C. 228, in which this court approved the construction which Danckwerts J. had put upon the words "*bona fide*" in section 8(a) of the Act which provides that "no registration of a trade mark shall interfere with (a) any *bona fide* use by a person of his own name. ..." The trial judge said that he understood that "*bona fide*" normally means "the honest use by the person of his own name, without any intention to deceive anybody or without any intention to make use of the goodwill which has been acquired by another trader". Mr Walton went on to submit that Parliament should be presumed to have intended that the words "*bona fide*" should have the same meaning whenever they were used in the Act and that if Danckwerts J.'s approved construction was applied to the plaintiffs' use of the mark "Nerit" that use had been honest and had not been intended to deceive anybody or to make use of anyone's goodwill. The defendants did not suggest otherwise. Mr Walton's submission, however, was fallacious. The context in which the qualifying words "*bona fide*" were used in section 26(1)(a) was entirely different from their use in section 8, so that a different meaning has to be given to the words as used in one section from their use in another. There is no conflict between the two decisions of this court.

I would dismiss the appeal.

Shaw and Brightman L.JJ. agreed. The order to expunge the mark was upheld.

5.2.5.4   *"Hermes" Trade Mark* [1982] R.P.C. 425 (Falconer J.)

The respondents purchased the registered mark "Hermes" for (inter alia) watches in 1954. They sold watches under it from 1960 to 1971 but not thereafter until September 1977. Before that the appellants, who had begun to import and sell "Hermes" watches in 1974, applied to expunge the appellants' mark under s.26(1)(b) on the ground that it had not, in the five years preceding 18 March 1977, been used by the proprietor or any registered user. By way of rebuttal the respondents relied upon their own conduct in two ways:

(i) entries each year in a trade publication referring to the mark and the proprietors by name – the annual entry being maintained during the years of non-use in order to guard against allegations of non-use or abandonment;
(ii) orders placed in October 1976 for parts to be supplied by manufacturers, including orders for dials bearing the word "Hermes". The orders were not completed until April 1977 but they were used to make up the watches that the respondents later marketed.

After pointing out that "Use of the mark . . . in relation to goods" is defined in s.68(2) to cover "references to the use thereof upon, or in physical or other relation to, goods", Falconer J. said of the trade publications entries:

Coming back to section 26(1)(b) – I am thinking about the advertisements which I was considering – if one has advertisements put out in the relevant period before the application for removal under section 26(1)(b), if the goods in question are on the market at the time, those advertisements would plainly constitute use of the mark in the course of trade. That is the position that Mr Faulkner in the *Radford* case was contemplating and I do not think that the possible use of advertisements for the purposes of section 26(1)(b) is restricted just to that case. I agree with the observation of Mr Myall, the Assistant Registrar, in the *REVUE* Trade Mark, [1979] R.P.C. 27 at 31, lines 12 to 14, where he said:

"I do not, however, think that it is necessary that the goods must exist concurrently with the advertisements".

Thus, if the registered proprietor should commence a series of advertisements featuring his mark as part of an introductory campaign, prior to putting his goods on the market under the mark, but before they were actually on the market, in my judgment such use would clearly be use of the mark in the course of trade, not upon the goods or in physical relation thereto, but it would be in other relation thereto, the point being that it would be use in the course of trade in those goods, albeit in advertisements.

The directory advertisements in the present case were not advertisements by the proprietors put out in the course of trade in the goods covered by the registration at all. That is plain from the evidence of Mr Crockett in his paragraph 12, which I have already read. That was not use in the course of trade and, therefore, in my judgment, the registered proprietors cannot rely upon these directory advertisements at all, either standing alone or as part of the use as a whole to be taken account with the use relied upon in the steps of the re-launch.

Of the orders for watch parts, Falconer J. said:

Counsel for the registered proprietors, Mr Wilson, put his case on this use in two ways. He submitted that the orders in exhibit AAC.3 – those are the orders to Louis Newmark to which Mr Greaves refers – themselves constituted a sufficient use of the mark in the course of trade in October 1976 and, therefore, in the relevant period, and he submitted that it did not matter that the goods were not then in existence. It was a use, he submitted, in their order to their suppliers to acquire the goods to be marketed by them under the mark and that, he contended, was use in the course of trade in relation to the watches in question.

In my judgment, he is right in that submission. Of course, in those orders it was not a use of the mark upon or in physical relation to the watches, but it was a use in other relation, to take the expression from the definition, that is to say, a non-physical use, as would be a use, for example, in advertisements or an order or an invoice, and it was a use in the course of trade in the watches – their acquisition for future sale.

In the second way that he put his case on this particular use, Mr Wilson based himself on a passage in the decision of Mr Myall, the Assistant Registrar, in the *REVUE* case, [1979] R.P.C. 27 at 31 lines 12 to 17. I have in fact read the first sentence of it, but I will read it again to make the whole passage clear.

> "I do not, however, think that it is necessary that the goods must exist concurrently with the advertisements. It seems to me that if the proprietor has, by the time an offer for sale is published, taken positive steps to acquire goods marked with the trade mark, he has done enough for his combined actions to constitute use on, or in relation to, goods within the meaning of s.68(2) and thus within section 26".

That passage was cited by Mr Wilson and he said that he relied on it to the extent that in October 1976 the registered proprietors were taking positive steps to acquire goods to be marketed under the trade mark and it was to be a *bona fide* use within section 26.

Accordingly the case for expunction under s.26 failed. If non-use had been shown, Falconer J. agreed with the Assistant Registrar that it would have been proper, under the discretion conferred by that section, to maintain the registration because: the proprietors had taken steps to revive the mark unprompted by the proceedings; they had proved some residual reputation in the mark; they had sold "Hermes" watches after the relevant period in continuation of conduct begun during it; the applicant's association with "Hermes" was not widely recognised and their sales were conceded to be infringing.

5.2.5.5   Trade Marks Act 1938, s.15(1),(2): Words becoming descriptive

S.15(1) The registration of a trade mark shall not be deemed to have become invalid by reason only of any use, after the date of registration, of a word or words which the trade mark contains, or of which it consists, as the name or description of an article or substance:

Provided that if it is proved either –

    (a) that there is a well-known and established use of the word or words as the name or description of the article or substance by a person or persons carrying on a trade therein, not being use in relation to goods connected in the course of trade with the proprietor or a registered user of the trade mark or (in the case of a certification trade mark) goods certified by the proprietor; or

    (b) that the article or substance was formerly manufactured under a patent (being a patent in force on, or granted after, the twenty-third day of December nineteen hundred and nineteen), that a period of two years or more after the cesser of the patent has elapsed, and that the word or words is or are the only practicable name or description of the article or substance;

the provisions of the next succeeding subsection shall have effect.

(2) Where the facts mentioned in the paragraph (a) or (b) of the proviso to the foregoing subsection are proved with respect to any word or words, then –

    (a) if the trade mark consists solely of that word or those words, the registration of the trade mark, so far as regards registration in respect of the article or substance in question or of any goods of the same description, shall be deemed for the purposes of section thirty-two of this Act to be an entry wrongly remaining on the register;

    (b) if the trade mark contains that word or those words and other matter, the Court or the Registrar, in deciding whether the trade mark shall remain on the register, so far as regards registration in respect of the article or substance in question and of any goods of the same description, may in case of a decision in favour of its remaining on the register require as a condition thereof that the proprietor shall disclaim any right to the exclusive use in relation to that article or substance and any goods of the same description of that word or those words, so, however, that no disclaimer on the register shall effect any rights of the proprietor of a trade mark except such as arise out of the registration of the trade mark in respect of which the disclaimer is made; and

    (c) for the purposes of any other legal proceedings relating to the trade mark –

        (i) if the trade mark consists solely of that word or those words, all rights of the proprietor, whether under the common law or by registration, to the exclusive use of the trade mark in relation to the article or substance in question or to any goods of the same description, or

        (ii) if the trade mark contains that word or those words and other matter, all such rights of the proprietor to the exclusive use of that word or those words in such relation as aforesaid;

    shall be deemed to have ceased on the date at which the use mentioned in paragraph (a) of the proviso to the foregoing subsection first became well known and established, or at the expiration of the period of two years mentioned in paragraph (b) of that proviso.

S.15(3) provides for the expunction of a mark which is the name of a chemical element or compound.

The form in which s.15 is applied to service marks is not given here. S.15(1)(a) does affect a word mark for services which becomes "the name or description of an activity". There is no equivalent to s.15(1)(b) or 15(3).

5.2.5.6   *"Daiquiri Rum" Trade Mark* [1969] R.P.C. 600 (H.L.)

United Rum Merchants owned the mark "Daiquiri Rum" for rum, originally registered in 1922 by a predecessor in title. At about that time "Daiquiri" was becoming used as the name of a cocktail, combining light rum, lime, sugar and ice. The applicants to remove the mark by virtue of section 15, Trade Marks Act 1938 were the agents importing "Bacardi" rum.

Lord Wilberforce (with whose speech the other members of the House agreed) set out the provisions of section 15 and continued:

Before I state the rival contentions of the parties it may be convenient to describe quite generally the purpose of section 15. Since the passing of the Patents, Designs and Trade Marks Act, 1888, it has been legitimate and possible to register as a trade mark a word or words in common use. The proposed mark has had to satisfy certain statutory tests, particularly those now set out in sections 9, 11 and 12 of the Act of 1938: for example, the word had to be distinctive of the applicant's goods, *Gramophone Co's Application* (1910) 2 Ch. 423; 27 R.P.C. 689. These tests related, and had to be applied by the Registrar, to the circumstances as existing at the date of the registration. But although registration might properly be admitted by the Registrar, and be maintained for a period, circumstances subsequently arising, in relation to the use of the word(s), might affect the propriety of allowing the mark to remain. Section 15 was evidently introduced to deal with this situation. A first reading of it shows clearly enough that it operates in two directions, one in favour of, the other against the interests of the registered proprietor. In his favour, it provides that use by the general public of the word(s) as the name or description of a article shall not affect the registration; against him it provides that a trade use may do so. The structure of the section requires first an answer to the question whether such a use in the trade as the section requires has been established after which it is necessary to proceed to consider the consequences of this established use under alternative heads. The appeal turns essentially, upon the words, appearing in the initial part of subsection (1), and in paragraph (a) of the proviso "as the name or description of an [the] article or substance".

The contending views may be summarised as follows. The proprietors' submission is that these words cannot be read in their apparent unqualified generality: they must, in the context, be understood to refer, and to refer only, to articles or substances within the registration, ie within the protection of the trade mark. It would be quite wrong, they say, to deprive the registered proprietor of the benefit of his mark by reason of a trade use relating to articles or substances outside the registration. He would, *ex hypothesi*, have no means of stopping this. The consequences of applying the section to such a case are particularly severe, since not only is the mark itself liable to be expunged, but, under subsection (2)(c), the proprietor is deprived of any pre-existing rights at common law as regards use of the word(s).

For the applicants for rectification it is said that the words "an article or substance" are of complete generality and unambiguous. Admittedly there must be some relation between the established trade use and the articles or substances covered by the registration, but this is achieved by subsection (2) through the words "or any goods of the same description". In effect the section, reading subsections (1) and (2) together, means that the registered mark may be affected by a use, in trade, in relation either to the articles or substances within the registration or to articles or substances of the same description as the first articles, "related goods" as the applicants describe them. This would, they say, be within the general policy of the Act of maintaining a neutral area round each registration into which no conflicting mark or descriptive term may penetrate, so preserving the distinctiveness of marks and avoiding confusion.

The proprietors' argument requires for its successful application to the facts of this case a decision, in their favour, of a further question, namely,, whether a Daiquiri cocktail is itself an article or substance within the registration of DAIQUIRI RUM. If it is, then even on their argument the section applies. Different views are possible on this point. Pennycuick J. said that he was by no means convinced that the cocktail was outside the registration: the Lords Justices thought it was, and I understand that some of your Lordships may be unwilling to differ from them. I record my own opinion that a Daiquiri cocktail, being simply a flavoured dilution of light rum, is within the registration, but, recognising that the contrary view is eminently tenable, I proceed, as did the learned trial judge, to deal with the case upon the basis that it is not. I shall return to the question whether a Daiquiri cocktail is "of the same description" as DAIQUIRI RUM.

On the first and important question how section 15 should be construed, I make two preliminary observations. First, I cannot think that the critical words are ambiguous, so as to permit us, even assuming that ambiguity would permit us, to look for guidance to the report of the Government committee which preceded the passing of the Act. Generality is not the same thing as ambiguity, otherwise ambiguity would be fatally easy to find. Nor is a phrase ambiguous because it requires to be construed, nor because judges differ as to its construction.

But, secondly, I do not think that the restricted application for which the proprietors contend necessarily involves the writing into the section of words not there. It seems within a normal process of construction of the section in its context to consider whether words apparently general are intended to bear a special or technical meaning; and if throughout the Act it were clear that in mentioning articles and substances the reference was to those within the registration and to none other, it might be wrong to attribute a general meaning. In this connection, though one section is only part of the context, I notice that section 26 (1), last line, explicitly adds the restrictive words "being goods in respect of which the trade mark is registered". Those words might well have been included in section 15, but they were not.

What, then, does a fair reading of the section require? The words are general; as they stand they do not, if accepted, produce absurdity. To read them at their face value may seem to press hardly on some registered proprietors, who may see a use developing which they cannot stop and which may deprive them of their mark. On the other hand, they may have acted unwisely or unluckily in their choice of the mark and there is certainly a public interest in preventing the appropriation of common words and in avoiding confusion. Indeed, the usefulness of the wider meaning is well exemplified by the present case for, without imputing anything discreditable to the proprietors, there would be little merit in permitting them to secure monopoly rights in a mark containing a word which, in relation to related goods, had acquired an independent trade reputation, which mark they could never have successfully registered (as I think they could not) at the date when they acquired it. On the other side, the proprietors' counsel were not able to give a convincing actual or hypothetical example of injustice or even anomaly if the general meaning were accepted.

In my opinion, no good reason exists why the general unrestricted meaning should not be accepted and, if this is so, the initial portion of section 15 fits the facts because it has been proved that there is a well-known and established use of the word or substance, viz, a Daiquiri cocktail, and it becomes necessary to inquire under subsection (2) whether DAIQUIRI RUM is "goods of the same description". This was answered negatively in the Court of Appeal.

The expression "goods of the same description" is used elsewhere in the Trade Marks Act, 1938, in particular sections 12 and 26, and no reason appears why it should not bear the same meaning throughout. The words are not perhaps self-explanatory. Taken by themselves, they would suggest that it is necessary to search for a description, by species, genus or wider category which would include all the goods in question. Taken in relation to the Act of 1938, they might suggest a grouping by reference to the classification of goods for trade mark purposes contained in the Third or Fourth Schedules to the Trade Marks Rules. But reference to the classification shows at once, that this cannot be the basis of "description", for there are many cases where a single class contains goods of different descriptions, while goods which one would think were of the same description may be found in different classes. Nor, on the more general test, is it sufficient to find a single trade description covering each of the goods in question. Thus, in *Lyons and Co Ltd's Application* [1959] R.P.C. 120, "sweets" though covering ice-cream and jellies was thought to be too wide a description to be suitable.

The variety of goods that have to be considered from the point of view of description is very great; there is a useful list in Kerly on Trade Marks, 9th edn., page 180. This shows that a considerable body of reasonably consistent practice has grown up under experience which it would be unwise to disturb.

I think that the test of sameness in description has rightly been taken to be a business and practical test, and I would accept the utility for most purposes of the matters stated as relevant by Romer J. in *Jellinek's Applications* (1946) 63 R.P.C. 59; these are the nature and composition of the goods, the respective uses of the articles and the trade channels through which the commodities are bought and sold: there may, and as business patterns change no doubt will, be others, but it is tests of this nature by which the Registrar should be guided. In the Court of Appeal, Danckwerts L.J. and Winn L.J. both decided that Daiquiri cocktails and DAIQUIRI RUM were not goods of the same description; indeed, Winn L.J. went further: he did not regard various intoxicating drinks, which he specified, as capable of being properly given the same description as rum. But I agree with learned counsel who appeared as *amicus curiae* on behalf of the Registrar of Trade Marks that the tests accepted in the Court of Appeal, however reasonable in the light of logic, and however acceptable they might be if the matters were *res integra*, represent a departure from the meaning which a considerable body of reported cases, as well as of decisions given by the Registrar over the years, has given with satisfactory and workable result, and I must therefore disagree with them.

Applying, as did Pennycuick J., a business test, I agree also with him that these goods were of the same description. So to decide is in fact well supported by observations expressed long ago in *Australian Wine Importers' Trade Mark* (1889) 41 Ch D. 278; 6 R.P.C. 311.

5.2.5.7   Trade Marks Act 1938, s.32(1): General power to rectify register

S.32(1) Any person aggrieved by the non-insertion in or omission from the register of any entry, or by any entry made in the register without sufficient cause, or by any entry wrongly remaining on the register, or by any error or

defect in any entry in the register, may apply in the prescribed manner to the Court or, at the option of the applicant and subject to the provisions of section fifty-four of this Act, to the Registrar, and the tribunal may make such order for making, expunging or varying the entry as the tribunal may think fit.

S.32(2)–(5) confer ancillary powers on the Registrar.

5.2.5.8 *General Electric Co. v General Electric Co. Ltd* [1970] R.P.C. 339 (C.A.); [1973] R.P.C. 297 (H.L.)

The American (appellant) and English (respondent) companies had originally adopted their very similar names honestly and each had built very large businesses in the UK and elsewhere. The English company applied to expunge the American company's mark – GE decoratively written in a rondel – which had been registered for various electrical goods since 1907 at which time the English company was only four years old. Until 1965 the American company made little use of its mark on the British market but then began to use it substantially in combination with other word marks. Both companies had recognised the possibility of confusion and had an understanding that they would do what they could to minimise it. The principal ground for expunction in the H.L. was that subsequent to registration the mark had become likely to cause confusion with the English company so that the mark was one wrongly remaining on the register (Section 32 (1)).

Lord Diplock:

The likelihood of confusion

Where the question of the likelihood of deception or confusion arises on an application to expunge a registered mark which has already been the subject of substantial use, the absence of evidence of actual confusion having occurred is a potent factor in determining whether or not the court should exercise its discretion to expunge the mark from the register. But it does not decide the relevant hypothetical question which must be answered in the affirmative before any question of discretion to expunge the mark arises: would any normal and fair future use of the mark in the course of trade be likely to cause deception or confusion? If actual confusion in the past is proved, this is a strong indication that continued confusion is likely; but the absence of evidence of past confusion may be accounted for by the small extent to which the mark has been used or by special circumstances affecting its past use which may not continue to operate to prevent confusion in the future.

After characterising the case as "a jury question", he continued:

It was also submitted by the American company that if the source of the confusion as to the origin of the goods which resulted from the use of the trade mark was due to the similarity of the names of two different manufacturers either of whom might be associated with the mark in the mind of a potential buyer of the goods, this was confusion "between name and name", not confusion "between mark and mark"; and that only the latter was relevant "confusion" within the meaning of that expression in Section 11 of the Act. I am unable to accept this argument. The essence of a trade mark is the association that it bears in the mind of a potential buyer of the goods to which it is applied. I can see no reason for differentiating between cases where the confusion arises because the trade mark is associated with the name of a manufacturer to which some other manufacturer's name is similar, and cases where it is associated with a design or with descriptive words and the confusion arises because some other manufacturer uses a similar design or similar descriptive words to indicate the origin of his goods. In my view, section 11 is wide enough to embrace "confusion" resulting from any of these kinds of association.

In the instant case all three members of the Court of Appeal were alert to the danger of relying on their own idiosyncratic knowledge and temperaments. All gave due weight to the evidence adduced on the issue at the hearing and to the criticisms of it by the trial judge. All were of opinion that they themselves would have been likely to be confused by the use of the rondel mark *simpliciter* on electrical consumer goods if, as had been the fact before the hearing of the appeal, they had known of the English company but had not known of the American company.

My Lords, I myself, as a member of the public in the United Kingdom, am idiosyncratic in that I have for many years known of both companies. I should not have been likely to be confused by the use of the rondel mark *simpliciter* on electrical consumer goods. Nevertheless, my common sense convinces me that there would be a likelihood of confusion among a substantial number of members of the public who did not share my idiosyncratic knowledge. On this issue I think the Court of Appeal was right.

The questions of construction

His Lordship set out Section 32 and continued:

For reasons which I shall develop later I reject the extreme submission of the American company that Section 32 is a mere procedural section prescribing the steps to be taken to give effect to an express power of removal conferred by other sections of the Act, such as section 15 (3), 26 (1) 27 (4) 28 (8) and (10), and 29 (4), and does not in itself confer any power to expunge otherwise than pursuant to those sections. I reject also the extreme submission of the English company that the words "wrongly remaining on the register" give to the court a discretion to remove from the register any entry the continued use of which the court considers would be contrary to the policy of the Act notwithstanding that it does not offend against any specific prohibition, express or implied, contained in the Act. In my opinion, an entry which was lawful at the time it was originally made can only be expunged under Section 32 (1) if, at the time of the application, its continued presence on the register is prohibited by virtue of some other provision of the Act. Such prohibitory provisions are not limited to those which also themselves confer an express power of removal. They include all provisions which, on their true construction, make unlawful the continued presence of the entry on the register.

The Court of Appeal, having held, as I think rightly, that the use of the rondel mark *simpliciter* as a trade mark on 20th July 1967 would have been likely to cause confusion, were of opinion that its continued presence as an entry on the register was prohibited by section 11 of the 1938 Act [and] they were also of opinion that its continued presence as an entry on the register was not excluded from that prohibition by section 13.

His Lordship set out the two sections.

The *ratio decidendi* of the Court of Appeal involves two questions as to the true construction of section 11. The first is as to the time to which the prohibition expressed in the words "It shall not be lawful to register" relates. The second is whether a limitation on the prohibition of the registration of a potentially deceptive or confusing trade mark is imposed by the requirement that its use "would ... be disentitled to protection in a court of justice". The words in which the proviso to section 13 is expressed are of assistance in answering the first question as to the construction of section 11, but throw no light on the answer to the second question.

Neither of these questions can be answered by linguistic analysis alone. The first depends on whether, in the context of section 11, the verb "to register" refers only to the act of making an entry on the register or whether it refers also to the retention of an entry on the register after it has been made. As a matter of ordinary usage of the English language either is a permissible meaning.

With regard to the second question, as a matter of syntax the dominant phrase in the relevant description of the disqualified matter is: matter "the use of which would ... be disentitled to protection in a court of justice". The words "by reason of its being likely to deceive or cause confusion or otherwise" constitute a subordinate clause of which the syntactic function is to restrict the amplitude of the disqualified matter. This it does by reference to the reasons for the disqualified matter's being disentitled to protection in a court of justice. But the inclusion in the subordinate clause of the words "or otherwise", if they are to be given a literal interpretation, has the consequence that the clause is wide enough to embrace any reason for the matter being disentitled to protection in a court of justice, and the clause thus becomes devoid of any restrictive effect and therefore performs no function at all. Furthermore, the use of the subjunctive mood in the dominant phrase gives rise to ambiguity as to the time to which the test of disentitlement to protect relates. Is the critical time at which the use of the mark would be disentitled to protection before it is entered on the register or after it has been entered on the register? Finally, whichever is the time to which the test relates, what meaning is to be ascribed to the words "disentitled to protection in a court of justice"?

My Lords, the meaning of particular sections in the 1938 Act can, in my view, only be ascertained by applying a purposive construction to the Act as a whole, and construing the actual words used in particular sections (unless it is linguistically impossible) so as to achieve and not so as to thwart the underlying policy to which the Act was intended to give effect.

The legislative history

The 1938 Act does not purport to be a self-contained code of the whole of the law relating to trade marks. As its long title discloses, it was an Act to consolidate three previous Acts of Parliament: the Trade Marks Act 1905, the Trade Marks Act 1919, and the Trade Marks (Amendment) Act 1937. Recourse must therefore be had to these Acts to ascertain the underlying point to which it was intended to give effect. The Act of 1905, however, was itself an Act to consolidate and amend the law relating to Trade Marks. Sections 11 and 41 of that Act are re-enacted in section 11 and 13 of the Act of 1938, the former *verbatim* and the latter with a minor amendment restricting its operations to marks in Part A of the register but with no other change of language. Section 11 of the Act of 1905 was, however, itself a re-enactment of section 73 of the Patents, Designs and Trademarks Act, 1883, with minor amendments, but without any alteration of any words or phrases which fall to be construed in the instant appeal. Section 41 of the Act of 1905 replaced part of section 76 of the Act of 1883, but with substantial amendments.

To ascertain the meaning of the language used in section 11 of the Act of 1938 one must go back beyond the Act of 1905 to the Act of 1883; but since the Act of 1883 was itself an act to amend and consolidate the law relating to trade marks and section 73 merely reproduced *verbatim* the language of the second part of section 6 of the Registration of

Trade Marks Act 1875, final recourse must be had to the Act of 1875.

In analysing the provisions of the initial Act of 1875 his Lordship referred in particular to section 6:

Section 6 imposed prohibitions on the registration of certain kinds of marks. These prohibitions are additional to the requirement that a trade mark should consist of distinctive matter as prescribed in section 10. The section reads as follows:

"The registrar shall not, without the special leave of the court, to be given in the prescribed manner, register in respect of the same goods or classes of goods a trade mark identical with one which is already registered with respect to such goods or classes of goods, and the registrar shall not register with respect to the same goods or classes of goods a trade mark so nearly resembling a trade mark already on the register with respect to such goods or classes of goods as to be calculated to deceive. It shall not be lawful to register as part of or in combination with a trade mark any words the exclusive use of which would not, by reason of their being calculated to deceive or otherwise, be deemed entitled to protection in a court of equity; or any scandalous designs".

The first part of the section deals with the act of making the original entry of a trade mark on the register. It imposes a prohibition on the registrar's acting on his own initiative but leaves it open to the court to permit the registration of identical marks notwithstanding the inherent risk of the public's being thereby deceived as to the origin of the goods. As a matter of judicial policy the court exercised this power under the Act so as to preserve the doctrine of honest concurrent user. Where honest concurrent user was established beyond what could be ignored under the *de minimis* rule (cf. *Re Hodson* (1881) 86 L.T. 188) the practice was to permit registration of identical or similar trade marks in respect of the same classes of goods up to the number of three but to refuse leave to register more than three on the ground that the mark would thereby cease to be distinctive (*Re Jelley, Son & Jones's Application* (1878) 46 L.T. 381).

The second part of the section introduced by the words: "It shall not be lawful to register", imposes an absolute prohibition on the registration of particular matter otherwise falling within the definition contained in section 10. It is clearly designed to prevent the proprietor obtaining by registration protection for a mark of such a character that a court of equity would have exercised its discretion to refuse to grant to its proprietor an injunction to restrain its being infringed by a usurper. Since the mere fact that the use of a mark involved a risk of deceiving the public was not enough to disentitle it to protection against infringement by a usurper provided that the risk of deception was due to honest concurrent user, there was no conflict between the first and the second parts of the section. The reference to the cause of disentitlement to protection, namely, "by reason of their being calculated to deceive or otherwise", does not restrict the ambit of the prohibition. The specific reference to deception is probably accounted for by the fact that up to 1875 misrepresentations as to the character of the goods, as in *Pidding v How* (1837) 8 Smi. 477, or as to their origin, as in *Perry v Truefitt* (1842) 6 Beav. 66, were the commonest reasons for the refusal of the Court of Chancery to grant injunctions. The addition of the words "or otherwise" may have been added *per majorem cautelam* or possibly to cover the cases of marks to which no title had been acquired by use or to which title had been lost by disuse as a trade mark.

In the context of section 6, as in the context of section 1, "to register" must, in my view, refer not only to the act of making an entry on the register but also to permitting the continuance of the entry of a trade mark on the register. It would not be reasonable to impute to Parliament in 1875 an intention that a mark, which truthfully described the character of the goods in respect of which it was registered at the time of its first being entered on the register, should continue to enjoy the protection accorded to registered trade marks even though the proprietor subsequently deliberately altered the character of the goods so that the registered mark told a lie about them.

It is difficult to conceive of a case where a mark which was not deceptive as to the character of goods at the time of original registration could become so subsequently except by some dishonest conduct of the proprietor himself. But deception as to the origin of the goods, in cases of honest concurrent user of identical or similar marks, could arise at any time during the period of concurrent use without any blameworthy conduct by any proprietor of the mark. In such cases, each of the proprietors remained entitled to protection of his mark against infringement by a usurper, though not against infringement by another *bona fide* proprietor of an identical or similar mark. Section 6 did not make the entry or continuance of such a mark on the register unlawful.

Lord Diplock then referred to sections 3 and 4 of the 1875 Act – the precursors of the present section 13 – which use "to register" in the passive in a manner plainly referring to the continuance of the registration.

In the Trade Marks Act 1905, sections 11 and 41 took the essential forms of the present sections 11 and 13. As to the former, Lord Diplock held that "it shall be lawful to register" and "the use of which would by reason of its being calculated to deceive [now: likely to deceive or cause confusion – words of similar meaning] or otherwise be disentitled to protection in a court of justice" must bear the same meaning as the corresponding words in the 1875 Act.

As to the latter he said:

The substantive rights conferred by section 41 are, however, limited to those which are the consequence of an "original registration" being valid. The insertion of the adjective "original" before "registration" in the description of what "shall . . . be taken to be valid in all respects" affords confirmation that the draftsman of the Act used the noun "registration" *simpliciter* and the corresponding verb "to register" as referring not only to the initial act of making an entry in the register but also to the continuance of it as an entry in the register. Thus, section 41 did not preclude removal of a trade mark from the register under any of the express powers of removal contained in other sections of the Act, nor did it preclude removal if the trade mark fell within the second exception laid down in section 41 itself in the words "unless the trade mark offends against the provisions of section eleven of this Act". The contrast between this language and the corresponding language of the first exception 'unless such original registration was obtained by fraud', and in particular the change of noun from original registration to trade mark and the change of tense of the verb from past to present, is a clear indication that the draftsman assumed that the words in section 11 "It shall not be lawful to register" imposed a prohibition on a trade mark's remaining on the register as well as on its original entry in the register.

What section 41 did was to preclude removal of a trade mark from the register after seven years on any ground of invalidity, such as lack of distinctiveness, which would have applied to the original registration. What it did not do was to preclude removal of a mark from the register if it had become likely to deceive as a result of blameworthy conduct by its proprietor since the date of its original registration. A *bona fide* proprietor whose trade mark had become likely to deceive through no fault of his own did not need to look to section 41 for his protection. Section 11 itself was sufficient protection to him whether or not seven years had elapsed since the original registration of the mark.

In *R Thorne & Sons Ltd v Pimms Ltd, Re Pimms's Trade Mark*, (1909) 26 R.P.C. 221 Neville J. construed section 11 as authorising the removal from the register of a mark which had become deceptive since the date of original registration as a result of the wrongful conduct of the proprietor. Graham J. is in error in supposing that the mark in question was not governed by section 41 because it had been registered before the passing of the 1905 Act. Section 41 was made expressly applicable to such marks by section 6 of the 1905 Act.

In *Re Woodward's Trade Mark, Woodward Ltd v Boulton Macro Ltd* (1915) 32 R.P.C. 173 Eve J. held that a mark, "Gripe-Water", which had become non-distinctive since its original registration because through no fault of its proprietor those words had come to be generally used as descriptive of any remedy for gripes, could not be removed from the register. Even assuming, as I think wrongly, that this non-distinctiveness also resulted in the mark having become "calculated to deceive" within the meaning of section 11, the actual decision was justified on the ground that it was excluded from the operation of section 11 because the deceptiveness resulted from circumstances over which the owner of the mark had no control and so was not disentitled to protection in a court of justice. Eve J.'s judgment was treated by Wynn-Parry J. in *Pan Press Publications Ltd's Applications* (1948) 65 R.P.C. 193 as being confined to cases where the subsequent deceptiveness of a mark resulted from events over which the proprietor of the mark had no control. Analysis of Eve J.'s reasoning, however, shows that his decision was based on the more general ground that, irrespective of the cause of any subsequent deceptiveness of a mark, it could not be removed as offending against section 11 because that section only applied to the moment of original registration of the mark. In this I think that he was wrong.

The particular mischief of allowing a mark to remain on the register after it has come into general public use as descriptive of the class of goods in respect of which it was originally registered has since been dealt with by successive amendments first introduced in section 6 of the 1919 Act and replaced and added to by section 15 of the 1938 Act. The right of such marks to remain on the register is no longer governed by section 11 of the 1938 Act (which corresponds to section 11 of the 1905 Act). ...

The question whether the American company is entitled to succeed on the main ground of appeal thus depends on whether the likelihood that the use of the rondel mark *simpliciter* on electrical goods would cause confusion on 20th July 1967, the date of the application to expunge, resulted from some blameworthy act of the American company. On the facts, it is only those which I have summarised earlier under head (7) which could be suggested as constituting blameworthy conduct on the part of the American company. On the findings of Graham J., which in my opinion are amply justified, as to the nature of the understanding between the two companies such as it was, it seems to me to be impossible to hold there was any such blameworthy conduct by the American company as would amount to an equitable ground for disentitling them to protection for the use of the mark. There is therefore no ground in law for expunging the mark and no question of the exercise of discretion of the court can arise.

Lord Diplock concluded that there was nothing essential in Bali Trade Mark *(above, 5.2.4.2) to prevent the House from adopting his proposed construction of sections 11 and 13.*

The case also raised a question of "muddying the mark", which was important on the question of unregistered licensing, as it was dealt with by the C.A. [1970] R.P.C. 339. The point is explained in the judgment of Cross L.J.:

This sufficed to dispose of the appeal but as the matter may be taken to the House of Lords, I ought, perhaps, to say something about some grounds of appeal looming very large in the particulars of objection which do not depend on any possible confusion between G.E. and G.E.C. They relate to the dealings of G.E. with the mark and would be just as strong or weak if no such company as G.E.C. had ever existed.

The facts which are alleged to be relevant in this connection are (1) that G.E. has authorised its wholly owned subsidiary "Housewares" to use the mark in combination with the word MONOGRAM in the form MONO-GE-GRAM otherwise than under a "registered user" agreement under section 28 of the Act; (2) that the registered user agreement entered into with Simplex G.E. extends to user of the mark on goods outside the scope of its registration; (3) that Simplex G.E. has in fact used the mark on goods not within the registration; (4) that the registered user agreement contained a clause which on its true construction precluded Simplex G.E. from using the G.E. mark in combination with the word Simplex and that they have in fact done so, and (5) that the user of the G.E. mark in combination with the words SIMPLEX and MONOGRAM has, to use the appellants' phrase, so "muddied" the mark that it ought to be expunged.

In order to estimate the strength of weakness of this line of attack one must, as I see it, view the matter historically.

When it was established – in the days before the first Trade Mark Act – that a trade mark was an item of property which could be assigned, it was also laid down that it could only be assigned together with the business in the goods to which the mark was affixed. This principle was given statutory force with regard to registered trade marks by section 2 of the 1875 Act and section 70 of the 1883 Act (see the judgment of Fry, L.J. in *Pinto v Badman* (1891) 8 R.P.C. 181 at 194, 195. By 1905 the conception of a trade mark had extended to include, as well as marks indicating the manufacturer of the goods, marks indicating other connections between the goods and the owner of the mark. This is shown by the definition of a "trade mark" in section 3 of the 1905 Act, which ran as follows:

"A 'trade mark' shall mean a mark used or proposed to be used upon or in connection with goods for the purpose of indicating that they are the goods of the proprietor of such trade mark by virtue of manufacture, selection, certification, dealing with, or offering for sale".

But this prohibition against assignment "in gross" was continued by section 22 of the Act.

In the *Bowden* case (1913) 30 R.P.C. 580 and (1914) 31 R.P.C. 385 the wire company had purported to grant to the brake company (over whose methods of manufacture it had no control), together with a licence of patent rights, a licence to use a trade mark of which they were the registered proprietors. It was held that this purported licence offended against section 22 of the 1905 Act (as being a partial assignment of the mark) and had taken the mark outside the statutory definition of a trade mark since it was no longer used for the purpose of indicating that the goods in question were the goods of the proprietor in any of the senses included in the definition. Consequently the court ordered the mark to be taken off the register.

In *"Radiation" Trade Mark* (1930) 47 R.P.C. 37 a company which was applying for registration of a mark did not itself manufacture or sell the goods in question which were made and sold by companies associated with it. The applicant, however, controlled the policy of these associated companies decided whether or not a particular article should be produced and sold maintained its own testing establishment and a staff to inspect the work of the associated companies and ensure that standards of manufacture which it approved were maintained. It was urged by those opposing the registration, on the authority of the *Bowden* case (above), that the applicants by licensing the associated companies to use the mark had deprived it of the quality of a trade mark and any right to protection in a court of law. The Comptroller General, however, distinguished the Bowden case on the ground that there the two companies were independent of each other so far as the manufacture and marketing of the goods was concerned and further expressed the view that the connection of the applicants with the goods fell within the words "selection" and "dealing with" in the definition in section 3 of the 1905 Act.

It is common ground between the parties that the 1938 Act to some extent relaxed the previous rules as to the assignment and licensing of registered marks. The question at issue – or, rather, one of the questions at issue – on this branch of the case is how far that relaxation went and what effect (if any) it had on the position of unregistered marks.

His Lordship set out section 22 (1), 28 and the definition of "trade mark" in section 68.

In *"Radiation" Trade Mark* it was held that "quality control" fell within the definition of the 1905 Act, and whether or not that was right, I think that a right to control the standards to be maintained in the manufacture of goods could, in the absence of some special context, be fairly described as a "connection in the course of trade" between the goods and the person having that right.

This view appears to me to be supported by what was said by Lord Macmillan in *Aristoc Ltd v Rysta Ltd* (1945) 62 R.P.C. 65 at page 80. It was held in that case that there could be no "connection in the course of trade" between the goods and the owner of the mark after the goods had been sold to the consumer, but Lord Macmillan remarked that the wording of the 1938 Act was wider than that of the 1905 Act and covered any association with the goods in the course of their production and preparation for the market.

Further it is clear that the existence or non-existence of adequate "quality control" is one of the matters which the Registrar is to have in mind in deciding whether or not to permit the registration of registered user agreement. Apart, therefore, from an argument based on the inclusion of the words "or as registered user" in the new definition, to which I will advert in a moment, I would have little hesitation in agreeing with the view of the effect of the 1938 Act on the licensing of marks expressed by Lloyd Jacob J. in *"Bostitch" Trade Mark* [1964] R.P.C. 183. This was, in substance, that, provided that "quality control" was maintained, licensing of a mark – whether registered or unregistered – did not deprive it of protection in a court of law or, if it was registered, afford a ground for its removal; that it was not necessary for the proprietor of a registered mark to avail himself of section 28 in order to grant a valid licence of it; but that if he chose to make use of the section (which was merely permissive) he would obtain certain advantages, for example the advantage of the Registrar's decision that the measure of "quality control" which he would retain was adequate to support the licence to use the mark.

The appellants, however, contended that "quality control", though it would justify the Registrar in sanctioning a registered user agreement, was not a "connection in the course of trade" within the definition in section 68 and that the grant of a licence to use a mark, even if accompanied by "quality control", still had the result, even after the Act, of depriving the mark of the character of a trade mark unless it was embodied in a registered user agreement under section 28.

In support of this contention the appellants relied strongly on the words in the definition "some person having the right either as proprietor or registered user to use the mark". If the respondents were right in saying that "quality control" was a connection in the course of trade between the goods and the proprietor of the mark, the definition would have said "a connection in the course of trade between the goods and the proprietor of the mark". It was just because "quality control" – though sufficient to support a registered user agreement – was not a connection in the course of trade that the definition referred to the right to use the mark possessed either by a proprietor who had not parted with his right to use it or by a registered owner who was the one person to whom the proprietor could grant a licence to use without destroying the character of the mark.

This argument is ingenious but, to my mind, it reads too much into the wording of the definition. The draftsman may well have said to himself "A mark on the register will cease to be a 'trade mark' if there is in fact no connection in the course of trade between the goods to which it is affixed and someone appearing on the register as having an interest in the mark, and now that the Act is providing for registered users as well as registered owners we had better mention them in the definition too".

On the whole, therefore, I see no sufficient reason for retracting the approval of what Lloyd-Jacob J. said in *"Bostitch" Trade Mark* which I expressed in *British Petroleum Co Ltd v European Petroleum Distributors Limited* [1968] R.P.C. 54 though the point was not argued then as fully as it has been on this appeal. I would add that in saying, as they did, in *Oertli A.G. v Bowman* (1950) 67 R.P.C. 1 that the grant of the licence had destroyed the validity of the mark, Lord Simonds and Lord Jenkins were clearly only recording what had been conceded in argument and not expressing considered views of their own.

Applying this conclusion to the facts of the case, I am of opinion, first, that the authority given by G.E. to the Housewares company to use the G.E. rondel was open to no objection (a) because as Housewares is a wholly owned subsidiary of G.E., the user might fairly be considered as user by G.E. itself, as in *"Radiation" Trade Mark* (above), and (b) because the licensing of a mark, whether registered or unregistered, does not deprive it of the character of a trade mark providing that the owner of the mark retains a sufficient connection in the course of trade with the relevant goods, which connection can be maintained.

Secondly, I am of opinion that even if Simplex G.E. has been using the G.E. mark on goods which do not fall within the registration, that fact in no way invalidates the mark since G.E. has in fact, as is indeed admitted, "quality control". The licensing agreement certainly envisaged that some of the goods on which the mark might be used might not be covered by the registration. Whether the switchgear, to which this question relates, was or was not in 1907 electrical apparatus included in class 6 (ie was machinery other than agricultural or horticultural machinery), is to my mind a question which hardly admits of an answer since apparatus of this sort was probably unknown in 1907. If I am right on the general point as to licensing, the question does not arise, I would say, however, that assuming that I am wrong on the general question of licensing, I am not satisfied that the inclusion in the licensing agreement and the user of the mark in relation to goods not covered by the registration would invalidate the registered mark.

. . .

That leaves only the question of the so-called "muddying" of the mark. The respondents could not succeed under this head unless the use of the G.E. rondel in combination with Simplex in the form SIMPLEX G.E. or in combination with Monogram in the form MONO-GE-GRAM caused confusion within the meaning of section 11. If one puts out of the way – as one must, for the purposes of this argument – confusion with G.E.C., then I do not think that any confusion such as is envisaged by section 11 is likely to arise. It is possible that some people looking at the marks may not get the message which G.E. intends them to get, but that would not, as I see it, invalidate the G.E. mark.

In the H.L. Lord Diplock dealt with the whole issue summarily:

There is, in my view, no logical ground for holding that the right of a proprietor to use a registered mark in respect of goods for which it is registered can be affected by his losing the right to use the same mark as an unregistered mark in respect of other goods. Since he would lose it in any event at common law by disuse, it would follow from this proposition that the owner of a mark registered in respect of a particular class of goods would lose his right as the proprietor of such mark if he failed to continue to use the mark as an unregistered mark in respect of any other class of goods for which he was using it at the time of first registration. This has only to be stated to be rejected.

5.2.6 Assignment and Licensing

5.2.6.1 Trade Marks Act 1938, s.22(1)–(4), 23(1)–(2): Assignment

Note: these provisions are given only in the version applicable to trade marks.

S.22(1) Notwithstanding any rule of law or equity to the contrary, a registered trade mark shall be, and shall be deemed always to have been, assignable and transmissible either in connection with the goodwill of a business or not.

(2) A registered trade mark shall be, and shall be deemed always to have been, assignable and transmissible in respect either of all the goods in respect of which it is registered, or was registered, as the case may be, or of some (but not all) of those goods.

(3) The provisions of the two foregoing subsections shall have effect in the case of an unregistered trade mark used in relation to any goods as they have effect in the case of a registered trade mark registered in respect of any goods, if at the time of the assignment or transmission of the unregistered trade mark it is or was used in the same business as a registered trade mark, and if it is or was assigned or transmitted at the same time and to the same person as that registered trade mark and in respect of goods all of which are goods in relation to which the unregistered trade mark is or was used in that business and in respect of which that registered trade mark is or was assigned or transmitted.

(4) Notwithstanding anything in the foregoing subsections, a trade mark shall not be, or be deemed to have been, assignable or transmissible in a case in which as a result of the assignment or transmission there would in the circumstances subsist, or have subsisted, whether under the common law or by registration, exclusive rights in more than one of the persons concerned to the use, in relation to –

(a) the same goods,
(b) the same description of goods, or
(c) goods and services or descriptions of goods and services which are associated with each other.

of marks nearly resembling each other or of identical marks, if, having regard to the similarity of the goods or the association of the goods and services or description of goods and services and to the similarity of the marks, the use of the marks in exercise of those rights would be, or have been, likely to deceive or cause confusion:

Provided that, where a trade mark is or has been, assigned or transmitted in such a case as aforesaid, the assignment or transmission shall not be deemed to be, or to have been, invalid under this subsection if the exclusive rights subsisting as a result thereof in the persons concerned respectively are, or were, having regard to limitations imposed thereon, such as not to be exercisable by two or more of those persons in relation to goods to be sold, or otherwise traded in, within the United Kingdom (otherwise than for export therefrom) or in relation to goods to be exported to the same market outside the United Kingdom.

S.22(5) provides for certification against subsequent attack on the validity of an assign-

ment. S.22(6) disallows assignments of trade or service marks where the effect will be to give equivalent rights to different persons in different areas of the UK; subject to an exception by which the Registrar can allow such an assignment if it is not contrary to the public interest.

(7) Where an assignment in respect of any goods of a trade mark that is at the time of the assignment used in a business in those goods is made, on or after the appointed day otherwise than in connection with the goodwill of that business, the assignment shall not take effect until the following requirements have been satisfied, that is to say, the assignee must, not later than the expiration of six months from the date on which the assignment is made or within such extended period, if any, as the Registrar may allow, apply to him for directions with respect to the advertisement of the assignment, and must advertise it in such form and manner and within such period as the Registrar may direct.

S.22(8) provides for appeal to the High Court.

S.23(1) Trade marks that are registered as, or that are deemed by virtue of this Act to be, associated trade marks shall be assignable and transmissible only as a whole and not separately, but they shall for all other purposes be deemed to have been registered as separate trade marks.

(2) Where a trade mark that is registered, or is the subject of an application for registration, in respect of any goods is identical with another trade mark that is registered, or is the subject of an application for registration, in the name of the same proprietor in respect of the same goods or description of goods, or so nearly resembles it as to be likely to deceive or cause confusion if used by a person other than the proprietor, the Registrar may at any time require that the trade marks shall be entered on the register as associated trade marks.

Any decision of the Registrar under this subsection shall be subject to appeal to the Board of Trade, or to the Court, at the option of the appellant.

S.23(2A) applies the same principle between marks for goods and for services associated with the goods, and vice versa. S.23(3),(4) treat marks registered as a series under s.21 as associated marks; s.23(5) provides for dissolution of the association where there is no resultant likelihood of deception or confusion.

S.24 gives the Registrar power to assign; s.25 provides for registration of assignments and transmissions.

5.2.6.2   Trade Marks Act, s.28(1)–(6): Registered User Agreements

Note: these provisions are given only in the version applicable to trade marks.

S.28(1) Subject to the provisions of this section, a person other than the proprietor of a trade mark may be registered as a registered user thereof in respect of all or any of the goods in respect of which it is registered (otherwise than as a defensive trade mark) and either with or without conditions or restrictions.

The use of a trade mark by a registered user thereof in relation to goods with

which he is connected in the course of trade and in respect of which for the time being the trade mark remains registered and he is registered as a registered user, being use such as to comply with any conditions or restrictions to which his registration is subject, is in this Act referred to as the 'permitted use' thereof.

(2) The permitted use of a trade mark shall be deemed to be use by the proprietor thereof, and shall be deemed not to be use by a person other than the proprietor, for the purposes of section twenty-six of this Act and for any other purpose for which such use is material under this Act or at common law.

(3) Subject to any agreement subsisting between the parties, a registered user of a trade mark shall be entitled to call upon the proprietor thereof to take proceedings to prevent infringement thereof, and, if the proprietor refuses or neglects to do so within two months after being so called upon, the registered user may institute proceedings for infringement in his own name as if he were the proprietor, making the proprietor a defendant.

A proprietor so added as a defendant shall not be liable for any costs unless he enters an appearance and takes part in the proceedings.

(4) Where it is proposed that a person should be registered as a registered user of a trade mark, the proprietor and the proposed registered user must apply in writing to the Registrar in the prescribed manner and must furnish him with a statutory declaration made by the proprietor, or by some person authorised to act on his behalf and approved by the Registrar –

(a) giving particulars of the relationship, existing or proposed, between the proprietor and the proposed registered user, including particulars showing the degree of control by the proprietor over the permitted use which their relationship will confer and whether it is a term of their relationship that the proposed registered user shall be the sole registered user or that there shall be any other restriction as to persons for whose registration as registered users application may be made;

(b) stating the goods in respect of which registration is proposed;

(c) stating any conditions or restrictions proposed with respect to the characteristics of the goods, to the mode or place of permitted use, or to any other matter; and

(d) stating whether the permitted use is to be for a period or without limit of period, and, if for a period, the duration thereof;

and with such further documents, information or evidence as may be required under the rules or by the Registrar.

(5) When the requirements of the last foregoing subsection have been compiled with, if the Registrar, after considering the information furnished to him under that subsection, is satisfied that in all the circumstances the use of the trade mark in relation to the proposed goods or any of them by the proposed registered user subject to any conditions or restrictions which the Registrar thinks proper would not be contrary to the public interest, the Registrar may register the proposed registered user as a registered user in respect of the goods as to which he is so satisfied subject as aforesaid.

(6) The Registrar shall refuse an application under the foregoing provisions of this section if it appears to him that the grant thereof would tend to

facilitate trafficking in a trade mark.

S.28(7) provides for confidential disclosure. S.28(8) provides for variation and cancellation and s.28(9)–(12) make various ancillary arrangements.

5.2.6.3   *"McGregor" Trade Mark* [1979] R.P.C. 36 (Whitford J.)

The registered proprietor of "McGregor" for clothing including dressing gowns never itself used the mark but in 1966 entered a registered agreement for Sterling Rubber to use it on dressing gowns, subject to the power of the proprietor to give directions as to materials and manufacture.

Some years later, Sterling sought but failed to buy the mark and then received advice that it might attack the registration for non-use on other clothing and even on dressing gowns. It began using the mark on other clothing and then launched proceedings for rectification under the Trade Marks Act 1938, section 26.

An American firm which used "McGregor" for clothing in the US and wished to acquire the right to use it in the UK also planned to attack the registration. But, knowing of Sterling's attack, it chose to purchase the existing registration and so intervened in the rectification proceedings to preserve the mark.

Whitford J. set out the terms of section 26(1) (above, 5.2.5.1) which he summarised thus:

If you are registered for a variety of articles of clothing, as the registered proprietors under this mark are, use in respect of one or more of the classes of clothing covered by the registration may be held to be sufficient to justify retaining the mark on the register for some or all of the other classes of clothing in respect of which there has been no use.

There was no dispute that it must be concluded on the evidence in this case that there was never any use of the mark for any goods by the registered proprietors during the relevant period. It was further accepted on the applicants' side that, if the use by them of their associates for dressing gowns was permitted use, the proviso may save the other goods.

I turn, therefore, to the question of whether such use as was made by the registered users can be relied upon for the purposes of defeating the claim under section 26 (1) (b).

He set out the terms of section 28 (1), (2) and said of their application to the facts before him:

There is no dispute that at all relevant times under the terms of the registered user agreements the registered proprietors had the right and were permitted or should have been permitted to take samples of or to inspect the goods and the methods of manufacturing them though they never did any such thing. The contention of the applicants that there never were any directions given by the registered proprietors as to the materials and methods of manufacture was not challenged. If this be the case, *prima facie*, in my view the conclusion must be that there never was any use complying with the conditions and restrictions on the register; and accordingly there was no permitted use.

Against this two submissions were made: first, on the principle that no man shall take advantage of his own wrong, it was said that the applicants cannot be heard to assert that their use was not in accordance with the registered user agreement. This point was put in an alternative way in that it was said that the conduct of the applicants in holding themselves out as registered users over a period of years should act as an estoppel against a suggestion upon their side that they never did act as registered users. I may say that, it this were purely an *inter-partes* matter, I would feel some sympathy with this approach. However, I do not propose to go into the merits of it in detail because it appears to me that I have to consider not only the commercial interests of the parties in connection with this mark, but also the public interest.

Registered trade marks, as is the case with trade marks at common law, serve to protect what may be a very valuable goodwill built up by some commercial enterprise. They also, however, serve as an indication to the public of the origin of the goods. If one buys a dressing gown bearing the trade mark "McGregor", one may never know and may not even be concerned to enquire who in fact made the dressing gown in question; but if one buys a dressing gown and finds it satisfactory one would feel, if one were buying another dressing gown bearing the same brand name at a later stage, that one could reasonably expect it to be of a similar quality to the first dressing gown. In the same way, it is customary for people to make recommendations to their friends by reference to brand names for goods; and upon a recommendation being made, the purchase is carried out in the confidence that the article purchased will be of a similar quality to that sold to the friend making the original recommendation.

It is for this reason that a bare licence under a trade mark has never been countenanced. A registered usership is accepted because in one way or another, by reason of financial control or express provisions in an agreement, a registered user is going to be subject to the control of the registered proprietor so far as the quality of the article made by the registered user is concerned. In this way, even if two persons are using a mark – the registered proprietor and the registered user – there is only one source controlling the question of quality; and if a member of the public were interested to find out who bore the ultimate responsibility for the quality of the goods, he or she would be able to do so by inspecting the relevant entries on the register.

In this case it is quite plain to me that the public have been misled since 1966. The mark "McGregor" has never been used by any registered proprietor at any relevant time. No registered proprietor has ever exercised any control over the activities of the registered user; and it appears to me that it was never intended that any such control should be exercised; but nonetheless the mark was maintained on the register and the present applicants, together with the registered proprietors, were prepared to present this mark as a registered mark being used by the applicants and their associates subject to the conditions of the registered user agreement. These are facts which, in consideration of the public interest, I must take into consideration. ...

The Assistant Registrar was, in my judgment, quite right to take into consideration the question of the public interest, but I confess that I am not myself satisfied that it would necessarily be in the public interest that the present applicants, who have been party to what must on the face of it be a use which was deceptive, although that may never have been their intention, should necessarily secure any registration. I would not, for my own part, assume that removal of the existing mark from the register would necessarily enable the applicants successfully to proceed with the registration in their own name, which is at present on file, with success. I certainly would not order rectification so as to frank what was initially a deliberate act of infringement by the applicants, and, as I have said, the applicants, whether innocently or otherwise, have been parties to a continued mis-representation as to the true facts relating to this mark for many years. I would certainly do nothing to assist them. The intervenors have gone into this with their eyes open as a commercial speculation; and in exercising my discretion I see no reason why I should refrain from rectifying the register merely to assist their enterprises.

Here is a mark in relation to which non-user is established. There is, to my mind, no good reason shown as to why it should not be removed from the register, and I think the order made by the Assistant Registrar was the correct order. The motion accordingly fails and must stand dismissed.

5.2.7 Infringement

5.2.7.1 Trade Marks Act 1938, s.4, 5, 7, 8: Rights under Parts A and B, Infringement and Defences

S.4(1) Subject to the provisions of this section, and of sections seven and eight of this Act, the registration (whether before or after the commencement of this Act) *after the coming into force of the Trade Marks (Amendment) Act 1984* of a person in Part A of the register as proprietor of a trade/*service* mark in respect of any goods/*services* shall, if valid, give to that person the exclusive right to the use of the trade/*service* mark in relation to those goods/*services* and, without prejudice to the generality of the foregoing words, that right shall be deemed to be infringed by any person who, not being the proprietor of the trade/*service* mark or a registered user thereof using by way of the permitted use, uses in the course of trade *in connection with the provision of any services* a mark identical with or nearly resembling it in relation to any goods/*services* in respect of which it is registered, and in such manner as to render the use of the mark likely to be taken either –

(a) as being used as a trade/*service* mark; or
(b) in a case in which the use is use upon goods or in physical relation thereto or in an advertising circular or other advertisement issued to the public, as importing a reference to some person having the right either as proprietor or as registered user to use the trade mark or to goods with which such a person as aforesaid is connected in the course of trade/
(b) *in a case in which the use is use at or near the place where the services are available for acceptance or performed or in an advertising circular or other advertisement issued to the public, as importing a reference to some person having a right either as proprietor or as registered user to use the mark or to services with the provision of which such a person as aforesaid is connected in the course of business.*

(2) The right to the use of a trade/*service* mark given by registration as aforesaid shall be subject to any conditions or limitations entered on the register, and shall not be deemed to be infringed by the use of any such mark as aforesaid in any mode, in relation to goods to be sold or otherwise traded/*services for use or available for acceptance in any place, country or territory* in relation to goods to be exported to any market, or in any other circumstances, to which, having regard to any such limitations, the registration does not extend.

(3) The right to the use of a trade/*service* mark given by registration as aforesaid shall not be deemed to be infringed by the use of any such mark as aforesaid by any person –

(a) in relation to goods connected in the course of trade with the proprietor or a registered user of the trade mark if, as to those goods or a bulk of which they form part, the proprietor of the registered user conforming to the permitted use had applied the trade mark and has not subsequently removed or obliterated it, or has at any time expressly or impliedly consented to the use of the trade mark; or/

    (a) *in relation to services to which the proprietor of the mark or a registered user conforming to the permitted use has applied the mark, where the purpose and effect of the use of the mark is to indicate, in accordance with the fact, that those services have been performed by the proprietor or a registered user of the mark; or*

    (b) in relation to goods adapted to form part of, or to be accessory to, other goods in relation to which the trade mark has been used without infringement of the right given as aforesaid or might for the time being be so used, if the use of the mark is reasonably necessary in order to indicate that the goods are so adapted and neither the purpose nor the effect of the use of the mark is to indicate otherwise than in accordance with the fact a connection in the course of trade between any person and the goods/

    (b) *in relation to services the provision of which is connected in the course of business with the proprietor or a registered user of the mark, where the proprietor or registered user has at any time expressly or impliedly consented to the use of the mark; or*

    (c) *in relation to services available for use with other services in relation to which the mark has been used without infringement of the right given by registration or might for the time being be so used, if –*

        (i) *the use of the mark is reasonably necessary in order to indicate that the services are available for such use, and*

        (ii) *neither the purpose nor the effect of the use of the mark is to indicate otherwise than in accordance with the fact a connection in the course of business between any person and the provision of those services.*

(4) The use of a registered trade/*service* mark, being one of two or more registered marks that are identical or nearly resemble each other, in exercise of the right to the use of that trade/*service* mark given by registration as aforesaid, shall not be deemed to be an infringement of the right so given to the use of any other of those trade/*service* marks.

S.5(1) Except as provided by subsection (2) of this section, the registration *after the commencement of the Trade Marks (Amendment) Act 1984* of a person in Part B of the register as proprietor of a trade/*service* mark in respect of any goods/*services* shall, if valid, give or be deemed to have given to that person the like right in relation to those goods/*services* as if the registration had been in Part A of the register, and the provisions of the last foregoing section shall have effect in like manner in relation to a trade/*service* mark registered in Part B of the register as they have effect in relation to a trade/*service* mark registered in Part A of the register.

(2) In any action for infringement of the right to the use of a trade mark given by registration as aforesaid in Part B of the register, otherwise than by an act that is deemed to be an infringement by virtue of the next succeeding section, no injunction or other relief shall be granted to the plaintiff if the defendant establishes to the satisfaction of the court that the use of which the plaintiff complains is not likely to deceive or cause confusion or to be taken as indicating a connection in the course of trade between the goods and some person having the right either as proprietor or as registered user to use the trade mark/

(2) *In any action for infringement of the right to the use of a service mark given by registration as aforesaid in Part B of the register, no injunction or other relief shall be granted to the plaintiff if the defendant establishes to the satisfaction of the court that the use of which the plaintiff complains is not likely to deceive or cause confusion or to be taken as indicating that a person having the right either as proprietor or as registered user to use the mark is connected in the course of business with the provision of the services.*

S.6 provides for infringement by failure to respect a written contract not to alter trade marked goods, the mark or connected material; or not to add another trade mark or injurious material.

S.7 Nothing in this Act shall entitle the proprietor or a registered user of a registered trade/*service* mark to interfere with or restrain the use by any person of a trade/*service* mark identical with or nearly resembling it in relation to goods/*services* in relation to which that person or a predecessor in title of his/*predecessor* of his in business has continuously used that trade mark from a date anterior –
  (a) **to the use of the first-mentioned trade mark in relation to those goods by the proprietor or a predecessor in title of his/*predecessor of his in business*; or**
  (b) **to the registration of the first-mentioned trade mark in respect of those goods in the name of the proprietor or a predecessor in title of his/ *predecessor of his in business*;**
whichever is the earlier, or to object (on such use being proved) to that person being put on the register for that identical or nearly resembling trade/*service* mark in respect of those goods/*services* under subsection (2) of section twelve of this Act.

S.8 No registration of a trade/*service* mark shall interfere with –
  (a) **any *bona fide* use by a person of his own name or of the name of his place of business, or of the name, or of the name of the place of business, of any of his predecessors in business; or**
  (b) **the use by any person of any *bona fide* description of the character or quality of his goods/*services*, not being a description that would be likely to be taken as importing any such reference as is mentioned in paragraph (b) of subsection (1) of section four, or in paragraph (b) of subsection (3) of section thirty-seven, of this Act.**

5.2.7.2   *Saville Perfumery v June Perfect* [1941] 58 R.P.C. 147 (C.A., H.L.)

The plaintiffs owned a trade mark of which the essential feature was the word "June", written in a special manner, and which was registered in Class 48 for perfumery. It sued both defendants for infringement and passing-off by the sale of articles within this class, under labels bearing the word "June" in conjunction with other words. They also claimed as against the first defendants an injunction to restrain them from trading in perfumery or toilet articles under their present name, June Perfect, or any name containing the word "June" and calculated to deceive the public into believing that they were in any way connected with the plaintiffs or their business.

In the Court of Appeal injunctions were granted against infringement and passing off and these injunctions were subsequently upheld by the House of Lords.

Sir Wilfred Greene M.R. (in the C.A.):

I will deal first with the case of alleged infringement. The trade mark which Respondents are said to have infringed is No. 489562 in Class 48. It consists of the word "June" written in characters of a special form across a bar with a garland of flowers depending from the bar. There is a disclaimer of the exclusive right to the floral device. It is not open to dispute that for the purposes of the present case, in order that the thing of which complaint is made may amount to an infringement, it must be used as a trade mark, that is, putting it shortly, for the purpose of indicating origin, or, to quote the words of the Trade Marks Act 1938, section 4, sub-section 1, used "in such a manner as to render the use of the mark likely to be taken as being used as a trade mark". It is said by the Appellants, and Bennett J. found the fact in their favour, that the word "June" is used by the Respondents in connection with all three articles as a brand name, that is, as a trade mark. I am in entire agreement with this finding. The way in which the word is presented to the eye would, by itself, have led me to this conclusion, and it is confirmed by the evidence given at the trial. Indeed, Mrs Coakley herself makes it clear that this is what she was aiming at. I had at one time some doubt with regard to the setting lotion. But I am satisfied that the printing of the word "June" in inverted commas shows that it was intended to be used as a trade mark. It is true that on a careful reading of the printed matter used in connection with the three articles it appears that the origin of the goods to indicate which the word "June" is used, is either the June Hair Curler Co or June Perfect Ltd. But this circumstance, relevant though it may be upon the question of passing-off, is immaterial upon the question of infringement. In an infringement action, once it is found that the defendant's mark is used as a trade mark, the fact that he makes it clear that the commercial origin of the goods indicated by the trade mark is some business other than that of the plaintiff avails him nothing, since infringement consists in using the mark as a trade mark, that is, as indicating origin. I may point out here that the Appellants' claim upon this part of the case, if successful, will not, as was suggested by Mr Lloyd-Jacob, in effect give them a monopoly in the use of the word "June" in connection with goods in Class 48. The most that it will do is to enable them to prevent the use of that word as a trade mark.

The question therefore is: "Does the mark 'June' used by the Respondents so nearly resemble the Appellants' registered mark as to be likely to deceive or cause confusion?" I use the language of section 4 (1) of the Trade Marks Act, 1938, which all Counsel agreed merely embodies the pre-existing law. It is possible that the words "or cause confusion" have in some measure altered the law. I do not pause to examine this question, since my conclusion would be the same if those words were omitted from the definition of infringement. The learned Judge answered this question adversely to the Appellants by an ocular comparison between the two marks. But the problem is not to be resolved by so simple a method. It is true that the ultimate question relates to the resemblance of one mark to the other, but before it can be answered certain relevant matters must be considered. The statute law relating to infringement of trade marks is based on the same fundamental idea as the law relating to passing-off. But it differs from that law in two particulars, namely (1) it is concerned only with one method of passing-off, namely the use of a trade mark, and (2), the statutory protection is absolute in the sense that once a mark is shown to offend, the user of it outside the actual mark itself he has distinguished his goods from those of the registered proprietor. Accordingly, in considering the question of infringement the Courts have held, and it is now expressly provided by the Trade Marks Act, 1938, section 4, that infringement takes place not merely by exact imitation, but by the use of a mark so nearly resembling the registered mark as to be likely to deceive. The questions therefore arise: First, is there a resemblance, and, second, is the resemblance so close as to be likely to cause deception? In answering these questions, ocular comparison is, of course, an important matter to be taken into consideration, in some cases it may be conclusive one way or the other. But if the Court were to confine itself to this test the protection afforded by the law of trade marks would in many cases prove illusory. It would be still more illusory if, as Mr Lloyd-Jacob contended, no witness could be listened to who was not prepared to say that when he saw the mark complained of he had in his mind the actual registered mark and made a comparison between the two. Propositions of this kind, if accepted, would, as it appears to me, divorce the law of trade marks from business realities. In the case of certain goods, traders, and perhaps the public too, may be expected to receive so strong an impression of the actual mark as to lead to the conclusion that nothing short of a degree of resemblance apparent to the eye will cause the necessary likelihood of deception. On the other hand, many articles do not fall within this category. In the present case, for example, the evidence makes it clear that traders who have to deal with a very large number of marks used in the trade in which they are interested, do not, in practice, and indeed cannot be expected to, carry in their heads the details of any particular mark, while the class of customer among the public which buys the goods does not interest itself in such details. In such cases the mark comes to be remembered by some feature in it which strikes the eye and fixes itself in the recollection. Such a feature is referred to sometimes as the distinguishing feature, sometimes as the essential feature, of the mark. I do not pause to examine these appellations, since the idea conveyed is free from ambiguity. In deciding whether or not a feature is of this class, not only ocular examination, but the evidence of what happens in practice in the particular trade is admissible. In the present case, the evidence leaves me in no doubt as to the word "June" being the distinguishing or essential feature of the Appellants' mark. It is by this word that traders and members of the public who see the mark on the goods which they purchase describe the Appellants' goods, and indeed I should have been surprised if it had been otherwise.

Now the question of resemblance and the likelihood of deception are to be considered by reference not only to the whole mark, but also to its distinguishing or essential features, if any. If authority be wanted for this proposition, it is to be found in the decision of this Court in *Bale and Church Ltd v Sutton Parsons and Sutton and Astrah Products*, (1934) 51 R.P.C. 129, where at page 141 Romer L.J. as he then was, quotes with approval what Counsel on both sides agreed was a correct statement of the test to be applied. The quotation was from page 445 of the late Sir Duncan Kerly's work on Trade Marks where he says: "Infringement is the use by the defendant for trade purposes upon or in connection with goods of the kind for which the plaintiff's right to exclusive use exists, not being the goods of the plaintiff, of a mark identical with the plaintiff's mark or comprising some of its essential features, or colourably resembling it so as to be calculated to cause goods to be taken by ordinary purchasers for the goods of the plaintiff". Applying this test and considering the evidence and the appearance of the two marks, I have come to the clear conclusion that the word "June" as used by the Respondents as a trade mark so nearly resembles the Appellants' mark as to be calculated to deceive and that infringement has taken place for which the Appellants are entitled to the appropriate remedies.

I now turn to the claim based on passing-off. It does not necessarily follow that a trader who uses an infringing mark upon goods is also guilty of passing-off. The reason is that in the matter of infringement, as I have already pointed out, once a mark is used as indicating origin, no amount of added matter intended to show the true origin of the goods can affect the question. In the case of passing-off, on the other hand, the defendant may escape liability if he can show that the added matter is sufficient to distinguish his goods from those of the plaintiff. Such proof may be very difficult, but theoretically at any rate the result may be as I have stated. In the present case there is to be found in connection with the three classes of goods of which complaint is made, added matter which refers their origin to the June Hair Curler Co or to June Perfect Ltd. But in my opinion, in view of the evidence in the case, this is not enough. The mere affirmative statement that the origin of the goods is one or other of those two concerns is, upon the facts of this case quite insufficient to prevent confusion arising. I do not enquire whether the addition of a negative statement to the effect that the goods were not the goods of the traders whose products are well known as "June" products would have been sufficient. It is enough to say that no such statement appears. There has been a great deal of confusion in fact, and I am satisfied that the Appellants have established a case of passing-off in respect of all three articles. The fact that they do not deal in setting lotion does not disentitle them to relief under this head since passing-off may occur in cases where the Plaintiffs do not in fact deal in the offending goods.

5.2.7.3   *Bismag v Amblins* [1940] Ch. 677 (C.A.)

The respondents produced medicines of the same composition as the appellants' well-known, high-priced products and sold them more cheaply after advertising the comparison. The appellants produced "Bisurated" magnesia tablets and powders for which the respondents' equivalent was called "Bismuthated". The latter's advertising presented comparative tables which enabled the reader to find the respondents' equivalent product and compare its price. The advertising also stated that the respondents offered for sale the products compared (including the appellants') as well as their own.

Despite the fact that "Bisurated" was the appellants' registered mark (in Part A) the respondents claimed that their advertisement did not constitute infringement under section 4 of the 1938 Act.

Greene M.R.:

The respondents have not used the registered trade marks of other persons as indicative of the origin of their own goods, and in default of use of this character no case of infringement could have been established against them under the law as it stood before the Act of 1938 came into force. It is said, however, on behalf of the appellants that the respondents' use of the appellants' registered trade mark "Bisurated" although not directed to indicate the origin of the respondents' goods, is nevertheless such as to fall within the definition of infringement in section 4 of the Act of 1938. This makes it desirable to examine further the implications of what the respondents have done in the poster and the booklet by referring to the appellants' remedies under their registered trade mark.

Here again the matter does not seem to me to be open to doubt. The respondents first of all are using the word "Bisurated" in a trade mark sense, that is, as indicative of the origin of the goods in relation to which reference is made to the trade mark. It is true that the reference is not to the respondents' goods but to the appellants' goods; nevertheless the word "Bisurated" is used in a trade mark sense and not in a descriptive sense as might have been the case if the word had had a descriptive as well as a distinctive significance.

Moreover, the respondents are using the appellants' trade mark as a convenient method of describing the merits of the respondents' own goods. They are in effect saying: "You, the public, are no doubt familiar with 'Bisurated Magnesia', and are aware of its virtues; the best method of describing the virtues of our 'Bismuthated Magnesia' is to tell you that they are precisely the same as those of 'Bisurated Magnesia' – that is all that you need to know". In short, the respondents are using the appellants' trade mark for the purpose of advertising and compendiously describing the virtues of their own goods and thus obtain for themselves a benefit from the reputation enjoyed by the appellants' goods sold under and identified by the appellants' registered trade mark.

Lastly must be noticed the fact that in the booklet the appellants' trade mark is used in relation to the appellants' own goods which the respondents stock and are willing to sell. This use of the mark considered by itself is, of course, unobjectionable. It was argued that this was the only use, but, for the reasons which I have endeavoured to explain, this argument in my view cannot be supported.

I now turn to consider the questions of law involved in the appeal. It is beyond dispute that under the law as it stood before the 1938 Act came into operation, the action of the respondents which I have described would not have amounted to an infringement of the appellants' trade mark. This results from the decision of the House of Lords in *Irving's Yeast-Vite Ltd v Horsenail* (1934) 51 R.P.C. 110, commonly called the "Yeast-Vite" case. In that case the defendant had exhibited in his shop window placards exhorting the public to purchase his preparations which he described as substitutes for named patent medicines (including Yeast-Vite) made up to the same formulae. He also sold bottles labelled "Yeast Tablets. A Substitute for Yeast-Vite". The plaintiffs were the registered proprietors of the trade mark Yeast-Vite and they claimed that the defendant's use of that word in the way described amounted to an infringement. This claim was rejected on the ground that the defendant's use of the mark was not for the purpose of indicating the origin of his goods and therefore did not infringe the right conferred upon the plaintiffs as registered proprietors of the trade mark under the statutes then in force. The definition of the right of the proprietor of a registered trade mark contained in section 4 of the Act of 1938 is quite different in language. The twenty-four words which I have quoted from section 39 of the Act of 1905 are replaced by the two hundred and fifty-five words of sub-section 1 if my addition is correct. Even this figure is vastly exceeded if the other sub-sections, which consist largely of definition, are included. So formidable an alteration may legitimately be supposed to have been intended by the Legislature to produce some concrete result. The definition in sub-section 1 falls into two parts; the first part gives a general definition of the exclusive right of the proprietor; the second part gives two special instances "without prejudice to the generality of the foregoing words" in which the right is to be deemed to be infringed. The first part of the definition is in the following words: "The exclusive right to the use of the trademark in relation to these goods", and by sub-section 2 of section 68 this reference to use in relation to goods is to be construed as a reference to use "upon or in physical or other relation to goods". If this had been the only alteration effected by the Act of 1938 I could have understood an argument to the effect that the law as laid down in the *Yeast-Vite* case remained unaffected in spite of the change in phraseology and in spite of the wide meaning given to the phrase "in relation to". But as will be seen there are provisions in the second part of the definition which are most relevant to the construction of the first part and make it in my opinion impossible to treat the language of the first part as identical in effect with that used in the earlier Act.

The second part of the definition gives two particular cases of use "in relation to" goods which are to be deemed to be infringements. Such use will be an infringement if it takes place "in such a manner as to render the use of the mark likely to be taken either (a) as being use as a trade mark; or (b) in a case in which the use is use upon the goods or in physical relation thereto or in an advertising circular or other advertisement issued to the public, as importing a reference to some person having the right either as proprietor or as registered user to use the trade mark or to goods with which such a person as aforesaid is connected in the course of trade".

Now the use mentioned under head (a) is quite clearly a use by the alleged infringer in relation to his own goods which is likely to be taken as being use as a trade mark for his own goods, that is, to use Lord Tomlin's words "as indicating in relation to" those goods "the origin of" them "in the user of the mark", that is, the alleged infringer. This, therefore, is the old type of infringement. But the use mentioned under head (b) is altogether different. It is expressed in the alternative and it would not be in accordance with any rule of construction to attribute to the language of head (b) a meaning identical with that of head (a). In my opinion it is clear that head (b) is intended to deal with a class of use which is not already covered by head (a); and as head (a) completely covers what I have called the old type of infringement, it follows that head (b) must be dealing with a type of use which is not a use indicating the origin of the goods in the infringer. Moreover, as this type of use is a use "in relation to" the goods of the infringer, it follows that the words "use in relation to" in both parts of the definition cannot be confined to a use in relation to those goods for the purpose of indicating their origin in the infringer. Once it appears that there may be a wrongful use of a trade mark "in relation to goods" (namely, the goods of the alleged infringer) which is not a use as a trade mark in reference to those goods, that is, as indicating the origin of those goods in the alleged infringer, all reason for giving a limited construction to the words "in relation to" disappears. I have already expressed the view that according to the ordinary meaning of the words apart from any special context, the respondents' use of the trade mark "Bisurated" which is complained of is a use "in relation to" the respondents' own goods. It is for the purpose of describing the virtues of those goods that the mark is used. The public is invited to compare "Bisurated" goods with "Bismuthated" goods and is told that the latter are identical with the former save in the matter of price.

I am of opinion therefore that the respondents have infringed the exclusive right of the appellants as defined in the first part of section 4, sub-section 1. But they have also in my judgment been guilty of infringement under paragraph (b) of the second part of the sub-section. The language of that paragraph is turgid and diffuse. But a patient examination makes it possible to discover its meaning. In order to bring himself within this paragraph there must be a use of "a mark" – not, be it observed, of a "trade mark" – "identical with the registered trade mark or so nearly resembling it as to be likely to deceive or cause confusion". The respondents have used the mark "Bisurated" in two ways, one a legitimate way as the trade mark of the appellants' goods, the other (with which we are now concerned) as a mark forming by reference part of the description of their own goods. Next the use must be in the course of trade. This condition is satisfied. Next the use must be "in relation to any goods in respect of which it is registered". The use complained of is in relation to the identical class of goods. Next the use must be "upon the goods or in physical relation thereto or in an advertising circular or other advertisement issued to the public" – this excludes all other forms of relationship covered by the definition of "in relation to" contained in section 68, sub-section 2. This condition has been compiled with. Next the mark must be used "in such manner as to render the use of the mark likely to be taken as importing a reference to some person having the right either as proprietor or as registered user to use the trade mark or to goods with which such a person as aforesaid is connected in the course of trade". The persons having the right as proprietors to use the trade mark "Bisurated" are the appellants. "Bisurated" goods are goods with which the appellants are connected in the course of trade. Does the use complained of import a reference to the appellants' "Bisurated" goods? Manifestly, since it is the whole object of that use that it should do so.

The language which I have just quoted is far from happy. In substance what is meant, as it appears to me, is that the mark must be used in what I may call a trade mark sense, not, of course, as a trade mark for the infringer's own goods (that is provided for by paragraph (a)), but as a trade mark identifying the complainant's goods, as the trade mark "Yeast-Vite" was used in the *Yeast-Vite* case, and as the trade mark "Bisurated" is used in the present case. The reason why it is only used in a trade mark sense which falls under paragraph (b) is, I think, fairly obvious. The use must be of a "mark" and a mark is defined in section 68, sub-section 1, as including among other things a "word". If paragraph (b) had not been confined to use of a mark in a trade mark sense it might well have followed that the use in a non-trade mark sense of a word which happened to be a trade mark would have been an infringement. Thus let it be supposed that a shoe manufacturer had succeeded in registering the word "Crocodile" as a trade mark. It might have been said that another manufacturer would have been unable to describe his shoes as "made of crocodile" skin. Under paragraph (b) as it stands such a description would be unobjectionable. But if he went on to say that his shoes were as good as the "Crocodile" brand shoes he would be using the word "Crocodile" in a different sense, namely, a trade mark sense and not a merely descriptive one. A similar example suggests itself in reference to the well known "Sheen" mark for sewing cotton: *In re J & P Coates Ltd's Application* (1936) 53 R.P.C. 355.

Another argument was founded upon the language of sub-section 3 (a) of section 4, which provides that certain acts shall not be deemed to be infringements. It was said that even if the language of section 4, sub-section 1, is wide enough in itself to cover what the respondents have done it is counteracted by paragraph (a) of sub-section 3 in that the use which the respondents have made of the appellants' mark is the use permitted by that paragraph. This argument in my opinion is founded on a fallacy. Paragraph (a) is a verbose piece of drafting, but its effect shortly stated appears to me to exclude from the category of infringing acts what would otherwise have fallen within the wide scope of sub-section 1, namely, the use of a trade mark upon the goods of the proprietor with his consent express or implied. The scheme of section 4 as a matter of drafting is I think clearly to include within the scope of sub-section 1 every use of a mark and then to exclude from its operation by the following sub-sections various types of use including the everyday type of use described in paragraph (a). There is no question that the respondents have used the appellants' trade mark in the way described in paragraph (a) for they sell the appellants' goods upon which the trade mark "Bisurated" has been placed by the appellants themselves. But as I have already pointed out this is only one use which the respondents have made of the appellants' mark and no complaint is or could be made with regard to it. The other use which the respondents have made of the mark is entirely different in character and purpose. The circumstances that the one use is made legitimate by paragraph (a) of sub-section 3 cannot possibly be treated as a justification for the other.

One last argument may be mentioned. It was said on behalf of the respondents that if the appellants are right, traders would find their activities outrageously circumscribed. For example, it was said that they could not advertise in one and the same catalogue or display in one and the same shop window their own goods and branded goods of similar qualities. This argument does not alarm me. Whether or not a particular use of the complainant's trade mark is a use "in relation to" the alleged infringer's goods within the meaning of the sub-section must in my view depend upon the facts of each individual case. In the present case the facts which I have analysed in the earlier part of this judgment present no difficulty to my mind.

I conclude, therefore, that the effect of this legislation is to alter the law as laid down in the Yeast-Vite case and to make what the respondents have done an infringement. It is interesting to observe that the first part of this conclusion agrees with the view taken by the respondents themselves and, I dare say, by traders in general. In their poster they say that "the Millionaire Patent Medicine Firms have secretly got an Act passed which makes it illegal for us to mention the names of Patent Medicines in comparison with our copies so that we cannot say for instance: '30 tablets Amblo 6d sold to compete with 10 tablets so-and-so at 6d'". They then proceed to state that they have found a "simple way" of showing the comparison. Unfortunately for them this "simple way" has not enabled them to circumvent the statute.

I do not add to the length of this judgment by examining in detail the reasoning of Simonds J. from whom, with all respect, I am differing. My reasons for disagreeing with the view which he took are, I hope, sufficiently apparent from what I have said. In my judgment the appeal should be allowed.

Clauson L.J. gave a concurring judgment. In dissenting, Mackinnon L.J. said:

In the course of three days hearing of this case I have I suppose, heard section 4 of the Act of 1938 read, or have read it for myself, dozens if not hundreds of times. Despite this iteration I must confess that, reading it through once again, I have very little notion of what the section is intended to convey, and particularly the sentence of two hundred and fifty-three words, as I make them, which constitutes sub-section 1. I doubt if the entire statute book could be successfully searched for a sentence of equal length which is of more fuliginous obscurity.

5.2.7.4   *Broad v Graham Building Supplies (No.1)* [1969] R.P.C. 286; [1969] F.S.R. 153 (Graham J.)

The plaintiffs owned "Broadstel" for metal drainage covers, registered in Part B. The defendants in supplying a substitute product which had been ordered from them invoiced it as "Broadstel 394F". In interlocutory proceedings Graham J. held that there was no prima facie case that customers had been led to believe that they were getting a Broadstel cover. He continued:

If in the present case the registration were in Part A of the register, it may well be that the plaintiffs could satisfy the court that the use by the defendants here comes within section 4 (1), but I do not decide the matter one way or the other because this is not a case of registration in Part A. As regards section 4 (1) (b) there is clearly here no document issued to the public by the defendants such as an advertisement or circular and the plaintiffs must bring themselves within the words "in physical relation thereto" as the mark BROADSTEL was admittedly not used upon the goods themselves. The onus is on the plaintiffs, and there is no evidence here that the invoices in question were used in physical relation to the goods. It can only be a matter of inference that they were sent with the goods on delivery and the plaintiffs ask the court to infer this.

Even if the necessary physical relationship is assumed, the plaintiffs here still have to overcome the provisions of section 5 (2) of the Act in the present case because their mark, as I have stated, is registered in Part B and not in Part A.

It is clear from what I have said previously in connection with passing off that in my judgment there is here no question of the use causing deception or confusion. Therefore there remains only the question whether the defendants can establish that the use complained of is or is not likely to be taken as indicating a connection in the course of trade between the goods and some person having the right as proprietor to use the trade mark, since in my judgment the word "or" is used in the section conjunctively and not disjunctively.

What "goods" are the words "the goods" in the sub-section referring to? Do those words mean the plaintiffs' goods? Do they mean generally any goods within the registration? Or do they mean the defendants' goods the subject of the plaintiffs' complaint? If the last is the proper meaning and if the defendant has used the plaintiffs' mark in reference to his own goods, then he cannot escape. In other words, if he is using the mark to describe his goods and is in effect "cashing in" on the plaintiffs' goodwill in order to sell his goods, it is right that he should be guilty of infringement of a mark registered in Part B. The point is to my mind not an easy one, but it seems to me that the expression "the goods" must be related back to the words "the use of which the plaintiff complains", and in my judgment this is the intention of the section fairly read and it should be so construed.

5.2.7.5   *Revlon v Cripps & Lee* [1980] F.S.R. 85 (C.A.)

Revlon, Inc. was the parent company of an international group, manufactured and sold in the U.S. an anti-dandruff shampoo and conditioner under the mark "Revlon Flex". For the U.K. this mark was owned by one subsidiary – "Suisse". It was used upon shampoos for the British market by two others, one of which – "Overseas" – manufactured the products in Wales, and the other – "International" (a registered user) – distributed them. The British products were not formulated to counteract dandruff.

Upon termination of the line in the U.S., Revlon Inc. disposed of surplus stock, partly to charity and partly by reduced price sale to wholesalers. Some of these U.S. products were brought into the U.K. for sale by parallel importers. In interlocutory proceedings for passing off and trade mark infringement, Dillon J. and the C.A. held that there was no serious issue to be tried.

On the question of passing off, Buckley L.J. stated:

It is common ground that the relevant reputation is a reputation in the United Kingdom. Mr Cullen for the first defendant has emphasised that Overseas and International have put the United Kingdom products on the United Kingdom market labelled, albeit in rather small type, "REVLON/New York-Paris-London" which he says draws attention to the international scope of the origin of the products. It is not disputed that identical goods are manufactured and marketed in the United States marked with the REVLON FLEX mark, nor that identical goods are marketed so marked in many countries in the world, although it is not clear where such goods which are sold elsewhere than in the United States and the United Kingdom are manufactured. It is no doubt true to say that the reputation in the United Kingdom of products of the Revlon group has been earned by the sale in the United Kingdom of the United Kingdom products, that is to say that, so far as shampoos and hair conditioners are concerned, it has been earned by sales under the REVLON FLEX mark of the three types of shampoo and the three associated types of conditioner which constitute the United Kingdom products.

It does not, in my judgment, follow from this that the mark REVLON FLEX is necessarily a signal to the British public that goods upon which it appears are goods made in this country or are the goods of either Overseas or International. I see nothing in the evidence to suggest that the general public in the United Kingdom is aware, or even that those in the trade are aware, that the United Kingdom products have all been made by Overseas or that they have all been put on the market in the United Kingdom by International. On the contrary it appears to me that the mark used in conjunction with a reference to New York, Paris and London is a signal that the goods are of a kind dealt with in the course of a business carried on in the United States and France as well as in the United Kingdom. It is a signal that the goods are goods of a kind dealt in by some concern or group which carries on its business at any rate in those three countries. Overseas and International do not manufacture or trade in the United States; so they cannot alone constitute the concern or group in question.

The United States products in question are products of that multi-national group produced in the United States. They appear to me to fall within the ambit of the relevant reputation. They are, like the United Kingdom products, preparations for imparting flexibility to the hair. They are further members of the group of products, designed for the washing and conditioning of various types of hair, to which the United Kingdom products and the identical American products belong. It has not been found inappropriate to deal in them in the United States for a period of about two years under the REVLON FLEX mark. In my judgment, the sale of the United States products in question in this country under that mark involves no more than a representation that those products are goods of the Revlon Group, as indeed they are. I consequently agree with the learned judge that the use of the mark in the United Kingdom or the United States products in question involves no misrepresentation of their commercial origin.

In relation to the differences in quality between the U.S. and the U.K. products, Buckley L.J. said:

The dandruff shampoo is clearly described upon its bottle as: "REVLON FLEX balsam and protein anti-dandruff shampoo. Helps control dandruff, and it adds shine, body, freshness". It would, in my view, be a mistake to imagine that any reasonably perspicacious member of the public (and even more so, any member of the trade) would suppose that a bottle so labelled contained the same product as one labelled in the way in which the United Kingdom product shampoo is labelled. The same applies to the associated conditioners.

There appears to me to be no evidence which suggests that the United States products in question are in any way inferior in quality – that is to say in excellence – compared with the United Kingdom products.

On the issue of trade mark infringement, the main question was whether s.4(3)(a) provided a defence because the trade mark proprietor had either (i) "applied" the mark to the goods, or (ii) "consented to the use" of the mark. As to the former, Buckley L.J. stated:

To use an expression employed in *Radiation Trade Mark* (1930) 47 R.P.C. 37, 43, line 36, the mark has become in effect a "house mark of the whole group". It has at all material times been intended for use, and has been used, to indicate that the goods to which it is applied are goods which originate from the Revlon Group, but not from any particular part of that Group. The exploitation of the mark and of the goods to which it relates is a world-wide exercise in which all the component companies of the Group who deal in these particular products are engaged in the course of trade. This view is, I think, reinforced by the condition attached to the registration of Overseas as a registered user of the mark. In these circumstances it seems right to say that the United States products in question are goods connected in the course of trade with Overseas. It might be said that, as Suisse carries on no trade, the products cannot be goods connected in the course of trade with Suisse, but I do not think that this would be right. Suisse holds trade marks for the purposes of the trade carried on by companies in the Group. In particular it holds the REVLON FLEX United Kingdom trade mark for the purposes of the trade of Overseas and International in the United Kingdom. This provides, in my view, a sufficient nexus with trade to lead to the conclusion that the United States products in question are goods connected with Suisse in the course of trade.

The mark was applied to the United States products in question by Revlon. For my part, I feel unable to take the view that in these circumstances the mark can be said to have been applied to the product by the proprietor of the registered user, notwithstanding the intimate relationship between Revlon, Suisse and Overseas. In *G.E. Trade Mark* [1970] R.P.C. 339, 395, line 18, the use of a mark by a wholly-owned subsidiary was regarded by Cross L.J. as user by its parent company. I find it more difficult to say that an act of the parent company can legitimately be regarded as the act of a wholly-owned subsidiary who cannot in any way control the parent company. An act of the hand may be caused or permitted by the brain, but the actions of the brain cannot be caused or controlled by the hand. At any rate, I prefer to base my decision on another ground which is, in my opinion, available.

Revlon deals with wholesalers in the United States to whom it sells its products without any condition against export. By so doing Revlon puts the purchasers of its products in the position of being able to export those goods with the mark upon them to the United Kingdom without any possibility of Revlon objecting. If Revlon were itself to export the United States products in question to the United Kingdom marked with the REVLON FLEX mark, none of the subsidiary companies could, in my opinion, object (a) because for reasons already stated they have, in my view, consented to Revlon's use of the mark to designate appropriate products of Revlon's own manufacture; and (b) because Revlon has the power by virtue of its control over the subsidiaries to overrule any objection by any of them.

In *Champagne Heidsieck et Cie v Buxton* (1930) 47 R.P.C. 28, a manufacturer in France of Champagne intended for the French market sold that wine to a wholesaler in France, who exported some of it to England where it came into competition with another type of champagne made by the same manufacturer for the English market. The wine intended for England was labelled "Champagne Dry Monopole" and that intended for France, but exported to England, was labelled "Champagne Dry Monopole" with the word "Brut" in black letters in the bottom righthand corner of the label. Both labels were put on by the manufacturer. Clauson J. held that the manufacturer could not object to the sale in England of the Brut wine under his own label. The use of that label made no misrepresentation. Just so in the present case Revlon itself could not object to any wholesaler to whom Revlon had sold any of the United States products in question marked with the REVLON FLEX mark exporting those goods to the United Kingdom under the mark; nor, in my opinion, can Suisse or Overseas object to any such wholesaler doing so because, for reasons which I have already indicated, Suisse and Overseas have both consented to Revlon doing what it has done by marking the goods with the mark in the United States. In my judgment, on the facts of the present case both Suisse and Overseas have consented to the use of the REVLON FLEX mark within the meaning of section 4(3)(a).

Bridge L.J. concurred with this judgment. Templeman L.J., in reaching the same conclusion, was prepared to find that the proprietor, "Suisse" had applied the mark to the United States products.

5.2.7.6 *Colgate-Palmolive v Markwell Finance* [1988] R.P.C. 283 (C.A.)

The plaintiff companies were United States parent and United Kingdom subsidiary of an international group which, inter alia, made and sold "Colgate" toothpaste. The parent company was the proprietor, and the UK subsidiary registered user, of six "Colgate" marks for the product in the United Kingdom.

In Brazil, a local Colgate subsidiary – "Limitada" – produced toothpaste and held a licence from the United States parent of the "Colgate" marks registered there. The Brazilian toothpaste was in numerous respects inferior to the United Kingdom product, notably, that some contained no fluoride, and some a less effective fluoride formulation than was present in the four British versions; and that the abrasives were not dical or silica but chalk. These differences resulted from production difficulties related to circumstances of Brazil. Another subsidiary – "Global" – directed local subsidiaries in the different countries how far they could export their products. Limitada was permitted to export to certain South American countries and to Nigeria.

The defendants secured supplies intended for Nigeria and imported them instead into the United Kingdom. In proceedings for passing off and registered mark infringement, they were held liable under both heads.

Passing Off

The plaintiffs claimed that the case concerned misrepresentations to the UK public as to the quality of its products and so was actionable in accordance with Spalding v Gamage *(above, 5.1.1) and* Wilts United Dairies v Robinson *(above, 5.1.4). The defendants pointed out that in those cases the plaintiffs were marketing only one product, whereas here they were responsible for the marketing of the Brazilian as well as the UK brands, and they relied upon* Champagne Heidsieck v Buxton *(1930) 47 R.P.C. 28 and the* Revlon *case (above, 5.2.7). In the* Champagne Heidsieck, *they placed particular emphasis upon Clauson J.'s remark:*

> I know of no case which would enable me to decide, or any principle on which I can decide, that a defendant who sells the Brut type of the plaintiffs' article under the very marks which the plaintiffs themselves think proper to use to distinguish that type can be accused of deception by the plaintiffs.

As to this Slade L.J. commented:

I would not dissent from that statement in so far as it was directed to an alleged misrepresentation concerning the origin (as opposed to the quality) of goods. A trader who places his mark on goods must be taken to do so for the purpose of indicating that he is the origin of the goods. "If there is one thing that may be described as fundamental in this branch of law it is that the function of a trade mark is to indicate the origin of the goods to which it is applied": see *Aristoc Ltd v Rysta Ltd* [1945] A.C. 68 at 96 per Lord Macmillan. It is not, in my judgment, open to a trader who has placed his mark on goods produced by him to complain that a person who resells those goods, without altering their contents or get-up, is misrepresenting the origin of the goods. In such circumstances the goods are "genuine goods" in the sense that their origin is in truth what the mark represents it to be.

However, in the passage under discussion, Clauson J. was not apparently directing his mind to the less common type of case, namely where a trader is offering by way of resale goods which are genuine goods in the sense just mentioned but nevertheless is doing so in circumstances which involve a representation that they are of a *quality* different from their true quality. Mr Hobbs drew our attention to a significant passage from the speech of Lord Phillimore delivering the opinion of the Privy Council in *Imperial Tobacco Company of India Ltd v Bonnan* [1924] A.C. 755 at 763:

> "The claim of the appellant company is that it can stop a trader, to whom goods have been lawfully sold under a particular description and by whom they have

been lawfully bought under that description, from reselling them under the same description. Such a claim sounds extravagant. It might, however, possibly be maintained, if it could be shown that the time, place or circumstances of the resale imported some representation, that the goods were other than what they were".

This general statement of principle is, in my opinion, clearly correct. In particular I can see no reason in principle why a trader who places the same mark on two distinct, readily identifiable, classes of article produced by him, a superior class and an inferior class, should not, in reliance on cases such as *Advocaat*, be entitled to bring a passing off action against a person who resells goods of the inferior class in circumstances which import a false representation that the goods are of the superior class, and thereby damages the trader's reputation.

Slade L.J. then analysed the Revlon *case at length and quoted three passages from the judgments of Buckley and Templeman L.JJ. on which the defendants here particularly relied. Of these, he said:*

None of these three statements, however, were made in the context of a case where the plaintiff member of a multinational group of companies, which has placed goods bearing a certain mark into circulation in another country, seeks to complain of a resale by a defendant of goods under the same mark in this country on the grounds that in the particular circumstances the resale will involve a misrepresentation that the foreign goods are of a character and quality superior to that which they in truth bear.

On the question of passing off, Lloyd L.J. delivered a concurring judgment and Sir George Waller agreed with both.

Registered Trade Marks
On this issue, the C.A. was principally concerned to distinguish Revlon *and hold that the plaintiffs had neither applied, nor consented to the application of, the UK trade marks, so that the 1938 Act, s.4(3)(a) had no effect.*

As to "application" of the mark, Mr Aikens, for the defendants, submitted that the physical application by Limitada was in pursuance of world-wide policy of standardised marking under the control of the US parent company, and should therefore be treated as an "application" by the parent, even though it took place outside the UK.

In response to this, Slade L.J. said:

I accept Mr Aikens' submission that in some circumstances a United Kingdom trade mark may properly be said to have been applied to goods by the proprietor, within the meaning of section 4(3)(a), even though the physical application took place outside this country. Nevertheless, in my judgment, Mr Hobbs was right in submitting that the defendants' argument overlooks the crucial distinction between United Kingdom and foreign trade marks. This distinction was clearly recognised for example by Tomlin J. in *Impex Electrical Ltd v Weinbaum* (1927) 44 R.P.C. 405 where he said (at p.410):

"... For the purpose of seeing whether the mark is distinctive, it is to the market of this country alone that one has to have regard. For that purpose foreign markets are wholly irrelevant, unless it be shown by evidence that in fact goods have been sold in this country with a foreign mark on them, and that the mark so used has thereby become identified with the manufacturer of the goods".

The 1938 Act is concerned only with U.K. trade marks and their use in this country. As is stated in *Kerly's Law of Trade Marks* (12th Edition) ("*Kerly*") para. 19–18:

"A trade mark registered in the United Kingdom has effect only within the territorial limits of the United Kingdom and the Isle of Man. Therefore, the use abroad only of a trade mark registered in the United Kingdom – even use by a person resident in the United Kingdom – does not constitute an infringement of the British trade mark. But a trade mark is used in the United Kingdom if goods bearing the mark are sold here, although the proprietor has applied the trade mark and sold the goods abroad only. . . .

The registration of a trade mark abroad does not give any rights, exclusive or otherwise, to use the trade mark in the United Kingdom".

Mr Hobbs relied strongly on the definition of "trade mark" in section 68(1) of the 1938 Act which defines the phrase as meaning, except in relation to a certification trade mark,

"a mark used or proposed to be used in relation to goods for the purpose of indicating, or so as to indicate, a connection in the course of trade between the goods and some person having the right either as proprietor or as registered user to use the mark, whether with or without any indication of the identity of that person . . ."

In his submission, "used or proposed to be used" means used or proposed to be used *in this country*. He referred us to the decision of Sargant J. in *In re Neuchatel Asphalte Company's Trade Mark* [1913] 2 Ch.291 (*"Neuchatel"*). That case related to section 3 of the Trade Marks Act 1905, which defined "trade mark" as meaning a mark

"used or proposed to be used upon or in connexion with goods for the purpose of indicating that they are the goods of the proprietor of such trade mark by virtue of manufacture, selection, certification, dealing with or offering for sale".

Sargant J. (at p.301) held that the world "used" must mean "used in this country", and (at p.302) that the words "proposed to be used" must import a present intention to use it in this country. Since the persons applying for the registration of a trade mark in that case had no more than a general desire to use it in this country, it was held that they were not entitled to registration. That decision is not binding on us. Nevertheless, I can see no relevant distinction between the definition of a "trade mark" considered by Sargant J. and that contained in the 1938 Act, and the correctness of his decision has not been challenged before us; its reasoning appears entirely consistent with the decision of Tomlin J. in *Impex* (above) and with the general pattern of the legislation.

Particularly in the light of the statutory definition of a "trade mark", as interpreted in *Neuchatel*, Mr Hobbs submitted that on the facts there had never been an application of the relevant U.K. *trade marks* by any person to the Brazilian goods complained of in the present case, since the Colgate mark applied to the goods in Brazil was neither used nor proposed to be used in the United Kingdom; the only application had been that of *Brazilian* trade marks, even though these happened to be the same as the relevant United Kingdom marks.

Slade L.J. held, following the view of Buckley and Bridge L.JJ. in Revlon, that in any case application by Limitada could not be treated as application by the US parent. With all this Sir George Waller L.J. agreed. Lloyd L.J. decided the issue in the same way, while reserving his position on this last point.

As to "consent to the application", Slade L.J. examined the various ways in which the defendants argued that this consent occurred, expressly or impliedly. He proceeded:

In these circumstances, it might have been arguable that Colgate U.S., despite the efforts of the Group to prevent exports of the Brazilian toothpastes to this country, should be treated as having impliedly consented to the use of the U.K. trade marks by persons offering the Brazilian toothpastes for sale in this country in circumstances *where such use did no more than make a representation as to the trade origin of the goods*. Some support for this argument might have been derived from *Revlon*. Buckley L.J. summarised the background thus (at p.106):

Slade L.J. referred to the judgments of Buckley and Templeman L.JJ. and to Kerly (12th ed.) para 14–30, and continued:

However, the facts of the present case are readily distinguishable from those of *Revlon*. Neither the members of this court in *Revlon*, nor (apparently) the editors of *Kerly* in the passage last cited were directing their minds to the special situation referred to Lord Phillimore in the *Imperial Tobacco* case where in particular circumstances the resale of goods under the particular marks and in the particular get-up imports a representation that the goods are other than what they are.

That, as I have already indicated in the section of this judgment dealing with passing off, is my view of the present case. As is recognised in *Aristoc v Rysta* [1945] A.C. 68, a trader by applying a U.K. registered trade mark to goods and thereby indicating their origin gives an assurance to consumers in this country that the goods are of the quality which they have come to expect from products bearing that trade mark. I accept Mr Hobbs' submission that there is nothing incongruous in holding that a U.K. registered trade mark is infringed in relation to goods which do not conform to an identifiable quality which purchasing members of the public in this country ordinarily receive by reference to that trade mark.

I can see no sufficient reason in principle or in the authorities why, in the absence of actual consent and indeed in the face of attempts to prevent the import of the Brazilian toothpastes to this country, this court should be obliged to treat Colgate U.S. as having impliedly consented to the use here of the U.K. trade marks in reaction to those toothpastes in circumstances where this would involve a misrepresentation to consumers as to the quality of the products. Section 4(3) of the 1938 Act is not, in my judgment, designed to sanction improper use of U.K. trade marks of this kind. In my judgment, no defence is available to the defendants under either limb of section 4(3).

With this conclusion Lloyd L.J. agreed and Sir George Waller concurred.

6
EEC LAW AND INTELLECTUAL PROPERTY

6.1 Treaty and Convention Provisions

6.1.1 Treaty of Rome (1957)

6.1.1.1 Treaty of Rome, Arts. 2, 3: Basic Principles

Art.2. The Community shall have as its task, by setting up a Common Market and progressively approximating the economic policies of Member States, to promote throughout the Community an harmonious development of economic activities, a continuous and balanced expansion, an increase in stability, an accelerated raising of the standard of living and closer relations between the Member States belonging to it.

Art.3. For the purposes set out in Article 2, the activities of the Community shall include, on the conditions and in accordance with the timetable provided in this Treaty:

- (a) the elimination, as between Member States, of customs duties and of quantitative restrictions in regard to the import and export of goods, as well as of all other measures having equivalent effect;
- (b) the establishment of a common custom tariff and of a common commercial policy towards third countries;
- (c) the abolition, as between Member States, of obstacles to freedom of movement for persons, services and capital;
- (d) the establishment of a common policy in the sphere of agriculture;
- (e) the adoption of a common policy in the sphere of transport;
- (f) the establishment of a system ensuring that competition in the Common Market is not distorted;
- (g) the application of procedures by which the economic policies of Member States can be co-ordinated and disequilibria in their balances of payments can be remedied;
- (h) the approximation of the laws of Member States to the extent required for proper functioning of the Common Market;
- (i) the creation of a European Social Fund in order to improve the possibilities of employment for workers and to contribute to the raising of their standard of living;
- (j) the establishment of a European Investment Bank to facilitate the economic expansion of the Community by opening up fresh resources; and
- (k) the association of overseas countries and territories with a view to increasing trade and to promoting jointly economic and social

development.

6.1.1.2   Treaty of Rome, Arts. 30, 34, 36: Elimination of Quantitative Restrictions

Art.30. Quantitative restrictions on imports and all measures having equivalent effect shall, without prejudice to the following provisions, be prohibited as between Member States.

Art.34(1) Quantitative restrictions on exports, and any measures having equivalent effect, are prohibited as between Member States.

Art.34(2) Member States shall, at least by the end of the first stage, abolish all quantitative restrictions on exports and any measures having equivalent effect which are in existence when this Treaty comes into force.

Art.36 The provisions of Articles 30 to 34 inclusive shall not preclude prohibitions or restrictions on imports, exports or goods in transit justified on the grounds of public morality; public policy (ordre public); public safety or security; the protection of health and life of humans, animals or plants; the protection of national treasures possessing artistic, historic or archaeological value; or the protection of industrial and commercial property. Such prohibitions or restrictions shall not, however, amount to a means of arbitrary discrimination not to a disguised restriction on trade between Member States.

6.1.1.3   Treaty of Rome, Art. 59: Freedom to Provide Services

Art.59 Within the framework of the provisions set out below, restrictions on freedom to provide services within the Community shall be progressively abolished during the transitional period in respect of nationals of Member States who are established in a State of the Community rather than that of the person for whom the services are intended. The Council, acting unanimously, on a proposal from the Commission, may extend the benefit of the provisions of the chapter to nationals of a third country who render services and who are established within the Community.

6.1.1.4   Treaty of Rome, Arts. 85, 86: Rules of Competition

Art.85(1) The following practices shall be prohibited as incompatible with the common market: all agreements between undertakings, all decisions by associations of undertakings and all concerted practices, which may affect trade between Member States and the object or effect of which is to prevent, restrict or distort competition within the common market, and in particular those which amount to:
  (a) the direct or indirect fixing of purchase or selling prices or of any other trading conditions;
  (b) the limiting or controlling of production, markets, technical development or capital investment;
  (c) the sharing of markets or sources of supply;
  (d) applying, in relation to customers in the trade unequal conditions

in respect of equivalent transactions, placing them thereby at a competitive disadvantage;

(e) making the conclusion of contracts subject to acceptance by the other parties of supplementary obligations, which, by their nature or according to commercial practice, have no connection with the subject of such contracts.

(2) Any agreements or decisions prohibited pursuant to this article shall automatically be null and void.

(3) The provisions of paragraph 1 may, however, be declared inapplicable in the case of:

any agreement or category of agreements between undertakings,

any decision or category of decisions of associations of undertakings,

and any concerted practice or category of concerted practices,

which contribute to improve the production or distribution of goods or to promote technical or economic progress, whilst allowing consumers a fair share of the resulting benefit and which does not:

(a) impose on the undertakings concerned restrictions which are not indispensable to the achievement of the above objectives;

(b) afford such undertakings the possibility of eliminating competition in respect of a substantial part of the products in question.

Art.86 It shall be incompatible with the common market and prohibited, in so far as trade between Member States is liable to be effected by it, for one or more undertakings to exploit in an improper manner a dominant position within the common market or within a substantial part of it. Such improper practices, may, in particular, consist in:

(a) the direct or indirect imposition of unfair purchase or selling prices or of other unfair trading conditions;

(b) the limitation of production, markets or technical development to the prejudice of consumers;

(c) applying in relation to like parties unequal conditions in respect of like transactions, placing them thereby at a competitive disadvantage;

(d) making the conclusion of contracts subject to agreement by the other parties to make additional payments, which, by their nature or according to commercial practice, have no connection with the subject of such contracts.

6.1.1.5   Treaty of Rome, Arts. 169, 173, 177: Community Institutions

Art.169 If the Commission considers that a Member State has failed to fulfil any of its obligations under this Treaty, it shall issue a reasoned opinion on the matter after giving the State concerned the opportunity to submit its comments. If the State does not comply with the terms of such opinion within the period laid down by the Commission, the latter may bring the matter before the Court of Justice.

Art.173 Supervision of the legality of acts taken by the Council and the Commission other than recommendations or opinions shall be a matter for the Court of Justice. It shall for this purpose have jurisdiction in proceedings instituted by a Member State, the Council or the Commission, on the grounds of lack of jurisdiction, infringements of important procedural rules, infringement of this Treaty or of any rule of law relating to its application, or misuse of powers.

Any natural or legal person may, subject to the same conditions, have recourse against a decision directed to him or it or against a decision which, although in the form of a regulation or a decision directed to another person, is of direct and individual concern to him or to it.

The proceedings provided for in this article shall be instituted within a period of two months, dating, as the case may be, either from the publication of the act concerned or from its notification to the complainant or, in default thereof, from the day on which the latter learnt of it.

Art.177 The Court of Justice shall have jurisdiction to give preliminary rulings concerning:
  (a) the interpretation of this Treaty;
  (b) the validity and interpretation of acts taken by the institutions of the Community;
  (c) the interpretation of the statutes of bodies set up by a formal measure of the Council, where those statutes so provide.

Where such a question is raised before any Court or tribunal of one of the Member states, that Court or tribunal may, if it considers that a decision on the question is necessary to enable it to give judgment, request the Court of Justice to give a ruling thereon.

Where such a question is raised in a case pending before a Court or tribunal of a Member State, from whose decisions there is no possibility of appeal under internal law, that Court or tribunal shall be bound to refer the matter to the Court of Justice.

6.1.2   Community Patent Convention (1975), Arts. 32, 46, 81: Exhaustion of Rights, Compulsory Licences

Art.32 The rights conferred by a Community patent shall not extend to acts concerning a product covered by that patent which are done within the territories of the Contracting States after that product has been put on the market in one of these States by the proprietor of the patent or with his express consent, unless there are grounds which, under Community law, would justify the extension to such acts of the rights conferred by the patent.

Art.46(1) Any provision in the law of a Contracting State for the grant of compulsory licences in respect of national patents shall be applicable to Community patents. The extent and effect of compulsory licences granted in respect of Community patents shall be restricted to the territory of the State concerned. Article 32 shall not apply.

(2) Each Contracting State shall, at least in respect of compensation under a compulsory licence, provide for a final appeal to a court of law.

(3) As far as practicable national authorities shall notify the European Patent Office of the grant of any compulsory licence in respect of a Community patent.

(4) For the purposes of this Convention, the term "compulsory licences" shall be construed as including official licences and any right to use patented inventions in the public interest.

Art.81(1) The rights conferred by a national patent in a Contracting State shall not extend to acts concerning a product covered by that patent which are done within the territory of that Contracting State after that product has been put on the market in any Contracting State by the proprietor of the patent or with his express consent, unless there are grounds which, under Community law, would justify the extension to such acts of the rights conferred by the patent.

(2) Paragraph 1 shall also apply with regard to a product put on the market by the proprietor of a national patent, granted for the same invention in another Contracting State, who has economic connections with the proprietor of the patent referred to in paragraph 1. For the purpose of this paragraph, two persons shall be deemed to have economic connections where one of them is in a position to exert a decisive influence on the other, directly or indirectly, with regard to the exploitation of a patent, or where a third party is in a position to exercise such an influence on both persons.

(3) The preceding paragraphs shall not apply in the case of a product put on the market under a compulsory licence.

6.2 Free Movement of Goods and Intellectual Property

6.2.1 General

6.2.1.1 *Consten and Grundig v EC Commission* [1966] E.C.R. 299; [1966] C.M.L.R. 418 (CJ EC)

The German electrical goods manufacturer, Grundig, appointed the French company, Consten, as its exclusive distributor in France. It likewise appointed other companies as national exclusive distributors in other countries of the Common Market and elsewhere. In support of this exclusivity, Grundig labelled its products not only with its own name but also with the mark, "Gint". It agreed with Consten that the latter would apply for registration of "Gint" in France, upon the understanding that, on termination of the distributorship, the mark would be assigned to Grundig. A parallel importer began importing Grundig products into France from elsewhere in the EEC and was sued for unfair competition and trade mark infringement by Consten.

In Article 85 proceedings, the EC Commission issued a decision that the entire exclusive distributorship agreement was void and refused to grant exemption under Article 85(3). The decision also enjoined Consten from using its trade mark right to obstruct parallel imports from another EC country.

In a path-breaking decision, the CJ EC agreed with the substance of the Commission's view of exclusive distributorships and Article 85. It only criticised the lower decision for declaring the entire agreement void, rather than just the provisions which offended Article 85(1); and over its approach in some respects to the application of Article 85(3).

On the basic issue, it held that Article 85 makes no distinction between horizontal and vertical agreements and may accordingly apply to an agreement between a manufacturer and its own distributor. Although the two are not themselves in competition, the agreement might have an adverse effect on competition between one of them and a third party (in this case, Consten and any other distributor of Grundig products in France). Thus it is distortive of competition to make agreements designed to insulate national markets within the Community for a widespread brand of products. Once this distortion is shown, it is not necessarily an answer that the improvement in the distribution of Grundig products, which the agreement would promote, would lead to an increase in competition with similar products of other producers.

On the question of Consten's use of its right to the "Gint" trade mark, the Court agreed with the Commission:

Consten's right under the contract to the exclusive user in France of the GINT trade mark, which may be used in a similar manner in other countries, is intended to make it possible to keep under surveillance and to place an obstacle in the way of parallel imports. Thus, the agreement by which Grundig, as the holder of the trade-mark by virtue of an international registration, authorised Consten to register it in France in its own name tends to restrict competition.

Although Consten is, by virtue of the registration of the GINT trade-mark, regarded under French law as the original holder of the rights relating to that trade-mark, the fact nevertheless remains that it was by virtue of an agreement with Grundig that it was able to effect the registration.

That agreement therefore is one which may be caught by the prohibition in Article 85(1). The prohibition would be ineffective if Consten could continue to use the trade-mark to achieve the same object as that pursued by the agreement which has been held to be unlawful.

Articles 36, 222 and 234 of the Treaty relied upon by the applicants do not exclude any influence whatever of Community law on the exercise of national industrial property rights.

Article 36, which limits the scope of the rules on the liberalisation of trade contained in Title I, Chapter 2, of the Treaty, cannot limit the field of application of Article 85. Article 222 confines itself to stating that the "Treaty shall in no way prejudice the rules in Member States governing the system of property ownership". The injunction contained in Article 3 of the operative part of the contested decision to refrain from using rights under national trade-mark law in order to set an obstacle in the way of parallel imports does not affect the grant of those rights but only limits their exercise to the extent necessary to give effect to the prohibition under Article 85(1). The power of the Commission to issue such an injunction for which provision is made in Article 3 of Regulation No 17/62 of the Council is in harmony with the nature of the Community rules on competition which have immediate effect and are directly binding on individuals.

Such a body of rules, by reason of its nature described above and its function, does not allow the improper use of rights under any national trade-mark law in order to frustrate the Community's law on cartels.

Article 234 which has the aim of protecting the rights of third countries is not applicable in the present instance.

6.2.1.2   *Deutsche Grammophon v Metro-SB-Grossmarkte*
[1971] E.C.R. 487; [1971] C.M.L.R. 631 (CJ EC)

At the time in question, resale prices could be maintained under German law provided that no retail selling below the set minimum price occurred. "Polydor" records, manufactured by Deutsche Grammophon or its subsidiaries, were subject to this r.p.m.; in West Germany their retail price was approximately double that in France, where there was no r.p.m. In addition, in West Germany, the manufacturer of sound recordings had a neighbouring right covering their making and distribution under the Copyright Law of 1965, Art. 85 (cf. CDPA 1988 (U.K.), s.5). There was no equivalent right in French law, though it may have been possible at that period to proceed against a record pirate under unfair competition law (subsequent legislation has strengthened the record companies' position in France).

Records originally manufactured by DG were marketed through its French subsidiary in France. They were apparently bought by a Swiss enterprise, then by a Hamburg wholesaler and finally by the defendant which retailed them in a Hamburg supermarket at cut price. In proceedings for infringement of Art. 85, the Hanseatische Obergericht, Hamburg, considered that the right under that Article had not been exhausted by the authorised sale in France, so that by German law the sale of the records by the defendant constituted infringement.

Under the Treaty of Rome, Art. 177, the Court raised two questions before the CJ EC. The first question asked whether this operation of the German copyright law was in conflict with Article 5(2) or 85(1) of the Treaty. After referring to those Articles, the CJ EC for the first time drew attention in this context to the terms of Article 36. It proceeded:

If a right related to copyright is relied upon to prevent the marketing in a Member State of products distributed by the holder of the right or with his consent on the territory of another Member State on the sole ground that such distribution did not take place on the national territory, such a prohibition, which would legitimise the isolation of national markets, would be repugnant to the essential purpose of the Treaty, which is to unite national markets into a single market.

That purpose could not be attained if, under the various legal systems of the Member States, nationals of those States were able to partition the market and bring about arbitrary discrimination or disguised restrictions on trade between Member States.

Consequently, it would be in conflict with the provisions prescribing the free movement of products within the common market for a manufacturer of sound recordings to exercise the exclusive right to distribute the protected articles, conferred upon him by the legislation of a Member State, in such a way as to prohibit the sale in that State of products placed on the market by him or with his consent in another Member State solely because such distribution did not occur within the territory of the first Member State.

The second question was treated asking whether an abuse of dominant position within Article 36 arose from the facts (i) that the price differential for the same records existed in different common market countries, and (ii) that the recording company had exclusive contracts with its performing artists. In answer, the CJ EC stated:

For it to fall within Article 86 a dominant position must further be abused. The difference between the controlled price and the price of the product reimported from another Member State does not necessarily suffice to disclose such an abuse; it may however, if unjustified by any objective criteria and if it is particularly marked, be a determining factor in such abuse.

6.2.1.3 *Centrafarm v Sterling Drug; Centrafarm v Winthrop*
[1974] E.C.R. 1147, 1183; [1974] 2 C.M.L.R. 480 (CJ EC)

The American parent of the Sterling Winthrop group, Sterling Drug, owned a patent for a urinary infection drug in a number of countries, including the UK and the Netherlands. In those two countries, the mark under which it was sold – "Negram" – was owned by a local marketing subsidiary of the group: in the UK, Sterling Winthrop Group Ltd; in the Netherlands, Winthrop BV.

Centrafarm obtained supplies of "Negram" in the UK and exported them for sale in the Netherlands, but was met by proceedings for infringement of the Dutch patent and trade mark. The Hoge Raad referred a number of interrelated questions to the CJ EC under Article 177. In each case the first of these concerned the compatibility of the intellectual property rights asserted with the rules concerning the free movement of goods.

In respect of the case concerning the patent, the Court stated:

As regards question I(a)

4 This question requires the Court to state whether, under the conditions postulated, the rules in the EEC Treaty concerning the free movement of goods prevent the patentee from ensuring that the product protected by the patent is not marketed by others.

5 As a result of the provisions inn the Treaty relating to the free movement of goods and in particular of Article 30, quantitative restrictions on imports and all measures having equivalent effect are prohibited between Member States.

6 By Article 36 these provisions shall nevertheless not include prohibitions or

restrictions on imports justified on grounds of the protection of industrial or commercial property.

7   Nevertheless, it is clear from this same Article, in particular its second sentence, as well as from the context, that whilst the Treaty does not affect the existence of rights recognised by the legislation of a Member State in matters of industrial and commercial property, yet the exercise of these rights may nevertheless, depending on the circumstances, be affected by the prohibitions in the Treaty.

8   Inasmuch as it provides an exception to one of the fundamental principles of the Common Market, Article 36 in fact only admits of derogations from the free movement of goods where such derogations are justified for the purpose of safeguarding rights which constitute the specific subject matter of this property.

9   In relation to patents, the specific subject matter of the industrial property is the guarantee that the patentee, to reward the creative effort of the inventor, has the exclusive right to use an invention with a view to manufacturing industrial products and putting them into circulation for the first time, either directly or by the grant of licences to third parties, as well as the right to oppose infringements.

10   An obstacle to the free movement of goods may arise out of the existence, within a national legislation concerning industrial and commercial property, of provisions laying down that a patentee's right is not exhausted when the product protected by the patent is marketed in another Member State, with the result that the patentee can prevent importation of the product into his own Member State when it has been marketed in another State.

11   Whereas an obstacle to the free movement of goods of this kind may be justified on the ground of protection of industrial property where such protection is invoked against a product coming from a Member State where it is not patentable and has been manufactured by third parties without the consent of the patentee and in cases where there exist patents, the original proprietors of which are legally and economically independent, a derogation from the principle of the free movement of goods is not, however, justified where the product has been put onto the market in a legal manner, by the patentee himself or with his consent, in the Member State from which it has been imported, in particular in the case of a proprietor of parallel patents.

12   In fact, if a patentee could prevent the import of protected products marketed by him or with his consent in another Member State, he would be able to partition off national markets and thereby restrict trade between Member States, in a situation where no such restriction was necessary to guarantee the essence of the exclusive rights flowing from the parallel patents.

13   The plaintiff in the main action claims, in this connection, that by reason by divergences between national legislations and practice, truly identical or parallel patents can hardly be said to exist.

14   It should be noted here that, in spite of the divergences which remain in the absence of any unification of national rules concerning industrial property, the identity of the protected invention is clearly the essential element of the concept of parallel patents which it is for the courts to assess.

15   The question referred should therefore be answered to the effect that the exercise, by a patentee, of the right which he enjoys under the legislation of a Member State to prohibit the sale, in that State, of a product protected by the patent which has

been marketed in another Member State by the patentee or with his consent is incompatible with the rules of the EEC Treaty concerning the free movement of goods within the Common Market.

In respect of the case concerning the trade mark, the Court repeated its general statement of the operation of Articles 30 and 36, and proceeded:

8 In relation to trade marks, the specific subject-matter of the industrial property is the guarantee that the owner of the trade mark has the exclusive right to use that trade mark, for the purpose of putting products protected by the trade mark into circulation for the first time, and is therefore intended to protect him against competitors wishing to take advantage of the status and reputation of the trade mark by selling products illegally bearing that trade mark.

9 An obstacle to the free movement of goods may arise out of the existence, within a national legislation concerning industrial and commercial property, of provisions laying down that a trade mark owner's right is not exhausted when the product protected by the trade mark is marketed in another Member State, with the result that the trade mark owner can prevent importation of the product into his own Member State when it has been marketed in another Member State.

10 Such an obstacle is not justified when the product has been put onto the market in a legal manner in the Member State from which it has been imported, by the trade mark owner himself or with his consent, so that there can be no question of abuse or infringement of the trade mark.

11 In fact, if a trade mark owner could prevent the import of protected products marketed by him or with his consent in another Member State, he would be able to partition off national markets and thereby restrict trade between Member States, in a situation where no such restriction was necessary to guarantee the essence of the exclusive right flowing from the trade mark.

12 The question referred should therefore be answered to the effect that the exercise, by the owner of a trade mark, of the right which he enjoys under the legislation of a Member State to prohibit the sale, in that State, of a product which has been marketed under the trade mark in another Member State by the trade mark owner or with his consent is incompatible with the rules of the EEC Treaty concerning the free movement of goods within the Common Market.

The Court also ruled as follows:

1. The applicable test for determining whether the Treaty provisions override a national intellectual property right is whether the goods have been placed on some part of the common market with the consent of the patentee or trade mark proprietor, not whether the right-owner and a licensee belong to the same group or not.

2. The applicable test applies even when the following further factors are present:

(a) price differences for the product exist because for price control measures taken by public authorities in the exporting country. (In the circumstances of the case, this arose because the Department of Health and Social Security in Britain could rely upon its Crown use powers under the Patents Act in negotiating favourable prices with the pharmaceutical companies. These powers allowed it, if it wished, to procure the drug from an alternative source and pay "reasonable" compensation to the patentee).

(b) in order to protect the public from the risk of receiving defective products, the right-owner needed to be able to control the distribution of a product between different

countries.

6.2.1.4   *Merck v Stephar* [1981] E.C.R. 2063; [1981] 3 C.M.L.R. 463 (CJ EC)

Merck held patents in all EC states save Luxembourg and Italy for a hypertension drug, "Moduretic". It marketed the product in Italy and Stephar purchased supplies there for importation into the Netherlands, where infringement proceedings were in consequence launched. On reference of the issue by the Arrondissementsrechtbank Rotterdam, the CJ EC quoted its own definition of the "specific subject-matter" of a patent right (see Centrafarm v Sterling Drug, *above, 6.2.1.3), and continued:*

7 Stephar and the Commission conclude that once the proprietor of the patent has himself placed the product in question on the open market in a Member State in which it is not patentable, the importation of such goods into the Member State in which the product is protected may not be prohibited because the proprietor of the patent has placed it on the market of his own free will.

8 In contrast Merck, supported by the French Government and the Government of the United Kingdom, maintains that the purpose of the patent, which is to reward the inventor, is not safeguarded if owing to the fact that the patent right is not recognised by law in the country in which the proprietor of the patent has marketed his product he is unable to collect the reward for his creative effort because he does not enjoy a monopoly in first placing the product on the market.

9 In the light of that conflict of views, it must be stated that in accordance with the definition of the specific purpose of the patent, which has been described above, the substance of a patent right lies essentially in according the inventor an exclusive right of first placing the product on the market.

10 That right of first placing a product on the market enables the inventor, by allowing him a monopoly in exploiting his product, to obtain the reward for his creative effort without, however, guaranteeing that he will obtain such a reward in all circumstances.

11 It is for the proprietor of the patent to decide, in the light of all the circumstances, under what conditions he will market his product, including the possibility of marketing it in a Member State where the law does not provide patent protection for the product in question. If he decides to do so he must then accept the consequences of his choice as regards the free movement of the product within the Common Market, which is a fundamental principle forming part of the legal and economic circumstances which must be taken into account by the proprietor of the patent in determining the manner in which his exclusive right will be exercised.

12 That is borne out, moreover, by the statements of the Court in its judgments of 22 June 1976 (*Terrapin*, Case 119/75 [1976] ECR 1039) and 20 January 1981 (*Musik-Vertrieb Membran and K-tel*, Joined Cases 55 and 57/80 not yet published) inasmuch as "the proprietor of an industrial or commercial property right protected by the law of a Member State cannot rely on that law to prevent the importation of a product which has been lawfully marketed in another Member State by the proprietor himself or with his consent".

13 Under those conditions to permit an inventor, or one claiming under him, to invoke a patent held by him in one Member State in order to prevent the importation of the product freely marketed by him in another Member State where that product is not patentable would bring about a partitioning of the national markets which would be

contrary to the aims of the Treaty.

6.2.1.5 *Keurkoop v Nancy Kean Gifts* [1982] E.C.R. 2853; [1983] 2 C.M.L.R. 47 (CJ EC)

A handbag, which was the subject of a U.S. design patent, had been marketed in the U.S. during the late 1970s. Nancy Kean Gifts, the Dutch subsidiary of an international group, purchased quantities of the bag through a Swiss enterprise from Taiwan. The bags were sent direct from Taiwan to the Netherlands for marketing there. Before launching them, Nancy Kean Gifts registered the design under the Benelux Designs Law of 1966, even though (as was alleged) it had no entitlement deriving from the American designer or his associates.

Keurkoop also procured a supply of Taiwanese bags to virtually the same design. The Dutch Court hearing design infringement proceedings was led to consider the impact of the Treaty of Rome if these bags were produced by the defendant in another Community country where the plaintiff had no protection for the design.

The Dutch Court raised two questions under Article 177 before the CJ EC:

(1) Whether it is compatible with the Rome Treaty provisions on free movement of goods for a regional Designs Law to confer a right on an applicant for that right without permitting others to challenge his entitlement by relying on the fact that he is not the author of the design or the person commissioning it or employing the author?

To this question the Court answered:

... national legislation having the characteristics of the Uniform Benelux Law on Designs falls within the scope of the provisions of Article 36 of the Treaty on the protection of industrial and commercial property. In the present state of its development Community law does not prevent the adoption of national provisions of the kind contained in the Uniform Benelux Law, as described by the national court.

(2) Whether the Dutch Court could enjoin the marketing of products within a Benelux registered design, if they were obtained by the defendant in another Common Market country where the Benelux design-owner has no equivalent right?

After referring to its earlier interpretation of Article 36, the Court answered:

... the proprietor of a right to a design acquired under the legislation of a Member State may oppose the importation of products from another Member State which are identical in appearance to the design which has been filed, provided that the products in question have not been put into circulation in the other Member State by, or with the consent of, the proprietor of the right or a person legally or economically dependent on him, that as between the natural or legal persons in question there is no kind of agreement or concerted practice in restraint of competition and finally that the respective rights of the proprietors of the right to the design in the various Member States were created independently of one another.

6.2.1.6 *EMI Electrola v Patricia* [1989] 2 C.M.L.R. 544 (CJ EC)

Sound recording right in recordings of songs by Cliff Richard had expired in Denmark but not in West Germany, because the pertinent period in each case was in the circumstances calculated from a different date.

The defendant company, Patricia, manufactured the recordings in question in West Germany for a Danish company which imported them to Denmark. Patricia then re-

purchased them in Denmark and re-imported them for marketing there. No assent to this conduct had been given by EMI or its German subsidiary (which as assignee of the German sound recording rights was plaintiff in the action for infringement of the rights). The Landgericht Hamburg referred the question whether enforcement of the rights would be compatible with Articles 30 and 36.

The CJ EC stated:

7   Pursuant to Article 36 of the Treaty, the provisions of Article 30 prohibiting all measures having an equivalent effect to quantitative restrictions on imports between member-States do not preclude prohibitions or restrictions on imports justified on grounds of the protection of industrial and commercial property. Such protection covers the protection of literary and artistic property including copyright, if it is exploited commercially. Therefore it also covers protection for exclusive rights of reproduction and distribution of sound recordings, if that is treated in the same way as copyright by the relevant national law.

8   Therefore the object of Articles 30 and 36 is to reconcile the requirements of the free movement of goods with upholding the lawful exercise of exclusive rights in literary and artistic property. In particular, that reconciliation means that protection must be refused to any improper exercise of those rights which would be likely to maintain or create artificial partitioning in the Common Market.

9   From this the Court's case law has inferred that a copyright owner cannot rely on the exclusive exploitation right conferred by his copyright to prevent or restrict the importation of sound recordings which have been lawfully marketed in another member-State by the owner himself or with his consent (Musik-Vertrieb Membran, Cases 55 and 57/80.)

10 However, that situation differs from the situation envisaged by the national court. The question before the Court shows that the fact that sound recordings were marketed lawfully in the market of another member-State is due, not to an act or consent of the copyright owner or his licensee, but to expiry of the protection period granted by the legislation of that member-State. Therefore the problem arises from the disparity between legislation of different countries regarding the protection period given by copyright and by similar rights. The disparity lies either in the duration of protection itself or the details or protection, such as the time when the protection period begins to run.

11 In this connection it should be observed that, in the present state of Community law, which is characterised by the absence of harmonisation or approximation of legislation on the protection of literary and artistic property, it is for national legislatures to specify the conditions and rules for such protection.

12 To the extent that the disparity between national laws is likely to create restrictions on sound recordings in the Community, such restrictions are justified by Article 36 of the Treaty if they arise from the difference in arrangements relating to the duration of protection and if the protection period is inseparably linked with the existence of the exclusive rights themselves.

13 There would be no justification if the restrictions on trade imposed or allowed by the national legislation on which the owner of exclusive rights or his licensee rely were such as to constitute a means of arbitrary discrimination or a disguised measure for restricting trade. However, there is nothing in the file which would permit the presumption that this situation could arise in a case such as the present.

6.2.1.7 *EMI Records v CBS UK* **[1976] E.C.R. 811; [1976] 2 C.M.L.R. 235 (CJ EC)**

The trade mark "Columbia" for records was originally used by the American Graphophone Co., predecessors of the CBS Group, in the US, UK and other countries. The marks passed to various companies, but ultimately in 1922, ownership of the US and UK marks was separated because there no longer existed any business connection between the Columbia undertakings in the two countries. Subsequently the British marks passed to EMI Records Ltd. It (or another EMI subsidiary) owned the "Columbia" mark for all countries of the EEC.

In the Americas, "Columbia" continued to be the principal trade mark of the CBS group, but in Europe it sold its records under different marks. Both CBS subsidiaries and independent retailers on occasion imported CBS "Columbia" records from America and some of these were then sold without changing the labelling to a different mark. Actions for trade mark infringement were in consequence commenced by EMI in England, Denmark and West Germany, which led to Article 177 proceedings from all three countries. The various questions from the national courts raised issues under both Arts. 30–36 and 85.

With regard to the free movement of goods, the CJ EC said:

9 Within the framework of the provisions of the Treaty relating to the free movement of goods and in accordance with Article 3(a), Article 30 *et seq.* on the elimination of quantitative restrictions and of measures having equivalent effect expressly provide that such restrictions and measures shall be prohibited "between Member States".

10 Article 36, in particular, after stipulating that Articles 30 to 34 shall not preclude restrictions on imports, exports or goods in transit justified *inter alia* on grounds of the protection of industrial and commercial property, states that such restrictions shall in no instance constitute a means of arbitrary discrimination or disguised restriction on trade "between Member States".

Consequently the exercise of a trade-mark right in order to prevent the marketing of products coming from a third country under an identical mark, even if this constitutes a measure having an effect equivalent to a quantitative restriction, does not affect the free movement of goods between Member States and thus does not come under the prohibitions set out in Article 30 *et seq.* of the Treaty.

11 In such circumstances the exercise of a trade-mark right does not in fact jeopardise the unity of the common market which Article 30 *et seq.* are intended to ensure.

With regard to competition, the Court said:

26 A trade-mark right, as a legal entity, does not possess those elements of contract or concerted practice referred to in Article 86(1).

27 Nevertheless, the exercise of that right might fall within the ambit of the prohibitions contained in the Treaty if it were to manifest itself as the subject, the means, or the consequence of a restrictive practice.

28 A restrictive agreement between traders within the common market and competitors in third countries that would bring about an isolation of the common market as a whole which, in the territory of the Community, would reduce the supply of products originating in third countries and similar to those protected by a mark within the Community, might be of such a nature as to affect adversely the

conditions of competition within the common market.

29   In particular if the proprietor of the mark in dispute in the third country has within the Community various subsidiaries established in different Member States which are in a position to market the products at issue within the common market such isolation may also affect trade between Member States.

30   For Article 85 to apply to a case, such as the present one, of agreements which are no longer in force it is sufficient that such agreements continue to produce their effects after they have formally ceased to be in force.

31   An agreement is only regarded as continuing to produce its effects if from the behaviour of the persons concerned there may be inferred the existence of elements of concerted practice and of coordination peculiar to the agreement and producing the same result as that envisaged by the agreement.

32   This is not so when the said effects do not exceed those flowing from the mere exercise of the national trade-mark rights.

33   Furthermore it is clear from the file that the foreign trader can obtain access to the common market without availing himself of the mark in dispute.

34   In those circumstances the requirement that the proprietor of the identical mark in a third country must, for the purposes of his exports to the protected market, obliterate this mark on the products concerned and perhaps apply a different mark forms part of the permissible consequences flowing from the protection of the mark.

6.2.1.8   *Polydor v Harlequin Records* [1982] E.C.R. 329; [1982] 1 C.M.L.R. 677 (CJ EC)

The plaintiffs were the owner and the exclusive licensee of the UK sound recording right in a recording made by the Bee-Gees. Copies of the recording made and sold in Portugal by companies associated with the plaintiffs, were imported by the defendants into the UK. In an action for infringement under the Copyright Act 1956, s. 16(2), the defendants relied upon provisions in the Agreement between the EEC and Portugal (itself an implementa- tion of the G.A.T.T.), equivalent to Arts. 30 and 36 of the Treaty of Rome. These Articles (14(2), 23) were said to have the same effect upon imports from Portugal as Arts. 30 and 36 have upon trade between Member States of the Community.

This argument was referred by the English Court of Appeal under Art. 177. The CJ EC stated:

The considerations which led to that interpretation of Articles 30 and 36 of the Treaty do not apply in the context of the relations between the Community and Portugal as defined by the Agreement. It is apparent from an examination of the Agreement that although it makes provision for the unconditional abolition of certain restrictions on trade between the Community and Portugal, such as quantitative restrictions and measures having equivalent effect, it does not have the same purpose as the EEC Treaty, inasmuch as the latter, as has been stated above, seeks to create a single market reproducing as closely as possible the conditions of a domestic market.

It follows that in the context of the Agreement restrictions on trade in goods may be considered to be justified on the ground of the protection of industrial and commercial property in a situation in which their justification would not be possible within the Community.

In the present case such a distinction is all the more necessary inasmuch as the instruments which the Community has at its disposal in order to achieve the uniform application of Community law and the progressive abolition of legislative disparities within the common market have no equivalent in the context of the relations between the Community and Portugal.

It follows from the foregoing that a prohibition on the importation into the Community of a product originating in Portugal based on the protection of copyright is justified in the framework of the free-trade arrangements established by the Agreement by virtue of the first sentence of Article 23. The findings of the national court do not disclose any factor which would permit the conclusion that the enforcement of copyright in a case such as the present constitutes a means of arbitrary discrimination or a disguised restriction on trade within the meaning of the second sentence of that article.

6.2.2 Application to Patents, Designs, Copyright and Other Rights against Misappropriation

6.2.2.1 *Dansk Supermarked v Imerco* [1981] E.C.R. 181; [1981] 3 C.M.L.R. 587 (CJ EC)

With a view to celebrating its fiftieth anniversary, the Danish hardware firm, Imerco, ordered from a British manufacturer, Broadhurst, a number of china services depicting Danish castles and referring to the Imerco anniversary. Very strict quality standards were prescribed by Imerco and Broadhurst was left with some 1,000 sub-standard sets, which Broadhurst was permitted to sell only outside Denmark. Nevertheless 300 of them found their way via a parallel importer from the UK to Dansk Supermarked, which retailed them in its stores.

Imerco sought relief against infringement of its Danish copyright and trade mark, and against conduct contrary to approved market usage (by virtue of the Danish Marketing Act of 1974). Under Article 177, the Danish court referred the question whether those Danish provisions could be applied, having regard to provisions of the Treaty of Rome. The CJ EC referred to its Terrapin decision (below, 6.2.3.3) and continued:

12 The first part of the reply to the question submitted must therefore be that Articles 30 and 36 of the EEC Treaty must be interpreted to mean that the judicial authorities of a Member State may not prohibit, on the basis of a copyright or of a trade mark, the marketing on the territory of that State of a product to which one of those rights applies if that product has been lawfully marketed on the territory of another Member State by the proprietor of such rights or with his consent.

13 The Danish Law of 14 June 1974 upon which Imerco relies, requires undertakings in their dealings to comply with the requirements of approved marketing usage. It authorises the competent courts to issue injunctions prohibiting all acts in breach of the provisions of the law and prescribes penalties for breach of such injunctions. As the Danish Government has explained, that Law is comparable in certain respects to the legislation in force in other Member States against unfair competition, but it has in addition other objectives in that sphere, in particular the protection of consumers.

14 The question submitted by the Højesteret is intended to establish whether it is possible to consider as contrary to approved marketing usage the sale in Denmark of goods marketed in another Member State with the agreement of a Danish undertaking but subject to the condition that the goods must not be exported to Denmark so as to compete there with goods marketed exclusively by the undertaking concerned.

15 In order to reply to that question it must first of all be remarked that Community law does not in principle have the effect of preventing the application in a Member State to goods imported from other Member States of the provisions on marketing in force in the State of importation. It follows that the marketing of imported goods may be prohibited if the conditions on which they are sold constitutes an infringement of the marketing usages considered proper and fair in the Member State of importation.

16 It must nevertheless be emphasised, as the Court of Justice has stressed in another context in its judgment of 25 November 1971 (*Béguelin*, Case 22/71, [1971] ECR 949), that the actual fact of the importation of goods which have been lawfully marketed in another Member State cannot be considered as an improper or unfair

act since that description may be attached only to offer or exposure for sale on the basis of circumstances distinct from the importation itself.

17 It must furthermore be remarked that it is impossible in any circumstances for agreements between individuals to derogate from the mandatory provisions of the Treaty on the free movement of goods. It follows that an agreement involving a prohibition on the importation into a Member State of goods lawfully marketed in another Member State may not be relied upon or taken into consideration in order to classify the marketing of such goods as an improper or unfair commercial practice.

18 The second part of the reply to the question submitted must thus be that Article 30 of the Treaty must be interpreted as meaning:

That the importation into a Member State of goods lawfully marketed in another Member State cannot as such be classified as an improper or unfair commercial practice, without prejudice however to the possible application of legislation of the State of importation against such practices on the ground of the circumstance or methods of offering such goods for sale as distinct from the actual fact of importation; and

That an agreement between individuals intended to prohibit the importation of such goods may not be relied upon or taken into consideration in order to classify the marketing of such goods as an improper or unfair commercial practice.

6.2.2.2 *Musik Vertrieb Membran v GEMA* [1981] E.C.R. 147; [1981] 2 C.M.L.R. 44 (CJ EC)

The GEMA, as well as being the performing right society of West Germany, licenses the mechanical recording rights of music in its repertoire. In the UK, this function is carried out for music copyright owners (mainly individual publishers) by an agency, the Mechanical Copyright Society (MCPS). Where MCPS licensed the production of records of copyright music in the UK its royalty was 6.25 per cent of the net retail selling price, the level set in the Copyright Act 1956, s. 8, for the statutory licence there conferred (a provision of the law abandoned in the CDPA 1988). On records exported from the UK to Germany, MCPS failed to secure payment of an additional royalty representing the difference between the royalty obtained there by the GEMA (over 8 per cent) and 6.25 per cent. GEMA accordingly sought to use its rights under German law to prevent the importation of such records into Germany. The importers' reliance on the free movement of goods Articles of the Treaty of Rome led the Bundesgerichtshof to refer this issue under Art. 177.

The CJ EC stated:

10 It is apparent from the well-established case-law of the Court and most recently from the judgment of 22 June 1976 in Case 119/75 *Terrapin Overseas Ltd* [1976] ECR 1039 that the proprietor of an industrial or commercial property right protected by the law of a Member State cannot rely on that law to prevent the importation of a product which has been lawfully marketed in another Member State by the proprietor himself or with his consent.

11 In the proceedings before the Court the French Government has argued that that case-law cannot be applied to copyright, which comprises *inter alia* the right of an author to claim authorship of the work and to object to any distortion, mutilation or other alteration thereof, or any other action in relation to the said work which would be prejudicial to his honour or reputation. It is contended that, in thus

conferring extended protection, copyright is not comparable to other industrial and commercial property rights such as patents or trade-marks.

12 It is true that copyright comprises moral rights of the kind indicated by the French Government. However, it also comprises other rights, notably the right to exploit commercially the marketing of the protected work, particularly in the form of licences granted in return for payment of royalties. It is this economic aspect of copyright which is the subject of the question submitted by the national court and, in this regard, in the application of Article 36 of the Treaty there is no reason to make a distinction between copyright and other industrial and commercial property rights.

13 While the commercial exploitation of copyright is a source of remuneration for the owner it also constitutes a form of control on marketing exercisable by the owner, the copyright management societies acting in his name and the grantees of licences. From this point of view commercial exploitation of copyright raises the same issues as that of any other industrial or commercial property right.

14 The argument put to the Court by the Belgian and Italian Governments that in the absence of harmonisation in this sector the principle of the territoriality of copyright laws always prevails over the principle of freedom of movement of goods within the Common Market cannot be accepted. Indeed, the essential purpose of the Treaty, which is to unite national markets into a single market, could not be attained if, under the various legal systems of the Member States, nationals of those Member States were able to partition the market and bring about arbitrary discrimination or disguised restrictions on trade between Member States.

15 It follows from the foregoing considerations that neither the copyright owner or his licensee, nor a copyright management society acting in the owner's or licensee's name, may rely on the exclusive exploitation right conferred by copyright to prevent or restrict the importation of sound recordings which have been lawfully marketed in another Member State by the owner himself or with his consent.

16 GEMA has argued that such an interpretation of Articles 30 and 36 of the Treaty is not sufficient to resolve the problem facing the national court since GEMA's application to the German courts is not for the prohibition or restriction of the marketing of the gramophone records and tape cassettes in question on German territory but for equality in the royalties paid for any distribution of those sound recordings on the German market. The owner of a copyright in a recorded musical work has a legitimate interest in receiving and retaining the benefit of his intellectual or artistic effort regardless of the degree to which his work is distributed and consequently it is maintained that he should not lose the right to claim royalties equal to those paid in the country in which the recorded work is marketed.

17 It should first be observed that the question put by the national court is concerned with the legal consequences of infringement of copyright. GEMA seeks damages for that infringement pursuant to the applicable national legislation and it is immaterial whether the quantum of damages which it seeks is calculated according to the difference between the rate of royalty payable on distribution in the national market and the rate of royalty paid in the country of manufacture or in any other manner. On any view its claims are in fact founded on the copyright owner's exclusive right of exploitation, which enables him to prohibit or restrict the free movement of the products incorporating the protected musical work.

18 It should be observed next that no provision of national legislation may permit an undertaking which is responsible for the management of copyrights and has a monopoly on the territory of a Member State by virtue of that management to charge a levy on products imported from another Member State where they were put into circulation by or with the consent of the copyright owner and thereby cause the Common Market to be partitioned. Such a practice would amount to allowing a private undertaking to impose a charge on the importation of sound recordings which are already in free circulation in the Common Market on account of their crossing a frontier; it would therefore have the effect of entrenching the isolation of national markets which the Treaty seeks to abolish.

19 It follows from those considerations that this argument must be rejected as being incompatible with the operation of the Common Market and with the aims of the Treaty.

On the effect of the UK Act, s.8, the Court stated:

24 As the Court held in another context in its judgment of 31 October 1974 in Case 15/74 *Centrafarm BV and Adriaan De Peijper v Sterling Drug Inc.* [1974] ECR 1147, the existence of a disparity between national laws which is capable of distorting competition between Member States cannot justify a Member State's giving legal protection to practices of a private body which are incompatible with the rules concerning free movement of goods.

25 It should further be observed that in a common market distinguished by free movement of goods and freedom to provide services an author, acting directly or through his publisher, is free to choose the place, in any of the Member States, in which to put his work into circulation. He may make that choice according to his best interests, which involve not only the level of remuneration provided in the Member State in question but other factors such as, for example, the opportunities for distributing his work and the marketing facilities which are further enhanced by virtue of the free movement of goods within the Community. In those circumstances, a copyright management society may not be permitted to claim, on the importation of sound recordings into another Member State, payment of additional fees based on the difference in the rates of remuneration existing in the various Member States.

26 It follows from the foregoing considerations that the disparities which continue to exist in the absence of any harmonisation of national rules on the commercial exploitation of copyrights may not be used to impede the free movement of goods in the Common Market.

The answer to the question put by the Bundesgerichtshof should therefore be that Articles 30 and 36 of the Treaty must be interpreted as precluding the application of national legislation under which a copyright management society empowered to exercise the copyrights of composers of musical work reproduced on gramophone records or other sound recordings in another Member State is permitted to invoke those rights where those sound recordings are distributed on the national market after having been put into circulation in that other Member State by or with the consent of the owners of those copyrights, in order to claim payment of a fee equal to the royalties ordinarily paid for marketing on the national market less the lower royalties paid in the Member State of manufacture.

6.2.2.3   *Pharmon v Hoechst* [1985] E.C.R. 2281;
[1985] 3 C.M.L.R. 775

Hoechst held patents in the UK and the Netherlands for the drug, frusemide. Under the former compulsory licensing provision of UK law, relating specifically to food and medicine patents (Patents Act 1949, s. 41; repealed in 1977), DDSA obtained authority to manufacture and sell frusemide in the UK; but the compulsory licence was subject to a prohibition against export. Despite this limitation, DDSA exported batches of frusemide to Pharmon in the Netherlands, claiming the right to do so under Article 30 of the Rome Treaty. On reference of questions by the Dutch Appeal Court, the CJ EC held as follows:

14   The Hoge Raad's first question asks in substance whether Articles 30 and 36 of the EEC Treaty preclude the application of legal provisions of a Member State which give a patent proprietor the right to prevent the marketing in that State of a product which has been manufactured in another Member State by the holder of a compulsory licence granted in respect of a parallel patent held by the same proprietor.

22   It must be recalled that the Court has consistently held that Articles 30 and 36 of the EEC Treaty preclude the application of national provisions which enable a patent proprietor to prevent the importation and marketing of a product which has been lawfully marketed in another Member State by the patent proprietor himself, with his consent, or by a person economically or legally dependent on him.

23   If a patent proprietor could preclude the importation of protected products marketed in another Member State by him or with his consent, he would be able to partition the national markets and thus restrict trade between the Member States, although such a restriction is not necessary to protect the substance of his exclusive rights under the parallel patents.

24   The Hoge Raad's question is therefore essentially intended to establish whether the same rules apply where the product imported and offered for sale has been manufactured in the exporting Member State by the holder of a compulsory licence granted in respect of a parallel patent held by the proprietor of the patent in the importing Member State.

25   It is necessary to point out that where, as in this instance, the competent tauthorities of a Member State grant a third party a compulsory licence which allows him to carry out manufacturing and marketing operations which the patentee would normally have the right to prevent, the patentee cannot be deemed to have consented to the operation of that third party. Such a measure deprives the patent proprietor of his right to determine freely the conditions under which he markets his products.

26   As the Court held most recently in its judgment of 14 July 1981 (*Merck v Stephar*), the substance of a patent right lies essentially in according the inventor an exclusive right of first placing the product on the market so as to allow him to obtain the reward for his creative effort. It is therefore necessary to allow the patent proprietor to prevent the importation and marketing of products manufactured under a compulsory licence in order to protect the substance of his exclusive rights under his patent.

27   Consequently, in reply to Question 1 it must be stated that Articles 30 and 36 of the EEC Treaty do not preclude the application of legal provisions of a Member State which give a patent proprietor the right to prevent the marketing in that state of a

product which has been manufactured in another Member State by the holder of a compulsory licence granted in respect of a parallel patent held by the same proprietor.

28 Questions 2 and 3 ask essentially whether the reply to Question 1 depends, in the first place, on whether the authorities of the Member State which granted the compulsory licence have attached to it a prohibition on exportation and, secondly, on whether the compulsory licence provides for a system of royalties for the patentee and whether he has actually accepted or received such royalties.

29 It is sufficient to state that the limits referred to above imposed by Community law on the application of the law of the importing Member State in no way depend on the conditions attached by the competent authorities of the exporting Member State to the grant of the compulsory licence.

30 It follows that in reply to Questions 2 and 3 it must be stated that it makes no difference to the reply to Question 1 whether a prohibition on exportation is attached to the compulsory licence, whether that licence fixes royalties payable to the patentee or whether the patentee has accepted or refused such royalties.

6.2.2.4 *Allen & Hanburys v Generics* [1988] 1 C.M.L.R. 701; [1988] 2 All E.R. 454 (CJ EC)

Under the Patents Act 1977, certain pre-1978 patents would have their terms extended from 16 to 20 years. However, during the additional four years they would be endorsed "licences of right" and a competitor seeking such a licence could have its terms set, if necessary, by the Comptroller-General of Patents, in accordance with s. 46. Allen & Hanburys held such a patent for an asthma treatment drug and Generics sought a licence of right under it. While applying to the Comptroller, Generics informed Allen & Hanburys of its intention to import the drug from Italy where it was unpatented; and this led to infringement proceedings.

S. 46(3) provided that if an alleged infringer undertook to obtain a licence of right under an endorsed patent no injunction against infringement should be granted; and any damages should be limited to at most double the amount payable under the licence. This however did not apply to an infringement by importation.

The principal question referred by the HL to the CJ EC concerned the double distinction drawn by s. 46(3) between the infringing acts of a competitor in the UK and those of a competitor importing from another Common Market country. As to this the CJ EC stated:

14 In those circumstances it must be considered that the power of national courts to prohibit the importation of the product in question may be justified under the provisions of Article 36 on the protection of industrial and commercial property only if that prohibition is necessary in order to ensure that the proprietor of such a patent has, vis-à-vis importers, the same rights as he enjoys as against producers who manufacture the product in the national territory, that is to say the right to a fair return from his patent.

15 That is therefore the test which must be applied in examining the merits of a number of arguments raised before the court, both by Allen & Hanburys and by the United Kingdom, in order to justify an injunction prohibiting imports granted against an importer-infringer.

16 It has been observed in the first place that an importer may have no substantial presence in the importing member state, in particular where his assets and

employees are not subject to the jurisdiction of that state. An injunction prohibiting him from importing the product is then justified until the patent proprietor has been guaranteed actual payment of the sums due to him.

17 However, that argument cannot be accepted in the case of a member state where, under the relevant legislation, the fact that manufacturers based in its territory do not have adequate assets cannot justify the grant of an injunction against them until they have offered guarantees of payment. For a manufacturer based in the territory of a member state as well as for an importer such guarantees of payment can only be included among the terms fixed in the licensing agreement or, in default of an agreement, by the competent national authority.

18 It has also been maintained that an injunction prohibiting imports may be justified by the difficulty of carrying out checks on the origin and quantities of goods imported, on the basis of which the royalties payable to the patent proprietor must be calculated.

19 However, it should be pointed out that it may also be difficult to check the quantity of goods marketed even where they are manufactured within the national territory and yet no injunction or interdict is possible in those circumstances. It is therefore a matter for the licensing agreement alone or, in default of agreement, for the competent national authority to lay down detailed rules to enable the patent proprietor to check the supporting documents produced by the importer regarding the purchase, import and sale of the product.

20 Finally, it has been maintained that an injunction prohibiting imports may be justified in order to enable the patent proprietor to check on the quality of an imported medicine in the interests of public health.

21 It must be observed, however, that that consideration has nothing to do with protection of the exclusive rights of the patent proprietor and, therefore, may not be relied on in order to justify, on grounds of protection of industrial and commercial property, a restriction on trade between member states.

22 It must therefore be concluded that an injunction issued against an importer-infringer in the circumstances described by the national court would constitute arbitrary discrimination prohibited by article 36 of the Treaty and could not be justified on grounds of the protection of industrial and commercial property.

In response to further questions from the HL the CJ EC also ruled:

(a) that Arts. 30–36 prohibited the Comptroller from restricting a licence of right so as to exclude importation from another member state;
(b) that it was irrelevant that the patented product was a pharmaceutical drug and that it came from a state where it was not patentable;
(c) that there were no imperative grounds of consumer protection or fair trading which could justify any exception being admitted under Art. 30 itself in the distinction between domestic and imported products created by s. 46.

6.2.2.5   *Thetford v Fiamma* [1989] 2 All E.R. 801 (CJ EC)

Under the Patents Act 1949, the novelty and inventiveness of a patent was to be judged against a state of the art which excluded the content of UK and other patent specifications published more than fifty years before the priority date in issue (s.50(1) – a provision which continues to affect "old" patents).

Thetford owned a patent for portable lavatories, which was arguably anticipated in 7 citations which were excluded from consideration by s. 50(1) in the UK even though they would have been a proper basis of objection in most other Community states.

Fiamma imported infringing lavatories from Italy. When sued it sought inter alia *to plead that it was not liable to an injunction because s. 50(1) operated in a manner which could not be justified under Art. 36 of the Rome Treaty.*

The English Court of Appeal first asked whether a UK patent which would have been anticipated but for the provisions of s. 50(1) constituted "industrial or commercial property" entitled to protection under Art. 36.

After referring in general terms to Arts. 30 and 36, the CJ EC continued:

11 Fiamma argues that the derogation provided for in Art 36 can apply only if a patent right granted pursuant to national legislation fulfils certain fundamental conditions. In particular, a patent granted in the absence of novelty or an inventive step cannot be regarded as being covered by the expression "protection of industrial and commercial property".

12 In that regard, it must be observed, as the court held in *Keurkoop BV v Nancy Kean Gifts BV* Case 144/81 [1982] ECR 2853 at 2871 (para 18) on the protection of designs, that –

> "in the present state of Community law and in the absence of Community standardisation or of a harmonisation of laws the determination of the conditions and procedures under which protection ... is granted is a matter for national rules ..."

13 However, Fiamma contends that the court's case law on designs may not be transposed to the field of patents in view of the higher degree of harmonisation of national legislation which has already been achieved in that field and the existence of international conventions based on the principle of absolute novelty.

14 That argument cannot be upheld. Firstly, no harmonisation of the patents legislation of the member states has yet been effected by virtue of measures of Community law. Secondly, none of the international conventions in force on patents is capable of supporting Fiamma's argument. The entry into force of the Convention on the Grant of European Patents (the European Patent Convention) (Munich, 5 October 1973; TS 20 (1978); Cmnd 7090), which is based on the principle of absolute novelty, did not affect the existence of national legislation on the granting of patents. Article 2(2) of that convention expressly provides that "The European patent shall, in each of the Contracting States for which it is granted, have the effect of and be subject to the same conditions as a national patent granted by that State". As for the Convention on the Unification of Certain Points of Substantive Law on Patents for Invention (Strasbourg, 27 November 1963; TS 70 (1980); Cmnd 8002), it must be pointed out that, since that convention entered into force after the patent in question had been granted, it cannot serve as a determining factor for the purposes of the interpretation of Community law. The only instrument the provisions of which might afford support for Fiamma's point of view with regard to the recognition in the Community legal order of the principle of absolute novelty is the Convention for the Patent for the Common Market (the Community Patent Convention) (Luxembourg, 15 December 1975; EC 18 (1976); Cmnd 6553), which has close links with the aforementioned Munich Convention but which has not yet entered into force.

15 It follows that, as the court held in *Parke Davis & Co v Probel* Case 24/67 [1968] ECR 55, since the existence of patent rights is at present a matter solely of national

law, a member state's patents legislation, such as the legislation at issue, is covered in principle by the derogations from Art 30 which are provided for in Art 36.

16 It must next be considered whether the application of the principle at issue may not constitute a means of arbitrary discrimination or a disguised restriction on trade between member states within the meaning of the second sentence of Art 36.

17 As regards the first possibility, namely whether a means of arbitrary discrimination is involved, it is sufficient, in order to refute that argument, to point out that before the court the agent of the United Kingdom stated, without being contradicted by the other parties, that the application of s. 50(1) of the Patents Act 1949 does not give rise to any discrimination. On the one hand, that rule prevents consideration from being given to a specification disclosing an invention whether it was filed in the United Kingdom or in another state; secondly, there is no discrimination based on the nationality of applicants for patents: foreign nationals applying for patents in the United Kingdom have the same rights as United Kingdom nationals.

18 It must further be considered whether the application of the principle in question may not give rise to a disguised restriction on trade between member states.

19 In that regard, the justification for the rule of relative novelty, as given in the documents before the court, discloses that the objective pursued by the United Kingdom legislature in introducing the "50-year rule" in 1902 was to foster creative activity on the part of inventors in the interest of industry. To that end, the 50-year rule aimed to make it possible to give a reward, in the form of the grant of a patent, even in cases in which an "old" invention was "rediscovered". In such cases the United Kingdom legislation was designed to prevent the existence of a former patent specification which had never been utilised or published from constituting a ground for revoking a patent which had been validly issued.

20 Consequently, a rule such as the 50-year rule cannot be regarded as constituting a disguised restriction on trade between member states.

21 In view of the foregoing considerations, the answer to the national court's first question must be that, in the present state of Community law, Art 36 must be interpreted as not precluding the application of a member state's legislation on patents which provides that a patent granted for an invention may not be declared invalid by reason only of the fact that the invention in question appears in a patent specification filed more than 50 years previously.

The question was also raised whether under Art. 36 it was permissible only to award monetary compensation but not to enjoin importation of infringing products from another member state.

23 Fiamma maintains in that connection that the "rule of proportionality" as defined in the case law of the court and, in particular, by *de Peijper* Case 104/75 [1976] ECR 613 should also be applied in the field of industrial and commercial property. In particular, in view of the particular features of the case at issue, in which the protection conferred by Art 36 relates to a patent obtained by virtue of the rule of relative novelty, the specific subject matter of the patent is already adequately protected by conferring on the proprietor of the patent the right to obtain reward for the marketing of the patented article without going so far as to give him the right to obtain an injunction.

24 However, it must be observed in that connection that according to the case law of the court (most recently in *Pharmon BV v Hoechst AG* Case 19/84 [1985]

ECR 2281) the right of the proprietor of a patent to prevent the importation and marketing of products manufactured under a compulsory licence is part of the substance of patents law. There is all the more reason for that conclusion to apply in a case such as this where no licence has been granted by the proprietor of the patent in the country of manufacture.

6.2.2.6 *Warner Brothers v Christiansen* (Note of Judgment, Proceedings of CJ EC, Week ending 7.10.88)

The Østre Landsret [Eastern Division of the High Court], Copenhagen, referred for a preliminary ruling a question on the interpretation of Articles 30 and 36 of the EEC Treaty, to establish in how far national copyright legislation on the hiring-out of video-cassettes is compatible with the free movement of goods.

The question was raised in the context of proceedings between, on the one hand, Warner Brothers and Metronome Video and, on the other, Mr Erik Viuff Christiansen. Warner, the owner in the United Kingdom of the copyright in the film "Never Say Never Again", which it produced in that country, assigned the management of the video production rights in Denmark to Metronome.

Since the video-cassette of the film was available for sale in the United Kingdom with Warner's consent, Mr Christiansen, who runs a video shop in Copenhagen, bought a copy of it in London in order to hire it out in Denmark, and imported it for that purpose into that Member State. Citing the Danish legislation which allows the author or producer of a musical or cinematographic work to restrain the hiring-out of videograms thereof until such time as he gives the appropriate consent, Warner and Metronome obtained an injunction from the Byret [District Court], Copenhagen, prohibiting Mr Christiansen from hiring out the video-cassettes in Denmark.

That prompted the Østre Landsret to refer to the Court a question which, in essence, seeks to ascertain whether Articles 30 and 36 of the EEC Treaty militate against the application of national legislation enabling the author to make the hiring-out of video-cassettes subject to his permission, when such video-cassettes have already been put into circulation with his consent in another Member State, whose legislation allows the author to control the first sale but without enabling him to prohibit hiring out.

The Court emphasised that in this case the prerogative conferred on the author by the national legislation in question was only applicable after importation had been carried out. None the less, the Court observed that the marketing of video-cassettes was achieved not only through sales but also, and increasingly, by way of hire to individuals owning video tape players. The right to prohibit such hiring-out in a Member State was thus likely to have an influence on the trade in video-cassettes within that State and thus to affect indirectly intra-Community trade in those goods. Legislation of the type which gave rise to the main proceedings should therefore be regarded as a measure having equivalent effect to a quantitative restriction on imports, prohibited under Article 30 of the Treaty.

The Court therefore turned to consider whether such legislation may be regarded as justified on the grounds of the protection of industrial and commercial property under Article 36 which covers literary and artistic property.

The Court noted that the national legislation in question applied without distinction to video-cassettes produced locally and video-cassettes imported from another Member State. The determining factor in its application was the type of transaction of which video-cassettes formed the subject-matter, not the origin of those video-cassettes. Such legislation did not therefore create any discrimination in trade between Member States.

Consideration should be given to the emergence of a specific market for the hiring-out of such recordings as distinct from their sale. The market for the hire of video-cassettes affected a wider public than the market for their sale, and now afforded a major potential source of revenue for the authors of films.

It was clear that authorisation to collect authors' fees only when sales were made either to individuals or to those hiring out video-cassettes could not ensure that authors of films received a remuneration which was commensurate with the number of occasions on which the video-cassettes were actually hired out and which guaranteed those authors a satisfactory share of the rental market. That explained why some national legislative systems had recently provided for the specific protection of the right to hire out video-cassettes.

Laws of that type were clearly justified on the grounds of the protection of industrial and commercial property under Article 36 of the Treaty.

6.2.2.7   *Basset v SACEM* [1987] E.C.R. 1747; [1987] 3 C.M.L.R. 173 (CJ EC)

French law does not grant to a record producer a neighbouring right in public perform-ance etc of a sound recording. Its Copyright Law of 1957, Art. 31, does require that, upon the transfer of a copy of a copyright work, the extent and purpose of its use should be defined. From this has grown the practice of selling recordings for private use only, the object being to require a separate, supplementary fee under the reproduction right (the so-called droit de destination) for public performance or broadcasting of the recording of the work in addition to a licence fee under the performing right in respect of the same use. Only in Belgium is there a similar practice. Thus the French collecting society for composers, SACEM, demanded of discothèque owners a licence fee of 8.25% of receipts, comprising 6.6% performance fee and 1.65% supplementary mechanical reproduction fee. This applied equally to legitimate recordings purchased in other EC countries and imported into France.

The Cour de Cassation raised the legitimacy of the second charge in relation to Arts. 30–36 of the Rome Treaty before the CJ EC, which held:

12   It appears from the judgment of the national court that the "supplementary mechanical reproduction fee" with which the preliminary questions are concerned is charged not on the importation or marketing of records or other sound recordings but by reason of their public use, for example by a radio station, in a discothèque or in a device such as a juke-box installed in a public place. The problem raised by the national court lies in the fact that in such circumstances that royalty is charged in addition to a performance royalty.

13   The national court asks whether Articles 30 and 36 or Article 86 of the Treaty prohibits the charging of such an aggregate fee where the sound recordings were manufactured and marketed in a Member State where there is no such aggregation of fees and only a performance royalty is charged on the public use of a recorded work. That is the hypothesis that must be examined.

14   It is undisputed that, as is normally the case with regard to copyright management, on the basis of the applicable international conventions, the aggregation of a performance fee and a supplementary mechanical reproduction fee charged on the public use in France of a recorded musical work takes place whether the records are of French origin or are manufactured or marketed in another Member State. It is true that public use in another Member State may give rise only to the collection of a performance royalty in favour of the author and the record manufacturer, but that circumstance does not imply that the amount of the royalty charged or its function are different from those of the royalties charged in France on such use.

15   In other words, disregarding the concepts used by French legislation and practice, the supplementary mechanical reproduction fee may thus be analysed as constitut-ing part of the payment for an author's rights over the public performance of a

recorded musical work. Moreover, the amount of that royalty, like that of the performance fee strictly so called, is calculated on the basis of the discothèque's turnover and not the number of records bought or played.

16 It follows that, even if the charging of the fee in question were to be capable of having a restrictive effect on imports, it does not constitute a measure having equivalent effect prohibited under Article 30 of the Treaty inasmuch as it must be regarded as a normal exploitation of copyright and does not constitute a means of arbitrary discrimination or a disguised restriction on trade between Member States for the purposes of Article 36 of the Treaty.

The Court proceeded to hold that the act of charging the second fee did not of itself amount to an abuse of SACEM's dominant position as the sole French collecting society for composers.

6.2.2.8 *Industrie Diensten Groep v Beele* [1982] E.C.R. 707; [1982] 3 C.M.L.R. 102 (CJ EC)

Beele was the sole importer into the Netherlands of a cable-duct system, MCT, produced by a Swedish firm and until 1975 protected by patent. After that year, a German firm began to produce a rival product, SVT, which was virtually identical in all aspects, including appearance. This was imported to the Netherlands by IDG, against whom Beele instituted proceedings for unfair competition based on a slavish imitation of products which would mislead purchasers as to source. The Dutch Court of Appeal raised the question whether an injunction against such conduct under Dutch law was compatible with the rules on free movement of goods in the Rome Treaty.

The CJ EC stated:

2 The question was raised in the context of an action between a Netherlands undertaking, the sole importer of cable ducts manufactured in Sweden which have been marketed in the Netherlands since 1963, and another Netherlands undertaking which since 1978 has marketed in the Netherlands cable ducts manufactured in the Federal Republic of Germany. The case-file shows that the Swedish cable ducts were previously protected by patent rights in the Federal Republic of Germany, the Netherlands and elsewhere, and that the German cable ducts were first made and imported into the Netherlands after the period of validity of those patents had expired.

3 The first-mentioned undertaking applied to the President of the Arrondissementsrechtbank [District Court], The Hague, for interlocutory relief against the second undertaking on the ground that the German cable ducts were a precise imitation of the Swedish cable ducts and sought an order from him restraining the defendant from marketing the German cable ducts or causing them to be marketed in the Netherlands.

4 The President of the Arrondissementsrechtbank granted the application whereupon the second undertaking appealed to the Gerechtshof, The Hague. According to the judgment making the reference for a preliminary ruling, that court arrived at the provisional view that the German manufacturer could have designed a cable-duct system different from the Swedish system without impairing the quality of its product economically or technically and by not doing so had caused the two products to be confused. The Gerechtshof accordingly considers that the President of the Arrondissementsrechtbank rightly decided that under Netherlands law the

German product is a precise imitation of the Swedish cable ducts. Since the appellant claimed that the cable ducts which it sold were lawfully marketed in another Member State and that the respondent's action was therefore contrary to Articles 30 to 36 of the EEC Treaty, the Gerechtshof decided to ask the Court the following question:

"Assuming that:

(a) A trader, A, markets products in the Netherlands which are no longer covered by any patent and which for no compelling reason are practically identical with products which have been marketed for a considerable period of time in the Netherlands by another trader, B, and which are different from similar kinds of articles, and in so doing trader A needlessly causes confusion:

(b) Under Netherlands law trader A is thereby competing unfairly with trader B and acting unlawfully;

(c) Netherlands law gives trader B the right to obtain an injunction on that ground restraining trader A from continuing to market the products in the Netherlands;

(d) The products of trader B are manufactured in Sweden and those of trader A in the Federal Republic of Germany;

(e) Trader A imports his products from the Federal Republic of Germany in which those products are lawfully put on the market by someone other than trader B, the Swedish manufacturer, someone who is associated with one of them or by someone who is authorised to do so by one of them,

do the rules contained in the EEC Treaty on the free movement of goods, notwithstanding the provisions of Article 36 thereof, then prevent trader B from obtaining such an injunction against trader A?"

5 The case-file shows that, just like protection against precise imitation in the law of most other Member States, the rule of Netherlands law to which the question refers has been developed chiefly by the courts. As the Commission has pointed out, no effort has been made hitherto at Community level to harmonise national rules against precise imitation. Therefore an examination of the question whether such protection accords with the rules of the Treaty on the free movement of goods should be confined to the way in which that protection is provided in Netherlands law, as described in the judgment of the Gerechtshof.

6 That judgment shows that, subject to the answer to be given to the question raised, the Gerechtshof is prepared to uphold the injunction against the marketing in the Netherlands of products which it presumes have been lawfully marketed in another Member State.

7 Such an injunction constitutes an obstacle to the free movement of goods between the Member States and in principle is caught by Article 30 which prohibits all measures having an effect equivalent to quantitative restrictions on imports. However, the Court has repeatedly held (for example, in the judgment of 20 February 1979 in Case 120/1978, the *Cassis de Dijon* case, [1979] ECR 649 and in the judgment of 17 June 1981 in Case 113/80 *Commission v Ireland* [1981] ECR 1625) that in the absence of common rules relating to the production and marketing of products, obstacles to movement within the Community resulting from disparities between national legislation must be accepted in so far as such legislation, applying without discrimination to both domestic and imported products, may be justified as being necessary in order to satisfy mandatory requirements relating in particular to the protection of consumers and fairness in commercial transactions. Therefore the protection against imitation provided in the way

described in the judgment making the reference for a preliminary ruling must be examined to determine whether it meets those conditions.

8 Although the main action concerns the protection of a product manufactured in a non-member country against the marketing of a product manufactured in a Member State, according to the national court the application of case-law does not depend on country of origin of the product imitated and country of origin of the imitation. What is more, there is nothing in the judgment of the national court from which it may be inferred that that case-law is applied in a manner adapted to the specific needs of national products thereby putting imported products as a disadvantage. Therefore it must be assumed that the case-law referred to by the national court applies without distinction to national and imported products.

9 National case-law prohibiting the precise imitation of someone else's product which is likely to cause confusion may indeed protect consumers and promote fair trading; these are general interests which, according to the decisions of the Court cited above, may justify the existence of obstacles to movement within the Community resulting from disparities between national laws relating to the marketing of products. That such a rule does meet mandatory requirements is moreover borne out by the fact that it accords with the principle underlying Article 10 bis of the Paris Convention for the Protection of Industrial Property, as last revised on 14 July 1967 at Stockholm, which prohibits *inter alia* all acts of such a nature as to create confusion with the goods of a competitor, and by the fact that this rule is recognised in principle in the case-law of most Member States.

10 In order to answer the question whether case-law such as that described in the judgment of the Gerechtshof is necessary to achieve the aforesaid objectives, or whether it goes beyond the limit which they may justify, the manner in which that case-law is applied, as described in the judgment, should be scrutinised.

11 As to that, the very wording of the question submitted shows first that in the provisional view of the national court the products which it intends to prohibit from being marketed are for no compelling reason practically identical to the products imitated and that the appellant in the main action thereby needlessly causes confusion. Furthermore, the judgment of the national court shows that the question whether or not such imitation is necessary was considered not only from the technical point of view, but also from the economic and commercial point of view.

12 Secondly, it is apparent from the wording of the question submitted and from the case-file that there is no indication of an agreement or of dependence between the Swedish manufacturer of the original product and the German manufacturer of the product which is supposed to be an imitation thereof and the marketing of which in the Netherlands is in dispute.

13 Where the circumstances mentioned by the national court are met a body of case-law prohibiting precise imitation of someone else's product may not be regarded as exceeding the scope of the mandatory requirements which the protection of consumers and the fairness of commercial transactions constitute.

14 The appellant in the main action has raised before the Court the question of spare parts. It points out that the cable ducts are installed not only in buildings but also in ships and an injunction against the marketing of the German product in the Netherlands would make it necessary to carry out repairs on ships in the Netherlands using spare parts for the Swedish product, even if the ship is fitted with

German cable ducts. Since this question has not been raised by the national court and the respondent in the main action has indicated during the procedure before the Court that the injunction which it seeks does not relate to spare parts for the repair of the German cable ducts, it is not necessary to resolve this question for which the foregoing considerations are not necessarily conclusive.

6.2.2.9   *Volvo v Veng* (CJ EC, Judgment, 5.10.88)

Volvo, the proprietor in the United Kingdom of a registered design for the front wings of Volvo series 200 cars, instituted proceedings against Veng before the High Court of Justice for infringement of its sole and exclusive rights. Veng imported the same body panels, manufactured without authority from Volvo, and marketed them in the United Kingdom.

Of three questions put to the CJ EC under Art. 177, the Court found it necessary to answer the second:

Is it prima facie *an abuse of such dominant position for such a manufacturer to refuse to license others to supply such body panels, even where they are willing to pay a reasonable royalty for all articles sold under the licence (such royalty to represent an award which is just and equitable having regard to the merits of the design and all the surrounding circumstances, and to be determined by arbitration or in such other manner as the national court shall direct)?*

The CJ EC stated:

7 It must first be observed, as the Court held in its judgment of 14 September 1982 (in Case 144/81, *Keurkoop v Nancy Kean Gifts*, (1982) ECR 2853) with respect to the protection of designs and models, that, as Community law stands at present and in the absence of Community standardisation or harmonisation of laws, the determination of the conditions and procedures under which protection of designs and models is granted is a matter for national rules. It is thus for the national legislatures to determine which products are to benefit from protection, even where they form part of a unit which is already protected as such.

8 It must also be emphasised that the right of the proprietor of a protected design to prevent third parties from manufacturing and selling or importing, without its consent, products incorporating the design constitutes the very subject-matter of his exclusive right. It follows that an obligation imposed upon the proprietor of a protected designs to grant to third parties, even in return for a reasonable royalty, a licence for the supply of products incorporating the design would lead to the proprietor thereof being deprived of the substance of his exclusive right, and that a refusal to grant such a licence cannot in itself constitute an abuse of a dominant position.

9 It must however be noted that the exercise of an exclusive right by the proprietor of a registered design in respect of car body panels may be prohibited by Article 86 if it involves, on the part of an undertaking holding a dominant position, certain abusive conduct such as the arbitrary refusal to supply spare parts to independent repairers, the fixing of prices for spare parts at an unfair level or a decision no longer to produce spare parts for a particular model even though many cars of that model are still in circulation, provided that such conduct is liable to affect trade between Member States.

10 In the present case no instance of any such conduct has been mentioned by the national court.

Note that in the similar case, CICRA v Renault *(CJ EC, Judgment, 5.10.88), the Court held, as in previous decisions that:*

With regard more particularly to the difference in price between the components sold by the car manufacturer and those sold by independent producers ... the fact that the price of the former was higher than that of the latter did not necessarily constitute an abuse, since the proprietor of protected rights in respect of an ornamental design could legitimately claim to be entitled to remuneration for the costs which he had incurred in perfecting the registered design.

6.2.3 *Application to Trade Mark and Related Cases*

6.2.3.1 *Sirena v Eda* [1971] E.C.R. 69; [1971] C.M.L.R. 260

Mark Allen, an American company, developed and built up an international market in "Prep" shaving cream before the second world war. In Italy it registered the mark in 1933 and in 1937 by agreement assigned it to Sirena. Thereafter, Sirena manufactured and marketed its own product under the mark, without receiving technical know-how from Mark Allen.

In Germany, Mark Allen apparently licensed use of the mark to a German company, whose products were exported to Italy by an import-export business, Novimpex. When they appeared on the Italian market, Sirena sued for infringement of its "Prep" marks. The questions submitted to the CJ EC by the Tribunale Civile e Penale di Milano referred to interpretation of Articles 85 and 86 of the EEC Treaty. Concerning Article 85 the Court stated:

5 In the sphere of provisions relating to the free movement of products, prohibitions and restrictions on imports justified on the grounds of protection of industrial and commercial property are allowed by Article 36, subject to the express condition that they "shall not, however, constitute a means of arbitrary discrimination or a disguised restriction on trade between Member States". Article 36, although it appears in the Chapter of the Treaty dealing with quantitative restrictions on trade between Member States, is based on a principle equally applicable to the question of competition, in the sense that even if the rights recognised by the legislation of a Member State on the subject of industrial and commercial property are not affected, so far as their existence is concerned, by Articles 85 and 86 of the Treaty, their exercise may still fall under the prohibitions imposed by those provisions.

The Court referred to provisions concerning trade mark use in the Commission Regulation 67/67 (Exclusive Distribution Agreement Block Exemption), and continued:

7 The exercise of a trade-mark right is particularly apt to lead to a partitioning of markets, and thus to impair the free movement of goods between States which is essential to the Common Market. Moreover, a trade-mark right is distinguishable in this context from other rights of industrial and commercial property, inasmuch as the interests protected by the latter are usually more important, and merit a higher degree of protection, than the interests protected by an ordinary trade-mark.

8 The request for interpretation is primarily directed to ascertaining in what circumstances the exercise of trade-mark rights may constitute infringement of the prohibition imposed by Article 85(1).

9 By virtue of this provision, "all agreements between undertakings, decisions by association of undertakings, and concerted practices" which may affect trade between Member States, and which have as their object or effect the distortion of competition, are prohibited as incompatible with the Common Market. A trade-mark right, as a legal entity, does not in itself possess those elements of contract or concerted practice referred to in Article 85(1). Nevertheless, the exercise of that right might fall within the ambit of the prohibitions contained in the Treaty each time it manifests itself as the subject, the means or the result of a restrictive practice. When a trade-mark right is exercised by virtue of assignments to users in one or more Member States, it is thus necessary to establish in each case whether such use leads to a situation falling under the prohibitions of Article 85.

10 Such situations may in particular arise from restrictive agreements between proprietors of trade-marks or their successors in title enabling them to prevent imports from other Member States. If the combination of assignments to different users of national trade-marks protecting the same product has the result of re-enacting impenetrable frontiers between the Member States, such practice may well affect trade between States, and distort competition in the Common Market. The matter would be different if, in order to avoid any partitioning of the market, the agreements concerning the use of national rights in respect of the same trade-mark were to be effected in such conditions as to make the general use of trade-mark rights at Community level compatible with the observance of the conditions of competition and unity of the market which are so essential to the Common Market that failure to observe them is penalised by Article 85 by a declaration that they are automatically void.

11 Article 85, therefore, is applicable to the extent to which trade-mark rights are invoked so as to prevent imports of products which originate in different Member States, which bear the same trade-mark by virtue of the fact that the proprietors have acquired it, or the right to use it, whether by agreements between themselves or by agreements with third parties. Article 85 is not precluded from applying merely because, under national legislation trade-mark rights may originate in legal or factual circumstances other than the abovementioned agreements, such as registration of the trade-mark, or its undisturbed use.

12 If the restrictive practices arose before the Treaty entered into force, it is both necessary and sufficient that they continue to produce their effects after that date.

13 Before restrictive practice can come under Article 85(1) it must affect trade between Member States to an appreciable extent, and restrict competition within the Common Market.

Concerning Article 86, the Court stated:

15 It is clear from the wording of this provision that what it prohibits is a combination of three elements: the existence of a dominant position, its abuse, and the possibility that trade between Member States may thereby be affected.

16 It should first be observed that the proprietor of a trade-mark does not enjoy a "dominant position" within the meaning of Article 86 merely because he is in a position to prevent third parties from putting into circulation, on the territory of a Member State, products bearing the same trade-mark. Since the article requires that the position in question should extend to at least a "substantial part" of the Common Market, it is also necessary that the proprietor should have power to impede the maintenance of effective competition over a considerable part of the relevant market, having regard in particular to the existence and position of any producers or distributors who may be marketing similar goods or goods which may be substituted for them.

17 As regards the abuse of a dominant position, although the price level of the product may not of itself necessarily suffice to disclose such an abuse, it may, however, if unjustified by any objective criteria, and if it is particularly high, be a determining factor.

6.2.3.2   *Van Zuylen v Hag* [1974] E.C.R. 731; [1974] 2 C.M.L.R. 127 (CJ EC)

The German company, Hag AG, developed a successful business in decaffeinated coffee early in this century, originally using a patented process. In 1927, it formed a Belgian subsidiary to supply the Belgian and Luxembourg markets and in 1934 transferred to it its "Hag" trade marks for those countries.

In 1946, the Belgian government administration which had taken over the subsidiary as enemy property, sold it to an unrelated buyer by an act of sequestration. Subsequently the business and marks were assigned to Van Zuylen.

Hag AG sought to enter these markets with the brand, "Decofa", but was not successful. It then secured the sale of "Hag" brand coffee in Luxembourg through an agent there. Trade mark infringement proceedings were launched against it, to which it pleaded a right of access under Arts. 30–36 and 85 of the Treaty of Rome.

The CJ EC said:

3 The file shows that the original holder, carrying on business in Germany, had assigned his trade mark as regards Belgium to a subsidiary established and controlled by him, but which became independent as a result of an act by a public authority.

4 As it is expressed in the question, there exists between the two present holders "no legal, financial, technical, or economic link".

5 Article 85 not being in these circumstances applicable, the question must be examined by reference only to the rules relating to the free movement of goods.

9 Inasmuch as it provides an exception to one of the fundamental principles of the Common Market, Article 36 in fact only admits derogations from the free movement of goods to the extent that such derogations are justified for the purpose of safeguarding rights that constitute the specific subject matter of this property.

10 Thus the application of the legislation relating to the protection of trade marks at any rate protects the legitimate holder of the trade mark against infringement on the part of persons who lack any legal title.

11 The exercise of a trade mark right tends to contribute to the partitioning off of the markets and thus to affect the free movement of goods between Member States, all the more so since – unlike other rights of industrial and commercial property – it is not subject to limitations in point of time.

12 Accordingly, one cannot allow the holder of a trade mark to rely upon the exclusiveness of a trade mark right – which may be the consequence of the territorial limitation of national legislations – with a view to prohibiting the marketing in a Member State of goods legally produced in another Member State under an identical trade mark having the same origin.

13 Such a prohibition, which would legitimise the isolation of national markets, would collide with one of the essential objects of the Treaty, which is to unite national markets in a single market.

14 Whilst in such a market the indication of origin of a product covered by a trade mark is useful, information to consumers on this point may be ensured by means other than such as would affect the free movement of goods.

15 Accordingly, to prohibit the marketing in a Member State of a product legally bearing a trade mark in another Member State, for the sole reason that an identical

trade mark having the same origin exists in the first state, is incompatible with the provisions providing for free movement of goods within the Common Market.

16 The second question asks whether the same would be the case if the marketing of the product covered by the trade mark were effected not by the holder of the trade mark in the other Member State but by a third party, who has duly acquired the product in that State.

17 If the holder of a trade mark in one Member State may himself market the product covered by the trade mark in another Member State, then this also applies to a third party who has duly acquired this product in the first State.

6.2.3.3 *Terrapin (Overseas) v Terranova Industrie* [1976] E.C.R. 1039; [1976] 2 C.M.L.R. 482

The German manufacturer, Terranova, was the registered proprietor in West Germany of trade marks, which included, "Terra" and "Terranova", for its well-known business in finished plaster for facades and other construction materials. The English company, Terrapin, manufactured prefabricated houses and components for their construction under its name. Terrapin was denied registration of its mark, and was sued for trade mark infringement by Terranova. In the latter proceedings the Oberlandesgericht, Munich, found infringement. In a subsequent appeal, the Bundesgerichtshof referred to the CJ EC the following question under Article 177:

"Is it compatible with the provisions relating to the free movement of goods (Articles 30 and 36 of the EEC Treaty) that an undertaking established in Member State A, by using its commercial name and trade-mark rights existing there, should prevent the import of similar goods of an undertaking established in Member State B if these goods have been lawfully given a distinguishing name which may be confused with the commercial name and trade-mark which are protected in State A for the undertaking established there, if there are no relations between the two undertakings, if their national trade-mark rights arose autonomously and independently of one another (no common origin) and at the present time there exist no economic or legal relations of any kind other than those appertaining to trade-marks between the undertakings?"

The CJ EC held:

It is for the court of first instance, after considering the similarity of the products and the risk of confusion, to enquire further in the context of this last provision whether the exercise in a particular case of industrial and commercial property rights may or may not constitute a means of arbitrary discrimination or a disguised restriction on trade between Member States. It is for the national court in this respect to ascertain in particular whether the rights in question are in fact exercised by the proprietor with the same strictness whatever the national origin of any possible infringer.

The Court then referred to its interpretation of Articles 30 and 36, and continued:

6 It follows from the above that the proprietor of an industrial or commercial property right protected by the law of a Member State cannot rely on that law to prevent the importation of a product which has lawfully been marketed in another Member State by the proprietor himself or with his consent. It is the same when the right relied on is the result of the subdivision, either by voluntary act or as a result of public constraint, of a trade-mark right which originally belonged to one and the same proprietor. In these cases the basic function of the trade-mark to guarantee to consumers that the product has the same origin is already undermined by the

subdivision of the original right. Even where the rights in question belong to different proprietors the protection given to industrial and commercial property by national law may not be relied on when the exercise of those rights is the purpose, the means or the result of an agreement prohibited by the Treaty. In all these cases the effect of invoking the territorial nature of national laws protecting industrial and commercial property is to legitimise the insulation of national markets without this partitioning within the common market being justified by the protection of a legitimate interest on the part of the proprietor of the trade-mark or business name.

7 On the other hand in the present state of Community law an industrial or commercial property right legally acquired in a Member State may legally be used to prevent under the first sentence of Article 36 of the Treaty the import of products marketed under a name giving rise to confusion where the rights in question have been acquired by different and independent proprietors under different national laws. If in such a case the principle of the free movement of goods were to prevail over the protection given by the respective national laws, the specific objective of industrial and commercial property rights would be undermined. In the particular situation the requirements of the free movement of goods and the safeguarding of industrial and commercial property rights must be so reconciled that protection is ensured for the legitimate use of the rights conferred by national laws, coming within the prohibitions on imports "justified" within the meaning of Article 36 of the Treaty, but denied on the other hand in respect of any improper exercise of the same rights of such a nature as to maintain or effect artificial partitions within the common market.

6.2.3.4 *Hoffmann-La Roche v Centrafarm* [1978] E.C.R. 1139; [1979] 3 C.M.L.R. 217 (CJ EC)

Hoffmann-La Roche sold their well-known tranquilliser, "Valium", in Britain in packets of 100 or 500 tablets. In Germany its packaging was in lots of 20 or 50 for individual use and 100 or 250 for hospitals. The British price was substantially lower than the German. Centrafarm accordingly purchased British supplies and repackaged them in batches of 1000 which were acceptable for the German market before reselling them there. It marked its own packages "Valium" and "Roche" – and stated its identity as the firm marketing the drug. This practice constituted an infringement of German trade-mark law. The issue was whether it was nonetheless permissible under Arts. 30–36.

The CJ EC held:

7 In relation to trade-marks, the specific subject-matter is in particular to guarantee to the proprietor of the trade-mark that he has the exclusive right to use that trade-mark for the purpose of putting a product into circulation for the first time and therefore to protect him against competitors wishing to take advantage of the status and reputation of the trade-mark by selling products illegally bearing that trade-mark. In order to answer the question whether that exclusive right involves the right to prevent the trade-mark being affixed by a third person after the product has been repackaged, regard must be had to the essential function of the trade-mark, which is to guarantee the identity of the origin of the trade-marked product to the consumer or ultimate user, by enabling him without any possibility of confusion to distinguish that product from products which have another origin. This guarantee of origin means that the consumer or ultimate user can be certain that a trade-marked product which is sold to him has not been subject at a previous stage of marketing to interference by a third person, without the authorisation of the

proprietor of the trade-mark, such as to affect the original condition of the product. The right attributed to the proprietor of preventing any use of the trade-mark which is likely to impair the guarantee of origin so understood is therefore part of the specific subject-matter of the trade-mark right.

8 It is accordingly justified under the first sentence of Article 36 to recognise that the proprietor of a trade-mark is entitled to prevent an importer of a trade-mark product, following repackaging of that product, from affixing the trade-mark to the new packaging without the authorisation of the proprietor.

9 It is, however, necessary to consider whether the exercise of such a right may constitute a "disguised restriction on trade between Member States" within the meaning of the second sentence of Article 36. Such a restriction might arise, *inter alia*, from the proprietor of the trade-mark putting onto the market in various Member States an identical product in various packages while availing himself of the rights inherent in the trade-mark to prevent repackaging by a third person even if it were done in such a way that the identity of origin of the trade-marked product and its original condition could not be affected. The question, therefore, in the present case is whether the repackaging of a trade-marked product such as that undertaken by Centrafarm is capable of affecting the original condition of the product.

10 In this respect the answer must vary according to the circumstances and in particular according to the nature of the product and the method of repackaging. Depending on the nature of the product repackaging in many cases inevitably affects its condition, while in others repackaging involves a more or less obvious risk that the product might be interfered with or its original condition otherwise affected. Nevertheless, it is possible to conceive of the repackaging being under-taken in such a way that the original condition of the product cannot be affected. This may be so where, for example, the proprietor of the trade-mark has marketed the product in a double packaging and the repackaging affects only the external packaging, leaving the internal packaging intact, or where the repackaging is inspected by a public authority for the purpose of ensuring that the product is not adversely affected. Where the essential function of the trade-mark to guarantee the origin of the product is thus protected, the exercise of his rights by the proprietor of the trade-mark in order to fetter the free movement of goods between Member States may constitute a disguised restriction within the meaning of the second sentence of Article 36 of the Treaty if it is established that the use of the trade-mark right by the proprietor, having regard to the marketing system which he has adopted, will contribute to the artificial partitioning of the markets between Member States.

11 Although this conclusion is unavoidable in the interests of freedom of trade, it amounts to giving the trader, who sells the imported product with the trade-mark affixed to the new packaging without the authorisation of the proprietor, a certain licence which in normal circumstances is reserved to the proprietor himself. In the interests of the proprietor as trade-mark owner and to protect him against any abuse it is therefore right to allow such licence only where it is shown that the repackaging cannot adversely affect the original condition of the product.

12 Since it is in the proprietor's interest that the consumer should not be misled as to the origin of the product, it is moreover right to allow the trader to sell the imported product with the trade-mark affixed to the new packaging only on condition that he gives the proprietor of the mark prior notice and that he states on the new packaging that the product has been repackaged by him.

13 It follows from what has been stated above that, subject to consideration of the facts of a particular case, it is irrelevant in answering the legal question raised regarding the substance of trade-mark law that the question referred by the national court is exclusively concerned with medicinal products.

14 The first question must therefore be answered to the effect that:

(a) The proprietor of a trade-mark right which is protected in two Member States at the same time is justified pursuant to the first sentence of Article 36 of the EEC Treaty in preventing a product to which the trade-mark has lawfully been applied in one of those States from being marketed in the other Member State after it has been repacked in new packaging to which the trade-mark has been affixed by a third party.

(b) However, such prevention of marketing constitutes a disguised restriction on trade between Member States within the meaning of the second sentence of Article 36 where:
  – It is established that the use of the trade-mark right by the proprietor, having regard to the marketing system which he has adopted, will contribute to the artificial partitioning of the markets between Member States;
  – It is shown that the repackaging cannot adversely affect the original condition of the product;
  – The proprietor of the mark receives prior notice of the marketing of the repackaged product; and
  – It is stated on the new packaging by whom the product has been repackaged.

The Court also held that there was no abuse of dominant position under Art. 86.

Note that in Pfizer v Eurim-Pharm [1981] E.C.R. 2913, [1982] C.M.L.R. 406, the Court considered the application of this judgment to a case where the parallel importer repackaged the 5-capsule blister strips put out by the manufacturer of a drug into larger packets; these were transparent so that the manufacturer's name and trade-mark for the drug could be seen within, the name and address of manufacturer and repacker were clearly stated and a leaflet to comply with German law was included. The Court stated:

10 No use of the trade mark in a manner liable to impair the guarantee of origin takes place in a case such as the one in point where, according to the findings of the national court and the terms of the question submitted by it, a parallel importer has re-packaged a pharmaceutical product merely by replacing the outer wrapping without touching the internal packaging and by making the trade mark affixed by the manufacturer on the internal packaging visible through the new external wrapping.

11 In such circumstances the re-packaging in fact involves no risk of exposing the product to interference or influences which might affect its original condition and the consumer or final user of the product is not liable to be misled as to the origin of the product, above all where, as in this case, the parallel importer has clearly indicated on the external wrapping that the product was manufactured by a subsidiary of the proprietor of the trade mark and has been re-packaged by the importer.

12 The fact that the parallel importer inserted in the external packaging a leaflet containing information relating to the medicinal product – a fact which is not even mentioned in the question submitted – does not affect this conclusion.

6.2.3.5 *American Home Products v Centrafarm* [1978] E.C.R. 1823; [1979] 1 C.M.L.R. 326 (CJ EC)

American Home Products marketed a drug containing the tranquillising constituent, oxazepamum, for which it had patents in the Netherlands and the UK. In the Netherlands, it used the registered Benelux mark, "Seresta" and in the UK the registered mark, "Serenid D". The two products had identical therapeutic effects, though they were not quite the same, differing particularly in taste. Centrafarm purchased supplies of "Serenid D" in the UK and marketed them as "Seresta" in the Netherlands, giving its own name in addition to this latter mark.

In infringement proceedings upon the Benelux registration, the Rotterdam court referred the question to the CJ EC, whether a finding of infringement in these circumstances would be consistent with the Rome Treaty rules concerning the free movement of goods.

After referring to its interpretation of Articles 30 and 36 in relation to intellectual property rights, the Court stated:

11 In relation to trade-marks, the specific subject-matter is in particular the guarantee to the proprietor of the trade-mark that he has the exclusive right to use that trade-mark for the purpose of putting a product into circulation for the first time and therefore his protection against competitors wishing to take advantage of the status and reputation of the mark by selling products illegally bearing that trade-mark.

12 In order to establish in exceptional circumstances the precise scope of that exclusive right granted to the proprietor of the mark regard must be had to the essential function of the trade-mark, which is to guarantee the identity of the origin of the trade-marked product to the consumer or ultimate user.

13 This guarantee of origin means that only the proprietor may confer an identity upon the product by affixing the mark.

14 The guarantee of origin would in fact be jeopardised if it were permissible for a third party to affix the mark to the product, even to an original product.

15 It is thus in accordance with the essential function of the mark that national legislation, even where the manufacturer or distributor is the proprietor of two different marks for the same product, prevents an unauthorised third party from usurping the right to affix one or other mark to any part whatsoever of the production or to change the marks affixed by the proprietor to different parts of the production.

16 The guarantee of the origin of the product requires that the exclusive right of the proprietor should be protected in the same manner where the different parts of the production, bearing different marks, come from two different Member States.

17 The right granted to the proprietor to prohibit any unauthorised affixing of his mark to his product accordingly comes within the specific subject-matter of the trade-mark.

18 The proprietor of a trade-mark which is protected in one Member State is accordingly justified pursuant to the first sentence of Article 36 in preventing a product from being marketed by a third party in that Member State under the mark in question even if previously that product has been lawfully marketed in another Member State under another mark held in the latter State by the same proprietor.

19 Nevertheless it is still necessary to consider whether the exercise of that right may constitute a "disguised restriction on trade between Member States" within the

meaning of the second sentence of Article 36.

6.2.3.6   *Kohl v Ringelhan & Rennett* [1984] E.C.R. 3651; [1985] 3 C.M.L.R. 340 (CJ EC)

Ringelhan & Rennett was a German supplier of pharmacy equipment with a well-known symbol, "r+r". In France it operated through a subsidiary. Upon it becoming insolvent in 1982, the French subsidiary was sold to a third party and the German business ceased. In 1983, Kohl, the other main supplier of such equipment in Germany, brought proceedings under the German Law against Unfair Competition, Art. 3, alleging that the French company and its new German agent were exporting and selling "r+r" equipment in Germany in a way which would lead purchasers to believe that they were buying from the old German company or its group.

The CJ EC answered an Art. 177 question concerning this as follows:

10   It should first be pointed out that in this case the undertaking seeking to restrain the use in the Federal Republic of Germany of the distinctive symbol in question does not rely on the fact that it is itself the proprietor of a similar distinctive symbol or of another industrial property right, such as a trade mark, and that the use of the symbol in question by the French undertaking might interfere with those rights or cause confusion in the mind of the German public between its own products and those of the French undertaking. It simply argues that the use of the symbol in question is misleading on the sole ground that it might be regarded by the German public as a reference to another German undertaking which has since been wound up.

11   Thus the question raised concerns the compatibility with the Treaty of a legal provision in one Member State making it possible to prohibit the use of a distinctive symbol by an undertaking established in another Member State where its use is lawful in that other Member State and was also lawful in the first Member State until the dissolution of the group which associated the undertaking in question with a company established in the first Member State.

12   Theodor Kohl KG, the plaintiff in the main proceedings, and the Government of the Federal Republic of Germany pointed out in that regard that the Court has held in previous judgments that, in the absence of common rules, obstacles to intra-Community trade resulting from disparities between national legislation must be accepted in so far as such legislation being applicable to domestic products and imported products without distinction, is necessary in order to satisfy imperative requirements relating *inter alia* to consumer protection and fair trading.

13   According to the Ringelhan companies, the defendants in the main proceedings, the Government of the French Republic and the Commission, that principle does not apply to a case such as this, where the obstacle to trade created by the application of national legislation is a result of the liquidation of a German company and the dissolution of the group composed of it and a French undertaking. It is contended that such circumstances cannot have the result of allowing a competitor on the German market to invoke consumer protection where he could not do so before the dissolution of the group.

14   It must first be considered whether national legislation of the type concerned in this case may be regarded, from the point of view of its effect on trade between Member States, as being applicable without distinction to domestic and imported products. That is in fact a precondition for the application of the principle laid down in the

judgments cited by Kohl and by the German Government, as the Court explained in particular in its judgment of 17 June 1981 (Case 113/80, *Commission v Ireland*, [1981] ECR 1625).

15 The facts established by the national court and set out in its order show that that condition is not fulfilled in a case such as the present. Even though a provision of national legislation on unfair competition applies without distinction to the marketing of domestic and imported goods, it cannot fulfil the condition referred to above if it is interpreted in such a way that it becomes possible to prohibit the use of a distinctive symbol for the sole reason that the public may be misled as to the domestic or foreign origin of the goods, without its being necessary to adduce evidence of other specific factors establishing the existence of unfair competition. In such a case, the provision in question in fact applies only to the marketing of imported products.

16 To the extent to which it makes it possible to impose such a prohibition, a provision of national law cannot be regarded as legislation applying in a uniform manner to the marketing of domestic products and imported products.

17 Such a provision makes it possible to erect barriers within the Common Market, amounting to a restriction on intra-Community trade prohibited by Article 30 of the Treaty.

18 The German Government further argued that even if the provision of national law in question was contrary to Article 30 it could be justified by reference to Article 36 of the Treaty, since consumer protection falls within a broad interpretation of the concept of public policy referred to in that article.

19 That argument cannot be accepted. Whatever interpretation is to be given to the term "public policy", it cannot be extended so as to include considerations of consumer protection. According to the aforesaid judgment of 17 June 1981, such considerations may in certain circumstances be taken into account in establishing whether national measures applicable without distinction to domestic and imported products are caught by the prohibitions laid down in Article 30; they cannot, however, serve to justify restrictions on imports under Article 36.

6.3 Free Provision of Services and Intellectual Property

6.3.1 *Coditel v Ciné Vog (No. 1)* [1980] E.C.R. 881; [1981] C.M.L.R. (CJ EC)

The copyright owner of the film "Le Boucher" granted the exclusive performing rights in Belgium (including the right of television transmission) to Ciné Vog for a period of seven years. By another licence, the German television channel, ARD, broadcast a German version of the film which the Coditel companies received off air in Belgium and transmitted to their cable subscribers. This amounted to a breach of Ciné Vog's rights for which they sued for damages. Coditel pleaded in defence that such a result would prejudice the free provision of services guaranteed by the Rome Treaty, Art. 59 (see above, 6.1.1) and this issue was referred to the CJ EC by two questions of which the Court found it necessary to answer only the second:

12 A cinematographic film belongs to the category of literary and artistic works made available to the public by performances which may be infinitely repeated. In this respect the problems involved in the observance of copyright in relation to the requirements of the Treaty are not the same as those which arise in connection with literary and artistic works the placing of which at the disposal of the public is inseparable from the circulation of the material form of the works, as in the case of books or records.

13 In these circumstances the owner of the copyright in a film and his assigns have a legitimate interest in calculating the fees due in respect of the authorisation to exhibit the film on the basis of the actual or probable number of performances and in authorising a television broadcast of the film only after it has been exhibited in cinemas for a certain period of time. It appears from the file on the present case that the contract made between Les Films la Boétie and Ciné Vog stipulated that the exclusive right which was assigned included the right to exhibit the film "Le Boucheur" publicly in Belgium by way of projection in cinemas and on television but that the right to have the film diffused by Belgian television could not be exercised until 40 months after the first showing of the film in Belgium.

14 These facts are important in two regards. On the one hand, they highlight the fact that the right of a copyright owner and his assigns to require fees for any showing of a film is part of the essential function of copyright in this type of literary and artistic work. On the other hand, they demonstrate that the exploitation of copyright in films and the fees attaching thereto cannot be regulated without regard being had to the possibility of television broadcasts of those films. The question whether an assignment of copyright limited to the territory of a Member State is capable of constituting a restriction on freedom to provide services must be examined in this context.

15 Whilst Article 59 of the Treaty prohibits restrictions upon freedom to provide services, it does not thereby encompass limits upon the exercise of certain economic activities which have their origin in the application of national legislation for the protection of intellectual property, save where such application constitutes a means of arbitrary discrimination or a disguised restriction on trade between Member States. Such would be the case if that application enabled parties to an assignment of copyright to create artificial barriers to trade between Member States.

16 The effect of this is that, whilst copyright entails the right to demand fees for any

showing or performance, the rules of the Treaty cannot in principle constitute an obstacle to the geographical limits which the parties to a contract of assignment have agreed upon in order to protect the author and his assigns in this regard. The mere fact that those geographical limits may coincide with national frontiers does not point to a different solution in a situation where television is organised in the Member States largely on the basis of legal broadcasting monopolies, which indicates that a limitation other than the geographical field of application of an assignment is often impracticable.

17 The exclusive assignee of the performing right in a film for the whole of a Member State may therefore rely upon his right against cable television diffusion companies which have transmitted that film on their diffusion network having received it from a television broadcasting station established in another Member State, without thereby infringing Community law.

18 Consequently the answer to the second question referred to the Court by the Cour d'Appel, Brussels, should be that the provisions of the Treaty relating to the freedom to provide services do not preclude an assignee of the performing right in a cinematographic film in a Member State from relying upon his right to prohibit the exhibition of that film in that State, without his authority, by means of cable diffusion if the film so exhibited is picked up and transmitted after being broadcast in another Member State by a third party with the consent of the original owner of the right.

Subsequently, a second issue was referred to the CJEC by the Cour d'Appel, Brussels: the right to show the film in Belgium had been licensed exclusively to Ciné Vog, subject to the condition that it would not be televised there within 40 months of its cinema release. This was alleged to constitute a contravention of Art. 85, which would also amount to a defence to the copyright infringement proceedings against Coditel.

The CJEC ruled that it was for the national court to ascertain whether, in a given case, the manner in which such an exclusive right conferred by contract is exercised is subject to a situation in the economic or legal sphere the object or effect of which is to prevent or restrict the distribution of films or to distort competition on the cinematographic market, regard being had to the specific characteristics of that market: Coditel v Ciné Vog (No.2) [1982] E.C.R. 3381.

6.4 Application of Rules of Competition to Intellectual Property

6.4.1 *Nungesser and Eisele v EC Commission* [1982] E.C.R. 2015; [1983] 1 C.M.L.R. 278 (CJ EC)

A French governmental research station, INRA, developed a new variety of maize seed and obtained plant variety rights for it in France. These it licensed in that country to a number of seed producers.

By a set of contractual arrangements INRA in effect granted an exclusive licence of the equivalent rights in West Germany to Eisele and his company, Nungesser. Parallel imports of seed produced in France were in consequence hindered by actions which included legal proceedings by Eisele against one particular parallel importer. In consequence complaints were lodged with the EC Commission, which investigated and decided that the contractual arrangements according Eisele his exclusive position on the German market contravened Art. 85(1) and were not capable of exemption under Art. 85(3). On the central issues in the decision, the West German licensee appealed to the CJ EC.

The Court found that plant variety rights were not distinguishable in basic character from other intellectual property:

43 It is therefore not correct to consider that breeders' rights are a species of commercial or industrial property right with characteristics of so special a nature as to require, in relation to the competition rules, a different treatment from other commercial or industrial property rights. That conclusion does not affect the need to take into consideration, for the purposes of the rules on competition, the specific nature of the products which form the subject-matter of breeders' rights.

Accordingly in relation to the exclusive licensing of plant variety rights, the Court proceeded to distinguish between two categories of obligation, even though the Commission had held that both these categories constituted infractions of Art. 85(1). These were the "open" and the "exclusive" elements in the contractual arrangements:

53 ... The first case concerns a so-called open exclusive licence or assignment and the exclusivity of the licence relates solely to the contractual relationship between the owner of the right and the licensee, whereby the owner merely undertakes not to grant other licences in respect of the same territory and not to compete himself with the licensee on that territory. On the other hand, the second case involves an exclusive licence or assignment with absolute territorial protection, under which the parties to the contract propose, as regards the products and the territory in question, to eliminate all competition from third parties, such as parallel importers or licensees for other territories.

In the contractual arrangements before the Court, the "open" aspects comprised INRA's obligation (and the obligations of those deriving rights from INRA) to refrain from producing or selling seeds in West Germany, or having them produced or sold by another licensee there. The "exclusive" aspects consisted of the obligations on INRA (and those deriving rights from it) to prevent third parties from exploiting the seeds to West Germany without Eisele's authority for use or sale there, and Eisele's concurrent use of his contractual rights and plant breeder's rights to prevent all imports into Germany or exports from there to other Member States.

Of the "open" aspects, the Court, disagreeing with the Commission, held:

56 An exclusive licence which forms the subject-matter of the contested decision concerns the cultivation and marketing of hybrid maize seeds which were developed by INRA after years of research and experimentation and were unknown to German farmers at the time when the cooperation between INRA and the applicants was taking shape. For that reason the concern shown by the interveners as regards the protection of new technology is justified.

57 In fact in the case of a licence of breeders' rights over hybrid maize seeds so developed in one Member State, an undertaking established in another Member State which was not certain that it would not encounter competition from other licensees for the territory granted to it, or from the owner of the right himself, might be deterred from accepting the risk of cultivating and marketing that product; such a result would be damaging to the dissemination of a new technology and would prejudice competition in the Community between the new product and similar existing products.

58 Having regard to the specific nature of the products in question, the Court concludes that, in a case such as the present, the grant of an open exclusive licence, that is to say a licence which does not affect the position of third parties, such as parallel importers and licensees for other territories, is not in fact incompatible with Article 85(1) of the Treaty.

Of the "exclusive" aspects, the Court, accepting the view of the Commission, held:

60 As regard to the position of third parties, the Commission in essence criticises the parties to the contract for having extended the definition of exclusivity to importers who are not bound to the contract, in particular parallel importers. Parallel importers or exporters, such as Louis David KG in Germany and Robert Bomberault in France who offered INRA seed for sale to German buyers, had found themselves subjected to pressure and legal proceedings by INRA, Frasema and the applicants, the purpose of which was to maintain the exclusive position of the applicants on the German market.

61 The Court has consistently held (cf. Joined Cases 56 and 58/64 *Consten and Grundig v Commission* [1966] ECR 299) that absolute territorial protection granted to a licensee in order to enable parallel imports to be controlled and prevented results in the artificial maintenance of separate national markets, contrary to the Treaty.

The Court also agreed with the Commission that, while the contracting parties sought to maintain these "exclusive" aspects of the arrangements, there could be no exemption under Art. 85(3):

74 [In the view of the Caisse de Gestion des Licences Végétales], the territorial protection enjoyed by the licensee in the present case was rather a relative protection on account of the presence on the market of numerous varieties of maize seed which could be substituted for INRA varieties and which could thus enter into direct competition with those varieties.

75 The Commission rightly stated in reply that that view ... concerns the problem of the demarcation of the market; that is a problem which arises when the Commission has to examine whether an agreement affords "the possibility of eliminating competition in respect of a substantial part of the products in question" (Article 85(3)(b)) but which is not relevant to the question whether an agreement is

capable of improving the production or distribution of goods.

76 It must be remembered that under the terms of Article 85(3) of the Treaty an exemption from the prohibition contained in Article 85(1) may be granted in the case of any agreement between undertakings which contributes to improving the production or distribution of goods or to promoting technical progress, and which does not impose on the undertakings concerned restrictions which are not indispensable to the attainment of those objectives.

77 It was a question of seeds intended to be used by a large number of farmers in the production of maize, which is an important product for human and animal foodstuffs, absolute territorial protection manifestly goes beyond what is indispensable for the improvement of production or distribution or the promotion of technical progress, as is demonstrated in particular in the present case by the prohibition, agreed to by both parties to the agreement, of any parallel imports of INRA maize seeds into Germany even if those seeds were bred by INRA itself and marketed in France.

78 It follows that the absolute territorial protection conferred on the licensee, as established to exist by the contested decision, constituted a sufficient reason for refusing to grant an exemption under Article 85(3) of the Treaty. It is therefore no longer necessary to examine the other grounds set out in the decision for refusing to grant such an exemption.

6.4.2 EC Commission Regulation 2349/84. Application of Art. 85(3) to certain Patent Licensing Agreements

In operation: 1.1.1985–31.12.1994: Art. 14.

The Preamble to the Regulation has been omitted. But its 27 Recitals contain statements concerning the objectives of the Regulation which are relevant to the interpretation of the substantive Articles. They should accordingly be referred to in making any complete analysis of the provisions.

Art.1(1) Pursuant to Article 85(3) of the Treaty and subject to the provisions of this Regulation, it is hereby declared that Article 85(1) of the Treaty shall not apply to patent licensing agreements, and agreements combining the licensing of patents and the communication of know-how, to which only two undertakings are party and which include one or more of the following obligations:

1 an obligation on the licensor not to license other undertakings to exploit the licensed invention in the licensed territory, covering all or part of the common market, in so far and as long as one of the licensed patents remains in force;

2 an obligation on the licensor not to exploit the licensed invention in the licensed territory himself in so far and as long as one of the licensed patents remains in force;

3 an obligation on the licensee not to exploit the licensed invention in territories within the common market which are reserved for the licensor, in so far and as long as the patented product is protected in those territories by parallel patents;

4 an obligation on the licensee not to manufacture or use the licensed product, or use the patented process or the communicated know-how, in territories within the common market which are licensed to other licensees in so far and as long as the licensed product is protected in those territories by parallel patents;

5 an obligation on the licensee not to pursue an active policy of putting the licensed product on the market in the territories within the common market which are licensed to other licensees, and in particular not to engage in advertising specifically aimed at those territories or to establish any branch or maintain any distribution depot there, in so far and as long as the licensed product is protected in those territories by parallel patents;

6 an obligation on the licensee not to put the licensed product on the market in the territories licensed to other licensees within the common market for a period not exceeding five years from the date when the product is first put on the market within the common market by the licensor or one of his licensees, in so far as and for as long as the product is protected in these territories by parallel patents;

7 an obligation on the licensee to use only the licensor's trade mark or the get-up determined by the licensor to distinguish the licensed product, provided that the licensee is not prevented from identifying himself as the manufacturer of the licensed product.

(2) The exemption of restrictions on putting the licensed product on the market resulting from the obligations referred to in paragraph 1(2),(3),(5) and (6) shall apply only if the licensee manufactures the licensed product himself or has it manufactured by a connected undertaking or by a subcontractor.

(3) The exemption provided for in paragraph 1 shall also apply where in a particular agreement the parties undertake obligations of the types referred to in that paragraph but with a more limited scope than is permitted by the paragraph.

Art.2(1) Article 1 shall apply notwithstanding the presence in particular of any of the following obligations, which are generally not restrictive of competition:

1 an obligation on the licensee to procure goods or services from the licensor or from an undertaking designated by the licensor, in so far as such products or services are necessary for a technically satisfactory exploitation of the licensed invention;

2 an obligation on the licensee to pay a minimum royalty or to produce a minimum quantity of the licensed product or to carry out a minimum number of operations exploiting the licensed invention;

3 an obligation on the licensee to restrict his exploitation of the licensed invention to one or more technical fields of application covered by the licensed patent;

4 an obligation on the licensee not to exploit the patent after termination of the agreement in so far as the patent is still in force;

5 an obligation on the licensee not to grant sub-licences or assign the licence;

6 an obligation on the licensee to mark the licensed product with an indication of the patentee's name, the licensed patent or the patent licensing agreement;

7 an obligation on the licensee not to divulge know-how communicated by the licensor; the licensee may be held to this obligation even after the agreement has expired;

8 obligations:
   (a) to inform the licensor of infringements of the patent,
   (b) to take legal action against an infringer,
   (c) to assist the licensor in any legal action against an infringer, provided that these obligations are without prejudice to the licensee's right to challenge the validity of the licensed patent;

9 an obligation on the licensee to observe specifications concerning the minimum quality of the licensed product, provided that such specifications are necessary for a technically satisfactory exploitation of the licensed invention, and to allow the licensor to carry out related checks;

10 an obligation on the parties to communicate to one another any experience gained in exploiting the licensed invention and to grant one

another a licence in respect of inventions relating to improvements and new applications, provided that such communication or licence is non-exclusive;

11 an obligation on the licensor to grant the licensee any more favourable terms that the licensor may grant to another undertaking after the agreement is entered into.

(2) In the event that, because of particular circumstances, the obligations referred to in paragraph 1 fall within the scope of Article 85(1), they shall also be exempted even if they are not accompanied by any of the obligations exempted by Article 1.

The exemption provided for in this paragraph shall also apply where in an agreement the parties undertake obligations of the types referred to in paragraph 1 but with a more limited scope than is permitted by that paragraph.

Art.3 Articles 1 and 2(2) shall not apply where:

1 the licensee is prohibited from challenging the validity of licensed patents or other industrial or commercial property rights within the common market belong to the licensor or undertakings connected with him, without prejudice to the right of the licensor to terminate the licensing agreement in the event of such a challenge;

2 the duration of the licensing agreement is automatically prolonged beyond the expiry of the licensed patents existing at the time the agreement was entered into by the inclusion in it of any new patent obtained by the licensor, unless the agreement provides each party with the right to terminate the agreement at least annually after the expiry of the licensed patents existing at the time the agreement was entered into, without prejudice to the right of the licensor to charge royalties for the full period during which the licensee continues to use know-how communicated by the licensor which has not entered into the public domain, even if that period exceeds the life of the patents;

3 one party is restricted from competing with the other party, with undertakings connected with the other party or with other undertakings within the common market in respect of research and development, manufacture, use or sales, save as provided in Article 1 and without prejudice to an obligation on the licensee to use his best endeavours to exploit the licensed invention;

4 the licensee is charged royalties on products which are not entirely or partially patented or manufactured by means of a patented process, or for the use of know-how which has entered into the public domain otherwise than by the fault of the licensee or an undertaking connected with him, without prejudice to arrangements whereby, in order to facilitate payment, the royalty payments for the use of a licensed invention are spread over a period extending beyond the life of the licensed patents or the entry of the know-how into the public domain;

5 the quantity of licensed products one party may manufacture or sell or

the number of operations exploiting the licensed invention he may carry out are subject to limitations;

6 one party is restricted in the determination of prices, components of prices or discounts for the licensed products;

7 one party is restricted as to the customers he may serve, in particular by being prohibited from supplying certain classes of user, employing certain forms of distribution or, with the aim of sharing customers, using certain types of packaging for the products, save as provided in Article 1(1)(7) and Article 2(1)(3);

8 the licensee is obliged to assign wholly or in part to the licensor rights in or to patents for improvements or for new applications of the licensed patents;

9 the licensee is induced at the time the agreement is entered into to accept further licences which he does not want or to agree to use patents, goods or services which he does not want, unless such patents, products or services are necessary for a technically satisfactory exploitation of the licensed invention;

10 without prejudice to Article 1(1)(5), the licensee is required, for a period exceeding that permitted under Article 1(1)(6), not to put the licensed product on the market in territories licensed to other licensees within the common market or does not do so as a result of a concerted practice between the parties;

11 one or both of the parties are required:
   (a) to refuse without any objectively justified reason to meet demand from users or resellers in their respective territories who would market products in other territories within the common market;
   (b) to make it difficult for users or resellers to obtain the products from other resellers within the common market, and in particular to exercise industrial or commercial property rights or take measures so as to prevent users or resellers from obtaining outside, or from putting on the market in, the licensed territory products which have been lawfully put on the market within the common market by the patentee or with his consent; or do so as a result of a concerted practice between them.

Art.4(1) The exemption provided for in Articles 1 and 2 shall also apply to agreements containing obligations restrictive of competition which are not covered by those Articles and do not fall within the scope of Article 3, on condition that the agreements in question are notified to the Commission in accordance with the provisions of Commission Regulation No. 27 as last amended by Regulation (EEC) No 1699/75, and that the Commission does not oppose such exemption within a period of six months.

Art. 4(2)–4(9) contain further provisions relating to the opposition procedure.

Art.5(1) This Regulation shall not apply:

1 to agreements between members of a patent pool which relate to the pooled patents;

2 to patent licensing agreements between competitors who hold interests in a joint venture or between one of them and the joint venture, if the licensing agreements relate to the activities of the joint venture;

3 to agreements under which one party grants to the other party a patent licence and that other party, albeit in separate agreements or through connected undertakings, grants to the first party a licence under patents or trade-marks or reciprocal sales rights for unprotected products or communicates to him know-how, where the parties are competitors in relation to the products covered by those agreements;

4 to licensing agreements in respect of plant breeder's rights.

(2) However, this Regulation shall apply to reciprocal licences of the types referred to in paragraph 1(3) where the parties are not subject to any territorial restriction within the common market on the manufacture, use or putting on the market of the products covered by these agreements or on the use of the licensed processes.

Art. 6 deals with pre-1962 agreements; Art. 7 with 1962–66 agreements; Art. 8 with pre-Accession agreements (UK, Ireland, Denmark, Greece).

Art.9 The Commission may withdraw the benefit of this Regulation, pursuant to Article 7 of Regulation No 19/65/EEC, where it finds in a particular case that an agreement exempted by this Regulation nevertheless has certain effects which are incompatible with the conditions laid down in Article 85(3) of the Treaty, and in particular where:

1 such effects arise from an arbitration award;

2 the licensed products or the services provided using a licensed process are not exposed to effective competition in the licensed territory from identical products or services or products or services considered by users as equivalent in view of their characteristics, price and intended use;

3 the licensor does not have the right to terminate the exclusivity granted to the licensee at the latest five years from the date the agreement was entered into and at least annually thereafter if, without legitimate reason, the licensee fails to exploit the patent or to do so adequately;

4 without prejudice to Article 1(1)(6), the licensee refuses, without objectively valid reason, to meet unsolicited demand from users or resellers in the territory of other licensees;

5 one or both of the parties;
   (a) without any objectively justified reason, refuse to meet demand from users or resellers in their respective territories who would market the products in other territories within the common market; or
   (b) make it difficult for users or resellers to obtain the products from other resellers within the common market, and in particular where they exercise industrial or commercial property rights or take measures so as to prevent resellers or users from obtaining outside, or from putting on the market in, the licensed territory products which have been lawfully put on the market within the common

market by the patentee or with his consent.

Art.10(1) This Regulation shall apply to:
  (a) patent applications;
  (b) utility models;
  (c) applications for registration of utility models;
  (d) "certificats d'utilité" and "certificats d'addition" under French law; and
  (e) applications for "certificats d'utilité" and "certificats d'addition" under French law; equally as it applies to patents.

(2) This Regulation shall also apply to agreements relating to the exploitation of an invention if an application within the meaning of paragraph 1 is made in respect of the invention for the licensed territory within one year from the date when the agreement was entered into.

Art.11 This Regulation shall also apply to:
(1) patent licensing agreements where the licensor is not the patentee but is authorised by the patentee to grant a licence or a sub-licence;
(2) assignments of a patent or of a right to a patent where the sum payable in consideration of the assignment is dependent upon the turnover attained by the assignee in respect of the patented products, the quantity of such products manufactured or the number of operations carried out employing the patented invention;
(3) patent licensing agreements in which rights or obligations of the licensor or the licensee are assumed by undertakings connected with them.

Art. 12 defines "connected undertakings" in terms virtually identical to those in the Know-How Agreements exemption (6.4.3 below) Art. 2.13.

6.4.3 EC Commission Regulation 556/89: Application of Art. 85(3) to certain Know-How Agreements

In operation: 1.4.1989 – 31.12.1999: Art. 12.

The Preamble (comprising 22 Recitals) is omitted; but see Introductory Note to 6.4.2 above.

Art.1(1) Pursuant to Article 85(3) of the Treaty and subject to the provisions of this Regulation, it is hereby declared that Article 85(1) of the Treaty shall not apply to pure know-how licensing agreements and to mixed know-how and patent licensing agreements not exempted by Regulation (EEC) No 2349/84, including those agreements containing ancillary provisions relating to trademarks or other intellectual property rights, to which only two undertakings are party and which include one or more of the following obligations:

1 an obligation on the licensor not to license other undertakings to exploit the licensed technology in the licensed territory;

2 an obligation on the licensor not to exploit the licensed technology in the licensed territory himself;

3 an obligation on the licensee not to exploit the licensed technology in territories within the common market which are reserved for the licensor;

4 an obligation on the licensee not to manufacture or use the licensed product, or use the licensed process, in territories within the common market which are licensed to other licensees;

5 an obligation on the licensee not to pursue an active policy of putting the licensed product on the market in the territories within the common market which are licensed to other licensees, and in particular not to engage in advertising specifically aimed at those territories or to establish any branch or maintain any distribution depot there;

6 an obligation on the licensee not to put the licensed product on the market in the territories licensed to other licensees within the common market;

7 an obligation on the licensee to use only the licensor's trademark or the get-up determined by the licensor to distinguish the licensed product during the term of the agreement, provided that the licensee is not prevented from identifying himself as the manufacturer of the licensed products;

8 an obligation on the licensee to limit his production of the licensed product to the quantities he requires in manufacturing his own products and to sell the licensed product only as an integral part of or a replacement part for his own products or otherwise in connection with the sale of his own products, provided that such quantities are freely determined by the licensee.

(2) The exemption provided for the obligations referred to in paragraph 1(1)(2) and (3) shall extend for a period not exceeding for each licensed

territory within the EEC 10 years from the date of signature of the first licence agreement entered into by the licensor for that territory in respect of the same technology.

The exemption provided for the obligations referred to in paragraph 1(4) and (5) shall extend for a period not exceeding 10 years from the date of signature of the first licence agreement entered into by the licensor within the EEC in respect of the same technology.

The exemption provided for the obligation referred to in paragraph 1(6) shall extend for a period not exceeding five years from the date of the signature of the first licence agreement entered into by the licensor within the EEC in respect of the same technology.

(3) The exemption provided for in paragraph 1 shall apply only where the parties have identified in any appropriate form the initial know-how and any subsequent improvements to it, which become available to the parties and are communicated to the other party pursuant to the terms of the agreement and for the purpose thereof, and only for as long as the know-how remains secret and substantial.

(4) In so far as the obligations referred to in paragraph 1(1) to (5) concern territories including Member States in which the same technology is protected by necessary patents, the exemption provided for in paragraph 1 shall extend for those Member States as long as the licensed product or process is protected in those Member States by such patents, where the duration of such protection exceeds the periods specified in paragraph 2.

(5) The exemption of restrictions on putting the licensed product on the market resulting from the obligations referred to in paragraph 1(2), (3), (5) and (6) shall apply only if the licensee manufactures or proposes to manufacture the licensed product himself or has it manufactured by a connected undertaking or by a subcontractor.

(6) The exemption provided for in paragraph 1 shall also apply where in a particular agreement the parties undertake obligations of the types referred to in that paragraph but with a more limited scope than is permitted by the paragraph.

(7) For the purposes of the present Regulation the following terms shall have the following meanings:

1 "know-how" means a body of technical information that is secret, substantial and identified in any appropriate form;

2 the term "secret" means that the know-how package as a body or in the precise configuration and assembly of its components is not generally known or easily accessible, so that part of its value consists in the lead-time the licensee gains when it is communicated to him; it is not limited to the narrow sense that each individual component of the know-how should be totally unknown or unobtainable outside the licensor's business;

3 the term "substantial" means that the know-how includes information which is of importance for the whole or a significant part of (i) a manufacturing process or (ii) a product or service, or (iii) for the

development thereof and excludes information which is trivial. Such know-how must thus be useful, ie can reasonably be expected at the date of conclusion of the agreement to be capable of improving the competitive position of the licensee, for example by helping him to enter a new market or giving him an advantage in competition with other manufacturers or providers of services who do not have access to the licensed secret know-how or other comparable secret know-how;

4 the term "identified" means that the know-how is described or recorded in such a manner as to make it possible to verify that it fulfils the criteria of secrecy and substantiality and to ensure that the licensee is not unduly restricted in his exploitation of his own technology. To be identified the know-how can either be set out in the licence agreement or in a separate document or recorded in any other appropriate form at the latest when the know-how is transferred or shortly thereafter, provided that the separate document or other record can be made available if the need arises;

5 "pure know-how licensing agreements" are agreements whereby one undertaking, the licensor, agrees to communicate the know-how, with or without an obligation to disclose any subsequent improvements, to another undertaking, the licensee, for exploitation in the licensed territory;

6 "mixed know-how and patent licensing agreements" are agreements not exempted by Regulation (EEC) No 2349/84 under which a technology containing both non-patented elements and elements that are patented in one or more Member States is licensed;

7 the terms "licensed know-how" or "licensed technology" mean the initial and any subsequent know-how communicated directly or indirectly by the licensor to a licensee by means of pure or mixed know-how and patent licensing agreements; however, in the case of mixed know-how and patent licensing agreements the term "licensed technology" also includes any patents for which a licence is granted besides the communication of the know-how;

8 the term "the same technology" means the technology as licensed to the first licensee and enhanced by any improvements made thereto subsequently, irrespective of whether and to what extent such improvements are exploited by the parties or the other licensees and irrespective of whether the technology is protected by necessary patents in any Member States;

9 "the licensed products" are goods or services the production or provision of which requires the use of the licensed technology;

10 the term "exploitation" refers to any use of the licensed technology in particular in the production, active or passive sales in a territory even if not coupled with manufacture in that territory, or leasing of the licensed products;

11 "the licensed territory" is the territory covering all or at least part of the common market where the licensee is entitled to exploit the licensed technology;

12 "territory reserved for the licensor" means territories in which the licensor has not granted any licences and which he has expressly reserved for himself;

13 "connected undertakings" means:
   (a) undertakings in which a party to the agreement, directly or indirectly;
       – owns more than half the capital or business assets, or
       – has the power to exercise more than half the voting rights, or
       – has the power to appoint more than half the members of the supervisory board, board of directors or bodies legally representing the undertaking, or
       – has the right to manage the affairs of the undertaking;
   (b) undertakings which directly or indirectly have in or over a party to the agreement the rights or powers listed in (a);
   (c) undertakings in which an undertaking referred to in (b) directly or indirectly has the rights or powers listed in (a);
   (d) undertakings in which the parties to the agreement or undertakings connected with them jointly have the rights or powers listed in (a): such jointly controlled undertakings are considered to be connected with each of the parties to the agreement.

Art.2(1) Article 1 shall apply notwithstanding the presence in particular of any of the following obligations, which are generally not restrictive of competition:

1 an obligation on the licensee not to divulge the know-how communicated by the licensor; the licensee may be held to this obligation after the agreement has expired;

2 an obligation on the licensee not to grant sublicences or assign the licence;

3 an obligation on the licensee not to exploit the licensed know-how after termination of the agreement in so far and as long as the know-how is still secret;

4 an obligation on the licensee to communicate to the licensor any experience gained in exploiting the licensed technology and to grant him a non-exclusive licence in respect of improvements to or new applications of that technology, provided that:
   (a) the licensee is not prevented during or after the term of the agreement from freely using his own improvements, in so far as these are severable from the licensor's know-how, or licensing them to third parties where licensing to third parties does not disclose the know-how communicated by the licensor that is still secret; this is without prejudice to an obligation on the licensee to seek the licensor's prior approval to such licensing provided that approval may not be withheld unless there are objectively justifiable reasons to believe that licensing improvements to third parties will disclose the licensor's know-how, and
   (b) the licensor has accepted an obligation, whether exclusive or not, to communicate his own improvements to the licensee and his right to

use the licensee's improvements which are not severable from the licensed know-how does not extend beyond the date on which the licensee's right to exploit the licensor's know-how comes to an end, except for termination of the agreement for breach by the licensee; this is without prejudice to an obligation on the licensee to give the licensor the option to continue to use the improvements after that date, if at the same time he relinquishes the post-term use ban or agrees, after having had an opportunity to examine the licensee's improvements, to pay appropriate royalties for their use;

5 an obligation on the licensee to observe minimum quality specifications for the licensed product or to procure goods or services from the licensor or from an undertaking designated by the licensor, in so far as such quality specifications, products or services are necessary for:
   (a) a technically satisfactory exploitation of the licensed technology, or
   (b) for ensuring that the production of the licensee conforms to the quality standards that are respected by the licensor and other licensees, and to allow the licensor to carry out related checks;

6 Obligations:
   (a) to inform the licensor of misappropriation of the know-how or of infringements of the licensed patents, or
   (b) to take or to assist the licensor in taking legal action against such misappropriation or infringements, provided that these obligations are without prejudice to the licensee's right to challenge the validity of the licensed patents or to contest the secrecy of the licensed know-how except where he himself has in some way contributed to its disclosure;

7 an obligation on the licensee, in the event of the know-how becoming publicly known other than by action of the licensor, to continue paying until the end of the agreement the royalties in the amounts, for the periods and according to the methods freely determined by the parties, without prejudice to the payment of any additional damages in the event of the know-how becoming publicly known by the action of the licensee in breach of the agreement;

8 an obligation on the licensee to restrict his exploitation of the licensed technology to one or more technical fields of application covered by the licensed technology or to one or more product markets;

9 an obligation on the licensee to pay a minimum royalty or to produce a minimum quantity of the licensed product or to carry out a minimum number of operations exploiting the licensed technology;

10 an obligation on the licensor to grant the licensee any more favourable terms that the licensor may grant to another undertaking after the agreement is entered into;

11 an obligation on the licensee to mark the licensed product with the licensor's name;

12 an obligation on the licensee not to use the licensor's know-how to construct facilities for third parties; this is without prejudice to the right of the licensee to increase the capacity of its facilities or to set up additional facilities for its own use on normal commercial terms, includ-

ing the payment of additional royalties.

(2) In the event that, because of particular circumstances, the obligations referred to in paragraph 1 fall within the scope of Article 85(1), they shall also be exempted even if they are not accompanied by any of the obligations exempted by Article 1.

(3) The exemption provided for in paragraph 2 shall also apply where in an agreement the parties undertake obligations of the types referred to in paragraph 1 but with a more limited scope than is permitted by that paragraph.

Art.3 Articles 1 and 2(2) shall not apply where:

1 the licensee is prevented from continuing to use the licensed know-how after the termination of the agreement where the know-how has meanwhile become publicly known, other than by the action of the licensee in breach of the agreement;

2 the licensee is obliged either:
   (a) to assign in whole or in part to the licensor rights to improvements to or new applications of the licensed technology;
   (b) to grant the licensor an exclusive licence for improvements to or new applications of the licensed technology which would prevent the licensee during the currency of the agreement and/or thereafter from using his own improvements in so far as these are severable from the licensor's know-how, or from licensing them to third parties, where such licensing would not disclose the licensor's know-how that is still secret; or
   (c) in the case of an agreement which also includes a post-term use ban, to grant back to the licensor, even on a non-exclusive and reciprocal basis, licences for improvements which are not severable from the licensor's know-how, if the licensor's right to use the improvements is of a longer duration than the licensee's right to use the licensor's know-how, except for termination of the agreement for breach by the licensee;

3 the licensee is obliged at the time the agreement is entered into to accept quality specifications or further licences or to procure goods or services which he does not want, unless such licences, quality specifications, goods or services are necessary for a technically satisfactory exploitation of the licensed technology or for ensuring that the production of the licensee conforms to the quality standards that are respected by the licensor and other licensees;

4 the licensee is prohibited from contesting the secrecy of the licensed know-how or from challenging the validity of licensed patents within the common market belonging to the licensor or undertakings connected with him, without prejudice to the right of the licensor to terminate the licensing agreement in the event of such a challenge;

5 the licensee is charged royalties on goods or services which are not entirely or partially produced by means of the licensed technology or for the use of know-how which has become publicly known by the action of

the licensor or an undertaking connected with him;

6 one party is restricted within the same technological field of use or within the same product market as to the customers he may serve, in particular by being prohibited from supplying certain classes of user, employing certain forms of distribution or, with the aim of sharing customers, using certain types of packaging for the products, save as provided in Article 1(1)(7) and Article 4(2);

7 the quantity of the licensed products one party may manufacture or sell or the number of operations exploiting the licensed technology he may carry out are subject to limitations, save as provided in Article 1(1)(8) and Article 4(2);

8 one party is restricted in the determination of process, components of prices or discounts for the licensed products;

9 one party is restricted from competing with the other party, with undertakings connected with the other party or with other undertakings within the common market in respect of research and development, production or use of competing products and their distribution, without prejudice to an obligation on the licensee to use his best endeavours to exploit the licensed technology and without prejudice to the right of the licensor to terminate the exclusivity granted to the licensee and cease communicating improvements in the event of the licensee's engaging in any such competing activities and to require the licensee to prove that the licensed know-how is not used for the production of goods and services other than those licensed;

10 the initial duration of the licensing agreement is automatically prolonged by the inclusion in it of any new improvements communicated by the licensor, unless the licensee has the right to refuse such improvements or each party has the right to terminate the agreement at the expiry of the initial term of the agreement and at least every three years thereafter;

11 the licensor is required, albeit in separate agreements, for a period exceeding that permitted under Article 1(2) not to license other undertakings to exploit the same technology in the licensed territory, or a party is required for periods exceeding those permitted under Articles 1(2) or 1(4) not to exploit the same technology in the territory of the other party or of other licensees;

12 one or both of the parties are required:
   (a) to refuse without any objectively justified reason to meet demand from users or resellers in their respective territories who would market products in other territories within the common market;
   (b) to make it difficult for users or resellers to obtain the products from other resellers within the common market, and in particular to exercise intellectual property rights or take measures so as to prevent users or resellers from obtaining outside, or from putting on the market in the licensed territory products which have been lawfully put on the market within the common market by the licensor or with his consent;
   or do so as a result of a concerted practice between them.

Art. 4 provides an Opposition Procedure for similar agreements in terms equivalent to those in the Patent Licence Exemption (above, 6.4.2.) Art. 4.

Art.5(1) This Regulation shall not apply to:

1 agreements between members of a patent or know-how pool which relate to the pooled technologies;

2 know-how licensing agreements between competing undertakings which hold interests in a joint venture, or between one of them and the joint venture, if the licensing agreements relate to the activities of the joint venture;

3 agreements under which one party grants the other a know-how licence and the other party, albeit in separate agreements or through connected undertakings, grants the first party a patent, trademark or know-how licence or exclusive sales rights, where the parties are competitors in relation to the products covered by those agreements;

4 agreements including the licensing of intellectual property rights other than patents (in particular trademarks, copyright and design rights) or the licensing of software except where these rights or the software are of assistance in achieving the object of the licensed technology and there are no obligations restrictive of competition other than those also attached to the licensed know-how and exempted under the present Regulation.

(2) However, this Regulation shall apply to reciprocal licences of the types referred to in paragraph 1(3) where the parties are not subject to any territorial restriction within the common market on the manufacture, use or putting on the market of the products covered by the agreements or on the use of the licensed technologies.

Art.6 This Regulation shall also apply to:

1 pure know-how agreements or mixed agreements where the licensor is not the developer of the know-how or the patentee but is authorised by the developer or the patentee to grant a licence or a sub-licence;

2 assignments of know-how or of know-how and patents where the risk associated with exploitation remains with the assignor, in particular where the sum payable in consideration of the assignment is dependent upon the turnover attained by the assignee in respect of products made using the know-how or the patents, the quantity of such products manufactured or the number of operations carried out employing the know-how or the patents;

3 pure know-how agreements or mixed agreements in which rights or obligations of the licensor or the licensee are assumed by undertakings connected with them.

Art. 7 gives the Commission power to withdraw the benefit of the Regulation in specified cases; these are equivalent to those in the Patent Licence Exemption (above 6.4.2) Art. 9. Art. 8 relates to pre-1962 agreements, Art. 9 to 1962–66 agreements, and Art. 10 to pre-Accession agreements. Art. 11 restricts the use of information acquired.

7 ENFORCEMENT PROCEDURES

7.1 Civil Actions

7.1.1 Interlocutory Injunction

7.1.1.1 *American Cyanamid v Ethicon* [1975] R.P.C. 513 (H.L.)

In an action for infringement of a patent for surgical sutures, the defendant denied that its product fell within the claims of the patent and contested validly on grounds of obviousness, lack of fair basis, ambiguity and inutility. In interlocutory proceedings for an injunction, the Court of Appeal refused relief. It required first to be satisfied that if the case went to trial upon no other evidence than is before the court at the hearing of the application the plaintiff would be entitled to judgment for a permanent injunction in the same terms as that being sought; only after this could it consider the balance of convenience. On appeal as to the correctness of this approach, Lord Diplock stated:

Your Lordships should in my view take this opportunity of declaring that there is no such rule. The use of such expressions as "a probability", "a *prima facie* case", or "a strong *prima facie* case" in the context of the exercise of a discretionary power to grant an interlocutory injunction leads to confusion as to the object sought to be achieved by this form of temporary relief. The court no doubt must be satisfied that the claim is not frivolous or vexatious; in other words, that there is a serious question to be tried.

It is no part of the court's function at this stage of the litigation to try to resolve conflicts of evidence on affidavit as to facts on which the claims of either party may ultimately depend nor to decide difficult questions of law which call for detailed argument and mature considerations. These are matters to be dealt with at the trial. One of the reasons for the introduction of the practice of requiring an undertaking as to damages upon the grant of an interlocutory injunction was that "it aided the court in doing that which was its great object, viz. abstaining from expressing any opinion, upon the merits of the case until the hearing" (*Wakefield v Duke of Buccleugh* (1865) 12 L.T. N.S. 628, at p.629). So unless the material available to the court at the hearing of the application for an interlocutory injunction fails to disclose that the plaintiff has any real prospect of succeeding in his claim for a permanent injunction at the trial, the court should go on to consider whether the balance of convenience lies in favour of granting or refusing the interlocutory relief that is sought.

As to that, the governing principle is that the court should first consider whether if the plaintiff were to succeed at the trial in establishing his right to a permanent injunction he would be adequately compensated by an award of damages for the loss he would have sustained as a result of the defendant's continuing to do what was sought to be enjoined between the time of the application and the time of the trial. If damages in the measure recoverable at common law would be adequate remedy and the defendant would be in a financial position to pay them, no interlocutory injunction should normally be granted, however strong the plaintiff's claim appeared to be at that stage. If, on the other hand, damages would not provide an adequate remedy for the plaintiff in the event of his succeeding at the trial, the court should then consider whether, on the contrary hypothesis that the defendant were to succeed at the trial in establishing his right to do that which was sought to be enjoined, he would be adequately compensated under the plaintiff's undertaking as to damages for the loss he would have sustained by being prevented from doing so between the time of the application and the time of the trial. If damages in the measure recoverable under such an undertaking would be an adequate remedy and the plaintiff would be in a financial position to pay them, there would be no reason upon this ground to refuse an interlocutory injunction.

It is where there is doubt as to the adequacy of the respective remedies in damages available to either party or to both, that the question of balance of convenience arises. It would be unwise to attempt even to list all the various matters which may need to be taken into consideration in deciding where the balance lies, let alone to suggest the relative weight to be attached to them. These will vary from case to case.

Where other factors appear to be evenly balanced it is a counsel of prudence to take such measures as are calculated to preserve the status quo. If the defendant is enjoined temporarily from doing something that he has not done before, the only effect of the interlocutory injunction in the event of his succeeding at the trial is to postpone the date at which he is able to embark upon a course of action which he has not previously found it necessary to undertake; whereas to interrupt him in the conduct of an established enterprise would cause much greater inconvenience to him since he would have to start again to establish it in the event of his succeeding at the trial.

Save in the simplest cases, the decision to grant or to refuse an interlocutory injunction will cause to whichever party is unsuccessful on the application some disadvantages which his ultimate success at the trial may show he ought to have been spared and the disadvantages may be such that the recovery of damages to which he would then be entitled either in the action or under the plaintiff's undertaking would not be sufficient to compensate him fully for all of them. The extent to which the disadvantages to each party would be incapable of being compensated in damages in the event of his succeeding at the trial is always a significant factor in assessing where the balance of convenience lies; and if the extent of the uncompensatable disadvantage to each party would not differ widely, it may not be improper to take into account in tipping the balance the relative strength of each party's case as revealed by the affidavit evidence adduced on the hearing of the application. This, however, should be done only where it is apparent upon the facts disclosed by evidence as to which there is no credible dispute that the strength of one party's case is disproportionate to that of the other party. The court is not justified in embarking upon anything resembling a trial of the action upon conflicting affidavits in order to evaluate the strength of either party's case.

I would reiterate that, in addition to those to which I have referred, there may be many other special factors to be taken into consideration in the particular circumstances of individual cases.

As to the fact that the proceedings concerned patent infringement, Lord Diplock said:

The instant appeal arises in a patent case. Historically there was undoubtedly a time when in an action for infringement of a patent that was not already "well established", whatever that may have meant, an interlocutory injunction to restrain infringement would not be granted if counsel for the defendant stated that it was intended to attack the validity of the patent.

Relics of this reluctance to enforce a monopoly that was challenged, even though the alleged grounds of invalidity were weak, are to be found in the judgment of Scrutton, L.J. as late as 1924 in *Smith v Grigg, Limited* ([1924] 1 K.B. 655); but the elaborate procedure for the examination of patent specifications by expert examiners before a patent is granted, the opportunity for opposition at that stage and the provisions for appeal to the Patent Appeal Tribunal in the person of a patent judge of the High Court, make the grant of a patent nowadays a good *prima facie* reason, in the true sense of that term, for supposing the patent to be valid, and have rendered obsolete the former rule of practice as respects interlocutory injunctions in infringement actions. In my view the grant of interlocutory injunctions in actions for infringement of patents is governed by the same principles as in other actions.

7.1.1.2   *BBC v Talbot* [1981] F.S.R. 228 (Megarry V.-C.)

The BBC was developing a traffic information system for cars under the name, Carfax. Although not yet on the market, it had been exhibited and had received considerable publicity. The Corporation accordingly sought to restrain the defendant from using Carfax for a vehicle spare parts service. In interlocutory proceedings, Megarry V.-C. referred to the legal elements needed to show passing off, and continued:

One other matter that I should mention at this stage is that this appears to be one of those cases in which, in applying the principles laid down in *American Cyanamid Co v Ethicon Ltd* [1975] A.C. 396, an important additional factor to be brought into considering the balance of convenience is the judge's estimation of the prospects of success that the plaintiff would have had if the case had gone to trial; for like so many passing off motions, this motion is one which may well prove decisive in one way or the other, without it being possible to go to trial. See generally *NWL Ltd v Woods* [1979] 1 W.L.R. 1294 at 1306, 1307; *Newsweek Inc v The British Broadcasting Corporation* [1979] R.P.C. 441. Here, the decision on the motion is going to produce one of two immediate results, it is said. If the BBC win, Talbot will have to call off the proposed launching of its CARFAX parts scheme in the middle of next January, and then, if they can surmount all the difficulties of obtaining the necessary funds, find another name, get all the requisite trade mark clearances for it, re-design all the publicity equipment and materials so as to use the new name, and get everything produced according to the new design. This, they say, will postpone the launching of their scheme for some six months, a period which Mr Morritt says is far longer than is necessary. If Talbot win, then the BBC, says Mr Morritt, will lose their only prospect of financial support and their scheme will be dead, a prospect which Mr Yorke controverts. At all events, the decision on the motion is going to have an immediate and serious effect on one side or the other. For either Talbot or the BBC, there is bound to be much wasted expenditure. I shall not attempt to analyse that expenditure, especially as I feel little doubt that there has been some degree of exaggeration on each side: but after all, these are proceedings for passing off.

Megarry V.-C. explored the evidence on motion, and assertions about its effects. He concluded in favour of granting an interlocutory injunction to preserve the status quo.

7.1.1.3   *Belfast Ropework v Pixdane* [1976] R.P.C. 337 (C.A.)

The defendant in an action for infringement of a patent for synthetic agricultural twine was beginning to import its product from Portugal. In interlocutory proceedings, the substantial issue concerned the balance of convenience.

Buckley L.J.:

The defendants are not manufacturers. They have no large capital sums tied up in plant or buildings, which would be sterilised by the grant of an injunction. They are merchants in agricultural equipment. It may be that at the present time their activities are substantially confined to the sale of baler twine. They have dealt in some other goods, although apparently not to any very substantial extent. But there seems to be no particular reason why they should not diversify their business into other goods. It is suggested in the evidence that if the injunction is granted, the defendant company will really have no alternative to going out of business. I am not altogether persuaded that that is a wholly justified view. But, even if it is so, their business has only been recently established, if it can yet be properly described as established at all, and it was initiated in circumstances in which the defendant company can I think reasonably be said to have been courting litigation. They may, of course, succeed in their counterclaim for the revocation of the patent, which would vindicate their conduct, and it is not for us at this stage to form any concluded opinion about that one way or the other. But, unless and until they do so, I do not think that they can feel aggrieved at being restrained until after the trial from continuing to pursue this newly and contentiously established business. If they are victorious in the outcome, they will be entitled to damages under the plaintiffs' undertaking, which will be a concomitant of the granting of an interlocutory injunction.

Mr Young has contended that the damage that the defendant company would suffer would be irretrievable damage and that they would never be able to re-establish themselves in this market. I do not think that that view is really justified on the evidence. I see no reason why a delay of one year or 18 months, or even two years, in the establishment of this new business should be regarded as something which will eventually shut them out of this market altogether. Nor do I see why, as has been suggested, if the injunction is granted, there will really be no alternative to the defendant company going into liquidation. It is said that if the injunction is granted, the defendant company will be unable to finance the defence of the action and that the action will go unfought. If that is the position, it is perhaps a misfortune which attends starting a venture of this kind in the circumstances in which this venture was started, knowing that it would almost inevitably involve the defendant company in litigation.

In these circumstances, will the trial judge, if and when the action comes to be tried, be better able to do justice as between the parties, whichever party wins, if the injunction is granted or if it is refused? If the injunction is refused, the plaintiffs will be at risk of having suffered damage to their established business considerably in excess of the sum of £15,000, which can I think be regarded as the only sum available to meet any claim for damages that they may have against the defendant company. If it is granted, the defendants will be at risk of having suffered damage by having been prevented from continuing for the time being in this infant business. But, whatever the measure of that damage may be, there is not I think any reason to suppose that the plaintiff company will not be of sufficient financial substance to meet it.

In these circumstances, in my judgment, the balance of convenience is clearly on the side of granting the injunction. Accordingly, I would allow this appeal and reverse the learned judge's decision.

The other members of the Court agreed.

7.1.1.4   *Catnic Components v Stressline* [1976] F.S.R. 157 (C.A.)

The plaintiffs' main business was in the patented steel lintel which was the subject of litigation elsewhere digested (see 1.2.1.4, 1.3.1.6). At the date of these proceedings it had a gross annual turnover of £6m. The defendants were introducing, as a small part of a similar business, a product which allegedly infringed the plaintiffs' patent. On the balance of convenience in interlocutory proceedings, Buckley L.J. said:

I take it to be the basis of the views expressed by the House of Lords in the *American Cyanamid* case that the function of an interlocutory junction is to ensure that the court, when the day comes to do final justice between the parties, will not find that something has happened in the meantime which puts it outside the power of the court then to do justice. However, on the facts of this case, if the plaintiffs succeed, it is unlikely that anything that happens between the present time and the trial of the action would so damage the plaintiffs as to make it impractical to compensate them by giving them damages. I can understand that, if the facts of the case are such that improper competition with an inventor in the exploitation of his invention would severely restrict his ability to lay the foundations of his own business in exploiting his invention and would stunt the expansion of that business, you might find that those circumstances were likely permanently to damage the plaintiff in the exploitation of his invention throughout the life of the patent because the early or formative years or even months of a business may be very important to the way in which the business will develop throughout its whole life. That sort of approach to the problem seems to me to have been in Lord Diplock's mind when he said what he will be found to have said at the foot of page 324 and at the top of page 325 in [1975] 2 W.L.R.

When I turn to consider the facts of the present case, with deference to the learned judge below, I find it difficult to believe that anything done by the defendant company in the way of selling metal lintels during the period – and I again repeat that it is likely to be a relatively short period – between now and the trial of this action could have so drastic an effect upon the plaintiffs' business in the exploitation of their metal lintels as to make damages an inadequate remedy. Any loss of business that the plaintiffs suffer as a result of competition by the defendants pending trial will be adequately compensated by damages calculated in relation to the number of lintels sold by the defendants; and, if it can then be shown that the plaintiffs have suffered in any respect in connection with their goodwill as a result of the defendants' action, I apprehend that that would be a perfectly proper head of damage to take into account in awarding damages to the plaintiffs for infringement down to the trial. I have not been satisfied that there is any likelihood in the present case of the plaintiff company's suffering any more drastic or far-reaching damage or that any damage which the plaintiff company is likely to suffer will be damage of a kind which could not be adequately recompensed in quantifiable damages.

7.1.2 Order to Obtain Discovery and Preserve Evidence and Assets

7.1.2.1 *Anton Piller v Manufacturing Processes* [1976] R.P.C. 719 (C.A.)

The plaintiff, a German company, sued the first defendant, its British agents and others for infringement of copyright, passing off and breach of confidence in respect of the design of sophisticated electrical components. On the basis of evidence that the first defendant was passing the plaintiff's drawings and other confidential material to third parties without authority, the plaintiff sought an order, ex parte and in camera, that it be permitted to enter the first defendant's premises in order to inspect documents and remove them or copies of them.

Lord Denning M.R.:

Let me say at once that no court in this land has any power to issue a search warrant to enter a man's house so as to see if there are papers or documents there which are of an incriminating nature, whether libels or infringements of copyright or anything else of the kind. No constable or bailiff can knock at the door and demand entry so as to inspect papers or documents. The householder can shut the door in his face and say "Get out". That was established in the leading case of *Entick v Carrington* (1765) 2 Wils. 275. None of us would wish to whittle down that principle in the slightest. But the order sought in this case is not a search warrant. It does not authorise the plaintiff's solicitors or anyone else to enter the defendant's premises against his will. It does not authorise the breaking down of any doors, nor the slipping in by a back door, nor getting in by an open door or window. It only authorises entry and inspection by the permission of the defendant. The plaintiff must get the defendant's permission. But it does do this: it brings pressure on the defendant to give permission. It does more. It actually orders him to give permission – with, I suppose, the result that if he does not give permission, he is guilty of contempt of court.

This may seem to be a search warrant in disguise. But it was fully considered in the House of Lords 150 years ago and held to be legitimate. The case is *East India Company v Kynaston* (1821) 3 Bli. 153. Lord Redesdale said at page 163:

> "The arguments for the appellants at the Bar are founded upon the supposition that the court has directed a forcible inspection. This is an erroneous view of the case. The order is to permit; and if the East India Company should refuse to permit inspection, they will be guilty of a contempt of the court ... It is an order operating on the person requiring the defendants to permit inspection, not giving authority of force, or to break open the doors of their warehouse".

That case was not, however, concerned with papers or things. It was only as to the value of a warehouse; and that could not be obtained without an inspection. But the distinction drawn by Lord Redesdale affords ground for thinking that there is jurisdiction to make an order that the defendant "do permit" when it is necessary in the interests of justice.

Accepting such to be the case, the question is in what circumstances ought such an order to be made. If the defendant is given notice beforehand and is able to argue the pros and cons, it is warranted by that case in the House of Lords and by Order 29, rule 2(1) and (5), of the Rules of the Supreme Court. But it is a far stronger thing to make such an order *ex parte* without giving him notice. This is not covered by the Rules of Court and must be based on the inherent jurisdiction of the court. There are one or two old precedents which give some colour for it, *Hennessey v Bohmann* (1877) W.N. 14, and *Morris v Howell* (1888) 22 L.R. Ir. 77, an Irish case in 1888. But they do not go very far. So it falls to us to consider it on principle. It seems to me that such an order can be made by a judge *ex parte*, but it should only be made where it is essential that the plaintiff should have inspection so that justice can be done between the parties: and when, if the defendant were forewarned, there is a grave danger that vital evidence will be destroyed, the papers will be burnt or lost or hidden, or taken beyond the jurisdiction, and so the ends of justice be defeated: and when the inspection would do no real harm to the defendant or his case.

Nevertheless, in the enforcement of this order, the plaintiffs must act with due circumspection. On the service of it, the plaintiffs should be attended by their solicitor, who is an officer of the court. They should give the defendant an opportunity of considering it and of consulting his own solicitor. If he wishes to apply to discharge the order as having been improperly obtained, he must be allowed to do so. If the defendant refuses permission to enter or to inspect, they must not force their way in. They must accept his refusal, and bring it to the notice of the court afterwards, if need be on an application to commit.

You might think that with all these safeguards against abuse, it would be of little use to make such an order. But it can be effective in this way: It services to tell the defendant that, on the evidence put before it, the court is of opinion that he ought to permit inspection – nay, it orders him to permit – and that he refuses at his peril. It puts him in peril not only of proceedings for contempt, but also of adverse inferences being drawn against him; so much so that his own solicitor may often advise him to comply. We are told that in two at least of the cases such an order has been effective. We are prepared, therefore, to sanction its continuance but only in an extreme case where there is grave danger of property being smuggled away or of vital evidence being destroyed.

Ormrod L.J.:

There are three essential pre-conditions for the making of such an order, in my judgment. First, there must be an extremely strong *prima facie* case. Secondly, the damage, potential or actual, must be very serious for the applicant. Thirdly, there must be clear evidence that the defendants have in their possession incriminating documents or things, and that there is a real possibility that they may destroy such material before any application *inter partes* can be made.

The form of the order makes it plain that the court is not ordering or granting anything equivalent to a search warrant. The order is an order on the defendant *in personam* to permit inspection. It is therefore open to him to refuse to comply with such an order, but at his peril either of further proceedings for contempt of court – in which case, of course, the court will have the widest discretion as to how to deal with it, and if it turns out that the order was made improperly in the first place, the contempt will be dealt with accordingly – but more important, of course, the refusal to comply may be the most damning evidence against the defendant at the subsequent trial. Great responsibility clearly rests on the solicitors for the applicant to ensure that the carrying out of such an order is meticulously, carefully done with the fullest respect for the defendant's rights, as my Lord has said, of applying to the court, should he feel it necessary to do so, before permitting the inspection.

Shaw L.J. agreed and the order was made, subject to a cross-undertaking in damages, supported in the circumstances by a bond of £10,000.

7.1.2.2 *Columbia Picture Industries v Robinson* [1986] F.S.R. 367 (Scott J.)

The plaintiffs secured an Anton Piller *order and* Mareva *injunction against Robinson and his company on the basis of evidence implicating him in illicit taping of films for hire to the public. On a subsequent application to discharge these, heard in conjunction with trial of the action, Scott J. dealt at length with the nature of the* Anton Piller *order:*

It is a fundamental principle of civil jurisprudence in this country that citizens are not to be deprived of their property by judicial or quasi-judicial order without a fair hearing. *Audi alterem partem* is one of the principles of natural justice and contemplates a hearing at which the defendant can, if so advised, be represented and heard. As was said by Slade L.J. in *Bank Mellat v Nikpour* [1985] F.S.R. 87 and cited by Whitford J. in *Jeffrey Rogers Knitwear Productions Limited v Vinola Knitwear Manufacturing Company* [1985] F.S.R. 184:

> "There is a primary precept governing the administration of justice, that no man is to be condemned unheard and, therefore, as a general rule, no order should be made to the prejudice of a party unless he has the opportunity of being heard in defence".

What is to be said of the *Anton Piller* procedure which, on a regular and institutionalised basis, is depriving citizens of their property and closing down their businesses by orders made *ex parte*, on applications of which they know nothing and at which they cannot be heard, by orders which they are forced, on pain of committal, to obey, even if wrongly made?

There are some possible answers to this criticism of *Anton Piller* orders and their effect. One is that every *Anton Piller* order records an undertaking by the applicants who have obtained it to compensate the respondent for any damage caused to him by the order and for which the court thinks the plaintiff ought to pay. This is theoretically a valuable safeguard. In the present case the defendants are seeking compensation under just such an undertaking. But, in my judgment, it does not meet the main objection to *Anton Piller* procedure. The main objection to the procedure is that the orders made produce for the respondents damaging and irreversible consequences without any hearing at which they can be heard. The respondents may lack the means or the strength of purpose to pursue the applicants for relief under the undertaking in damages. And even villains ought not to be deprived of their property by proceedings at which they cannot be heard.

The second comment is that which Mr Cumberland gave in the course of his cross-examination. *Anton Piller* orders, he said, are not sought by his firm against innocent persons. Mr Hoffman, too, emphasised in his evidence the care with which Hamlins satisfy themselves that the proposed objects of *Anton Piller* procedure were engaged in piratical activities before applying for *Anton Piller* orders. This comment serves, in my opinion, not to mitigate but to underline the dangers inherent in *ex parte* procedure and, *a fortiori*, *ex parte* procedure where the object is to obtain a mandatory order intended for immediate execution. . . .

The draconian and essentially unfair nature of *Anton Piller* orders from the point of view of respondents against whom they are made requires, in my view, that they be so drawn as to extend no further than the minimum extent necessary to achieve the purpose for which they are granted, namely, the preservation of documents or articles which might otherwise be destroyed or concealed. Anything beyond that is, in my judgment, impossible to justify. For example, I do not understand how an order can be justified that allows the plaintiffs' solicitors to take and retain all relevant documentary material and correspondence. Once the plaintiffs' solicitors have satisfied themselves what material exists and have had an opportunity to take copies thereof, the material ought, in my opinion, to be returned to its owner. The material need be retained no more than a relatively short period of time for that purpose.

Secondly, I would think it essential that a detailed record of the material taken should always be required to be made by the solicitors who execute the order before the material is removed from the respondent's premises. So far as possible, disputes as to what material was taken, the resolution of which depends on the oral testimony and credibility of the solicitors on the one hand and the respondent on the other hand, ought to be avoided. In the absence of any corroboration of a respondent's allegation that particular material (for instance, divorce papers) was taken, a solicitor's sworn and apparently credible denial is likely always to be preferred. This state of affairs is unfair to respondents. It ought to be avoided so far as it can be.

Thirdly, no material should, in my judgment be taken from the respondent's premises by the executing solicitors unless it is clearly covered by the terms of the order. In particular, I find it wholly unacceptable that a practice should have grown up whereby the respondent to the order is procured by the executing solicitors to give consent to additional material being removed. In view of the circumstances in which *Anton Piller* orders are customarily executed (the execution is often aptly called "a raid"), I would not, for my part, be prepared to accept that an apparent consent by a respondent had been freely and effectively given unless the respondent's solicitor had been present to confirm and ensure that the consent was a a free and informed one.

Fourthly, I find it inappropriate that seized material the ownership of which is in dispute, such as allegedly pirate tapes, should be retained by the plaintiffs' solicitors pending the trial. Although officers of the court, the main role of solicitors for plaintiffs is to act for the plaintiffs. If the proper administration of justice requires that material taken under an *Anton Piller* order from defendants should, pending trial, be kept from the defendants, then those responsible for the administration of justice might reasonably be expected to provide a neutral officer of the court charged with the custody of the material. In lieu of any such officer, and there is none at present, the plaintiffs' solicitors ought, in my view, as soon as solicitors for the defendants are on the record, be required to deliver the material to the defendants' solicitors on their undertaking for its safe custody and production, if required, in court.

Finally, the nature of *Anton Piller* orders requires that the affidavits in support of applicants for them ought to err on the side of excessive disclosure. In the case of material falling into the grey area of possible relevance, the judge, not the plaintiffs' solicitors, should be the judge of relevance. Whitford J., whose experience in these matters probably exceeds that of any other first instance judge, has recently drawn attention to the particular importance of full disclosure on *Anton Piller* applications. In the *Jeffrey Rogers Knitwear* case the learned judge said this at page 189:

> "I wholly reject the suggestion . . . that when seeking an *Anton Piller* order, there is no need to investigate the question whether or not in the absence of an order there is a real possibility that infringing material or evidence will be done away with. Any plaintiff seeking an *Anton Piller* order must place before the court all the information they have relating to the circumstances of the defendant which they can suggest points to the probability that in the absence of an *Anton Piller* order material which should be available will disappear".

Scott J. proceeded to find that the plaintiff's solicitors had permitted infractions to occur under each of his five criteria. While he found substantially for the plaintiffs in trial of the action, he also found that the preliminary orders had been improperly obtained. He accordingly awarded £10,000 compensatory and aggravated damages to the defendants on the plaintiffs' cross-undertaking.

7.1.2.3 Supreme Court Act 1981, s.72: Withdrawal of privilege against incrimination of self or spouse in certain proceedings

S.72(1) In any proceedings to which this subsection applies a person shall not be excused, by reason that to do so would tend to expose that person, or his or her spouse, to proceedings for a related offence or for the recovery of a related penalty –
    (a) from answering any question put to that person in the first-mentioned proceedings; or
    (b) from complying with any order made in those proceedings.

(2) Subsection (1) applies to the following civil proceedings in the High Court, namely –
    (a) proceedings for infringement of rights pertaining to any intellectual property or for passing off;
    (b) proceedings brought to obtain disclosure of information relating to any infringement of such rights or to any passing off; and
    (c) proceedings brought to prevent any apprehended infringement of such rights or any apprehended passing off.

(3) Subject to subsection (4), no statement or admission made by a person –
    (a) in answering a question put to him in any proceedings to which subsection (1) applies; or
    (b) in complying with any order made in any such proceedings,
shall, in proceedings for any related offence or for the recovery of any related penalty, be admissible in evidence against that person or (unless they married after the making of the statement or admission) against the spouse of that person.

(4) Nothing in subsection (3) shall render any statement or admission made by a person as there mentioned inadmissible in evidence against that person in proceedings for perjury or contempt of court.

(5) In this section –
    "intellectual property" means any patent, trade mark, copyright, registered design, technical or commercial information or other intellectual property;
    "related offence", in relation to any proceedings to which subsection (1) applies, means –
    (a) in the case of proceedings within subsection (2)(a) or (b) –
        (i) any offence committed by or in the course of the infringement or passing off to which those proceedings relate; or
        (ii) any offence not within sub-paragraph (i) committed in connection with that infringement or passing off, being an offence involving fraud or dishonesty;
    (b) in the case of proceedings within subsection (2)(c), any offence revealed by the facts on which the plaintiff relies in those proceedings;
    "related penalty", in relation to any proceedings to which subsection (1)

applies means –
(a) in the case of proceedings within subsection (2)(a) or (b), any penalty incurred in respect of anything done or omitted in connection with the infringement or passing off to which those proceedings relate;
(b) in the case of proceedings within subsection (2)(c), any penalty incurred in respect of any act or omission revealed by the facts on which the plaintiff relies in those proceedings.

(6) Any reference in this section to civil proceedings in the High Court of any description includes a reference to proceedings on appeal arising out of civil proceedings in the High Court of that description.

7.1.2.4 *CBS United Kingdom v Lambert* [1983] F.S.R. 123 (C.A.)

In copyright infringement proceedings against two large-scale distributors of private tapes, plaintiffs representing the British Phonographic Industry Ltd sought an Anton Piller order coupled with a Mareva injunction. The defendants appeared to have no assets from which judgment could be satisfied other than a number of expensive cars and one object of the order was to identify these and have them seized pending the outcome of the proceedings.

The Mareva injunctions were permitted by the C.A. to stand part of the order on the particular facts, the Court formulating the following guidelines:

Lawton L.J.:

First, there should be clear evidence that the defendant is likely, unless restrained by order, to dispose of or otherwise deal with his chattels in order to deprive the plaintiff of the fruits of any judgment he may obtain. Moreover, the court should be slow to order the delivery up of property belonging to the defendant unless there is some evidence or inference that the property has been acquired by the defendant as a result of his alleged wrongdoing. In the present case, for example, the inference is that the motor vehicles which the defendants own could only have been purchased out of the proceeds of sale by the defendants of articles which infringe the plaintiff's copyright. The inference is also that, if the defendants are forewarned or left in possession of the motor vehicles, those vehicles will be sold on and the proceeds of sale dissipated or hidden so that the plaintiffs would be deprived not only of damages but also of the proceeds of sale of infringing articles which belong to the plaintiffs.

Second, no order should be made for the delivery up of a defendant's wearing apparel, bedding, furnishings, tools of his trade, farm implements, live stock or any machines (including motor vehicles) or other goods such as materials or stock in trade, which it is likely he uses for the purposes of a lawful business. Sometimes furnishings may consist of objets d'art of great value. If the evidence is clear that such objects were bought for the purposes of frustrating judgment creditors they could be included in an order.

Third, all orders should specify as clearly as possible what chattels or classes of chattels are to be delivered up. A plaintiff's inability to identify what he wants delivered up and why is an indication that no order should be made.

Fourth, the order must not authorise the plaintiff to enter on the defendant's premises or to seize the defendant's property save by permission of the defendant. In *Anton Piller K.G. v Manufacturing Processes Ltd* and others [1976] Ch. 55, at 60, Lord

Denning emphasised that the order in that case:

> "... does not authorise the plaintiffs' solicitors or anyone else to enter the defendants' premises against their will ... It only authorises entry and inspection by the permission of the defendants. The plaintiffs must get the defendants' permission. But it does do this: It brings pressure on the defendants to give permission. It does more. It actually orders them to give permission – with, I suppose, the result that if they do not give permission, they are guilty of contempt of court".

The order in the present case was in the same form.

Fifth, no order should be made for delivery up to anyone other than the plaintiff's solicitor or a Receiver appointed by the High Court. The court should appoint a Receiver to take possession of the chattels unless satisfied that the plaintiff's solicitor has, or can arrange, suitable safe custody for what is delivered to him.

Sixth, the court should follow the guidelines set out in the *Z Ltd* case insofar as they are applicable to chattels in the possession, custody or control of third parties.

Finally, provision should always be made for liberty to apply to stay, vary or discharge the order.

Guidelines are guidelines; they are not Rules of Court and the spirit of them and not the letter should be kept in mind.

Costs reserved to the trial of the action.

7.1.2.5   *Norwich Pharmacal v Commissioners of Customs and Excise* [1974] R.P.C. 101 (H.L.)

The first plaintiff, patentee of the drug, furazolidone, learned that it was being imported by unauthorised persons. Since the Customs held records of who those persons were, the plaintiff applied to know the names but their request was refused. The plaintiff accordingly brought an action, inter alia, for discovery of the names and inspection of the relevant documents.

Lord Reid:

Discovery as a remedy in equity has a very long history. The chief occasion for its being ordered was to assist a party in an existing litigation. But this was extended at an early date to assist a person who contemplated litigation against the person from whom discovery was sought, if for various reasons it was just and necessary that he should have discovery at that stage. Such discovery might disclose the identity of others who might be joined as defendants with the person from whom discovery was sought. Indeed in some cases it would seem that the main object in seeking discovery was to find the identity of possible other defendants. It is not clear to me whether in all these cases the plaintiff had to undertake in some way to proceed against the person from whom he sought discovery if he found on discovery being ordered that it would suit him better to drop his complaint against that person and concentrate on his cause of action against those whose identity was disclosed by the discovery. But I would think that he was entitled to do this if he chose.

But it is argued for the respondents that it was an indispensable condition for the ordering of discovery that the person seeking discovery should have a cause of action against the person from whom it was sought. Otherwise it was said the case would come within the "mere witness" rule.

I think that there has been a good deal of misunderstanding about this rule. It has been clear at least since the time of Lord Hardwicke that information cannot be obtained by discovery from a person who will in due course be compellable to give that information either by oral testimony as a witness or on a *subpoena duces tecum*. Whether the reasons justifying that rule are good or bad it is much too late to enquire: the rule is settled. But the foundation of the rule is the assumption that eventually the testimony will be available either in an action already in progress or in an action which will be brought later. It appears to me to have no application to a case like the present case. Here if the information in the possession of the respondents cannot be made available by discovery now, no action can ever be begun because the appellants do not know who are the wrongdoers who have infringed their patent. So the appellants can never get the information.

To apply the mere witness rule to a case like this would be to divorce it entirely from its proper sphere. Its purpose is not to prevent but to postpone the recovery of the information sought. It may sometimes have been misapplied in the past but I see no reason why we should continue to do so.

But that does not mean, as the appellants contend, that the discovery will be ordered against anyone who can give information as to the identity of a wrongdoer. There is absolutely no authority for that. A person injured in a road accident might know that a bystander had taken the number of the car which ran him down and have no other means of tracing the driver. Or a person might know that a particular person is in possession of a libellous letter which he has good reason to believe defames him but the author of which he cannot discover. I am satisfied that it would not be proper in either case to order discovery in order that the person who has suffered damage might be able to find and sue the wrongdoer. Neither authority, principle nor public policy would justify that.

So discovery to find the identity of a wrongdoer is available against anyone against whom the plaintiff has a cause of action in relation to the same wrong. It is not available against a person who has no other connection with the wrong than that he was a spectator or has some document relating to it in his possession. But the respondents are in an intermediate position. Their conduct was entirely innocent; it was in execution of their statutory duty. But without certain action on their part the infringements could never have been committed. Does this involvement in the matter make a difference?

On the view which I take of the case I need not set out in detail the powers and duties of the respondents with regard to imported goods. From the moment when they enter the port until the time when the consignee obtains clearance and removes the goods, they are under the control of the Customs in the sense that the Customs authorities can prevent their movement or specify the places where they are to be put, and in the event of their having any suspicions they have full powers to examine or test the goods. When they are satisfied and the appropriate duty has been paid the consignee or his agent is authorised to remove the goods. No doubt the respondents are never in possession of the goods, but they do have considerable control of them during the period from entry into the port until removal by the consignee. And the goods cannot get into the hands of the consignee until the respondents have taken a number of steps and have released them.

My noble and learned friends, Lord Cross of Chelsea and Lord Kilbrandon, have dealt with the authorities. They are not very satisfactory, not always easy to reconcile and in the end inconclusive. On the whole I think they favour the appellants, and I am particularly impressed by the views expressed by Lord Romilly and Lord Hatherley in *Upmann v Elkan* (1871) 12 Eq. 140; 7 Ch. App. 130. They seem to me to point to a very reasonable principle that if through no fault of his own a person gets mixed up in the tortious acts of others so as to facilitate their wrongdoing he may incur no personal liability but he comes under a duty to assist the person who has been wronged by giving him full information and disclosing the identity of the wrongdoers. I do not think that it matters whether he became so mixed up by voluntary action on his part or because it was his duty to do what he did. It may be that if this causes him expense the person seeking the information ought to reimburse him. But justice requires that he should co-operate in righting the wrong if he unwittingly facilitated its perpetration.

I am the more inclined to reach this result because it is clear that if the person mixed up in the affair has to any extent incurred any liability to the person wronged, he must make full disclosure even though the person wronged has no intention of proceeding against him. It would I think be quite illogical to make his obligation to disclose the identity of the real offenders depend on whether or not he has himself incurred some minor liability. I would therefore hold that the respondents must disclose the information now sought unless there is some consideration of public policy which prevents that.

Apart from public policy the respondents say that they are prevented by law from making this disclosure. I agree with your Lordships that that is not so. If it were they could not even disclose such information in a serious criminal case, but their counsel were, quite rightly, not prepared to press their argument so far as that.

So we have to weigh the requirements of justice to the appellants against the considerations put forward by the respondents as justifying non-disclosure. They are twofold. First it is said that to make such disclosures would or might impair or hamper the efficient conduct of their important statutory duties. And secondly it is said that such disclosure would or might be prejudicial to those whose identity would be disclosed.

There is nothing secret or confidential in the information sought or in the documents which came into the hands of the respondents containing that information. Those documents are ordinary commercial documents which pass through many different hands. But it is said that those who do not wish to have their names disclosed might concoct false documents and thereby hamper the work of the Customs. That would require at least a conspiracy between the foreign consignor and the importer and it seems to me to be in the highest degree improbable. It appears that there are already arrangements in operation by the respondents restricting the disclosure of certain matters if the importers do not wish them to be disclosed. It may be that the knowledge that a court might order discovery in certain cases would cause somewhat greater use to be made of these arrangements. But it was not suggested in argument that that is a matter of any vital importance. The only other point was that such disclosure might cause resentment and impair good relations with other traders: but I find it impossible to believe that honest traders would resent failure to protect wrongdoers.

Protection of traders from having their names disclosed is a more difficult matter. If we could be sure that those whose names are sought are all tort feasors, they do not deserve any protection. In the present case the possibility that any are not is so remote that I think it can be neglected. The only possible way in which any of these imports could be legitimate and not an infringement would seem to be that someone might have exported some furazolidone from this country and then whoever owned it abroad might have sent it back here. Then there would be no infringement. But again that seems most unlikely.

But there may be other cases where there is much more doubt. The validity of the patent may be doubtful and there could well be other doubts. If the respondents have any doubts in any future case about the propriety of making disclosures they are well entitled to require the matter to be submitted to the court at the expense of the person seeking the disclosure. The court will then only order discovery if satisfied that there is no substantial chance of injustice being done.

Lords Morris, Dilhorne, Cross and Kilbrandon delivered concurring speeches.

7.1.2.6 *British Steel v Granada Television* [1981] A.C. 1096 (H.L.)

Granada obtaining access to secret documents of the plaintiff, which related to important facts affecting a current, much discussed strike by the British Steel workforce. The documents were revealed by a source within British Steel without solicitation or payment, but on condition that the source's identity would not be revealed. Granada used the documents in order to confront the Chairman of British Steel in a broadcast. In response to an order for delivery up, it returned the documents but took steps to remove any indication of who the source was. An order was accordingly sought to compel Granada to reveal the name. Against this Granada sought to establish a public interest immunity in favour of journalists and other media workers.

Lord Wilberforce reviewed case-law which established that journalists in general enjoy no privilege against disclosure in litigation. He then considered whether a Norwich Pharma- *cal order could be made against a journalist or similar worker:*

But Mr Neill Q.C., for Granada, argued that the remedy of, in effect, a bill of discovery ought not to be applied to a case such as the present. His grounds were, I think, as follows. Historically there is no case of such an action having been brought against a newspaper, or in a breach of confidence case. Yet, in the 18th to 19th centuries many opportunities must have arisen for doing so, if the action lay. The press was, then as now, eager to publish any information, the more sensational the better, which it had obtained from confidential sources, and, then as now, breaches of confidence or leaks were of common occurrence. The failure or abstinence to invoke such proceedings must, it is said, be taken to reflect an *opinio juris* that no such proceedings could be brought.

Lord Wilberforce reviewed cases and the Newspaper Stamp Act 1836, which (it was argued) gave support to this contention. He continued:

But in the end I am not persuaded that we ought to deny the plaintiffs their remedy. The cases are indecisive and only support an argument *a silentio*: the statute of 1836 seems to have been passed for a different purpose. Abstinence from using this weapon hitherto can be explained by the fact that it is only exceptionally that the aggrieved person would have, and could demonstrate, a real interest in suing the source. If the present is such a case (and I think it is), it is to that extent exceptional and decision on it would not open floodgates to actions against newspapers, still less support any general argument that the confidence existing between journalists and their sources is something which the courts will not respect, still less stifle investigation. To succeed in proceedings aimed at compelling disclosure the plaintiff will always have to satisfy the court that he has a real grievance, even after suing the newspaper, which, in the interest of justice, he ought to be allowed to pursue, and that this ought, in the particular case, to outweigh whatever public interest there may be in preserving the confidence. It is possible that, if the plaintiff succeeds here, fewer "leaks" will occur, though that must be speculation. But I do think that judicially we are able to place a value on this. "Leaks" may vary all the way from mere gossip or scandal to matters of national or international importance. A general proposition that leaks should be encouraged, or at least not discouraged, cannot be made without weighing the detriments in loss of mutual confidence and co-operation which they involve. The public interest involved in individual leaks can be taken account of and weighed by the court in deciding whether to grant the remedy in a particular case.

Lord Wilberforce also held that the order should be granted even though British Steel's primary objective may have been to be able to dismiss the source. He refused to find sufficient countervailing public interest in the information given to the public to justify protecting the source by not making the order. Lords Dilhorne, Fraser and Russell gave concurring speeches; Lord Salmon dissented.

7.1.3 Threats to Sue

7.1.3.1 Patents Act 1977, s.70: Groundless threats of infringement proceedings

S.70(1) Where a person (whether or not the proprietor of, or entitled to any right in, a patent) by circulars, advertisements or otherwise threatens another person with proceedings for any infringement of a patent, a person aggrieved by the threats (whether or not he is the person to whom the threats are made) may, subject to subsection (4) below, bring proceedings in the court against the person making the threats, claiming any relief mentioned in subsection (3) below.

(2) In any such proceedings the plaintiff or pursuer shall, if he proves that the threats were so made and satisfies the court that he is a person aggrieved by them, be entitled to the relief claimed unless –
   (a) the defendant or defender proves that the acts in respect of which proceedings were threatened constitute or, if done, would constitute an infringement of a patent; and
   (b) the patent alleged to be infringed is not shown by the plaintiff or pursuer to be invalid in a relevant respect.

(3) The said relief is –
   (a) a declaration or declarator to the effect that the threats are unjustifiable;
   (b) an injunction or interdict against the continuance of the threats; and
   (c) damages in respect of any loss which the plaintiff or pursuer has sustained by the threats.

(4) Proceedings may not be brought under this section for a threat to bring proceedings for an infringement alleged to consist of making or importing a product for disposal or of using a process.

(5) It is hereby declared that a mere notification of the existence of a patent does not constitute a threat of proceedings within the meaning of this section.

The Registered Designs Act 1949, s.26 and the Copyright, Designs and Patents Act 1988, s.253, provide a threats action in similar terms, respectively concerning registered designs and (unregistered) design right. There is no equivalent statutory action in respect of other intellectual property.

7.1.3.2 *Granby Marketing Services v Interlego* [1984] R.P.C. 209 (Vinelott J.)

The plaintiff operated as an agent for the promotion of products, including Kellogg's cereals. For a Kellogg's campaign, the plaintiff undertook to procure kits of toy bricks from an Australian supplier. These were to be distributed in the promotion but Interlego wrote claiming that the bricks infringed copyright in their drawings for "Lego" bricks and threatening proceedings. In consequence, Kellogg's refused to take delivery of their bricks and ended their contract with the plaintiff by a small ex gratia payment.

Even on the assumption that the plaintiff could demonstrate that Interlego's action was intended to induce Kellogg to break its contract with the plaintiff, the defendant asserted that no cause of action had been disclosed and applied to strike out.

Vinelott J.:

It appears that there is no clear decision, at least of the English courts, whether a defendant who in good faith asserts a legal right which he claims would be infringed by the performance of a contract between the plaintiff and a third party, intending that the contract be not performed, can be made liable in an action brought by the plaintiff for unjustified interference with his contractual relationship with the third party. Mr Hoffman submits that, although there is no clear decision that no such action will lie, it has been assumed sub silentio in a very long series of cases that it will not.

Vinelott J. referred to Pitt v Donovan *(1813) 1 M & S 639;* Green v Button *(1835) 2 Cromp. M & R 707 and* Wren v Weild *(1869) L.R. 4 Q.B. 730. He continued:*

Mr Lightman points out that that case was decided not long after the decision in *Lumley v Gye* when the limits of the tort of wrongful interference with contractual relations were perhaps imperfectly defined. That cannot however be said of *Halsey v Brotherhood* (1880) 15 Ch. D. 514, another case concerning a patent. The plaintiff and the defendant both manufactured steam engines. The defendant owned certain patents and claimed that the plaintiff's engines infringed them. He told customers of the plaintiff what he genuinely believed to be true; that is, that the plaintiff's engines infringed his patent and that, if they dealt with the defendant, he would obtain an injunction. Sir George Jessel M.R. said at page 517:

> "The defendant alleges that the plaintiff is making and selling engines which are infringements of his patent. It is said that he is not entitled to tell persons buying the plaintiff's engines that they are infringements and that those persons are liable to an action; and that he is not entitled even to give a notice that these engines are infringements of his patent rights unless he follows up that notice by some legal proceedings. I must entirely dissent from that proposition. There is, as far as I am aware, no law in this country compelling a man to assert his legal right by action. He may, if he thinks fit, give notice to persons, the notices being given *bona fide*, that they are infringing his legal rights: in many cases it is his duty to do so before bringing an action, and in some cases the legislature has compelled him to do so before bringing an action. Take, for example, those cases of infringement of copyrights and designs, and so on, where the seller is only liable if he knows that the right has been infringed; there you must let him know before bringing an action, or your action would fail".

Then, after observing that in many contexts a person who proposes to assert a legal right is bound not by law but by propriety to give notice of his intention to assert it, he said at page 518:

> "If a man, with a view to preventing another man from carrying on his business, knowing he himself has no patent, or knowing that he has an invalid patent, or knowing that the thing manufactured by the other man is not an infringement for the purpose of injuring the other man in his trade, threatens the purchasers or advertises that the thing is an infringement, of course he is liable like any other person who makes a false assertion to the injury of another in his trade, because it is an untrue assertion and not made *bona fide*. The mere fact of a man mentioning he has a right, and that something is an infringement of it, does not *per se* give a ground of action. It is obvious that such a course of conduct, adopted *bona fide*, does not constitute a case in which an action could be maintained, for the essence

of the case is the falsity of the assertion and the want of good faith in making it. That is, the assertion is made, not for the purpose of preserving the alleged legal right, but for a different purpose, and has injured the plaintiff in his trade".

That decision was affirmed in the Court of Appeal: see (1884) 19 Ch. D. 386.

Vinelott J. referred to the consequent change introduced for patents and designs in 1883 by the creation of the special "threats action"; to the restricted scope of this provision revealed in Ellis v Pogson *(1923) 40 R.P.C. 62, which was dealt with by statutory amendment in 1932; and to the restrictive general rule at common law to which this development was an admitted exception. He referred for the same approach to* James v Commonwealth *(1939) 62 C.L.R. 339 at 367, per Dixon J.; and to the Second U.S. Restatement of Law of Torts, s.773. He continued:*

However, Mr Lightman founds his submission on a passage in the judgment of Whitford J. in *Jaybeam Limited v Abru Aluminium Limited* [1976] R.P.C. 308. In that case, the defendant owned a copyright in drawings relating to a lightweight step-ladder and a registered design relating to it. The plaintiff manufactured a similar step-ladder. The defendant's solicitors wrote to a customer of the plaintiff making certain demands. Implicit in the letter was a claim that the defendant owned the copyright in drawings for their step-ladder which was infringed by the plaintiff's step-ladder. They added:

"Notwithstanding the above and as a separate matter we would also draw your attention to the fact that Abru are registered proprietors of registered design number 940,140".

As regards the claim to be the proprietor of a registered design, the case fell within the threats section in the 1949 Act. As to that, Whitford J. said at page 314 that:

"the plaintiffs are undoubtedly entitled to relief in respect of the issue of the threat, more particularly because, although I am prepared to accept for present purposes that there may be an arguable case or possibly an arguable case that what the IPC were selling and what the plaintiffs were making is an infringement of the registered design, the ground of justification is not so thoroughly made out that relief pending the trial should be withheld. Threats of this kind are of tremendous potential damage. Nobody wants to be involved in litigation, let alone litigation about registered designs and patents, which is no doubt why provisions of this sort have been specifically enacted".

He then went on to deal with the copyright claim in a passage which I shall read in full. He said:

"The copyright position is in an entirely different position. So far as threats of proceedings on registered designs are concerned, there is specific statutory provision, a prohibition against threats. So far as copyright is concerned, there is no such statutory provision. The importance of that has perhaps not been quite so acute until in recent years people have come to realise, as the defendants have, that under the provisions of the existing Act manufactured articles which could previously have only been protected under a registered design can confidently be asserted to be an infringement of copyright in drawings. The penalties which may be secured under the Act, particularly by way of damages for conversion, are enormous and threat of proceedings in respect of infringement of copyright may in the end be even more persuasive than the threat of proceedings in respect of infringement of patents or registered designs. However that may be, counsel for the plaintiffs quite rightly accepted there is no statutory provision prohibiting threats and that if he is to succeed in this action he has to succeed on some other basis. That is why he advances the alternative bases of malicious falsehood on the one hand or interference with business relations – possibly interference with contractual relations – on the other".

I do not think I need read the next paragraph, but he continues:

"Let me assume for the moment that the case so far as infringement of copyright is concerned when the action comes may go the one way or the other. Can the plaintiffs succeed in restraining the sending out of letters of this character on the basis of malicious falsehood or some sort of interference with business relations? Once again counsel for the defendants did not argue that it was impossible that the plaintiffs should succeed on one or other of these heads. I myself take the view that it is indeed possible that they may succeed on one or other of these heads. Counsel for the defendants accepts that at the trial of the action the plaintiffs might be entitled to some sort of relief of the kind which they seek in this motion, though he said for interlocutory purposes the relief sought goes much too wide".

That passage seems to me to afford flimsy support for Mr Lightman's submission. Whitford J. clearly thought that the plaintiff might succeed at the trial in establishing that the threats were made maliciously. Moreover the ground on which he thought the plaintiff might, even in the absence of malice, succeed on the other of the heads he mentions namely interference with business relations, referred to earlier as including "possibly interference with contractual relations", is not examined, no doubt because it was conceded in argument that the plaintiff's case in inducing breach of contract was arguable but not strong. None of the relevant authorities were cited to him. I do not therefore feel constrained by the respect which is due to a decision of Whitford J. on a matter relating to copyright law to hold that the facts relied on in the statement of claim can found a possible cause of action.

7.1.3.3   *Mentmore v Fomento* (1955) 72 R.P.C. 157 (C.A.)

The defendant sued another enterprise for patent infringement and succeeded before the Court of Appeal, which however stayed the injunction and order for delivery up pending further appeal to the House of Lords. The defendants' legal representative (a solicitor) allegedly said to a buyer from Selfridge's that the decision applied equally to Mentmore pens and that she had until Friday to remove them from the shelves if there were not to be "a little court job again": it was also claimed that he said nothing about suspension of the order. Mentmore then sued the defendants for threats concerning patent infringement and for injurious falsehood. On the latter basis alone, Roxburgh J. made an interlocutory order restraining the defendants from making misleading statements of the kind alleged.

Evershed M.R.:

I have said that the amendment of the writ had been such as to raise the cause of action known as "injurious falsehood"; and, in order that such an action may succeed, it appears that two characteristics must be established, namely, first, that representations have been made which are false and, second, that the representations were not only false but made as it is said, maliciously. The precise significance of the word "maliciously" in that context may be a subject which hereafter will have to be further considered and debated. According to the language of Scrutton L.J. which was quoted by Roxburgh J. himself in an earlier case of *Joyce v Motor Surveys Ltd* [1948] Ch. 252, at 255, "'Maliciously' (is used), not in the sense of illegality, but in the sense of being made with some indirect or dishonest motive. Honest belief in an unfounded claim is not malice; but the nature of the unfounded claim may be evidence that there was not an honest belief in it".

Without pursuing the matter further, if it is eventually found, when all the witnesses have been heard, that a statement here was made which was not only false but was put forward by or on behalf of the Defendants not honestly believing it to be true, and with the primary object of damaging the Defendants' rivals in business, it would appear to me, *prima facie*, that a case of injurious falsehood has been established.

Accordingly, the C.A. refused to interfere with the judge's order.

7.2 Criminal Offences

7.2.1 Trade Descriptions Act 1968, s.1(1), 2(1), 14(1), 34

S.1(1) Prohibition of false trade descriptions
Any person who, in the course of a trade or business –
  (a) applies a false trade description to any goods; or
  (b) supplies or offers to supply any goods to which a false trade description is applied;
shall, subject to the provisions of this Act, be guilty of an offence.

S.2(1) Trade Description
A trade description is an indication, direct or indirect, and by whatever means given of any of the following matters with respect to any goods or parts of goods, that is to say –
  (a) quantity, size or gauge;
  (b) method of manufacture, production, processing or reconditioning;
  (c) composition;
  (d) fitness for purpose, strength, performance, behaviour or accuracy;
  (e) any physical characteristics not included in the preceding paragraphs;
  (f) testing by any person and results thereof;
  (g) approval by any person or conformity with a type approved by any person;
  (h) place or date of manufacture, production, processing or reconditioning;
  (i) person by whom manufactured, produced, processed or reconditioned;
  (j) other history, including previous ownership or use.

S.2(2)–(5) contain a variety of definitions relating to s.2(1).

S.3 further defines broadly the concept of a false trade description; S.4 likewise defines what constitutes applying a trade description to goods; S.5 deals with case where the description is applied in an advertisement; S.6 gives broad meaning to "offering to supply".

S.14(1) False or misleading statements as to services, etc
It shall be an offence for any person in the course of any trade or business –
  (a) to make a statement which he knows to be false; or
  (b) recklessly to make a statement which is false; as to any of the following matters, that is to say –
    (i) the provision in the course of any trade or business of any services, accommodation or facilities;
    (ii) the nature of any services, accommodation or facilities provided in the course of any trade or business;
    (iii) the time at which, manner in which or persons by whom any services, accommodation or facilities are so provided;
    (iv) the examination, approval or evaluation by any person of any services, accommodation or facilities so provided; or
    (v) the location or amenities of any accommodation so provided.

S.14(2)–(4) provide definitions, notably of what constitutes "falsity". S.23 makes it an offence to cause another to commit an offence under the Act; S.24 gives a defence relating to mistake, reliance on information from another and accident, which a defendant may rely upon if he can show that he exercised all due diligence to avoid commission.

34 Trade marks containing trade descriptions

The fact that a trade description is a trade mark, or part of a trade mark, within the meaning of the Trade Marks Act 1938 does not prevent it from being a false trade description when applied to any goods, except where the following conditions are satisfied, that is to say –

(a) that it could have been lawfully applied to the goods if this Act had not been passed; and

(b) that on the day this Act is passed the trade mark either is registered under the Trade Marks Act 1938 or is in use to indicate a connection in the course of trade between such goods and the proprietor of the trade mark; and

(c) that the trade mark as applied is used to indicate such a connection between the goods and the proprietor of the trade mark or a person registered under section 28 of the Trade Marks Act 1938 as a registered user of the trade mark; and

(d) that the person who is the proprietor of the trade mark is the same person as, or a successor in title of, the proprietor on the day this Act is passed.

7.2.2   *Bulmer v Bollinger* [1978] R.P.C. 79 (C.A.)

Two British drink manufacturers sought a declaration that they were entitled to call products "Champagne Cider" and "Champagne Perry". Amongst the objections raised by the French champagne producers was a claim that, under the Trade Descriptions Act 1968, s.1, they had a civil cause of action against the British manufacturers. On this aspect of the case, Buckley L.J. stated:

I now come to the claim under the Trade Descriptions Act 1968. Section 1 of that Act makes it a criminal offence for any person to apply a false trade description to any goods or to supply or offer to supply any goods to which a false trade description is applied. There is no provision in the Act expressly conferring upon anyone a civil right of action in relation to a false trade description. Mr Sparrow contends, however, that by implication the Act is capable of giving rise to a civil cause of action. In *Cutler v Wandsworth Stadium Ltd* [1949] A.C. 398, Lord Simonds pointed out at page 407 that it is often a difficult question whether, where a statutory obligation is placed on A, B who conceives himself to be damnified by A's breach of it has a right of action against him. Lord Simonds went on to say: "The only rule which in all circumstances is valid is that the answer must depend on a consideration of the whole Act and the circumstance, including the pre-existing law, in which it was enacted". Lord Simonds then proceeded to consider certain authorities, including *Black v Fife Coal Co Ltd* [1912] A.C. 149, where Lord Kinnear said at page 165: "We are to consider the scope and purpose of the Statute and in particular for whose benefit it is intended. Now the object of the present Statute is plain. It was intended to compel mine owners to make due provision for the safety of the men working in their mines, and the persons for whose benefit all these Rules are to be enforced are the persons exposed to danger. But when a duty of this kind is imposed for the benefit of particular persons, there arises at common law a correlative right in those persons who may be injured by its contravention". So we have to consider whether the defendants can successfully assert that the Trade Descriptions Act 1968 was intended for the protection of the Champagne Houses or of any class of which the Champagne Houses form part.

A similar question arose in respect of the Merchandise Marks Act 1887 to 1953 in the *Spanish Champagne* Case in which Danckwerts J. reached the conclusion that it was impossible to regard those Acts as giving civil rights of action to rival traders [1960] R.P.C. 16 at 34, line 7. Mr Sparrow has placed reliance upon an observation of Lord Goddard, C.J., in *Kat v Diment* [1951] 1 K.B. 34 at 42 where he said: "It should be borne in mind that this Act" (The Merchandising Marks Act 1887) "is intended to protect not only the public or traders who may purchase the goods, but also the proprietors of trade marks and those who manufacture and deal in the genuine article". Lord Goddard was not in that case concerned with any question about civil liability, but in any case his language seems to me to be directed to emphasising the wide and general nature of the protection afforded by the Act and not to any suggestion that the Act was intended to protect any particular class of the public. In my judgment, there is no sound basis for suggesting that the Trade Descriptions Act 1968 was passed for the protection of any particular class of the public, and accordingly I think that it cannot give rise to any civil cause of action. Nor, in my opinion, have the defendants established any ground for relief by way of injunction upon any such principle as is adumbrated by Lord Denning, M.R. in *Acrow Ltd v Rex Chainbelt Inc* [1971] 1 W.L.R. 1676 at 1682 G.

The other members of the Court agreed.

7.2.3   *Scott v Metropolitan Police Commissioner* [1975] A.C. 819 (H.L.)

The defendant temporarily obtained copies of films from cinema staff in order to make and distribute copies in infringement of copyright. He was charged inter alia *with conspiracy to defraud at common law. No deceit was involved and it was argued (relying on Buckley J.,* re London and Globe Finance *[1903] 1 Ch. 728 at 732) that this was a necessary element of the offence.*

Viscount Dilhorne reviewed a number of cases which he considered to be inconsistent with this proposition and continued:

What conclusions are to be drawn from the cases to which I have referred? I think they are these:

1. There is no separate and distinct class of criminal conspiracy called conspiracy to effect a public mischief.
2. That description has in the past been applied to a number of cases which might have been regarded as coming within well-known heads of conspiracy, eg conspiracy to defraud, to pervert the course of justice, etc: see *Brailsford* [1905] 2 K.B. 730: *Porter* [1910] 1 K.B. 369; *Bassey* 22 Cr.App.R. 160; *Young* 30 Cr.App.R. 57; *Newland* [1954] 1 Q.B. 158 and *Bailey* [1956] N.I. 15.
3. It is far too late to hold that a conspiracy of the kind that occurred in those cases was not criminal and Lord Goddard C.J.'s observations in *Newland* should be understood in that sense.
4. The judges have no power to create new offences.
5. Where a charge of conspiracy to effect a public mischief has been preferred, the question to be considered is whether the objects or means of the conspiracy are in substance of such a quality or kind as has already been recognised by the law as criminal.
6. If there are, then one has to go on to consider, on an appeal, whether the course the trial took in consequence of the reference to public mischief was such as to vitiate the conviction.

Relating these conclusions to this appeal, it may be that, if the references to public mischief had been omitted from counts 1 and 2 of the indictment, the case might have proceeded on the basis that the conspiracy charged in each count was conspiracy to defraud, and if the accused had been then convicted, that by applying the reasoning of Lord Radcliffe in *Welham v Director of Public Prosecutions* [1961] A.C. 103, 123 *et seq.* and the *dictum* of Lord Tucker in *Board of Trade v Owen* [1957] A.C. 602, 621, which I have cited, the convictions could have been upheld.

I express no firm opinion on this though at one time I thought that it might become necessary to do so in order to determine whether or not this appeal should be dismissed on the ground that no miscarriage of justice had actually occurred: Criminal Appeal Act 1968, section 2(1).

7.2.4   *DPP v Withers* [1975] A.C. 852 (H.L.)

The defendants, operating an investigation agency, deceived banks, building societies and government agencies into providing personal information about customers, etc. by representing themselves as other branches or agencies. They were charged on two counts of conspiracy to effect a public mischief.

Viscount Dilhorne reviewed the line of cases which allowed charges to be preferred on this basis. He continued:

In *Welham v Director of Public Prosecutions* [1961] A.C. 103 this House had to consider the meaning of "intent to defraud" in relation to forgery. In the course of his speech Lord Radcliffe said, at pp.123, 124:

> "Now, I think that there are one or two things that can be said with confidence about the meaning of this word 'defraud'. It requires a person as its object: that is, defrauding involves doing something to someone. Although in the nature of things it is almost invariably associated with the obtaining of an advantage for the person who commits the fraud, it is the effect upon the person who is the object of the fraud that ultimately determines its meaning. ... Secondly, popular speech does not give, and I do not think ever has given, any sure guide as to the limits of what is meant by 'to defraud'. It may mean to cheat someone. It may mean to practise a fraud upon someone. It may mean to deprive someone by deceit of something which is regarded as belonging to him or, though not belonging to him, as due to him or his right".

Later, Lord Radcliffe said, at p.126, that he was unable to accept Buckley J.'s observations in *In re London and Globe Finance Corporation Ltd* [1903] 1 Ch. 728, which he said were *obiter*, as an authoritative exposition of words employed in a subsequent statute.

While the meaning to be given to words may be affected by their context and Lord Radcliffe was only considering the meaning of intent to defraud in section 4 of the Forgery Act 1913, the passages which I have cited from his speech are, I think, of general application; and certainly those passages and his speech lend no support to the contention that there cannot be a conspiracy to defraud which does not involve deceit.

In the course of delivering the judgment of the Court of Appeal in *Reg. v Sinclair* [1968] 1 W.L.R. 1246, where the defendants had been convicted of conspiracy to cheat and defraud a company, its shareholders and creditors by fraudulently using its assets for purposes other than those of the company and by fraudulently concealing such use, James J. said, at p.1250: "To cheat and defraud is to act with deliberate dishonesty to the prejudice of another person's proprietary right". Again, one finds in this case no support for the view that in order to defraud a person that person must be deceived.

One must not confuse the object of a conspiracy with the means by which it is intended to be carried out. In the light of the cases to which I have referred, I have come to the conclusion that Mr Blom-Cooper's main contention must be rejected. I have not the temerity to attempt an exhaustive definition of the meaning of "defraud". As I have said, words take colour from the context in which they are used, but the words "fraudulently" and "defraud" must ordinarily have a very similar meaning. If, as I think, and as the Criminal Law Revision Committee appears to have thought, "fraudulently" means "dishonestly", then "to defraud" ordinarily means, in my opinion, to deprive a person dishonestly of something which is his or of something to which he is or would or might but for the perpetration of the fraud be entitled.

The other members of the House agreed that the convictions should be quashed.

7.3 Customs Authorities

7.3.1 Trade Marks Act 1938, s.64A; Restrictions on importation of goods bearing infringing trade marks

S.64A (1) The person who is registered as the proprietor or registered user of a trade mark in respect of any goods may give notice in writing to the Commissioners of Customs and Excise (in this section referred to as the Commissioners) –

    (a) that he is the proprietor or registered user of that trade mark, and

    (b) that such goods bearing the trade mark are expected to arrive in the United Kingdom at a time and place and by a consignment specified in the notice, and

    (c) that the use within the United Kingdom of the trade mark in relation to the goods would infringe the proprietor's exclusive right to that use, and

    (d) that he requests the Commissioners to treat the goods as prohibited goods.

(2) Where a notice has been given under this section in respect of any goods bearing a trade mark and has not been withdrawn and the requirements of any regulations made under this section are complied with, then, subject to the following provisions of this section, the importation into the United Kingdom of the goods shall, if the condition of paragraph (c) of the preceding subsection is satisfied, be deemed to be prohibited unless the importation is for the private and domestic use of the person importing the goods.

(3) The Commissioners may make regulations prescribing the form in which notices are to be given under this section, and requiring a person giving such a notice, either at the time of giving the notice or at the time when the goods in question are imported, or at both those times, to furnish the Commissioners with such evidence, and to comply with such other conditions (if any), as may be specified in the regulations, and any such regulations may include such incidental and supplementary provisions as the Commissioners consider expedient for the purposes of this section.

(4) Without prejudice to the generality of the preceding subsection, regulations made under that subsection may include provision for requiring a person who has given a notice under subsection (1) of this section, or a notice purporting to be a notice under that subsection –

    (a) to pay such fees in respect of the notice as may be prescribed by the regulations;

    (b) to give to the Commissioners such security as may be so prescribed, in respect of any liability or expense which they may incur in consequence of the detention of any goods to which the notice relates, or in consequence of anything done in relation to goods so detained;

    (c) whether any such security is given or not, to keep the Commissioners indemnified against any such liability or expense as is mentioned in the preceding paragraph.

(5) For the purposes of section 17 of the Customs and Excise Management Act 1979 (which relates to the disposal of duties) any fees paid in pursuance of regulations made under this section shall be treated as money collected on account of duties (whether of customs or excise) charged on imported goods.

(6) Regulations under subsection (3) of this section shall be made by statutory instrument, which shall be subject to annulment in pursuance of a resolution of either House of Parliament.

Note that a similar provision operates in respect of infringing copies of literary, dramatic and musical works, sound recordings and films which are the subject of copyright: Copyright, Designs and Patents Act 1988, s.111, 112. Other intellectual property is not so treated.